This Dictionary Belongs To

_____

THE BEST DICTIONARY FOR STUDENTS

© 2010, The Dictionary Project, Inc.
  Sullivan's Island, SC 29482
ISBN 0-9771777-3-4

ISBN 0-9771777-3-4

ABCDEFGHIJKLMNOPQRSTUVWXYZ

Table of Contents

Introduction…………………………………………….2

Parts of Speech……………………………………….3

Punctuation…………………………………………...4

Guide to the Dictionary……………………………….6

Dictionary…………………………………………….7

Weights and Measures.......................................362

Words for Large Numbers………………………...364

Roman Numerals…………………………………….365

Map of the United States………………………..366

abcdefghijklmnopqrstuvwxyz

Aa Bb Cc Dd Ee Ff Gg Hh Ii Jj Kk
Ll Mm Nn Oo Pp Qq Rr Ss Tt Uu
Vv Ww Xx Yy Zz

ABCDEFGHIJKLMNOPQRSTUVWXYZ

This dictionary is one of your most valuable, interesting, and fun learning tools. Keep it handy! It will help you do your very best work in school, and you will also learn many new words to use every day. Communication is the key to learning, and this dictionary was written to help you use words to share your thoughts and articulate your feelings so that you can share them with other people. A dictionary this size cannot contain the 300,000 words in our language. This book has more than 35,000 words and their meanings that will help you better understand our world.

To succeed in school and in life, you must be able to use the English language effectively. You simply cannot learn all that you need to know without being able to understand the words you hear and read, and without knowing how to use the right words to convey your thoughts and ideas clearly. A dictionary is an essential tool for a quality education; you cannot do your best work without one. Use it to look up the spelling, meaning, and pronunciation of words. You will also find that it is fun spending time looking for new and useful words to expand your vocabulary. Learning new words gives you a feeling of satisfaction.

The English language is a living language that is constantly changing, and dictionaries must change, too. Our technology is driven by words that weren't in the dictionary ten years ago. If there are words or meanings you would like to see added to our new dictionaries, please send them to The Dictionary Project for consideration. You can help us make sure that this dictionary is the best dictionary for students.

www.The Dictionary Project.com

NINE PARTS OF SPEECH

Three little words you often see,
Are Articles – *a, an,* and *the*.
A Noun's the name of anything,
As *school*, or *garden*, *hoop,* or *swing*.
Adjectives tell the kind of Noun,
As *great, small, pretty, white,* or *brown*.
Instead of Nouns the Pronouns stand-
Her head, *his* face, *your* arm, *my* hand.
Verbs tell of something to be done –
To *read*, *count*, *sing*, *laugh*, *jump,* or *run*.
How things are done, the Adverbs tell,
As *slowly, quickly, ill,* or *well*.
Conjunctions join the words together
As man *and* woman, wind *or* weather.
The Preposition stands before
A noun, as *in*, or *through* a door.
The Interjection shows surprise,
As *oh!* How pretty – *ah*! How wise.
The whole are called Nine Parts of Speech,
Which reading, writing, speaking teach.

Dr. Chase , 1867

Punctuation

Punctuation marks and pauses are used to separate written or printed information into sentences and parts of sentences to assist the reader in understanding the meaning of the writer.

A **Period (.)** is placed at the end of a sentence; as,
> *I admit I made a mistake.*
> Or is used after an abbreviation; as
> *Dr. Johnson   Jan. 1, 2004*

A **question mark (?)** indicates a question; as
> *What is your opinion?*

An **Exclamation Point (!)** denotes humor or strong feeling; as,
> *Facing it—always facing it – that's the way to get through it.*
> *Face it!* Joseph Conrad, 1924

The **Comma (,)**, **Semicolon (;)**, and **Colon (:)** mark grammatical division in a sentence; as,
> *There are three genders: feminine, masculine, and neuter; in language they are referred to as she, he, and it, respectively.*

A **comma** is used to list items in a series. The **colon** may separate two clauses when the second explains the first, and is also used before an explanatory list.The **semicolon** is used to separate two independent clauses when there is no conjunction. Sometimes it is called a weak period.

A **Hyphen (-)** is used between syllables in a word divided at the end of a line; as,
> *knowl-edge   pow-er*
> And between the parts of a compound word, as
> *self-improvement   absent-minded*

The **Dash (--)** is used where there is a sudden break or pause in a sentence; as,

Individual commitment to a group effort-- that is what makes a team work, a company work, a society work, a civilization work.
Vince Lombardi, 1970

Quotation marks (" ") denote the words of another; as

"My name is Margalo," said the little bird softly in a musical voice. "I come from fields once tall with wheat, from pastures deep in fern and thistle; I come from vales of meadow-sweet, and I love to whistle." Stuart Little, E.B. White, 1985

An **apostrophe (')** denotes that a letter or letters are left out; as,

I'd be better off if I had gone to school longer, and so will you.
Joe Louis

And is also used to show ownership; as

There are spaces between our fingers so that another person's fingers can fill them in. Anonymous

Pronunciation Key

a̧,	for	ŏ,	as in	want	y̆,	for	ĭ, as in	chlorophyll
ê,	"	â,	"	tear	c,	"	k,	"	character
ȩ,	"	ā,	"	eight	ç,	"	s,	"	city
ï,	"	ē,	"	police	çh,	"	sh,	"	chivalry
ī,	"	ē̆,	"	sir	eh,	"	k,	"	chorus
ȯ,	"	ŭ,	"	ton	ġ,	"	j,	"	general
o̱,	"	ōo,	"	do	ṉ,	"	ng,	"	sang
ọ,	"	ŏŏ,	"	book	s̱,	"	z,	"	hands
ô,	"	a̧,	"	pork	s,	"	sh,	"	sure
õ,	"	û,	"	worm	x̱,	"	ḡz,	"	example
u̧,	"	ŏŏ,	"	pull	gh,	"	f,	"	laugh
u̱,	"	ōo,	"	rule	ph,	"	f,	"	phone
ȳ,	"	ī,	"	try	qu,	"	k.	"	plaque

qu, for kw, as in quiet

A schwa "ə" in the pronunciation guide indicates an
unstressed vowel, as in "the" or "someone"

Guide to the Dictionary

entry word	**re-spect** [rĭ-spĕkt′] *noun*, 1) an aspect
	2) consideration for someone, *verb*, 3) to have a good opinion of someone, to look up to, to hold in esteem
spelling	**cour-te-ous** [kûr′tē-əs] *adjective*, showing good manners, polite
meaning	**com-pas-sion** [kəm-păsh′ən] *noun*, kindness, tenderness, pity, sympathy for suffering
more than one meaning	**char-ac-ter** [kăr′ək-tər] *noun* 1) the moral makeup of a person 2) a person in a book or movie or play 3) a symbol, sign, or written letter used in a language
part of speech	**hon-or** [ŏn′ər] *noun*, 1) fame or a rank of high esteem, *verb*, 2) to hold in high respect 3) to keep an agreement
no plural	**cour-age** [kûr′ĭj] *noun*, *no plural*, the strength to face danger when overwhelmed by fear

guide words	# persevere phrase

per-se-vere [pûr′sə-vîr′] *verb*, to work to accomplish a goal despite difficulty

per-sist [pər-sĭst′] *verb*, to keep doing something, to persevere

phrase [frāz] *noun*, 1) a part of a sentence 2) an expression, a saying, *verb*, 3) to express in words or a particular way

syllabic pronunciation	**in-teg-ri-ty** [ĭn-tĕg′rĭ-tē] *noun*, honesty, uprighteousness
phonetic spelling	**in-spire** [ĭn-spīr′] *verb*, to stimulate to think and to act, to influence

6

A

a [ă] *article*, used to indicate one before a noun

a-ba-cus [ăb′ə-kəs] *noun*, a frame holding parallel rods with beads, used for doing arithmetic

ab-a-lo-ne [ăb′ə-lō′nē] *noun*, a shell sea mollusk animal whose shell is lined with mother-of-pearl

a-ban-don [ə-băn′dən] *verb*, to leave or give up completely, to walk away from

a-bash [ə-băsh′] *verb*, to cause to feel embarrassed or ashamed

a-bate [ə-bāt′] *verb*, to gradually become less in amount or degree

ab-bre-vi-ate [ə-brē′vē-āt′] *verb*, to shorten, to cut down, to contract

ab-di-cation [ăb′dĭ-kā-shŭn] *noun*, a surrender, abandonment

ab-do-men [ăb′də-mən] *noun*, the digestive system in the body, belly

ab-duct [ăb-dŭkt′] *verb*, to kidnap

ab-er-ra-tion [ăb′ə-rā′shən] *noun*, a departure from what is right, correct or natural

a-bet [ə-bĕt′] *verb*, to encourage or assist, especially in wrongdoing

ab-hor [ăb-hôr′] *verb*, to withdraw in disgust or horror

a-bide [ə-bīd′] *verb*, 1) to put up with, tolerate 2) to wait patiently

a-bil-i-ty [ə-bĭl′ĭ-tē] *noun*, 1) skill, expertise 2) capability or power

a-ble [ā′bəl] *adjective*, having the strength or knowledge to do something

ab-nor-mal [ăb-nôr′məl] *adjective*, irregular, unusual, peculiar

a-board [ə-bôrd′] *preposition*, on, in, upon (a ship)

a-bode [ə-bōd′] *noun*, home; a place of residence; a habitation

a-bol-ish [ə-bŏl′ĭsh] *verb*, to do away with entirely

ab-o-li-tion [ăb′ə-lĭsh′ən] *noun*, complete destruction

a-bom-i-na-ble [ə-bŏm′ə-nə-bəl] *adjective*, detestable, odious

Ab-o-rig-i-ne [ăb′ə-rĭj′ə-nē] *noun*, a person, animal or plant that has been in a country or region from earliest times

a-bor-tive [ə-bôr′tĭv] *adjective*, unsuccessful, fruitless, unfinished

a-bound [ə-bound′] *verb*, to exist in large numbers, to overflow

a-bout [ə-bout′] *adverb*, 1) concerning 2) approximately 3) here or there, everywhere

a-bove [ə-bŭv′] *adverb*, 1) at a higher level, *preposition*, 2) over, in a higher place

a-bra-sion [ə-brā′zhən] *noun*, a wearing away or rubbing that causes scratches

a-bridge [ə-brĭj′] *verb*, to shorten by using fewer words

a-bridg-ment [ə-brĭj′mənt] *noun*, abbreviation, shortening

a-broad [ə-brôd′] *adverb*, in a foreign country, overseas

ab-rupt [ə-brŭpt′] *adjective*, suddenly, without warning

ab-scess [ăb′sĕs′] *noun*, an accumulation of pus due to an infection from bacteria

ab-sence [ăb′səns] *noun*, 1)the state of being away from someplace or someone 2) lack

ab-sent [ăb′sənt] *adjective*, missing, not present, unavailable

ab-sent-mind-ed [ăb′səntmĭn′dĭd] *adjective*, forgetful, not paying attention

ab-so-lute [ăb′sə-lōot′] *adjective*, complete, perfect, total

ab-solve [əb-zŏlv′, -sŏlv′] *verb*, to pardon, to forgive

ab-sorb [əb-sôrb′, -zôrb′] *verb*, 1) to soak up a fluid or moisture 2) to hold someone's attention 3) to dissolve a debt completely and accept the loss 4) to assimilate information

ab-sorb-ent [əb-sôr′bənt] *adjective*, absorbing moisture, fluid or light rays

ab-stain [ăb-stān′] *verb*, to deliberately avoid doing something

ab-sti-nence [ăb′stə-nəns] *noun*, the act of depriving oneself of some indulgence, voluntary denial

ab-stract [ăb-străkt′] *adjective*, difficult to describe or qualify

ab-surd [əb-sûrd′, -zûrd′] *adjective*, outrageous, silly, untrue

ab-surd-i-ty [əb-sûrd′ĭt ē] *noun*, that which is ridiculous or unreasonable

a-bun-dance [ə-bŭn′dəns] *noun*, large quantity, plenty

a-bun-dant [ə-bŭn′dənt] *adjective*, plentiful, more than enough

a-buse [ə-byōo′s] *noun*, 1) hurtful treatment, *verb*[ə-byōoz′], 2) to hurt someone or something intentionally

a-bu-sive [ə-byōo′sĭv, -zĭv] *adjective*, using insulting words or bad treatment

a-but [ə-bŭt′] *verb*, to border upon, to be next to or touching

a-bys-mal [ə-bĭz′məl] *adjective*, 1) immeasurably bad 2) bottomless

a-byss [ə-bĭs′] *noun*, a very deep crack in the earth, a bottomless gulf, a deep chasm

ac-a-dem-ic [ăk′ə-děm′ĭk] *adjective*, 1) of or relating to an education in the arts 2) having no practical importance

a-cad-e-my [ə-kăd′ə-mē] *noun*, a school offering specialized training and education

ac-cel-er-a-tion [ăk-sĕl′ə-rā′shən] *noun*, an increase in the speed of something

ac-cent [ăk′sĕnt′] *noun*, 1) the sound and tone of a foreign language, *verb*, 2) to emphasize a sound or letter when pronouncing a word 3) to emphasize something

ac-cept [ăk-sĕpt′] *verb*, 1) to agree with 2) to receive

ac-cep-tance [ăk-sĕp′təns] *noun*, the act of receiving something graciously

ac-cess [ăk′sĕs] *noun*, a way to get to a person, place, or thing

ac-ces-si-ble [ăk-sĕs′ə-bəl] *adjective*, easy to reach or use, approachable

ac-ces-so-ry [ăk-sĕs′ə-rē] *noun*, 1) an accomplice, connected as a subordinate 2) an article or decoration worn to complete an outfit, such as a belt, scarf, hat, etc.

ac-ci-dent [ăk′sĭ-dənt] *noun*, 1) an incident involving bodily injury or death 2) a mistake

ac-claim [ə-klām′] *verb*, to applaud, to announce with great approval

ac-cli-mate [ə-klī′mĭt] *verb*, to change or adjust to a different temperature or environment

ac-com-mo-date [ə-kŏm′ə-dāt′] *verb* 1) to adapt or make fit 2) to do a favor 3) to provide lodging

ac-com-mo-da-tion [ə-kŏm′ə-dā′shən] *noun*, an adaptation, an adjustment made to assist someone

ac-com-pa-ny [ə-kŭm′pə-nē] *verb*, to go with, to join

ac-com-plice [ə-kŏm′plĭs] *noun*, someone who goes along with something, usually something wrong

ac-com-plish [ə-kŏm′plĭsh] *verb*, to finish, to complete a task or reach a goal

ac-com-plish-ment [ə-kŏm′plĭsh-mənt] *noun*, something done, a goal that has been reached, a finished task

ac-cord [ə-kôrd′] *noun*, 1) mutual agreement, *verb*, 2) to be in harmony, to conform

ac-cor-di-on [ə-kôr′dē-ən] *noun*, a musical instrument that is played by fingering a keyboard on one side and squeezing bellows in and out on the other side

ac-cost [ə-kôst′] *verb*, to approach abruptly and speak to first

ac-count [ə-kount′] *noun*, 1) an explanation, a statement of money or inventory, *verb*, 2) to give a reason, to explain

ac-crue [ə-krōō′] *verb*, to be added on to, to increase

ac-cu-mu-late [ə-kyōōm′yə-lāt′] *verb*, to collect, to amass

ac-cu-mu-la-tion [ə-kyōōm′yə-lā′shən] *noun*, gathering a quantity of something

ac-cu-ra-cy [ăk′yər-ə-sē] *noun*, exactness, correctness, precision

ac-cu-rate [ăk′yər-ĭt] *adjective*, having no mistakes

ac-cu-sa-tion [ăk′yōō-zā′shən] *noun*, a claim that someone has done something wrong

ac-cuse [ə-kyōōz′] *verb*, to say someone has committed an offense or crime

ac-cus-tom [ə-kŭs′təm] *verb*, to become familiar with something through use or habit

ace [ās] *noun*, 1) a playing card 2) a fighter pilot who was shot down

ache [āk] *noun*, 1) a painful or sore spot, *verb*, 2) to hurt, to feel pain

a-chieve [ə-chēv′] *verb*, to do what one sets out to do

a-chieve-ment [ə-chēv′mənt] *noun*, something that a person has done to reach a goal

ac-id [ăs′ĭd] *noun*, a chemical substance soluble in water, sour in taste, that reddens litmus paper

ac-knowl-edge [ăk-nŏl′ĭj] *verb*, 1) to look at someone and speak to him or her 2) to admit the truth

ac-knowl-edg-ment [ăk-nŏl′ĭj-mənt] *noun*, 1) admission, recognition of an achievement 2) an expression of thanks

a-corn [ā′kôrn′, ā′kərn] *noun*, the seed of an oak tree

a-cous-tic [ə-kōō′stĭk] *adjective*, of or relating to the ability to carry a sound without distortion

ac-quaint [ə-kwānt′] *verb*, to cause to know or be aware of someone or something

ac-quaint-ance [ə-kwān′təns] *noun*, a person with whom one is familiar

ac-qui-esce [ăk′wē-ĕs′] *verb*, to submit, to consent, to agree

ac-quire [ə-kwīr′] *verb*, to get or to buy, to gain possession of

ac-qui-si-tion [ăk′wĭ-zĭsh′ən] *noun*, something gained or acquired

ac-quit [ə-kwĭt′] *verb*, to render a verdict that an accused person is not guilty of a crime, to exonerate

ac-quit-tal [ə-kwĭt′l] *noun*, a setting free from a charge, a finding of "not guilty"

a-cre [ā′kər] *noun*, a plot of land measuring 43,560 square feet

ac-ri-mo-ny [ăk′rə-mō′nē] *noun*, bitterness or caustic temper or speech, bad feelings

ac-ro-bat [ăk′rə-băt′] *noun*, a person skilled in tumbling or in using gymnastics equipment

ac-ro-nym [ăk′rə-nĭm′] *noun*, a word formed from the initial letters of a series of words, e.g. AIDS: *Acquired Immune Deficiency Syndrome*

a-cross [ə-krôs′, ə-krŏs′] *adverb*, 1) from one side of a place to the other, *preposition*, 2) on the opposite side from something

act [ăkt] *noun*, 1) something that has been done, a deed 2) a part of a play containing different scenes, *verb*, 3) to pretend to be something or someone 4) to behave 5) to carry out, to perform

ac-tion [ăk′shən] *noun*, 1) something done 2) the process of doing

ac-tive [ăk′tĭv] *adjective*, 1) always busy doing something 2) taking part

ac-tiv-i-ty [ăk-tĭv′ĭ-tē] *noun*, state of action, energy, a task

ac-tor [ăk′tər] *noun*, a male or female performer in a play, a film or television program

ac-tu-al [ăk′chōō-əl] *adjective*, real, existing in fact

ac-tu-al-ly [ăk′chōō-əl-ē] *adverb*, really, truly, in reality

a-cu-i-ty [ə-kyōō′ĭ-tē] *noun*, keenness, as of thought and vision

a-cute [ə-kyōōt′] *adjective*, 1) sharp, pointed, keen, sensitive 2) describing an angle formed by intersecting lines that is less than 90 degrees

A.D. abbreviation for the Latin words **Anno Domini**, the time after the birth of Christ

ad-age [ăd′ĭj] *noun*, a proverb or a saying with a moral message

ad-a-mant [ăd′ə-mənt] *adjective*, inflexible, unyielding

a-dapt [ə-dăpt′] *verb*, to change to fit the environment

ad-ap-ta-tion [ăd′ăp-tā′shən] *noun*, a change to improve the way things work

add [ăd] *verb*, 1) to put together with something else 2) to count

ad-der [ăd′ər] *noun*, a snake with a poisonous bite, a viper

ad-dict [ə-dĭkt′] *noun*, someone who has a strong habit or a physical despendency, as for drugs

ad-dic-tion [ə-dĭk′shən] *noun*, a dependency, such as a physical craving for a drug

ad-di-tion [ə-dĭsh′ən] *noun*, 1) the act of putting or joining things together 2) an annexation

ad-di-tion-al [ə-dĭsh′ən-əl] *adjective*, added on, extra

ad-dress [ə-drĕs′] *noun*, 1) the location of something, usually the street number, city, and state, *verb*, 2) to speak or write to someone 3) to direct in writing, as in a letter 4) to speak to an audience, as in a speech

a-dept [ə-dĕpt′] *adjective*, proficient, expert, highly skilled

ad-e-quate [ăd′ĭ-kwĭt] *adjective*, just enough, sufficient, all right

ad-here [ăd-hîr′] *verb*, to hold, to be attached, to stick to

ad-her-ent [ăd-hîr′ənt] *adjective*, 1) sticking securely, *noun*, 2) a supporter or follower

ad-he-sive [ăd-hē′sĭv, -zĭv] *noun*, a sticky substance that holds things in place

a-dieu [ə-dyōō′, ə-dōō′] *noun and interjection*, farewell, goodbye

ad in-fi-ni-tum [ăd ĭn′fə-nī′təm] *adverb*, to infinity, endlessly

ad-ja-cent [ə-jā′sənt] *adjective*, next to, lying near or touching

ad-jec-tive [ăj′ĭk-tĭv] *noun*, a word that describes a person, place or thing

ad-join [ə-join′] *verb*, to be next to and connected to something

ad-journ [ə-jûrn′] *verb*, to put off a meeting until later, to postpone

ad-just [ə-jŭst′] *verb*, to reposition or reset something

ad-just-a-ble [ə-jŭst′ə-bəl] *adjective*, capable of being arranged or altered

ad-just-ment [ə-jŭst′mənt] *noun*, a minor modification or change

ad lib [ăd lĭb′] *verb*, to make up words or actions at the moment, not before

ad-min-is-ter [ăd-mĭn′ĭ-stər] *verb*, 1) to look after or tend 2) to distribute, to disperse 3) to manage, to run

ad-min-is-tra-tion [ăd-mĭn′ĭ-strā′shən] *noun*, those who are empowered to make decisions, management

ad-min-is-tra-tor [ăd-mĭn′ĭ-strā′tər] *noun*, a person authorized to carry out certain duties

ad-mi-ra-ble [ăd′mər-ə-bəl]*adjective*, excellent, deserving the highest praise

ad-mi-ral [ăd′mər-əl] *noun*, the highest ranking officer in the navy

ad-mi-ra-tion [ăd′mə-rā′shən] *noun*, appreciation, esteem

ad-mire [ăd-mīr′] *verb*, 1) to look up to someone, to revere 2) to look at with pleasure

ad-mis-si-ble [ăd-mĭs′ə-bəl] *adjective*, that may be allowed

ad-mis-sion [ăd-mĭsh′ən] *noun*, 1) access, admittance 2) acknowledgment, confession

ad-mit [ăd-mĭt′] *verb*, 1) to allow someone to enter 2) to acknowledge as true

a-do [ədoō] *noun*, fuss, excitment

a-do-be [ə-dō'bē] *noun*, 1) a type of clay or the sun-dried bricks made from it, 2) a home made with baked mud, usually in the Southwest

ad-o-les-cent [ăd'l-ĕs'ənt] *noun*, a teenager

a-dopt [ə-dŏpt'] *verb*, 1) to use someone else's idea 2) to make someone a member of your family, legally

a-dore [ə-dôr', ə-dōr'] *verb*, to like or love very much

a-dorn [ə-dôrn'] *verb*, to decorate, to add beauty, to embellish

a-drift [ə-drĭft'] *adverb*, out in water or space without means of control, drifting

a-dult [ə-dŭlt'] *noun*, a grown person or animal

ad-vance [ăd-văns'] *adjective*, 1) ahead of time, done beforehand, *noun*, 2) a positive change, progress *verb*, 3) to move forward

ad-van-tage [ăd-văn'tĭj] *noun*, something that helps a person

ad-van-ta-geous [ăd'văn-tā'jəs,] *adjective*, profitable, useful, beneficial, favorable

ad-vent [ăd'vĕnt'] *noun*, the arrival of someone or something

ad-ven-ture [ăd-vĕn'chər] *noun*, 1) a bold or hazardous undertaking, 2) an exciting or extraordinary experience

ad-verb [ăd'vûrb] *noun*, a word that tells how, when, or where something is done

ad-ver-sar-y [ăd'vər-sĕr'ē] *noun*, a rival, foe, or opponent

ad-verse [ăd-vûrs'] *adjective*, opposed, hostile

ad-ver-si-ty [ăd-vûr'sĭ-tē] *noun*, hard times, trouble

ad-ver-tise [ăd'vər-tīz'] *verb*, 1) to announce publicly 2) to try to sell something by promoting it

ad-ver-tise-ment [ăd'vər-tīz'mənt] *noun*, a notice or short film about something that is for sale

ad-vice [ăd-vīs'] *noun*, counsel, opinion given for acceptable conduct, guidance

ad-vis-a-ble [ăd-vī'zə-bəl] *adjective*, proper, recommended, prudent

ad-vise [ăd-vīz'] *verb*, to suggest to someone what to do, to inform, to recommend, to counsel

ad-vis-er [ăd-vī'zər] *noun*, one who advises, one who gives counsel or information

ad-vo-cate [ăd'və-kt t'] *noun*, 1) one who pleads the cause of another or himself, [ăd'və-kāt'] *verb*, 2) to defend, to urge, to support, to endorse

aer-i-al [âr'ē-əl] *adjective*, pertaining to or inhabiting the air

aer-o-bic [â-rō'bĭk] *adjective*, requiring the presence of free oxygen to live

aer-o-dy-nam-ics [âr'ō-dī-năm'ĭks] *noun*, the science of the movement of flying bodies in air

aer-o-sol [âr'ə-sôl'] *noun*, a gaseous suspension of fine particles, a mist

aer-o-space [âr'ō-spās'] *adjective*, having to do with the atmosphere and space

aes-thet-ic [ĕs-thĕt'ĭk] *adjective*, relating to beauty or the arts

af-fair [ə-fâr′] *noun*, matter, concern, business of any kind

af-fect [ə-fĕkt′] *verb*, 1) to act upon to bring about a change 2) to move the feelings of someone 3) to pretend to do something

af-fec-ta-tion [ăf′ĕk-tā′shən] *noun*, insincerity, pretense

af-fec-tion [ə-fĕk′shən] *noun*, tenderness, warmth, love, devotion, kindness

af-fec-tion-ate [ə-fĕk′shə-nĭt] *adjective*, feeling or showing love

af-fec-tion-ate-ly [ə-fĕk′shə-nĭt-lē] *adverb*, showing love and care

af-fi-da-vit [ăf′ĭ-dā′vĭt] *noun*, a written declaration, an oath

af-fil-i-ate [ə-fĭl′ē-āt′] *verb*, to closely connect or associate with someone or groups of people

af-fil-i-a-tion [ə-fĭl-ē-ā′shən] *noun*, an association, a connection

af-fin-i-ty [ə-fĭn′ĭ-tē] *noun*, a feeling of attraction to a person or thing

af-firm [ə-fûrm′] *verb*, to approve, to confirm, to endorse

af-fir-ma-tion [ăf′ər-mā′shən] *noun*, a solemn pledge

af-firm-a-tive [ə-fûr′mə-tĭv] *adjective*, 1) being positive and helpful, *noun*, 2) a word or phrase expressing a positive reply

af-flict [ə-flĭkt′] *verb*, to hurt, to torment, to cause pain

af-flic-tion [ə-flĭk′shən] *noun*, state or cause of distress, pain or misery

af-flu-ence [ăf′lōō-əns] *noun*, an abundant supply, wealth

af-ford [ə-fôrd′] *verb*, to have enough money to buy something

a-float [ə-flōt′] *adjective*, on or above the water, buoyant

a-fraid [ə-frād′] *adjective*, scared

Af-ri-ca [ăf′rĭ-kə] *noun*, one of the seven continents, surrounded by the Atlantic and Indian Oceans, containing 12.7% of the world's population

af-ter [ăf′tər] *adverb*, 1) following, next, *preposition*, 2) behind

af-ter-math [ăf′tər-măth′] *noun*, the end result, outcome, consequence

af-ter-noon [ăf′tər-nōōn′] *noun*, time between noon and evening

af-ter-ward [ăf′tər-wərd] *adverb*, later

a-gain [ə-gĕn′] *adverb*, once more

a-gainst [ə-gĕnst′] *preposition*, 1) in opposition to 2) in contact with, touching 3) in the other direction, opposite

age [āj] *noun*, 1) the amount of time something has lived 2) a particular period of time, *verb*, 3) to grow or cause to become old

aged [ā′jĭd] *adjective*, old

a-gen-cy [ā′jən-sē] *noun*, an organization designed to distribute funds and services to people

a-gen-da [ə-jĕn′də] *noun*, a list of items that need attention

a-gent [ā′jənt] *noun*, 1) a person who represents a group 2) a force of change

ag-gran-dize [ə-grăn′dīz′] *verb*, to make greater in power, rank or riches

ag-gra-vate [ăg′rə-vāt′] *verb*, to make worse, to annoy

aggregate

ag-gre-gate [ăg′rĭ-gĭt] *noun*, the sum total of a group of things

ag-gres-sion [ə-grĕsh′ən] *noun*, anger in an attack

ag-gres-sive [ə-grĕs′ĭv] *adjective*, forceful, likely to attack

ag-ile [ăj′əl, -īl′] *adjective*, swift, nimble, able to move easily

ag-i-tate [ăj′ĭ-tāt′] *verb*, to shake up

ag-i-ta-tion [ăj′ĭ-tā′shən] *noun*, confusion, frenzy, excitement

ag-nos-tic [ăg-nŏs′tĭk] *noun*, a person who believes that the human mind cannot comprehend the beginning of the universe or the existence of God

a-go [ə-gō′] *adverb*, in the past

ag-o-ny [ăg′ə-nē] *noun*, very bad physical or emotional pain

a-gree-a-ble [ə-grē′ə-bəl] *adjective*, easy to get along with

a-gree-ment [ə-grē′mənt] *noun*, a mutual understanding

ag-ri-cul-ture [ăg′rĭ-kŭl′chər] *noun*, the science and art of cultivating soil and growing crops

a-head [ə-hĕd′] *adverb*, 1) in front, preceding 2) into the future

aid [ād] *noun*, 1) a form of help 2) assistance, support, *verb*, 3) to help or assist

aide [ād] *noun*, an assistant, a helper

ail-ment [āl′mənt] *noun*, a sickness,

aim [ām] *noun*, 1) target, direction 2) intention, purpose, goal, *verb*, 3) to point toward a target when ready to throw something, fire something, or take a picture

air [âr] *noun* 1) the mixture of gases surrounding the earth 2) an appearance or atmosphere, *verb*, 3) to refresh or ventilate

air-borne [âr′bôrn′] *adjective*, carried by or through the air

air-craft [âr′krăft′] *noun*, a machine capable of flying

air force [âr′fôrs′] *noun*, a group of soldiers trained to fight and destroy using aircraft

air-plane [âr′plăn′] *noun*, a flying machine used to transport people or cargo moving through the air by means of motor driven propellers or engines and kept aloft by the upward thrust of the air on its fixed wings

air pol-lu-tion [âr - pə-lōō′shən] *noun*, particles that contaminate the air and make it unsafe to breathe

air-port [âr′pôrt′] *noun*, a place where aircraft land and take off

aisle [īl] *noun*, the passageway between seats in a bus, auditorium, church, etc., or between shelves in a store

a-jar [ə-jär′] *adjective and adverb*, slightly open

Al-a-bama [ăl′ə-băm′ə] *noun*, one of the southern United States the capital is Montgomery. The state flower for **Alabama** is the camellia and the motto is "We dare to defend our rights."

a-lac-ri-ty [ə-lăk′rĭ-tē] *noun*, 1) cheerful willingness or readiness 2) speed

a-larm [ə-lärm′] *noun*, 1) a feeling of fear or danger 2) a programmed sound to awaken persons from sleep or warn of danger, *verb*, 3) to worry or frighten

a-las [ə-lăs′] *interjection*, an expression of pity or concern

Alas-ka [ə-lăs′kə] *noun*, one of the 50 United States located in the north. The capital city is Juneau. The state flower of **Alaska** is the forget me-not, and the motto is "North to the Future."

al-ba-tross [ăl′bə-trôs′] *noun*, a large bird with long narrow wings found near the ocean, especially in the South Seas

al-bi-no [ăl-bī′nō] *noun*, a person or animal lacking pigmentation, and therefore extraordinarily pale

al-bum [ăl′bəm] *noun*, 1)a book that holds a collection of pictures, stamps or autographs 2) a collection of recordings

al-che-my [ăl′kə-mē] *noun*, medieval chemistry that attempted to turn ordinary things into gold

al-co-hol [ăl′kə-hôl′] *noun*, 1) an intoxicating beverage, such as wine, beer or liquor, the result of fermentation 2) an organic compound used as an antiseptic

al-co-hol-ic [ăl′kə-hô′lĭk] *adjective*, 1) containing alcohol as an ingredient, *noun*, 2) a person with the disease of alcoholism

al-der-man [ôl′dər-mən] *noun*, a member of a city council

a-lert [ə-lûrt′] *adjective*, 1) awake and ready to act, *noun*, 2) a warning of danger

al-fal-fa [ăl-făl′fə] *noun*, a plant in the pea family

al-ga [ăl′gə] *noun*, *plural*, **algae**, an organism, often one-celled, that continuously divides itself, with no root or stem that lives in water

al-ge-bra [ăl′jə-brə] *noun*, a branch of mathematics in which the expressions of quantity are in symbols that express general relationships

a-li-as [ā′lē-əs] *noun*, an assumed name, a fake name, incognito

al-i-bi [ăl′ə-bī′] *noun*, the plea of having been elsewhere at the time a crime was committed

al-ien [ā′lē-ən] *adjective*, 1) strange, wholly different in nature, *noun*, 2) a person from another country

al-ien-ate [āl′yə-nāt′] *verb*, to separate, to make hostile

a-light [ə-līt′] *verb*, to come from, to get off

a-lign-ment [ə-līn′mənt] *noun*, 1) arrangement in a line 2) the condition of cooperation

a-like [ə-līk′] *adjective*, 1) similar, *adverb*, 2) in the same manner

al-i-men-ta-ry [ăl′ə-měn′tə-rē] *adjective*, supplying nourishment

al-i-mo-ny [ăl′ə-mō′nē] *noun*, an allowance given to a spouse for his or her support after a divorce

a-live [ə-līv′] *adjective*, 1) living, not dead 2) active, moving

al-ka-li [ăl′kə-lī′] *noun*, any soluble substance having marked basic qualities as a mineral salt or mixture of salts that can neutralize acids and turns litmus blue

all [ôl] *adjective*, the whole of, any, 2) *adverb*, 2) completely, totally, *pronoun*, 3) everyone, the whole thing

al-lay [ə-lā′] to ease, to calm, to appease

al-le-ga-tion [ăl′ĭ-gā′shən] *noun*, the statement of something that is to be proved, an accusation

al-lege [ə-lĕj′] *verb*, to urge as a reason, to assert, to suggest

al-le-giance [ə-lē′jəns] *noun*, strong support of something, an obligation to a government or ruler, loyal support

al-le-go-ry [ăl′ĭ-gôr′ē] *noun*, a story with a moral in which characters are used as symbols, a fable

al-ler-gy [ăl′ər-jē] *noun*, an abnormal reaction to substances in the environment such as pollen, dust or insect bites

al-le-vi-ate [ə-lē′vē-āt′] *verb*, to lighten or lessen pressure

al-ley [ăl′ē] *noun*, a very narrow road between buildings

al-li-ance [ə-lī′əns] *noun*, a partnership based on trust, common objectives, etc.

al-li-ga-tor [ăl′ĭ-gā′tər] *noun*, a large reptile that lives near water and is a carnivore

al-lit-er-a-tion [ə-lĭt′ə-rā′shən] *noun*, repetition of the beginning sound, e.g., *Peter Piper picked a peck of pickled peppers*

al-lo-cate [ăl′ə-kāt′] *verb*, to set something aside for a special use

al-lot [ə-lŏt′] *verb*, to divide something and then to give someone his or her portion

al-lot-ment [ə-lŏt′mənt] *noun*, the portion given to each

al-low [ə-lou′] *verb*, to permit someone to do something

al-low-ance [ə-lou′əns] *noun*, a definite sum granted, an abatement or deduction

al-loy [ăl′oi′] *noun*, a substance composed of two or more metals mixed together

al-lude [ə-lōōd′] *verb*, to hint or suggest indirectly

al-lu-sion [ə-lōō′zhən] *noun*, an indirect reference, knowledge of something not actually mentioned

al-ly [ə-lī′] *noun*, 1) someone who helps you fight against someone else, a person or group who has the same purpose or cause, *verb*, 2) to unite, to join

al-ma ma-ter [ăl′mə mä′tər] *noun*, a school from which a person has graduated

al-ma-nac [ôl′mə-năk′] *noun*, a book containing a calendar and certain statistics

al-might-y [ôl-mī′tē] *adjective*, having very great power

al-mond [ä′mənd] *noun*, a nut-like kernel of the fruit of the almond tree

al-most [ôl′mōst′] *adverb*, nearly, not quite

alms [ämz] *noun*, *plural*, money or items given to charity

a-lo-ha [ə-lō-ha′] *noun and interjection*, Hawaiian word used for greeting or parting

a-lone [ə-lōn′] *adjective and adverb* without others, singular

a-long [ə-lông′] *adverb*, 1) following the length of something from end to end 2) moving forward 3) as a companion, *preposition*, 4) over, through, by the course of

a-loof [ə-l ōōf] *adjective*, 1) reserved in social relationships, *adverb* 2) away in place or time

a-loud [ə-loud′] *adverb*, in a clear voice that can be easily heard

al-pha-bet [ăl′fə-bĕt′] *noun*, the letters of a language arranged in customary order

al-pha-bet-i-cal [ăl′fə-bĕt′ĭ-kəl] *adjective*, arranged in the same order as the letters of the alphabet

al-read-y [ôl-rĕd′ē] *adverb*, even now, before a certain time

al-so [ôl′sō] *adverb*, in addition, too

al-tar [ôl′tər] *noun*, a table in a holy place where religious rites are performed

al-ter [ôl′tər] *verb*, to change

al-ter-a-tion [ôl′tə-rā′shən] *noun*, a change or an adjustment

al-ter-nate [ôl′tər-nāt′] *verb*, to take turns, to switch off

al-ter-na-tive [ôl-tûr′nə-tĭv] *adjective*, 1) other, *noun*, 2) something you can choose

al-though [ôl-thō′] *conjunction*, supposing that, notwithstanding

al-ti-tude [ăl′tĭ-tood′] *noun*, extent upward, the height of something measured in relation to a reference level, such as sea level

al-to [ăl′tō] *noun*, a singing voice between tenor and soprano

al-to-geth-er [ôl′tə-gĕth′ər] *adverb*, wholly, completely, including everyone, united

al-tru-is-tic [ăl′troo-ĭs′tĭk] *adjective*, unselfish, concerned about others

al-u-mi-num [ə-loo′mə-nəm] *noun*, a very soft silver metal made chiefly of bauxite ore

al-ways [ôl′wāz] *adverb*, at all times, forever

am [ăm] *verb*, the part of the verb **be** used with **I**

a.m. in the morning, the hours between midnight and noon, from the Latin ante meridiem "before midday"

a-mass [ə-măs′] *verb*, to collect, to accumulate

am-a-teur [ăm′ə-tûr′] *adjective*, 1) for enjoyment rather than money, not professional, *noun*, 2) someone who is not paid for doing something but does it for pleasure

a-maze [ə-māz′] *verb*, to surprise or bewilder

a-maze-ment [ə-māz′mənt] *noun*, a state of surprise, awe, wonder

am-a-zon [ăm′ə-zŏn′] *noun*, a mythical female warrior

am-bas-sa-dor [ăm-băs′ə-dər] *noun*, an appointed official who represents his or her country in another country

am-ber [ăm′bər] *noun*, the fossilized sap from a pine tree

am-bi-dex-trous [ăm′bĭ-dĕk′strəs] *adjective*, capable of using either hand with equal ease

am-bi-ence [ăm′bē-əns] *noun*, the environment, the atmosphere in a room or building

am-big-u-ous [ăm-bĭg′yoo-əs] *adjective*, capable of more than one interpretation, unclear

am-bi-tion [ăm-bĭsh′ən] *noun*, a strong desire to achieve

am-bi-tious [ăm-bĭsh′əs] *adjective*, wanting to have power, driven to achieve

am-biv-a-lent [ăm-bĭv′ə-lənt] *adjective,* having mixed feelings, conflicting emotional attitudes

am-bul-ance [ăm′byə-ləns] *noun,* a vehicle equipped to carry the injured or sick

am-bush [ăm′bŏŏsh] *noun,* a surprise attack

a-mel-io-rate [ə-mēl′yə-rāt′] *verb,* to improve a deplorable condition

A-men [ā-měn′, ä-měn′] *interjection,* an expression of approval, to say I agree

a-mend [ə-měnd′] *verb,* to correct, to change generally for the better

a-mend-ment [ə-měnd′mənt] *noun,* a change made in a bill or motion

a-men-i-ty [ə-měn′ĭ-tē] *noun,* a courtesy, a thoughtful action of consideration, a convenience

A-mer-i-ca [ə-měr′ĭ-kə] *noun,* a country in North America with a democratic form of government

A-mer-i-can In-di-an [ə-měr′ĭ-kən ĭn′dē-ən] *noun,* the people whose ancestors lived in North America for thousands of years

am-e-thyst [ăm′ə-thĭst] *noun,* a purple or bluish-violet stone

a-mi-a-ble [ā′mē-ə-bəl] *adjective,* friendly, easy to get along with

a-mid [ə-mĭd′] *preposition,* among, surrounded by

am-mo-nia [ə-mōn′yə] *noun,* a colorless compound of hydrogen and nitrogen

am-mu-ni-tion [ăm′yə-nĭsh′ən] *noun,* rockets, bombs and bullets used in loading or charging guns and rifles

am-ne-sia [ăm-nē′zhə] *noun,* loss of memory

am-nes-ty [ăm′nĭ-stē] *noun,* a pardon that absolves or discounts past offenses

a-mok [əmə′k] *adverb,* behave uncontrollably and disruptively

a-mong [ə-mŭng′] *preposition,* between, surrounded by

a-mount [ə-mount′] *noun,* 1) a sum, the total number 2) quantity, mass, *verb,* 3) to add up

am-phib-i-an [ăm-fĭb′ē-ən] *noun,* 1) a cold-blooded animal living both on land and in the water 2) an airplane designed to take off on the water or on land

am-phib-i-ous [ăm-fĭb′ē-əs] *adjective,* able to live or operate on land or in water

am-phi-the-a-ter [ăm′fə-thē′ə-tər] *noun,* a theater with seats all around the stage or arena

am-ple [ăm′pəl] *adjective,* abundant, plentiful, more than enough

am-pli-fy [ăm′plə-fī′] *verb,* to increase in size, to make louder

am-pu-tate [ăm′pyŏŏ-tāt′] *verb,* to cut off

am-u-let [ăm′yə-lĭt] *noun,* a good luck charm, a talisman

a-muse [ə-myŏŏz′] *verb,* to entertain or delight, to make someone smile

a-muse-ment [ə-myŏŏz′mənt] *noun,* entertainment, a distraction

an [ən; ăn when stressed] *article,* used instead of a in front of a vowel

an-aer-o-bic [ăn′ə-rō′bĭk] *adjective,* able to live only in the absence of free oxygen

a-nal-o-gous [ə-năl′ə-gəs] *adjective,* similar, comparable, resembling

a-nal-o-gy [ə-năl′ə-jē] *noun*, an explanation based on resemblances between different objects or cases

a-nal-y-sis [ə-năl′ĭ-sĭs] *noun*, a thorough examination

an-a-lyze [ăn′ə-līz′] *verb*, to examine critically elements or constituent parts

an-ar-chist [ăn′ər-kĭst] *noun*, a person who rebels against the established order or laws

an-ar-chy [ăn′ər-kē] *noun*, a lawless condition of society, chaos

a-nat-o-my [ə-năt′ə-mē] *noun*, the study of the structure of people, animals or plants

an-ces-tor [ăn′sĕs′tər] *noun*, a person from whom one is descended

an-ces-try [ăn′sĕs′trē] *noun*, family members or ethnic descent

an-chor [ăng′kər] *noun*, 1) a heavy piece of metal on the end of a rope or chain lowered into the water to keep a boat from drifting, *verb*, 2) to secure or fasten firmly, to fix in place

an-cient [ān′shənt] *adjective*, belonging to a remote period of time, very old

and [ənd, ən; ănd when stressed] *conjunction*, a word that adds or joins other words

an-ec-dote [ăn′ĭk-dōt′] *noun*, a short story or fact of an interesting nature

a-ne-mi-a [ə-nē′mē-ə] *noun*, a condition marked by a low red blood cell count

an-e-mom-e-ter [ăn′ə-mŏm′ĭ-tər] *noun*, an instrument to measure the force or speed of wind

an-es-the-sia [ăn′ĭs-thē′zhə] *noun*, the loss of sensation or consciousness, especially when caused by anesthetic

an-es-thet-ic [ăn′ĭs-thĕt′ĭk] *noun*, a substance that causes loss of sensation or consciousness

an-gel [ān′jəl] *noun*, 1) a messenger of God 2) a kind, loveable person

an-ger [ăng′gər] *noun*, feelings of hostility and hurt, a desire to fight or argue

an-gle [ăng′gəl] *noun*, 1) the shape made when two lines or planes intersect 2) a point of view, *verb*, 3) to fish with a hook and line

an-gry [ăng′grē] *adjective*, feeling extreme emotion due to hurt feelings, hostile

an-guish [ăng′gwĭsh] *noun*, extreme pain either of body or mind, acute suffering, deep sadness

an-i-mal [ăn′ə-məl] *noun*, a living creature that is not a plant

an-i-mate [ăn′ə-māt′] *verb*, to inspire with energy, to enliven

an-i-mos-i-ty [ăn′ə-mŏs′ĭ-tē] *noun*, a feeling of hatred leading to opposition, hostility

an-kle [ăng′kəl] *noun*, the joint connecting the foot to the leg

an-nals [ăn′əlz] *noun*, records, history, chronicles, accounts

an-neal [ə-nēl′] *verb*, to subject to high heat, with subsequent cooling, for the purpose of softening thoroughly and making less brittle

an-nex [ə-něks′] *noun*, 1) a building added onto a larger building, *verb*, 2) to add on, to attach a smaller thing to something larger

an-nex-a-tion [ăn′ĭk-sā′shən] *noun*, the territory or thing that has been added

an-ni-hi-late [ə-nī′ə-lāt′] *verb*, to reduce to nothing, to destroy entirely, to obliterate

an-ni-ver-sa-ry [ăn′ə-vûr′sə-rē] *noun*, a day celebrated each year to remember something important from the past

an-no-tate [ăn′ō-tāt′] *verb*, to write comments or explanatory notes

an-nounce [ə-nouns′] *verb*, to give notice of the arrival of something, to proclaim, to declare

an-nounce-ment [ə-nouns′mənt] *noun*, 1) act of making something publicly known 2) a printed notice

an-noy [ə-noi′] *verb*, to disturb or irritate, to bother

an-noy-ance [ə-noi′əns] *noun*, anything that irritates

an-nu-al [ăn′yōō-əl] *adjective*,
1) occurring once a year, *noun,*
2) a plant that lives for one year

a-noint [ə-noint′] *verb*, to baptize, to purify, to sprinkle with oil or holy water

a-nom-a-ly [ə-nŏm′ə-lē] *noun*, an irregularity, a deviation from the normal, one of a kind

a-non-y-mous [ə-nŏn′ə-məs] *adjective*, of unknown name

an-o-rex-i-a [ăn′ə-rĕk′sē-ə] *noun*, a lack of appetite and inability or refusal to consume food

an-oth-er [ə-nŭth′ər] *adjective, and pronou*n, 1) an additional, one more 2) someone else

an-swer [ăn′sər] *noun*, 1) a reply to a question, *verb*, 2) to make a response, to reply

ant [ănt] *noun*, a small insect that lives in colonies, known for its social order and industry

an-tag-o-nist [ăn-tăg′ə-nĭst] *noun*, one who opposes with active resistance, an opponent

Ant-arc-ti-ca [ănt-ärk′tĭ-kə] *noun*, one of the seven continents in the world, the area containing the South Pole

an-te-ced-ent [ăn′tĭ-sēd′nt] *adjective*, going before, preceding

an-te-lope [ăn′tl-ōp′] *noun*, a wild animal, similar to a deer, which runs fast and usually has antlers

an-ten-na [ăn-tĕn′ə] *noun*, *plural*, **antennae**, 1) the sensory organ of an insect or crustacean 2) wire supported in the air for directly transmitting and receiving electromagnetic waves

an-them [ăn′thəm] *noun*, a song or hymn of praise

an-thro-po-log-ist [ăn′thrə-pŏl′ə-jĭst] *noun*, a student of the history and science of mankind

an-thro-po-mor-phic [ăn′thrə-pə-môr′-fĭk] *adjective*, having human form or characteristics

an-ti-bi-ot-ic [ăn′tĭ-bī-ŏt′ĭk] *noun*, a substance such as penicillin, effective in fighting destructive microorganisms and used for treatment of diseases

an-tic-i-pate [ăn-tĭs′ə-pāt′] *verb*, to look forward to

an-ti-dote [ăn′tĭ-dōt′] *noun*, 1) a remedy to counteract poison 2) anything that counteracts evil

an-tip-a-thy [ăn-tĭp′ə-thē] *noun*, a strong dislike, a natural aversion

an-ti-quat-ed [ăn′tĭ-kwā′tĭd] *adjective*, old-fashioned, obsolete

an-tique [ăn-tēk′] *adjective*, 1) old-fashioned, from another time, *noun*, 2) something made long ago and valued for its age

an-ti-sep-tic [ăn′tĭ-sĕp′tĭk] *adjective*, 1) clean, sterile, *noun*, 2) a substance that tends to prevent harmful effects of bacteria growth

an-tith-e-sis [ăn-tĭth′ĭ-sĭs] *noun*, the exact opposite

ant-ler [ănt′lər] *noun*, one of a pair of branched horns on the head of a deer

an-to-nym [ăn′tə-nĭm′] *noun*, a word that has the opposite meaning to another

anx-i-e-ty [ăng-zī′ĭ-tē] *noun*, uneasiness of mind, concern about future events

anx-ious [ăngk′shəs] *adjective*, worried, concerned, nervous

any [ĕn′ē] *adjective*, 1) some, an uncertain number, quantity, volume or degree 2) every 3) one

an-y-bod-y [ĕn′ē-bŏd′ē] *pronoun*, any person

an-y-one [ĕn′ē-wŭn′] *pronoun*, anybody

an-y-thing [ĕn′ē-thĭng′] *noun*, something

an-y-way [ĕn′ē-wā′] *adverb*, 1) no matter what happens, in any case, 2) haphazardly, in any fashion

an-y-where [ĕn′ē-hwâr′] *adverb*, in, at, or to any place

a-part [ə-pärt′] *adverb*, separately in place or time

a-part-ment [ə-pärt′mənt] *noun*, rooms or a part of a building where someone lives

ap-a-thy [ăp′ə-thē] *noun*, lack of interest or concern

ape [āp] *noun*, 1) a large mammal similar to a monkey without a tail, for example, a gorilla, chimpanzee, etc., *verb*, 2) to copy, to imitate

aph-o-rism [ăf′ə-rĭz′əm] *noun*, a statement of truth, an adage

a-poc-a-lyp-tic [ə-pŏk′ə-lĭp′tĭk] *adjective*, prophetic, pertaining to revelations about the end of the world

a-pol-o-gize [ə-pŏl′ə-jīz′] *verb*, to say you're sorry for what you have done, to express regret

a-pol-o-gy [ə-pŏl′ə-jē] *noun*, an explanation by way of asking for forgiveness

a-pos-tle [ə-pŏs′əl] *noun*, any person zealously advocating a cause

a-pos-tro-phe [ə-pŏs′trə-fē] *noun*, a mark (') used to indicate an omission of a letter, i.e. *I'll*, or letters, or to denote the possessive case i.e. *Kara's*

ap-o-thegm [ăp′ə-thĕm′] *noun*, a pithy, compact saying, a proverb

a-poth-e-o-sis [ə-pŏth′ē-ō′sĭs] *noun*, deification, glorification, making into a god

ap-pall [ə-pôl'] *verb*, to fill with horror or dismay, to shock

ap-pa-rat-us [ăp'ə-ră'təs] *noun*, equipment, a collection or set of implements for a specific purpose

ap-par-el [ə-păr'əl] *noun*, clothing, garments

ap-par-ent [ə-păr'ənt] *adjective*, capable of seeming or appearing to be evident, easily understood

ap-par-ent-ly [ə-păr'ənt] *adverb*, clearly, evidently, obviously

ap-pa-ri-tion [ăp'ə-rĭsh'ən] *noun*, a ghost, a phantom

ap-peal [ə-pēl'] *noun*, 1) the proceeding by which a case is brought to a superior court for reexamination or review 2) a request, *verb*, 3) to plead, to ask urgently 4) to seem attractive

ap-pear [ə-pîr'] *verb*, 1) to come into view unexpectedly 2) to seem to be

ap-pear-ance [ə-pîr'əns] *noun*, 1) the act of appearing or becoming visible 2) the way something or someone looks

ap-pease [ə-pēz'] *verb*, to satisfy or often by granting demands

ap-pel-lant [ə-pĕl'ənt] *noun*, one who asks for a judicial decree

ap-pel-la-tion [ăp'ə-lā'shən] *noun*, a name or title

ap-pen-di-ci-tis [ə-pĕn'dĭ-sī'tĭs] *noun*, inflammation of the appendix

ap-pen-dix [ə-pĕn'dĭks] *noun*, 1) information added to a section at the end of a book 2) a small tube-like part growing out from the intestine

ap-pe-tite [ăp'ĭ-tīt'] *noun*, craving, the desire for food

ap-plaud [ə-plôd'] *verb*, to show approval especially by clapping hands together in praise

ap-plause [ə-plôz'] *noun*, praise for someone, usually expressed by clapping hands

ap-ple [ăp'əl] *noun*, the firm-fleshed, round, juicy fruit of an apple tree

ap-pli-ance [ə-plī'əns] *noun*, an apparatus or device, a machine

ap-pli-ca-ble [ăp'lĭ-kə-bəl] *adjective*, relevant, appropriate

ap-plic-ant [ăp'lĭ-kənt] *noun*, one who makes a request, a petitioner

ap-pli-ca-tion [ăp'lĭ-kā'shən] *noun*, 1) work or effort 2) a use 3) a form used to make a request

ap-pli-que [ăp'lĭ-kā'] *noun*, ornamental patterns put on textiles

ap-ply [ə-plī'] *verb*, 1) to seek or ask 2) to put on 3) to pertain to

ap-point [ə-point'] *verb*, to choose for a job

ap-point-ment [ə-point'mənt] *noun*, 1) a meeting, a date, a rendezvous 2) a selection, a nomination

ap-prais-al [ə-prā'zəl] *noun*, value or worth, assessment

ap-praise [ə-prāz'] *verb*, to evaluate something to establish its worth

ap-pre-ci-ate [ə-prē'shē-āt'] *verb*, 1) to recognize the value of something, 2) to increase in value

ap-pre-ci-a-tion [ə-prē'shē-ā'shən] *noun*, grateful recognition

ap-pre-hend [ăp'rĭ-hĕnd'] *verb*, 1) to arrest a criminal 2) to anticipate

with anxiety, dread, or, fear,
3) to understand

ap-pre-hen-sion [ăp'rĭ-hĕn'shən]
noun, 1) the ability to understand
2) fear, anxiety, dread

ap-pren-tice [ə-prĕn'tĭs] *noun*, a
novice or learner who works with
a master to learn a skill

ap-prise [ə-prīz'] *verb*, to give notice
to, to inform

ap-proach [ə-prōch'] *noun*, 1) a way
of dealing with something, 2) the
way that leads to a place, *verb*, 3)
to move toward

ap-proach-able [ə-prō'chə-bəl]
adjective, friendly, easy to talk to

ap-pro-pri-ate [ə-prō'prē-ĭt]
adjective, 1) suitable, proper, [ə-
prō'prē-āt]*verb*, 2) to allocate, to
set aside for a purpose

ap-pro-pri-a-tion [ə-prō'prē-ā'shən]
noun, a setting apart for a
particular purpose

ap-prov-al [ə-prōō'vəl] *noun*,
1) praise, 2) the go-ahead or okay
to proceed, permission

ap-prove [ə-prōōv'] *verb*, to say that
something is favorable

ap-prox-i-mate [ə-prŏk'sə-mĭt]
adjective, 1) almost accurate or
exact, near, [ə-prŏk'sə-māt]*verb*,
2) to estimate or guess

ap-prox-i-mate-ly [ə-prŏk'sə-mĭt-lē]
adverb, closely, nearly

ap-pur-te-nance [ə-pûr'tn-əns]
noun, something connected but
not as important, accessory

A-pril [ā'prəl] *noun*, the fourth
month of the year, having 30 days

a-pron [ā'prən] *noun*, a cover worn
over the front of one's clothing to
protect it

ap-ro-pos [ăp'rə-pō'] *adjective*,
appropriate, pertinent

apt [ăpt] *adjective*, 1) suited to,
fitting, 2) likely or almost certain

ap-ti-tude [ăp'tĭ-tōōd'] *noun*, natural
ability, fitness, talent

a-quar-i-um [ə-kwâr'ē-əm] *noun*, a
container, usually with glass sides,
to keep animals or plants in water

a-quat-ic [ə-kwăt'ĭk] *adjective*,
occurring on or in the water

aq-ue-duct [ăk'wĭ-dŭkt'] *noun*, a
passage used to bring water from
a distant source

aq-ui-fer [ăk'wə-fər] *noun*, an
underground geologic formation
in which the cracks in rock, sand,
soil, or gravel are filled with water

Ar-ab [ăr'ə-b] 1) an inhabitant of
Arabia, 2) any of a Semitic people
originating in Arabia

Ar-a-bic [ăr'ə-bĭk] *adjective*, 1)
relating to the Arab language and
culture, *noun*, 2) the Semitic
language of the Arabs

ar-a-ble [ăr'ə-bəl] *adjective*, suitable
to be used for growing crops

ar-bi-ter [är'bĭ-tər] *noun*, a judge, an
umpire or referee, a mediator

ar-bi-trar-y [är'bĭ-trĕr'ē] *adjective*,
chosen without any qualifications

ar-bi-tra-tion [är'bĭ-trā'shən] *noun*,
the hearing and determination of a
matter in dispute by a third party

ar-bor [är'bər] *noun*, a place shaded
by trees or shrubs

ar-bo-re-tum [är'bər 'ē-təm] *noun,* a
botanical garden devoted to trees

arc [ärk] *noun*, a segment of a circle,
a curve in an arch

ar-cade[är'kād]*noun*, a covered walk
with stores along one or both sides

arch [ärch] *noun*, a curved part of a structure sometimes supporting weight above it, as in bridges, doorways, etc

ar-chae-ol-o-gist [är'kē-ŏl'ə-jĭst] *noun*, an expert in the study of past civilizations and ancient cultures, mainly through digging up remains

ar-chae-ol-o-gy [är'kē-ŏl'ə-jē] *noun*, the study of ancient things made by man from an earlier civilization

ar-cha-ic [är-kā'ĭk] *adjective*, antiquated, ancient, very old

arch-bish-op [ärch-bĭsh'əp] *noun*, the chief bishop in the Christian church

ar-cher-y [är'chə-rē] *noun*, the practice or art of shooting with a bow and arrow

ar-chi-pel-a-go [är'kə-pĕl'ə-gō'] *noun*, a group or chain of islands

ar-chi-tect [är'kĭ-tĕkt'] *noun*, one who draws plans and specifications for buildings

ar-chi-tec-ture [är'kĭ-tĕk'chər] *noun*, the art and study of building design and structure

ar-chive [är'kīv'] *noun*, a place in which public records and historic documents are kept

arc-tic [ärk'tĭk, är'tĭk] *adjective*, relating to the area around the North Pole

ar-dent [är'dnt] *adjective*, zealous, passionate, very excited

ar-dor [är'dər] *noun*, passion, zeal, enthusiasm, great excitement

ar-du-ous [är'jōō-əs] *adjective*, difficult, attended with great labor or exertion, strenuous

are [är] *verb*, the part of the *verb* is used with we, you and they

ar-e-a [âr'ē-ə] *noun*, 1) a location or vicinity, 2) a surface measured by multiplying the width times the length

a-re-na [ə-rē'nə] *noun*, a playing field or a stadium surrounded by seats used for sports or entertainment

aren't [ärnt, är'ənt] the *contraction*, for the two words **are** and **not**

ar-gon [är'gŏn'] *noun*, one of the noble gases, a colorless, odorless, inert gas

ar-gue [är'gyōō] *verb*, to fight by using words, to disagree, to debate, to dispute

ar-gu-ment [är'gyə-mənt] *noun*, a disagreement, a dispute

ar-id [är'ĭd] *adjective*, dry, parched, dusty

a-rise [ə-rīz'] *verb*, to come up, to issue, to spring forth, to get up

a-ris-to-crat [ə-rĭs'tə-krăt'] *noun*, a man or woman of fashion, a member of the nobility

a-rith-me-tic [ə-rĭth'mĭ-tĭk] *noun*, the science of numbers

Ar-i-zo-na [ăr'ĭ-zō'nə] *noun*, one of the 50 United States, located in the Southwest, the capital is Phoenix. The state flower of **Arizona** is the blossom of the saguaro cactus and the motto is "God enriches."

ark [ärk] *noun*, a large flat-bottomed ship

Ar-kan-sas [är'kən-sô'] *noun*, a state in the southern part of the United States, the capital is Little Rock. The **Arkansas** state flower is the apple blossom and the motto is "The people rule."

arm [ärm] *noun*, 1) the part of the body between the shoulder and the hand, *verb*, 2) to provide with weapons, to prepare for combat

ar-ma-ments [är′mə-mənts] *noun*, *plural*, military forces and weapons

ar-mi-stice [är′mĭ-stĭs] *noun*, a treaty of peace, a truce

ar-mor [är′mər] *noun*, a covering of metal worn by soldiers for protection

ar-mor-y [är′mə-rē] *noun*, a military storehouse

arms [ärmz] *noun*, *plural*, weapons, such as bombs and guns

ar-my [är′mē] *noun*, a large number of soldiers training for war on land, ground troops

a-ro-ma [ə-rō′mə] *noun*, smell, scent, fragrance

a-round [ə-round′] *adverb*, 1) in a circle, surrounding all sides, 2) nearby 3) approximately, *preposition*, 4) on every side

a-rouse [ə-rouz′] *verb*, 1) to awaken, to animate, to coax 2) to excite, to provoke, to stimulate

ar-raign [ə-rān′] *verb*, to call to account, to bring into court to answer charges, to accuse publicly

ar-range [ə-rānj′] *verb*, to put in proper order or sequence

ar-range-ment [ə-rānj′mənt] *noun*, 1) the act of putting in an orderly condition 2) a plan

ar-ray [ə-rā′] *noun*, 1) a display, an exhibition, *verb*, 2) to arrange in a display, to place, to order

ar-rest [ə-rĕst′] *noun*, 1) the act of taking someone into custody, *verb*, 2) to stop the movement or progress of 3) to seize by legal

authority and charge with breaking the law

ar-ri-val [ə-rī′vəl] *noun*, the moment when a place or object is reached

ar-rive [ə-rīv′] *verb*, to reach a destination or a goal

ar-ro-gance [ăr′ə-gəns] *noun*, an overbearing sense of self-importance. excessive pride

ar-ro-gant [ăr′ə-gənt] *adjective*, having a high opinion of oneself

ar-row [ăr′ō] *noun*, 1) a pointed stick that is shot from a bow 2) a mark shaped like an arrow that shows direction

ar-se-nal [är′sə-nəl] *noun*, a collection of weapons, a storehouse of ammunition

ar-son [är′sən] *noun*, the crime of purposely setting property on fire

art [ärt] *noun*, the creation of beautiful or significant things through music, drawing, painting, sculpture, cooking, dancing, etc.

art-ful [ärt′fəl] *adjective*, a clever or skillful person or action, typically in a crafty or cunning way

ar-ter-y [är′tə-rē] *noun*, the thick blood vessels that carry blood from the heart

ar-te-sian well [är-tē′zhən] *noun*, a well that taps ground water that is under pressure and therefore does not require a pump, so called from Artois, France

ar-thri-tis [är-thrī′tĭs] *noun*, inflammation of the joints

ar-ti-cle [är′tĭ-kəl] *noun*, 1) a particular thing 2) a section, provision, item 3) a brief written composition, as in a newspaper or magazine 4) one of the limiting articles, *a*, *an*, or *the*

ar-tic-u-late [är-tĭk′yə-lĭt]
adjective, 1) effective, distinct,
able to express ideas clearly, [är-
tĭk′yə-lāt] *verb*, 2) to speak
clearly to express an idea

ar-ti-fact [är′tə-făkt′] *noun*,
something made by humans
from an earlier civilization

ar-ti-fice [är′tə-fĭs] *noun*, skill,
scheme, ability, trick

ar-ti-fi-cial [är′tə-fĭsh′əl] *adjective*,
1) made of or contrived by art
2) not natural, not made by
nature, made by humans 3)
assumed, affected

ar-t-il-ler-y [är-tĭl′ə-rē] *noun*, the
mounted guns in an army, the
soldiers in charge of such guns

art-ist [är′tĭst] *noun*, a person
skilled in the techniques of the
fine arts, such as painting,
dancing, drama, etc.

as [ăz] *conjunction*, 1) when, while
2) because, *preposition*, 3) in
such a way, like

ascend [ə-sĕnd′] *verb*, to climb, to
go upward, to rise

as-cen-sion [ə-sĕn′shən] *noun*, the
act of going up, a rising

as-cent [ə-sĕnt′] *noun*, the act of
climbing up an incline, a slope

as-cer-tain [ăs′ər-tān′] *verb*, to
determine, to establish

as-cet-ic [ə-sĕt′ĭk] *adjective*, self-
denying, austere, disciplined

ash [ăsh] *noun*, 1) the gray powder
residue left after something has
burned 2) a tree of the olive
family, with hard wood

a-shamed [ə-shāmd′] *adjective*,
upset because you have done

something that you think is silly,
not good enough or wrong,
embarrassed, feeling inadequate

a-shore [ə-shôr′] *adverb*, on to land

A-sia [ā′zhə] *noun*, one of the
seven continents in the world,
holding 57% of the population

a-side [ə-sīd′] *adverb*, 1) to or
toward one side, away, *noun*,
2) departure from the main topic,
3) a whisper

ask [ăsk] *verb*, 1) to pose or speak
a question, to inquire 2) to
request something

a-skew [ə-skyoō′] *adjective*, out of
line, crooked

a-sleep [ə-slēp′] *adjective*,
sleeping, not awake

as-pect [ăs′pĕkt] *noun*,
1) appearance, look 2) part, or
point of view

as-phalt [ăs′fôlt′] *noun*, a tar like
material mixed with sand or
gravel for highway surfaces or
pavement,

as-phyx-i-a-tion [ăs-fĭk′sē-ā′-shən]
noun, death by lack of oxygen

as-pi-ra-tion [ăs′pə-rā′shən] *noun*,
an ambition, a strong desire

as-pire [ə-spīr′] *verb*, to desire, to
strive, to hope for

as-pi-rin [ăs′pər-ĭn, -prĭn] *noun*, a
medicine used to relieve pain,
acetylsalicylic acid

as-sas-si-nate [ə-săs′ə-nāt′] *verb*,
to murder a public official or
other important person

as-sault [ə-sôlt′] *noun*, 1) an attack,
verb, 2) to strike, to hit

as-sem-ble [ə-sĕm′bəl] *verb*, to
gather or put together

as-sem-bly [ə-sĕm′blē] *noun*, 1) a gathering, for educational, religious, or entertainment programs of students and teachers 2) a legal body such as Congress or a legislature

as-sert [ə-sûrt′] *verb*, to declare, to state forcefully

as-sess [ə-sĕs′] *verb*, to evaluate

as-sess-ment [ə-sĕs′mənt] *noun*, an appraisal, an estimation

as-set [ăs′ĕt′] *noun*, something of value or worth

as-sign [ə-sīn′] *verb*, 1) to give out or allot 2) to delegate a task

as-sign-ment [ə-sīn′mənt] *noun*, homework, an obligation, work given to someone to accomplish

as-sim-i-late [ə-sĭm′ə-lāt′] *verb*, to take in food or knowledge, to make part of oneself

as-sist [ə-sĭst′] *verb*, to aid or help

as-sis-tance [ə-sĭs′təns] *noun*, help or aid given

as-sis-tant [ə-sĭs′tənt] *noun*, a helper, an aide, a subordinate,

as-so-ci-ate *noun*, [ə-sō′shē-ĭt] 1) a colleague or co-worker, [ə-sō′shē-āt′] *verb*, 2) to think of something in relation with something else 3) to keep company, to socialize with someone

as-so-ci-a-tion [ə-sō′sē-ā′shən,] *noun*, a group of people joined together for one purpose

as-sort-ment [ə-sôrt′mənt] *noun*, a variety of things

as-suage [ə-swāj′] *verb*, to lessen, to ease, to comfort

as-sume [ə-sōōm′] *verb*, to think something is true without proof

as-sump-tion [ə-sŭmp′shən] *noun*, something taken for granted

as-sur-ance [ə-shōōr′əns] *noun*, a promise, a pledge

as-sure [ə-shōōr′] *verb*, to tell someone firmly, to promise

as-ter-isk [ăs′tə-rĭsk′] *noun*, the sign *

as-ter-oid [ăs′tə-roid′] *noun*, small planets, most of which are located between Mars and Jupiter, that revolve around the sun

asth-ma [ăz′mə] *noun*, a respiratory disorder that causes difficulty in breathing accompanied by wheezing

a-stig-ma-tism [ə-stĭg′mə-tĭz′əm] *noun*, an eye defect that prevents proper focus

as-ton-ish [ə-stŏn′ĭsh] *verb*, to give a feeling of surprise, amaze

as-ton-ish-ment [ə-stŏn′ĭsh-mənt] *noun*, complete surprise, amazement

as-tound [ə-stound′] *verb*, to amaze, to shock, to surprise

as-tral [ăs′trəl] *adjective*, relating to the stars

a-stray [ə-strā′] *adverb*, off course, in error

as-trin-gent [ə-strĭn′jənt] *adjective*, capable of drawing tissue together

as-tro-naut [ăs′trə-nôt′] *noun*, a person who travels in space

as-trol-o-gy [ə-strŏl′ə-jē] *noun*, the study of the assumed influence of planets and stars on the course of human affairs

as-tron-o-mer [ə-strŏn′ə-mər] *noun*, a person who studies the stars and the heavens

as-tro-nom-i-cal [ăs′trə-nŏm′ĭ-kəl] *adjective*, enormously large or extensive, huge

as-tron-o-my [ə-strŏn′ə-mē] *noun*, the study of the sun, moon, stars, and the heavens

as-tute [ə-stoōt′] *adjective*, having a clever, shrewd, or cunning mind, perceptive, insightful

a-sy-lum [ə-sī′ləm] *noun*, protection from persecution

at [ăt] *preposition*, 1) showing where 2) showing when 3) showing how much

ate [āt] *verb*, the *past tense* of **eat**

a-the-ism [ā′thē-ĭz′əm] *noun*, the belief that there is no God

ath-lete [ăth′lēt′] *noun*, someone who is good at sports

ath-let-ic [ăth-lĕt′ĭk] *adjective*, strong, vigorous, having to do with sports

at-las [ăt′ləs] *noun*, a book or section of a book that has maps

at-mos-phere [ăt′mə-sfîr′] *noun*, 1) the mass of air surrounding the earth 2) the mood or feeling of a place, a tone conveyed

at-om [ăt′əm] *noun*, the smallest particle of an element

a-tom-ic [ə-tŏm′ĭk] *adjective*, tiny, infinitesimal, having to do with atoms

at-om-iz-er [ăt′ə-mī′zər] *noun*, an instrument for reducing a liquid to a fine spray

a-tri-um [ā′trē-əm] *noun*, **atria** or **atriums**, *plural*, 1) one of the chambers of the heart 2) the central court in a Roman building

a-tro-cious [ə-trō′shəs] *adjective*, very bad, outrageously cruel

a-troc-i-ty [ə-trŏs′ĭ-tē] *noun*, a brutal deed, a cruel act

a-tro-phy [ăt′rə-fē] *verb*, to stop the development of an organ, to wither from lack of use

at-tach [ə-tăch′] *verb*, 1) to connect something with something else 2) to feel affection toward someone 3) to ascribe

at-tach-ment [ə-tăch′mənt] *noun*, 1) an affection, fondness 2) an additional part for a machine

at-tack [ə-tăk′] *noun*, 1) fight, an attempt to harm someone, *verb*, 2) to assail, to try to injure someone, to assault

at-tain [ə-tān′] *verb*, to succeed in getting something done, to reach a goal

at-tempt [ə-tĕmpt′] *noun*, 1) a try, an endeavor, *verb*, 2) to try, to endeavor, to make an effort

at-tend [ə-tĕnd′] *verb*, 1) to be present at 2) to take care of 3) to pay attention to

at-tend-ance [ə-tĕn′dəns] *noun*, the act of showing up or putting in an appearance, presence

at-tend-ant [ə-tĕn′dənt] *noun*, one who accompanies or attends, as a companion, a servant

at-ten-tion [ə-tĕn′shən] *noun*, application of the mind to something, concentration

at-ten-tive [ə-tĕn′tĭv] *adjective*, careful to notice little things

at-tic [ăt′ĭk] *noun*, the top floor of a house, right under the roof

at-tire [ə-tīr′] *noun*, anything that dresses or adorns, clothing

at-ti-tude [ăt′ĭ-tōod′] *noun*, a mood or feeling, a way of thinking

at-tor-ney [ə-tûr′nē] *noun*, one legally authorized to act for another, a lawyer

at-tract [ə-trăkt′] *verb*, 1) to draw the attention of someone or something 2) to cause someone or something to come near

at-trac-tion [ə-trăk′shən] *noun*, 1) the power to bring things together 2) a fascination that holds someone's attention

at-trac-tive [ə-trăk′tĭv] *adjective*, pleasing to look at, appealing

at-trib-ute *noun*, [ə-trăb′yŏot] 1) a distinguishing feature that belongs to someone, [ətrĭb′yŏot] *verb*, 2) to explain how one thing is associated with another

at-tri-tion [ə-trĭsh′ən] *noun*, a gradual wearing down

auc-tion [ôk′shən] *noun*, a public sale at which buyers bid on items to be sold

auc-tion-eer [ôk′shə-nîr′] *noun*, one licensed to hold a public sale at which items go to the highest bidder

au-dac-i-ty [ô-dăs′ĭ-tē] *noun*, impertinence, boldness, self-assurance, daring

au-di-ble [ô′də-bəl] *adjective*, capable of being heard

au-di-ence [ô′dē-əns] *noun*, 1) a group gathered to watch or listen to a performance 2) a formal hearing

au-di-o [ô′dē-ō′] *adjective*, relating to sound or sound reproduction

au-dit [ô′dĭt] *noun*, 1) a special examination of accounting records, *verb*, 2) to examine or investigate, to evaluate

au-di-tion [ô-dĭsh′ən] *noun*, a tryout for a performance

au-di-to-ri-um [ô′dĭ-tôr′ē-əm] *noun*, an assembly hall with a stage and seats

au-ger [ô′gər] *noun*, a tool for making holes, a drill

aug-ment [ôg-mĕnt′] *verb*, to make larger, to increase, to add on to

au-gur [ô′gər] *verb*, to foretell, to see into the future, to portend, to be an omen

Au-gust [ô′gəst] *noun*, the eighth month of the year, having 31 days

aunt [ănt, änt] *noun*, the sister of one of your parents or the wife of the brother of one parent

aus-pices [ô′spĭ-sēz′] *noun, plural*, 1) patronage, protection 2) omens

aus-pi-cious [ô-spĭsh′əs] *adjective*, fortunate, showing signs that promise success

aus-tere [ô-stîr′] *adjective*, 1) severe or strict in judging, harsh, rough or bitter acting, 2) very plain, simple, bare, ascetic

Aus-tra-lia [ô-strāl′yə] *noun*, one of the seven continents in the world, the only continent that is also a country containing .5% of the world's population

au-then-tic [ô-thĕn′tĭk] *adjective*, genuine, known to be true

au-then-ti-cate [ô-thĕn′tĭ-kāt′] *verb*, to prove genuine

au-thor [ô′thər] *noun*, a person who writes books, articles, etc.

au-thor-i-ta-tive [ə-thôr′ĭ-tā′tĭv] *adjective*, reliably accurate

au-thor-i-ty [ə-thôr′ĭ-tē] *noun*, 1) a person who runs something or controls it 2) command, prestige, influence, control 3) an expert

au-thor-ize [ô′thə-rīz′] *verb*, 1) to empower 2) to make legal 3) to give permission to act

au-to-bi-og-ra-phy [ô′tō-bī-ŏg′rə-fē] *noun*, a story written about the author's life

au-to-crat [ô′tə-krăt′] *noun*, a ruler with supreme power

au-to-graph [ô′tə-grăf′] *noun*, a person's signature

au-to-mat-ic [ô′tə-măt′ĭk] *adjective*, acting mechanically without human direction

au-to-mat-i-cal-ly [ô′tə-măt′ĭk-lē] *adverb*, 1) by a machine 2) without trying or thinking first

au-tom-a-tion [ô′tə-mā′shən] *noun*, a machine that imitates the actions of humans, a robot

au-to-mo-bile [ô′tə-mō-bēl′] *noun*, a vehicle on wheels, powered by an engine to transport people on roads, a car

au-ton-o-mous [ô-tŏn′ə-məs] *adjective*, self-governing, acting independently from government

au-top-sy [ô′tŏp′sē] *noun*, the dissection of a dead body to determine the cause of death

au-tumn [ô′təm] *noun*, the third season of each year, between summer and winter, September 22-December 21, known as fall

aux-il-ia-ry [ôg-zĭl′yə-rē] *adjective*, additional, serving alongside another, supporting

a-vail-a-ble [ə-vā′lə-bəl] *adjective*, capable of being used, accessible

av-a-lanche [ăv′ə-lănch′] *noun*, a large overwhelming quantity of snow, rocks, or mud that falls from a mountain suddenly, gaining size as it falls

av-a-rice [ăv′ə-rĭs] *noun*, greed for money or power

a-venge [ə-vĕnj′] *verb*, to punish in kind, to retaliate, to get even

av-e-nue [ăv′ə-nōō′] *noun*, a wide road, often with many roads intersecting at right angles

av-er-age [ăv′ər-ĭj] *adjective*, 1) ordinary, usual, typical, *noun*, 2) the mean value of a set of numbers, *verb*, 3) to find the mean

a-ver-sion [ə-vûr′zhən] *noun*, a dislike, antipathy, opposition

a-vert [ə-vûrt′] *verb*, to avoid, to prevent or turn away

a-vi-a-tion [ā′vē-ā′shən, ăv′ē-] *noun*, air transportation

a-vi-a-tor [ā′vē-ā′tər] *noun*, an airplane or helicopter pilot

av-id [ăv′ĭd] *adjective*, eager, enthusiastic, excited

av-o-ca-tion [ăv′ō-kā′shən] *noun*, a hobby

a-void [ə-void′] *verb*, to stay away from, to evade, to shun

a-wait [ə-wāt′] *verb*, to expect, to wait, to anticipate

a-wake [ə-wāk′] *adjective*, not sleeping, alert

a-ward [ə-wôrd′] *noun*, 1) a prize or an honor to recognize exceptional service, achievement, etc., *verb*, 2) to present a certificate or plaque or trophy in recognition of an honor

a-ware [ə-wâr′] *adjective*, knowing, conscious, informed

a-way [ə-wā′] *adverb*, 1) off in a different direction 2) from one's possession

awe [ô] *noun*, a solemn wonder

aw-ful [ô′fəl] *adjective*, very bad, appalling, frightful, horrible

awk-ward [ôk′wərd] *adjective*, 1) clumsy, ungraceful 2) embarrassing

awl [ôl] *noun*, a pointed tool used to make holes in wood or leather

awn-ing [ô′nĭng] *noun*, a sunshade, a canvas covering for a porch, patio, deck, etc.

a-wry [ə-rī′] *adjective*, 1) amiss, crooked, wrong, *adverb*, 2) distorted, twisted to one side

ax or axe [ăks] *noun*, a tool with a metal blade fixed onto a handle, used for chopping

ax-i-om [ăk′sē-əm] *noun*, a self-evident truth or principle

ax-is [ăk′sĭs] *noun*, a real or imaginary line around which something rotates

ax-le [ăk′səl] *noun*, the rod on which a wheel revolves

B

ba-by [bā′bē] *noun*, an infant, a very young child or animal

bach-e-lor [băch′ə-lər] *noun*, a man who has never been married

back [băk] *adverb*, 1) to or in a place where something or someone was before 2) toward the back part, away from the front, *noun*, 3) the part of the body opposite the face, extending from the neck to the hips, *verb*, 4) to move in the opposite direction from 5) to give support to

back-ground [băk′ground′] *noun*, 1) the surroundings behind something 2) past experience, culture

back-ward [băk′wərd] *adjective*, 1) having the part designed for the back in the front 2) following tradition and resisting progress, *adverb*, 3) in reverse 4) beginning at the end

ba-con [bā′kən] *noun*, meat from the back and sides of a pig, salted and smoked

bac-te-ri-um [băk-tîr′ē-əm] *noun*, **bacteria**, *plural*, a single-celled living thing that cannot be seen without a microscope, reproducing rapidly and sometimes causing diseases

bad [băd] *adjective*, 1) not good, rotten 2) severe, unpleasant

badge [băj] *noun*, a pin or emblem worn to show authority or accomplishment

baf-fle [băf′əl] *verb*, to mix up, to confuse, to puzzle

bag [băg] *noun*, a container made of paper, cloth, plastic, or leather that has an opening at the top or in the side

bag-gage [băg'ĭj] *noun*, *no plural*, suitcases, bags, or trunks one takes along on a journey

bail [bāl] *noun*, 1) a bond or pledge backed with money or property, *verb*, 2) to ladle or empty out

bail-iff [bā'lĭf] *noun*, an official who keeps order in the court

bait [bāt] *noun*, 1) food used to lure or entice fish or animals, *verb*, 2) to annoy or taunt

bake [bāk] *verb*, to cook by dry heat, usually in an oven

bak-er [bā'kər] *noun*, someone who makes pastries, cakes and breads for a living

bak-er-y [bā'kə-rē] *noun*, a place where pastries, cakes, and breads are made and sold

bal-ance [băl'əns] *noun*, 1) steadiness 2) an instrument used to weigh something 3) the difference between the debits and credits of an account, *verb*, 4) to keep oneself steady 5) to make equal and stable, to compensate for

bal-co-ny [băl'kə-nē] *noun*, a porch outside of a building and above the first floor

bald [bôld] *adjective*, having no hair

bale [bāl] *noun*, 1) a large amount of materials bundled tightly together, *verb*, 2) to bundle into a package

balk [bôk] *verb*, 1) to hesitate, to refuse to act 2) to hinder

ball [bôl] *noun*, 1) a round object used in games or as a toy 2) a large party for dancing

bal-lad [băl'əd] *noun*, a poem or song that tells a story

bal-last [băl'əst] *noun*, 1) heavy material carried by a ship to balance it 2) crushed stones

bal-let [bă-lā'] *noun*, a play without speech in which the story is told through dance

bal-loon [bə-loon'] *noun*, a rubber bag that expands as it is filled with air or gas

bal-lot [băl'ət] *noun*, 1) a printed ticket used in voting to make a choice 2) the whole vote cast

balm [bäm] *noun*, 1) something that relieves pain 2) a soothing ointment

balm-y [bä'mē] *adjective*, mild, refreshing, soft and warm

bam-boo [băm-boo'] *noun*, a woody grass with hollow stems, abundant in the tropics

ban [băn] *noun*, 1) an order that does not allow something, *verb*, 2) to not allow something or to prevent it from taking place

ba-nal [bə-năl', bā'nəl] *adjective*, ordinary, commonplace, trite

ba-nan-a [bə-năn'ə] *noun*, a long yellow tropical fruit having a tasty soft pulp

band [bănd] *noun*, 1) a group of musicians who get together to play their instruments, usually brass, percussion, and woodwinds 2) a strip of something 3) a group 4) a piece that wraps around something, *verb*, 5) to join together

band-age [băn′dĭj] *noun*, 1) a piece of cloth or adhesive strip put over a wound, *verb*, 2) to cover a wound with a cloth or adhesive strip

ban-dan-na [băn-dăn′ə] *noun*, a cotton scarf or handkerchief

ban-dit [băn′dĭt] *noun*, a robber

ban-dy [băn′dē] *verb*, to exchange, to pass to and fro

bane [bān] *noun*, the cause of ruin

bane-ful [bān′fəl] *adjective*, ruinous, having poisonous qualities, causing misery

bang [băng] *noun*, 1) a startling loud sound, *verb*, 2) to produce a loud sound by striking one thing against another

ban-ish [băn′ĭsh] *verb*, 1) to send away, to dismiss 2)2 to exile as a form of punishment

ban-is-ter [băn′ĭ-stər] *noun*, a railing that guards the edges of stairs to prevent someone from falling

ban-jo [băn′jō] *noun*, a stringed musical instrument, like a ukulele or guitar, but with a circular sound box

bank [băngk] *noun*, 1) the land along a body of water, the side of a hill 2) a commercial institution where money is kept and loaned

bank-er [băng′kər] *noun*, one who conducts the business of a bank

bank-rupt [băngk′rŭpt] *adjective*, broke, out of business

ban-ner [băn′ər] *noun*, a flag, a cloth bearing an emblem

ban-quet [băng′kwĭt] *noun*, a feast or ceremonious dinner

ban-ter [băn′tər] *noun*, 1) good-natured ridiculing or teasing 2) to speak or to address in a witty or teasing manner

bap-tism [băp′tĭz′əm] *noun*, the ceremony of initiation into Christianity

bap-tize [băp-tīz′] *verb*, to sprinkle someone with holy water and bestow a name

bar [bär] *noun*, 1) a counter where drinks are sold 2) a long solid object made of wood or metal 3) the legal profession, *verb*, 4) to exclude or block

barb [bärb] *noun*, the sharp projections from a fishhook, arrow, etc.

bar-ber [bär′bər] *noun*, a person who cuts men's hair

bare [bâr] *adjective*, 1) uncovered, naked 2) unadorned, empty

bare-ly [bâr′lē] *adverb*, almost, not, hardly, only, scarcely

bar-gain [bär′gĭn] *noun*, 1) something bought at a lower price than expected 2) an agreement or compact between two parties, *verb*, 3) to haggle for a lower price

barge [bärj] *noun*, a large boat with a flat bottom, used to carry things on a river or a canal

bar-i-um [bâr′ē-əm] *noun*, one of the elements of the alkaline earth group

bark [bärk] *noun*, 1) the outer covering of a tree trunk and branches 2) a sound made by a

dog or a brusque voice, *verb*,
3) to speak like a dog

bar-ley [bär′lē] *noun*, one of the
cereal grains

barn [bärn] *noun*, a farm building
where animals and harvested
crops are kept

bar-na-cle [bär′nə-kəl] *noun*, a
marine crustacean that attaches
itself to rocks and boats

ba-rom-e-ter [bə-rŏm′ĭ-tər] *noun*,
a device that measures air
pressure in the atmosphere

bar-on [băr′ən] *noun*, a nobleman,
an aristocrat, a tycoon

ba-roque [bə-rōk′] *adjective*, an
ornate style of the 17ᵗʰ and 18ᵗʰ
centuries

bar-racks [băr′əks] *noun*, *plural*,
buildings for lodging soldiers

bar-rage [bär′ĭj] *noun*, an artillary
attack covering a wide area

bar-rel [băr′əl] *noun*, 1) a large
container shaped like a cylinder
2) the long metal tube forming
part of a gun

bar-ren [băr′ən] *adjective*,
1) bleak, lacking in good things
2) unable to bear children,
unable to support growth

bar-ri-cade [băr′ĭ-kād] *noun*,
1) an obstruction or means of
defense, a barrier, *verb*, 2) to
block, to fortify, to bar

bar-ri-er [băr′ē-ər] *noun*, 1) a
stumbling block, a deterrent, an
obstacle, something blocking the
way 2) a fence or wall to mark
the limits of a place

bar-ris-ter [băr′ĭ-stər] *noun*, in
England, a counselor at law, a
lawyer

bar-ter [bär′tər] *verb*, to trade

base [bās] *adjective*, 1) low,
menial, inferior, *noun*, 2) the
bottom on which something
stands 3) an area designated
safe, in baseball one of four
sandbags

base-ball [bās′bôl′] *noun*, a game
played with a bat and a ball by
two teams with nine players on a
side, on a field with four bases at
the corners of a diamond

base-ment [bās′mənt] *noun*,
storage or living space in the
foundation of a building

ba-sic [bā′sĭk] *adjective*,
1) forming a starting point,
fundamental 2) plain, simple

ba-sin [bā′sĭn] *noun*, 1) a low,
bowl-shaped area, a depression in
the land 2) a shallow sink

ba-sis [bā′sĭs] *noun*, the starting
point or central idea of
something, the core

bask [băsk] *verb*, to lay in the sun

bas-ket [băs′kĭt] *noun*, a container
woven from reeds or twigs and
used to carry things

bas-ket-ball [băs′kĭt-bôl′] *noun*, a
game in which two teams of five
players each compete to throw a
ball through a hoop

bass [bās] *adjective*, 1) the lowest
range of the male voice, as in
sound, [băs] *noun*, 2) a fresh-
water fish

bas-tion [băs′chən] *noun*, a
fortress, a defense

bat [băt] *noun*, 1) a piece of wood
used to hit a ball in a game 2) a
flying mammal, *verb*, 3) to hit a
ball with a piece of wood

batch [băch] *noun*, a number of things in a group

bath [băth, bäth] *noun*, 1) a container large enough to hold water to wash a body 2) the act of washing one's body

bathe [bāth] *verb*, to wash with water, usually a part of a body

bath-room [băth'rōōm] *noun*, a room with a toilet and a sink where people wash

ba-ton [bə-tŏn] *noun*, a wand, a night-stick, a rod, a stick used for conducting an orchestra

bat-tal-ion [bə-tăl'yən] *noun*, a large group of army soldiers ready for battle

bat-ter [băt'ər] *noun*, 1) the person holding the bat in baseball 2) a mixture of flour, eggs, and milk, *verb*, 3) to hit repeatedly

bat-ter-y [băt'ə-rē] *noun*, an apparatus for storing chemical energy and converting it to electrical power

bat-tle [băt'l] *noun*, 1) a fight or skirmish between people or different groups, *verb*, 2) to fight

bay [bā] *adjective*, 1) reddish-brown, *noun*, 2) part of a sea that stretches into land 3) a recess in a room 4) a tree or shrub of the laurel family, *verb*, 5) to howl, to bark at

bay-o-net [bā'ə-nĭt] *noun*, a blade on the end of a rifle

ba-zaar [bə-zär'] *noun*, a marketplace where miscellaneous articles are sold

B.C., signifying a time before the birth of Christ

be [bē] *verb*, 1) used to give information about people or things and to join words for people or things to the qualities or position they have 2) the present indicative of verb **be**

Singular	Plural
I **am**	We **are**

   *I **am** proud of you.*
   *We **are** happy to see you.*

You **are**   You **are**

   *You **are** what you eat.*
   *You **are** the students in the class.*

He/she/it **is**   They **are**

   *He **is** a gentleman, he **is** kind.*
   *They **are** all our friends.*

Past Tense

I **was**   We **were**

   *I **was** waiting for you.*
   *We **were** hoping you could stay.*

You **were**   You **were**

   *You **were** a true friend.*
   *You **were** good children.*

He/she it **was**   They **were**

   *It **was** time to go.*
   *They **were** our heroes.*

beach [bēch] *noun*, a shore of sand or pebbles along a lake or ocean

bea-con [bē'kən] *noun*, a lantern, a beam of light, a signal

bead [bēd] *noun*, a small ball of glass or other material, with a small hole for string or wire to pass through

beak [bēk] *noun*, the hard, pointed mouth of a bird

beak-er [bē'kər] *noun*, 1) a deep, open-mouthed, thin, glass vessel with a lip 2) a tall wide-mouthed cup

beam [bēm] *noun*, 1) a large piece of timber used to brace or support a ceiling 2) a ray, a shaft of light, *verb*, 3) to smile happily 4) to send or transmit, to shine

bean [bēn] *noun*, the seed of any bean plant, often used for food

bear [bâr] *adjective*, 1) referring to unfavorable market conditions. *noun*, 2) a large, furry mammal with four feet, *verb*, 3) to carry 4) to suffer or endure 5) to produce, to bring forth, to yield 6) to exhibit, to show, to relate

beard [bîrd] *noun*, hair on the face below the mouth

beast [bēst] *noun*, an animal, especially a savage animal

beat [bēt] *noun*, 1) a stroke or movement that is part of a rhythm, *verb*, 2) to pound, to tap 3) to conquer, to defeat

beau-ti-ful [byōō′tə-fəl] *adjective*, charming and delightful to the senses, very pretty, lovely

beau-ty [byōō′tē] *noun*, qualities pleasing to the eye or ear, charm

bea-ver [bē′vər] *noun*, an amphibious rodent with brown fur that builds dams as homes

be-cause [bĭ-kôz] *conjunction*, since, for the reason that

beck-on [bĕk′ən] *verb*, to signal, call or summon to come over by motioning silently

be-come [bĭ-kŭm′] *verb*, to change or to grow to be, to suit

bed [bĕd] *noun*, 1) a piece of furniture on which someone sleeps 2) the bottom of something 3) a garden plot

bed-lam [bĕd′ləm] *noun*, confusion, noise, uproar

bed-room [bĕd′rōōm] *noun*, the room for sleeping in

bee [bē] *noun*, an insect with a stinger and wings that makes honey and carries pollen from flower to flower

beech [bēch] *noun*, a family of hardwood trees that includes oak and elm

beef [bēf] *noun*, the meat from cattle

bee-hive [bē′hīv′] *noun*, a house made for bees to live in

been [bĭn] the *past tense* of the *verb* **to be**

beer [bîr] *noun*, an alcoholic beverage made of grain and hops

beet [bēt] *noun*, a purplish root vegetable, used for dye and eaten like a turnip

bee-tle [bēt′l] *noun*, an insect whose outside wings make a hard, protective cover for its body

be-fore [bĭ-fôr] *adverb*, 1) happening in advance of, earlier than, *preposition*, 2) in front of, ahead of

be-fore-hand [bĭ-fôr′hănd] *adverb*, ahead of, in advance

beg [bĕg] *verb*, to ask as a favor

be-gan [bĭ-găn′] *verb*, *past tense* of **begin**

beg-gar [bĕg′ər] *noun*, one who asks for favors or money

be-gin [bĭ-gĭn′] *verb*, to start, to commence

be-gin-ning [bǐ-gǐn′ǐng] *noun*, the start of something, the origin

be-guile [bǐ-gīl′] *verb*, to divert or to entertain, to trick, to charm

be-gun [bǐ-gǔn′] *verb, past tense* of **begin**

be-half [bǐ-hǎf] *noun*, interest, side

be-have [bǐ-hāv′] *verb*, to act, to conduct yourself

be-hav-ior [bǐ-hāv′yər] *noun*, manner of acting or bearing oneself, conduct

be-he-moth [bǐ-hē′məth] *noun*, a huge creature

be-hind [bǐ-hīnd′] *adverb*, 1) further away from, late, *preposition*, 2) following, at the back of, remaining after

be-hoove [bǐ-hōōv′] *verb*, to be fitting or proper, to require

be-ing [bē′ǐng] *noun*, 1) a living thing, *verb*, 2) *present participle of the verb* to **be**

be-la-bor [bǐ-lā′bər] *verb*, to repeat over and over

be-lat-ed [bǐ-lā′tǐd] *adjective*, too late, delayed, tardy

be-lea-guered [bǐ-lē′gərd] *adjective*, in a difficult position, besieged, attacked

bel-fry [bĕl′frē] *noun*, a tower where bells hang above a building

be-lie [bǐ-lī′] *verb*, to contradict, to give a false impression

be-lief [bǐ-lēf′] *noun*, faith, acceptance, conviction

be-lieve [bǐ-lēv′] *verb*, 1) to have faith or confidence 2) to think

be-lit-tle [bǐ-lǐt′l] *verb*, to tease, to make fun of

bell [bĕl] *noun*, a round, hollow object of metal or glass that sounds when it is struck

bel-li-cose [bĕl′ǐ-kōs′] *adjective*, warlike, ready to fight

bel-lig-er-ent [bə-lǐj′ər-ənt] *adjective*, hostile, pugnacious, preparing to fight, aggressive

bel-low [bĕl′ō] *verb*, to make a loud deep sound like a bull

bel-lows [bĕl′ōz] *noun, plural*, a machine that draws air through a valve and expels it through a tube by alternate expansion and contraction, used in an organ or to blow air on a fire

bel-ly [bĕl′ē] *noun*, stomach, gut,

be-long [bǐ-lông] *verb*, 1) to be a part of, to be a member 2) to own or have possession of

be-long-ings [bǐ-lông′ǐngs] *noun, plural*, one's personal possessions

be-lov-ed [bǐ-lǔv′ǐd] *adjective*, cherished, highly valued, adored

be-low [bǐ-lō′] *adverb*, 1) at a lower level, *preposition*, 2) at a lower place or rank

belt [bĕlt] *noun*, 1) a band worn around the waist,, often made of cloth or leather 2) a band or strip indicating a region or zone, *verb*, 3) to hit or smack, to clobber 4) to strap, to surround, to attach by wrapping a cord around something

bench [bĕnch] *noun*, 1) a long seat often wooden 2) the table at which someone works 3) a judge's seat in court

bend [bĕnd] *noun*, 1) a curve, *verb*, 2) to shape into a curve or make crooked 3) to stoop

be-neath [bĭ-nēth′] *preposition*, below, under, at a lower level than

ben-e-dic-tion [bĕn′ĭ-dĭk′shən] *noun*, a blessing

ben-e-fac-tor [bĕn′ə-făk′tər] *noun*, a gift-giver, a patron

be-nef-i-cent [bə-nĕf′ĭ-sənt] *adjective*, performing acts of kindness and charity, generous

ben-e-fi-cial [bĕn′ə-fĭsh′əl] *adjective*, useful, profitable

ben-e-fi-ci-ar-y [bĕn′ə-fĭsh′ē-ĕr′ē] *noun*, one who is going to receive something valuable

ben-e-fit [bĕn′ə-fĭt] *noun*, 1) an advantage, 2) a fundraiser *verb*, 3) to be helpful, to aid

be-nev-o-lence [bə-nĕv′ə-ləns] *noun*, goodwill or kindness, charity given, generosity

be-nev-o-lent [bə-nĕv′ə-lənt] *adjective*, generous, kind-hearted

be-nign [bĭ-nīn′] *adjective*, harmless, not cancerous

bent [bĕnt] *past tense* of **bend**

be-quest [bĭ-kwĕst′] *noun*, the act of leaving by a written will, a legacy for the next generation

be-rate [bĭ-rāt′] *verb*, to criticize or scold vigorously

be-reave-ment [bĭ-rēv′-mĕnt] *noun*, the state of being deprived of something, sorrow, mourning

be-reft [bĭ-rĕft′] *adjective*, lacking, deprived of, doing without

ber-ry [bĕ-rē′] *noun*, a small, round fruit from a bush

ber-serk [bər-sßrk] *adjective*, frenzied with rage, crazy

be-seech [bĭ-sēch′] *verb*, to ask or entreat, to implore, to beg

be-side [bĭ-sīd′] *preposition*, next to, at the side of, adjacent

be-sides [bĭ-sīdz′] *adverb*, also, in addition to, as an extra

be-siege [bĭ-sēj′] *verb*, to surround with armed forces, to harass, to encircle, to crowd around

best [bĕst] *adjective*, finest, exceeding all others in quality

be-stow [bĭ-stō′] *verb*, to give something, to confer

bet [bĕt] *noun*, 1) an agreement to risk money on the odds of winning, *verb*, 2) to risk money on a gamble, to wager

be-tray [bĭ-trā′] *verb*, to break a trust, to reveal a secret

bet-ter [bĕt′ər] *adjective*, 1) superior, *adverb*, 2) more, larger, *verb*, 3) to improve

bet-ween [bĭ-twēn′] *adverb*, 1) showing where in relation to things or places on either side 2) showing when in relation to events before and after, *preposition*, 3) showing how things are joined 4) showing how things are divided

bev-er-age [bĕv′ər-ij] *noun*, a drink, a liquid refreshment

bev-y [bĕv′ē] *noun*, 1) a large group, 2) a group of birds

be-ware [bĭ-w r ′] *verb*, to be wary, to be careful, to be on guard of

be-wild-er-ed [bĭ-wĭl′dərd] *adjective*, confused, puzzled, perplexed

be-witch [bǐ-wǐch′] *verb* to charm, to put under a magic spell

be-yond [bē-ŏnd] *preposition*, at a distance farther away, on the other side of, past

bi-as [bī′əs] *adjective*, 1) in a slanting manner, obliquely, diagonally, *noun*, 2) inclination, tendency, *verb*, 3) to influence, to show prejudice, to sway

Bi-ble [bī′bəl] *noun*, the religious book of the Christian and Jewish faiths

bib-li-og-ra-phy [bǐb′lē-ŏg′rə-fē] *noun*, a list of books on any subject usually found at the end of a manuscript

bick-er [bǐk′ər] *verb*, to quarrel about petty things

bi-cy-cle [bī′sǐk′əl] *noun*, a two wheeled vehicle propelled by pedals

bid [bǐd] *noun*, 1) an offer to buy something, *verb*, 2) to offer a price for something 3) to ask, plea 4) to utter a greeting

bi-en-ni-al [bī-ĕn′ē-əl] *adjective*, happening every two years

big [bǐg] *adjective*, large in size, weight, importance, etc.

big-ot [bǐg′ət] *noun*, a person filled with stubborn hatred

big-ot-ry [bǐg′ə-trē] *noun*, prejudice, intolerance

bi-lin-gual [bī-lǐng′gwəl] *adjective*, capable of speaking two languages

bill [bǐl] *noun*, 1) a piece of paper stating what you owe 2) a plan for a new law 3) the beak of a bird, *verb*, 4) to send a list of charges to someone

bil-liards [bǐl′yərdz] *noun*, *plural*, a game similar to pool

bil-lion [bǐl′yən] *noun*, *adjective*, a thousand million, written 1,000,000,000

bil-low [bǐl′ō] *noun*, 1) a wave, a surge of water or smoke, *verb*, 2) to surge, to swell

bin [bǐn] *noun*, a large container with a lid, for flour, grain, etc.

bind [bīnd] *verb*, 1) to tie with rope or string 2) to constrict 3) to put under an obligation

bind-er [bīn′dər] *noun*, that which fastens or binds together, such as a notebook with large rings to hold paper

binge [bǐnj] *noun*, a spree, uncontrolled eating

bin-oc-u-lars [bə-nŏk′yə-lərz] *noun*, *plural*, a pair of special glasses that make things in the distance look closer

bi-o-de-grad-a-ble [bī′ō-dǐ-grā′də-bəl] *adjective*, capable of being broken down by microorganisms into simple, stable compounds such as carbon dioxide and water

bi-og-ra-phy [bī-ŏg′rə-fē] *noun*, a written history of a person's life

bi-ol-o-gy [bī-ŏl′ə-jē] *noun*, the branch of knowledge that studies all living things

birch [bûrch] *noun*, a hardwood tree known for its thin, peeling bark and yellow leaves in the fall

bird [bûrd] *noun*, any of a class of warm-blooded, two-legged, egg-laying vertebrates with feathers and wings

birth [bûrth] *noun*, the act of being born, the beginning of existence

birth-day [bûrth′dā′] *noun*, the day someone is born

bis-cuit [bĭs′kĭt] *noun*, a small soft bread

bish-op [bĭsh′əp] *noun*, a senior member of the Christian clergy

bi-son [bī′sən, -zən] *noun*, a large mammal native to North America and Europe, including the buffalo

bit [bĭt] *noun*, 1) a very small amount 2) the metal mouthpiece on a bridle used to control a horse 3) the cutting edge of a tool, *verb*, 4) *past tense* of **bite**

bite [bīt] *noun*, 1) a wound made by biting or stinging, *verb*, 2) to seize or cut with teeth

bit-ter [bĭt′ər] *adjective*, 1) having a sharp, sour taste 2) grievous, painful 3) piercingly cold

bi-zarre [bĭ-zär′] *adjective*, very strange or unusual, weird

black [blăk] *adjective*, 1) lacking color or light, the opposite of white, *noun*, 2) a Negro or person of African descent

black-mail [blăk′māl′] *noun*, 1) compliance with another person's terms, hush money, *verb*, 2) to threaten to reveal a secret unless money is paid or favors given

blad-der [blăd′ər] *noun*, a sack attached to the kidneys to hold urine

blade [blād] *noun*, 1) the flat cutting part of anything sharp 2) a long flat leaf of grass, or anything with such a shape

blame [blām] *noun*, 1)responsibility for something bad, *verb*, 2) to say that someone is the cause of something unfortunate

blanch [blănch] *verb*, 1) to bleach, to whiten, to fade 2) to cook briefly in boiling water

bland [blănd] *adjective*, mild, almost tasteless, neutral

blank [blăngk] *adjective*, 1) without writing or other marks 2) without expression

blan-ket [blăng′kĭt] *noun*, a warm cloth cover used on a bed

blas-phe-my [blăs′fə-mē] *noun*, speech or actions that are disrespectful to God or sacred things

blast [blăst] *noun*, 1) a strong gust of wind 2) an explosion, *verb*, 3) to launch into space 4) to use explosions to break something apart 4) to make a loud sound

bla-tant [blāt′nt] *adjective*, loudly offensive, very obvious

blaze [blāz] *noun*, 1) a strong fire, *verb*, 2) to burn, to burst into flame 3) to shine brightly

blaz-er [blā′zər] *noun*, a light sports jacket of wool or silk

bleach [blēch] *noun*, 1) a substance used to whiten or remove color, *verb*, 2) to make white, to remove color

bleach-ers [blē′chərs] *noun*, *plural*, seats for spectators

bleak [blēk] *adjective*, cold and unpleasant, empty

bleed [blēd] *verb*, 1) to lose blood 2) to become mixed or run (e.g., dyes in wet cloth)

blem-ish [blĕm′ĭsh] *noun*, a flaw, an imperfection, a pimple

blend [blĕnd] *noun*, 1) a thorough mixture, *verb*, 2) to mix together into one 3) to go together

bless [blĕs] *verb*, to make holy, to ask God's favor, to praise

bless-ing [blĕs′ĭng] *noun*, 1) words that thank God for His gifts 2) good fortune

blew [bloo] *verb*, *past tense* of **blow**

blight [blīt] *noun*, 1) a disease on plants that makes the leaves dry up, *verb*, 2) to injure, to damage, to ruin a crop

blind [blīnd] *adjective*, 1) unable to see, without the sense of sight 2) concealed, hard to see 3) oblivious, unaware, ignorant, *noun*, 4) a window covering to keep out light, *verb*, 5) to make unable to see

blink [blĭngk] *noun*, 1) the quick opening and closing of an eyelid, *verb*, 2) to open and shut the eyes quickly

bliss [blĭs] *noun*, complete joy, happiness, or delight

blis-ter [blĭs′tər] *noun*, a sack under the skin filled with water or blood, from a burn or rubbing

bliz-zard [blĭz′ərd] *noun*, a snow storm with strong winds and cold temperatures

block [blŏk] *noun*, 1) a cube, a chunk 2) the area bounded by four city streets 3) something that stands in the way and prevents movement, *verb*, 4) to hinder, clog or jam, to impede, prevent, stop, or obstruct 5) to form, shape, or press

block-ade [blŏ′kād] *noun,* the closure of an area , port, etc.

blond or blonde [blŏnd] *adjective*, a light hair color the shade of straw or wheat

blood [blŭd] *noun*, a red fluid in the veins of people and animals

blood ves-sel [blŭd vĕs′əl] *noun*, any of the tubes in the body that carry blood, veins, arteries, capillaries

bloom [bloom] *noun*, 1) a flower, *verb*, 2) to have a flower

blos-som [blŏs′əm] *noun*, 1) a flower, *verb*, 2) to bloom or open from a bud to come in to a flower

blot [blŏt] *noun*, 1) a spot or stain, *verb*, 2) to absorb a liquid with cloth or a sponge to remove it

blouse [blous] *noun*, a garment similar to a shirt covering the top of a woman's body, from the neck to the waist

blow [blō] *noun*, 1) a sudden strike with a hand or weapon, *verb*, 2) to force air into a current, to expel air from the mouth

blue [bloo] *adjective*, 1) having the color of a cloudless sky, 2) unhappy, depressed, *noun*, 3) one of the three primary colors: red, blue, yellow 3) a feeling of unhappiness, sadness

bluff [blŭf] *noun*, 1) a high, steep bank, *verb,* 2) to try to trick or fool someone 3) to pretend

blun-der [blŭn′dər] *noun*, a stupid mistake, an error

blunt [blŭnt] *adjective*, 1) not sharp 2) frank, candid, abrupt, *verb*, 3) to deaden, insensitize, dull

blur [blûr] *verb*, to make unreadable or indistinct, to obscure

blush [blŭsh] *verb*, to become red in the face from embarrassment

board [bôrd] *noun*, 1) a long flat piece of wood 2) a group of directors who act as a body 3) a piece of cardboard or wood on which a game is played, *verb*, 4) to cover with wood 5) to climb onto a vessel or vehicle

board-er [bôr′dər] *noun*, a paying guest who receives meals

boast [bōst] *verb*, to brag, to praise oneself, to show off

boat [bōt] *noun*, a small ship or vessel that floats on water

bode [bōd] *verb*, to predict, to portend, to foretell

bod-y [bŏd′ē] *noun*, 1) the form of a person or animal or object 2) a group of persons who act as a unit 3) a corpse

bog [bôg] *noun*, a swamp, a marsh

boil [boil] *noun*, 1) a painful sore under the skin, *verb*, 2) to heat to 212 degrees Fahrenheit 3) to be angered, to be enraged

bold [bōld] *adjective*, brave, assertive, forward, fearless

bolt [bōlt] *noun*, 1) a metal screw used with a nut to hold something in place, a metal bar 2) a stroke of lightning, a thunderbolt, *verb*, 3) to lock with a bar across a doorway 4) to run quickly from the scene

bomb [bŏm] *noun*, 1) a device of explosive materials, *verb*, 2) to bombard with explosives

bom-bard [bŏm-bärd] *verb*, to attack repeatedly

bond [bŏnd] *noun*, 1) a mutual feeling of trust that joins people together 2) a written promise to pay money, *verb*, 3) to join together, to unite

bond-age [bŏn′dĭj] *noun*, confinement, servitude

bone [bōn] *noun*, a hard white substance forming the skeleton of an animal

bon-fire [bŏn′fīr′] *noun*, a large controlled fire

bo-nus [bō′nəs] *noun*, a sum paid in addition to a salary

book [bŏŏk] *noun*, 1) sheets of paper bound together for reading or writing, a long work of literature, etc., in electronic form, *verb*, 2) to make reservations for a future date

book-keep-ing [bŏŏk′kē′pĭng] *noun*, a systematic record of business transactions

boo-mer-ang [bŏŏ′mə-răng′] *noun*, an angular shaped object that returns after it is thrown

boor [bŏŏr] *noun*, a rude person, a jerk, a brash individual

boost [bŏŏst] *noun*, 1) a lift, a helping hand, *verb*, 2) to support, to encourage

boot [bŏŏt] *noun*, 1) a shoe that covers above the ankle, *verb*, 2) to kick 3) to load the operating system on a computer

booth [bŏŏth] *noun*, an enclosure, a cubicle, a compartment

bor-der [bôr′dər] *noun*, 1) the dividing line between two countries or territories 2) an edge or trim, *verb*, 3) to lie along the edge of a geographic boundary

bore [bôr] *noun*, 1) a tiresome person, a nuisance, *verb*, 2) to drill a hole, to penetrate 3) to make someone feel disinterested

bore-dom [bôr'dəm] *noun*, dullness, lack of interest

boring [bôr'ĭng] *adjective*, not interesting, dull, tedious

born [bôrn] *adjective*, having been given life, existing as a result of birth

bor-ough [bûr'ō] *noun*, a self-governing incorporated town

bor-row [bôr'ō] *verb*, 1) to use a thing that does not belong to you, then return it 2) to adopt or use as one's own

bos-om [bŏoz'əm] *adjective*, 1) relating to the closeness between friends or family, *noun*, 2) chest area 3) a woman's breast

boss [bôs] *noun*, 1) the person in charge, someone in control, the employer, *verb*, 2) to give orders in a domineering way

bot-a-nist [bŏt'n-ĭst] *noun*, one who studies plants

bot-a-ny [bŏt'n-ē] *noun*, the science of plants

both [bōth] *adjective*, *pronoun*, the two together in conjunction

both-er [bŏth'ər] *noun*, *no plural*, 1) trouble or difficulty, a nuisance, *verb*, 2) to trouble or annoy, to harass or pester

bot-tle [bŏt'l] *noun*, 1) a container with a narrow neck, usually made of glass or plastic, used to hold liquids *verb*, 2) to store in a glass container

bot-tom [bŏt'əm] *noun*, 1) the lowest part or end of something 2) the buttocks, seat

bough [bou] *noun*, a tree branch

bouil-lon [bŏol'yŏn', -yən] *noun*, a broth, consommé

boul-der [bōl'dər] *noun*, a very large stone or rock

bounce [bouns] *verb*, to spring back from a surface, to jump

bound [bound] *adjective*, 1) constrained, restricted, confined 2) going to, destined for, *noun*, 3) a jump, a leap

bound-a-ry [boun'də-rē] *noun*, a real or imaginary limit, especially between two properties

boun-ti-ful [boun'tə-fəl] *adjective*, generous, plentiful, provided freely, abundant

bow [bō] *noun*, 1) a ribbon worn as a hair ornament 2) a piece of wood bent with a string, used to shoot arrows 3) a piece of wood with hairs fastened, to create vibrations when pulled across the strings of an instrument, such as a violin, [bou] 4) the front of a boat, *verb*, 5) to bend the body forward to show respect 6) to submit to another, to consent

bowl [bōl] *noun*, a round deep dish

box [bŏks] *noun*, 1) a container like a cube, constructed from wood, cardboard, metal, etc. *verb*, 2) to fight with clenched fists

boy [boi] *noun*, a male child

boy-cott [boi'kŏt'] *noun*, 1) the refusal to purchase the products of an individual, corporation, or nation as a way to bring

43

economic pressure for social or political change, *verb*, 2) to refuse to deal with or trade with, to desert, to abandon

brace [brās] *noun*, 1) a support, a vise, 2) two like items, a pair, *verb*, 3) to fortify

brack-et [brăk′ĭt] *noun*, 1) a shelf supported against a wall 2) one of the signs [ ] in a sentence that encloses additional information

brack-ish [brăk′ĭsh] *adjective*, a mixture of fresh and salt water

brag [brăg] *verb*, to praise oneself, to sound conceited, to boast

braid [brād] *noun*, 1) a rope, twine, *verb*, 2) to weave hair or rope

Braille [brāl] *noun*, a system of writing for people who are blind using raised dots as letters and numbers to be read with the fingertips

brain [brān] *noun*, 1) the mass of nerve tissue in the heads of people and animals, the center of the nervous system 2) the intellect, where we get our thoughts and ideas

brake [brāk] *noun*, 1) a mechanical device used to stop a bicycle, car, train, etc., *verb*, 2) to stop with the help of a mechanical device

branch [brănch] *noun*, 1) a part of a tree that extends from the trunk 2) an office that is located some distance from the headquarters 3) a stream or river that flows into a larger one, *verb*, 4) to move away or divide from the main body into branches

brand [brănd] *noun*, 1) a label indicating the name of a product and the manufacturer, *verb*, 2) to make a permanent mark on an animal to identify it

brass [brăs] *noun*, 1) a yellow metal that is a copper and zinc alloy 2) musical instruments, such as a trumpet, that are made out of metal and that give a loud sound when blown

bra-va-do [brə-vä′dō] *noun*, an air of defiance, fake bravery

brave [brāv] *adjective*, willing to make a personal sacrifice

brav-er-y [brā′və-rē] *noun*, courage, daring, boldness

brawl [brôl] *noun*, 1) a fight, an altercation, a dispute, *verb*, 2) to argue and wrestle or fight

breach [brēch] *noun*, the breaking of a contract, a gap in a fence

bread [brĕd] *noun*, a food made of flour, water, and yeast that is baked

breadth [brĕdth] *noun*, the distance from one side to the other, width

break [brāk] *noun*, 1) an opening made when something is torn or broken, 2) a pause, a rest, a time away from school or work, *verb*, 3) to cause to fall apart 4) to violate, to disobey

break-fast [brĕk′fəst] *noun*, the first meal of the day, eaten in the morning

breast [brĕst] *noun*, 1) one of the two parts on the front of a woman's body that can give milk 2) the top part of the front of the body

breath [brĕth] *noun*, air inhaled and exhaled in respiration

breathe [brēth] *verb*, to inhale air into the lung and then exhale

bred [brĕd] *verb*, *past tense and past participle* of **breed**

breed [brēd] *noun*, 1) a type or group of animals descended from a common ancestor, *verb*, 2) to reproduce, to multiply 3) to train and raise animals

breed-ing [brē'dĭng] *noun*, values a person learns, upbringing

breeze [brēz] *noun*, a gentle wind

brev-i-ty [brĕv'ĭ-tē] *noun*, shortness, ability to say something briefly, succinctly

brew [broo] *verb*, to make drinks such as tea, coffee, or beer

bribe [brīb] *noun*, 1) money given to buy cooperation, *verb*, 2) to get someone's cooperation by paying them, to pay off

brick [brĭk] *noun*, a block of baked clay used in construction

brid-al [brīd'əl]*adjective*, referring to the bride in a wedding

bride [brīd] *noun*, a woman about to be married, is in the process of being married, or who has just been married

bride-groom [brīd'groom] *noun*, a man who is going to be married, is in the process of being married, or has just been married

bridge [brĭj] *noun*, 1) an elevated structure such as a viaduct or an overpass that crosses over water or a highway 2) a card game 3) a link, a connection, *verb*, 4) to join, connect, bring together

bri-dle [brīd'l] *noun*, 1) a leather band on the head of a horse used for control, *verb*, 2) to show anger or resentment

brief [brēf] *adjective*, 1) for a short period of time, *noun*, 2) a summary of a case for the court, *verb*, 3) to inform

bri-er [brī'ər] *noun* prickly vegetation

bri-gade [brĭ-gād'] *noun*, a large group of soldiers

bright [brīt] *adjective*, 1) giving light 2) shining, not dull 3) smart, intelligent 4) cheerful

bril-liant [brĭl'yənt] *adjective*, 1) very bright, glittering, splendid 2) very clever

brim [brĭm] *noun*, 1) the edge of a cup, glass, or bowl 2) the part of the hat that is the edge

bring [brĭng]*verb*, to carry something or to lead someone

brink [brĭngk] *noun*, the edge of a steep slope, the verge

brisk [brĭsk] *adjective*, 1) quick and active, energetic 2) curt

bris-tle [brĭs'əl] *noun*, 1) a coarse brush, *verb*, 2) to feel irritated or annoyed, to show indignation

brit-tle [brĭt'l] *adjective*, hard but easily broken or snapped

broach [brōch] *verb*, to bring up, to begin discussion of

broad [brôd] *adjective*, 1) wide, extensive 2) tolerant

broad-cast [brôd'kăst'] *noun*, 1) a program aired on television or radio, *verb*, 2) to convey a message through radio or television or other electronic media

broad-en [brôd'n] *verb*, to expand

bro-chure [brō-shŏŏr′] *noun*, a pamphlet dealing with a subject of passing interest, a leaflet

broc-co-li [brŏk′ə-lē] *noun*, a plant with dense green flowers eaten as a vegetable

broil [broil] *verb*, to cook by exposing to direct, intense heat

broke [brōk] *adjective*, 1) without money, bankrupt, *verb,* 2) *past tense* of **break**

bro-ker [brō′kər] *noun*, an agent who buys and sells for others

bron-chi-tis [brŏn-kī′tĭs] *noun*, an inflammation of the lungs that causes chronic coughing

bronze [brŏnz] *noun*, a hard metal made by mixing copper and tin

brooch [brōch] *noun*, an ornamental dress-clasp, a decorative pin

brood [brōōd] *noun*, 1) a group of animals born together, or the children of a family, *verb,* 2) to think deeply and sadly about something

brook [brŏŏk] *noun*, 1) a small river or stream, *verb*, 2) to allow

broom [brōōm] *noun*, a brush with a long handle

broth [brŏth] *noun*, watery soup, bouillon

broth-er [brŭth′ər] *noun*, a boy or man with the same parents as another person

brought [brôt*]* *verb*, *past tense* of **bring**

brow [brou] *noun*, the part of the face between the eyes and the hair, the forehead

brown [broun] *adjective*, a dark color like coffee or earth

browse [brouz] *verb*, to leaf through, to scan, to pass over

bruise [brōōz] *noun*, 1) a red or blue mark left on damaged skin caused by blood vessels breaking beneath the skin, *verb*, 2) to injure in such a way that the blood vessels beneath the skin are broken

brunch [brŭnch]*noun*, a meal between breakfast and lunch

bru-nette [brōō-nĕt′] *noun*, a woman with brown hair

brush [brŭsh] *noun*, 1) a device with wires or plastic bristles spread from a handle for combing, or cleaning, or painting, *verb*, 2) to clean, straighten, or paint with a brush

brusque [brŭsk] *adjective*, rough and short in manner, blunt,

bru-tal [brōōt′l] *adjective*, fierce, harsh, destructive

brute [brōōt] *noun*, a cruel person who acts like a wild animal

bub-ble [bŭb′əl] *noun*, 1) a sphere containing liquid or gas, *verb*, 2) to boil, to froth

buck [bŭk] *noun*, a male deer, goat, or rabbit

buck-et [bŭk′ĭt] *noun*, a container, usually with a curved handle to carry something, a pail

buck-le [bŭk′əl] *noun*, a device for uniting two loose ends of a belt or to fasten shoes, etc.

bu-col-ic [byōō-kŏl′ĭk] *adjective*, rustic, pastoral, in the country

bud [bŭd] *noun*, a sprout on a stem that becomes a flower or branch

Bud-dhism [bōō'dĭz'əm] *noun*, one of the world's major religions, practiced primarily in Asia and taught by monks

budge [bŭj] *verb*, to make something heavy move a little

budg-et [bŭj'ĭt] *noun*, a plan that indicates how money will be spent

buf-fa-lo [bŭf'ə-lō'] *noun*, a large, shaggy, wild ox

buff-er [bŭf'ər] *noun*, 1) a solution that neutralizes different substances 2) a person or thing between two opposing forces that softens the impact of their collision, *verb*, 3) to lessen

buf-fet [bə-fā'] *noun*, 1) a counter or table for refreshments, [bə-fĭt] *verb*, 2) to batter, to flap, to hit

buf-foon [bə-fōōn'] *noun*, one who clowns around

bug [bŭg] *noun*, 1) an insect that drinks juices from plants or animals 2) an error in data, *verb*, 3) to eavesdrop electronically

bug-gy [bŭg'ē] *noun*, 1) a hand-pushed carriage for babies 2) a one-horse carriage for two people

bu-gle [byōō'gəl] *noun*, a musical instrument, a horn used mainly in the military

build [bĭld] *verb*, 1) to create or construct 2) to increase

build-ing [bĭl'dĭng] *noun*, a structure with a foundation, roof, and walls

built [bĭlt] *verb*, *past tense* of **build**

bulb [bŭlb] *noun*, 1) the underground part of a plant formed by thick leaves, which

separates and becomes a new plant 2) any object of this shape, such as a light bulb

bulge [bŭlj] *noun*, 1) a swelling shape, *verb*, 2) to swell outwards

bulk-head [bŭlk'hĕd'] *noun*, a partition separating the compartments of a vessel

bull [bōōl] *adjective*, 1) describing the stock market when prices are going up and the economy is strong, *noun*, 2) male animal of the ox, cow, whale, or other animals

bull-doz-er [bōōl'dō'zər] *noun*, a heavy machine that moves earth

bul-let [bōōl'ĭt] *noun*, a piece of metal fired from a gun

bul-le-tin [bōōl'ĭ-tn] *noun*, an announcement made by an organization, a newsletter

bul-lion [bōōl'yən] *noun*, a block of metal such as gold or silver

bul-ly [bōōl'ē] *noun*, 1) a person who likes to hurt or tease weaker people, *verb*, 2) to intimidate someone, to make someone feel afraid or overpowered

bul-wark [bōōl'wərk] *noun*, protection, a defensive wall

bum-ble-bee [bŭm'bəl-bē'] *noun*, a large yellow and black hairy social bee

bump [bŭmp] *noun*, 1) a sudden blow 2) a raised round lump due to swelling 3) an elevated place in the road or on a surface, *verb*, 4) to knock against, to strike

bun [bŭn] *noun*, 1) a small sweet roll or dinner roll 2) a hairstyle in which the hair is lifted off the neck and wrapped into a circle

bunch [bŭnch] *noun*, 1) a cluster of similar things grouped together, *verb*, 2) to gather together in a mass

bun-dle [bŭn′dl] *noun*, 1) a group of things tied together to make a package, *verb*, 2) to make into a bunch by tying things together

bu-oy [boo′ē] *noun*, an anchored floating device used as a navigation marker

buoy-ant [boi′ənt] *adjective*, 1) having the quality of rising or floating in fluid 2) light-hearted

bur-den [bûr′dn] *noun*, 1) a heavy thought or object that is carried, *verb*, 2) to load

bu-reau [byoor′ō] *noun*, 1) a chest of drawers 2) a satellite office for a news agency

bu-reauc-ra-cy [byoo-rŏk′rə-sē] *noun*, a system of government through agencies to which tasks and authority are delegated

bur-geon [bûr′jən] *verb*, to grow and develop rapidly

bur-glar [bûr′glər] *noun*, one who breaks into other people's property to rob them

bur-i-al [bĕr′ē-əl] *noun*, the act of putting a dead body in the ground, internment

burn [bûrn] *noun*, 1) a wound caused by fire or heat, or friction, *verb*, 2) to be destroyed by fire, heat or acid

burnt [bûrnt] *adjective*, showing damage by fire

burr [bûr] *noun*, a round seed covered with spurs or barbs

bur-ro [bûr′ō] *noun*, a donkey

bur-row [bûr′ō] *noun*, 1) a tunnel or hole dug by an animal as a den, *verb*, 2) to dig or hide in a hole

burst [bûrst] *noun*, 1) a sudden action, *verb*, 2) to break due to force from inside, to combust

bury [bĕr′ē] *verb*, to dig a hole to conceal something underground, to cover, to conceal

bus [bŭs] *noun*, a large vehicle that carries many people to a destination by a road

bush [boosh] *noun*, a shrub

bush-el [boosh′əl] *noun*, dry measure equal to 64 pints or 32 quarts

busi-ness [bĭz′nĭs] *noun*, 1) regular occupation, work, profession 2) something to be transacted 3) affairs involving money

bust [bŭst] *noun*, a sculpture of a person from the chest up

bus-y [bĭz′ē] *adjective*, 1) having a lot to do, *verb*, to work actively

but [bŭt; bət when unstressed] *adverb*, 1) only, merely, *conjunction,* 2) yet, however, *preposition,* 3) except, save 4) other than

butch-er [booch′ər] *noun*, a person who cuts meat for sale

but-ter [bŭt′ər] *noun*, a substance made from churning cream

but-ter-fly [bŭt′ər-flī′] *noun*, an insect with four colorful wings and a slender body

but-ton [bŭt′n] *noun*, 1) a variety of forms or materials used to fasten a dress, pants, shirt, etc. 2) a badge, a form of identification, 3) a knob pressed to operate a device, *verb*, 4) to secure with a button or snap

but-ton-hole [bŭt′n-hōl′] *noun*, the hole in a piece of clothing that a button goes through in order to fasten two sides together

but-tress [bŭt′rĭs] *noun*, a support projecting outwards to strengthen the walls of a building

buy [bī] *verb*, to acquire something by giving an accepted price, to purchase with money

buy-er [bī′ər] *noun*, a customer, one who makes a purchase

by [bī] *adverb*, 1) near, aside, past *preposition*, 2) near, beside 3) through, by way of, via 4) before 5) past

by-pro-duct [bī′prŏd′əkt] *noun*, anything produced in the process of making something else

byte [bīt] *noun*, 1) a small unit of information 2) a fixed number of bits (usually eight)

C

cab [kăb] *noun*, 1) a vehicle for hire, a taxi 2) the part of a truck or train where the driver sits

cab-bage [kăb′ĭj] *noun*, a vegetable with a short stem and thick green or purple overlapping leaves that form a dense head

cab-in [kăb′ĭn] *noun*, 1) a small wooden house 2) a room for living quarters on a ship 3) the passenger area on an airplane

cab-i-net [kăb′ə-nĭt] *noun*, 1) a cupboard with drawers or

shelves for keeping items 2) a group of people who advise the head of state

ca-ble [kā′bəl] *noun*, 1) a strong, large diameter wire or rope 2) a bundle of insulated wires that carry electrical current 3) a system delivering television signals by cable

ca-boose [kə-bōōs′] *noun*, the last car used on a freight train, containing facilities for the crew

cache [kăsh] *noun*, 1) a hiding place for food or treasures, *verb*, 2) to hide or store something

cack-le [kăk′əl] *noun*, 1) a loud laugh, *verb*, 2) to laugh loudly to sound like a hen

ca-coph-o-ny [kə-kŏf′ə-nē] *noun*, harsh or dissonant noise, a discordant mixture of sounds

cac-tus [kăk′təs] *noun*, *plural*, **cacti or cactuses**, a prickly, succulent plant with thick stems that grows in hot, dry climates

ca-dav-er [kə-dăv′ər] *noun*, a dead body

ca-det [kə-dĕt′] *noun*, a student at a military school

caf-e-te-ri-a [kăf′ĭ-tîr′ē-ə] *noun*, a place to eat where customers select food from a serving line

caf-feine [kă-fēn] *noun*, a stimulant found especially in coffee, tea, or some sodas

cage [kāj] *noun*, a box-like enclosure with bars in which birds or animals are kept, a pen

cake [kāk] *noun*, 1) a sweet, baked food made of flour, fat, and eggs, *verb*, 2) to harden from a wet substance into a solid crust

ca-lam-i-ty [kə-lăm′ĭ-tē] *noun*, an unfortunate event, a disaster

cal-ci-um [kăl′sē-əm] *noun*, a silver-white, rather soft metal that occurs in bones, shells, etc.

cal-cu-late [kăl′kyə-lāt′] *verb*, to find the answer using arithmetic, to plan using reasoning

cal-cu-la-tion [kăl′kyə-lā′shən] *noun*, the result of numbers added together, subtracted, etc.

cal-cu-la-tor [kăl′kyə-lā′tər] *noun*, a small computer used to perform math problems

cal-cu-lus [kăl′kyə-ləs] *noun*,

1) a branch of mathematics that provides a method for describing change 2) a buildup of materials within the body, such as a gallstone

cal-en-dar [kăl′ən-dər] *noun*, a table of the days and the months of the year

calf [kăf] *noun*, 1) the newborn or young of any large mammal, such as a cow, whale, or elephant 2) part of the leg between the knee and the ankle, the back of the shin

cal-i-ber [kăl′ə-bər] *noun*, 1) the diameter of a cylinder or tube 2) a person's degree of ability

Cal-i-for-nia [kăl′ĭ-fôr′nyə] *noun*, a state on the Pacific coast of the United States, the capital is Sacramento. The state flower of **California** is the golden poppy and the motto is "Eureka!"

cal-lis-then-ics [kăl′ĭs-thĕn′ĭks] *noun, plural*, exercise to promote strength and grace

call [kôl] *noun*, 1) the act of reaching someone on the telephone or paying a visit 2) a shout or plea, *verb*, 3) to name 4) to shout 5) to ask someone to come 6) to telephone 7) to visit

cal-lig-ra-phy [kə-lĭg′rə-fē] *noun*, beautiful writing, the art of hand lettering

cal-lous [kăl′əs] *adjective*,

1) lacking feeling, hard-hearted, feeling no pity 2) thick skinned

cal-lus [kăl′əs] noun, a hard thickened spot (of skin)

calm [käm] *adjective*, quiet, not excited

cal-o-rie [kăl′ə-rē] *noun*, a unit used to measure the amount of energy produced

cam-el [kăm′əl] *noun*, a large animal with one or two humps on its back, used for transportation

cam-e-o [kăm′ē-ō′] *noun*, a piece of jewelry with a stone or shell on which figures are carved

cam-er-a [kăm′ər-ə] *noun*, an instrument used to take photographs or film pictures

cam-ou-flage [kăm′ə-fläzh] *noun*, 1) special clothing for people or colors in an animal that help them blend into their surroundings, *verb*, 2) an organism's ability to blend in with the environment

camp [kămp] *noun*, 1) a place with tents or cabins for temporary shelter, *verb*, 2) to live outdoors and sleep in a tent under the stars, etc.

cam-paign [kăm-pān′] *noun*,
1) activities organized to gain or win something, *verb*, 2) to create a connected series of operations to achieve a desired result

cam-pus [kăm′pəs] *noun*, the grounds surrounding a college, school, or organization

can [kăn] *noun*, 1) a metal container, *verb*, 2) able to, to know how to 3) to preserve food in a can

ca-nal [kə-năl′] *noun*, 1) an artificial waterway designed for navigation 2) a duct in the body

ca-nar-y [kə-nâr′ē] *noun*, a songbird, usually yellow

can-cel [kăn′səl] *verb*, to annul, to revoke, to end or stop

can-cel-la-tion [kăn′sə-lā′shən] *noun*, a stop or end to something, withdrawal

can-cer [kăn′sər] *noun*, a serious illness in which abnormal cells multiply rapidly

can-di-date [kăn′dĭ-dāt′] *noun*, one who is being considered or who applies for a certain job

can-dle [kăn′dl] *noun*, a cylinder of wax with a wick embedded in it designed to burn to give off light

can-dor [kăn′dər] *noun*, the quality of being fair, unprejudiced, and honest

cane [kān] *noun*, 1) a hollow stick made from some plants 2) a stick with a curved handle used for support when walking

ca-nine [kā′nīn] *adjective*, relating to dogs

can-is-ter [kăn′ĭ-stər] *noun*, a small box or container, often of metal, for holding tea, coffee, etc.

can-ni-bal [kăn′ə-bəl] *noun*, **a** person who eats people or an animal who eats one of its own kind

can-non [kăn′ən] *noun*, a mounted gun or piece of artillery

can-not [kăn′ŏt] unable to

ca-noe [kə-nōō′] *noun*, a narrow light boat tapered at the ends, moved with paddles

can-o-py [kăn′ə-pē] *noun*, a covering from the sun, an awning or umbrella

cant [kănt] *noun*, 1) empty talk, deceit, 2) jargon, slang, *verb*, 3) to speak insincerely

can't [kănt] the *contraction* of the words **can** and **not**

can-ta-loupe [kăn′tl-ōp′] *noun*, a variety of muskmelon with an orange-red color fruit

can-tan-ker-ous [kăn-tăng′kər-əs] *adjective*, irritable, cross

can-vas [kăn′vəs] *noun*, 1) a strong, coarse, water-repellant cloth used to make tents, sails, etc. 2) a piece of heavy cloth, stretched over a frame, on which pictures are painted

can-vass [kăn′vəs] *verb*, 1) to examine thoroughly, scrutinize 2) to solicit votes or opinions

can-yon [kăn′yən] *noun*, a valley with high, steep sides between hills or mountains

cap [kăp] *noun*, 1) a soft hat 2) the covering for a bottle or tube

ca-pa-ble [kā′pə-bəl] *adjective*, able to do things well, having ability, competent or efficient

ca-pac-i-ty [kə-păs′ĭ-tē] *noun*, 1) the maximum amount of liquid a container can hold, 2) the ability or aptitude for a specified task

cape [kāp] *noun*, 1) a piece of land that goes out into the sea 2) a coat without sleeves that covers shoulders, arms, and back

cap-il-lar-y [kăp′ə-lĕr′ē] *noun*, one of the tiniest blood vessels

cap-i-tal [kăp′ĭ-tl] *adjective*, 1) first, chief, 2 punishable by death, *noun*, 3) resources, means or money 4) the city where the rules for a state or county or country are made 5) a letter that begins a sentence or a proper noun

cap-i-tal-ism [kăp′ĭ-tl-ĭz′əm] *noun*, an economic system based on profit and private ownership

cap-i-tal-ize [kăp′ĭ-tl-īz′] *verb*, 1) to finance or invest in for profit 2) to use a capital letter

Cap-i-tol [kăp′ĭ-tl] *noun*, 1) the building in which the Congress of the United States meets to create laws, **capitol** 2) the building in which a state legislature meets to create laws

ca-price [kə-prēs′] *noun*, a silly thought, a notion, whimsy

cap-size [kăp′sīz′] *verb*, to upset or overturn as of a boat

cap-sule [kăp′səl] *noun*, 1) a container with a matching top and bottom that holds medicine 2) a small spacecraft

cap-tain [kăp′tən] *noun*, the leader of a team or a company of soldiers, or the commander of a ship or aircraft

cap-tion [kăp′shən] *noun*, 1) a short title heading 2) text under an illustration

cap-tive [kăp′tĭv] *adjective*, 1) unable to escape, *noun*, 2) a prisoner

cap-ture [kăp′chər] *verb*, 1) to seize and hold as a prisoner 2) to take hold of something

car [kär] *noun*, an automobile, a form of transportation with four wheels and an engine, usually fueled by gasoline

ca-rafe [kə-răf′] *noun*, a glass bottle, a decanter

car-at [kăr′ət] *noun*, a unit of weight for precious stones

car-a-van [kăr′ə-văn′] *noun*, 1) a group of people traveling together with vehicles or animals 2) a mobile home

car-bo-hy-drate [kär′bō-hī′drāt′] *noun*, a class of foods, that supply energy to the body

car-bon [kär′bən] *noun*, a nonmetallic element, symbolized as C, the required common substance in organic chemistry

car-bo-nate [kär′bə-nāt′] *noun*, a salt of carbonic acid

car-bon di-ox-ide [kär′bən dī-ŏk′sīd] *noun*, a colorless, odorless gas that is absorbed by plants

car-bon mon-ox-ide [kär′bən mə-nŏk′sīd′] *noun*, a colorless, odorless poisonous gas

car-cass [kär′kəs] *noun*, the dead body of an animal or bird

car-cin-o-gen [kär-sĭn′ə-jən] *noun*, a substance that causes cancer

card [kärd] *noun*, a small, flat piece of thick, stiff paper (e.g., a playing card, a postcard, a greeting or business card)

car-di-ac [kär′dē-ăk′] *adjective*, pertaining to the heart, stimulating the heart action

car-di-gan [kär′dĭ-gən] *noun*, a sweater that buttons or opens down the front

car-di-nal [kär′dn-əl] *adjective*, 1) chief, most important, *noun*, 2) an important leader of the Roman Catholic church, appointed by the pope as one of his advisors 3) a bright red bird common in North America

care [kâr] *noun*, 1) thought or interest 2) worry, anxiety, *verb*, 3) to show concern for others 4) to look after someone and tend to his or her needs 5) to show affection or love

ca-reen [kə-rēn′] *verb*, to sway or lean over to one side

ca-reer [kə-rîr′] *noun*, a profession, a chosen pursuit

care-ful [kâr′fəl] *adjective*, cautious, watchful

care-ful-ly [kâr′fə-lē] *adverb*, cautiously, with much care

care-less [kâr′lĭs] *adjective*, neglectful, reckless

ca-ress [kə-rĕs′] *noun*, 1) a tender or loving touch, *verb*, 2) to stroke with affection, to touch in a loving way

car-et [kăr′ĭt] *noun*, a mark used by writers to indicate something – like a word – to be inserted

car-go [kär′gō] *noun*, the goods or freight carried by a ship, train, plane, or any vehicle

car-i-bou [kăr′ə-bōō′] *noun*, a type of reindeer

car-i-ca-ture [kăr′ĭ-kə-chŏŏr′] *noun*, a representation of a person or thing in which the peculiarities are exaggerated to produce a ridiculous effect

car-nage [kär′nĭj] *noun*, the killing of many people, a massacre

car-na-tion [kär-nā′shən] *noun*, a garden flower of the pink family

car-ni-val [kär′nə-vəl] *noun*, a festival with parades and dancing, a fair

car-ni-vore [kär-nĭv′ər] *adjective*, a meat-eating mammal

car-ol [kăr′əl] *noun*, a song of joy

ca-rouse [kə-rouz′] *verb*, to drink and be merry, especially with a group

carp [kärp] *noun*, 1) a kind of fish, *verb*, 2) to find fault, to criticize

car-pen-ter [kär′pən-tər] *noun*, a builder or repairer of wooden structures or objects

car-pen-try [kär′pən-trē] *noun*, the art of making things out of wood

car-pet [kär′pĭt] *noun*, a woven or felted floor covering of wool, cotton, or a synthetic, a rug

car-riage [kăr′ĭj] *noun*, 1) a wheeled vehicle 2) a manner of bearing or posture

car-ri-er [kăr′ē-ər] *noun*, 1) a messenger 2) one engaged in the business of carrying goods for others for hire

car-rot [kăr′ət] *noun*, a plant with an edible root of orange color used as a vegetable

car-ry [kăr′ē] *verb*, 1) to transport something, to convey, to move, to haul 2) to support a weight

cart [kärt] *noun*, a small wagon used to carry goods

car-ti-lage [kär′tl-ĭj] *noun*, elastic animal tissue attached to bones near the joints

car-tog-ra-pher [kär-tŏg′rə-fûr] *noun*, a maker of maps or charts

car-ton [kär′tn] *noun*, a box or container made of cardboard

car-toon [kär-tōōn′] *noun*, a comical drawing of a person, event, or place

car-tridge [kär′trĭj] *noun*, a case holding something that is dispensed mechanically

cart-wheel [kärt′hwēl′] *noun*, a sideways flip that is done by springing the body onto one hand and then the other, followed by the feet

carve [kärv] *verb*, 1) to reshape in an artistic or decorative manner by cutting 2) to cut meat for serving

cas-cade [kă-skād′] *noun*, a small waterfall, a profusion

case [kās] *noun*, 1) a container to hold things 2) a condition, an example of an illness 3) a question of law decided in court 4) something that has happened, an instance

cash [kăsh] *noun*, 1) money consisting of dollars or loose change, *verb*, 2) to receive bills and coins in exchange for a check

cash-ier [kă-shîr′] *noun*, one who has charge of payments, etc., as at a store

cas-ket [kăs′kĭt] *noun*, a coffin

cas-se-role [kăs′ə-rōl′] *noun*, a dish consisting of several different foods combined together

cas-sette [kə-sĕt′, kă-] *noun*, a magnetic tape used for electronic recording enclosed in a plastic case that can fit directly into a recorder

cast [kăst] *noun*, 1) the performers in a play 2) a plaster dressing used to hold surgery in place, *verb*, 3) to direct a glance at someone or something 4) to assign a role in a play 5) to form a shape from clay on a potter's wheel 6) to throw or toss 7) the act of throwing a fishing line 8) to overshadow 9) to register a vote 10) to discard or shed

caste [kăst] *noun*, 1) one of the hereditary classes in Hindu society 2) any exclusive social class

cas-tle [kăs′əl] *noun*, 1) a fortress or palace usually the residence of nobility 2) a chess piece also known as the rook

cas-u-al [kăzh′ōō-əl] *adjective*, 1) not planned or prearranged 2) informal 3) careless

cas-u-al-ty [kăzh′ōō-əl-tē] *noun*, one injured or killed, as in a battle

cat [kăt] *noun*, a furry animal kept in the house as a pet or to catch mice

cat-a-combs [kăt′ə-kōmz′] *noun*, *plural*, a burial ground of underground rooms

cat-a-log [kăt′l-ôg′] *noun*, 1) a list of names, titles, or articles arranged in order, *verb*, 2) to list names and objects with a description of each one

cat-a-lyst [kăt′l-ĭst] *noun*, an agitator or force of change

cat-a-pult [kăt′ə-pŭlt′] noun, 1) a device that uses tension to throw objects, a weapon, *verb*, 2) to hurl or make an object go as far as possible

cat-a-ract [kăt′ə-răkt′] *noun*, 1) a great waterfall 2) an eye abnormality, cloudiness on the lens of the eye resulting in blurry vision

ca-tas-tro-phe [kə-tăs′trə-fē] *noun*, a sudden calamity, a disaster

catch [kăch, kĕch] *noun* 1) something that has been captured 2) the metal clasp that connects a door to a door frame, *verb*, 3) to get hold of something and not let go, to grasp 4) to get someone's attention 5) to trap

cat-e-chism [kăt′ĭ-kĭz′əm] *noun*, a set of questions and answers, especially for teaching about religion

cat-e-go-ry [kăt′ĭ-gôr′ē] *noun*, division or class to which something belongs

ca-ter [kā′tər] *verb*, to provide food or personal attention, to serve up

ca-ter-pil-lar [kăt′ər-pĭl′ər] *noun*, the larva of a butterfly

ca-thar-sis [kə-thär′sĭs] *noun*, 1) purging or cleansing of any part of the body 2) a release of tension or strong feelings

ca-the-dral [kə-thē′drəl] *noun*, a very large church, the main church of a diocese

Cath-o-lic [kăth′ə-lĭk] *noun*, a member of the church that recognizes the pope as its leader

cat-tle [kăt′l] *noun*, livestock such as cows, bulls, or steer kept for meat, milk, or skins

cau-cus [kô′kəs] *noun*, a group of politicians who gather to decide a policy or select a candidate

caught [kôt] *verb*, *past tense* of **catch**

caulk [kôk] *verb*, to make watertight, to seal cracks

cause [kôz] *noun*, 1) the reason, the thing that made something happen 2) something you believe in strongly enough to take action, *verb*, 3) to bring about, to make something happen

caus-tic [kô′stĭk] *adjective*, 1) burning 2) sarcastically biting

cau-tion [kô′shən] *noun*, care and watchfulness, a warning

cau-tious [kô′shəs] *adjective*, wary, prudent, careful, watchful

cave [kāv] *noun*, a hollow place under the ground or in the side of a mountain or rock, sheltered from the elements

ca-ve-at [kā′vē-ăt′] *noun*, an indication of limitations

cav-ern [kăv′ərn] *noun*, a hollow place in a rock, a cave

cav-i-ar [kăv′ē-är′] *noun*, the prepared and salted eggs of the sturgeon or other large fish

cav-i-ty [kăv′ĭ-tē] *noun*, 1) a hollow place or a hole 2) a hole in the tooth caused by decay

cease [sēs] *verb*, to end, to stop

cease-less [sēs/lĭs] *adjective*, without end or interruption

ce-dar [sē/dər] *noun*, a large evergreen tree with reddish, fragrant wood

ceil-ing [sē/lĭng] *noun*, 1) the covering of a room 2) the top of a space 3) upper limit

cel-e-brate [sĕl/ə-brāt/] *verb*, to do certain things because of a special occasion, to rejoice

cel-e-bra-tion [sĕl/ə-brā/-shən] *noun*, a festive occasion

ce-leb-ri-ty [sə-lĕb/rĭ-tē] *noun*, fame, renown, a famous person

ce-ler-i-ty [sə-lĕr/ĭ-tē] *noun*, speed,

cel-er-y [sĕl/ə-rē] *noun*, a plant of the parsley family, whose leaf - stalks are eaten raw or cooked

ce-les-tial [sə-lĕs/chəl] *adjective*, in the stars, heavenly

cel-i-ba-cy [sĕl/ə-bə-sē] *noun*, the state of being unmarried

cell [sĕl] *noun*, 1) a small room where a prisoner is kept or where a nun or monk lives 2) a small, microscopic piece of a living organism

cel-lar [sĕl/ər] *noun*, a room under a house, partly or completely underground, a basement

cel-lu-lar [sĕl/yə-lər] *adjective*, 1) formed of cells 2) relating to a mobile telephone system

Cel-si-us [sĕl/sē-əs] *noun*, a scale on which the freezing point is 0

ce-ment [sĭ-mĕnt/] *noun*, a substance that consists of burned lime and clay, which is mixed with water and sand to make concrete

cem-e-ter-y [sĕm/ĭ-tĕr/ē] *noun*, a burial place, a graveyard

cen-sor [sĕn/sər] *noun*, 1) one who filters inappropriate material from books, movies, etc., before they are published or released *verb*, 2) to filter out information considered unsuitable

cen-sus [sĕn/səs] *noun*, an official count of a population

cent [sĕnt] *noun*, a metal coin equal to one penny or 1/100 of a dollar

cen-ten-ni-al [sĕn-tĕn/ē-əl] *adjective*, of or pertaining to a hundredth anniversary

cen-ter [sĕn/tər] *noun*, 1) the middle, a point equidistant from all sides 2) a place where people gather 3) a hub of activity

cen-ti-grade [sĕn/tĭ-grād/] *noun*, the temperature scale in which 0 degrees is the freezing point and 100 degrees is the boiling point of water

cen-ti-me-ter [sĕn/tə-mē/tər] *noun*, a measure of length somewhat less than ½ an inch, a standard unit in the metric system

cen-tral [sĕn/trəl] *adjective*, located in the middle

cen-trif-u-gal [sĕn-trĭf/yə-gəl] *adjective*, relating to forces caused by rotation directed outward from the center

cen-trip-e-tal [sĕn-trĭp/ĭ-tl] *adjective*, directed toward the center

cen-tu-ry [sĕn/chə-rē] *noun*, a period of one hundred years

ce-re-al [sîr′ē-əl] *noun*, any edible grain, including oats, rye, rice

cer-e-bel-lum [sĕr′ə-bĕl′əm] *noun*, the part of the brain related to muscular movements and coordination

ce-re-bral [sĕr′ə-brəl] *adjective*, appealing to the intellect and not the emotions

cer-e-mo-ni-al [sĕr′ə-mō′nē-əl] *adjective*, following a tradition or certain rituals, formal

cer-e-mo-ny [sĕr′ə-mō′nē] *noun*, a special occasion that honors traditions or rituals

cer-tain [sûr′tn] *adjective*, 1) sure 2) unquestionable 3) not named, but thought to be known

cer-tain-ty [sûr′tn-tē] *noun*, a state of being sure of something

cer-tif-i-cate [sər-tĭf′ĭ-kĭt] *noun*, a document verifying qualification or ability or fact

cer-ti-fy [sûr′tə-fī′] *verb*, to authorize the validity of something, to guarantee

chafe [chāf] *verb*, 1) to rub together leaving a sore 2) to annoy

chaff [chăf] *noun*, 1) a worthless or trivial thing 2) the outer coating of wheat

cha-grin [shə-grĭn′] *noun*, a feeling of embarrassment because one has failed, deep disappointment

chain [chān] *noun*, 1) links or rings joined together, *verb*, 2) to hold with a chain, to restrain

chair [châr] *noun*, furniture with four legs and a back used to seat someone

chal-ice [chăl′ĭs] *noun*, a goblet

chalk [chôk] *noun*, a soft white limestone substance used to write on a blackboard

chal-lenge [chăl′ənj] *noun*, 1) an offer to test ability or skill 2) a formal objection, *verb*, 2) to call or invite to a contest of any kind

cham-ber [chām′bər] *noun*, 1) a room 2) a space surrouded by walls 3) a compartment in a firearm that holds the ammunition

cham-pi-on [chăm′pē-ən] *noun*, the winner of a competition

cham-pi-on-ship [chăm′pē-ən-shĭp′] *noun*, a competition among people or teams to decide who is best

chance [chăns] *noun*, 1) luck, fate 2) possibility or probability 3) risk 4) a turn to do something, an opportunity 5) a coincidence

chan-de-lier [shăn′də-lîr′] *noun*, a branched lighting fixture that hangs from the ceiling in a frame

change [chānj] *noun*, 1) a transformation, the process of becoming different 2) loose coins, *verb*, 3) to make or become different 4) to transform

change-a-ble [chān′jə-bəl] *adjective*, variable, adaptable

chan-nel [chăn′əl] *noun*, 1) a narrow stream of flowing water that connects two large bodies of water, *verb*, 2) to make something, such as energy or water, flow in a certain direction

chant [chănt] *noun*, 1) words repeated in rhythm, *verb*, 2) to speak in a singing way

cha-os [kā'ŏs'] *noun*, disorder, confusion, upheaval

chap-el [chăp'əl] *noun*, a small room within a larger building set aside for religious purposes

chap-er-one [shăp'ə-rōn'] (also **chaperon**) *noun*, an older person who accompanies as a protector

chap-lain [chăp'lĭn] *noun*, a clergyman, minister priest or rabbi serving in a hospital, the armed forces, etc.

chap-ter [chăp'tər] *noun*, a division of a book

char [chär] *verb*, to burn, to scorch

char-ac-ter [kăr'ək-tər] *noun*, 1) the moral makeup of a person 2) a person in a book or movie or play 3) a symbol, sign, or written letter used in a language

char-ac-ter-is-tic [kăr'ək-tə-rĭs'tĭk] *noun*, a trait, an attribute

char-ac-ter-ize [kăr'ək-tə-rīz'] *verb*, to describe, to indicate details or traits of someone or something

char-ac-ter-i-za-tion [kăr'ək-tə-rīz'ā'-shən] *noun*, a description of someone or something

char-coal [chär'kōl'] *noun*, a black porous material made by partially burning wood

charge [chärj] *noun*, 1) an accusation 2) care or instruction given 3) the cost, expense, *verb*, 4) to request money 5) to accuse someone of doing something wrong 6) to rush or attack 7) to fill with power 8) to control

char-i-ot [chăr'ē-ət] *noun*, a horse-drawn cart

cha-ris-ma [kə-rĭz'mə] *noun*, attraction, charm, and allure, having a strong effect on others

char-i-ta-ble [chăr'ĭ-tə-bəl] *adjective*, 1) giving freely and generously 2) lenient, kind

char-i-ty [chăr'ĭ-tē] *noun*, 1) goodness, generosity, and kindness 2) an agency that provides a service to those in need, especially the poor

charm [chärm] *noun*, 1) a pleasant, courteous manner 2) a thing like a talisman or a group of words spoken to cause good luck, *verb*, 3) to please someone

charm-ing [chär'mĭng] *adjective*, pleasing, beautiful, enchanting

chart [chärt] *noun*, 1) a piece of paper or spreadsheet with information on it indicating, patterns, information, or changes, *verb*, 2) to plan a route on a map of the ocean or other large area

char-ter [chär'tər] *noun*, 1) a document establishing the creation of an entity 2) a reservation of a vehicle, ship, etc., *verb*, 3) to hire a ship, bus, plane, etc.

chase [chās] *noun*, 1) the act of running after someone, *verb*, 2) to follow someone while trying to capture them, to pursue

chasm [kăz'əm] *noun*, a deep hole

chas-sis [shăs'ē] *noun*, the under part of a car, consisting of the frame with the wheels and machinery

chaste [chāst] *adjective*, 1) pure, celibate 2) simple in style

chat [chăt] *noun*, 1) a pleasant conversation, *verb*, 2) to make conversation or small talk

chat-tel [chăt/təl]*noun*, a moveable article of personal property

chauf-feur [shō/fər] *noun*, a person employed as a driver of a car

chau-vin-ist [shō/və-nĭst] *noun*, a belief in the superiority of your own race, sex, etc.

cheap [chēp] *adjective*, low in price, inexpensive, poorly made

cheat [chēt] *verb*, to do something that is not honest, to deceive

check [chĕk] *noun*, 1) an order for money, *verb*, 2) to make sure everything is in order

check-ers [chĕk/ərz] *noun*, *plural*, a board game played by two people, each with twelve pieces

cheek [chēk] *noun*, 1) the fleshy skin covering the bone beneath the eye socket on both sides of the face 2) impudent speech

cheer [chîr] *noun*, 1) a shout of support 2) gladness, a joyful state of mind, *verb*, 3) to make happy 4) to encourage with shouts

cheese [chēz] *noun*, the consolidated curd of milk, used as food

chee-tah [chēɴt/ə]*noun*, a swift, animal of Africa and Asia, like a leopard, with a small head, long legs, and black-spotted, tan coat

chef [shĕf] *noun*, a head cook

chem-i-cal [kĕm/ĭ-kəl] *noun*, a substance or mixture of substances used in or produced by changes in atoms or molecules

chem-ist [kĕm/ĭst] *noun*, a person who studies matter such as gases, metal, and liquids to see what they do and what they are made of

chem-is-try [kĕm/ĭ-strē] *noun*, the study of the composition, properties, and reactions of matter, particularly at the level of atoms and molecules

cher-ish [chĕr/ĭsh] *verb*, to love dearly, to adore

cher-ry [chĕr/ē] *noun*, an edible, fleshy, red fruit containing a pit

chess [chĕs] *noun*, a game of skill played on a checkered board by two players each with 16 pieces

chest [chĕst] *noun*, 1) the front of the body between the shoulders and the waist 2) a large box made of metal, wood, etc.

chew [choō] *verb*, to grind food between the teeth

chic [shēk*]* *noun*, great artistic cleverness or skill, style

chick-en [chĭk/ən] *noun*, fowl kept for eggs or meat

chide [chīd] *verb*, to scold

chief [chēf] *adjective*, 1) highest in office or rank, *noun* 2) the leader of a group or organization

chif-fon [shĭ-fŏn/] *noun*, 1) a soft gauzy silk material used for dresses 2) a light airy dessert made with egg whites

child [chīld] *noun*, *plural* **children**, a young person, offspring

child-ish [chīl/dĭsh] *adjective*, to be selfish and inconsiderate

chil-i or chili con carne[chĭl/ē] *noun*, a dish of tomatoes, meat, and sometimes beans, flavored with hot spices

chill [chĭl] *adjective*, 1) cold, frosty, *noun*, 2) coldness, freezing, *verb*, 3) to make or become cold

chime [chīm] *verb*, to make a tinkling sound like a bell

chim-ney [chĭm′nē] *noun*, a structure by which smoke passes from a building to the outdoors

chim-pan-zee [chĭm′păn-zē′] *noun*, an ape native to Africa larger than a monkey, without a tail

chin [chĭn] *noun*, the part of the face below the lips

chi-na [chī′nə] *noun*, *no plural*, dishes, such as plates, cups, and saucers, made of fine clay or porcelain, used to serve a meal

chip [chĭp] *noun*, 1) a small piece of something that has broken off 2) a cracker or a thinly sliced fried food 3) the small silicon object that enables the computer to process information, *verb*, 4) to break off small pieces from the main part

chip-munk [chĭp′mŭngk′] *noun*, a tan rodent like a small squirrel with a black stripe from its head to the tip of its tail

chirp [chûrp] *noun*, 1) a high pitched sound, *verb*, 2) to warble, to tweet like a bird

chis-el [chĭz′əl] *noun*, 1) a metal tool with a cutting edge at the end of a blade, *verb*, 2) to carve a sculpture or use a chisel as a tool 3) to swindle, to cheat

chiv-al-ry [shĭv′əl-rē] *noun*, bravery, heroism, courtesy,

chlo-ride [klôr′īd] *noun*, a compound of chlorine with another substance

chlo-rine [klôr′ēn′] *noun*, a yellow-green gas added to water supplies as a disinfectant

chlo-ro-form [klôr′ə-fôrm′] *noun*, a colorless, sweetish liquid used as an anesthetic

chlo-ro-phyll [klôr′ə-fĭl] *noun*, a green pigment in plants, essential for photosynthesis

choc-o-late [chô′kə-lĭt] *noun*, a candy made from cocoa, the roasted seeds of cacao

choice [chois] *adjective*, 1) first rate, *noun*, 2) an act of making a selection or choosing

choir [kwīr] *noun*, a band of singers, especially in church

choke [chōk] *verb*, 1) to feel suffocated because the throat is obstructed 2) to repress

chol-er [kŏl′ər] *noun*, anger

choose [chōōz] *verb*, to pick or select from a group, to make a choice

chop [chŏp] *noun*, 1) a piece of meat near the bone, *verb*, 2) to cut with a sharp blade

cho-ral [kôr′əl] *adjective*, for or relating to a chorus

chord [kôrd] *noun*, a combination of three or more tones sounded together in harmony

chore [chôr] *noun*, a job or distasteful task

cho-re-og-ra-phy [kôr′ē-ŏg′rə-fē, kōr′-] *noun*, 1) the plan of the steps and movements in dancing 2) the creation of ballets or dances

chor-tle [chôr′tl] *verb*, to make a chuckling or snorting noise

cho-rus [kôr′əs] *noun*, 1) a company of singers singing in concert 2) the part of a song that is repeated, the refrain

chow-der [chou′dər] *noun*, a thick soup or stew usually featuring fish, corn, etc.

chris-ten [krĭs′ən] *verb*, to give a name to someone who is baptized into the Christian faith

Chris-tian [krĭs′chən] *noun*, a person who believes in Jesus Christ

chromosome [krō′mə-sōm′] *noun*, a thread-like structure in the nucleus of a cell that carries the genes

chron-ic [krŏn′ĭk] *adjective*, continuing for a long time, habitual, prolonged

chron-i-cle [krŏn′ĭ-kəl] *noun*, 1) a historical register of facts in order of their occurrence, *verb*, 2) to record in a factual and detailed way

chron-o-log-i-cal [krŏn′ə-lŏj′ĭ-kəl] *adjective*, documented according to the order of time

chuck-le [chŭk′əl] *noun*, 1) a quick laugh or giggle, *verb*, 2) to laugh softly, in a gentle manner

chunk [chŭngk] *noun*, a thick piece of something, a block, a slab

church [chûrch] *noun*, a building in which Christians meet to worship and pray

churn [chûrn] *verb*, to move about with force, to turn violently

ci-der [sī′dər] *noun*, a drink made from pressed apples

ci-gar [sĭ-gär′] *noun*, tobacco leaves rolled together in paper for smoking

cig-a-ret-te [sĭg′ə-rĕt′] *noun*, a cylinder of finely cut tobacco rolled in paper

cin-der [sĭn′dərz] *noun*, a hot coal, an ember

cin-e-ma [sĭn′ə-mə] *noun*, 1) a building where films are shown 2) the movie business

cin-na-mon [sĭn′ə-mən] *noun*, the bark of an East Indian tree, ground into a spice

cir-cle [sûr′kəl] *noun*, 1) a closed curve in which all points are equidistant from the center, a ring 2) a group of people

cir-cuit [sûr′kĭt] *noun*, the circumference or distance around an area

cir-cuit-ous [sər-kyōō′ĭ-təs] *adjective*, roundabout, indirect, meandering, winding

cir-cu-lar [sûr′kyə-lər] *adjective*, 1) round, *noun*, 2) a leaflet, a pamphlet, a newsletter

cir-cu-late [sûr′kyə-lāt′] *verb*, to move about or around

cir-cu-la-tion [sûr′kyə-lā′shən] *noun*, 1) the act of moving around, especially of blood through the body 2) the extent or amount of distribution, dissemination

cir-cum-fer-ence [sər-kŭm′fər-əns] *noun*, the distance around a circle or circular figure

cir-cum-lo-cu-tion [sûr′kəm-lō-kyōō′shən] *noun*, an indirect or roundabout way of expressing something

cir-cum-spec-tion [sûr′kəm-spĕk′shən] *noun*, caution, care, forethought

cir-cum-stance [sûr′kəm-stăns′] *noun*, a particular incident, a state of affairs, events

cir-cum-stan-tial [sûr′kəm-stăn′shəl] *adjective*, relating to evidence that tends to prove a fact at issue by proving other basic events

cir-cum-vent [sûr′kəm-věnt′] *verb*, to find a way around, to evade a difficulty

cir-cus [sûr′kəs] *noun*, a traveling show usually performed by clowns and acrobats and tamed animals presented in an arena

cit-a-del [sĭt′ə-dəl] *noun*, fortress

ci-ta-tion [sī-tā′shən] *noun*, 1) a summons to appear in court, a ticket 2) a quote or reference to a document 3) honorary mention to receive an award or degree for meritorious service

cite [sīt] *verb*, 1) to quote or refer to a document 2) to recognize someone for commendable service 3) to write a ticket for violating the law

cit-i-zen [sĭt′ĭ-zən] *noun*, a person whose legal home is a certain place or nation

cit-i-zen-ship [sĭt′ĭ-zən-shĭp′] *noun*, 1) the fact of being a citizen 2) community participation

cit-y [sĭt′ē] *noun*, a large important town, a metropolis

civ-ic [sĭv′ĭk] *adjective*, pertaining to a community or city

civ-il [sĭv′əl] *adjective*, 1) polite 2) relating to a government employee who is not in the armed forces

ci-vil-ian [sĭ-vĭl′yən] *noun*, a person not in the armed forces

ci-vil-i-ty [sĭ-vĭl′ĭ-tē] *noun*, good manners, courtesy

civ-i-li-za-tion [sĭv′ə-lĭ-zā′shən] *noun*, 1) the condition of being civilized or having culture 2) people sharing their way of life and living in one place at a time, any human society

civ-i-lize [sĭv′ə-līz′] *verb*, to reclaim from a savage state

civ-il war *noun*, a war fought in a country between two different groups of the same nation

claim [klām] *noun*, 1) a statement, an assertion *verb*, 2) to say and demand possession of something by demonstrating ownership

claim-ant [klā′mənt] *noun*, a person submitting an application or making a claim

clair-voy-ant [klâr-voi′ənt] *adjective*, having foresight

clam [klăm] *noun*, a shellfish similar to an oyster

clam-or [klăm′ər] *noun*, 1) a loud steady noise, an outcry, *verb*, 2) to make a lot of noise

clan [klăn] *noun*, a group of people sharing one ancestor

clan-des-tine [klăn-děs′tĭn] *adjective*, secret, concealed

clang [klăng] *noun*, the sound of one piece of metal hitting another, a ringing sound

clap [klăp] *noun*, 1) a loud noise, as in thunder, *verb*, 2) to make a sound by hitting your hands together, applause

clar-i-fy [klăr′ə-fī′] *verb*, to make or become clear, to explain

clar-i-on [klăr′ē-ən] *adjective*, shrill, loud and clear

clar-i-ty [klăr′ĭ-tē] *adjective*, clearness

clash [klăsh] *noun*, 1) a fight or angry dispute 2) the sound of metal on metal, *verb*, 3) to hit or fight 4)of colors, to look awful together 5) to collide noisily

clasp [klăsp] *noun*, 1) a fastening, *verb*, 2) to hold tightly

class [klăs] *noun*, 1) a group of similar things or people 2) students meeting together for instruction, *verb*, 3) to classify

clas-sic [klăs′ĭk] *adjective*, showing excellence, exemplary

clas-si-cal [klăs′ĭ-kəl] *adjective*, 1)pertaining to ancient Greeks and Romans 2)excellent in a traditional style, esp. of music

clas-si-fi-ca-tion [klăs′ə-fĭ-kā′shən] *noun*, categorizing, grouping

clas-si-fy [klăs′ə-fī′] *verb*, to sort, to form into classes or groupings

clause [klôz] *noun*, 1) a group of words in a sentence that contains a subject and a verb 2) a single part in a contract, law, or treaty

claus-tro-pho-bi-a [klô′strə-fō′bē-ə] *noun*, a fear of being in a close space

claw [klô] *noun*, 1) the sharp, hard nails on the foot of an animal or bird, *verb*, 2) to tear or scratch with the hand or nails

clay [klā] *noun*, a common earth used for making pottery and bricks when baked

clean [klēn] *adjective*, 1) free from dirt, neat, *verb*, 2) to remove dirt and soil or impurities

clean-li-ness [klĕn′lē-nĭs] *noun*, the state of being clean, neatness of person, good hygiene

cleanse [klĕnz] *verb*, 1) to scrub, to wash, to disinfect 2) to absolve

clear [klîr] *adjective*, 1) easily understood 2) transparent 3) distinct or easy to hear, *verb*, 4) to remove items 5) to remove an obstacle, to bring into focus

clear-ance [klîr′əns] *noun*, 1) the act of removing whatever may obstruct 2) permission

clear-ly [klîr′lē] *adverb*, plainly

cleave [klēv] *verb*, 1) to cling, to adhere to 2) to separate or split

cleft [klĕft] *noun*, a space or opening made by or as if by splitting, a crack, a fissure

clem-en-cy [klĕm′ən-sē] *noun*, mildness, leniency, mercy

clench [klĕnch] *verb*, to hold tightly, to grip, to grasp

cler-gy [klûr′j*noun*, ministers of the church as a group

clerk [klûrk] *noun*, a person who does office work, a salesperson

cle-ver [klĕv′ər] *adjective*, quick at learning, smart, good at doing things, resourceful, intelligent

cli-ché [klē-shā′] *noun*, a phrase repeated often, e.g. *down and out*

click [klĭk] *verb*, 1) to make a small noise like a tick on a clock 2) to press the mouse button once

cli-ent [klī′ənt] *noun*, a customer who uses the professional help of another, a patron

cliff [klĭf] *noun*, a high, steep wall of rock or bank on a coast

cli-mate [klī′mĭt] *noun*, the typical weather or atmosphere of a place year after year

cli-max [klī′mǎks′] *noun*, the crucial point when everything comes together, culmination

climb [klīm] *noun*, 1) the distance traveled up a hill or mountain, *verb*, 2) to go up, to ascend

clime [klīm] *noun*, region, climate

cling [klĭng] *verb*, to hold on tightly, to clutch, to grip

cling-ing [klĭng′ĭng] *adjective*, 1) devoted 2) holding fast 3) dependent

clin-ic [klĭn′ĭk] *noun*, a place that provides medical treatment

clin-ic-al [klĭn′ĭ-kəl] *adjective*, 1) related to observation and treatment of patients 2) scientific and observable

clip [klĭp] *noun*, 1) an object used to fasten things 2) a brisk pace, *verb*, 3) to cut or trim

clique [klēk] *noun*, a small group with joint interests, an exclusive set of friends, a gang

cloak [klōk] *noun*, 1) a loose piece of clothing, usually sleeveless, worn as an outer garment, *verb*, 2) to conceal

clock [klŏk] *noun*, an instrument used to measure time

clog [klôg] *noun*, 1) a blockage 2) a thick-soled shoe with an open back, *verb*, 3) to dance in the shoes 4) to hinder or obstruct, to be blocked up

close [klōs] *adjective*, 1) near 2) alike, similar, *verb*, 3) to shut out 4) to bring or come to an end

clos-et [klŏz′ĭt] *noun*, a small room or space where clothes are hung and items are stored

clot [klŏt] *noun*, a thickened mass of blood tissue

cloth [klôth] *noun*, a piece of fabric made of natural or synthetic fibers, such as cotton or rayon

cloth-ing [klō′thĭng] *noun*, *no plural*, garments, apparel, things worn as clothes, articles of dress

cloud [kloud] *noun*, 1) a visible mass of water droplets floating in the sky 2) a mass of dust

cloud-y [klou′dē] *adjective*, filled with clouds, overcast

clown [kloun] *noun*, a person who has the ability to turn himself or herself into a comical character that brings happiness and joy; especially to children, the sick, and sad

club [klŭb] *noun*, 1) a group of people who meet for a common purpose 2) a heavy stick

clue [kloō] *noun*, information or evidence that helps you find the answer to a puzzling question

clum-sy [klŭm′zē] *adjective*, awkward, unhandy, unwieldy

clus-ter [klŭs′tər] *noun*, 1) a clump, a bunch, a small, close group, *verb*, 2) to gather together into a small group

clutch [klŭch] *noun*, 1) the part of a machine that connects and disconnects the power from the rest of the machine, *verb*, 2) to hold something tightly, to grip, to cling to

clut-ter [klŭt′ər] *noun*, things lying about, a mess

coach [kōch] *noun*, 1) one who trains athletes, actors, or singers 2) a part of a train or bus that carries passengers 3) a carriage drawn by horses, *verb*, 4) to assist talented people develop their capability, to train

co-ag-u-late [kō-ăg′yə-lāt′] *verb*, to form into a dense mass, solidify from a liquid, to congeal

coal [kōl] *noun*, a fossil fuel in solid form that gives off heat when burned

co-a-lesce [kō′ə-lĕs′] *verb*, to combine, to fuse, to join together

co-a-li-tion [kō′ə-lĭsh′ən] *noun*, a union of people of differing views in a single body or group

coarse [kôrs, kōrs] *adjective*, 1) rough in surface or texture 2) crude, ill-mannered

coast [kōst] *noun*, 1) the edge of land that touches the ocean, *verb*, 2) to slide or glide

coat [kōt] *noun*, a piece of clothing with sleeves, worn over everything else, a jacket

coax [kōks] *verb*, to gently persuade

cob-bler [kŏb′lər] *noun*, someone who makes and repairs shoes

cob-web [kŏb′wĕb′] *noun*, threads woven by a spider in which it catches insects

co-caine [kō-kān′] *noun*, a bitter, crystalline alkaloid used as a local anesthetic and illegally as a stimulant

cock [kŏk] *noun*, a male bird

cock-pit [kŏk′pĭt′] *noun*, the compartment in a vehicle where the driver of a race car or the pilot of an airplane sits

co-co-nut [kō′kə-nŭt′] *noun*, the fruit of a variety of palm tree

co-coon [kə-kōōn′] *noun*, the silky case insects live in during the pupa stage

cod [kŏd] *noun*, *no plural*, a family of sea fish used for food

cod-dle [kŏd′l] *verb*, to treat gently, to pamper, to spoil

code [kōd] *noun*, 1) a collection of laws 2) a system of symbols given certain meanings

co-erce [kō-ûrs′] *verb*, to persuade by force

co-er-cion [kō-ûr′zhən] *noun*, persuasion by force or threats, pressuring

cof-fee [kô′fē] *noun*, the hot beverage made from the seeds of a coffee plant, a pale brown color

cof-fin [kô′fĭn] *noun*, a box in which a dead body is placed

cog [kŏg] *noun*, the tooth projecting from a wheel rim or a bar

cog-ni-zant [kŏg′nĭ-zənt] *adjective*, conscious, aware, knowledgeable

co-her-ent [kō-hîr′ənt] *adjective*, 1) able to be understood 2) forming a connection

co-he-sion [kō-hē′zhən] *noun*, the act of sticking together

coil [koil] *noun*, 1) a wire in a continuous circling shape, *verb*, 2) to wrap up around in a ring

coin [koin] *noun*, 1) a piece of money made of metal, legally authorized by a government 2) a quantity of value, *verb*, 3) to make coins 4)to invent

co-in-cide [kō'ĭn-sīd'] *verb*, to occur at the same time, to correspond exactly

co-in-cid-ence [kō-ĭn'sĭ-dəns] *noun*, random events that happen at the same time, chance, luck

col-an-der [kŭl'ən-dər] *noun*, a bowl-shaped container that is perforated for use as a strainer

cold [kōld] *adjective*, 1) feeling no heat, not warm 2) unfriendly, *noun*, 3) a virus with symptoms of a sore throat and runny nose

col-lab-o-rate [kə-lăb'ə-rāt'] *verb*, to work together as a group

col-lab-o-ra-tion [kə-lăb'ə-rā'shən] *noun*, a project that includes ideas from two or more people working together

col-lapse [kə-lăps'] *noun*, 1) any sudden or complete breakdown, *verb*, 2) to break down suddenly 3) to fall down

col-lar [kŏl'ər] *noun*, 1) a band worn around the neck of an animal 2) the part of a shirt around the neck

col-late [kə-lāt'] *verb*, 1) to examine in order to verify a special authenticity 2) to combine and arrange in order

col-lat-er-al [kə-lăt'ər-əl]*adjective*, 1)secondary, *noun*, 2) security in the form of property for repayment of a loan

col-league [kŏl'ēg'] *noun*, an associate from work, a friend or a peer, a co-worker

col-lect [kə-lĕkt'] *verb*, 1) to accumulate, to compile, to scrape together 2) to gather, to meet, to flock, to convene

col-lec-tion [kə-lĕk'shən] *noun*, an accumulation of things of a similar nature

col-lec-tive [kə-lĕk'tĭv] *adjective*, gathered, compiled, joint

col-lege [kŏl'ĭj] *noun*, a place where people study after high school that gives degrees

col-lide [kə-līd'] *verb*, to come together with great force

col-li-sion [kə-lĭzh'ən] *noun*, the act of striking or dashing together, a crash

co-lon [kō'lən] *noun*, 1) the sign [:] which is used before a listing or examples 2) the part of the large intestine extending to the rectum

colo-nel [kûr'nəl] *noun*, the commanding officer of a regiment, below brigadier general

co-lo-ni-al [kə-lō'nē-əl] *adjective*, relating to a period in America before independence

col-o-nist [kŏl'ə-nĭst] *noun*, someone who settles a territory

col-o-ni-za-tion [kŏl'ə-nĭ-zā'shən] *noun*, the act of setting up homes and starting a community in a new place with the purpose of living there a long time

col-o-ny [kŏl'ə-nē] *noun*, a country, area, etc.under the jurisdiction of another country and occupied by settlers

col-or [kŭl'ər] *noun*, 1) any of the hues of the rainbow, including white, *verb*, 2) to paint, dye, tint, to change the hue 3) to affect

Col-o-ra-do [kŏl'ə-răd'ō] *noun*, one of the United States, the capital city is Denver. The state flower of Colorado is the rocky mountain columbine, and the motto is "Nothing without the divine will."

co-los-sal [kə-lŏs'əl] *adjective*, huge, gigantic, immense

colt [kōlt] *noun*, a young male horse

col-umn [kŏl'əm] *noun*, 1) a supporting pillar 2) a perpendicular set of lines of a text in a book or periodical

col-um-nist [kŏl'əm-nĭst] *noun*, a writer who is featured regularly in a newspaper, or magazine

co-ma [kō'mə] *noun*, state of being unresponsive, unconsciousness

comb [kōm] *noun*, 1) a piece of plastic, wood, or metal with teeth to smooth and adjust hair, *verb*, 2) to tidy hair with a comb

com-bat [kəm-băt'] *noun*, 1) an armed battle, *verb*, 2) to fight

com-bi-na-tion [kŏm'bə-nā'shən] *noun*, the act or result of combining, a union, a mixture

com-bine [kəm-bīn'] *verb*, to mix together, to blend, to unite

com-bus-ti-ble [kəm-bŭs'tə-bəl] *adjective*, apt to catch fire and burn, flammable

come [kŭm] *verb*, 1) to arrive, to approach 2) to happen

com-e-dy [kŏm'ĭ-dē] *noun*, a funny performance that makes the audience laugh, humor

come-ly [kŭm'lē] *adjective*, attractive, beautiful, or handsome

com-et [kŏm'ĭt] *noun*, a celestial object of a frozen mass of dust that vaporizes as it nears the sun

com-fort [kŭm'fərt] *noun*, 1) consolation in trouble, *verb*, 2) to show kindness to someone, to console

com-fort-a-ble [kŭm'fər-tə-bəl] *adjective*, relaxed, content

com-ic [kŏm'ĭk] *adjective*, funny, humorous

com-ma [kŏm'ə] *noun*, a punctuation mark (,) used to indicate pauses and to separate elements within a sentence

com-mand [kə-mănd'] *noun*, 1) an order 2) mastery, rule, *verb*, 3) to be in charge of, to order someone to do something

com-man-deer [kŏm'ən-dîr'] *verb*, to take, often for military use

com-mem-o-rate [kə-mĕm'ə-rāt'] *verb*, to honor, to memorialize

com-mence-ment [kə-mĕns'mənt] *noun*, 1) the beginning 2) the ceremony of graduation

com-mend [kə-mĕnd'] *verb*, to praise, to compliment, to support

com-men-su-rate [kə-mĕn'sər-ĭt] *adjective*, equal in extent, in proportion, corresponding

com-ment [kŏm'ĕnt] *noun*, 1) a remark or something said, *verb*, 2) to make a remark about something, to express an opinion

com-ment-ary [kŏm'ĕntrĕr'ē] *noun*, remarks or observations about something, an explanation

com-merce [kŏm'ərs] *noun*, business, the buying and selling of goods, all forms of trade

com-mer-cial [kə-mûr'shəl] *adjective*,
1) for business purposes, having
profit as an aim, *noun*, 2) an
advertisement on television or radio

com-mis-er-ate [kə-mĭz'ə-rāt']
verb, to feel or express sorrow

com-mis-sion [kə-mĭsh'ən] *noun*,
1) a committee or board that
studies an issue 2) the
percentage paid to an agent

com-mit [kə-mĭt'] *verb*, 1) to
entrust 2) to pledge 3) to act out,
to perform 4) to put into custody

com-mit-ment [kə-mĭt'mənt] *noun*, a
pledge, a promise, a responsibility

com-mit-tee [kə-mĭt'ē] *noun*, a
group appointed or formed to
consider or accomplish some
matter or business

com-mod-i-ty [kə-mŏd'ĭ-tē] *noun*,
an item that can be bought and
sold, merchandise

com-mon [kŏm'ən] *adjective*,
1) ordinary, found everywhere,
general 2) joint, shared, *noun*,
3) a public outdoor space

com-mon-wealth [kŏm'ən-wĕlth']
noun, 1) a group of independent
states in a country 2) a self-
governed nation or state

com-mo-tion [kə-mō'shən] *noun*,
noise, confusion, disruption,

com-mune [kŏm'yōon'] *noun*,
a living arrangement in which
everyone shares possessions,
work, etc.

com-mu-ni-ca-ble
[kə-myōo'nĭ-kə-bəl] *adjective*,
contagious, infectious

com-mu-ni-cate [kə-myōo'nĭ-kāt']
verb, 1) to give or exchange
information 2) to transmit

com-mu-ni-ca-tion
[kə-myōo'nĭ-kā'shən] *noun*,
1) exchange of information
between people 2) that which is
made known 3) transmission

com-mun-ion [kə'myōonyən]
noun, 1) the mutual sharing of
feelings and thoughts 2) a
religious fellowship among
members of a church

com-mu-nism [kŏm'yə-nĭz'əm]
noun, a political system in which
property is owned by the state

com-mu-nist [kŏm'yə-nĭst] *noun*, a
person who believes the state
should own all industry and land

com-mu-ni-ty [kə-myōo'nĭ-tē]
noun, a town, city, suburb, or
other place where people live
and work, a society

com-mute [kə-myōot'] *verb*, 1) to
make a sentence of punishment
less severe 2) to travel, to go back
and forth to work

com-pact [kəm-păkt'] *adjective*,
1) taking up a small amount of
space, *noun*, 2) a small case
with makeup and a mirror 3) an
agreement, *verb*, 4) to press
close together

com-pan-ion [kəm-păn'yən] *noun*,
a friend or associate, one who
accompanies another

com-pa-ny [kŭm'pə-nē] *noun*,
1) an association for business or
social purposes 2) a corporation
or firm 3) guests, visitors 4) a
subdivision of a regiment

com-pa-ra-ble [kŏm'pər-ə-bəl]
adjective, similar, equivalent

com-pare [kəm-pâr'] *verb*, to look
at similarities and differences

com-par-i-son [kəm-păr′ĭ-sən] *noun*, an examination of two or more objects with the view to discovering the similarities or differences, contrast

com-pass [kŭm′pəs] *noun*, 1) an instrument using a magnetic needle that always points to the north 2) a tool used to draw a circle 3) a range, scope, or limits

com-pas-sion [kəm-păsh′ən] *noun*, sympathy for suffering, kindness

com-pat-i-ble [kəm-păt′ə-bəl] *adjective*, in harmony with something, well-suited

com-pel [kəm-pĕl′] *verb*, 1) to drive or urge with force 2) to coerce

com-pen-di-um [kəm-pĕn′dē-əm] *noun*, an abridgement, collection, summary of information

com-pen-sate [kŏm′pən-sāt′] *verb*, to make up for something, to make amends, to pay

com-pen-sa-tion [kŏm′pən-sā′shən] *noun*, an amount paid to make up for something, payment

com-pete [kəm-pēt′] *verb*, to try to win a race, contest, etc.

com-pe-tent [kŏm′pĭ-tənt] *adjective*, capable, qualified, adequate, proficient, able

com-pe-ti-tion [kŏm′pĭ-tĭsh′ən] *noun*, 1) rivalry, free market conditions 2) a contest to see who performs better, a game

com-pet-i-tor [kəm-pĕt′ĭ-tər] *noun*, a rival, one who competes

com-pile [kəm-pīl′] *verb*, to gather information

com-pla-cen-cy [kəm-plā′sən-sē] *noun*, self-satisfaction, smugness

com-plac-ent [kəm-plā′sənt] *adjective*, 1) self-satisfied, smug 2) agreeable, lazy

com-plain [kəm-plān′] *verb*, 1) to express unhappiness or dissatisfaction or resentment 2) to make a formal accusation

com-plaint [kəm-plānt′] *noun*, 1) a criticism, reproach 2) an illness

com-ple-ment [kŏm′plə-mənt] *noun*, that which fills up, completes, or balances

com-plete [kəm-plēt′] *adjective*, 1) lacking nothing, full, whole, 2) finished, *verb*, 3) to finish

com-plex [kəm-plĕks′] *adjective*, 1) complicated, puzzling 2) consisting of connected parts, *noun*, 3) a group of buildings

com-plex-ion [kəm-plĕk′shən] *noun*, 1) the color or hue of the skin of the face 2) general appearance or aspect

com-pli-ance [kəm-plī′əns] *noun*, the act of yielding to demand, consent, agreement

com-plic-ate [kŏm′plĭ-kāt′] *verb*, to confuse, to perplex, to make more difficult or complex

com-pli-ment [kŏm′plə-mənt] *noun*, 1) nice words said about someone, praise, *verb*, 2) to express admiration, to laud

com-ply [kəm-plī′] *verb*, to follow, to conform, to go along with an order or a rule

com-po-nent [kəm-pō′nənt] *noun*, an essential part, a fundamental piece, a constituent part

com-port [kəm-pôrt′] *verb*, to carry oneself in a specified way

com-pose [kəm-pōz′] *verb*, 1) to write or create music, literature, etc. 2) to blend the ingredients or components of something

com-pos-ite [kəm-pŏz′ĭt] *adjective*, 1) made up of separate distinctive parts 2) relating to a combination of the Corinthian and Ionic styles of architecture

com-po-si-tion [kŏm′pə-zĭsh′ən] *noun*, 1) something written, such as a story or music 2) a creation

com-post [kŏm′pōst′] *noun*, the product from the decomposition of organic materials, such as yard waste or dead plants

com-po-sure [kəm-pō′zhər] *noun*, a settled state, calmness

com-pound [kŏm-pound′] *noun*, 1) a composite, a mixture 2) a fenced-in area with one or more buildings in it, *verb*, 3) to make by mixing together 4) to increase

com-pre-hend [kŏm′prĭ-hĕnd′] *verb*, to understand

com-pre-hen-sive [kŏm′prĭ-hĕn′sĭv] *adjective*, thorough, all-inclusive

com-press [kŏm′prĕs′] *noun*, 1) a bandage, a pad, *verb*, [kŭm′prĕs] 2) to pack, to squeeze

com-prise [kəm-prīz′] *verb*, to include, consisting of

com-pro-mise [kŏm′prə-mīz′] *noun*, 1)the result of adjustments made by concessions to make a mutual agreement, *verb* 2) to adjust by making concessions

com-pul-sion [kəm-pŭl′shən] *noun*, 1) duress, urgency, duty 2) an obsession, a fixation

com-pul-so-ry [kəm-pŭl′sə-rē] *adjective*, required, mandatory

com-pute [kəm-pyōōt′] *verb*, to figure mathematically

com-put-er [kəm-pyōōt′ər] *noun*, an electronic device for storing and processing data, typically in binary form, according to instructions given to it in a software program

com-rade [kŏm′răd′] *noun*, a faithful friend, a colleague

con-cave [kŏn-kāv′] *adjective*, sunken, as the inside of a sphere or a spoon

con-ceal [kən-sēl′] *verb*, to hide , to disguise, to keep from sight

con-cede [kən-sēd′] *verb*, to surrender, to grant, to allow

con-ceit [kən-sēt′] *noun*, vanity, an exaggerated opinion of oneself, self-importance

con-ceive [kən-sēv′] *verb*, 1) to imagine, to take into one's mind 2) to become pregnant

con-cen-trate [kŏn′sən-trāt′] *verb*, 1) to focus all one's thoughts and efforts on 2) to bring or come together in one place to increase the strength of

con-cen-tra-tion [kŏn′sən-trā′shən] *noun*, 1) density, consistency 2) close attention, intense thought

con-cen-tric [kən-sĕn′trĭk] *adjective*, having a common center

con-cept [kŏn′sĕpt′] *noun*, an abstract idea, a thought

con-cep-tion [kən-sĕp′shən] *noun*, 1) the act of conceiving life 2) the beginning or understanding of an idea

con-cern [kən-sûrn′] *noun*,
1) anxiety 2) something that involves a person or people, *verb*, 3) to be about, to interest 4) to trouble or worry

con-cert [kŏn′sûrt′] *noun*, 1) music played for an audience, [kŏn′sûrt] *verb* 2) to plan or arrange together

con-ces-sion [kən-sĕsh′ən] *noun*, the act of yielding, a grant

con-cil-i-ate [kən-sĭl′ē-āt]*verb*, to gain goodwill, to placate

con-cil-i-a-to-ry [kən-sĭl′ē-ə-tôr′ē] *adjective*, making less angry or hostile to overcome animosity

con-cise [kən-sīs′] *adjective*, short, to the point, brief, succinct

con-clude [kən-klōōd′] *verb*, 1) to form an opinion after thinking about something 2) to finish to bring or come to an end

con-clu-sion [kən-klōō′zhən] *noun*, 1) the end, an outcome 2) a decision, a judgment

con-coct [kən-kŏkt′] *verb*, 1) to prepare by combining different ingredients 2) to devise a plan or scheme, to invent

con-cor-dant [kən-kôr′dant] *adjective*, in agreement, harmonious

con-crete [kŏn-krēt′] *adjective*, 1) not abstract, particular, *noun*, 2) a compound mass of cement, sand, gravel, and water used for building

con-cus-sion [kən-kŭsh′ən] *noun*, a head injury that is the result of a blow or a fall, a shock

con-demn [kən-dĕm′] *verb*, 1)to pronounce sentence against someone 2) to disapprove of or censure, to denounce

con-dem-na-tion [kŏn′dĕm-nā′shən] *noun*, criticism, blame, an objection

con-den-sa-tion [kŏn′dĕn-sā′shən] *noun*, 1) the act, process, or state of compressing or being compressed into a smaller enclosed space 2) the process by which a substance changes from its gaseous state to a liquid state 3) the liquid formed by this process

con-dense [kən-dĕns′] *verb*, to shorten or compress

con-de-scend [kŏn′dĭ-sĕnd′] *verb*, to act superior to someone else

con-di-ment [kŏn′də-mənt] *noun*, a type of relish or seasoning

con-di-tion [kən-dĭsh′ən] *noun*, 1) a stipulation or provision 2) the state in which a person or thing exists, *verb*, 3) to prepare, to adapt, to train, to influence

con-di-tion-ing [kən-dĭsh′ən-ing] *noun*, preparation, training

con-dol-ence [kən-dō′ləns] *noun*, an offering of sympathy, an expression of regret

con-done [kən-dōn′] *verb*, to pardon, to forgive, to overlook

con-du-cive [kən-dōō′sĭv] *adjective*, tending to promote, helpful, beneficial

con-duct *noun*, [kən-dŭkt′] 1) behavior, [kən-dŭkt′] *verb*, 2) to lead or guide 3) to direct

con-duc-tor [kən-dŭk′tər] *noun*, 1) someone who sells tickets on a train 2) something that transmits energy 3) the leader of a musical ensemble

con-duit [kŏn′dōō-ĭt] *noun*, a channel or passage through which electrical wires run

cone [kōn] *noun*, 1) a cylinder that tapers to a point at the end 2) the reproductive structures of the conifer trees, a pine cone 3) a cylindrical wafer on which a scoop of ice cream is placed

con-fed-er-ate [kən-fĕd′ər-ĭt] *noun*, 1) an ally, an accomplice **Confederate** 2) someone who fought for the Confederacy during the Civil War

con-fed-er-a-tion [kən-fĕd′ə-rā′shən] *noun*, a coalition, a group of people working together, an alliance

con-fer [kən-fûr′] *verb*, 1) to give as a gift 2) to meet and discuss

con-fer-ence [kŏn′fər-əns] *noun*, a meeting for an exchange of ideas, a conversation with someone to share information

con-fess [kən-fĕs′] *verb*, to acknowledge or admit a fault

con-fes-sion [kən-fĕsh′ən] *noun*, an admission of guilt or wrongdoing

con-fet-ti [kən-fĕt′ē] *noun*, small pieces of colorful paper

con-fi-dant [kŏn′fĭ-dănt′] *noun*, one to whom secrets are entrusted, a friend

con-fide [kən-fīd′] *verb*, to trust, to disclose a secret, to reveal

con-fi-dence [kŏn′fĭ-dəns] *noun*, complete trust, a secret

con-fi-dent [kŏn′fĭ-dənt] *adjective*, assured beyond doubt, certain

con-fi-den-tial [kŏn′fĭ-dĕn′shəl] *adjective*, secret, private, trusted

con-fine [kən-fīn′] *verb*, to restrain within a specific place, to limit

con-firm [kən-fûrm′] *verb*, to give proof of something, to ratify

con-fir-ma-tion [kŏn′fər-mā′shən] *noun*, 1) proof, collaboration 2) a ceremony recognizing a member of the church

con-fis-cate [kŏn′fĭ-skāt′] *verb*, to seize, to take without consent

con-flict [kŏn′flĭkt′] *noun*, 1) a fight or argument, a disagreement, *verb*, 2) to disagree or clash

con-form [kən-fôrm′] *verb*, to comply, to obey social norms

con-form-i-ty [kən-fôr′mĭ-tē] *noun*, harmony, agreement

con-front [kən- frŭnt] *verb*, to face boldly or defiantly

con-fuse [kən-fyōōz′] *verb*, to mix up in the mind, to perplex

con-fu-sion [kən-fyōō′zhən] *noun*, a state of disorder, chaos, bewilderment

con-geal [kən-jēl′] *verb*, 1) to change from a fluid state to a solid state 2) to thicken

con-gen-ial [kən-jēn′yəl] *adjective*, naturally adapted, pleasant and sympathetic, good-natured

con-gen-i-tal [kən-jĕn′ĭ-tl] *adjective*, existing at birth

con-ges-tion [kən-jĕs′shən] *noun*, 1) a gathering or accumulation 2) an overcrowded state

con-glom-er-a-tion [kən-glŏm′ə-rā′shən] *noun*, material sticking together

con-grat-u-la-tions [kən-grăch′ə-lā′shənz] *noun, plural*, expressions of good wishes for a happy event or achievement

con-gre-gate [kŏng′grĭ-gāt′] *verb*, to gather together, to assemble

con-gre-ga-tion [kŏng′grĭ-gā′shən] *noun*, a gathering or assembly

con-gress [kŏng′grĭs] *noun*, 1) a meeting of a group of people **Congress** 2)the legislature of the United States consisting of the Senate and the House of Representatives

con-gru-ent [kŏng′grōō-ənt] *adjective*, in agreement, exactly alike, matching, equal

con-jec-ture [kən-jĕk′chər] *noun*, theory, an unfounded remark

con-ju-gate [kŏn′jə-gāt′] *verb*, to change the form of a verb depending on the subject and the tense, e.g. *I am, you are, he is, we are, you are, they are*

con-junc-tion [kən-jŭngk′shən] *noun*, a word that joins two other words or phrases together

con-jure [kŏn′jər] *verb*, 1) to seem to create out of thin air as if by magic 2) to entreat, to summon

con-nect [kə-nĕkt′] *verb*, to join or bring together, to link, to unite

Con-nect-i-cut [kə-nĕt′ĭ-kət] *noun*, one of the 50 United States, the capital is Hartford. The state flower of **Connecticut** is the mountain laurel, and the motto is "He who transplanted still sustains."

con-nec-tion [kə-nĕk′shən] *noun*, the act of joining, a relationship

con-nive [kə-nīv′] *verb*, to cooperate in a crime or fault, to secretly allow, to deceive

con-nois-seur [kŏn′ə-sûr′] *noun*, one who is an expert judge of art and style or taste

con-no-ta-tion [kŏn′ə-tā′shən] *noun*, suggested meaning

con-quer [kŏng′kər] *verb*, 1) to gain or acquire by force, to be victorious, to win, to defeat 2) to master, to overcome

con-quest [kŏn′kwĕst′] *noun*, a takeover, a triumph, a victory

con-science [kŏn′shəns] *noun*, a sense of moral goodness

con-sci-en-tious [kŏn′shē-ĕn′shəs] *adjective*, influenced by conscience, careful, thoughtful

con-scious [kŏn′shəs] *adjective*, aware of, awake, alert

con-scious-ly [kŏn′shəs-lē] *adverb*, after thorough consideration, with full awareness

con-se-crate [kŏn′sĭ-krāt′] *verb*, to dedicate, to declare sacred

con-sec-u-tive [kən-sĕk′yə-tĭv] *adjective*, one after another

con-sen-sus [kən-sĕn′səs] *noun*, agreement in opinion, custom, or function, the popular choice

con-sent [kən-sĕnt′] *noun*, 1) an agreement, permission, *verb*, 2) to agree, to comply

con-se-quence [kŏn′sĭ-kwĕns′] *noun*, 1) that which follows as a result, outcome 2) importance

con-se-quen-tial [kŏn′sĭ-kwĕn′shəl] *adjective*, significant, very important

con-ser-va-tion [kŏn′sûr-vā′shən] *noun*, the planned management of natural resources to prevent loss, destruction, or waste

con-serv-a-tive [kən-sûr′və-tĭv]
adjective, 1) opposed to change or innovation 2) traditional 3) a low estimated number

con-ser-va-tor-y [kən-sûr′və-tôr′ē]
noun, 1) a small greenhouse for growing plants 2) a college of music, an academy

con-serve [kən-sûrv′] *verb*, to keep from loss or waste, to preserve

con-sid-er [kən-sĭd′ər] *verb*, 1) to think about carefully, 2) to take into account 3) to believe

con-sid-er-a-ble [kən-sĭd′ər-ə-bəl]
adjective, important, great, large

con-sid-er-ate [kən-sĭd′ər-ĭt]
adjective, caring about a person's feelings, courteous

con-sid-er-a-tion
[kən-sĭd′ə-rā′shən] *noun*,
1) thought and attention
2) a payment

con-sign [kən-sīn′] *verb*, 1) to ship something to an agent in another place, to deliver 2) to assign

con-sign-ment [kən-sīn′mənt]
noun, 1) the entrusting of something to another's care 2) a quantity of goods for delivery

con-sist [kən-sĭst′] *verb*, to be made of or composed of

con-sist-ent [kən-sĭs′tənt]
adjective, sticking to the same principles, the same throughout

con-so-la-tion [kŏn′sə-lā′shən]
noun, comfort, sympathy

con-sole [kən-sōl′] *verb*, to comfort, to calm, to soothe

con-sol-i-date [kən-sŏl′ĭ-dāt′] *verb*, to unite, to bring together , to strengthen, to make solid

con-so-nant [kŏn′sə-nənt]
adjective, 1) in agreement, *noun*,
2) a letter in the alphabet other than a vowel

con-spic-u-ous [kən-spĭk′yōō-əs]
adjective, plainly visible, prominent, attracting attention

con-spir-a-cy [kən-spîr′ə-sē] *noun*, a combination of people often for an evil purpose, a secret plan

con-stant [kŏn′stənt] *adjective*, continuous, unceasing, faithful

con-stel-la-tion [kŏn′stə-lā′shən]
noun, an arrangement of stars that resembles a figure

con-sti-tute [kŏn′stĭ-tōōt′] *verb*, to make up, to empower

con-sti-tu-tion [kŏn′stĭ-tōō′shən]
noun, the fundamental law of a nation, state, or society

con-sti-tu-tion-al[kŏn′stĭtōō′shənl]
adjective, according to law

con-strain [kən-strān′] *verb*, to force, to restrain unnaturally

con-struct [kən-strŭkt′] *verb*, to build a structure, to erect

con-struc-tion [kən-strŭk′shən]
noun, 1) something that is built, a structure 2) the arrangement of words in parts of a sentence

con-struc-tive [kən-strŭk′tĭv]
adjective, helpful, useful, productive, beneficial

con-strue [kən-strōō′] *verb*, to interpret, to try to understand

con-sult [kən-sŭlt′] *verb*, to ask for help looking for more information, to confer

con-sult-ant [kən-sŭl′tənt] *noun*, an expert hired to study data to resolve a problem or give advice

con-sume [kən-sōōm′] *verb*, 1) to eat
2) to exhaust, to expend 3) to make
use of, to apply 4) to destroy

con-sum-er [kən-sōō′mər] *noun*,
1) a higher level organism that gets
its food from other living things
2) someone who buys products, a
customer

con-sum-mate [kŏn′sə-māt′] *verb*, to
bring to completion, to perfect

con-sump-tion [kən-sŭmp′shən]
noun, 1) the use of goods 2) a
disease of the lungs, such as
tuberculosis 3) the eating of food

con-tact [kŏn′tăkt′] *noun*, 1) a
physical touch 2) a connection
through writing or speaking, *verb*,
3) to talk or write to, to touch

con-ta-gi-ous [kən-tā′jəs] *adjective*,
of a disease passed from one person
to another by touch or proximity

con-tain [kən-tān′] *verb*, 1) to have
inside, to hold 2) to include

con-tain-er [kən-tā′nər] *noun*,
anything that can hold and carry
something, eg., a box, jar, basket

con-tam-i-nant [kən-tăm′ə-nənt]
noun, a compound that pollutes,
making the original substance
impure, a poison, a toxin

con-tam-i-nate [kən-tăm′ə-nāt′]
verb, to soil, to stain or corrupt
by contact, to pollute, to infect

con-tam-i-na-tion
[kən-tăm′ə-nā′shən] *noun*, the act
of making a substance impure
or unusable

con-tem-plate [kŏn′təm-plāt′]
verb, to consider with continued
attention, to think about, to
ponder

con-tem-po-rar-y [kən-tĕm′pə-
rĕr′ē] *adjective*, 1) of the present
day, current, *noun*, 2) a person
of the same age, a peer

con-tempt [kən-tĕmpt′] *noun*, a
feeling that someone or
something is bad

con-tempt-i-ble [kən-tĕmp′tə-bəl]
adjective, despicable, vile

con-tent [kən-tĕnt′] *adjective*,
1) happy, satisfied, [kŏn′-tĕnt]
noun, 2) that which is inside
3) the subject matter of a book

con-ten-tion [kən-tĕn′shən] *noun*, a
struggle, an argument, a dispute

con-ten-tious [kən-tĕn′shəs]
adjective, argumentative, quarrelsome, causing disagreement

con-test [kŏn′tĕst] *noun*, 1) a game
in which there is a winner
[kən-tĕst′]*verb*, 2) to disagree, to
object to, to challenge

con-text [kŏn′tĕkst′] *noun*, the words
or actions that provide a necessary
link or explanation to the meaning
of a word or event

con-tig-u-ous [kən-tĭg′yōō-əs]
adjective, adjoining, touching

con-ti-nent [kŏn′tə-nənt] *noun*, a
major land area in the world
unbroken by major oceans

con-tin-gent [kən-tĭn′jənt]
adjective, conditional, relying
on chance or something
happening

con-tin-u-al [kən-tĭn′yōō-əl]
adjective, happening repeatedly

con-tin-ue [kən-tĭn′yōō] *verb*, 1) to
go on, to resume 2) to persevere

con-tin-u-ous [kən-tĭn′yōō-əs]
adjective, uninterrupted

con-tor-tion [kən-tôr′shən] *noun,*
something bent or twisted out of
shape, a distortion

con-tour [kŏn′tŏŏr′] *noun,* the
outline of a figure, body, hill,
coastline, etc.

con-tra-band [kŏn′trə-bănd′]
noun, illegal goods, smuggled
materials

con-tract [kŏn′trăkt′] *noun,* 1) a
written agreement between two
or more persons that has the
force of law, [kən′-trăkt′] *verb,*
2) to draw closer together 3) to
make a binding agreement

con-trac-tion [kŏn′trăk′ shən]
noun, 1) the shortening of a
word or group of words by
omitting a letter or letters and
replacing them with an
apostrophe, e.g. y*ou'll* 2) the act
of drawing together like muscles

con-tra-dict [kŏn′trə-dĭkt′] *verb,* to
say the opposite, to oppose in
words, to conflict with

con-trar-y [kŏn′trĕr′ē] *adjective,*
opposite, perverse, wayward

con-trast [kən-trăst′] *noun,* 1) the
difference, *verb,* 2) to compare
in order to show the differences
between two things

con-trib-ute [kən-trĭb′yŏŏt] *verb,*
to give as part of a group effort,
to help in causing

con-tri-bu-tion [kŏn′trĭ-byŏŏ′shən]
noun, an offering, a donation

con-trite [kən-trīt′] *adjective,*
asking forgiveness, remorseful

con-trive [kən-trīv′] *verb,* to invent
or make a clever device

con-trol [kən-trōl′] *noun,* 1)
power, guidance, *verb,* 2) to
manage or oversee a situation or
machine

con-tro-ver-sy [kŏn′trə-vûr′sē]
noun, a disagreement or debate

con-tu-sion [kən-tŏŏ′zhən] *noun,* a
wound or bruise that does not
break the skin

con-va-les-cent [kŏn′və-lĕs′ənt]
adjective, recovering from
sickness

con-vene [kən-vēn′] *verb,* to
assemble, to call together

con-ven-ience [kən-vēn′yəns]
noun, the state of being easily
used or immediately available

con-ven-ient [kən-vēn′yənt]
adjective, adapted to one's
comfort or ready use, handy

con-vent [kŏn′vənt] *noun,* a home
where nuns live

con-ven-tion [kən-vĕn′shən] *noun,*
1) an assembly of members of a
delegation 2) a practice or
custom 3) a formal agreement

con-ven-tion-al [kən-vĕn′shə-nəl]
adjective, contemporary

con-verge [kən-vûrj′] *verb,* to
come together, to assemble

con-ver-sant [kən-vûr′sənt]
adjective, familiar with

con-ver-sa-tion [kŏn′vər-sā′shən]
noun, an informal discourse, a
chat or familiar talk

con-verse *noun,* [kən- vûrs′]
1) the contrary or opposite,
[kŏn′vûrs′] *verb,* 2) to talk or
exchange ideas

con-ver-sion [kən-vûr′zhən] *noun*, a change from one thing, state, or religion to another

con-vert [kən-vûrt′] *verb*, to change into something else

con-vex [kŏn′vĕks′] *adjective*, curved out like the outside of a sphere or ball or spoon

con-vey [kən-vā′] *verb*, 1) to take or transport, to carry 2) to communicate, to pass on, to impart, to give 3) to transmit

con-vict [kən-vĭkt′] *noun*, 1) a person who has been judged guilty of a crime, and sentenced *verb*, 2) to decide in court that someone has committed a crime

con-vic-tion [kən-vĭk′shən] *noun*, a strong belief, the state of being convinced, complete confidence

con-vince [kən-vĭns′] *verb*, to satisfy by proof

con-vo-lut-ed [kŏn′və-loo′tĭd] *adjective*, coiled around, intricate, complicated

con-vul-sions [kŏn′və-loo′shənz] *noun*, *plural*, strong and uncontrolled involuntary muscle contractions

cook [kŏok] *noun*, 1) someone who prepares food to eat, *verb*, 2) to prepare food for eating on the stove or in an oven, to bake

cool [kool] *adjective*, 1) moderately cold 2) calm, *verb*, 3) to lower temperature 4) to calm down

coop [koop] *noun*, a pen, a hen-house, a cage for poultry

co-op-er-ate [kō-ŏp′ə-rāt′] *verb*, to work together, to collaborate

co-op-er-a-tion [kō-ŏp′ə-rā′shən] *noun*, the process of working together toward a common goal

co-op-er-a-tive [kō-ŏp′ər-ə-tĭv] *adjective*, willing to join together to help other people

co-or-di-nate [kō-ôr′dn-āt′] *verb*, to make the parts of something work together, to harmonize

co-or-di-na-tion [kō-ôr′dn-ā′shən] *noun*, 1)the organization of separate elements working together 2) dexterity

cope [kōp] *verb*, to deal successfully with something

cop-per [kŏp′ər] *noun*, a common metal of a reddish color, a good conductor of heat and electricity

cop-y [kŏp′ē] *noun*, 1) an imitation, reproduction, *verb*, 2) to make something that is the same as something else

cop-y-right [kŏp′ē-rīt′] *noun*, the exclusive right to publish and sell the matter and form of a literary or artistic work

cor-al [kôr′əl] *noun*, 1) a pink reddish color, salmon 2) a stony substance formed from the skeletons of tiny animals that live on reefs in the ocean

cord [kôrd] *noun*, thin rope

cor-dial [kôr′jəl] *adjective*, sincere, friendly, encouraging, gracious

core [kôr] *noun*, 1) the heart, essence 2) the center of focus

cork [kôrk] *noun*, a light substance that comes from the outer bark of a tree

corn [kôrn] *noun*, 1) a sore that sometimes grows on toes when shoes are tight 2) a grain grown on a stalk as an ear (maize)

cor-ner [kôr′nər] *noun*, 1) a nook, a niche 2) where two lines, edges or streets meet, *verb*, 3) to put

someone in a place they cannot
escape 4) to monopolize

cor-nu-co-pi-a [kôr′nə-kō′pē-ə]
noun, 1) a horn containing an
abundantly overflowing supply
of food 2) abundance, plenty

cor-ol-lary [kôr′ə-lĕr-ē] *noun*, what
follows logically, the
consequence or effect

cor-o-na-tion [kôr′ə-nā′shən]
noun, a ceremony to crown a
king or queen

cor-po-ra-tion [kôr′pə-rā′shən]
noun, a business that operates as
a person under the law

corps [kôr] *noun*, a troop, a main
subdivision of an army

corpse [kôrps] *noun*, a dead body

cor-pu-lent [kôr′pyə-lənt]
adjective, very fat

cor-pus-cle [kôr′pə-səl] *noun*, a
minute particle of matter, a cell,
a red or white blood cell

cor-ral [kə-rǎl′] *noun*, a pen for
livestock

cor-rect [kə-rĕkt′] *adjective*, 1)
without error, *verb*, 2) to point
out an error 3) to make right

cor-rec-tion [kə-rĕk′shən] *noun*, a
change or revision, to remove
error, to make right

cor-rel-ate [kôr′ə-lāt′] *verb*, to be
linked to something

cor-re-la-tion [kôr′ə-lā′shən] *noun*,
a mutual relationship, a
connection

cor-re-spond [kôr′ĭ-spŏnd′] *verb*,
1) to communicate by writing
and receiving letters 2) to fit in
with, to match, to agree

cor-re-spond-ence [kôr′ĭ-spŏn′dəns]
noun, an exchange of letters

cor-ri-dor [kôr′ĭ-dər] *noun*, a
hallway connecting rooms or
apartments opening onto it

cor-rob-o-rate [kə-rŏb′ə-rāt′] *verb*,
to confirm or support with facts,

cor-ro-sive [kə-rō′sĭv] *adjective*,
1) eating away gradually by
chemicals 2) sarcastic

cor-ru-gat-ed [kôr′ə-gā′tĭd]
adjective, bent into a series of
alternate ridges and grooves for
added stiffness

cor-rupt [kə-rŭpt′] *adjective*,
1) crooked, dishonest, *verb*,
2) to cause to become dishonest

cor-rup-tion [kə-rŭp′shən] *noun*,
dishonesty, depravity

cort-ege [kôr-tĕzh′] *noun*, a funeral
procession

cos-met-ic [kŏz-mĕt′ĭk] *noun*, a
beauty product

cos-mic [kŏz′mĭk] *adjective*,
universal, vast

cost [kôst] *noun*, 1) the price you
pay when you buy something,
verb, 2) to have as a price

cos-tume [kŏs′tōōm′] *noun*, clothes
worn for a special occasion to
represent a particular period in
history, traditions of a country,
or an assumed character

cot [kŏt] *noun*, a lightweight
collapsible bed that usually folds
up to a smaller size

cot-tage [kŏt′ĭj] *noun*, a small
country house, a bungalow

cot-ton [kŏt′n] *noun*, 1) the white
part of the cotton plant used to

make cloth 2) the fabric made from this

couch [kouch] *noun*, an upholstered piece of furniture that seats several people

cough [kôf] *noun*, 1) a hacking sound made when air is expelled from the lungs, *verb*, 2) to make a sharp noise when air comes up from the lungs

could [kŏŏd]*verb past tense* of **can**

could-n't [kŏŏd′nt] the *contraction* of the words **could** and **not**

coun-cil [koun′səl] *noun*, an assembly of men and women convened for consultation

coun-sel [koun′səl] *noun*, 1) an attorney, a lawyer 2) an interchange of opinions, advice, *verb*, 3) to advise

coun-se-lor [koun′sə-lər] *noun*, someone who helps you make the best choice

count [kount] *noun*, 1) the total number added together, *verb*, 2) to add up 3) to recite numbers in the correct order 4) to list

coun-te-nance [koun′tə-nəns] *noun*, a facial expression, aspect, appearance, composure

coun-ter [koun′tər] *noun*, 1) the table between customers and workers in a business, *verb*, 2) to make an offer against another

coun-ter-act [koun′tər-ăkt′] *verb*, to act against, to neutralize, to prevent the effects of

coun-ter-clock-wise [koun′tər-klŏk′wīz] *adjective*, in the opposite direction from the movement of the hands of a clock

coun-ter-feit [koun′tər-fĭt′] *noun*, 1) an imitation intended to deceive, *verb*, 2) to imitate or make a copy of

coun-ter-part [koun′tər-pärt′] *noun*, a thing that completes another, a mate

coun-try [kŭn′trē] *noun*, 1) the land ruled by a government, a nation 2) the land outside of a city, usually farmland or forests

coun-ty [koun′tē] *noun*, an administrative division of a state

coup [kōō] *noun*, a successful sudden attack to seize power

coupe [kōōp] *noun*, a sports car with a sloping back

cou-ple [kŭp′əl] *noun*, 1) two people or things that are usually thought of together, a pair, *verb*, 2) to fasten

cou-pon [kōō′pŏn′] *noun*, a certificate that gives a discount on a purchase, a rebate

cour-age [kûr′ĭj] *noun, no plural*, the strength to face danger when overwhelmed by fear

cou-ra-geous [kə-rā′jəs] *adjective*, brave or bold in danger

cour-i-er [kŏŏr′ē-ər] *noun*, a messenger who carries documents

course [kôrs] *noun*, 1) the path of something, the sequence of events 2) a portion of a meal 3) a series of lessons in a school

court [kôrt] *noun*, 1) a place where judges decide how people who break laws should be punished and civil cases heard 2) an open space next to a house in an enclosed area 3) the members of a royal family 4) a royal palace *verb*, 5) to date

cour-te-ous [kûr′tē-əs] *adjective*, showing good manners, polite

cour-te-sy [kûr′tĭ-sē] *noun*, politeness, civility, consideration

court-ship [kôrt′shĭp′] *noun*, going steady, a period of dating before marriage

cous-in [kŭz′ĭn] *noun*, the son or daughter of your uncle or aunt

cove [kōv] *noun*, an inlet

cov-e-nant [kŭv′ə-nənt] *noun*, 1) a legal undertaking to do or to refrain from doing some act or thing 2) a contract under seal

cov-er [kŭv′ər] *noun*, 1) something that is placed over something to protect it, *verb*, 2) to protect by placing a lid, wrapping, etc., around or on top of 3) to hide 4) to go over

co-vert [kŭv′ərt] *adjective*, concealed, hidden, or sheltered

cov-et [kŭv′ĭt] *verb*, to want to have a thing belonging to another person

cow [kou] *noun*, a grown female cattle or certain other large animals

cow-ard [kou′ərd] *noun*, someone who is easily frightened, a person who lacks courage

cow-ard-ice [kou′ər-dĭs]*noun*, lack of courage to face danger, timidity, fearfulness

cow-ard-ly [kou′ərd-lē] *adjective*, timid, afraid, scared, fearful

cow-boy [kou′boi′] *noun*, a man who rides a horse and looks after livestock on a ranch

cow-er [kou′ər] *verb*, to shrink from as if from fear, to tremble

coy-o-te [kī-ō′tē] *noun*, a North American, wolflike dog

co-zy [kō′zē] *adjective*, snug, warm

crab [krăb] *noun*, a sea animal with eight legs, a pair of pincers and a hard shell that lives in a hole

crack [krăk] *noun*, 1) a line showing where something is broken, a crevice 2) a sharp noise, such as a gunshot or thunder, *verb*, 3) to break while separating

cra-dle [krād′l] *noun*, 1) a small bed for an infant 2) the holder for a telephone, *verb*, 3) to rock or shelter an infant or comfort a crying baby

craft [krăft] *noun*, 1) something made by hand to be used as a decoration 2) a boat or plane 3) guile, slyness, skill

cram [krăm] *verb*, to fill or force in

cramp [krămp] *noun*, 1) a painful muscle spasm, *verb*, 2) to keep within narrow limits, to confine

crane [krān] *noun*, a machine designed to lift heavy loads from one place to another

cra-ni-um [krā′nē-əm] *noun*, the skull of a vertebrate animal

crank [krăngk] *noun*, a handle that is attached to a machine and that turns, causing motion

crash [krăsh] *noun*, 1) a loud noise caused by a collision or something falling, *verb*, 2) to shatter violently, scattering pieces everywhere

crass [krăs] *adjective*, grossly insensible, rude coarse

crate [krāt] *noun*, a large usually wooden box or container, a case

cra-ter [krā'tər] *noun*, a bowl-shaped cavity, a hole

crave [krāv] *verb*, to want something badly

crawl [krôl] *verb*, to move on one's hands and knees, to move slowly

cray-on [krā'ŏn'] *noun*, a small pencil of colored wax used for drawing or writing

craze [krāz] *noun*, a fad, a popular idea, a trend

cra-zy [krā'zē] *adjective*, insane, wild, daft, very foolish

creak [krēk] *verb*, to make the sound of a door that has not been oiled, a long squeak

cream [krēm] *adjective*, 1) the color yellowish white, ivory 2) a thick lotion, *noun*, 3) the fatty part of milk

crease [krēs] *noun*, the mark or line left by a fold, a wrinkle, a furrow

cre-ate [krē-āt'] *verb*, to make, to bring into being, to produce for the first time

cre-a-tion [krē-ā'shən] *noun*, the act of causing to exist, that which is produced

cre-a-tive [krē-ā'tĭv] *adjective*, having new or original ideas

cre-a-tiv-i-ty [krē-ā'tĭv-ĭ-tē] *noun*, the ability to make or invent things, originality

crea-ture [krē'chər] *noun*, an animal or insect or person

cre-den-tials [krĭ-dĕn'shəlz] *noun*, a document verifying a person's ability or authority, references

cred-i-ble [krĕd'ə-bəl] *adjective*, 1) believable 2) reliable or trustworthy

cred-it [krĕd'ĭt] *noun*, 1) a system in which merchandise is given with the understanding that it will be paid for later 2) attention and praise received for doing something

cred-o [krē'dō] *noun*, creed, a belief

cred-u-lous [krĕj'ə-ləs] *adjective*, easily imposed upon, gullible

creed [krēd] *noun*, a statement of religious or ethical beliefs, principles

creek [krēk, krĭk] *noun*, a stream smaller than a river and larger than a brook, an inlet of water

creep [krēp] *verb*, to move slowly and quietly, to move furtively

cre-o-sote [krē'ə-sōt'] *noun*, an oily liquid obtained from coal tar and used as a wood preservative

cre-scen-do [krə-shĕn'dō] *noun*, a musical direction used to indicate increasing loudness

cres-cent [krĕs'ənt] *noun*, a curved shape like a new moon

crest [krĕst] *noun*, 1) the feathers that stick up on top of a bird's head 2) the top of something

crev-ice [krĕv'ĭs] *noun*, a narrow opening in a surface resulting from a split, a cleft, a gap

crew [krōō] *noun*, a group of people who work together

crib [krĭb] *noun*, 1) a bed made for an infant 2) a container for grain

crick-et [krĭk'ĭt] *noun*, 1) a ball game played with two teams of eleven players 2) a small brown

insect that makes a shrill
chirping noise at night

cried [krīd] *verb*, *past tense* of **cry**

crime [krīm] *noun*, something that
is against the law, illegal acts

crim-i-nal [krĭm′ə-nəl] *adjective*,
1) illegal, wrong, *noun*, 2) one
who has broken the law and is
guilty of a crime

cringe [krĭnj] *verb*, to shrink back
in fear, to cower in fear

crip-ple [krĭp′əl] *verb*, to disable or
make lame

cri-sis [krī′sĭs] *noun*, *plural*, **crises**
[krī′-sēz], a stressful time when
something serious is happening

crisp [krĭsp] *adjective*, 1) dry,
brittle, easily broken 2) firm and
fresh 3) very clean and pressed

criss cross [krĭs′krôs′] *noun* , a
pattern of intersecting lines

cri-te-ri-on [krī-tîr′ē-ən] *noun*,
plural, **criteria**, a standard for
judgment, a benchmark

crit-ic [krĭt′ĭk] *noun*, 1) a person
who is paid to review a
performance or art 2) one who
finds faults

crit-i-cal [krĭt′ĭ-kəl] *adjective*,
1) very important, able or
inclined to pass judgment
2) crucial, pivotal, key

crit-i-cism [krĭt′ĭ-sĭz′əm] *noun*,
faultfinding, review

crit-i-cize [krĭt′ĭ-sīz′] *verb*, to
examine as a critic, to censure

croak [krōk] *noun*, 1) a hoarse
sound like that made by frogs,
verb, 2) to make a low hoarse
sound in the throat

croc-o-dile [krŏk′ə-dīl′] *noun*, a
large reptile, like an alligator,
that lives in tropical climates

crook-ed [krŏŏk′ĭd] *adjective*,
1) bent, not straightened
2) dishonest, deceitful

crop [krŏp] *noun*, food that is
planted and grown in a field

cross [krôs] *adjective*, 1) irritated,
angry, *noun*, 2) a shape with four
arms, *verb*, 3) to go over, to
extend across

crouch [krouch] *verb*, to stoop

crow [krō] *noun*, 1) any of a genus
of large black birds including
the raven, *verb*, 2) to make a
sound like a rooster

crowd [kroud] *noun*, 1) a large
gathering of people or things,
verb, 2) to press or cram

crown [kroun] *noun*, 1) a circular
head covering, often made of
metal with precious stones, worn
by royalty, *verb*, 2) to top, to
culminate, to climax

cru-cial [krōō′shəl] *adjective*,
important or essential as decisive
in determining a doubtful crisis

cru-ci-ble [krōō′sə-bəl] *noun*, a
vessel used for melting substances

cru-ci-fix-ion [krōō′sə-fĭk′shən]
noun, the killing of someone by
nailing them to a cross

crude [krōōd] *adjective*, 1) roughly
made 2) rude, ill-mannered

cru-el [krōō′əl] *adjective*, mean,
deliberately causing pain

cru-el-ty [krōō′əl-tē] *noun*,
unkindness, oppression

cruise [krōōz] *noun*,1) a holiday on
ship, *verb*, 2) to sail or drive around

crum-ble [krŭm′bəl] *verb*, to fall or break apart into small pieces

cru-sade [krōō-sād′] *noun*, 1) a campaign conducted by a band of people devoted to advancing a cause, *verb*, 2) to battle for a cause

crush [krŭsh] *verb*, to hurt or flatten by applying pressure

crust [krŭst] *noun*, a hard surface on the outside of something that often preserves what is inside, such as bread, pie, or the earth

crutch [krŭch] *noun*, a piece of wood or metal extending from under the arm to the ground, to support a person who cannot walk unaided

crux [krŭks] *noun*, the crucial point

cry [krī] *noun*, 1) a shout or call for help, *verb*, 2) to call out loudly 3) tears flowing from the eyes

crypt [krĭpt] *noun*, a vault where bodies are buried, a tomb

cryp-tic [krĭp′tĭk] *adjective*, having a hidden meaning, puzzling

crys-tal [krĭs′təl] *adjective*, 1) clear, transparent, *noun*, 2) a clear mineral 3) a high-quality clear glass

crys-tal-lize [krĭs′tə-līz′] *verb*, 1) to form crystals 2) to become clear

cub [kŭb] *noun*, a young animal of certain mammals, such as a bear, lion, or fox

cube [kyōōb] *noun*, a solid shape with six equal square sides

cu-bic-le [kyōō′bĭ-kəl] *noun*, a small space for work partitioned off in a larger room

cu-cum-ber [kyōō′kŭm′bər] *noun*, a long, green-skinned fruit, pickled or eaten green as a salad

cue [kyōō] *noun*, 1) a signal or hint 2) a rod used to hit a billiard ball

cul-de-sac [kŭl′dĭ-săk′] *noun*, a small dead end off the main road

cu-li-nar-y [kyōō′lə-nĕr′ē] *adjective*, relating to cooking

cull [kŭl] *verb*, to select or gather, to pick out from others

cul-mi-nate [kŭl′mə-nāt′] *verb*, to reach the highest point of altitude, power, climax

cul-pa-ble [kŭl′pə-bəl] *adjective*, deserving blame, liable

cul-prit [kŭl′prĭt] *noun*, a person charged with or found guilty of a crime or misdeed

cul-ti-vate [kŭl′tə-vāt′] *verb*, 1) to improve or develop, to refine 2) to foster and promote healthy growth, as in crops, to farm

cul-tur-al [kŭl′chər-əl] *adjective*, relating to culture, the arts, good taste, etc.

cul-ture [kŭl′chər] *noun*, 1) advancement of knowledge of a civilization 2) a level of education that appreciates art and style 3) a growth of micro-organisms and bacteria

cum-ber-some [kŭm′bər-səm] *adjective*, heavy, hard to manage, unwieldy

cu-mu-la-tive [kyōōm′yə-lā′tĭv] *adjective*, increasing by successive additions

cun-ning [kŭn′ĭng] *noun*, cleverness, craftiness, skill

cup [kŭp] *noun*, 1) a bowl-shaped drinking container with a handle 2) a unit of measure equal to 8 ounces

cup-board [kŭb′ərd] *noun*, a small closet or recessed shelf

cu-ra-tor [kyŏŏ-rā′tər] *noun*, one who has the care of a museum, a custodian, keeper

curb [kûrb] *noun*, 1) control, restraint 2) a ledge, a boundary, especially that along a street

cur-dle [kûr′dl] *verb*, to sour and coagulate from liquid to a solid, e.g., milk to cheese

cure [kyŏŏr] *noun*, 1) the remedy that made someone who was sick well again, *verb*, 2) to make someone who is ill, healthy, to heal

cur-few [kûr′fyŏŏ] *noun*, a set time enforced by law when people are to be off the streets

cu-ri-os-i-ty [kyŏŏr′ē-ŏs′ĭ-tē] *noun*, 1) the feeling of wanting to know about something 2) something that is strange or unusual

cu-ri-ous [kyŏŏr′ē-əs] *adjective*, 1) eager to know about all things 2) singular, unusual, odd

curl [kûrl] *noun*, 1) a ringlet or spiral shape, *verb*, 2) to make straight hair wavy and curly

cur-mudg-eon [kər-mŭj′ən] *noun*, a mean, bad-tempered person

cur-rant [kûr′ənt] *noun*, a small berry, similar to a raisin

cur-ren-cy [kûr′ən-sē] *noun*, money in circulation

cur-rent [kûr′ənt] *adjective*, 1) up to date, pertaining to the present, *noun*, 2) the powerful flow of water or electricity or air

cur-ric-u-lum [kə-rĭk′yə-ləm] *noun*, the classes that a school requires or offers

cur-ry [kûr′ē, kŭr′ē] *noun*, 1) a yellow powder containing several spices, including turmeric, used to flavor cooking, *verb*, 2) to seek favor by flattery 3) to brush or groom a horse

curse [kûrs] *noun*, 1) something said hoping harm will come to someone, *verb*, 2) to wish bad luck or injury on someone 3) to use profanity

cur-sive [kûr′sĭv] *adjective*, characteristic of handwriting in which the letters flow together

cur-tail [kər-tāl′] *verb*, to cut short, to reduce, to decrease

cur-tain [kûr′tn] *noun*, a piece of cloth hung over a window or doorway as a screen or cover

cur-tsy [kûrt′sē] *noun*, 1) a formal bow made with bent knees by a woman, *verb*, 2) to make a bow with one foot forward, as a gesture of respect

cur-va-ture [kûr′və-chŏŏr′] *noun*, a curve, a bend

curve [kûrv] *noun*, a bend or arch

curv-ed [kûrvd] *adjective*, having a line with no part straight or flat

cush-ion [kŏŏsh′ən] *noun*, a case or bag stuffed with some soft and elastic material

cus-tard [kŭs′tərd] *noun*, a pudding made of milk and eggs

cus-to-di-an [kŭ-stō′dē-ən] *noun*, a caretaker or porter, a janitor

cus-to-dy [kŭs′tə-dē] *noun*, safe-keeping under penalty or under a judge's ruling, imprisonment

cus-tom [kŭs′təm] *noun*, a tradition passed on from one generation to the next

cus-tom-ar-y [kŭs′tə-měr′ē] *adjective*, established by common usage, habitual

cus-tom-er [kŭs′tə-mər] *noun*, one who makes regular purchases from a business, a patron

cut [kŭt] *noun*, 1) a wound or injury that may cause the skin to bleed 2) an insult, a derogatory remark 3) something that has been made shorter, *verb*, 4) to break with a knife or blade

cute [kyōōt] *adjective*, lovable, adorable, delightful

cu-ti-cle [kyōō′tĭ-kəl] *noun*, the skin surrounding the fingernail

cy-cle [sī′kəl] *noun*, 1) events that happen in the same order over and over again 2) a bicycle, *verb*, 3) to move in a circuit controlled by alternating negative and positive currents

cy-clone [sī′klōn′] *noun*, a violent windstorm, sometimes called a typhoon or hurricane, depending on location and intensity

cyl-in-der [sĭl′ən-dər] *noun*, a solid spherical figure with two faces that are circles

cy-lin-dri-cal [sə-lĭn′drĭ-kəl] *adjective*, a circular or spherical shape with straight sides

cym-bal [sĭm′bəl] *noun*, a large round metal plate used as a percussion instrument

cyn-ic [sĭn′ĭk] *noun*, a doubter, a skeptic, an unbeliever

cyn-i-cism [sĭn′ĭ-sĭz′əm] *noun*, an attitude given to sneering at honesty or virtue, a belief that people are self-interested

cy-press [sī′prĭs] *noun*, an evergreen tree with scale-like needles

cyst [sĭst] *noun*, a fluid-filled pouch attached to a body part

czar [zär, tsär] *noun*, the supreme ruler of an empire, especially the ruler of Russia before 1917

D

dad [dăd] *noun*, father

daf-fo-dil [dăf′ə-dĭl] *noun*, a spring flowering bulb, yellow or white, with a trumpet-like center

dag-ger [dăg′ər] *noun*, a weapon used specifically for stabbing, a knife

dai-ly [dā′lē] *adjective*, done or occurring every day

dain-ty [dān′tē] *adjective*, delicate, fragile, small, pretty, refined

dair-y [dâr′ē] *noun*, a place where milk is produced and pasteurized

da-is [dā′ĭs] *noun*, a raised platform for honored guests

dai-sy [dā′zē] *noun*, a flower with a yellow or brown center surrounded by petals

dal-ly [dăl′ē] *verb*, to loiter, to fiddle around, to flirt

dam [dăm] *noun*, 1) a wall built across a river or lake that controls water flow, *verb*, 2) to construct a wall in a lake to retain the water and to regulate its flow

dam-age [dăm′ĭj] *noun*, 1) loss or detriment due to injury or harm, *verb*, 2) to hurt or cause harm or injury to something, to destroy

damp [dămp] *adjective*, humid, somewhat wet, moist

dance [dăns] *noun*, 1) a set of movements designed to accompany music, *verb*, 2) to move in rhythm with music, to skip or leap, to perform

dan-de-li-on [dăn′dl-ī′ən] *noun*, a bitter herb with yellow flowers, often cooked and eaten

dan-ger [dān′jər] *noun*, the possibility of harm

dan-ger-ous [dān′jər-əs] *adjective*, full of risk, perilous, hazardous, likely to harm

dan-gle [dăng′gəl] *verb*, to hang, to suspend loosely

dap-pled [dăp′əld] *adjective*, spotted with color or shade

dare [dâr] *verb*, to be brave, bold

dark [därk] *adjective*, 1) without light, not reflecting light, shadowy, *noun*, 2) a space without light

dark-ness [därk′nĕs] *noun*, *no plural*, a lack of light

darl-ing [där′lĭng] *adjective*, 1) a term of affection for someone who is loved, *noun*, 2) a sweetheart, the favorite

darn [därn] *verb*, to mend socks

dart [därt] *noun*, 1) a small weapon like a tiny arrow that can be

thrown by hand, *verb*, 2) to move quickly or suddenly

dash [dăsh] *noun*, 1) a punctuation mark used to indicate a pause 2) a small amount, *verb*, 3) to move quickly 4) to hit, to shatter, to break, to strike

da-ta [dā′tə, dăt′ə, dä′tə] *noun*, information collected on a subject for reference

da-ta-base [dā′tə-bās′, dăt′ə-] *noun*, information arranged for computer access

date [dāt] *noun*, 1) the date, month, and year 2) a small, sweet, brown fruit grown in tropical climates, *verb*, 3) to measure, to mark 4) to court

daub [dôb] *verb*, to dab, to smear, to spread paint or another liquid

daugh-ter [dô′tər] *noun*, a human female considered with reference to her parents

daunt [dônt] *verb*, to intimidate

daunt-less [dônt′lĭs] *adjective*, bold

daw-dle [dôd′l] *verb*, to dilly dally, to waste time

dawn [dôn] *noun*, the break of day when the sun rises

day [dā] *noun*, 1) the period of 24 hours when the earth completes one rotation on its axis 2) the opposite of night, when the sun is in the sky

daze [dāz] *noun*, 1) a stupor, amazement, *verb*, 2) to cause to feel stunned

daz-zle [dăz′əl] *verb*, to awe, to impress with splendor

dead [dĕd] *adjective*, 1) not alive, inactive, *noun*, 2) referring to people who are no longer alive

dead-line [dĕd′lĭn′] *noun*, a set time when an assignment is to be finished, a time limit

dead-lock [dĕd′lŏk′] *noun*, a stalemate, a state in which no progress can be made

dead-ly [dĕd′lē] *adjective*, dangerous, possibly fatal, causing death, mortal

deaf [dĕf] *adjective*, 1) not able to hear 2) not listening

deal [dēl] *noun*, 1) a business agreement 2) an unspecified amount 3) a bargain, *verb*, 4) to barter, or buy and sell 5) to be concerned, to cope 6) to pass out or to distribute, i.e. playing cards

deal-er [dē′lər] *noun*, 1) a person who buys and sells things 2) in a card game, the person who holds the cards and passes them out

dear [dîr] *adjective*, 1) beloved 2) costly

dear-ly [dîr′lē] *adverb*, very much

death [dĕth] *noun*, the end of life

de-ba-cle [dĭ-bä′kəl] *noun*, a sudden downfall

de-bat-a-ble [dĭ-bā′tə-bəl] *adjective*, disputable, open to question

de-bate [dĭ-bāt′] *noun*, 1) a public discussion of a topic in which opposing points of view are presented, *verb*, 2) to argue different points of view

de-bil-i-tate [dĭ-bĭl′ĭ-tāt′] *verb*, to weaken

deb-it [dĕb′ĭt] *noun*, an entry on an account for a sum owed

de-bris [də-brē′, dā′brē′] *noun*, rubbish, especially such as results from destruction

debt [dĕt] *noun*, money owed

debt-or [dĕt′ər] *noun*, one who owes something, especially money

de-but [dā-byōō′] *noun*, 1) a beginning 2) first public appearance

dec-ade [dĕk′ād′] *noun*, a period of ten years

de-cay [dĭ-kā′] *noun*, 1) the condition of being rotten or degenerating, *verb*, 2) to rot, to decompose 3) to decline

de-ceased [dĭ-sēst′] *adjective*, dead, defunct, without life

de-ceit [dĭ-sēt′] *noun*, fraud, trickery, deception, lie

de-ceit-ful [dĭ-sēt′fəl] *adjective*, dishonest, deceptive, false

de-ceive [dĭ-sēv′] *verb*, to lead into error, to mislead, to delude, to lie to

De-cem-ber [dĭ-sĕm′bər] *noun*, the twelfth month of the year, having 31 days

de-cen-cy [dē′sən-sē] *noun*, behavior that is proper and moral

de-cent [dē′sənt] *adjective*, honorable, good, fitting, ethical

de-cep-tion [dĭ-sĕp′shən] *noun*, the act of deceiving, fraud, false representation, dishonesty

de-cide [dĭ-sīd′] *verb*, to determine, to make a choice, to resolve, to choose

de-cid-u-ous [dĭ-sĭj′ōō-əs] *adjective*, falling out at a certain stage of development (as some leaves, antlers, insect wings, or milk teeth)

dec-i-mal [dĕs′ə-məl] *adjective*, pertaining to or founded on the number ten

de-ci-pher [dĭ-sī′fər] *verb*, 1) to translate from coded characters 2) to make out or read

de-ci-sion [dĭ-sĭzh′ən] *noun*, act or result of deciding or settling, a conclusion, a resolution

de-ci-sive [dĭ-sī′sĭv] *adjective*, positive, able to decide quickly

de-ci-sive-ly [dĭ-sī′sĭv-lē] *adverb*, in a clean manner, precisely

deck [dĕk] *noun*, 1) the floor on each level of a ship 2) a pack of playing cards 3) a flat structure without a roof attached to a house

dec-la-ra-tion [dĕk′lə-rā′shən] *noun*, an announcement or statement, a proclamation

de-clare [dĭ-klâr′] *verb*, to formally announce, to state firmly and solemnly

de-cline [dĭ-klīn′] *noun*, 1) a gradual lessening of strength or numbers, *verb*, 2) to refuse 3) to steadily become less

de-com-pose [dē′kəm-pōz′] *verb*, 1) to rot or decay 2) to separate a chemical into constituent parts

de-com-po-si-tion [dē-kŏm′pə-zĭsh′ən] *noun*, the process of decay

dec-o-rate [dĕk′ə-rāt′] *verb*, to beautify, to adorn, to enhance

dec-o-ra-tion [dĕk′ə-rā′shən] *noun*, 1) an ornament 2) an award such as a ribbon or a medal

dec-o-rous [dĕk′ər-əs] *adjective*, proper, correct, polite

de-coy [dē′koi′] *noun*, something used as a lure or bait

de-crease [dĭ-krēs′] *noun*, 1) the amount by which something has been made smaller, *verb*, 2) to diminish and lessen the amount, to reduce

de-cree [dĭ-krē′] *noun*, 1) a pronouncement, a declaration, *verb*, 2) to proclaim, to order

de-crep-it [dĭ-krĕp′ĭt] *adjective*, broken down with age, feeble, worn out, dilapidated

de-cry [dĭ-krī′] *verb*, to discredit, to denounce publicly

ded-i-cate [dĕd′ĭ-kāt′] *verb*, 1) to recognize in a solemn ceremony 2) to devote oneself to something 3) to inscribe a message in the front of a book

ded-i-ca-tion [dĕd′ĭ-kā′shən] *noun*, 1) devotion to something 2) an acknowledgement of another person by an author

de-duce [dĭ-dōōs′] *verb*, to reach a conclusion by reasoning

de-duct [dĭ-dŭkt′] *verb*, to subtract, to take away

deed [dĕd] *noun*, 1) an action taken, something someone has done 2) a legal document proving that someone owns a piece of land or property

deep [dēp] *adjective*, 1) extending or reaching a long distance beneath the surface of the earth 2) intense, heart-felt, feelings

deer [dîr] *noun*, an animal with hooves that eats grass and leaves; the males have antlers

de-face [dĭ-fās′] *verb*, to mar, to vandalize, to destroy the appearance of

def-a-ma-tion [děf'ə-mā'shən] *noun*, harm to a person's good reputation, slander, libel

de-fault [dǐ-fôlt'] *noun*, 1)failure to fulfill an obligation 2) a computer setting that is used if the user does not make another choice

de-feat [dǐ-fēt'] *noun*, 1) a loss to be overcome, *verb*, 2) to beat, to conquer, to cause to fail

de-fect [dē'fěkt'] *noun*, 1) a fault, a failing, a drawback, *verb*, 2) to desert your country or cause

de-fec-tive [dǐ-fěk'tǐv] *adjective*, faulty, broken, imperfect

de-fend [dǐ-fěnd'] *verb*, to fight to protect something, to guard

de-fend-ant [dǐ-fěn'dənt] *noun*, a person required to make an answer in a lawsuit or a criminal case

de-fense [dǐ-fěns'] *noun*, 1) protection from harm 2) justification for an action 3) protection of the goal in sports

de-fen-sive [dǐ-fěn'sǐv] *adjective*, guarding, protective

de-fer [dǐ-fûr'] *verb*, 1) to put off, to postpone 2) to submit respectfully

de-fer-ence [děf'ər-əns] *noun*, a yielding of judgment with respect to another, courtesy

de-fi-ance [dǐ-fī'əns] *noun*, a state of open opposition, a challenge

de-fi-ant [dǐ-fī'ənt] *adjective*, opposing or resisting power or authority, disobedient

def-i-cit [děf'ǐ-sǐt] *noun*, an amount that falls short of a goal or perfect balance

de-fine [dǐ-fīn'] *verb*, 1) to determine the boundaries of something 2) to give the meaning of

def-i-nite [děf'ə-nǐt] *adjective*, fixed, having certain limits, precise, clearly defined

def-i-nite-ly [děf'ə-nǐt-lē] *adverb*, precisely, clearly stated, certainly

def-i-ni-tion [děf'ə-nǐsh'ən] *noun*, an explanation of the meaning of a word or term

de-fin-i-tive [dǐ-fǐn'ǐ-tǐv] *adjective*, final, conclusive, decisive

de-flate [dǐ-flāt'] *verb*, 1) to let the air out 2) to dishearten, to discourage

de-flect [dǐ-flěkt'] *verb*, 1) to turn aside 2) to cause something to change direction

de-form-i-ty [dǐ-fôr'mǐ-tē] *noun*, a lack of proper form or symmetry, distortion

de-fraud [dǐ-frôd'] *verb*, to deprive someone of a right or property through deceit, to swindle

de-fray [dǐ-frā'] *verb*, to meet the cost of something, to pay

de-frost [dē-frôst'] *verb*, to melt, to thaw, to remove ice by melting

deft [děft] *adjective*, able, skillful,

de-funct [dǐ-fŭngkt'] *adjective*, ended, dead, no longer existing

de-fy [dǐ-fī'] *verb*, to challenge a stronger force, to disobey

de-gen-er-ate [dǐ-jěn'ər-āt'] *verb*, to become worse physically, mentally or morally, to decay

de-grade [dǐ-grād'] *verb*, to lower someone's reputation or character, to treat disrespectfully

de-gree [dǐ-grē′] *noun*, 1) a unit for measuring temperature or angles 2) a grade or rank conferred by colleges or un graduates or other scholars 3) a measured portion determined on a scale 4) a proportion

de-i-fy [dē′ə-fī′] *verb*, to idolize or worship as a god

de-jec-tion [dǐ-jěk′shən] *noun*, sadness, depression, low spirits

Del-a-ware [děl′ə-wâr′] *noun*, a state on the east coast of the United States; the capital is Dover. The state flower of **Delaware** is the peach blossom and the motto is "Liberty and Independence."

de-lay [dǐ-lā′] *noun*, 1) a period of waiting, *verb*, 2) to postpone, to make something take longer

de-lec-ta-ble [dǐ-lěk′tə-bəl] *adjective*, delicious

del-e-gate [děl′ǐ-gāt′] *noun*, 1) one sent and empowered to act for another, a deputy, *verb*, 2) to entrust a duty or task to another, to assign

de-lete [dǐ-lēt′] *verb*, to erase, to mark for omission, to remove

de-lib-er-ate [dǐ-lǐb′ər-ǐt] *adjective*, 1) planned or done on purpose, *verb*, [dǐ-lǐb′ər-āt] 2) to think carefully in or to make up one's mind, to consider reasons for and against

de-lib-er-ate-ly [dǐ-lǐb′ər-ǐt-lē] *adverb*, after mature consideration, consciously, intentionally, on purpose

del-i-ca-tes-sen [děl′ǐ-kə-těs′ən] *noun*, a shop where meat, cheese, and salads are sold

del-i-ca-cy [děl′ǐ-kə-sē] *noun*, 1) good taste, tact 2) choice food

de-li-cious [dǐ-lǐsh′əs] *adjective*, giving pleasure to the senses, especially taste

de-light [dǐ-līt′] *noun*, 1) a joy, *verb*, 2) to please, to cause joy or happiness

de-light-ful [dǐ-līt′fəl] *adjective*, pleasing, causing pleasure and satisfaction

de-lin-quent [dǐ-lǐng′kwənt] *adjective*, 1) failing to do what is required 2) past due, *noun*, 3) a child who persistently breaks the law

de-lir-i-ous [dǐ-lǐr′ē-əs] *adjective*, wandering in mind, light-headed

de-liv-er [dǐ-lǐv′ər] *verb*, 1) to carry or take to a person to whom something is addressed 2) to assist in the birth of a baby 3) to utter, to speak 4) to rescue or set free

de-liv-er-y [dǐ-lǐv′ə-rē] *noun*, the act of delivering goods, a letter, etc. 2) goods that have been brought to be handed over

del-ta [děl′tə] *noun*, a fan-shaped area of land where a river splits into channels at its mouth

de-lude [dǐ-lōōd′] *verb*, to deceive, to fool, to mislead

de-lu-sion [dǐ-lōō′zhən] *noun*, 1) a mirage, a fantasy 2) a mistake, a misconception, a false belief

delve [dělv] *verb*, to examine, to probe, to look through, to search

dem-a-gogue [děm′ə-gôg′] *noun*, a person who wins support by appealing to popular feelings and prejudices especi

de-mand [dǐ-mǎnd'] *noun,*
1) a strong request, *verb,* 2) to
ask for something very strongly,
to insist or require, to claim

de-mean [dǐ-mēn'] *verb,* to
humiliate, to lower

de-mean-or [dǐ-mē'nər] *noun,* a
person's posture or conduct,
behavior, attitude

de-mise [dǐ-mīz'] *noun,* the death
of a person, the end of
something, a failure

de-moc-ra-cy [dǐ-mŏk'rə-sē] *noun,*
a form of government in which
people exercise power by
electing representatives

Dem-o-crat [dĕm'ə-krăt'] *noun,* a
person who advocates
democracy, one who believes in
government in which all people
have a vote

dem-o-crat-ic [dĕm'ə-krăt' ĭk]
adjective, 1) favoring equality,
considerate of humanity
2) representative

de-mol-ish [dǐ-mŏl'ĭsh] *verb,* to
destroy, to ruin, to take down

dem-o-li-tion [dĕm'ə-lĭsh'ən]
noun, destruction

dem-on-strate [dĕm'ən-strāt']
verb, to establish beyond doubt,
to show

dem-on-stra-tion
[dĕm'ən-strā'shən] *noun,* 1) a
presentation of evidence, proof
2) an exhibit, a display 3) a
peaceful march, a protest

de-mor-al-ize [dǐ-môr'ə-līz'] *verb,*
1) to corrupt, to destroy the
morals of someone 2) to
discourage 3) to confuse

de-mur [dǐ-mûr'] *noun,*
1) hesitation, objection, refusal,
verb, 2) to make an objection, to
delay

de-mure [dǐ-myo͝or'] *adjective,*
quietly modest, reserved

den [dĕn] *noun,* 1) a place in which
a wild animal lives, a lair 2) a
quiet, private room

den-i-grate [dĕn'ĭ-grāt'] *verb,* to
ridicule, to belittle, to defame

den-im [dĕn'ĭm] *noun,* a heavy
cotton fabric, usually blue, used
to make clothing such as jeans

de-nom-i-na-tion
[dǐ-nŏm'ə-nā'shən] *noun,*
1) classification, identification,
2) a branch of a religion 3) the
value of a banknote, stamp, etc.

de-nom-i-na-tor [dǐ-nŏm'ə-nā'tər]
noun, the number base or the
quantity below the line of a
fraction

de-nounce [dǐ-nouns'] *verb,* to
attack as deserving of
punishment or censure

dense [dĕns] *adjective,* compact,
closely packed together

den-si-ty [dĕn'sǐ-tē] *noun,* 1) mass
per unit of volume 2) the number
of people in a specified area

dent [dĕnt] *noun,* 1) an indentation,
a nick, *verb,* 2) to make a gouge

den-tal [dĕn'tl] *adjective,* referring
to teeth or dentistry

de-nun-ci-a-tion
[dǐ-nŭn'sē-ā'shən] *noun,* a public
accusation, condemnation

de-ny [dǐ-nī'] *verb,* to declare
something untrue

de-part [dǐ-pärt'] *verb,* to leave, to
go away from 2) deviate, to
withdraw 3) to die

de-part-ment [dǐ-pärt′mənt] *noun*, a separate division of a government or a business

de-par-ture [dǐ-pär′chər] *noun*, the act of leaving a place or the subject

de-pend [dǐ-pĕnd′]*verb*, to be determined, to be a result of 2) to need, to trust, to rely on

de-pend-a-ble [dǐ-pĕnd′ā′bəl] *adjective*, reliable

de-pend-ant or de-pend-ent [dǐ-pĕn′dənt] *noun*, a person supported by another

de-pend-ent [dǐ-pĕn′dənt] *adjective*, relying on something else for support, contingent

de-pict [dǐ-pǐkt′] *verb*, to portray

de-plete [dǐ-plēt′] *verb*, to use up

de-plor-able [dǐ-plôr′ə-bəl] *adjective*, shockingly bad, vile, horrible, unfortunate

de-plore [dǐ-plôr′] *verb*, to feel or express disapproval

de-ploy [dǐ-ploi′] *verb*, to move troops to the battle line to make it stronger, to position strategically

de-port [dǐ-pôrt′] *verb*, to force someone to leave a country

de-pose [dǐ-pōz′] *verb*, 1)to remove from office or power 2) to testify under oath

de-pos-it [dǐ-pŏz′ǐt] *noun*, 1) money placed in a bank for safekeeping 2) money to hold something until the full price is paid 3) sediment that has settled on the bottom, *verb*, 4) to put aside for safekeeping

de-po-si-tion [dĕp′ə-zǐsh′ən] *noun*, testimony under oath

de-pot [dē′pō] *noun*, a railroad or bus station 2) a warehouse

de-praved [dǐ-prāvd′] *adjective*, morally corrupt

de-pre-ci-ate [dǐ-prē′shē-āt′] *verb*, to diminish in value

de-pre-ci-a-tion [dǐ-prē′shē-ā′shən] *noun*, a decrease in value

dep-re-da-tion [dĕp′rǐ-dā′shən] *noun*, stealing, pillage, plundering, destruction

de-press [dǐ-prĕs′] *verb*, 1) to make someone feel sad and despondent 2) to hold down

de-pres-sion [dǐ-prĕsh′ən] *noun*, 1) a feeling of sadness 2) a mental illness characterized by hopelessness and despair 3)a low place or hole or basin 4) a major slump in the economy, a long recession

de-prive [dǐ-prīv′] *verb*, to deny, to keep from having, to prevent from enjoying something

depth [dĕpth] *noun*, 1) wisdom, intellect 2)the distance from the top downward

de-ranged [dǐ-rānjd′] *adjective*, insane, mad, crazy

der-by [dûr′bē] *noun*, 1) a contest or race, a horserace 2) a round hat with a narrow brim

der-e-lict [dĕr′ə-lǐkt′] *adjective*, 1) abandoned 2) failing in one's duty, *noun* 3) a vagrant

de-ride [dǐ-rīd′] *verb*, to scoff at

de-ri-sion [dǐ-rǐzh′ən] *noun*, ridicule, scorn, mockery

de-riv-a-tive [dǐ-rǐv′ə-tǐv] *noun*, something derived from another source

de-rive [dĭ-rīv′] *verb*, to obtain or issue from a source

de-rog-a-to-ry [dĭ-rŏg′ə-tôr′ē] *adjective*, negative, mean, detracting, disparaging

der-rick [dĕr′ĭk] *noun*, 1) a tall tower that fits over an oil well, that supports drilling machinery 2) a large hoisting crane

dearth [dûrth] *noun*, a scarcity, lack, too small a supply

de-scend [dĭ-sĕnd′] *verb*, to go or move down, to fall, to drop

de-scend-ant [dĭ-sĕn′dənt] *noun*, a person descended from a particular ancestor, such as a child or a grandchild

de-scent [dĭ-sĕnt′] *noun*, a change from higher to lower, a downward movement

de-scribe [dĭ-skrīb′] *verb*, 1) to set forth in words, to tell about, to recount 2) to mark out, to draw

de-scrip-tion [dĭ-skrĭp′shən] *noun*, act or result of representing by words, a narration

des-e-crate [dĕs′ĭ-krāt′] *verb*, to destroy something sacred or of religious significance

des-ert [dĕz′ərt] *noun*, 1) a dry region that is sandy and without trees, [dĭ-zûrt′] *verb*, 2) to leave, to leave the armed forces without permission, to abandon

de-ser-tion [dĭ-zûr′shən] *noun*, 1) abandonment 2)the act of leaving service in the armed forces without permission

de-serve [dĭ-zûrv′] *verb*, to merit or be worthy of, to earn by service

de-sign [dĭ-zīn′] *noun*, 1) a plan, 2) a pattern, *verb*, 3) to conceive, to invent 4) to create a plan for something, to scheme

des-ig-nate [dĕz′ĭg-nāt′] *verb*, 1) to point out, to indicate 2) to give a name 3) to appoint

de-sign-er [dĭ-zī′nər] *noun*, a person who creates plans for clothes, buildings, products, etc.

de-sire [dĭ-zīr′] *noun*, 1) a want, wish, craving, *verb*, 2) to long for, to set your heart on

desk [dĕsk] *noun*, a work table usually with drawers for paper, pencils, etc.

des-o-late [dĕs′ə-lĭt] *adjective*, deserted, forsaken, comfortless, dismal, abandoned

des-o-la-tion [dĕs′ə-lā′shən] *noun*, 1) emptiness, extinction 2) extreme sadness

de-spair [dĭ-spâr′] *noun*, 1) the state of being without hope, sadness, *verb*, 2) to have no hope or optimism

des-per-ate [dĕs′pər-ĭt] *adjective*, hopeless, downcast, frantic, reckless because of despair

des-per-a-tion [dĕs′pə-rā′shən] *noun*, a great need, an anxious feeling out of hopelessness

de-spise [dĭ-spīz′] *verb*, to look down upon with contempt, to consider unworthy of respect

de-spite [dĭ-spīt′] *preposition*, 1)in spite of, notwithstanding, *noun* 2) insult, injury

de-spoil [dǐ-spoil′] *verb*, to plunder

de-spond-ent [dǐ-spŏn′dənt] *adjective*, discouraged, without hope

des-pot-ic [dǐ-spŏt′ĭk] *adjective*, 1)possessing unlimited power 2) tyrannical

des-pot-ism [dĕs′pə-tĭz′əm] *noun*, tyranny, dictatorship, repression

des-sert [dǐ-zûrt′] *noun*, usually sweet, the last course of a meal

des-ti-na-tion [dĕs′tə-nā′shən] *noun*, the place someone is going, a goal, the end of a journey

des-ti-ny [dĕs′tə-nē] *noun*, fate, a condition predetermined by divine will, providence

des-ti-tute [dĕs′tǐ-tōot′] *adjective*, without means of existence, extremely poor, penniless

de-stroy [dǐ-stroi′] *verb*, to put an end to, to ruin or annihilate

de-struc-tion [dǐ-strŭk′shən] *noun*, the act of tearing down, causing harm or damage

de-struc-tive [dǐ-strŭk′tǐv] *adjective*, harmful, ruinous, causing damage

de-tach [dǐ-tăch′] *verb*, to separate, to remove, to disconnect, to undo

de-tail [dǐ-tāl′] *noun*, a small part of a larger whole, an item

de-tain [dǐ-tān′] *verb*, 1) to restrain, to confine, to hold back, 2) to delay, to hinder, to impede

de-tect [dǐ-tĕkt′] *verb*, to discover the presence of, to find

de-tec-tive [dǐ-tĕk′tǐv] *noun*, 1) a special policeman who is trained to investigate crimes 2) a person

whose job it is to obtain information for clients

de-ter-gent [dǐ-tûr′jənt] *noun*, a chemical substance like soap used to wash clothes or dishes

de-te-ri-o-rate [dǐ-tîr′ē-ə-rāt′] *verb*, to grow worse, to rot, to decay

de-te-ri-o-ra-tion [dǐ-tîr′ē-ə-rā′shən] *noun*, a process of getting worse

de-ter-mi-na-tion [dǐ-tûr′mə-nā′shən] *noun*, a firm purpose, resolve, willpower

de-ter-mine [dǐ-tûr′mǐn] *verb*, to come to a decision, to realize

de-test [dǐ-tĕst′] *verb*, to hate

de-tour [dē′tŏŏr′] *noun*, a temporary way around a blockage in the road

de-tract [dǐ-trăkt′] *verb*, to belittle, to take away from

det-ri-men-tal [dĕt′rə-mĕn′tl] *adjective*, harmful, injurious

dev-as-tate [dĕv′ə-stāt′] *verb*, 1) to lay waste, to destroy 2) to cause someone sorrow

de-vel-op [dǐ-vĕl′əp] *verb*, unfold gradually, to evolve, to mature

de-vel-op-ment [dǐ-vĕl′əp-mənt] *noun*, 1) expansion, growth 2) a new piece of information

de-vi-ate [dē′vē-āt′] *verb*, to turn away from an accepted course of action or standard, to stray

de-vice [dǐ-vīs′] *noun*, 1) an instrument used for a particular purpose 2) a scheme, a trick

dev-il [dĕv′əl] *noun*, 1) an evil spirit, thought to cause destruction and bad things 2) a wicked or mischievous person

de-vi-ous [dē′vē-əs] *adjective*, crafty, dishonest, gone astray

de-vise [dǐ-vīz′] *verb*, to contrive, to invent, to plan, to create

de-void [dǐ-void′] *adjective*, empty, entirely without, lacking

de-vote [dǐ-vōt′] *verb*, to dedicate , to give entirely, to use for a specific purpose

de-vo-tion [dǐ-vō′shən] *noun*, 1) dedication, affection, love 2) religious worship

de-vour [dǐ-vour′] *verb*, to consume greedily, to eat

de-vout [dǐ-vout′] *adjective*, sincere, dedicated, having religious feeling

dew-drop [dōō′drŏp′] *noun*, drops of water that form on anything exposed to air overnight

dex-ter-i-ty [dĕk-stĕr′ĭ-tē] *noun*, the ability to operate skillfully by hand, adroitness

di-a-be-tes [dī′ə-bē′tǐs] *noun*, a metabolic disorder in which one is very thirsty, produces excessive urine, and is unable to produce or use sufficient insulin

di-a-bol-ic-al [dī′ə-bŏl′ĭ-kəl] *adjective*, evil, devilish

di-ag-no-sis [dī′əg-nō′sǐs] *noun*, an identification of a disease based on signs or symptoms

di-ag-o-nal [dī-ăg′ə-nəl] *adjective*, a line extending from one corner of a polygon to another corner, that is not adjacent

di-a-gram [dī′ə-grăm′] *noun*, 1) a figure, or plan drawn to show how something works, *verb*, 2) to represent by a drawing

di-al [dī′əl] *noun*, a round face on a machine, often with numbers on it, that sets the instrument to perform a specific task 2) the face of a clock, watch, etc.3) to make a telephone call

di-a-lect [dī′ə-lĕkt′] *noun*, a form of speech characterized by local peculiarities

di-a-logue [dī′ə-lôg′] *noun*, 1) a conversation between two or more people, especially in a play or narrative 2) a discussion

di-am-e-ter [dī-ăm′ĭ-tər] *noun*, any straight line passing from side to side, through the center of a figure or body

dia-mond [dī′ə-mənd] *noun*, 1) a hard clear stone that is very precious 2) a plane shape with four equal sides with two acute angles and two obtuse angles 3) a baseball field

di-a-phragm [dī′ə-frăm′] *noun*, the muscle for breathing located between the lungs and the stomach

di-ar-rhe-a [dī′ə-rē′ə] *noun*, a purging or looseness of the bowels

di-a-ry [dī′ə-rē] *noun*, a journal in which a person makes daily entries of observations and personal experiences

di-a-tribe [dī′ə-trīb′] *noun*, a tirade, a scolding, a forceful and bitter verbal attack against someone or something

dice, [dīs] *noun, plural* 1) a small square cube with a different number of dots on each side ranging from 1-6, often used in games of chance, 2) *verb*, to cut into small cubes

dichotomy

di·chot·o·my [dī-kŏt′ə-mē] *noun*,
a division into two parts

dic·tate [dĭk′tāt′] *verb*, 1) to speak
into a recording device or so that
someone else can write or type
what is said 2) to impose, to
decree, to command

dic·ta·tor [dĭk′tā′tər] *noun*, an
absolute ruler, a tyrant

dic·tion [dĭk′shən] *noun*,
enunciation of words

dic·tion·ar·y [dĭk′shə-nĕr′ē] *noun*,
a word list, usually with
definitions, pronunciations, etc.

did [dĭd] *past tense* of **do**

did·n't [dĭd′nt] the *contraction* of
the words **did** and **not**

die [dī] *verb*, 1) to stop living or
existing 2) to fade away

die·sel [dē′zəl, -səl] *noun*, 1) an
engine that burns oil instead of
gasoline 2) the petroleum fuel
used in a diesel engine

di·et [dī′ĭt] *noun*, 1) the food
someone eats, *verb*, 2) to reduce
the intake of food

dif·fer [dĭf′ər] *verb*, to be unlike, to
vary, to disagree

dif·fer·ence [dĭf′ər-əns] *noun*,
1) contrast, unlikeness
2) disagreement, dissension
3) the answer in subtraction

dif·fer·ent [dĭf′ər-ənt] *adjective*,
1) not alike 2) not the same as
the rest, strange 3) separate

dif·fer·en·tial [dĭf′ə-rĕn′shəl]
adjective, 1) showing or making
a difference, *noun* 2) a gear that
allows two wheels to rotate at
different speeds

dif·fi·cult [dĭf′ĭ-kŭlt′] *adjective*,
hard to manage or please, tough

dif·fi·cul·ty [dĭf′ĭ-kŭl′tē] *noun*, a
hardship, a problem

dif·fuse *adjective*, [dĭ-fyo͞o′ s′]
1) not concentrated, [dĭ-fyo͞oz′]
verb, 2) to spread or circulate 3)
to cause to flow on all sides

dif·fu·sion ən] *noun*, the process of
spreading in all directions like gas

dig [dĭg] *verb*, 1) to unearth dirt
with tools or a machine to make
a hole 2) to search, to probe

di·gest [dī-jĕst′] *noun*, 1) a
condensed literary work, article,
etc. *verb*, 2) to convert food into
an absorbable form 3) to think
over and arrange in the mind

di·ges·tion [dī-jĕs′chən] *noun*, the
process by which food is converted
into a source of energy that can be
assimilated by the body

di·ges·tive tract *noun*, the
alimentary canal where food is
processed and broken down into
sugars for energy and wastes are
eliminated

dig·it [dĭj′ĭt] *noun*, 1) a finger or
toe 2) any number 0 through 9

dig·it·al [dĭj′ĭtəl] *adjective*, using
signals or information
represented by values of a
physical quantity, such as
voltage or magnetic polarization,
to represent arithmetic numbers
from logical expressions

dig·ni·fy [dĭg′nə-fī] *verb*, to give
honor to

dig·ni·tar·y [dĭg′nĭ-tĕr′ē] *noun*,
1) a person who is well-known
and respected 2) a person
holding high rank or position

dig·ni·ty [dĭg′nĭ-tē] *noun*, 1) an
office or rank 2) nobleness of
manner 3) the quality of being
respected and respecting oneself

di·gres·sion [dī-grĕsh′ən, dĭ-]
noun, an act or instance of
wandering away from the
subject temporarily

dike [dīk] *noun*, a dam or wall that holds back water

di-lap-i-dat-ed [dǐ-lăp′ǐ-dā′tǐd] *adjective*, falling into ruin, decaying, in disrepair

di-late [dī-lāt′] *verb*, to expand, to enlarge or become wider

dil-a-to-ry [dǐl′ə-tôr′ē] *adjective*, delaying, wasting time

di-lem-ma [dǐ-lĕm′ə] *noun*, a case in which a person must make a difficult choice, a quandary

dil-i-gence [dǐl′ə-jəns] *noun*, careful attention and application to work, a constant effort to accomplish something

dil-i-gent [dǐl′ə-jənt] *adjective*, careful, tireless in work

di-lute [dī-lōōt′] *verb*, to make thinner or weaker by mixing in something else

dim [dǐm] *adjective*, 1) poorly lit, 2) less bright or distinct

dime [dīm] *noun*, a coin worth ten cents in the United States

di-men-sion [dǐ-mĕn′shən] *noun*, size in a particular direction such as length or width, scope, extent

di-min-ish [dǐ-mǐn′ǐsh] *verb*, to make or grow less, to reduce

dim-i-nu-tion [dǐm′ə-nōō′shən] *noun*, a lessening, a reduction in size or duration

dim-ple [dǐm′pəl] *noun*, a small dent in a surface

din-gy [dǐn′jē] *adjective*, dirty, soiled, dull and drab, shabby

din-ner [dǐn′ər] *noun*, the main meal of the day served in the evening

di-no-saur [dī′nə-sôr′] *noun*, extinct gigantic reptiles of the Mesozoic era that were either herbivores, carnivores, or omnivores

dip [dǐp] *noun*, 1) a decline 2) a plunge, a soaking, an immersion 3) a mixture into which foods are dunked, *verb*, 4) to put something into a liquid and then take it out again 5) to slope

diph-thong [dǐf′thông′] *noun*, a combination of two vowels forming a compound sound

di-plo-ma [dǐ-plō′mə] *noun*, a document under seal attesting a degree conferred on a person

di-plo-ma-cy [dǐ-plō′mə-sē] *noun*, the business of conducting international negotiations

dip-lo-mat [dǐp′lə-mǎt′] *noun*, 1) an ambassador 2) a tactful person

dire [dīr] *adjective*, disastrous, serious, threatening

di-rect [dǐ-rĕkt′, dī-] *adjective*, 1) straight to something without stopping, *verb*, 2) to aim 3) to guide, to control, to manage

di-rec-tion [dǐ-rĕk′shən] *noun*, 1) the way in which someone is going or pointing 2) **di-rec-tions** instructions explaining how to do something

di-rect-ly [dǐ-rĕkt′lē] *adverb*, 1)at once, immediately 2) in a forthright manner

di-rec-to-ry [dǐ-rĕk′tə-rē] *noun*, 1) a list of people and their addresses 2) a computer file listing other files

dirge [dûrj] *noun*, sorrowful music, a lament for someone who has died

dir-i-gi-ble [dĭr'ə-jə-bəl] *noun*, an airship, a blimp

dirt [dûrt] *noun*, loose soil, something which causes filth

dirt-y [dûr'tē] *adjective*, 1) not clean, soiled 2) obscene

dis-a-bil-i-ty [dĭs'ə-bĭl'ĭ-tē] *noun*, a physical or mental incapacity, an inability to do something

dis-a-ble [dĭs-ā'bəl] *verb*, to impair the activity of something, to make incapable

dis-ad-van-tage [dĭs'əd-văn'tĭj] *noun*, something that makes things more difficult, a detriment

dis-a-gree [dĭs'ə-grē'] *verb*, to be of a different opinion, to differ

dis-a-gree-a-ble [dĭs'ə-grē'ə-bəl] *adjective*, unpleasant, irritating, obnoxious, bad-tempered

dis-a-gree-ment [dĭs'ə-grē'mənt] *noun*, an argument, a dispute

dis-ap-pear [dĭs'ə-pîr'] *verb*, to vanish, to go away or become hidden, to fade away

dis-ap-point [dĭs'ə-point'] *verb*, to frustrate the hopes of someone

dis-ap-point-ment [dĭs'ə-point'mənt] *noun*, failure, frustration, a feeling of being let down

dis-ap-prove [dĭs'ə-prōōv'] *verb*, to object, to have a bad opinion of

dis-arm [dĭs-ärm'] *verb*, 1) to take weapons away from someone, to subdue 2) to win over

dis-as-ter [dĭ-zăs'tər] *noun*, something very bad that happens, a catastrophe

dis-be-lief [dĭs'bĭ-lēf'] *noun*, doubt, skepticism

dis-burse [dĭs-bûrs'] *verb*, to pay out money

dis-burse-ment [dĭs-bûrs'mənt] *noun*, 1) the act of paying out money 2) money paid out

dis-card [dĭ-skärd'] *verb*, to shed, to eliminate, to throw away

dis-cern [dĭ-sûrn'] *verb*, to distinguish, to perceive

dis-charge [dĭs-chärj'] *noun*, 1) something that is sent out from its source, *verb*, 2) to unload 3) to send away, to dismiss from duty or a job

dis-ci-ple [dĭ-sī'pəl] *noun*, a follower, an apostle

dis-ci-pline [dĭs'ə-plĭn] *noun*, 1) strict training to teach self-control 2) an advanced area of knowledge *verb*, 3) to instruct, to prepare 4) to punish

dis-close [dĭ-sklōz'] *verb*, to reveal, to make known, to uncover

dis-com-fort [dĭs-kŭm'fərt] *noun*, 1) annoyance, embarrassment 2) ache

dis-con-nect [dĭs'kə-nĕkt'] *verb*, to cut off, to detach, to sever

dis-con-tent [dĭs'kən-tĕnt'] *noun*, dissatisfaction, restlessness, unhappiness

dis-con-tin-ue [dĭs'kən-tĭn'yōō] *verb*, to cease, to stop

dis-cord [dĭs'kôrd'] *noun*, a conflict, opposition, differences

dis-count [dĭs'kount'] *noun*, 1) a reduction in the price of something , *verb,* 2) to disregard or disbelieve someone

dis-cour-age [dĭ-skûr′ĭj] *verb,* to dishearten, to deter

dis-course [dĭs′kôrs′] *noun,* a talk, a long written or verbal discussion

dis-cov-er [dĭ-skŭv′ər] *verb,* 1) to make known the existence of something 2) to find out through study or observation

dis-cov-er-y [dĭ-skŭv′ə-rē] *noun,* something seen or learned for the first time

dis-cred-it [dĭs-krĕd′ĭt] *verb,* to destroy confidence in, to cause to disbelieve

dis-creet [dĭ-skrēt′] *adjective,* prudent, careful, tactful, unobtrusive

dis-crep-an-cy [dĭ-skrĕp′ən-sē] *noun,* inconsistency between facts or figures, failure to match

dis-cre-tion [dĭ-skrĕsh′ən] *noun,* discernment, wise conduct and management, freedom to decide something, the act of being discreet

dis-crim-i-nate [dĭ-skrĭm′ə-nāt′] *verb,* to make a difference or distinction, to treat differently

dis-crim-i-na-tion [dĭ-skrĭm′ə-nā′shən] *noun, no plural,* 1) the ability to make fine distinctions 2) treatment based on differences, prejudice

dis-cuss [dĭ-skŭs′] *verb,* to talk about, to exchange ideas

dis-cus-sion [dĭ-skŭsh′ən] *noun,* the exchange of ideas, a debate

dis-dain [dĭs-dān′] *noun,* scorn or contempt

dis-ease [dĭ-zēz′] *noun,* 1) any mental or physical disorder 2) any quality or social condition considered harmful

dis-en-gage [dĭs′ĕn-gāj′] *verb,* to release, to detach, to become free

dis-fig-ure [dĭs-fĭg′yər] *verb,* to deform, to injure, to spoil

dis-grace [dĭs-grās′] *noun,* 1) something to feel ashamed of *verb,* 2) to shame, to discredit

dis-grace-ful [dĭs-grās′fəl] *adjective,* causing shame

dis-grunt-led [dĭs-grŭn′tld] *adjective,* resentful, annoyed, discontented, angry

dis-guise [dĭs-gīz′] *noun,* 1) things worn to change the appearance, *verb,* 2) to change the appearance of someone or something, to cover up

dis-gust [dĭs-gŭst′] *noun,* 1) a strong feeling of dislike, revulsion, *verb,* 2) to cause someone a strong feeling of dislike or offense

dish [dĭsh] *noun,* 1) a container used at a meal to serve food 2) food served

dis-hon-est [dĭs-ŏn′ĭst] *adjective,* deceitful, lying, corrupt

disk [dĭsk] *noun,* any flat round object, a circular plate

dis-like [dĭs-līk′] *noun,* 1) distaste, hostility *verb,* 2)to detest, to hate

dis-mal [dĭz′məl] *adjective,* dark or gloomy, dreary, depressing

dis-man-tle [dĭs-măn′tl] *verb,* to take apart, to break down to basic parts to see how something is made

dis-may [dĭs-mā′] *noun*, 1) an uneasy feeling of alarm, *verb*, 2) to feel alarm and distress

dis-miss [dĭs-mĭs′] *verb*, to send away, to cause or permit to go

dis-obe-di-ent [dĭs′ə-bē′dē-ənt] *adjective*, refusing to obey

dis-o-bey [dĭs′ə-bā′] *verb*, not to do what you are told, to resist

dis-or-der [dĭs-ôr′dər] *noun*, 1) sickness, ailment 2) confusion, chaos

dis-or-gan-ized [dĭs-ôr′gə-nīzd′] *adjective*, not properly planned

dis-par-age [dĭ-spăr′ĭj] *verb*, to belittle, to criticize

dis-pa-rate [dĭs′pər-ĭt] *adjective*, very different in kind, containing unrelated elements

dis-par-i-ty [dĭ-spăr′ĭ-tē] *noun*, a noticeable difference, inequality

dis-patch [dĭ-spăch′] *noun*, 1) a message 2) promptness, *verb*, 3) to send off to a destination

dis-pel [dĭ-spĕl′] *verb*, to drive or clear away

dis-pense [dĭ-spĕns′] *verb*, to distribute, to give out medicine

dis-perse [dĭ-spûrs′] *verb*, to scatter, to distribute in different directions, to disseminate

dis-per-sion [dĭ-spûr′zhən] *noun*, scattering, diffusion, distribution

dis-place [dĭs-plās′] *verb*, 1) to rearrange, to move around 2) to force people from their homes 3) to take the place of

dis-play [dĭ-splā′] *noun*, 1) a show, an exhibit, *verb*, 2) to show or exhibit something, to present

dis-pose [dĭ-spōz′] *verb*, 1) to get rid of 2) to adjust, to settle 3) to place or arrange 4) to influence in favor of

dis-po-si-tion [dĭs′pə-zĭsh′ən] *noun*, 1) nature, personality, makeup 2) arrangement

dis-pro-por-tion-ate [dĭs′prə-pôr′shə-nĭt] *adjective*, relatively too large or too small, uneven, out of proportion

dis-prove [dĭs-prōōv′] *verb*, to refute, to prove false

dis-pute [dĭ-spyōōt′] *noun*, 1) an argument, a strong difference of opinion, *verb*, 2) to call into question, to debate

dis-qual-i-fy [dĭs-kwŏl′ə-fī′] *verb*, to invalidate, to judge ineligible

dis-re-gard [dĭs′rĭ-gärd′] *noun*, 1) indifference, disrespect, neglect, *verb*, 2) to fail to notice

dis-re-spect-ful [dĭs′rĭ-spĕkt′fəl] *adjective*, rude, lacking respect

dis-rupt [dĭs-rŭpt′] *verb*, to interrupt, to disturb

dis-sat-is-fac-tion [dĭs-săt′ĭs-făk′shən] *noun*, discontent, uneasiness

dis-sat-is-fied [dĭs-săt′ĭs-fīd′] *adjective*, displeased, fed up, disgruntled, unhappy

dis-sect [dĭ-sĕkt′] *verb*, 1) to divide into separate parts 2) to analyze

dis-sec-tion [dĭ-sĕk′shən] *noun*, analysis, the act of cutting apart in order to examine internal structure

dis-sem-i-nate [dĭ-sĕm′ə-nāt′] *verb*, to scatter, to spread around

dis-sem-i-na-tion [dĭ-sĕm′ə-nā′shən] *noun*, a scattering or spreading around, diffusion

dis-sen-sion [dĭ-sĕn'shən] *noun*, a disagreement causing strife

dis-sent [dĭ-sĕnt'] *noun*, disagreement, a quarrel

dis-sim-i-lar [dĭ-sĭm'ə-lər] *adjective*, not alike, different

dis-si-pate [dĭs'ə-pāt'] *verb*, 1) to lessen, to diminish, to scatter 2) to fritter away

dis-solve [dĭ-zŏlv'] *verb*, 1) to make a solid disappear into a liquid solution 2) to break up an assembly, to end an agreement

dis-so-nance [dĭs'ə-nəns] *noun*, discord, noise, harsh sounds

dis-suade [dĭ-swād'] *verb*, to discourage by persuasion, to deter

dis-tance [dĭs'təns] *noun*, 1) the space between two points, an interval 2) a place far away

dis-tant [dĭs'tənt] *adjective*, 1) far 2) cool, reserved in manner

dis-tend [dĭ-stĕnd'] *verb*, to expand, to bloat, to stretch

dis-tinct [dĭ-stĭngkt'] *adjective*, 1) distinguished by nature or station 2) individual, unique 3) well-defined, very clear

dis-tinc-tion [dĭ-stĭngk'shən] *noun*, 1) notable difference as in a feature 2)excellence, recognition of an accomplishment

dis-tin-guish [dĭ-stĭng'gwĭsh] *verb*, 1) to stand out, to be different 2) to recognize as different

dis-tort [dĭ-stôrt'] *verb*, to twist out of shape, to bend, to falsify

dis-tract [dĭ-străkt'] *verb*, to take one's attention from something

dis-trac-tion [dĭ-străk'shən] *noun*, 1) mental distress 2) something that distracts or amuses

dis-traught [dĭ-strôt'] *adjective*, very worried, disturbed, overcome with anxiety, upset

dis-tress [dĭ-strĕs'] *noun*, 1) a feeling of worry, sadness or difficulty, *verb*, 2) to make someone sad or worried

dis-trib-ute [dĭ-strĭb'yo͞ot] *verb*, 1) to allot or divide among several 2) to spread out over an area, to give out

dis-tri-bu-tion [dĭs'trə-byo͞o'shən] *noun*, the passing out of things, circulation

dis-trict [dĭs'trĭkt] *noun*, 1) a division of territory 2) a defined portion of a state, county, or city

dis-trust [dĭs-trŭst'] *noun*, 1) suspicion, doubt, *verb*, 2) to lack confidence or trust in

dis-turb [dĭ-stûrb'] *verb*, to bother or interrupt, to make anxious

ditch [dĭch] *noun*, 1) a long narrow channel, a shallow waterway *verb*, 2) to discard

dive [dīv] *noun*, 1) a downward plunge, *verb*, 2) to plunge head first into water 3) to move downward, to drop sharply

div-er [dī'vər] *noun*, 1) a person who dives into water 2) a person who works underwater

di-verge [dĭ-vûrj'] *verb*, to go off in different directions from the same starting point

di-verse [dĭ-vûrs'] *adjective*, various, many and different

di-ver-sion [dĭ-vûr'zhən] *noun*, amusement, play, distraction

di-ver-si-ty [dĭ-vûr'sĭ-tē] *noun*, variety, a wide range

di-vert [dǐ-vûrt′] *verb*, to distract, to draw aside, to entertain, to change the course of

di-vest [dǐ-věst′] *verb*, to strip, to take away from, to get rid of

di-vide [dǐ-vīd′] *verb*, 1) to calculate how many times one number can go into another 2) to separate
3) to share or distribute

div-i-dend [dǐv′ǐ-děnd′] *noun*, 1) the share of profits earned by any policy or company 2) a number to be divided by another number 3) a benefit from an action

di-vine [dǐ-vīn′] *adjective*, of or relating to God, holy, sacred

di-vis-i-ble [dǐ-vǐz′ə-bəl] *adjective*, capable of being divided or separated

di-vi-sion [dǐ-vǐzh′ən] *noun*, 1) the act or result of separating anything into parts 2) a difference in opinion or feeling 3) an operation on two numbers that results in a quotient 4) a military group 5) a section of a company

di-vorce [dǐ-vôrs′] *noun*, 1) a legal end of a marriage, *verb*, 2) to arrange by law for a husband and wife to separate and end their marriage

di-vulge [dǐ-vǔlj′] *verb*, to reveal

do [dōō] *verb*, 1) to act, to produce 2) to travel 3) to be enough 4) to give 5) used with another verb to ask a question

doc-ile [dŏs′əl] *adjective*, easy to control, gentle, submissive

dock [dŏk] *noun*, 1) a pier where ships load and unload cargo, *verb*, 2) to tie a ship up at a port or wharf or boat landing 3) to deduct from someone's wages

doc-tor [dŏk′tər] *noun*, a person trained and licensed to practice medicine

doc-trine [dŏk′trǐn] *noun*, a tenet, a principle of faith or religion

doc-u-ment [dŏk′yə-mənt] *noun*, 1) an original or official paper 2) any writing that conveys information, *verb*, 3) to write down or put on paper 4) to provide information as proof

dodge [dŏj] *verb*, to avoid something by moving out of the way, to evade, to escape

doe [dō] *noun*, a female deer

does [dǔz] *verb*, the part of the verb **do** used with he, she and it

does-n't [dǔz′ənt] the *contraction* of the words **does** and **not**

dog [dôg] *noun*, a domesticated mammal four legs that eats meat

dog-ma [dôg′mə] *noun*, 1)opinion or beliefs widely held but not based on facts 2) doctrine

dol-drums [dōl′drəmz′] *noun*, 1) listlessness, an inactive period, depression 2) an ocean region near the equator with calm waters and little wind

dol-lar [dŏl′ər] *noun*, 1) currency used in the United States and Canada, valued at 100 cents 2) the basic unit of currency used in many countries

dol-phin [dŏl′fǐn] *noun*, 1) any of various small cetaceans with the snout in the shape of a beak and the neck vertebrae partially fused like a whale 2) any of various fish

do-main [dō-mān′] *noun*, specialty, area ruled over, jurisdiction, field

dome [dōm] *noun*, a roof that resembles a half circle

do-mes-tic [də-měs′tĭk] *adjective*, found in the home or in one's home land

dom-i-nant [dŏm′ə-nənt] *adjective*, governing, controlling, bossy

dom-i-nate [dŏm′ə-nāt′] *verb*, to have control over someone

dom-i-no [dŏm′ə-nō′] *noun*, a game played with uniform blocks with one side divided into two halves, each half showing any number from 0 to 6

do-nate [dō′nāt′] *verb*, to make a contribution, to bestow, to give

do-na-tion [dō-nā′shən] *noun*, a gift of money or goods given to a charitable organization

done [dŭn] *adjective*, 1) finished or complete 2) cooked, *verb*, 3) the *past tense* of **do**

don-key [dŏng′kē] *noun*, an animal like a small horse with long ears

do-nor [dō′nər] *noun*, a person who gives money or something of value

don't [dōnt] the *contraction* of the words **do** and **not**

doom [dōōm] *noun*, 1) a grim fate, *verb*, 2) to make certain that something fails or is destroyed

door [dôr] *noun*, the moveable piece of wood or metal standing at an entrance, a portal

door-way [dôr′wā′] *noun*, the opening for an entrance to a building or a room

dor-mant [dôr′mənt] *adjective*, sleeping, inactive, inert

dor-mi-to-ry [dôr′mĭ-tôr′ē] *noun*, a building containing rooms for sleeping, a residence hall 2) a large room with many beds

dor-sal [dôr′səl] *adjective*, of or on the back of an animal

dose [dōs] *noun*, the amount of medicine that is to be taken at one time to be effective

dot [dŏt] *noun*, a very small round spot or mark, a point, a fleck

dou-ble [dŭb′əl] *adjective*, 1) twice as much, *noun,* 2) a stand in or look alike 3) a two-base hit in baseball, *verb*, 4) to make twice as much, to fold in two

doubt [dout] *noun*, 1) a question, a feeling of uncertainty, mistrust, *verb*, 2) to question, to wonder 3) to hesitate, to ponder

doubt-ful [dout′fəl] *adjective*, 1) questionable, unlikely 2) feeling uncertain

dough [dō] *noun*, a mixture of mostly flour and a liquid to be baked to make bread or cake

douse [dous] *verb*, to drench, to saturate, to put out a light

dove [dŭv] *noun*, 1) one of many of a small type of pigeon, *verb*, [dōv] 2) *past tense* of **dive**

down [doun] *adverb*, 1) toward the ground, *noun*, 2) soft feathers, *preposition*, 3) in or to a lower place

down-stairs [doun′stârz′]*adverb*, 1) on or to a lower floor, *noun*, 2) a lower floor of a building

downtown [doun′toun′] *noun*, the main business area of a city or town

down-ward [doun′wərd] *adverb*, descending from a higher to a lower level, moving toward the ground

doze [dōz] *verb*, to take a nap, to sleep for a brief time, to sleep lightly

doz-en [dŭz′ən] *noun*, twelve

Dr. the abbreviation of doctor

drab [drăb] *adjective*, dull in color, dreary, dingy, not interesting

draft [drăft] *noun*, 1) the first unedited copy of a manuscript 2) an order for payment of money 3) a current of air 4) forced military service

drag [drăg] *verb*, to pull along with effort, to haul

drag-on [drăg′ən] *noun*, a mythical creature that breathes fire

drain [drān] *noun*, 1) a pipe used to transport water into a sewer, *verb*, 2) to relieve the pressure of fluid in a wound 3) to become dry as water flows away 4) to make weak

dra-ma [drä′mə] *noun*, 1) a story that can be performed on stage 2) excitement

dra-mat-ic [drə-măt′ĭk] *adjective*, theatrical, exciting, stirring

dra-mat-i-cal-ly [drə-măt′ĭk-lē] *adverb*, in a sudden or alarming way, impressively

drank [drăngk] *past tense* of **drink**

drape [drāp] *noun*, 1) a heavy curtain, *verb*, 2) to cover with a piece of cloth

dra-per-y [drā′pə-rē] *noun*, a heavy curtain or fabric designed to cover a window

dras-tic [drăs′tĭk] *adjective*, forceful, severe, extreme

draw [drô] *noun*, 1) a tie score, *verb*, 2) to get, to take, to understand 3) to pull along 4) to make a picture with a writing instrument 5) to choose at random 6) to formulate, to prepare 7) to suck

draw-bridge [drô′brĭj′] *noun*, a bridge that can be raised or turned to allow boats and ships to pass

drawl [drôl] *noun*, a manner of speaking that stretches out the sound of a word or vowels

drawn [drôn] *adjective*, thin, gaunt

dread [drĕd] *noun*, 1) fear, horror, terror, *verb*, 2) to anticipate with anxiety, to fear greatly

dream [drēm] *noun*, 1) images seen while you sleep 2) desires, goals, *verb*, 3) to picture something with your imagination 4) to see images while sleeping

drear-y [drîr′ē] *adjective*, gloomy, depressing

dredge [drĕj] *verb*, 1) to remove something from deep water 2) to cover food with sugar, flour, etc.

drench [drĕnch] *verb*, to make completely wet, to soak

dress [drĕs] *noun*, 1) a piece of clothing that covers the bust, waist and thighs 2) a general term for clothing or attire, *verb*, 3) to put clothes on 4) to adorn

dress-er [drĕs′ər] *noun*, 1) a chest of drawers, a bureau 2) a person who helps another to dress 3) a person who dresses a certain way

drew [drōō] *past tense* of **draw**

drift [drĭft] *noun*, 1) the general meaning 2) a pile of snow, leaves, etc. *verb*, 3) to float

drill [drĭl] *noun*, 1) a tool made of hard material used to make holes in something 2) a practice, an exercise, *verb*, 3) to make a hole in something with a special machine 4) to be trained

drink [drĭngk] *noun*, 1) liquid refreshment, a beverage, *verb*, 2) to consume liquid through the mouth, to swallow, to imbibe

drip [drĭp] *verb*, to fall in drops

drive [drīv] *noun*, 1) a short journey or trip made in a vehicle, *verb*, 2) to steer and control a moving vehicle 3) to force to go, to push through 4) to make, to compel, to urge

driv-er [drī'vər] *noun*, 1)the person steering and controlling a moving vehicle 2) a golf club for hitting long shots

droll [drōl] *adjective*, odd, strange and amusing

drone [drōn] *noun*, 1) a male bee with no stinger that mates with the queen bee, *verb*, 2) to talk dully, to buzz or murmur like a bee

drop [drŏp] *noun*, 1) a small amount of a liquid, *verb*, 2) to let something fall 3) to decrease

dross [drŏs] *noun*, waste, impurity

drought [drout] *noun*, a long period without rain

drown [droun] *verb*, to suffocate by immersion under water

drow-sy [drou'zē] *adjective*, sleepy, sluggish

drudg-er-y [drŭj'ə-rē] *noun*, dull routine work

drug [drŭg] *noun*, 1) a substance that changes the body's chemistry, medicine 2)a narcotic

drug-gist [drŭg'ĭst] *noun*, a pharmacist, one who is licensed to sell drugs

drum [drŭm] *noun*, 1) a percussion instrument consisting of a hollow cylinder with a taut covering 2) a cylindrical metal container, *verb*, 3) to make music or beat on a drum

drunk [drŭngk] *adjective*, showing the effect of too much alcohol, losing control of one's movement or speech because of alcohol

dry [drī] *adjective*, 1) without moisture or water, *verb*, 2) to expel or remove moisture

dry-er [drī'ər] *noun*, a machine that adds heat and tumbles clothes to evaporate and remove moisture

dual [dōō'əl] *adjective*, having two purposes or parts

duch-ess [dŭch'ĭs] *noun*, the wife or widow of a duke

duck [dŭk] *noun*, 1) a bird that swims and is hunted for its eggs and meat, *verb*, 2) to crouch or lower one's head to avoid something, to dodge

duct [dŭkt] *noun*, a tube or channel, a ventilation shaft

due [dōō] *adjective*, 1) owed, unpaid 2) expected, appropriate, *noun*, 3) a charge or fee for membership

duel [dōō'əl] *noun*, 1) a fight or competition, *verb*, 2) to fight

du-et [do͞o-ĕt′] *noun*, a song or a piece of music for two people

duke [do͞ok] *noun*, the title of a man who is a high-ranking nobleman

dull [dŭl] *adjective*, 1) not sharp, blunt 2) boring, slow, dim

dumb [dŭm] *adjective*, 1) unable to speak, mute, silent 2) unintelligent, stupid

dump [dŭmp] *noun*, 1) a public place where garbage is collected and usually buried, *verb*, 2) to leave, to drop or throw away

dune [do͞on] *noun*, a rounded hill of sand heaped up by the wind

dun-geon [dŭn′jən] *noun*, a close, dark prison, an underground cell

dupe [do͞op] *verb*, to fool, to trick

du-pli-cate [do͞o′plĭ-kĭt] *adjective*, 1) alike, twin, *noun*, 2) a copy, a reproduction, [do͞o′pl ĭ-kāt′]*verb*, 3) to reproduce, to remake, to do again

du-ra-ble [do͞or′ə-bəl] *adjective*, able to endure, lasting

du-ra-tion [do͞o-rā′shən] *noun*, the length of time something continues or exists

dur-ing [do͞or′ĭng] *preposition*, in the course of a period of time, throughout the course of

dusk [dŭsk] *noun*, evening, the time just after the sun has set, twilight

dust [dŭst] *noun*, 1) fine particles or powder of matter, *verb*, 2) to remove the powder by cleaning or wiping

du-ty [do͞o′tē] *noun*, 1) an obligation or a commitment 2) the responsibilities of one's job 3) a tax on goods, especially imports and exports

dwarf [dwôrf] *noun*, 1) an unusually small person, *verb*, 2) to make something look small by comparison

dwell [dwĕl] *verb*, 1) to inhabit, to live in 2) to emphasize, to think about for a long time, to ponder

dwell-ing [dwĕl′ĭng] *noun*, a home to live in, a residence, an abode

dwin-dle [dwĭn′dl] *verb*, to reduce

dye [dī] *noun*, 1) a substance used to color cloth, hair, etc. *verb*, 2) fixing colors permanently in the fibers of materials, to change the color

dy-na-mic [dī-năm′ĭk] *adjective*, relating to the forces producing motion, forceful, energetic

dy-na-mite [dī′nə-mīt′] *noun*, an explosive of nitroglycerin absorbed in porous matter

dy-nas-ty [dī′nə-stē] *noun*, a series of rulers from the same family

dys-func-tion-al [dĭs-fŭngk′shən-əl] *adjective*, functioning abnormally

E

each [ēch] *adjective*, every, one of two or more things, all

ea-ger [ē′gər] *adjective*, very willing to do something, enthusiastic

ea-gle [ē′gəl] *noun*, a very large keen-sighted bird of prey

ear [îr] *noun*, 1) the organ, one on each side of the head, used to hear 2) the sleeve in a cereal plant used to hold seeds or flowers

ear-ly [ûr′lē] *adjective*, 1) near the beginning of a time period, *adverb*, 2) before the set time

earn [ûrn] *verb*, 1) to get something through work, to achieve, to gain money 2) to achieve by one's own efforts

ear-nest [ûr′nĭst] *adjective*, fervent, serious, sincere

ear-ring [îr′rĭng, îr′ĭng] *noun*, an ornament worn on the earlobe

Earth [ûrth] *proper noun*, 1) the name of the planet on which we live, our world, , 2) **earth** *common noun*, soil, dirt, ground

earth-quake [ûrth′kwāk′] *noun*, a shaking movement of the earth caused by underground movement

ease [ēz] *noun*, 1) relaxation, relief, *verb*, 2) to move carefully 3) to make less painful or difficult

ea-sel [ē′zəl] *noun*, a tripod frame used to support an artist's canvas

eas-i-ly [ē′zə-lē] *adverb*, without difficulty, effortlessly

east [ēst] *noun*, one of the four points of a compass, pointing right of north, where the sun rises

east-ern [ē′stərn] *adjective*, 1) belonging to or characteristic of the east 2) Asian

eas-y [ē′zē] *adjective*, 1) effortless, not difficult 2) relaxed, comfortable 3) free from pain or worry 4) not strict

eat [ēt] *verb*, 1) to put food in the mouth, chewing it and swallowing it 2) to corrode

eaves [ēvz] *noun*, *plural*, the lower edges of a roof that overhang a building

ebb [ĕb] *noun*, 1) the receding of the tide, *verb*, 2) to fall back

eb-on-y [ĕb′ə-nē] *adjective*, 1) black, *noun*, 2) a hard, heavy and durable wood 3) a tropical Asian tree

ec-cen-tric [ĭk-sĕn′trĭk] *adjective*, 1) off-center from the regular or normal, *noun*, 2) an odd person

ec-cle-si-as-tic [ĭ-klē′zē-ăs′tĭk] *adjective*, pertaining to the Christian church or clergy

ech-o [ĕk′ō] *noun*, 1) a series of reflected sound waves that repeat as they bounce back from an object, repeating the sound *verb*, 2) to reverberate, to reflect a sound back

e-clipse [ĭ-klĭps′] *noun*, 1) a period of time when the light from one celestial object is blocked another, *verb*, 2) to overshadow and cause a loss of light

e-col-o-gy [ĭ-kŏl′ə-jē] *noun*, the study of how plants and animals interact with the environment

e-co-nom-ic [ĕk′ə-nŏm′ĭk] *adjective*, related to business and the production of goods

e-co-nom-i-cal [ĕk′ə-nŏm′ĭ-kəl] *adjective*, affordable, inexpensive

e-co-nom-ics [ĕk′ə-nŏm′ĭks] *noun*, the study of the way people secure goods and services and the necessities of life

e-con-o-my [ĭ-kŏn′ə-mē] *noun*, 1) the careful or thrifty management of resources 2) a system for the management of resources, money, and jobs

ec·o·sys·tem [ĕk′ō-sĭs′təm] *noun*, living things that work together and their environment

ec·u·men·i·cal [ĕk′ə- mĕn′ĭ′-kəl] *adjective*, representing a number of different Christian churches

ec·sta·sy [ĕk′stə-sē] *noun*, an overwhelming feeling of delight

ec·ze·ma [ĕk′sə-mə] *noun*, a rash, inflammatory disease of the skin

edge [ĕj] *noun*, 1) the segment where two surfaces meet 2) the rim or brink of something 3) the sharp blade of a cutting instrument such as a knife 4) the point farthest from the middle of a surface 5) an advantage, *verb*, 6) to take small, cautious steps 7) to put a border on something

ed·i·ble [ĕd′ə-bəl] *adjective*, fit to be eaten as food

ed·i·fice [ĕd′ə-fĭs] *noun*, a large, imposing building or structure

ed·i·fy [ĕd′ə-fī′] *verb*, to educate, to instruct, to guide spiritually

ed·it [ĕd′ĭt] *verb*, to revise and correct, to prepare something for publication, to cut a part of

e·di·tion [ĭ-dĭsh′ən] *noun*, an issue of a book, newspaper or magazine

ed·i·tor [ĕd′ĭ-tər] *noun*, one who reads and revises books or newspapers before they are published

ed·u·cate [ĕj′ə-kāt′] *verb*, to teach people, to provide knowledge

ed·u·ca·tion [ĕj′ə-kā′shən] *noun*, the process of teaching and learning, acquired knowledge

eel [ēl] *noun*, a long fish that looks like a snake that lives in freshwater and the sea

ee·rie [îr′ē] *adjective*, spooky, strange, causing dread

ef·fect [ĭ-fĕkt′] *noun*, a result, consequence, outcome

ef·fec·tive [ĭ-fĕk′tĭv] *adjective*, having a positive result, helpful

ef·fer·ves·cence [ĕf′ər-vĕs′sĭns] *noun,* 1) the process of gas escaping in innumerable small bubbles 2) vivacious, enthusiasm

ef·fi·ca·cious [ĕf′ĭ-kā′shəs] *adjective*, producing a desired result, effective, efficient

ef·fi·cien·cy [ĭ-fĭsh′ən-sē] *noun*, productivity with little or no wasted effort

ef·fi·cient [ĭ-fĭsh′ənt] *adjective*, working well with no waste of money or effort, capable

ef·fi·gy [ĕf′ə-jē] *noun*, a likeness in the form of a dummy, an image of a hated person usually hung

ef·fort [ĕf′ərt] *noun*, an attempt, an action, strenuous exertion

ef·fu·sion [ĭ-fyoō′zhən] *noun*, a pouring forth of liquid, light, etc.

e.g. for example

egg [ĕg] *noun*, 1) a shell covered fetus of a baby bird, fish or insect 2) an ovum, a female reproductive cell

e·go [ē′gō, ĕg′ō] *noun*, a person's self-importance, self-esteem

e·go·tist [ē′gə-tĭst] *noun*, one who is excessively interested in herself or himself

eight [āt] *noun*, the number 8

eight·een [ā-tēn′] *noun*, the number 18, ten plus eight

eight·eenth [ā-tēnth′] *noun*, *adjective*, the number eighteen in order, 18th

eighth [ātth] *noun, adjective,* the number eight in order, one of eight equal parts

eight-i-eth [ā'tē-ĭth] *noun,* the number 80 in order, one of eighty equal parts

eight-y [ā'tē] *adjective, noun,* the number 80, eight times ten

ei-ther [ē'thər, ī'thər] *adjective, pronoun,* one or the other of two

e-ject [ĭ-jĕkt'] *verb,* to exit suddenly and forcefully, to expel

e-lab-o-rate [ĭ-lăb'ər-ĭt] *adjective,* 1) made with great care, carefully planned, complicated, [ĭ-lă-bə-rāt']*verb,* 2) to explain in detail

e-lapse [ĭ-lăps'] *verb,* to pass by

e-las-tic [ĭ-lăs'tĭk] *adjective,* 1) able to return to an original size and shape after having been stretched completely, *noun,* 2) fabric with fine strings of rubber woven in it

e-la-tion [ĭ-lā' shən] *noun,* excitement, joy

el-bow [ĕl'bō'] *noun,* the joint in the arm that allows it to bend in the middle

eld-er [ĕl'dər] *adjective,* 1)older, more aged, *noun,* 2) one who is older than others 3) an influential older person

e-lect [ĭ-lĕkt'] *verb,* to choose by vote, to decide a course of action or representative

e-lec-tion [ĭ-lĕk'shən] *noun,* the process of making a choice by voting

e-lec-tor-ate [ĭ-lĕk'tər-ĭt] *noun,* the people qualified to vote

e-lec-tric [ĭ-lĕk'trĭk] *adjective,* relating to or powered by electricity

e-lec-tri-cian [ĭ-lĕk-trĭsh'ən] *noun,* one who is licensed to install and repair electrical equipment

e-lec-tric-i-ty [ĭ-lĕk-trĭs'ĭ-tē] *noun,* a form of energy resulting from the activity of electrons and protons

e-lec-tro-cute [ĭ-lĕk'trə-kyoot']*verb,* to kill by electric shock

e-lec-trode [ĭ-lĕk'trōd'] *noun,* a conductor by which an electric unit enters or leaves a region or object

e-lec-tron [ĭ-lĕk'trŏn'] *noun,* a particle smaller than an atom and having a negative electric charge

e-lec-tron-ic [ĭ-lĕk'trŏnĭk] *adjective,* operating by transistors, microchips, etc. that control an electric current

el-e-gant [ĕl'ĭ-gənt] *adjective,* lovely, gorgeous, refined

el-e-ment [ĕl'ə-mənt] *noun,* 1) a basic substance of which the universe is composed, *plural,* 2) the forces that constitute the weather

el-e-men-ta-ry [ĕl'ə-mĕn'tə-rē] *adjective,* of or related to the first principles or basic facts of a subject

el-e-phant [ĕl'ə-fənt] *noun,* a huge, herbivore mammal that lives in Africa and India, weighs 3-7 tons, stands 8-13 feet high, has thick skin, two tusks and a long nose called a trunk

el-e-vate [ĕl'ə-vāt'] *verb,* to raise to a higher level, to lift up

el-e-va-tion [ĕl′ə-vā′shən] *noun*, the altitude, the height of something from a reference point such as sea level

el-e-va-tor [ĕl′ə-vā′tər] *noun*, a machine with hoisting equipment for conveying persons, goods, etc. to or from different levels

e-lev-en [ĭ-lĕv′ən] *noun*, the number 11, one plus ten

e-lev-enth [ĭ-lĕv′ənth] *noun*, the number 11 in order, 11th

elic-it [ĭ-lĭs′ĭt] *verb*, to draw forth, to evoke a response

el-i-gi-ble [ĕl′ĭ-jə-bəl] *adjective*, qualified to be chosen

e-lim-i-nate [ĭ-lĭm′ə-nāt′] *verb*, to get rid of, to exclude from consideration, to leave out

e-lite [ĭ-lēt′] *adjective*, choice, select, superior, considered best

elk [ĕlk] *noun*, an animal similar to a moose, a large deer

elm [ĕlm] *noun*, a tall hardwood shade tree

e-lope [ĭ-lōp′] *verb*, to run away to marry secretly

el-o-quence [ĕl′ə-kwəns] *noun*, persuasive use of language

else [ĕls] *adverb*, 1) otherwise, instead of 2) more, in addition

else-where [ĕls′hwâr′] *adverb*, in some other place

e-lude [ĭ-lōōd′] *verb*, to get away from, to avoid, to escape

e-lu-sive [ĭ-lōō′sĭv] *adjective*, hard to grasp or catch, hard to remember

em-a-nate [ĕm′ə-nāt′] *verb*, to flow out, to radiate, to come out

e-man-ci-pate [ĭ-măn′sə-pāt′] *verb*, to set free from restrictions or slavery

e-man-ci-pa-tion [ĭ-măn′sə-pā′shən] *noun*, the act or condition of being freed from oppression or slavery

em-bar-go [ĕm-bär′gō] *noun*, a law that prevents a country from trading with another

em-bark [ĕm-bärk′] *verb*, 1) to board an airplane or boat 2) to begin an undertaking

em-bar-rass [ĕm-băr′əs] *verb*, to make ill at ease or self-conscious

em-bar-rass-ment [ĕm-băr′əs-mənt] *noun*, a feeling of self-consciousness, distress or shame

em-bas-sy [ĕm′bə-sē] *noun*, the building in which people work to represent their own country in another country

em-bed [ĕm-bĕd′] *verb*, to implant into something, to fix firmly

em-bel-lish [ĕm-bĕl′ĭsh] *verb*, to adorn, to make beautiful by adding decoration

em-bez-zle [ĕm-bĕz′əl] *verb*, to steal money from one's company or from savings accounts entrusted to one

em-blem [ĕm′bləm] *noun*, a badge or symbol of something

em-bod-y [ĕm-bŏd′ē] *verb*, 1) to include as a part of a whole 2) to represent

em-brace [ĕm-brās′] *verb*, 1) to hold closely in one's arms, to hug 2) to accept something, to include 3) to take up seriously

em-broi-der [ĕm-broi′dər] *verb*,
1) to sew ornamental patterns on
fabric 2) to embellish, to add
false details

em-bry-o [ĕm′brē-ō′] *noun*, an
early stage of development of an
animal or plant organism

em-bry-on-ic [ĕm′brē-ŏn′ĭk]
adjective, in an early stage of
development of an organism

em-er-ald [ĕm′ər-əld] *noun*, a
precious stone of rich, bright
green color, a variety of beryl

e-merge [ĭ-mûrj′] *verb*, to come out
or become visible, to appear

e-mer-gen-cy [ĭ-mûr′jən-sē] *noun*,
an unexpected event that calls
for immediate action, a crisis

em-i-grant [ĕm′ĭ-grənt] *noun*, a
person leaving one country to
live in another

em-i-grate [ĕm′ĭ-grāt′] *verb*, to
leave one country to go and live
in another

em-i-nent [ĕm′ə-nənt] *adjective*,
high, lofty, noted, famous

e-mis-sion [ĭ-mĭsh′ən] *noun*, a
substance given off into the air

e-mo-tion [ĭ-mō′shən] *noun*,
feelings, passion, excitement

e-mo-tion-al [ĭ-mō′shə-nəl]
adjective, excitable, showing
emotions more than usual,
fervent

em-pa-thize [ĕm′pə-thīz′] *verb*, to
relate to the feelings of others

em-pa-thy [ĕm′pə-thē] *noun*, the
ability to share the feelings of
another person

em-per-or [ĕm′pər-ər] *noun*, the
male ruler of a country or empire

em-pha-sis [ĕm′fə-sĭs] *noun*,
importance or stress given to
something

em-pha-size [ĕm′fə-sīz′] *verb*, to
call to someone's attention, to
bring out clearly, to stress

em-pire [ĕm′pīr′] *noun*, a group of
nations or states united under a
single sovereign power

em-pir-i-cal [ĕm-pîr′ĭ-kəl] *adjective*,
based on observation and
experience rather than theory

em-ploy [ĕm-ploi′] *verb*, to put into
use, to engage, to hire for work

em-ploy-ee [ĕm-ploi′ē] *noun*, one
who works for another for wages

em-ploy-er [ĕm-ploi′ər] *noun*, a
person or business that employs
or hires one or more persons

em-ploy-ment [ĕm-ploi′mənt]
noun, a job, an occupation

em-pow-er [ĕm-pou′ər] *verb*, to
authorize, to enable

emp-ty [ĕmp′tē] *adjective*,
1) having nothing inside, without
content or meaning, *verb*, 2) to
remove the contents completely,
to make vacant, to unload

em-u-late [ĕm′yə-lāt′] *verb*, to
follow or copy in the hope of
equaling

en-a-ble [ĕ-nā′bəl] *verb*, to make
possible, to empower

en-act [ĕn-ăkt′] *verb*, 1) to make
into law 2) to act, to perform

e-nam-el [ĭ-năm′əl] *noun*, 1) a
smooth glossy surface finish 2)
a hard glassy colored substance
fused to metal, glass or pottery
3) the outer covering of the teeth

en-chant [ĕn-chănt′] *verb*, 1) to put a spell on 2)to captivate, to delight

en-chant-ment [ĕn-chănt′mənt] *noun*, 1) a magical spell, 2) a fascination, appeal, charm

en-clave [ĕn′klāv′] *noun*, territory enclosed in a foreign land

en-close [ĕn-klōz′] *verb*, to put something inside of something else, to shut in on all sides

en-clo-sure [ĕn-klōz′hər] *noun*, something that surrounds on all sides

en-com-pass [ĕn-kŭm′pəs] *verb*, 1)to enclose in a circle, to surround 2)to include as a part of

en-core [ŏn′kôr′] *noun*, an additional performance given in response to calls from the audience, as by applause

en-coun-ter [ĕn-koun′tər] *noun*, 1) a casual meeting 2) a skirmish, *verb*, 3) to meet by chance 4) to confront in battle

en-cour-age [ĕn-kûr′ĭj] *verb*, to give praise or hope to someone, to urge

en-cour-age-ment [ĕn-kûr′ĭj-mənt, -kŭr′-] *noun*, support, assurance

en-croach-ment [ĕn-krōch′mənt] *noun*, the act of overstepping boundaries or someone's rights

en-cy-clo-pe-di-a [ĕn-sī′klə-pē′dē-ə] *noun*, a comprehensive summary of knowledge on many subjects or a specialilzed subject written in a set of volumes

end [ĕnd] *noun*, 1) the farthest point or edge of anything 2) completion, finish 3) the aim, reason, design, *verb*, 4) to finish

en-dan-ger [ĕn-dān′jər] *verb*, to put in danger, to hazard

en-deav-or [ĕn-dĕv′ər] *noun*, 1) an attempt, a serious effort, *verb*, 2) to try, to make an earnest effort, to strive

end-less [ĕnd′lĭs] *adjective*, without end, infinite, ceaseless

en-dorse [ĕn-dôrs′] *verb*, 1) to write on the back of a check to cash it or give it to another person 2) to sanction, to declare approval of

en-dow [ĕn-dou′] *verb*, 1) to provide or bestow income or property 2) to give a quality to

en-dow-ment [ĕn-dou′mənt] *noun*, giving of money to provide a regular income

en-dur-ance [ĕn-dŏŏr′əns] *noun*, the ability to survive, the will to persevere

en-dure [ĕn-dŏŏr′] *verb*, to bear, to put up with, to tolerate, to suffer

en-e-my [ĕn′ə-mē] *noun*, a hostile person or group or country, a foe

en-er-gize [ĕn′ər-jīz′] *verb*, to make active, to invigorate, to give energy to

en-er-gy [ĕn′ər-jē] *noun*, 1) the capacity for performing work 2) power that makes machines work

en-fold [ĕn-fōld′] *verb*, to envelope, to enclose

en-force [ĕn-fôrs′] *verb*, to impose by force, to require compliance

en-gage [ĕn-gāj′] *verb*, 1) to put in gear 2) to fight 3) to hire 4) to become involved 5) to be busy or occupied 6) to promise

en-gage-ment [ĕn-gāj′mənt] *noun*, 1) an encounter, a military action 2) a promise by two people to marry 3) an appointment

en-gen-der [ĕn-jĕn′dər] *verb*, to cause, to give rise to

en-gine [ĕn′jĭn] *noun*, 1) a machine that converts energy into motion 2) a locomotive 3) a source of power

en-gi-neer [ĕn′jə-nîr′] *noun*, 1) one who designs machines 2) one who drives an engine, *verb*, 3) to bring about an event

Eng-lish [ĭng′glĭsh] *adjective*, 1) the language of the people of Britain, America, Canada, Australia, and other countries 2) relating to or belonging to the people of England

en-grave [ĕn-grāv′] *verb*, 1) to cut into a surface 2) to leave an impression

en-gulf [ĕn-gŭlf′] *verb*, to cover completely, to close over

en-hance [ĕn-hăns′] *verb*, to make better, to increase the value or quality of something

e-nig-ma [ĭ-nĭg′mə] *noun*, something hard to explain, a puzzle, a mysterious person

en-joy [ĕn-joi′] *verb*, to take pleasure in

en-joy-ment [ĕn-joi′mənt] *noun*, delight, satisfaction, happiness, pleasure

en-large [ĕn-lärj′] *verb*, to increase,

en-light-en [ĕn-līt′n] *verb*, to educate, to inform, to give spiritual insight

en-list [ĕn-lĭst′] *verb*, to sign up, to enroll in the armed forces

en-mi-ty [ĕn′mĭ-tē] *noun*, hatred

e-nor-mous [ĭ-nôr′məs] *adjective*, monstrous, huge, immense

e-nough [ĭ-nŭf′] *adjective*, 1) as much as is needed, ample, *adverb*, 2) to an adequate or sufficient degree, *noun*, 3) the required amount

en-rage [ĕn-rāj′] *verb*, to anger, to inflame, to make furious

en-rich [ĕn-rĭch′] *verb*, to improve, to make rich, to enhance

en-roll [ĕn-rōl′] *verb*, to register in a list or as a student in a school, to become a member

en-roll-ment [ĕn-rōl′mənt] *noun*, the total number registered

en-sem-ble [ŏn-sŏm′bəl] *noun*, the whole, all the parts taken together as a group

en-sue [ĕn-sōō′] *verb*, to make sure or certain, to follow up

en-sure [ĕn-shōōr′] *verb*, to guarantee, to make sure of, to insure

en-ter [ĕn′tər] *verb*, to go into, to become involved in

en-ter-prise [ĕn′tər-prīz′] *noun*, a bold undertaking, a project or business activity, a venture

en-ter-tain [ĕn′tər-tān′] *verb*, 1) to hold the interest of the people you are talking to or performing for, 2) to amuse, to delight 3) to have in mind

en-ter-tain-ment [ĕn′tər-tān′mənt] *noun*, a performance that tries to interest an audience

en-thrall [ĕn-thrôl′] *verb*, to fascinate, to mesmerize

en-thu-si-asm [ĕn-thōō′zē-ăz′əm] *noun*, eager interest, excitement

en-thu-si-as-tic [ĕn-thoō′zē-ăs′tĭk]
adjective, showing a passionate
and devoted interest in a belief
or idea

en-tice [ĕn-tīs′] *verb*, to lure, to
attract, to tempt, to persuade

en-tire [ĕn-tīr′] *adjective*, whole,
complete, with no parts missing

en-ti-tle [ĕn-tīt′l] *verb*, 1) to give as
a right 2) to give a title to

en-ti-ty [ĕn′tĭ-tē] *noun*, a being, an
individual, an existence

en-trance [ĕn′trəns] *noun*, 1) a
means of entry or access 2) the
act of coming in

en-tree [ŏn′trā] *noun*, the main dish
of a meal

en-tre-pre-neur [ŏn′trə-prə-nûr′]
noun, a person who starts a
business and assumes financial
risk for it

en-trust [ĕn-trŭst′] *verb*, to
confide, to give to for
safekeeping

en-try [ĕn′trē] *noun*, 1) entrance, a
way in 2) an item in a log

e-nun-ci-ate [ĭ-nŭn′sē-āt′] *verb*, to
pronounce, to state clearly

en-vel-op [ĕn-věl′əp] *verb*, to
cover, to enclose, to surround

en-vel-ope [ĕn′və-lōp′] *noun*, a
folded paper cover like a pocket
for a letter

en-vi-ous [ĕn′vē-əs] *adjective*,
jealous, full of envy

en-vi-ron-ment [ĕn-vī′rən-mənt]
noun, the surroundings or place
in which something lives

en-vy [ĕn′vē] *noun*, 1) a feeling of
anger or bitterness because
someone has more of something,

or a better life, *verb*, 2) to want
something someone has, to be
jealous

e-on [ē′ŏn′, ē′ən] *noun*, a billion
years, a long time

e-phem-er-al [ĭ-fĕm′ər-əl]
adjective, short-lived, fleeting

ep-ic [ĕp′ĭk] *noun*, a long poem
about a hero and his deeds

ep-i-dem-ic [ĕp′ĭ-dĕm′ĭk]
adjective, 1) affecting many in
the community, widespread,
noun, 2) a contagious disease
infecting many among the
population

ep-i-der-mis [ĕp′ĭ-dûr′mĭs] *noun*,
the outer layer of the skin

ep-i-gram [ĕp′ĭ-grăm′] *noun*, a
pithy phrase, a witty saying

ep-i-lep-sy [ĕp′ə-lĕp′sē] *noun*, a
disorder of the nervous system
accompanied by convulsions and
loss of consiousness

ep-i-logue [ĕp′ə-lôg′] *noun*, a short
conclusion added to the end of a
book, play, etc.

ep-i-sode [ĕp′ĭ-sōd′] *noun*, 1) a
distinctive occurrence 2) a
separate incident in a longer
story or poem

ep-i-taph [ĕp′ĭ-tăf′] *noun*, an
inscription on a monument in
memory of a dead person who is
buried there

e-pit-o-me [ĭ-pĭt′ə-mē] *noun*, a
typical or perfect example of a
group or type

ep-och [ĕp′ək] *noun*, 1) a time
period characterized by a
distinctive development 2) a date
marking the beginning of a new
period of history 3) a division of
geological time

e-qual [ē′kwəl] *adjective*, 1) being the same as 2) alike, *noun*, 3) something valued as the same 4) a symbol = that shows both sides have the same value, *verb*, 5) to be as good as someone or something else

e-qual-i-ty [ĭ-kwŏl′ĭ-tē] *noun*, the state of being the same as

e-qual-ize [ē′kwə-līz′] *verb*, to make even, to balance

e-qual-ly [ē′kwə-lē] *adverb*, in an equal way, to an equal degree

e-qua-tion [ĭ-kwā′shən] *noun*, 1) the act or process of considering or making equal 2) a statement that the values of two mathematical expressions are equal (=)

e-qua-tor [ĭ-kwā′tər] *noun*, the imaginary band circling the middle of the earth, at an equal distance from the North and South Poles

e-ques-tri-an [ĭ-kwĕs′trē-ən] *adjective,* 1) relating to horseback riding, *noun*, 2) a rider on horseback

e-qui-lib-ri-um [ē′kwə-lĭb′rē-əm] *noun*, a state of balance between opposing forces

e-qui-lat-er-al tri-angle [ē′kwə-lăt′ər-əl trī′ăng′gəl] *noun*, a triangle with 60 degree angles and three equal sides

e-qui-nox [ē′kwə-nŏks′] *noun*, either of two times in the year when night and day are of equal length: March 20; September 22

e-quip [ĭ-kwĭp′] *verb*, to provide what is needed, to outfit

e-quip-ment [ĭ-kwĭp′mənt] *noun*, tools, supplies, etc., needed for a job or a special activity

eq-ui-ty [ĕk′wĭ-tē] *noun*, 1)the value of property or stock after subtracting liens against it 2) just, impartial, fairness

e-quiv-a-lent [ĭ-kwĭv′ə-lənt] *noun*, 1) equal in value or worth 2) similar in force, measure, meaning or effect, identical

e-quiv-o-cate [ĭ-kwĭv′ə-kāt′] *verb*, to use deliberately evasive language

e-ra [îr′ə, ĕr′ə] *noun*, a distinct period of time, or history

e-rad-i-cate [ĭ-răd′ĭ-kāt′] *verb*, to destroy completely, to get rid of

e-rase [ĭ-rās′] *verb*, to rub out, to remove all traces of

e-rect [ĭ-rĕkt′] *adjective*, 1) standing straight, upright, *verb*, 2) to build or construct

er-mine [ûr′mĭn] *noun*, a small weasel with white fur and black-tipped tail in winter

e-rode [ĭ-rōd′] *verb*, 1) to wear away gradually 2) to destroy slowly

e-ro-sion [ĭ-rō′zhən] *noun*, the process of wearing down, breaking up, and carrying off land, soil, and rock, by wind and water

err [ûr, ĕr] *verb*, to be mistaken

er-rand [ĕr′ənd] *noun*, a short trip to accomplish a task

er-rat-ic [ĭ-răt′ĭk] *adjective*, irregular, inconsistent

er-ro-ne-ous [ĭ-rō′nē-əs] *adjective*, false, incorrect

er-ror [ĕr′ər] *noun*, 1) a belief in
what is untrue 2) an act
involving a departure from truth
and accuracy, a mistake

er-satz [er′säts] *adjective*, 1) made
or used as a substitute 2) not real
or genuine

er-u-dite [ĕr′yə-dīt] *adjective*,
learned, well-educated, scholarly

e-rupt [ĭ-rŭpt′] *verb*, 1) to burst out
suddenly, to explode 2) to
express an emotion suddenly and
forcefully

es-ca-la-tor [ĕs′kə-lā′tər] *noun*,
moving stairs attached to a
circulating belt

es-cape [ĭ-skāp′] *noun*, 1) a means
to get away from danger or
unpleasantness, *verb*, 2) to free
oneself

es-chew [ĕs-chōō′] *verb*, to avoid,
to keep away from, to evade

es-cort [ĕs′kôrt′] *noun*, 1) a guide,
an attendant, *verb*, 2) to
accompany someone, to go with
them as protection or an honor

es-crow [ĕs′krō′] *noun*, money, a
bond or a deed held by a third
person until a specified
condition is met

Es-ki-mo [ĕs′kə-mō′] *noun*, a
member of a people living in
Russia, Alaska, Canada, and
Greenland, the Inuit

e-soph-a-gus [ĭ-sŏf′ə-gəs] *noun*,
the tube that leads from the
pharynx to the stomach

es-o-ter-ic [ĕs′ə-tĕr′ĭk] *adjective*,
understood only by a chosen few

es-pe-cial-ly [ĕ-spĕsh′ə-lē] *adverb*,
particularly, to a great extent

es-pi-o-nage [ĕs′pē-ə-näzh′] *noun*,
of spying, the practice of spying

es-say [ĕs′ā′, ĕ-sā′] *noun*, 1) a
literary composition expressing
personal observations, *verb*,
2) to try out, to test, to attempt

es-sence [ĕs′əns] *noun*, 1) the real
character or nature of something
2) perfume, scent

es-sen-tial [ĭ-sĕn′shəl] *adjective*,
1) indispensable 2) of or pertaining
to the essential nature, *noun*, 3) a
necessity, the basic elements

es-tab-lish [ĭ-stăb′lĭsh] *verb*, 1) to
make stable or firm, to settle or
set up, *verb*, 2)to prove to be true

es-tab-lish-ment [ĭ-stăb′lĭsh-mənt]
noun, 1) a place of business or
residence 2) an organization

es-tate [ĭ-stāt′] *noun*, 1) a property
2) property left at someone's death

es-teem [ĭ-stēm′] *noun*, 1) respect,
honor, *verb*, 2) to regard favorably

es-ti-mate [ĕs′tə-mĭt′] *noun*, 1) an
educated guess, an approximation,
[ĕs′tə-māt′]*verb*, 2) to calculate
the approximate value or amount
of something 3) to give an
approximate rather than an exact
answer, to guess

et cet-er-a [ĕt sĕt′ər-ə] *abbr.* **etc.**,
and so on

etch [ĕch] *verb*, to engrave by biting
out with an acid

e-ter-nal [ĭ-tûr′nəl] *adjective*,
endless, infinite, forever

e-ter-ni-ty [ĭ-tûr′nĭ-tē] *noun*, forever

eth-i-cal [ĕth′ĭ-kəl] *adjective*, having
or relating to morals

eth-ics [ĕth′ĭks] *noun*, *plural*, rules
of moral principles governing a
group

eth-nic [ĕth′nĭk] *adjective*, relating to different races, ancestry, or culture

eth-nol-o-gy [ĕth-nŏl′ə-jē] *noun*, the study of different races and their characteristics

et-i-quette [ĕt′ĭ-kĕt′] *noun*, good manners, the rules for polite behavior

et-y-mol-o-gy [ĕt′ə-mŏl′ə-jē] *noun*, the study of the origin and derivation of words

eu-gen-ics [yōō-jĕn′ĭks]*noun*, the study of genetic traits by controlling breeding

eu-lo-gy [yōō′lə-jē] *noun*, a speech or written tribute lauding a deceased person

eu-phe-mism [yōō′fə-mĭz′əm] *noun*, a mild expression to replace an offensive remark

eu-re-ka [yōō-rē′kə] *exclamation*, an expression of triumph concerning a discovery

Eu-rope [yōōr′əp] *noun*, one of the seven continents, the second smalles continent

eu-tha-na-sia [yōō′thə-nā′zhə] *noun*, mercy killing

e-vac-u-ate [ĭ-văk′yōō-āt′] *verb*, to abandon, to empty out

e-vade [ĭ-vād′] *verb*, to avoid, to escape by cleverness

e-val-u-ate [ĭ-văl′yōō-āt′] *verb*, to measure the value, to appraise

e-vap-o-rate [ĭ-văp′ə-rāt′] *verb*, 1) to turn from solid or liquid into vapor 2) to lose moisture, to dry up 3) to vanish

e-vap-o-ra-tion [ĭ-văp′ə-rā′shən] *noun*, the process in which water disappears from a surface as it becomes vapor, the loss of water into the air

e-va-sive [ĭ-vā′sĭv] *adjective*, 1) avoiding something, elusive 2) intentionally not answering

eve [ēv] *noun*, the night before

e-ven [ē′vən] *adjective*, 1) level, flat, smooth 2) able to be divided by two 3) equal, *adverb*, 4) more than expected 5) indeed 6) exactly

eve-ning [ēv′nĭng] *noun*, the time between the end of the afternoon and bedtime, dusk

e-ven-ly [ē′vən-lē] *adverb*, in an equal way, smoothly

e-vent [ĭ-vĕnt′] *noun*, something that takes place, an activity

e-ven-tu-al-ly [ĭ-vĕn′chōō-ə-lē] *adverb*, at long last, after the passing of some time

ev-er [ĕv′ər] *adverb*, 1) always, at all times 2) at any time

ev-er-green [ĕv′ər-grēn′] *noun*, a plant that keeps its leaves all year long, including holly, rhododendrons, pine trees, and others

eve-ry [ĕv′rē] *adjective*, each, all possible

eve-ry-bod-y [ĕv′rē-bŏd′ē] *pronoun*, every person

eve-ry-day [ĕv′rē-dā′] *adjective*, ordinary, commonplace, normal

eve-ry-one [ĕv′rē-wŭn′] *pronoun*, each person, everybody

eve-ry-thing [ĕv′rē-thĭng′]*pronoun*, all together, all things

eve-ry-where [ĕv′rē-hwâr′] *adverb*, in every place

ev-i-dence [ĕv′ĭ-dəns] *noun*, 1) one or more facts or items 2) testimony 3) the basis on which one believes something to be true

ev-i-dent [ĕv′ĭ-dənt] *adjective*, clear, apparent, obvious

e-vil [ē′vəl] *adjective*, very bad, corrupt, immoral, wicked

e-voke [ĭ-vōk′] *verb*, 1) to call forth, 2) to bring to mind

ev-o-lu-tion [ĕv′ə-lōō′shən] *noun*, the natural process of growth and change, development

e-volve [ĭ-vŏlv′] *verb*, to come into being, to develop gradually

ex-ac-er-bate [ĭg-zăs′ər-bāt′] *verb*, to make worse

ex-act [ĭg-zăkt′] *adjective*, precise, correct, completely accurate

ex-ag-ger-ate [ĭg-zăj′ə-rāt′] *verb*, to enlarge beyond the bounds of truth, to overstate

ex-alt [ĭg-zôlt′] *verb*, to praise, to elevate, to raise in rank

ex-am-i-na-tion [ĭg-zăm′ə-nā′shən] *noun*, scrutiny, inquiry, a test

ex-am-ine [ĭg-zăm′ĭn] *verb*, 1) to inspect carefully, to look at every point 2) to scrutinize 3) to question

ex-am-ple [ĭg-zăm′pəl] *noun*, 1) a model, a sample of what others are like 2) a person punished as a warning to others

ex-as-per-ate [ĭg-zăs′pə-rāt′] *verb*, to irritate, to provoke, to enrage

ex-ceed [ĭk-sēd′] *verb*,1) to pass beyond the measure of something, 2) to surpass

ex-cel [ĭk-sĕl′] *verb*, to be better than others at something, to do well

ex-cel-lent [ĕk′sə-lənt] *adjective*, superior, very good

ex-cel-si-or [ĕk′sə-l′sē′ər] *adjective,* higher, always upward

ex-cept [ĭk-sĕpt′] *preposition*, 1) apart from, not including, *verb*, 2) to exclude

ex-cep-tion [ĭk-sĕp′shən] *noun*, 1) a circumstance not conforming to the general rule 2) an omission

ex-cep-tion-al [ĭk-sĕp′shə-nəl] *adjective*, superior, unusually good

ex-cerpt [ĕk′sûrpt′] *noun*, section that has been removed from a longer text

ex-cess [ĭk-sĕs′] *adjective*, 1) extra, more than expected, *noun,* 2) an amount that is more than enough 3) immoderate behaivor

ex-change [ĭks-chānj′] *noun*, 1) the process of settling accounts or trading items between parties, *verb*, 2) to change something for something else, to replace, to trade

ex-cise [ĕk′sīz′]*noun*, a tax levied upon specific articles and services within a country

ex-cite [ĭk-sīt′] *verb*, to be energized or to have strong feeling

ex-cit-ement [ĭk-sīt′mənt] *noun*, 1) ado, commotion 2) a thrill

ex-claim [ĭk-sklām′] *verb*, to speak suddenly and with strong feeling

ex-cla-ma-tion mark [ĕk′sklə-mā′shən märk] *noun*,

the sign ! used to show surprise, humor, or strong feeling

ex-clude [ĭk-sklo̅o̅d′] *verb*, to keep out

ex-clu-sive [ĭk-sklo̅o̅′sĭv] *adjective*, restricted to particular group of people

ex-cru-ci-at-ing [ĭk skro̅o̅′shē-ā′tĭng] *adjective*, very painful, agonizing

ex-cur-sion [ĭk-skûr′zhən] *noun*, a journey chiefly for recreation, a brief tour, an outing

ex-cuse [ĭk′skyo̅o̅s] *noun*, 1) a reason, a defense, [ĭk-skyo̅o̅z′] *verb*, 2) to free, to allow an interruption 3) to give a reason for a fault

ex-e-cute [ĕk′sĭ-kyo̅o̅t′] *verb*, 1) to kill someone legally as punishment for a crime 2) to take action

ex-e-cu-tion [ĕk′sĭ-kyo̅o̅′shən] *noun*, 1) accomplishment, implementation 2) the act of putting to death a condemned person

ex-ec-u-tive [ĭg-zĕk′yə-tĭv] *noun*, 1) a business person responsible for making decisions, a manager 2) one of the three branches of the United States government

ex-em-pla-ry [ĭg-zĕm′plə-rē] *adjective*, commendable, serving as a desirable model

ex-em-pli-fy [ĭg-zĕm′plə-fī′] *verb*, to show or illustrate by example

ex-empt [ĭg-zĕmpt′] *verb*, to excuse from an obligation or rule, to make immune

ex-er-cise [ĕk′sər-sīz′] *noun*, 1) an activity used to train the body,

verb, 2) to train the body by using one's muscles

ex-ert [ĭg-zûrt′] *verb*, 1) to make an effort 2) to bring to bear

ex-er-tion [ĭg-zûr′shən] *noun*, hard work, a strong effort

ex-hale [ĕks-hāl′] *verb*, to breathe out, to blow, to emit

ex-haust [ĭg-zôst′] *verb*, 1) to be thorough covering all points 2) to use up 3) the waste fumes from an engine

ex-haus-tion [ĭg-zôs′chən] *noun*, fatique, tiredness

ex-haus-tive [ĭg-zô′stĭv] *adjective*, complete, thorough, attending to every detail, comprehensive

ex-hib-it [ĭg-zĭb′ĭt] *noun*, 1) a display of a collection, *verb*, 2) to display

ex-hi-bi-tion [ĕk′sə-bĭsh′ən] *noun*, a public display of art or other items

ex-hil-a-ra-tion [ĭg-zĭl′ə-rā′shən] *noun*, a feeling of excitement and joy

ex-i-gen-cy [ĕk′sə-jən-sē] *noun*, a pressing necessity, a case demanding immediate action

ex-ile [ĕg′zīl′] *noun*, 1) one who is not allowed to live in his or her own country as a form of punishment, *verb*, 2) to be forced out of a place and not allowed to return

ex-ist [ĭg-zĭst′] *verb*, 1) to be, to live, to be present, to occur

ex-ist-ence [ĭg-zĭs′təns] *noun*, 1) state of being actual, life 2) reality 3) all that which lives

ex-it [ĕg′zĭt] *noun*, 1) a way to go out, the door leading out of a building 2) the ramp leading off a major highway, *verb*, 3) to leave, to go out, to depart

ex-o-dus [ĕk'sə-dəs] *noun*, mass departure of people, migration

ex-o-skel-e-ton [ĕk'sō-skĕl'ĭ-tn] *noun*, an outer structure that provides protection to an insect, shellfish, turtle, etc.

ex-ot-ic [ĭg-zŏt'ĭk] *adjective*, strange, interesting, or unusual

ex-pand [ĭk-spănd'] *verb*, to grow or make larger, to extend

ex-panse [ĭk-spăns'] *noun*, a large open space, an area of land

ex-pa-tri-ate [ĕk-spā'trē-āt'] *noun*, someone who left his native land

ex-pect [ĭk-spĕkt'] *verb*, to wait for something that is supposed to happen, to anticipate

ex-pec-ta-tion [ĕk'spĕk-tā'shən] *noun*, anticipation, calculation

ex-pe-di-en-cy [ĭk-spē'dē-ən-sē] *noun*, that which is practical

ex-pe-di-tion [ĕk'spĭ-dĭsh'ən] *noun*, a journey or excursion for a specific purpose, a trip

ex-pe-di-tious [ĕk'spĭ-dĭsh'əs] *adjective*, efficient and speedy

ex-pel [ĭk-spĕl'] *verb*, to drive out

ex-pend-i-ture [ĭk-spĕn'də-chər] *noun*, a laying out, as of money or labor, the cost

ex-pense [ĭk-spĕns'] *noun*, 1) cost, payment 2) detriment, sacrifice

ex-pen-sive [ĭk-spĕn'sĭv] *adjective*, costing a lot of money

ex-pe-ri-ence [ĭk-spîr'ē-əns] *noun*, 1) an encounter that provokes a reaction 2) knowledge gained by observation or trial, *verb*, 3) to live, to feel by participating

ex-per-i-ment [ĭk-spĕr'ə-mənt] *noun*, 1) a test done to see if something is valid or true, *verb*, 2) to carry out a plan in order to test a prediction

ex-pert [ĕk'spûrt'] *noun*, a very knowledgeable person in his or her particular field, an authority

ex-per-tise [ĕk'spûr-tēz'] *noun*, specialized knowledge or skill

ex-pi-ra-tion [ĕk'spə-rā'shən] *noun*, 1) a coming to a close 2) death, the end

ex-pire [ĭk-spīr'] *verb*, 1) to end, to cease to exist 2) to breath out

ex-plain [ĭk-splān'] *verb*, to clarify or to give a reason, to account for

ex-pla-na-tion [ĕk'splə-nā'shən] *noun*, the act of interpreting an action or giving a description

ex-ple-tive [ĕk'splĭ-tĭv] *noun*, a curse word, an obscenity

ex-plic-it [ĭk-splĭs'ĭt] *adjective*, plain, definite, expressed clearly

ex-plode [ĭk-splōd'] *verb*, 1) to release energy with a loud noise as something is destroyed by bursting outward 2) to increase suddenly

ex-ploit [ĕk'sploit'] *noun*, 1) a deed or act, of renown, *verb*, 2) to make use of for one's own profit

ex-plo-ra-tion [ĕk'splə-rā'shən] *noun*, a search in order to discover, an investigation

ex-plore [ĭk-splôr'] *verb*, 1) to look into closely, to examine or investigate 2) to go into new or unknown places to find new things and learn about them

ex-plo-sion [ĭk-splō'zhən] *noun*, a blast, a bomb bursting

ex-plo-sive [ĭk-splō′sĭv] *adjective*,
1) likely to explode, *noun*, 2) a
substance that explodes

ex-port [ĭk-spôrt′] *noun*, 1) goods
sold abroad as part of
international trade, *verb*,
2) to convey merchandise to
another country for sale

ex-pose [ĭk-spōz′] *verb* 1) to make
easy to see 2) to reveal
something hidden, to make
known 3) to leave unprotected

ex-po-si-tion [ĕk′spə-zĭsh′ən]
noun, 1) a statement of intent,
2) a public exhibition or display

ex-po-sure [ĭk-spō′zhər] *noun*, the
state of not being sheltered from
the elements, such as cold, sun,
rain, wind, etc.

ex-press [ĭk-sprĕs′] *adjective*,
1) by the fastest means
available, without many stops
verb, 2) to show, to state

ex-pres-sion [ĭk-sprĕsh′ən] *noun*,
1) the look on someone's face, a
facial gesture 2) a remark, a
cliché 3) voice, articulation,
4) wording language, 5)a way of
showing feelings or emotion

ex-pul-sion [ĭk-spŭl′shən] *noun*, a
driving or forcing out

ex-punge [ĭk-spŭnj′] *verb*, to erase,
to remove

ex-quis-ite [ĕk′skwĭ-zĭt] *adjective*,
1) carefully crafted or executed,
delicate 2) lovely, very beautiful

ex-tend [ĭk-stĕnd′] *verb*, 1) to stretch
out, to lengthen 2) to offer

ex-ten-sion [ĭk-stĕn′shən] *noun*, 1)
the act of extending 2) a part
added on

ex-ten-sive [ĭk-stĕn′sĭv] *adjective*,
having wide reach, broad

ex-tent [ĭk-stĕnt′] *noun*, the area
covered or affected by
something, the amount or degree

ex-ten-u-ate [ĭk-stĕn′yōō-āt′] *verb*,
to make something seem less
serious

ex-te-ri-or [ĭk-stîr′ē-ər] *adjective*,
1) external, outward, 2) of the
surface or appearance,
noun, 3) the outer surface

ex-ter-mi-nate [ĭk-stûr′mə-nāt′]
verb, to destroy completely

ex-ter-nal [ĭk-stûr′nəl] *adjective*,
1) on or relating to the outside of
the subject 2) outward

ex-tinct [ĭk-stĭngkt′] *adjective*, no
longer existing or living

ex-tin-guish [ĭk-stĭng′gwĭsh] *verb*,
to put out, to suppress, to kill

ex-tort [ĭk-stôrt′] *verb*, to get by
making threats and by
intimidation or coercion

ex-tor-tion [ĭk-stôr′shən] *noun*, the
act of demanding money by
making threats, blackmail

ex-tra [ĕk′strə] *adjective*, 1) more
than needed, *noun* 2) a surplus ,
adverb, 3) unusually

ex-tract [ĭk-străkt′] *verb*, 1) to take
out 2) to distill or remove

ex-tra-di-tion [ĕk′strə-dĭsh′ən]
noun, the surrender of a prisoner
by a country or state to another

ex-tra-ne-ous [ĭk-strā′nē-əs]
adjective, not essential

ex-traor-di-nar-y [ĭk-strôr′dn-ĕr′ē,
ĕk′strə-ôr′-] *adjective*, beyond
the common order, unusual, rare

ex-tra-ter-res-tri-al [ĕkstrətə′
restrēəl] *adjective*, 1) of or from
outside the earth's atmosphere 2)
a person from another planet

ex·trav·a·gant [ĭk-străv′ə-gənt]
adjective, wasteful, exceeding
reasonable limits, spending too
much, very expensive

ex·treme [ĭk-strēm′] *adjective*,
1) to the highest or a very high
degree 2) to or of the utmost
limit or degree, radical 3) final

ex·trem·i·ty [ĭk-strĕm′ĭ-tē] *noun*,
1) farthest point or part 2) an
appendage such as a hand or foot

ex·tri·cate [ĕk′strĭ-kāt′] *verb*, to
free, to untangle

ex·trin·sic [ĭk-strĭn′sĭk] *adjective*,
from outside, nonessential

ex·u·ber·ant [ĭg-zōō′bər-ənt]
adjective, displaying high spirits

ex·ude [ĭg-zōōd′] *verb*, 1) to ooze,
to discharge 2) to display a
strong feeling

ex·ul·ta·tion [ĕk′səl-tā′shən] *noun*,
joy, celebration, delight

eye [ī] *noun*, 1) either of the pair of
organs located in the head used
to see 2) the tiny hole at the end
of a needle

eye·lash [ī′lăsh′] *noun*, one of the
hairs growing on the eyelid

eye·lid [ī′lĭd′] *noun*, the skin that
covers the eye

F

fa·ble [fā′bəl] *noun*, a fictitious
short story with a moral, often
with animals that talk

fab·ric [făb′rĭk] *noun*, 1) any cloth
that is woven or knit from fibers
2) make up, substance

fab·ri·cate [făb′rĭ-kāt′] *verb*, 1) to
build, to construct 2) to lie

fab·u·lous [făb′yə-ləs] *adjective*,
marvelous, wonderful, amazing

fa·cade [fə-säd′] *noun*, the
decorated front of a building

face [fās] *noun*, 1) the front of the
head, with the eyes, nose and
mouth 2) the front of something
3) a flat surface of an object,
verb, 4) to stand in front of or
turn to confront

fac·et [făs′ĭt] *noun*, 1) one of the
polished plane surfaces of a
precious stone 2) an aspect of a
subject, a feature

fa·ce·tious [fə-sē′shəs] *adjective*,
joking, sportive, not serious

fac·ile [făs′əl] *adjective*, 1) easy,
superficial 2) speaking fluently

fa·cil·i·tate [fə-sĭl′ĭ-tāt′] *verb*, to
make easier, to aid, to help

fac·sim·i·le [făk-sĭm′ə-lē] *noun*, a
reproduction or a likeness

fact [făkt] *noun*, an indisputable
piece of information, a certainty

fac·tion [făk′shən] *noun*, a
dissenting party, an inner circle,
a clique, a group within a group

fac·tious [făk′shəs] *adjective*,
relating to internal dissension

fac·tor [făk′tər] *noun*, 1) a
condition that contributes to a
result 2) the numbers multiplied
to give a product

fac·to·ry [făk′tə-rē] *noun*, a
building where products are
manufactured

fac·ul·ty [făk′əl-tē] *noun*, 1) the
teachers in an institution of
learning 2) a physical or mental
ability, talent, capacity

fad [făd] *noun*, temporary fashion
or style, the "in" thing

fade [fād] *verb*, 1) to lose light or color 2) to become dim or less visable

Fahr-en-heit [făr′ən-hīt′] *adjective*, of or relating to the temperature scale on which the freezing point of water is 32 degrees and the boiling point of water is 212 degrees under normal atmospheric pressure

fail [fāl] *verb*, 1) to not accomplish what you set out to 2) to stop working

fail-ure [fāl′yər] *noun*, 1) lack of success 2) state of not working

faint [fānt] *adjective*, 1) hard to see, dim 2) inaudible, indistinct, soft, *noun*, 3) a loss of consciousness, *verb*, 4) to collapse unconscious

fair [fâr] *adjective*, 1) treating everyone equally, not favoring one more than another, 2) so-so, mediocre 3) pale, light-skinned *noun*, 4) a place for buying and selling goods 5) an entertainment with rides, games, and food

fair-y [fâr′ē] *noun*, an imaginary person with magical powers

faith [fāth] *noun*, 1) a belief in something that is not seen, relying on trust 2) belief in a religion

faith-ful [fāth′fəl] *adjective*, loyal, trustworthy, full of faith

fake [fāk] *noun*, 1) a forgery, an imitation, *verb*, 2) to pretend, to falsify 3) to counterfeit

fall [fôl] *noun*, 1) autumn, @) a dropping downward, *verb*, 3) to come down, to tumble or topple, 4) to lose power

fal-lacy [făl′ə-sē] *noun*, an error in reasoning, an erroneous idea

fal-li-ble [făl′ə-bəl] *adjective*, liable to err

false [fôls] *adjective*, 1) not true 2) artificial, not real

fal-ter [fôl′tər] *verb*, to hesitate

fame [fām] *noun*, *no plural*, wide recognition, renown

fa-mil-iar [fə-mĭl′yər] *adjective*, having some knowledge of something or someone

fam-i-ly [făm′ə-lē] *noun*, 1) a parent or parents and children 2) all of a person's relatives

fam-ine [făm′ĭn] *noun*, 1) general scarcity of food 2) extreme scarcity of something

fam-ish-ed [făm′ĭshd] *adjective*, extremely hungry

fa-mous [fā′məs] *adjective*, well known, celebrated, noted

fan [făn] *noun*, 1) a device designed to circulate air 2) an ardent follower or supporter, *verb*, 3) to move air, to cool with a fan 4) to spread out

fa-nat-ic [fə-năt′ĭk] *adjective*, 1) carrying an interest or enthusiasm to extremes, *noun*, 2) a person with a very strong enthusiasm for something

fan-cy [făn′sē] *adjective*, elaborate, unusually decorated, not plain

fang [făng] *noun*, 1) a long sharp tooth 2) the often hollow tooth through which a snake injects poison

fan-tas-tic [făn-tăs′tĭk] *adjective*, 1) imaginary, fanciful, unreal 2) very good

fan-ta-sy [făn′tə-sē] *noun*, a daydream, an imaginary situation, make-believe

far [făr] *adjective*, 1) at a great distance, not near or close by, *adverb*, 2) exceedingly 3) at or to or by a great distance in time or space

fare [făr] *noun*, 1) money paid for a trip by bus or train 2) food and drink, *verb* 3) to get along well

fare-well [făr-wĕl'] *noun*, a goodbye, the act of parting

farm [färm] *noun*, buildings and land where people grow food or raise animals to sell

farm-er [făr'mər] *noun*, a person who cultivates crops or raises animals for sale

far-ther [făr'thər]*adjective*, 1)more distant in time, space or degree *adverb*, 2) to or at a greater distance in space or time

fas-ci-nate [făs'ə-nāt'] *verb*, to attract and hold interest, to captivate

fas-ci-na-tion [făs'ə-nā'shən] *noun*, personal attraction, infatuation

fash-ion [făsh'ən] *noun*, 1) clothing or articles that are in style, *verb*, 2) to shape or form

fast [făst] *adjective*, 1) quick, rapid 2) fixed in place, unable to move, *verb*, 3) to go for a long period of time without eating

fas-tid-i-ous [făst'ĭd'ē-əs]*adjective*, hard to please, very critical

fat [făt] *adjective*, 1) having a wide round shape 2) thick, *noun*, 3) a greasy substance in meat

fa-tal [fāt'l] *adjective*, resulting in death, lethal

fate [fāt] *noun*, an invisible hand that seems to cause certain things to happen over which people have no control, destiny

fa-ther [fä'thər] *noun*, the male parent

fa-ther-in-law [fä'thər-ĭn-lô'] *noun*, the father of your wife or husband

fath-om [făth'əm] *noun*, 1) a measurement of water depth, *verb*, 2) to understand, to comprehend

fa-tigue [fə-tēg'] *noun*, 1) the condition of being very tired or exhausted, *verb*, 2) to become or make tired

fau-cet [fô'sĭt] *noun*, a fixture for drawing liquid from a pipe and regulating the flow

fault [fôlt] *noun*, 1) mistake, failure 2) a defect, 3) responsibility for a failure, 4) a fracture in the earth's surface causing a displacement

fa-vor [fā'vər] *noun*, 1) an act of kindness, *verb*, 2) to prefer, to patronize, to fancy, to like

fa-vor-ite [fā'vər-ĭt] *adjective*, something preferred above others, liked the best

fawn [fôn] *noun*, a young deer less than a year old

fear [fîr] *noun*, 1) expecting harm, *verb*, 2) to dread or be afraid of

fear-ful [fîr'fəl] *adjective*, afraid

fea-si-ble [fē'zə-bəl] *adjective*, capable of being done, practical, possible, achievable

feast [fēst] *noun*, 1) an elaborate meal, a banquet, *verb*, 2) to eat large amounts of food and drink

feat [fēt] *noun*, an accomplishment, a remarkable achievement

feath-er [fĕth'ər] *noun*, a soft thing which covers birds, like a toothpick covered with fine hairs

fea-ture [fē′chər] *noun*, 1) a distinctive aspect of a person's face, a characteristic 2) an article in the newspaper

Feb-ru-ar-y [fĕb′rōō-ĕr′ē] *noun*, the second month in the year, usually having 28 days but 29 every four years on the leap year

fed [fĕd] *past tense* of **feed**

fed-er-al [fĕd′ər-əl] *adjective*, belonging or pertaining to a state formed by the consolidation of several states

fed-er-a-tion [fĕd′ə-rā′shən] *noun*, an alliance, an association in which members retain autonomy

fee [fē] *noun*, money charged for something, the cost or expense

fee-ble [fē′bəl] *adjective*, frail

feed [fēd] *noun*, 1) food for animals, *verb*, 2) to give someone food, to nourish

feel [fēl] *verb*, 1) to perceive in a way other than your five senses, to sense with emotions 2) to examine with the sense of touch 3) to form an opinion

feign [fān] *verb*, to pretend

feist-y [fī′stē] *adjective*, 1) spirited, lively, exuberant 2) quarrelsome

fell [fĕl] *adjective*, 1) cruel, deadly, *verb*, 2) *past tense* of **fall**

fel-low [fĕl′ō] *noun*, 1) a man 2) a companion, a comrade

fel-on [fĕl′ən] *noun*, a person convicted of a serious crime

fel-o-ny [fĕl′ə-nē] *noun*, any offense that is punishable by confinement in prison for one year or more or death

felt [fĕlt] *noun*, 1) a soft synthetic fabric of compressed, matted animal fibers, such as wool 2) the *past tense* of **feel**

fe-male [fē′māl′] *adjective*, 1) referring to a woman, feminine, *noun*, 2) a woman, a person who belongs to the sex that can have babies

fem-i-nine [fĕm′ə-nĭn] *adjective*, of or pertaining to the female sex

fence [fĕns] *noun*, 1) a partition that encloses an area made of wood or wire 2) a person who receives stolen goods, *verb*, 3) to put in an enclosure 4) to duel with a sword

fend-er [fĕn′dər] *noun*, the strip of metal over the wheels of a car, bicycle, or other vehicle to protect against mud or water

fer-ment [fər-mĕnt′] *verb*, to change chemically with bacteria or yeast

fern [fûrn] *noun*, a plant that does not have flowers or seeds that grows in shady places

fer-ret [fĕr′ĭt] *noun*, 1) a small mammal of the weasel family, *verb*, 2) to drive or hunt out of hiding 3) to find something out by persistent investigation

fer-ry [fĕr′ē] *noun*, a boat used to transport people or goods across a body of water

fer-tile [fûr′tl] *adjective*, fruitful, able to produce abundantly

fer-ti-lize [fûr′tl-īz′] *verb*, to make ready for planting or encourage growth by providing proper amounts of nitrogen, potash, etc.

fer-vent [fûr′vənt] *adjective*, hot, showing intense feeling

fes-ter [fĕs′tər] *verb*, to become worse due to infection or anger

fes-ti-val [fĕs′tə-vəl] *noun*, 1) a big party that takes place on a holiday or at another special time 2) a program of cultural events 3) a carnival

fetch [fĕch] *verb*, 1) to go after something and bring it back, to retrieve 2) to bring a certain price

fet-ish [fĕt′ĭsh] *noun*, 1) a quirky habit based on a belief in magic 2) a compulsion 3) an object believed to be magical

feud [fyōōd] *noun*, 1) a prolonged fight, a quarrel, lasting hostility

fe-ver [fē′vər] *noun*, a body temperature higher than 98.6 degrees, often because the body is trying to fight off infection

few [fyōō] *adjective*, *noun*, *pronoun*, three or more

fi-an-cé [fē′än-sā′, fē-än′sā′] *noun*, a man engaged to be married

fi-an-cée [fē′än-sā′] *noun*, a woman engaged to be married

fi-as-co [fē-ăs′kō] *noun*, a total failure, an upheaval, a collapse

fi-ber [fī′bər] *noun*, 1) thread-like structures combined with others to create tissue 2) a filament 3) material in food that is not easily digested

fick-le [fĭk′əl] *adjective*, moody, inconsistent, not loyal, flighty

fic-tion [fĭk′shən] *noun*, that which is not true or based in fact, make-believe literature that is based on imagination

fic-ti-tious [fĭk-tĭsh′əs] *adjective*, imaginary, unreal, false

fid-dle [fĭd′l] *noun*, 1) another word for a violin, *verb*, 2) to tinker with something

fid-dler [fĭd′l-ər] *noun*, a person who plays a hand-held stringed instrument

fi-del-i-ty [fĭ-dĕl′ĭ-tē, fī-] *noun*, 1) faithfulness, loyalty, honesty 2) degree to which electronics accurately reproduce sound

field [fēld] *noun*, 1) land put to special use for sports or farming 2) a sphere or range of activities, *verb*, 3) to receive a ball in a game and pass it to another player

fiend [fēnd] *noun*, 1) a person who is wicked, cruel, or malicious 2) an evil sprit, a demon

fierce [fîrs] *adjective*, furious, violent or aggressive, intense

fier-y [fīr′ē] *adjective*, burning, heated, impassioned

fif-teen [fĭf-tēn′] *adjective*, *noun*, the number 15, ten plus five

fif-teenth [fĭf-tēnth′] *adjective*, *noun*, number 15 in order, 15th

fifth [fĭfth] *adjective*, *noun*, number five in order, 5th

fif-ti-eth [fĭf′tē-ĭth] *adjective*, *noun*, the ordinal of fifty, 50th

fif-ty [fĭf′tē] *adjective*, *noun*, the number 50, 5 times 10

fig [fĭg] *noun*, a small fruit grown in warm climates, full of seeds

fight [fīt] *noun*, 1) the use of the body or weapons against someone, *verb*, 2) to engage in a physical struggle 3) to quarrel 4) to struggle in any way

fig-ment [fĭg′mənt] *noun*, an imaginary thing

fig-ur-a-tive [fĭg′yər-ə-tĭv] *adjective*, 1) not literal, metaphorical 2) featuring human or animal figures

fig-ure [fĭg'yər] *noun*, 1) shape or outline of something, 2) digits or numbers in an equation, *verb*, 3) to calculate numbers or simplify something hard to understand

fig-ure-head [fĭg'yər-hĕd'] *noun*, 1) a carved figure set at the front of a sailing ship 2) a leader in name only who has no authority

fil-a-ment [fĭl'ə-mənt] *noun*, a slender threadlike structure, fiber, or wire

filch [fĭlch] *verb*, to steal

file [fīl] *noun*, 1) a drawer for papers 2) a metal tool with a rough edge for making things smooth 3) a line of people 4) a stored collection of data, *verb*, 5) to organize papers or other items into a system 6) to make a surface smooth through friction with a tool 7) to walk in a straight and orderly line 8) to register with a public agency

fil-i-al [fĭl'ē-əl] *adjective*, referring to having a relationship like a son or daughter

fill [fĭl] *verb*, 1) to occupy as much as possible 2) to make full

fil-let or fi-let [fĭl'ĭt] *noun*, 1) a boneless piece of meat or fish, *verb*, 2) to remove bones from and slice into fillets

film [fĭlm] *noun*, 1) a sensitized material that receives photographic impressions 2) a movie shown in a theater or on television, *verb*, 3) to photograph something on film 4) to make a movie using a camera

filth-y [fĭl'thē] *adjective*, 1) very dirty, nasty, squalid 2) obscene

fil-tra-tion [fĭl-trā'shən] *noun*, purification of a liquid by passing it through a filter

fin [fĭn] *noun*, part of a fish that sticks out, may be fan-shaped, used for steering or balance

fi-nal [fī'nəl] *adjective*, last, not to be changed

fi-na-le [fə-năl'ē] *noun*, the last part of a show or musical composition

fi-nal-ly [fī'nə-lē] *adverb*, at last, reaching the end, concluding

fi-nance [fə-năns'] *noun*, 1) money management of, *verb*, 2) to use money to pay for something

find [fīnd] *verb*, to uncover or see something after a search

fine [fīn] *adjective*, 1) pleasant, nice 2) having small grains or particles, *noun*, 3) a penalty, *verb*, 4) to punish someone by making them pay money

fin-esse [fə-nĕs'] *noun*, 1) a delicate skill, dexterity 2) tact, grace

fin-ger [fĭng'gər] *noun*, 1) one of five digits on a hand, *verb*, 2) to handle, to touch or feel

fin-ger-nail [fĭng'gər-nāl'] *noun*, the horny protective material on the end of a finger

fin-ick-y [fĭn'ĭ-kē] *adjective*, fussy

fin-ish [fĭn'ĭsh] *noun*, 1) a surface appearance or texture, *verb*, 2) to end or complete 3) to use up

fi-nite [fī'nīt'] *adjective*, 1) limited in number 2) having boundaries

fir [fûr] *noun*, an evergreen tree

fire [fīr] *noun*, 1) excitement 2) the state or process of burning, *verb*, 3) to dismiss from a job 4) to discharge from a gun

firm [fûrm] *adjective*, 1) solid, hard, *noun*, 2) a company managing a business

firm-ly [fûrm'lē] *adverb*, solidly, resolutely, unwaveringly

first [fûrst] *adjective*, 1) initial, beginning, *noun*, 2) the most important, the highest

first aid [fûrst'ād'] *noun*, the emergency help given someone who has been hurt or who suddenly becomes ill

fish [fĭsh] *noun*, 1) any cold-blooded vertebrate that lives in water, *verb*, 2) to try to catch a fish 3) to try to get something from someone

fis-sure [fĭsh'ər] *noun*, a crack, a narrow groove, a cleft

fist [fĭst] *noun*, the hand with fingers closed tightly together and folded into the palm

fit [fĭt] *adjective*, 1) healthy, active, vibrant 2) good enough, *verb*, 3) to be the right size 4) to conform in shape and size

five [fĭv] *adjective*, *noun*, the number 5, one plus four

fix [fĭks] *noun*, 1) a dilemma, a predicament, *verb*, 2) to repair 3) to set, to arrange, to put in place 4) to focus on

fix-ture [fĭks'chər] *noun*, that which is attached to something permanently, apparatus

flac-cid [flăk'sĭd, flăs'ĭd] *adjective*, flabby, hanging loosely

flag [flăg] *noun*, 1) cloth with a special pattern on it, used as the sign of a country, club, etc., *verb*, 2) to wave to someone as a signal to stop 3) to droop

flag-rant [flā'grənt] *adjective*, plainly wicked, unashamed

flail [flāl] *verb*, to move wildly as if beating something, to thrash

flair [flâr] *noun*, an aptitude or talent for doing something well

flake [flāk] *noun*, 1) a small sliver of something, *verb*, 2) to peel off in shavings or tiny bits

flam-boy-ant [flăm-boi'ənt] *adjective*, showy, flashy

flame [flām] *noun*, burning gas seen in a fire

flam-ma-ble [flăm'ə-bəl] *adjective*, capable of igniting easily and burning quickly

flank [flăngk] *noun*, a side of the body between the ribs and the hip, *verb*, 2) to be on one or either side of something

flan-nel [flăn'əl] *noun*, a very soft woolen or cotton cloth

flap [flăp] *noun*, 1) the covering of an opening, that hangs loose, *verb*, 2) to wave to and fro

flare [flâr] *noun*, 1) a torch or brilliant light, *verb*, 2) to shine, to burn brightly 3) to spread out like a fan, to expand outward

flash [flăsh] *noun*, 1) a split second, an instant, 2) a burst of light, *verb*, 3) to show a bright light

flash-back [flăsh'băk] *noun*, an interruption in the continuity of a story, play, etc. by the presentation of an earlier episode

flat [flăt] *adjective*, level and horizontal, smooth

flat-ter-y [flăt'ə-rē] *noun*, *no plural*, excessive compliments

flaunt [flônt] *verb*, to show off

fla-vor [flā'vər] *noun*, 1) seasoning of food, the taste of something, *verb*, 2) to give a taste to food

flaw [flô] *noun*, a defect, a weak spot, an imperfection

flax [flăks] *noun*, a slender plant with blue flowers whose stalks are used to make thread

flay [flā] *verb*, to whip or beat so as to strip off the skin

flea [flē] *noun*, a small jumping insect that sucks blood from people and animals

fled [flĕd] *verb*, *past tense* of **flee**

flee [flē] *verb*, to run away

fleece [flēs] *noun*, 1) the wool on sheep 2) a soft fabric with a deep pile, *verb*, 3) to shake someone down for money 4) to swindle

fleet [flēt] *noun*, a group of ships sailing together, or vehicles, or aircraft under one command

fleet-ing [flē′tĭng] *adjective*, swift in motion, passing quickly

flex [flĕks]*verb*,to bend, to contract

flex-i-ble [flĕk′sə-bəl] *adjective*, 1) willing to change a course of action, easily adaptable 2) moving or bending easily

flick-er [flĭk′ər] *verb*, 1) to change unsteadily from bright to dim light, *noun*, 2) a brief sensation

flight [flīt] *noun*, 1) flying, a trip by plane 2) an act of fleeing

flim-sy [flĭm′zē] *adjective*, 1) weak and easily broken 2) ineffectual, without substance

flinch [flĭnch] *verb*, to hesitate, to make a nervous movement away

flint [flĭnt] *noun*, a kind of quartz

flip [flĭp] *adjective*, 1) sarcastic, kidding, joking, *noun*, 2) a somersault in the air, *verb*, 3) to turn swiftly in the air

flip-pant [flĭp′ənt] *adjective*, glib, sarcastic, disrespectful

flirt [flûrt] *verb*, to show romantic interest, to tease affectionately

float [flōt] *noun*, 1) a portable display in a parade, 2) a soda with ice cream in it, *verb*, 3) to be supported by liquid or gas

flock [flŏk] *noun*, 1) a company of birds, animals, or people 2) to gather, to congregate, to huddle

flood [flŭd] *noun*, 1) water that stays on land that is normally dry, *verb*, 2) to cover or overflow with water

floor [flôr] *noun*, 1) the part of the room you walk on 2) a level of a building, *verb*, 3) to knock down 4) to surprise

flo-ral [flôr′əl] *adjective*, decorated with or containing flowers

Flor-i-da [flôr′ĭ-də] *noun*, one of the 50 United States, located in the Southeast, the capital is Tallahassee. The **Florida** state flower is the orange blossom, the motto: "In God we trust."

floss [flôs] *noun*, 1) a soft silky substance found in the husks of some plants 2) a thin silk thread used for embroidery 3) a thread covered with wax used to clean between the teeth, *verb*, 4) to run thread through the teeth to remove food and tartar

flo-til-la [flō-tĭl′ə] *noun*, a small fleet of ships

floun-der [floun′dər] *noun*, 1) a member of the flatfish family, *verb*, 2) to flail about

flour [flour] *noun*, the finely ground meal of wheat or other cereal plants like oats, rice, corn

flour-ish [flûr′ĭsh] *noun*, 1) a handwritten decoration, 2) a sweeping, showy gesture, *verb*, 3) to prosper, to grow well

flout [flout] *verb*, to scoff at, to ridicule, to disobey a law

flow [flō] *noun*, *no plural*, 1) a current, a steady stream, *verb*, 2) to move in the manner of gases or fluid

flow-er [flou′ər] *noun*, the part of a plant that bears the seeds, the blossom where fruit develops

flu [floo] *noun*, an illness caused by a virus and characterized by fever, body aches and coughing, influenza

fluc-tu-ate [flŭk′choo-āt′] *verb*, 1) to move back and forth like a wave, 2) to vary in degree or value

fluc-tu-a-tion [flŭk′choo-ā′ shən] *noun*, 1) wavering 2) the change of the level or degree of something

flu-ent [floo′ənt] *adjective*, able to speak smoothly and easily

flu-id [floo′ĭd] *adjective*, 1) not fixed or settled, able to flow, *noun*, 2) a liquid that flows

fluo-res-cent [floo-rĕs′ənt] *adjective*, giving off light after absorbing radiation from another source

flur-ry [flûr′ē] *noun*, 1) a brief, quick movement, 2) a light, windy snowfall

flush [flŭsh] *adjective*, 1) even, *noun*, 2) in poker, five cards of the same suit, *verb*, 3) to turn red in the face 4) to wash out

flust-er [flŭs′tər] *verb*, to confuse

flute [floot] *noun*, a musical instrument, a woodwind, like a pipe with keys to control the flow of air

flut-ter [flŭt′ər] *verb*, to flap, to move up and down or back and forth hurriedly

flux [flŭks] *noun*, a flowing series of continuous changes

fly [flī] *noun*, 1) a small flying insect, *verb*, 2) to move through the air 3) to move very fast

foam [fōm] *noun*, 1) froth formed on the surface of liquids by agitation, 2) a soft material produced by putting gas bubbles into a solid

fo-cal [fō′kəl] *adjective*, central

fo-cus [fō′kəs] *noun*, 1) a central point, 2) the clarity of a photograph or other optical object, *verb*, 3) to concentrate, to pay attention to something

foe [fō] *noun*, an enemy, an adversary, an opponent

fog [fôg] *noun*, a cloud of fine water drops of vapor found close to the ground or sea

foil [foil] *noun*, 1) a paper-like sheet of metal, 2) a long, thin sword used in fencing, *verb*, 3) to throw off someone's plans

fo-li-age [fōlē′ĭj] *noun*, ,the leaves of trees and other plants

fold [fōld] *noun*, 1) a part of something that has been wrapped or doubled over, *verb*, 2) to double or bend over, to envelope 3) to quit

fol-low [fŏl′ō] *verb*, 1) to go after, to pursue 2) to come after or behind 3) to pay close attention

fond [fŏnd] *adjective*, having feelings of affection

fon-dle [fŏn′dl]*verb*, to caress, to stroke lovingly

food [food] *noun*, a source of nourishment, what you eat

fool [fool] *noun*, 1) a silly person, *verb*, 2) to trick or deceive

fool-ish [foo′lĭsh] *adjective*, unwise, silly, senseless

foot [fŏŏt] *noun*, *plural*, **feet**, 1) the part of the leg that touches the ground 2) a measure of length equal to 12 inches 3) any base that resembles a foot

foot-ball [fŏŏt'bôl'] *noun*, 1) a game in which two teams of eleven players try to score points by passing a ball to each other in a period of time 2) an oval-shaped inflated ball 3) soccer used outside of the US

for [fôr, fər when unstressed] *conjunction*, 1) because, *preposition*, 2) in favor of 3) on behalf of or used by 4) at a certain price 5) having as a destination 6) showing the meaning of as in an example

for-age [fôr'ĭj] *verb*, to look for food or supplies

for-ay [fôr'ā'] *noun*, a raid, an attempt at something unfamiliar

for-bear [fôr-bâr'] *verb*, to hold back, to wait, to refrain from

for-bear-ance [fôr-bâr'əns] *noun*, the act of refraining from anything, self-restraint

for-bid [fər-bĭd'] *verb*, to prohibit, to order someone not to do something

force [fôrs, fōrs] *noun*, 1) power, energy 2) police or military personel, *verb*, 3) to cause to happen by strength or compulsion

fore-bod-ing [fôr-bō'dĭng] *noun*, a sense of evil to come

fore-cast [fôr'kăst'] *noun*, 1) a prediction that something will happen, especially in reference to the weather, *verb*, 2) to anticipate, or expect

fore-close [fôr-klōz'] *verb*, to take away property from a person who owes money on it

for-eign [fôr'ĭn] *adjective*, belonging to another country

for-eign-er [fôr'ə-nər] *noun*, someone from another country

fore-man [fôr'mən] *noun*, 1) the overseer of a set of workers 2) the spokesman of a jury

fore-most [fôr'mōst'] *adjective*, first in importance, time or place

fo-ren-sic [fə-rĕn'sĭk] *adjective*, suitable for argument in court

fore-see-a-ble [fôr-sē'ə-bəl] *adjective*, predictable, able to be seen as likely to occur

fore-sight [fôr'sīt'] *noun*, the ability to foresee future happenings or needs

for-est [fôr'ĭst] *noun*, a large place where trees grow together

fore-stall [fôr-stôl'] *verb*, to prevent by taking action first

fore-tell [fôr-tĕl'] *verb*, to predict, to make a prophecy, to forecast

for-ev-er [fôr-ĕv'ər] *adverb*, until the end of time, always

for-feit [fôr'fĭt] *verb*, to lose the right, to surrender, to give up

forge [fôrj] *noun*, 1) a furnace where metal is worked, *verb*, 2) to move ahead deliberately and steadily 3) to mold metal with heat and then hammer it into shapes 4) to invent or create something 5) to counterfeit with intent to defraud

for-ger-y [fôr'jə-rē] *noun*, a false or altered document, art object or other item for the purpose of fraud, counterfeit

for-get [fər-gĕt'] *verb*, 1) to fail to
recall or remember 2) to neglect

for-give [fər-gĭv'] *verb*, to accept
an apology, to get rid of a
grudge, to cease to feel angry

for-got [fər-gŏt'] *verb*, *past tense*
of **forget**

for-got-ten [fər-gŏt'n] *adjective*,
left behind

fork [fôrk] *noun*, 1) a utensil with
prongs on the end used to stab
food 2) a place in a road where it
separates in different directions

for-lorn [fər-lôrn'] *adjective*, sad
and unhappy, lonely

form [fôrm] *noun*, 1) the shape of
something 2) a document with
questions that need to be
answered, *verb*, 3) to shape or
create, to develop, to mold

for-mal [fôr'məl] *adjective*,
following the customs of an
occasion, ceremonious

for-mal-i-ty [fôr-măl'ĭ-tē] *noun*,
adherence to established rules of
etiquette and convention

for-ma-tion [fôr-mā'shən] *noun*,
1) a creation, the process of
being formed 2) an arrangement

form-er [fôr'mər] *noun*, the first
mentioned of two

for-mi-da-ble [fôr'mĭ-də-bəl]
adjective, 1) causing
apprehension, feared 2)
impressive because of excellence
3) difficult to overcome

for-mu-la [fôr'myə-lə] *noun*, 1) a
representation using chemical
symbols of substances mixed
together in specific amounts to
create something 2) a
mathematical statement using
symbols

for-mu-late [fôr'myə-lāt'] *verb*, to
prepare using a formula 2) to
give form to 3) to express
precisely in words

fort [fôrt] *noun*, a place for
protecting soldiers, a fortified
structure

forte [fôrt] *noun*, one's strength

for-ti-eth [fôr'tē-ĭth] *noun*, the
ordinal of forty, 40th

for-ti-fy [fôr'tə-fī'] *verb*, 1) to
make stronger or more secure
2) to strengthen against attack
3) to add nutrients

for-ti-tude [fôr'tĭ-tōōd'] *noun*,
courage, strength of mind, the
ability to withstand hardship

for-tu-nate [fôr'chə-nĭt] *adjective*,
lucky, favorable, advantageous

for-tune [fôr'chən] *noun*,
1) whatever good or bad happens
to people, luck 2) a large amount
of money, wealth, riches

for-ty [fôr'tē] *noun*, the number 40

fo-rum [fôr'əm] *noun*, a public
meeting place and market square

for-ward [fôr'wərd] *adjective*,
1) near or at the front part, ahead
2) onward 3) bold, aggressive

fos-sil [fŏs'əl] *noun*, the impression
or remains in a rock of a
petrified plant or animal

fos-ter [fô'stər] *verb*, to help, to
raise children not related to you,
to encourage

fought [fôt] *past tense* of **fight**

foul [foul] *adjective*, 1) dirty,
filthy, *noun*, 2) an action in a
sport that is against the rules

found [found] *verb*, 1) to establish,
to lay a foundation 2) *past tense*
of **find**

foun-da-tion [foun-dā'shən] *noun*, 1) the base of a building 2)fundamental assumptions 3) a charitable institution

found-er [foun'dər] *noun*, 1) one who begins or establishes an organization, *verb*, 2) to sink

found-ry [foun'drē] *noun*, a plant refining metal or glass, a factory

foun-tain [foun'tən] *noun*, a device that sprays water into the air or pumps it for drinking

four [fôr] *adjective*, *noun*, the number 4, one plus three

four-teen [fôr-tēn'] *noun*, the number 14, four plus ten

four-teenth [fôr-tēnth'] *adjective*, *noun*, number 14 in order, 14th

fourth [fôrth] *adjective*, *noun*, the ordinal number after third, 4th

fowl [foul] *noun*, a bird eaten as food or kept for its eggs

fox [fŏks] *noun*, a carnivorous mammal, the size of a dog with a pointed muzzle and bushy tail

foy-er [foi'ər] *noun*, the entry way in a hall, a hotel lobby

frac-tion [frăk'shən] *noun*, 1) a piece of something 2) a number that names part of a whole or part of a group using equal parts

frac-ture [frăk'chər] *noun*, 1) a break, a fissure, *verb*, 2) to break

frag-ile [frăj'əl, -īl'] *adjective*, easily broken, delicate

frag-ment [frăg'mənt] *noun*, a piece broken off, a particle

fra-grance [frā'grəns] *noun*, a sweet smell, perfume, aroma

frail [frāl] *adjective*, weak, fragile

frame [frām] *noun*, 1) the structure that supports something 2) the outline of something encasing something, *verb*, 3) to enclose in a frame 4) to make someone appear guilty of a crime by arranging false evidence

fran-chise [frăn'chīz'] *noun*, an agreement granted by a company to do business under their name

frank [frăngk] *adjective*, candid, honest in expressing your thoughts

fran-tic [frăn'tĭk] *adjective*, wild with emotion, characterized by nervous activity

fra-ter-ni-ty [frə-tûr'nĭ-tē] *noun*, a fellowship of men in a college

fraud [frôd] *noun*, 1) an imposter, a fake 2) criminal deception

fraud-u-lent [frô'jə-lənt] *adjective*, tricky, deceitful, dishonest

fray [frā] *noun*, 1) a conflict, a commotion, *verb*, 2) to unravel

freak [frēk] *noun*, a strange event or person, an aberration

freck-le [frĕk'əl] *noun*, a small, brownish spot on the skin

free [frē] *adjective*, 1) able to do as you please, unrestrained 2) not costing any money 3) available, *verb*, 4) to release something from captivity

free-dom [frē'dəm] *noun*, liberty, independent, the state of being free

freeze [frēz] *verb*, to become chilled by cold, to change to ice

freez-er [frē'zər] *noun*, an appliance that preserves food by keeping it frozen

freight [frāt] *noun*, transportation of products in bulk, cargo

freight-er [frā'tər] *noun*, a ship or aircraft laden with cargo

fren-zy [frĕn'zē] *noun*, craziness, wild excitement, violent agitation

133

fre-quen-cy [frē′kwən-sē] *noun*, the number of times something, especially a sound wave, occurs during a particular period of time

fre-quent [frē′kwənt] *adjective*, 1) happening often, repeated many times, *verb,* 2) to go to a place often for visits

fresh [frĕsh] *adjective*, new, unused, arrived recently

fresh-man [frĕsh′mən] *noun*, a person in his first year of high school or college

fret [frĕt] *verb*, to feel anxious

fric-tion [frĭk′shən] *noun*, 1) the force that resists movement between two things that are in contact with each other 2) an argument caused by differences of opinion, rivalry

Fri-day [frī′dē, -dā′]*noun*, the sixth day of the week

friend [frĕnd] *noun*, a person who knows and likes another

friend-ship [frĕnd- shĭp] *noun*, mutual respect, companionship

fright [frīt] *noun*, sudden fear

fright-en [frīt′n] *verb*, to scare or alarm, to fill with fear

frig-id [frĭj′ĭd] *adjective*, very cold

frill [frĭl] *noun*,1) a doodad, an unnecessary extra feature or luxury 2) a pleated piece of fabric used as a trim

fringe [frĭnj] *noun*, 1) an edge made of short lengths of thread, used to decorate clothes, curtains, etc. 2) an outside edge

frisk-y [frĭs′kē] *adjective*, playful

frit-ter [frĭt′ər] *noun*, 1) fried batter containing fruit, vegetables, or meat, *verb*, 2) to waste

friv-o-lous [frĭv′ə-ləs] *adjective*, 1) of little weight or importance 2) given to trifling, silly

frog [frôg] *noun*, 1) a jumping amphibian that can swim in water or live on land 2) a tool designed to sit in the bottom of a bowl or vase to hold flower stems 3) a decorative braid used to fasten a piece of clothing

frol-ic [frŏl′ĭk] *noun*, 1) merry making *verb*, 2) to play happily

from [frŭm] *preposition*, 1) used to show a starting point 2) used to show a point of separation 3) used to show material source or cause, given by

front [frŭnt] *adjective*, 1) located ahead of the others, *noun*, 2) the face or the part of something that faces forward 3) the facade

fron-tier [frŭn-tîr′] *noun*, 1) the part of a country facing another country 2) a new field of learning, undiscovered territory, 3) a region at the edge of settled territory

frost [frôst] *noun*, the frozen water that covers the surface of everything outdoors when the temperature goes below freezing

froth [frôth] *noun*, 1) fine bubbles, foam, *verb*, 2) to cause to foam

frown [froun] *noun*, 1) facial expression in which the brow is furrowed and the lips turn down at the edges, *verb*, 2) to look unhappy, to show disapproval

froze [frōz] *past tense* of **freeze**

fro-zen [frō′zən] *adjective*, cooled to the point that liquid turns to solid, icy

fru-gal [frōō′gəl] *adjective*, careful with resources, thrifty

fruit [froot] *noun*, 1) an edible product of a plant, bearing seeds 2) the results, the outcome

fruit-ful [froot′fəl] *adjective*, successful, productive

fru-i-tion [froo-ĭsh′ən] *noun*, fulfillment, realization

frus-trate [frŭs′trāt′] *verb*, to prevent from attaining a purpose

fry [frī] *verb*, to cook in hot oil or other fat

fudge [fŭj] *noun*, a soft candy usually made with sugar, milk and flavoring 2) chocolate candy or sauce, *verb* 3) to deal with in an inadequate or evasive way

fuel [fyoo′əl] *noun*, something that gives off heat when it is burned

fu-gi-tive [fyoo′jĭ-tĭv] *noun*, one who flees pursuit by the law

ful-fill [fool-fĭl′] *verb*, 1) to satisfy a contract 2) to complete

full [fool] *adjective*, 1) leaving no empty space, holding as much as possible, *adverb*, 2) entirely

fumes [fyoomz] *noun, plural*, gases

fu-mi-gate [fyoo′mĭ-gāt′] *verb*, to apply smoke or vapor as a means of disinfecting or killing bugs

fun [fŭn] *noun, no plural*, amusement, enjoyment

func-tion [fŭngk′shən] *noun*, 1) the natural and proper action of anything 2) a service, duty, purpose 3) the way in which something works 4) a large social gathering

fund [fŭnd] *noun*, 1) a sum of money collected for a special purpose, *verb*, 2) to provide money to support a cause

fun-da-men-tal [fŭn′də-měn′tl] *adjective*, 1) of first importance, essential 2) elementary, basic

fu-ner-al [fyoo′nər-əl] *noun*, a ceremony honoring the life of someone who died

fun-gus [fŭng′gəs] *noun*, a plant that lacks chlorophyll, leaves, and a flower, e.g., mushrooms, mold, yeast

fun-nel [fŭn′əl] *noun*, an open cone wide at the top with a smaller end to pour liquids from one container to another

fun-ny [fŭn′ē] *adjective*, 1) amusing, entertaining, making someone laugh 2) strange, unusual, odd

fur [fûr] *noun*, a soft hair covering on some animals, the pelt

fu-ri-ous [fyoor′ē-əs] *adjective*, very angry, violent

fur-nace [fûr′nĭs] *noun*, 1) an enclosed place in which heat is produced by the combustion of fuel 2) a large appliance containing a very hot fire

fur-nish [fûr′nĭsh] *verb*, to supply, to stock or provide, to give

fur-ni-ture [fûr′nĭ-chər] *noun, no plural*, the articles in a home that make it more comfortable, such as beds, chairs, tables, etc.

fu-ror [fyoor′ôr′] *noun*, frenzy, a state of great public excitement

fur-ther [fûr′thər] *adverb*, at a greater distance, beyond

fur-tive [fûr tĭv] *adjective*, done in a sneaky way, hoping to be unnoticed

fu-ry [fyoor′ē] *noun*, great anger

fur-ry [fûr′ē] *adjective*, covered with hair, like fur

fuse [fyōōz] *noun*, 1) a combustible cord that is lit to ignite an explosive device 2) a device to protect an electrical circuit from an electrical surge, *verb*, 3) to combine, to melt together

fu-sion [fyōō'zhən] *noun*, 1) the process of joining two or more things together as one 2) a nuclear reaction

fuss [fŭs] *noun*, 1) complaint, commotion, *verb*, 2) to behave in an excited, worried way

fu-tile [fyōōt'l, fyōō'tĭl'] *adjective*, ineffective, fruitless, pointless

fu-ture [fyōō'chər] *adjective*, 1) coming after the present, *noun*, 2) a time that has not yet arrived

G

gadg-et [găj'ĭt] *noun*, a mechanical device or tool, a thingamajig

gag [găg] *noun*, 1) something put in the mouth to keep people from talking, *verb*, 2) to restrain someone from speaking 3) to choke or retch

gai-e-ty [gā'ĭ-tē] *noun*, merriment

gain [gān] *noun*, 1) an increase, *verb*, 2) to win, to acquire

gait [gāt] *noun*, a manner of walking, skipping, or running

gal-ax-y [găl'ək-sē] *noun*, a group of billions of stars held together by mutual gravitation

gale [gāl] *noun*, a strong wind

gall [gôl] *noun*, 1) bitterness, anger, 2) nerve, rudeness, *verb*, 3) to annoy, to anger, to infuriate

gal-lant [găl'ənt] *adjective*, brave, bold, daring, chivalrous

gal-le-on [găl'ē-ən] *noun*, a large sailing ship of earlier times

gal-ler-y [găl'ə-rē] *noun*, 1) a long, narrow, room-like corridor or passageway 2) a room for the exhibition of works of art

gal-ley [găl'ē] *noun*, 1) an oblong tray to hold type which has been set 2) the part of a ship where food is prepared

gal-lon [găl'ən] *noun*, a unit of liquid measure equal to 4 quarts or 128 ounces

gal-lop [găl'əp] *verb*, to trot

gal-lows [găl'ōz] *noun*, apparatus from which criminals are hung

gal-va-nize [găl'və-nīz'] *verb*, 1) to stimulate with shock, to stir up 2) to cover with zinc

gam-ble [găm'bəl] *verb*, to try to win money by betting

gam-bler [găm'blər] *noun*, a bettor

game [gām] *noun*, a form of entertainment played with rules that tests skill, knowledge, or athletic ability

gam-ut [găm'ət] *noun*, the entire range from beginning to end

gan-der [găn'dər] *noun*, male goose

gang [găng] *noun*, 1) an organized group of people who intimidate and harass 2) a group of workers

gan-grene [găng'grēn'] *noun*, the death of body tissue because of infection

gap [găp] *noun*, 1) a hole, an opening 2) the difference between two numbers

ga-rage [gə-räzh'] *noun*, 1) a place for housing automobiles 2) a place where motor vehicles are repaired

gar-bage [gär′bǐj] *noun*, another word for solid waste, especially household waste, trash

gar-den [gär′dn] *noun*, 1) a plot of land where flowers or vegetables grow, *verb*, 2) to look after the plants by watering and pruning

gar-den-er [gärd′nər] *noun*, one who makes and tends a garden

gar-gle [gär′gəl] *verb*, to rinse the throat with a liquid kept in motion by air forced through it from the lungs

gar-goyle [gär′goil′] *noun*, grotesque figures of people or animals carved as a roof spout

gar-ish [gâr′ĭsh, gär′-] *adjective*, in bad taste, gaudy, showy

gar-lic [gär′lĭk] *noun*, a plant like an onion with a strong taste and smell, used to season food

gar-ment [gär′mənt] *noun*, a piece of clothing

gar-ner [gär′nər] *verb*, to gather up, to accumulate, to amass

gar-net [gär′nĭt] *noun*, a semiprecious stone of a red color

gar-nish [gär′nĭsh] *noun*, 1) a decoration for food, *verb*, 2) to adorn 3) to take funds from someone a little at a time by order of the court to pay a debt

gar-ri-son [găr′ĭ-sən] *noun*, troops stationed in a fort or fortified town, a military post

gas [găs] *noun*, 1) a state of matter in which a substance like air is capable of infinitely expanding, has no fixed form or volume and takes the shape of its container 2) the short word for gasoline

gas-e-ous [găs′ē-əs, găsh′əs] *adjective*, in vapor form

gas-ket [găs′kĭt] *noun*, a piece of rubber sealing a joint between metal surfaces

gas-o-line [găs′ə-lēn′] *noun*, petroleum refined and used as motor fuel

gasp [găsp] *noun*, 1) a short intake of breath, *verb*, 2) to pant with a short, excited breath

gas-tron-o-my [gă-strŏn′ə-mē] *noun*, the art of preparing and serving good food

gate [gāt] *noun*, a a hinged door that closes an opening in a wall or fence

gath-er [găth′ər] *noun*, 1) a fold or pucker in a piece of cloth, *verb*, 2) to bring together or accumulate, to harvest 3) to infer from what someone has said

gauche [gōsh] *adjective*, clumsy, lacking social grace, awkward

gaud-y [gô′dē] *adjective*, showy in a tasteless way, ostentatious

gauge [gāj] *noun*, 1) an instrument used to measure, *verb*, 2) to measure or estimate

gaunt [gônt] *adjective*, 1) thin, lean 2) emaciated as from illness

gauze [gôz] *noun*, 1) a cotton bandage 2) a thin fabric

gaze [gāz] *verb*, to look at steadily, and intently, to stare

gaz-et-teer [gaezə′tir] *noun*, a geographical dictionary

gear [gîr] *noun*, 1) a toothed wheel that passes motion and power along 2) equipment, supplies

gel-a-tin [jĕl′ə-tn] *noun*, a tasteless, transparent substance, obtained from animal tissue such as skin, bones, or horns

gem [jĕm] *noun*, a precious or semiprecious stone used as an ornament

gen-der [jĕn'dər] *noun*, 1) a set of categories applied to nouns as masculine or feminine 2) the state of being male or female

ge-ne-al-o-gy [jē'nē-ŏl'ə-jē] *noun*, a record of family history, a family tree

gen-er-al [jĕn'ər-əl] *adjective*, 1) not particular or definite of or from the whole 2) usual or customary, common, lacking detail, *noun*, 3) the title of the commander in an army

Gen-er-al As-sem-bly *noun*, 1) the law-making body of some of the US states 2) the assembly of the representatives of the United Nations

gen-er-al-i-ty [jĕn'ə-răl'ĭ-tē] *noun*, a vague, nonspecific statement

gen-er-al-ize [jĕn'ər-ə-līz'] *verb*, to make a broad statement

gen-er-al-ly [jĕn'ər-ə-lē] *adverb*, usually, as a rule, normally

gen-er-ate [jĕn'ə-rāt'] *verb*, to make or create, to produce

gen-er-a-tion [jĕn'ə-rā'shən] *noun*, 1) the average time interval between the birth of parents and the birth of their offspring 2) all of the people born at about the same time 3) the act or process of producing something

gen-er-a-tor [jĕn'ə-rā'tər] *noun*, a machine by which mechanical energy is changed into electrical energy

gen-er-os-i-ty [jĕn'ə-rŏs'ĭ-tē] *noun*, the trait of giving freely to others, unselfishness

gen-er-ous [jĕn'ər-əs] *adjective*, liberal, open-handed, abundant

ge-ni-al [jēn'yəl] *adjective*, kind

gen-ius [jēn'yəs] *noun*, mental or creative superiority

gen-re [zhän'rə] *noun*, a category, art or music characterized by a particular style, class

gen-til-i-ty [jĕn-tĭl'ĭ-tē] *noun*, men or women who have high social standing and refined manners

gen-tle [jĕn'tl] *adjective*, 1) kind, courteous, amiable 2) soft and mild 3) not steep, moderate

gen-tle-man [jĕn'tl-mən] *noun*, a well-mannered man

gent-ly [jĕnt'lē] *adverb*, carefully

gen-u-flect [jĕn'yə-flĕkt'] *verb*, to bend one knee and bow in worship or reverence

gen-u-ine [jĕn'yōō-ĭn] *adjective*, real, not false, not pretended

gen-u-ine-ly [jĕn'yōō-ĭn-lē] *adverb*, truly, really

ge-og-ra-phy [jē-ŏg'rə-fē] *noun*, the science that describes the physical surface of the earth, and the effects of human activity on it

ge-ol-o-gist [jē-ŏl'ə-jĭst] *noun*, a person who studies the structure of the earth, its physical changes, and the causes producing these

ge-ol-o-gy [jē-ŏl'ə-jē] *noun*, the science that studies the history and structure of the earth, its physical changes, and the causes producing these changes

ge-om-e-try [jē-ŏm'ĭ-trē] *noun*, the branch of mathematics that studies the relations, properties, and measurement of solids, surfaces, lines, and angles

Geor-gia [jôr′jə] *noun*, a state in the southeastern United States. The capital city is Atlanta. The state flower of **Georgia** is the Cherokee rose and the motto is "Wisdom, justice, and moderation."

ge-ra-ni-um [jə-rā′nē-əm] *noun*, a flower with pink, red, or white blooms and velvety leaves

germ [jûrm] *noun*, a micro-organism that causes disease

ger-mi-nate [jûr′mə-nāt′] *verb*, to cause to grow, develop or sprout

ges-ta-tion [jĕ-stā′shən] *noun*, the period of time a new life is in the womb until it is born, pregnancy

ges-tic-u-late [jĕ-stĭk′yə-lāt′] *verb*, to make a motion, to gesture emphatically

ges-ture [jĕs′chər] *noun*, 1) any action of the hand or head that shows feeling, *verb*, 2) to make a movement, to signal

get [gĕt] *verb*, 1) to receive, have, or buy, to acquire 2) to become or attain

gey-ser [gī′zər] *noun*, a natural hot spring that throws out a spray of steam and water occasionally

ghet-to [gĕt- tō] *noun*, any section of a city in which many members of a minority group live, or to which they are restricted by discrimination

ghost [gōst] *noun*, the appearance of a dead person, an apparition believed to haunt the living

gi-ant [jī′ənt] *adjective*, 1) very large, huge, *noun*, 2) a legendary person or animal who is huge

gift [gĭft] *noun*, 1) a present 2) a person's inborn ability to do something well, talent

gi-gan-tic [jī-găn′tĭk] *adjective*, very big, large, huge, titanic

gig-gle [gĭg′əl] *verb*, to laugh in a silly, undignified way

gill [gĭl] *noun*, respiratory organs in fish that separate dissolved oxygen from water

gi-raffe [jə-răf′] *noun*, a tall African animal with a very long neck and very long legs and large brown spots on its coat

gird-er [gûr′dər] *noun*, an iron or steel beam to span an opening or carry the weight of a building

girl [gûrl] *noun*, a female child

gist [jĭst] *noun*, the main point

give [gĭv] *verb*, 1) to present, to donate, to hand-over 2) to impart something 3) to provide or assign 4) to yield to pressure

giv-en [gĭv′ən] *adjective*, 1) stated, typical 2) habitually inclined

gla-cier [glā′shər] *noun*, a body of ice, formed in a region of perpetual snow, moving slowly across land

glad [glăd] *adjective*, 1) feeling pleasure or joy 2) very willing

glad-i-o-lus [glăd′ē-ō′ləs] *noun*, *plural*, **gladioli**, a native bulb from Africa of the iris family, with sword-shaped leaves and stems of brightly colored flowers

glad-ly [glăd′lē] *adverb*, happily, willingly, joyfully

glam-or [glăm′ər] *noun*, beauty, attraction, alluring charm

glance [glăns] *noun*, 1) a quick or a brief look, *verb*, 2) to look quickly or briefly, to glimpse

gland [glănd] *noun*, a part of a living organism that secretes a vital substance

glare [glâr] *noun*, 1) a bright light reflecting shine or a gleam 2) an angry stare, *verb*, 3) to stare disapprovingly, to glower

glass [glăs] *noun*, *no plural*, 1) a hard clear substance that is easily shattered, used for windows 2) a drinking container *plural*, **glass-es** [glăs'ez] *noun*, 3) specially cut lenses made of plastic or glass held in a frame to adjust vision so that a person can see better, spectacles

glaze [glāz] *noun*, 1) a coating that creates a smooth, shiny surface, *verb*, 2) to cover with material or substance that creates a thin shiny surface

gleam [glēm] *noun*, 1) a brief flash of light, *verb*, 2) to shine brightly, to glisten, to glitter

glean [glēn] *verb*, to gather leftovers, to collect

glee [glē] *noun*, joy, merriment

glib [glĭb] *adjective*, flippant, speaking freely, persuasive

glide [glīd] *verb*, to move smoothly and effortlessly, to slide

glid-er [glī'dər] *noun*, an aircraft that flies without an engine

glimpse [glĭmps] *noun*, 1) a brief look at something, *verb*, 2) to get a quick look at something

glit-ter [glĭt'ər] *noun*, 1) something that sparkles or twinkles, *verb*, 2) to sparkle or twinkle as a reflection of light, to shimmer

gloat [glōt] *verb*, to brag, to boast

globe [glōb] *noun*, 1) the round replica of the Earth marked with countries, continents and oceans 2) anything round like a ball

gloom [glōom] *noun*, 1) near or total darkness 2) a feeling of sadness, dejection, dispondency

glo-ri-fy [glôr'ə-fī'] *verb*, to exalt, to acclaim, to worship

glo-ri-ous [glôr'ē-əs] *adjective*, exhibiting qualities that deserve or receive glory or praise

glory [glôr'ē] *noun*, praise given to someone who has accomplished something extraordinary, a state of honor

glos-sa-ry [glô'sə-rē] *noun*, a list of specialized words used in a given text with definitions

gloss-y [glô'sē] *adjective*, smooth and shiny, gleaming bright

glove [glŭv] *noun*, a covering for the hand with separate sections for the fingers and the thumb

glow [glō] *noun*, 1) gentle radiance, light and warmth, *verb*, 2) to radiate, steady, even light or heat

glu-cose [glōo'kōs'] *noun*, 1) sugar created in the body by processing starch 2) a syrup made by processing corn

glue [glōo] *noun*, 1) a substance used to make things stick together, *verb*, 2) to fasten with an adhesive, to attach closely

glut-ton [glŭt'n] *noun*, someone who is greedy for food

glyc-er-in [glĭs'ər-ĭn] *noun*, syrupy liquid used as a softening agent for skin, solvent, and in foods

gnarled [närld] *adjective*, twisted in a knotted form

gnat [năt] *noun*, a very small flying insect that bites

gnaw [nô] *verb*, to bite so as to wear away persistently

go [gō] *noun*, 1) a try, an effort, *verb*, 2) to move along 3) to depart 4) to proceed

goad [gōd] *verb*, 1) to use some object to make an animal move 2) to provoke into an argument

goal [gōl] *noun*, 1) an intended or desired achievement 2) the cage, line or basket at the end of a playing field that the opposite team tries to penetrate 3) a score in some athletic contests 4) an objective

goat [gōt] *noun*, a small, horned ruminant animal, sometimes raised for its milk, meat, and fur

gob-ble [gŏb'əl] *verb*, 1) to consume, to eat fast 2) to make the sound a make turkey makes

gob-lin [gŏb'lĭn] *noun*, in folklore, an ugly, grotesque creature that makes trouble

god [gŏd] *noun*, a being to whom people pray and that has control of the forces in the world

God [gŏd] *proper noun*, the supreme being, the creator of the universe

god-dess [gŏd'ĭs] *noun*, a female deity

goes [gōz] *present tense* of **go** used in the singular, with *he*, *she*, or *it*

gog-gles [gŏg'əlz] *noun*, large spectacles for protecting the eyes

gold [gōld] *adjective*, 1)having a bright deep yellow color, *noun*, 2) a precious metallic element

golf [gŏlf] *noun*, a game played by two or more people in which a small ball is hit into 9 or 18 holes arranged on a large piece of land called a course

gone [gôn] *past tense* of **go,**

gong [gông] *noun*, a percussion instrument consisting of a large piece of metal hung up and hit to make a loud noise

good [gŏŏd] *adjective*, 1) right, not wrong 2) appropriate, suitable, useful 3) well-behaved 4) nice, pleasant, *noun*, *no plural*, 5) what is virtuous and kind

good-ness [gŏŏd'nĭs] *noun*, generosity, kindness, virtue

goods [gŏŏdz] *noun*, merchandise, things made by people

good-will [gŏŏd wĭl] *noun*, the value of kindness in business and relationships

goose [gŏŏs] *noun*, *plural*, **geese**, a large web-footed aquatic bird

gore [gôr] *noun*, clotted blood

gorge [gôrj]*verb*, to stuff yourself

gor-geous [gôr'jəs] *adjective*, strikingly beautiful

go-ril-la [gə-rĭl'ə] *noun*, a very large animal similar to a monkey, the largest ape

gos-pel[gŏs'pəl]*noun*, the first four books of the New Testament of the Bible, which tell the life and teachings of Jesus

gos-sa-mer [gŏs'ə-mər] *adjective*, sheer, like cobwebs

gos-sip [gŏs'əp] *noun*, 1) rumors about people that are often unkind or untrue 2) a person who divulges personal information about others, *verb*, 3) to talk about other people

got [gŏt] *past tense* of **get**

gouge [gouj] *noun*, 1) a chisel with a troughlike blade 2) a groove or hole, *verb*, 3) to cut, scoop, or tear out

gourd [gôrd] *noun*, a large fruit related to squash, with a shell often made into a container

gour-met [gŏŏr-mā′]*noun*, a person who understands and enjoys the finest food and drink

gov-ern [gŭv′ərn] *verb*, to lead or control by authority; to make and enforce laws

gov-ern-ment [gŭv′ərn-mənt] *noun*, the offices, agencies, and people who control a nation, state, or city by making laws and seeing that they are followed

gov-er-nor [gŭv′ər-nər] *noun*, 1) the elected or appointed leader who controls a colony, state, or country 2) an attachment to an engine for controlling its speed

gown [goun] *noun*, 1) a dress worn by a woman that reaches to the floor 2) a covering over the body so that a doctor can examine you without your clothes on or worn by a surgeon during operations

grab [grăb] *verb*, to seize, to clutch, to snatch suddenly

grace [grās] *noun*, 1) elegance, refinement, charm 2) kindness, 3) holiness, devotion, love 4) mercy, pardon, 5) a blessing, giving thanks, *verb*, 6) to beautify, to enhance, to adorn

grace-ful [grās′fəl] *adjective*, having beauty of movement

gra-cious [grā′shəs] *adjective*, kindly, pleasing, courteous

grade [grād] *noun*, 1) a rating of evaluation or class, *verb*, 2) to rate or rank in a group according to size, quantity, or aptitude

grad-u-al [grăj′ŏŏ-əl] *adjective*, progressing slowly, step by step

grad-u-al-ly [grăj′ŏŏ-ə-lē] *adverb*, progressively, in a piecemeal way

grad-u-ate [grăj′ŏŏ-ĭt′] *noun*, 1) someone who has received a diploma to document that he or she has completed a required course of study 2) a cup or cylinder marked for measuring liquid, [grăj′ŏŏ-āt′]*verb*, 3) to get one's degree by finishing school

grad-u-a-tion [grăj′ŏŏ-ā′shən] *noun*, a ceremony to award diplomas to graduates

graf-fi-to [grə-fē′tō] *noun*, *plural*, **graffiti**, words or images drawn or painted in public places to deface a building or surface

graft [grăft] *noun*, 1) a bud or a shoot of a tree inserted into another tree to grow 2) a piece of transplanted living skin, tissue, or an organ 3) use of one's position to make dishonest gains

grain [grān] *noun*, 1) a very small piece of something, a particle 2) seed from a cereal plant such as wheat, corn, or rice 3) the design or pattern of wood

gram [grăm] *noun*, the metric unit of weight used to measure small objects equal to one thousandth of a kilogram

gram-mar[grăm′ər]*noun*, *no plural* 1) the study of how words make sentences 2) rules that govern the correct use of language

grand [grănd] *adjective*, very large and fine, impressive in size

grand-child [grănd′chīld′] *noun*, *plural* **grandchildren**, the child of someone's son or daughter

grand-daugh-ter [grăn′dô′tər] *noun*, the daughter of a person's son or daughter

gran-deur [grăn′jər] *noun*, magnificence, greatness

grand-son [grănd′sŭn′] *noun*, the son of a person's daughter or son

gran-ite [grăn′ĭt] *noun*, a hard igneous rock, consisting of feldspar, mica, and quartz, used in monuments or buildings

grange [g rānj] *noun*, 1) a farm with its dwelling house, barns, etc. 2) an association of farmers founded in 1867 for mutual welfare and advancement

grant [grănt] *noun*, 1) money donated by the government or a charitable foundation, *verb*, 2) to allow, to confer, to give

gran-u-late [grăn′yə-lāt′] *verb*, to process a dense solid into grains

grape [grāp] *noun*, a small, round, edible, juicy fruit that grows in clusters on a vine

grape-fruit [grāp′frōōt′] *noun*, a large, round, sour citrus fruit

graph [grăf] *noun*, 1) a picture indicating measurements to show change 2) a drawing used to show information

graph-ic [grăf′ĭk] *adjective*, 1) pertaining to the arts of painting and drawing 2) clearly and vividly described

graph-ite [grăf′ĭt′] *noun*, a soft, black crystallized form of carbon

grap-ple [grăp′əl] *noun*, 1) a tool with several hooks, usually attached to a rope and thrown *verb*, 2) to grab and struggle, to seize in a firm grip

grasp [grăsp] *noun*, 1) a clasp with the hand, *verb*, 2) to hold or seize 3) to understand or learn

grass [grăs] *noun*, 1) a fine ground cover with thin leaves that animals eat 2) a lawn

grass-hop-per [grăs′hŏp′ər] *noun*, an insect that lives in the grass with strong back legs for jumping and wings for flying

grate [grāt] *noun*, 1) a metal frame with wires or bars laid in the shape of a grid, *verb*, 2) to shred or shave into small pieces by rubbing on a jagged surface 3) to irritate, to annoy

grate-ful [grāt′fəl] *adjective*, thankful, appreciative

grat-i-fy [grăt′ə-fī′] *verb*, to please

grat-i-tude [grăt′ĭ-tōōd′] *noun*, *no plural*, a feeling of thankfulness

gra-tu-i-tous [grə-tōō′ĭ-təs] *adjective*, 1) given freely or without charge 2) unnecessary

gra-tu-i-ty [grə-tōō′ĭ-tē] *noun*, a tip

grave [grāv] *adjective*, 1) serious, *noun*, 2) a hole in the ground where a dead person is buried

grav-el [grăv′əl] *noun*, a mixture of pebbles and rock fragments

grav-i-ty [grăv′ĭ-tē] *noun*, 1) the force that draws everything to the earth's center or toward any large body that has mass 2) solemnity, of a serious nature

gra-vy [grā′vē] *noun*, a sauce made with flour and meat drippings

gray [grā] *noun*, a color between white and black

graze [grāz] *verb*, 1) to eat grass or vegetation 2) to rub against something and scrape against the surface

grease [grēs] *noun*, 1) a soft animal fat 2) any oily matter, *verb*, 3) to

143

lubricate or make slippery with oils, to coat with grease

great [grāt] *adjective*, 1) large in size, quantity, duration 2) eminent, remarkable

great-er [grā'tər] *adjective*, more than something in comparison to it, bigger, larger, better

great-est [grā'tĭst] *adjective*, most, superior, best, largest

greed [grēd] *noun*, *no plural*, the feeling that you want more than you need, desire for wealth

green [grēn] *noun*, 1) a color made by combining yellow and blue 2) a plot of grass

green-house [grēn'hous'] *noun*, a house made of glass or clear plastic used to grow plants in a controlled environment all year

greet [grēt] *verb*, to welcome, to say hello

greet-ing [grē'tĭng] *noun*, a friendly expression when meeting someone

gre-gar-i-ous [grĭ-gâr'ē-əs] *adjective*, very social

grew [grōō] *past tense* of **grow**

grey [grā] see **gray**, *noun*, a mixture of black and white

grid [grĭd] *noun*, 1) grate, a metal plate with perforations 2) a network of horizontal and vertical lines used to locate a particular point on a map 3) a system of electrical wires for distributing power in an area

grid-dle [grĭd'l] *noun*, a flat surface used for cooking

grief [grēf] *noun*, very deep sorrow, sadness caused by someone's death

griev-ance [grē'vəns] *noun*, cause of complaint, a protest expressing resentment

grieve [grēv] *verb*, to be very sorry and upset about something lost or done, to be filled with sadness

grill [grĭl] *noun*, 1) a cooking unit with a metal rack or a flat heated surface used for broiling food 2) a system of bars forming a lattice, *verb*, 3) to broil food 4) to question intensely

grim [grĭm] *adjective*, dreadful

grin [grĭn] *noun*, 1) a big smile, *verb*, 2) to smile broadly

grind [grīnd] *verb*, to crush something so hard that it becomes powder

grip [grĭp] *noun*, 1) a hold, a grasp, *verb*, 2) to hold or clench something tightly

gris-ly [grĭz'lē] *adjective*, ghastly, horrible, gruesome, shocking

grist [grĭst] *noun*, grain that is to be or has been ground

grit [grĭt] *noun*, 1) courage, fortitude, bravery 2) sand, gravel, coarse sandstone

grits [grĭts] *noun*, *plural*, coarsely ground hulled corn

griz-zly [grĭz'lē] *noun*, a big brown bear found in western North America

groan [grōn] *noun*, 1) a moan, a complaint, a cry of distress, *verb*, 2) to emit a low cry in disapproval or pain

groom [grōōm] *noun*, 1) a man about to be or just having been married 2) a person who takes care of horses, *verb*, 3) to make oneself presentable, neat and trim 4) to train someone for a career

groove [grōōv] *noun*, 1) a channel or furrow cut into something, *verb*, 2) to move to a rhythm

grope [grōp] *verb*, to feel your way blindly or uncertainly

gross [grōs] *adjective*, 1) bulky, coarse, unrefined 2) very fat, *noun*, 3) twelve dozen 4) income earned before deductions

gro-tesque [grō-tĕsk'] *adjective*, strange-looking in shape, bizarre

ground [ground] *noun*, *no plural*, 1) the surface of the earth, *verb*, 2) past tense of **grind**

ground-wa-ter [ground'wô'tər] *noun*, water beneath the earth's surface that supplies wells and springs

group [grōōp] *noun*, 1) people or things classed together because of similar qualities 2)people who share the same needs and interests

grove [grōv] *noun*, a group of trees without undergrowth

grov-el [grŏv'əl] *verb*, to lie prone, crawl, or creep, to beg

grow [grō] *verb*, 1) to become larger, to increase in size or maturity 2) to change and become 3) to sprout, to germinate, to develop 4) to cultivate plants

growl [groul] *noun*, a low angry or unfriendly noise coming from the throat made by a dog, other animal or person

grown [grōn] *adjective*, having reached maturity or full growth

growth[grōth]*noun* 1) development 2) tumor or other form of swelling

grub [grŭb] *noun*, 1) the larva of certain insects, a maggot, *verb*, 2) to dig, to uproot

grudge [grŭj] *noun*, hatred, lasting resentment

gruel-ing [grōō'ə-lĭng] *adjective*, exhausting, very difficult

grue-some [grōō'səm] *adjective*, ghastly, frightening, horrible

grum-ble [grŭm'bəl] *verb*, to complain in a low voice

grunt [grŭnt] *verb*, to make a guttural sound, to snort like a pig

guar-an-tee [găr'ən-tē'] *noun*, 1) a pledge, *verb* 2) to make a promise

guard [gärd] *noun*, 1) a person or thing that provides security or a defense, *verb*, 2) to watch over, to prevent an escape

guard-i-an [gär'dē-ən] *noun*, someone who takes care of another or their property

guer-ril-la [gə-rĭl'ə] *noun*, a member of an irregular military group that carries out surprise attacks and harasses the enemy

guess [gĕs] *noun*, 1) a conjecture, *verb*, 2) to imagine, to think or believe 3) to give an answer without being sure

guest [gĕst] *noun*, 1) a person invited to stay with someone else, a visitor 2) a customer

guid-ance [gīd'ns] *noun*, *no plural*, help, the act or result of guiding

guide [gīd] *noun*, 1) someone or something that shows the way to find something, *verb*, 2) to show the way or lead 3) to counsel

guile [gīl] *noun*, the ability to trick others, cunning, deceit

guilt [gĭlt] *noun*, *no plural*, the knowledge that you have done wrong, the acceptance of blame for a wrongdoing

guilt-y [gĭl′tē] *adjective*, 1) legally convicted of a crime 2) full of shame, feeling remorse

guise [gīz] *noun*, general, external appearance, manner, pretense

gui-tar [gĭ-tär′] *noun*, a musical instrument with six strings that you pluck or strum

gulf [gŭlf] *noun*, 1) part of a sea partially surrounded by land, larger and deeper than a bay 2) a large empty space or chasm

gul-li-ble [gŭl′ə-bəl] *adjective*, easily tricked or cheated

gul-ly [gŭl′ē] *noun*, a deep channel made by running water

gulp [gŭlp] *noun*, 1) a mouthful that is swallowed, *verb*, 2) to swallow quickly 3) to choke or gasp nervously

gum [gŭm] *noun*, 1) the tissue in your mouth above or below the teeth to protect the roots of each tooth 2) a sticky substance, like glue, used to hold things together, 3) a soft substance, flavored like candy that can be chewed but it does not dissolve in the mouth

gun [gŭn] *noun*, a weapon consisting of a metal tube used to shoot bullets under pressure

gust [gŭst] *noun*, a sudden rush of wind or strong blast of air

gut [gŭt] *noun*, 1) the stomach, the belly 2) the intestine

gut-ter [gŭt′ər] *noun*, 1) a drainage ditch, a channel along the side of the road 2) a trough along the eaves that drains water from a roof

gym-na-si-um [jĭm-nā′zē-əm] *noun*, a place where athletic exercises are performed or sports are played

gym-nas-tics [jĭm-năs′tĭks] *noun*, *plural*, exercises that develop and train the body and the muscles

gyp-sy [jĭp′sē] *noun*, a group of wandering people originally from Central Asia

H

hab-it [hăb′ĭt] *noun*, a pattern of behavior acquired through repetition

hab-i-tat [hăb′ĭ-tăt′] *noun*, the natural environment in which an animal or plant lives

hab-i-ta-tion [hăb′ĭ-tā′shən] *noun*, home, abode, dwelling

hab-it-u-al [hə-bĭch′ōō-əl] *adjective*, customary, regular, according to habit

hack-les [hăk′əlz] *plural*, *noun*, hairs on the back of the neck of a dog

hack-neyed [hăk′nēd] *adjective*, common, dull, overused

had [hăd] *past tense* of **have**

hag-gle [hăg′əl] *verb*, to argue about price, to bargain

hai-ku [hī′kōō] *noun*, a form of Japanese poetry consisting of 3 lines of 5, 7, and 5 syllables each

hail [hāl] *noun*, 1) precipitation in the form of ice pellets, *verb*, 2) to shout with enthusiasm, to call out in a greeting, to welcome

hair [hâr] *noun*, a strand of filament that grows out of the skin of mammals

hal-cy-on [hăl′sē-ən] *adjective*, calm, peaceful, happy

half [hăf] *adverb*, 1) partially, *noun*, 2) one of two equal parts of a whole

half-dol-lar [hăf'dŏl'ər] *noun*, a coin equal to fifty cents

half-way [hăf'wā'] *adjective*, midway between two points

hal-i-but [hăl'ə-bət] *noun*, the largest species of marine flatfish

hall [hôl] *noun*, 1) the corridor in a building 2) a large room for entertaining 3) a building at a college or university

hal-low [hăl'ō] *verb*, to bless or make holy or sacred

hal-lu-ci-na-tion [hə-lōō'sə-nā'shən] *noun*, something that is seen or heard but is not actually happening, a delusion, a vision

halt [hôlt] *verb*, to cause to stop, to come to a stop

halt-er [hôl'tər] *noun*, 1) a rope or leather straps used to lead or secure a horse 2) a woman's top tied behind the neck and across the back 3) a hangman's noose

halve [hăv] *verb*, to divide in two

ham [hăm] *noun*, 1)the meat from a pig's leg, preserved with salt or smoke 2) an actor who overacts

ham-burg-er [hăm'bûr'gər] *noun*, ground beef often served as a patty on a sandwich

ham-mer [hăm'ər] *noun*, 1) a tool used for driving nails, *verb*, 2) to hit or pound with a hammer or mallet, to strike

ham-mock [hăm'ək] *noun*, a bed of canvas cord hanging between two supports and easily swinging

ham-per [hăm'pər] *noun*, 1) a basket usually with a cover, *verb*, 2) to obstruct, to hinder

ham-ster [hăm'stər]*noun*, a rodent similar to a rat, with large cheek pouches often kept as a pet

hand [hănd] *noun*, 1) the part at the end of the arm used to hold something, *verb*, 2) to deliver or pass on

hand-i-cap [hăn'dē-kăp'] *noun*, an impediment, a physical defect

hand-ker-chief [hăng'kər-chĭf] *noun*, a cloth carried for wiping hands, the face, or the nose

han-dle [hăn'dl] *noun*, 1) the part of a tool or instrument held in the hand, *verb*, 2) to touch, feel, or examine with the hand 3) to control, manage or deal with

han-dle-bar [hăn'dl-bär'] *noun*, the part of a bicycle used to steer when you ride it

hand-shake [hănd'shāk'] *noun*, a greeting made by shaking hands

hand-some [hăn'səm] *adjective*, good-looking, attractive, manly

hand-writ-ing [hănd'rī'tĭng] *noun*, penmanship, writing done with a pen and usually in cursive

hand-y [hăn'dē] *adjective*, 1) easy to use, convenient 2) skillful with one's hands

hang [hăng] *verb*, 1) to fasten so that something can swing freely, to suspend 2) to suspend from a rope until dead 3) to linger, to wait 4) to be contingent

hang-ar [hăng'ər] *noun*, a building for storing aircraft

hang-er [hăng'ər] *noun*, a device on which something hangs

hap-haz-ard [hăp-hăz'ərd] *adjective*, random, by chance

hap-less [hăp'lĭs] *adjective*, unfortunate, unlucky

hap-pen [hăp′ən] *verb*, 1) to occur by chance, 2) to come to pass

hap-pi-ly [hăp′ə-lē] *adverb*, 1) in a joyous way 2) fortunately

hap-pi-ness [hăp′ē-nĭs] *noun*, conscious enjoyment of good fortune, contentment

hap-py [hăp′ē] *adjective*, content, delighted, or pleased

ha-rangue [hə-răng′] *noun*, a loud address to a multitude, a noisy, ranting speech

ha-rass [hăr′əs] *verb*, to trouble by repeated attacks, to annoy

har-bor [här′bər] *noun*, 1) a port where ships or boats can dock safely, *verb*, 2) to hide, to protect or conceal

hard [härd] *adjective*, 1) difficult to understand 2) firm, solid, impenetrable 3) difficult, fatiguing, challenging, *adverb*, 4) intensely, diligently

hard drive [hard-drĭv] *noun*, a nonremovable storage device in a computer

hard-en [här′dn] *verb*, 1) to make solid 2) to become unfeeling to become used to

hard-ly [härd′lē] *adverb*, barely, almost never, scarcely

hard-ship [härd′shĭp′] *noun*, something that causes suffering, extreme privation

hard-ware [härd′wâr′] *noun*, 1) the pieces of equipment that make up a computer 2) the items such as nuts, bolts, tools, and machinery needed to put something together or to do repairs

hare [hâr] *noun*, an animal similar to a rabbit, but larger, and with young born covered with fur

harm [härm] *noun*, 1) injury, damage, *verb*, 2) to hurt or injure

harm-ful [härm′fəl] *adjective*, able or likely to cause damage or injury

harm-less [härm′lĭs] *adjective*, causing no harm or damage

har-mon-i-ca [här-mŏn′ĭ-kə] *noun*, a hand-held rectangular musical instrument played by exhaling and inhaling through a row of metal reeds

har-mo-ni-ous [här-mō′nē-əs] *adjective*, symmetrical, congruous, in agreement

har-mo-nize [här′mə-nīz′] *verb*, 1) to sing in harmony 2) to go together, to coordinate

har-mo-ny [här′mə-nē] *noun*, 1) a pleasing combination of musical chords 2) agreement, accord

har-ness [här′nĭs] *noun*, the working gear of a horse used to attach it to a cart

harp [härp] *noun*, 1) a large stringed instrument, plucked with fingers, *verb*, 2) to nag

har-poon [här-pōōn′] *noun*, 1) a barbed spear, that is thrown, *verb*, 2) to spear with a harpoon

harsh [härsh] *adjective*, 1) hard to bear, severe, cruel 2) inharmonious, jarring, dissonant

har-vest [här′vĭst] *noun*, 1) the season's crop, the amount gathered, *verb*, 2) to gather or pick a crop, to reap, to gain

has [hăz] the part of the *verb* **have** used with *he*, *she*, and *it*

haste [hāst] *noun*, hurry

hast-i-ly [hāst′ĭ-lē] *adverb*, hurriedly, quickly, fast

hast-y [hā′stē] *adjective*, swift

hat [hăt] *noun*, a clothing accessory used to cover the head often with a crown and a brim

hatch [hăch] *noun*, 1) a small doorway or opening in a wall or a floor or the deck of a ship, *verb*, 2) to emerge from an egg when born

hatch-et [hăch′ĭt] *noun*, a small ax with a short handle

hate [hāt] *verb*, to dislike, to detest

hate-ful[hāt′fəl]*adjective*, arousing, deserving, or full of hate

ha-tred [hā′trĭd] *noun*, hostility

haugh-ty [hô′tē] *adjective*, snobbish, proud, arrogant

haul [hôl] *verb*, 1) to pull or draw with force, to drag 2) move from one place to another in a vehicle

haunt [hônt] *noun*, 1) a frequently visited place, *verb*, 2) to intrude upon continually, to annoy

have [hăv] *verb*, 1) to hold possession of or keep 2) a word used to indicate the *past tense* 3) need to, must

ha-ven [hā′vən] *noun*, a safe place

hav-oc [hăv′ək] *noun*, widespread destruction, confusion

Ha-waii [hə-wä′ē] *noun*, one of the 50 United States located in the Pacific Ocean, the capital city is Honolulu. The state flower of **Hawaii** is the red hibiscus, and the motto is "The life of the land is preserved in righteousness."

hawk [hôk] *noun*, 1) a large bird of prey that kills birds and small animals for food, *verb*, 2) to peddle, to sell on the street

hay [hā] *noun*, grass cut and dried that is eaten by farm animals such as cows, goats, and horses

haz-ard [hăz′ərd] *noun*, a danger

haz-ard-ous [hăz′ər-dəs] *adjective*, dangerous, risky

haze [hāz] *noun*, *no plural*, widely dispersed dust, smoke, and moisture particles in the air that cloud the view

ha-zel [hā′zəl]*noun*, a color that combines gray, brown, and brownish-yellow

he [hē] *pronoun*, *plural*, **they**, the male person or animal, who is the subject of the sentence

head [hĕd] *noun*, 1) the bony structure at the top of humans and animals that contains the brain, face, ears, eyes, mouth, and nose, 2) the seat of reason 3) the leader, 4) the top of something, *verb*, 5) to move in the direction of something, 6) to lead, to be the chief of

head-ache [hĕd′āk′]*noun*, 1)pain in the head 2) a dispute, a nuisance

head-ing [hĕd′ĭng] *noun*, the title or caption at the top of a piece of writing

head-line [hĕd′līn′] *noun*, 1) a line of type displayed conspicuously at the top of a page or column of a newspaper, etc.

head-quar-ters [hĕd′kwôr′tərz] *noun*, the center of operations from which orders are issued

heal [hēl] *verb*, to cure, to treat an illness, to remedy, to repair

health [hĕlth] *noun*, 1)the condition of the body or mind free from sickness or disease

health-y [hĕl′thē] *adjective*, 1) having a sound mind and body, strong, vibrant, robust 2) wholesome, nutritious

heap [hēp] *noun*, 1) a pile of things, *verb*, 2) to put into a large pile, to stack

hear [hîr] *verb*, to receive sound through the ears

heard [hûrd] *past tense* of **hear**

hear-ing [hîr′ĭng] *noun*, 1) the ability to hear 2) an opportunity to be heard

hearse [hûrs] *noun*, a car used to carry a coffin to a church or the cemetery

heart [härt] *noun*, 1) an organ in the chest that pumps the blood around the body, 2) a feeling of tenderness, compassion, or sympathy, affection, emotions

hearth [härth] *noun*, the floor of a fireplace

heat [hēt] *noun*, *no plural*, 1) the feeling of warmth from a fire, furnace, or caused by friction, *verb*, 2) to raise the temperature to become hot, to make warmer

heat-er [hē′tər] *noun*, an appliance that warms

heath-en [hē′thən] *noun*, a person who does not acknowledge the god of Christianity, Judaism, or Islam

heave [hēv] *verb*, to lift or pull something of great weight

heav-en [hĕv′ən] *noun*, 1) the home of God, where the saved go to live after death 2) a state of supreme happiness or bliss

heav-en-ly [hĕv′ən-lē] *adjective*, divine, very nice or pleasant

heav-i-er [hĕv′ē-ər] *adjective*, having more weight

heav-y [hĕv′ē] *adjective*, 1) having a lot of weight 2) burdensome

heck-ler [hĕk′əl- ər] *noun*, a person who shouts and bothers a public speaker by asking impertinent questions

hec-tic [hĕk′tĭk] *adjective*, unsettled, confused, frenzied

hedge [hĕj] *noun*, a dense row of shrubs or bushes to make a wall or border

heed [hēd] *verb*, to notice, to pay careful attention to

heel [hēl] *noun*, 1) the back part of a foot, below the ankle 2) the back, bottom part of a shoe 3) an unpleasant, immoral person, *verb*, 4) to follow closely behind

heif-er [hĕf′ər] *noun*, a young cow

height [hīt] *noun*, distance upwards, how tall something is

hei-nous [hā′nəs] *adjective*, hateful, odious, wicked

heir [âr] *noun*, one who inherits, or has the right to inherit, property after the death of its owner

heir-ess [âr′ĭs] *noun*, a woman who inherits, especially one who inherits a fortune

heir-loom [âr′lōōm′] *noun*, a valued family possession that is given to a new generation

held [hĕld] *past tense* of **hold**

hel-i-cop-ter [hĕl′ĭ-kŏp′tər] *noun*, a flying machine propelled by rotating blades without supporting wings

he-li-um [hē′lē-əm] *noun*, an inert, gaseous element the lightest of the noble gasses

hell [hĕl] *noun*, a place where Satan lives, and where the wicked are said to go when they die according to Christian belief

helm [hĕlm] *noun*, 1)the wheel or other device by which a ship is steered, 2) a position of control

hel-met [hĕl′mĭt] *noun*, a hard protective head covering

help [hĕlp] *noun*, 1)assistance, support, guidance, *verb*, 2) to do something for someone, to assist

help-ing [hĕl′pĭng] *adjective*, 1) willing to assist, *noun*, 2) a portion of food, a serving

help-less [hĕlp′lĭs] *adjective*, unable to help oneself

help-ful [hĕlp′fəl] *adjective*, ready to give help, useful

hem [hĕm] *noun*, 1) the edge of a garment that has been folded over and sewn to keep it from fraying and to hang on the body at the correct length, *verb*, 2) to sew the bottom of a garment, 3)to confine, to enclose

hem-i-sphere [hĕm′ĭ-sfîr′] *noun*, one of the halves of the Earth

hem-or-rhage [hĕm′ər-ĭj] *noun*, excessive discharge of blood, heavy bleeding

hen [hĕn] *noun*, a female bird

her [hər, ər; hûr when stressed] *pronoun*, 1) belonging to a female, 2) referring to a female previously mentioned

her-ald [hĕr′əld] *noun*, 1) a bearer of news, *verb*, 2) to announce publicly, to proclaim

herb [ûrb] *noun*, a plant used for medicine or adding flavor to food or aromatherapy

her-biv-o-rous [hûr-bĭv′ər-əs] *adjective*, plant eating

herd [hûrd] *noun*, 1) a group of animals eating, traveling, or living together, *verb*, 2) to control or steer a group of animals, 3) to congregate

here [hîr] *adverb*, in this place

he-red-i-tar-y [hə-rĕd′ĭ-tĕr′ē] *adjective*, transmitted genetically

he-red-i-ty [hə-rĕd′ĭ-tē] *noun*, inherited characteristics or traits passed from parents to offspring

her-e-sy [hĕr′ĭ-sē] *noun*, dissenting religious view, nonconformity

her-e-tic [hĕr′ĭ-tĭk] *noun*, a person who holds beliefs opposed to church dogma

her-it-age [hĕr′ĭ-tĭj]*noun*, practices, attributes or possessions handed down from ancestors, traditions

her-mit [hûr′mĭt] *noun*, a recluse

he-ro [hîr′ō] *noun*, a person of great strength or courage

her-o-ine [hĕr′ō-ĭn] *noun*, a woman admired for her brave deeds

her-o-ism [hĕr′ō-ĭz′əm] *noun*, courage, boldness, bravery

her-on [hĕr′ən] *noun*, a large wading bird with long legs, a long neck, and a pointed bill

her-ring [hĕr′ĭng] *noun*, a small food fish abundant in the ocean

hers [hûrz] *pronoun*, indicating something belonging to a woman or girl

her-self [hûr-sĕlf′] *pronoun*, *plural*, **themselves**, the reflexive form of **she**, belonging to her

hes-i-tate [hĕz′ĭ-tāt′] *verb*, to act slowly, as if in doubt, or uncertain, to falter

hes-i-ta-tion [hĕz′ĭ-tā′shən] *noun*, pausing because of doubt or uncertainty

hew [hyōō] *verb*, to cut with an ax

hex-a-gon [hĕk′sə-gŏn′] *noun*, a plane figure having six sides

hi-a-tus [hī-ā′təs] *noun*, a gap, an interval in time, a pause

hi-ber-nate [hī′bər-nāt′] *verb*, to sleep or be dormant in winter

hic-cup [hĭk′əp]*noun*, a noise made by contraction of the diaphragm and closing of the glottis

hid-den [hĭd′n] *adjective*, concealed from sight

hide [hīd] *noun*, 1) the skin of an animal, *verb*, 2) to put out of sight or keep a secret

hid-e-ous [hĭd′ē-əs] *adjective*, horribly ugly, shocking

hi-er-ar-chy [hī′ə-rär′kē] *noun*, a pecking order, ranking

hi-er-o-glyph-ics [hī′ər-ə-glĭf′ĭks] *noun*, *plural*, characters in the picture writing of the ancient Egyptians

high [hī] *adjective*, 1) tall, far above the ground, 2) expensive 3) shrill in pitch 4) elated, happy

high-land [hī′lənd] *noun*, land that is high up in the hills

high-ness [hī′nĭs] *noun*, a title of a member of the royal family

high-way [hī′wā′] *noun*, a main road especially one connecting two towns

hi-jack [hī′jăk′] *verb*, to force the driver of a vehicle to go somewhere, to commandeer

hike [hīk] *noun*, 1) a walk, a trek, *verb*, 2) to go on an extended walk

hi-lar-i-ous [hĭ-lâr′ē-əs] *adjective*, very funny, boisterously merry

hill [hĭl] *noun*, a natural elevation

him [hĭm] *pronoun*, a man or boy previously named

him-self [hĭm-sĕlf′] *pronoun*, referring to a man or boy as the object of a verb or preposition or reflexively used of the subject *plural*, **themselves**

hind [hīnd] *adjective*, 1) situated in the rear, back, posterior 2) a female deer

hind-er [hĭn′dər] *verb*, to make it more difficult for someone to do something, to obstruct

hind-rance [hĭn′drəns] *noun*, an impediment, something that slows you down

Hin-du [hĭn′dōō] *noun*, 1) a native of India or Hindustan 2) an adherent of Hinduism, religion in the culture of India

hinge [hĭnj] *noun*, 1) a joint on which a door or gate turns or swings, *verb*, 2) to hang on or attach to something

hint [hĭnt] *noun*, 1) a suggestion, a clue 2) a slight trace

hip [hĭp] *noun*, the part of your body below the waist where your legs are connected to the rest of your body

hip-po-pot-a-mus[hĭp′ə-pŏt′ə məs] *noun*, a large mammal native to Africa that eats plants and lives mostly in water, with a thick skin and short legs

hire [hīr] *verb*, to pay someone to do work or perform services

his [hĭz] *pronoun*, belonging to a man or a boy, the possessive case of **he**

hiss [hĭs] *noun*, 1) a sound made by forcing air through the teeth, *verb*, 2) to make a sound like a defensive cat to express displeasure

his-tol-o-gy [hĭ-stŏl′ə-jē] *noun*, the science that treats of the microscopic structure of animal and vegetable tissues

his-to-ri-an [hĭ-stôr′ē-ən] *noun*, an authority of events in history

his-tor-ic [hĭ-stôr′ĭk] *adjective*, something important in or belonging to the past

his-to-ry [hĭs′tə-rē] *noun*, the story and knowledge of the past

hit [hĭt] *noun*, 1) a blow, 2) contact between the ball and the bat, 3) a smash, a wow, a success, *verb*, 4) to bring something down hard onto something else, to smack, to strike with the hand

hitch [hĭch] *verb*, to tie something to something else, to attach to a vehicle for hauling

hive [hīv] *noun*, 1) a place in which bees live, 2) any place busy with activity, 3) a variety of allergic reactions marked by itching welts or a rash

hoard [hôrd] *noun*, 1) a hidden store of something, *verb*, 2) to collect and save, to accumulate, to set aside and hide away

hoarse [hôrs] *adjective*, sounding husky and rough or harsh

hoax [hōks] *noun*, a deceitful trick

hob-by [hŏb′ē] *noun*, an activity outside work that is done for relaxation and pleasure

hock-ey [hŏk′ē] *noun*, a game played on ice (ice hockey) or grass (field hockey) by two teams of several players who use curved sticks to hit a puck or a ball into a net or goal

hoe [hō] *noun*, 1) a tool with a flat blade used to lift and loosen the earth, *verb*, 2) to turn the soil over with a hoe

hog [hôg, hŏg] *noun*, a large pig, warthog, or boar

hoist [hoist] *verb*, to lift up, especially with a pulley

hold [hōld] *noun*, 1) the part of the ship that holds cargo, *verb*, 2) to grasp, 3) to contain, 4) to host an event, 5) to restrain, to keep back, 6) to possess, 7) to embrace

hole [hōl] *noun*, an empty space in something, a gap, a cavity

hol-i-day [hŏl′ĭ-dā′] *noun*, 1) a day on which a particular event is celebrated, 2) a period of time that involves relaxation not work

hol-low [hŏl′ō] *adjective*, 1) not solid, empty inside, 2) without significance, *noun*, 3) a valley

hol-ly [hŏl′ē] *noun*, an evergreen tree or shrub, with red berries and prickly and glossy leaves

hol-o-caust [hŏl′ə-kôst′] *noun*, great or total destruction by fire

ho-ly [hō′lē] *adjective*, of God or the gods, divine, sacred

hom-age [hŏm′ĭj] *noun*, honor, public tribute given to a person

home [hōm] *noun*, a place where someone lives, a residence

home-less [hōm′lĭs] *adjective*, 1) without a home *noun, plural* 2) (the homeless) people who do not have a home and who live on the streets of a city

home-ly [hōm′lē] *adjective*, unattractive, plain looking, ugly

ho-me-op-a-thy [hō′mē -ə-păth′ ē] *noun*, a system of medical treatment based on the practice of giving patients small doses of a drug or natural substance that, in healthy persons, would produce symptoms of the disease being treated

home run [hōm rŭn′] *noun*, a run scored on a hit that enables the batter to touch all four bases

home-stead [hōm′stĕd′] *verb*, to claim land by settling on it according to US law

home-work [hōm′wûrk′] *noun*, material from school to be completed at home

hom-i-cide [hŏm′ĭ-sīd′] *noun*, the killing of a person by another

hom-i-ly [hŏm′ə-lē] *noun*, a sermon, a moral lesson

ho-mo-ge-neous [hō′mə-jē′nē-əs] *adjective*, 1) of the same kind or nature 2) consisting of similar parts throughout

ho-mog-e-nize [hə-mŏj′ə-nīz′] *verb*, to reduce particles in liquids such as milk or paint to the same size by mixing and distributing them evenly

hom-o-phone [hŏm′ə-fōn′] *noun*, a word that sounds the same as another, but is spelled differently, and has a different meaning, e.g. *see* and *sea*

hone [hōn] *verb*, to sharpen

hon-est [ŏn′ĭst] *adjective*, truthful, not deceitful, trustworthy

hon-est-ly [ŏn′ĭst-lē] *adverb*, truthfully, openly, candidly

hon-es-ty [ŏn′ĭ-stē] *noun*, the quality of telling the truth, integrity, truthfulness

hon-ey [hŭn′ē] *noun*, a syrup made by bees with nectar gathered from flowers

hon-ey-comb [hŭn′ē-kōm′] *noun*, six-sided wax cells made by bees to store honey or larvae

hon-or [ŏn′ər]*noun*, 1)high esteem, 2)good reputation, 3)an award for bravery or achievement, *verb*, 4) to hold in high respect, 5) to keep an agreement

hon-or-a-ble [ŏn′ər-ə-bəl] *adjective*, respectable, honest

hood [hŏŏd] *noun*, 1) a covering for the head, often attached to another piece of clothing, 2) an engine cover

hoof [hŏŏf] *noun*, *plural,* **hooves**, the horny, hard covering on the foot of a horse, cow, goat, etc.

hook [hŏŏk] *noun*, 1) a bent piece of metal or plastic used to catch or hang something, *verb*, 2) to clasp, to hang or fasten with a hook

hoop [hŏŏp] *noun*, a hard circular band, such as a hoola hoop or a basketball hoop

hop [hŏp] *noun*, 1) a short jump, *verb*, 2) to move on one foot, 3)to jump with both feet together

hope [hōp] *noun*, 1) a feeling of confidence, expectation, *verb*, 2) to look forward to something believing that it will happen

horde [hôrd] *noun*, crowd, a mob, a large multitude, a swarm

ho-ri-zon [hə-rī′zən] *noun*, the line where the earth appears to intersect the sky

hor-i-zon-tal [hôr′ĭ-zŏn′tl] *adjective*, 1) parallel to the horizon 2) flat, level

horn [hôrn] *noun*, 1) one of two hard growths growing out from the heads of some animals such as deer, elk, etc. 2) the device on a car or bicycle used to warn people 3) a musical wind instrument in the brass family with valves to regulate the flow of air

hor-net [hôr'nĭt] *noun*, a large wasp

hor-o-scope [hôr'ə-skōp'] *noun*, 1) a chart of the positions of the stars at the time of someone's birth, 2) an astrological prediction

hor-ri-ble [hôr'ə-bəl] *adjective*, shocking, hideous, terrible

hor-rid [hôr'ĭd] *adjective*, vile, disgusting, vulgar, frightful

hor-ri-fy [hôr'ə-fī'] *verb*, to frighten, to terrify, to petrify

hor-ror [hôr'ər] *noun*, great fear and shock caused by something terrible, a feeling of terror

horse [hôrs] *noun*, a mammal with long legs that eats grass and can pull a cart or carry people

horse-back [hôrs'băk'] *adverb*, on the back of a horse

horse-pow-er [hôrs'pou'ər] *noun*, a unit of power, 33,000 foot pounds of work per minute or about 746 watts

horse-shoe [hôrs'shoō'] *noun*, a strip of iron conformed to the rim of a horse's hoof

hor-ti-cul-ture [hôr'tĭ-kŭl'chər] *noun*, the study of growing fruits, vegetables, flowers, or plants

hose [hōz] *noun*, 1) a rubber or plastic tube used to transfer liquid, 2)socks, stockings, and tights, *verb*, 3) to water with a hose

hos-pi-tal [hŏs'pĭ-tl] *noun*, a facility where the sick or injured are treated and given medicine

hos-pi-tal-i-ty [hŏs'pĭ-tăl'ĭ-tē] *noun*, *no plural*, a warm welcome or reception to visitors

host [hōst] *noun*, 1) a man who entertains guests, 2) an organism harboring a parasite, 3) the communion wafer, representing the bread of the last supper, *verb*, 4) to receive guests, to entertain, 5) to serve as a master of ceremonies

hos-tage [hŏs'tĭj] *noun*, a person or thing taken prisoner to ensure that others meet specified demands

host-ess [hō'stĭs] *noun*, a woman who entertains guests

hos-til-i-ty [hŏ-stĭl'ĭ-tē] *noun*, unfriendliness, antagonism, ill will, rancor

hot [hŏt] *adjective*, 1) having a very high temperature 2) having a very spicy taste

ho-tel [hō-tĕl'] *noun*, a building where travelers can pay for a place to sleep and other services

hound [hound] *noun*, a breed of dog used for hunting or racing

hour [our] *noun*, 1)sixty minutes, a measure of time, 1/24th of a day, 2) a particular time of day

house [hous] *noun*, a building or part of one, where people live

House of Representatives *noun*, the lower house of the legislature of the United States

hov-el [hŭv′əl] *noun*, a shack

hov-er [hŭv′ər] *verb*, to stay in one place flying or floating in the air

hov-er-craft [hŭv′ər-krăft′] *noun*, a vehicle that travels over land or water by floating on air pushed out by its engines

how [hou] *adverb*, 1) used in questions about time, amount, or size, 2) used to ask about health, 3) used to show surprise or pleasure, 4) used to show the way something is done

how-ev-er [hou-ev′ər] *adverb*, 1) nonetheless, despite, though, 2) yet, after all, 3) in whatever manner

howl [houl] *verb*, 1) to make a long wailing cry like a wolf, 2) to moan loudly in pain

hub [hŭb] *noun*, 1) the center of activity, 2) the center part of a wheel or propeller

hud-dle [hŭd′l] *verb*, to cluster

hue [hyōō] *noun*, a shade of a color

hug [hŭg] *noun*, 1) a close embrace with arms around the body, *verb*, 2) to put arms around someone, to hold them closely, to embrace

huge [hyōōj] *adjective*, very large

hulk [hŭlk] *noun*, 1) a bulky body, a big clumsy person or thing, 2) a ship that has been wrecked

hull [hŭl] *noun*, 1) the body of a ship, 2) a shell or a husk of fruit, grain, or a seed

hum [hŭm] *noun*, 1) a low, buzzing sound like a bee, *verb*, 2) to sing a melody to yourself with lips closed

hu-man [hyōō′mən] *noun*, a person, *Homo sapiens*

hu-mane [hyōō-mān′] *adjective*, kind, compassionate, merciful

hu-man-i-ty [hyōō-măn′ĭ-tē] *noun*, mankind, people, the human race

hum-ble [hŭm′bəl] *adjective*, 1) modest, not proud, 2) plain, 3) respectful, courteous, *verb*, 4) to bring down to defeat, to humiliate

hu-mid-i-ty [hyōō-mĭd′ĭ-tē] *noun*, moisture in the air, dampness

hu-mil-i-ate [hyōō-mĭl′ē-āt′] *verb*, to treat in a way that takes away a person's pride or self-respect

hu-mil-i-a-tion [hyōō-mĭl′ē-ā′shən] *noun*, embarrassment, shame

hu-mil-i-ty [hyōō-mĭl′ĭ-tē] *noun*, the state of being modest, meek

hu-mor [hyōō′mər] *noun*, *no plural*, 1) the ability to make others laugh, *verb*, 2) to indulge

hu-mor-ous [hyōō′mər-əs] *adjective*, full of or characterized by humor, funny, comical

hump [hŭmp] *noun*, a round lump or protuberance

hu-mus [hyōō′məs] *noun*, 1) organic material consisting of decayed vegetable matter, 2) a thick dip made from mashed chickpeas and flavorings

hunch [hŭnch] *noun*, 1) a premonition or suspicion, *verb*, 2) to sit or stand with the back bent or arched

hun-dred [hŭn′drĕd] *noun*, the number 100, ten times ten

hun-dreth [hŭn′drĭdth] *noun*, 1) the ordinal number after 99th 2) the number two digits to the right of the decimal point

hung [hŭng] *past tense* of **hang**

hun-ger [hŭng′gər] *noun*,
1) the desire for food, craving,
verb, 2) to feel a strong desire
for something, 3) to yearn

hun-gry [hŭng′grē] *adjective*,
desiring food

hunt [hŭnt] *verb*, 1) seek out to
capture for food or sport, 2) to
search for something

hur-dle [hûr′dl] *noun*, 1) a barrier
that can be jumped over, 2) an
obstacle to overcome, *verb*,
3) to jump over, to vault

hurl [hûrl] *verb*, to throw hard

hur-ri-cane [hûr′ĭ-kān′] *noun*, a
severe tropical storm with high
winds

hur-ry [hûr′ē] *noun*, 1) haste, *verb*,
2) to move quickly, to rush

hurt [hûrt] *verb*, 1) to injure, to
inflict pain or damage, 2) to
offend, 3) to ache, to throb

hur-tle [hûr′tl] *verb*, to move at
great speed, to rush headlong

hus-band [hŭz′bənd] *noun*, the
male spouse in a marriage

hus-band-ry [hŭz′bən-drē] *noun*,
1) cultivation of plants or
animals in a scientific way,
2) home management, careful
attention to spending money

hush [hŭsh] *noun*, 1) calm, silence,
verb, 2) to muffle, to quiet down

hus-tle [hŭs′əl] *verb*, 1) to hurry,
2) to trick someone in business

hy-brid [hī′brĭd] *noun*, a new breed
created by breeding two
different varieties or species

hy-drant [hī′drənt] *noun*, a pipe
located at a curb with a valve for
fire engines to connect a hose to
a source of water to fight fire

hy-drau-lic [hī-drô′lĭk] *adjective*,
operated or moved by means of
water or fluid under pressure

hy-dro-gen [hī′drə-jən] *noun*, an
element that is normally a
tasteless, odorless, and
inflammable gas

hy-dro-pho-bi-a [hī′drə-fō′bē-ə]
noun, 1) fear of water, 2) a
symptom of rabies

hy-dro-plane [hī′drə-plān′] *noun*,
1) a boat that glides on the
surface of water, *verb*, 2) to lose
control and slide on a wet road
because a vehicle has lost
traction

hy-e-na [hī-ē′nə] *noun*, a
carnivorous wild doglike
mammal that lives in Africa and
Asia

hy-giene [hī′jēn′] *noun*, practices
that keep people clean and
healthy, cleanliness

hymn [hĭm] *noun*, a religious song

hy-per-bo-le [hī-pûr′bə-lē] *noun*, a
figure of speech using extravagant
exaggeration, e.g., *I've told you at
least a million times.*

hy-phen [hī′fən] *noun*, the mark -,
used to separate syllables, as at
the end of a line e.g. *enthusiasm*, or to join the parts of
compound words e.g.
self-confidence, self-reliant

hyp-no-tize [hĭp′nə-tīz′] *verb*, to
put in a trance in which the
subject is susceptible to
suggestion, to mesmerize

hy-po-chon-dri-ac
[hī′pə-kŏn′drē-ăk′] *noun*, a
person always worrying about
the state of their health,
especially one with imaginary
illnesses

hy-poc-ri-sy [hĭ-pŏk′rĭ-sē] *noun*, the act or practice of feigning to be what one is not, especially the false assumption of virtue or religion

hyp-o-crite [hĭp′ə-krĭt′] *noun*, someone who says one thing especially in regard to values and morals, and does another

hy-poth-e-sis [hĭ-pŏth′ĭ-sĭs] *noun*, a theory that has not been proven

hy-po-thet-i-cal [hī′pə-thĕt′ĭ-kəl] *adjective*, an assumption based on theory or conjecture

hys-ter-i-cal [hĭ-stĕr′ĭ-kəl] *adjective*, showing excessive or uncontrollable emotion

I

I [ī] *pronoun*, *plural*, **we**, first person singular, the individual speaking

ice [īs] *noun*, 1) frozen water, *verb*, 2) to put frosting on a cake

ice-berg [īs′bûrg′] *noun*, a large mass of ice floating in the sea

ice cream [īs′krēm′] *noun*, cream, sugar, milk, flavoring, and eggs mixed together to make a frozen dessert

i-ch-thy-ol-o-gy [ĭk′thē-ŏl′ə-jē] *noun*, the study of fish

i-ci-cle [ī′sĭ-kəl] *noun*, a piece of ice in the form of a spike made by water dripping and freezing

i-con [ī′kŏn′] *noun*, 1) a religious image painted on wood, found especially in the Eastern Christian Church, 2) a graphic symbol used in computing

I'd [īd] the *contraction* of the words **I** and **would**

Ida-ho [ī′də-hō′] *noun*, one of the United States, located in the northwest, the capital city is Boise. The state flower of **Idaho** is the syringa, and the motto is "May it endure forever."

i-de-a [ī-dē′ə] *noun*, 1) a concept, a thought, an impression, 2) a belief, an opinion, 3)an intention

i-de-al [ī-dē′əl] *adjective*, 1) perfect, ultimate, *noun*, 2) an image of something in its perfect form, a model

i-den-ti-cal [ī-dĕn′tĭ-kəl] *adjective*, being the very same in every way

i-den-ti-fi-ca-tion [ī-dĕn′tə-fĭ-kā′shən] *noun*, the means to verify who someone is

i-den-ti-fy [ī-dĕn′tə-fī′] *verb*, 1) to classify or name, 2) to equate

i-den-ti-ty [ī-dĕn′tĭ-tē] *noun*, who someone is, individuality

i-de-ol-o-gy [ī′dē-ŏl′ə-jē] *noun*, a system of beliefs, political ideas

id-i-om [ĭd′ē-əm] *noun*, a group of words that when used together have a special meaning, different from what they mean individually, e.g., *raining cats and dogs*

id-i-o-syn-cra-sy [ĭd′ē-ō-sĭng′krə-sē] *noun*, a peculiar habit, a quirk

i-dle [īd′l] *adjective*, not busy, unoccupied, inactive, lazy

i-dol [īd′l] *noun*, 1) an image that is worshipped, 2) a person that is adored

i.e. an abbreviation, that is…

if [ĭf] *conjunction*, 1) on condition that, 2) whether

ig-loo [ĭg′loo] *noun*, an Eskimo home made of blocks of ice and snow

ig-ne-ous [ĭg′nē-əs] *adjective*, produced by fire, volcanic

ig-nite [ĭg-nīt′] *verb*, 1) to set on fire, to begin to burn, 2) to inspire, to inflame

ig-no-ble [ĭg-nō′bəl] *adjective*, unworthy, of low character

ig-no-rance [ĭg′nər-əns] *noun*, *no plural*, lack of knowledge

ig-no-rant [ĭg′nər-ənt] *adjective*, uneducated, lacking knowledge

ig-nore [ĭg-nôr′] *verb*, to pretend something is not there

ill [ĭl] *adjective*, feeling unhealthy

I'll [īl] the *contraction* of the words **I** and **will**

il-le-gal [ĭ-lē′gəl] *adjective*, against the law, prohibited, criminal

il-leg-i-ble [ĭ-lĕj′ə-bəl] *adjective*, so poorly written as to be unreadable

il-le-git-i-mate [ĭl′ĭ-jĭt′ə-mĭt] *adjective*, 1) unlawful, illegal, 2) born of unmarried parents

il-lic-it [ĭ-lĭs′ĭt] *adjective*, not according to law, not permitted or allowed, forbidden

il-lim-it-a-ble [ĭ-lĭm′ĭ-tə-bəl] *adjective*, infinite, vast, limitless

Il-li-nois [ĭl′ə-noi′] *noun*, one of the United States, located in the midwest, the capital is Springfield. The state flower of **Illinois** is the meadow violet, and the motto is "State sovereignty, national union."

il-lit-er-ate [ĭ-lĭt′ər-ĭt] *adjective*, unable to read and write

il-log-i-cal [ĭ-lŏj′ĭ-kəl] *adjective*, not observing the rules of correct reasoning, unreasonable

il-lu-mi-nate [ĭ-loo′mə-nāt′] *verb*, 1) to fill with light 2) to make understandable, to clarify

il-lu-sion [ĭ-loo′zhən] *noun*, a false idea, a fallacy, a delusion

il-lu-sive [ĭ-loo′sĭv] *adjective*, false, deceptive, evasive, hard to grasp

il-lus-trate [ĭl′ə-strāt′] *verb*, 1) to explain by examples or verbal images, 2) to provide with pictures or designs, to show

il-lus-tra-tion [ĭl′ə-strā′shən] *noun*, 1) a picture or drawing that makes something written clearer, 2) an explanation

il-lus-tri-ous [ĭ-lŭs′trē-əs] *adjective*, distinguished, well known, acclaimed, celebrated

I'm [īm] the *contraction* of the words **I** and **am**

im-age [ĭm′ĭj] *noun*, 1) a picture in the mind or in a mirror or on television, etc., 2) a figure made of stone, wood, etc.

im-age-ry [ĭ-măj′ĕr′ē] *noun*, 1) mental images, 2) descriptions and figures of speech

im-ag-i-nar-y [ĭ-măj′ə-nĕr′ē] *adjective*, unreal, fanciful, existing only in the mind

im-ag-i-na-tion [ĭ-măj′ə-nā′shən] *noun*, 1) fantasy, dreams, 2) the creative part of the mind

im-ag-ine [ĭ-măj′ĭn] *verb*, 1) to develop an idea in your mind or mental picture, 2) to suppose

im-bue [ĭm-byoo′] *verb*, 1) to saturate with moisture or color 2) to teach, to inspire

im-i-tate [ĭm′ĭ-tāt′] *verb*, to do something the same way as someone else, to emulate

im-i-ta-tion [ĭm′ĭ-tā′shən] *adjective*, 1) artificial, synthetic, counterfeit, *noun*, 2) a copy of something, a fake, a replica

im-mac-u-late [ĭ-măk′yə-lĭt] *adjective*, without stain or blemish, spotlessly clean

im-ma-te-ri-al [ĭm′ə-tîr′ē-əl] *adjective*, not applicable, irrelevant, not important

im-ma-ture [ĭm′ə-tyŏŏr′] *adjective*, not grown up, childish

im-meas-ur-a-ble [ĭ-mĕzh′ər-ə-bəl] *adjective*, vast, limitless, endless, infinite

im-me-di-ate [ĭ-mē′dē-ĭt] *adjective*, right away

im-me-di-ate-ly [ĭ-mē′dē-ĭt-lē] *adverb*, at once, without interval of time or delay, now

im-mense [ĭ-mĕns′] *adjective*, huge, very large, enormous

im-men-si-ty [ĭ-mĕn′sĭ-tē] *noun*, enormity, endlessness

im-mi-grant [ĭm′ĭ-grənt] *noun*, a settler from another country

im-mi-gra-tion [ĭm′ĭ-grā′shən] *noun*, the process of traveling to another country to settle there

im-mi-grate [ĭm′ĭ-grāt′] *verb*, to go to a country of which one is not a native to live as a resident

im-mi-nent [ĭm′ə-nənt] *adjective*, impending, near at hand, likely to occur at any moment

im-mo-bil-i-ty [ĭ-mō-bĭl′-ĭ-tē] *noun*, the state of being unable to move, motionlessness

im-mortal [ĭ-môr′tl] *adjective*, undying, everlasting, perpetual

im-mor-tal-i-ty [ĭm′ôr-tăl′ĭ-tē] *noun*, eternal life, unending fame

im-mune [ĭ-myoōn′] *adjective*, 1) not affected by disease 2) exempt from an influence

im-mu-ni-ty [ĭ-myoō′nĭ-tē] *noun*, 1) the ability to resist a disease or infection, 2) freedom from legal prosecution

im-mu-nize [ĭm′yə-nīz′] *verb*, to protect the body from diseases by injecting an inactive form of the virus or bacteria

im-mu-ni-za-tion [ĭm′yə-nĭ-zā′shən] *noun*, an injection that protects the body from a virus or disease

im-pact [ĭm′păkt′] *noun*, 1) personal contact, 2) a forceful impression, a strong effect

im-pair [ĭm-pâr′] *verb*, to weaken, to diminish in value, make worse

im-pale [ĭm-pāl′] *verb*, to pierce with something pointed

im-part [ĭm-pärt′] *verb*, to tell, to reveal, to make known, to give

im-par-tial [ĭm-pär′shəl] *adjective*, fair, just, not favoring one more than another, not biased

im-pas-sa-ble [ĭm-păs′ə-bəl] *adjective*, unable to be passed or traversed

im-passe [ĭm′păs′] *noun*, 1) a road with no outlet, a blind alley or dead end, 2) a situation in which no progress can be made or resolution reached

im-pa-tience [ĭm-pā′shəns] *noun*, *no plural*, anticipation, anxious expectancy, feeling anxious

im-pa-tiens [ĭm-pā′shəns] *noun*, a flower with white or red flowers that bloom in summer

im-pa-tient [ĭm-pā′shənt] *adjective*, not wanting to wait

im-peach [ĭm-pēch′] *verb*, to charge with a crime while in office, to discredit

im-pec-ca-ble [ĭm-pĕk′ə-bəl] *adjective*, faultless, perfect, without sin

im-pede [ĭm-pēd′] *verb*, to hinder or obstruct, to slow action

im-ped-i-ment [ĭm-pĕd′ə-mənt] *noun*, hindrance, obstacle

im-pel [ĭm-pĕl′] *verb*, to push, to motivate, to drive forward

im-pend-ing [ĭm-pĕn′dĭng] *adjective*, about to happen

im-per-a-tive [ĭm-pĕr′ə-tĭv] *adjective*, 1) expressive of command 2) binding, obligatory

im-per-fect [ĭm-pûr′fĭkt] *adjective*, 1) flawed, defective, faulty, *noun*, 2) a verb tense used for action that is continuing

im-per-fec-tion [ĭm′pər-fĕk′shən] *noun*, 1) a flaw, a defect 2) a failing, a shortcoming, a fault

im-pe-ri-al [ĭm-pîr′ē-əl] *adjective*, relating to an empire and its ruler

im-per-il [ĭm-pĕr′əl] *verb*, to put in danger or peril

im-pe-ri-ous [ĭm-pîr′ē-əs] *adjective*, bossy, domineering

im-per-me-a-ble [ĭm-pûr′mē-ə-bəl] *adjective*, not allowing other substances, especially liquid, to pass through

im-per-son-al [ĭm-pûr′sə-nəl] *adjective*, detached, withdrawn

im-per-son-ate [ĭm-pûr′sə-nāt′] *verb*, to pretend to be someone by assuming their identity, often with the intent to defraud

im-per-ti-nent [ĭm-pûr′tn-ənt] *adjective*, 1) rude, 2) irrelevant

im-per-vi-ous [ĭm-pûr′vē-əs] *adjective*, 1) impenetrable, not admitting entrance or passage through 2) unaffected, unharmed

im-pet-u-ous [ĭm-pĕch′ōō-əs] *adjective*, impulsive, rash

im-pe-tus [ĭm′pĭ-təs] *noun*, a driving force, motive, incentive

im-plau-si-ble [ĭm-plô′zə-bəl] *adjective*, unlikely, unbelievable

im-ple-ment [ĭm′plə-mənt] *noun*, 1) a tool, a device, *verb*, 2) to complete, to accomplish, to make good on an idea

im-pli-ca-tion [ĭm′plĭ-kā′shən] *noun*, something that is implied, hinted at or suggested

im-plic-it [ĭm-plĭs′ĭt] *adjective*, 1) implied although unsaid, understood, 2) without doubt

im-plore [ĭm′plôr] *verb*, to plead with much feeling

im-ply [ĭm-plī′] *verb*, 1) to suggest a meaning not spoken, to hint 2) to include or suggest as a necessary condition

im-po-lite [ĭm′pə-līt′] *adjective*, rude, discourteous, disrespectful

im-port [ĭm-pôrt′] *noun*, 1) merchandise brought into another country 2) the significance, the meaning, *verb*, 3) to bring goods into another country 4) to signify

im-por-tance [ĭm-pôr′tns] *noun*, *no plural*, great significance or consequence, prominence

im-por-tant [ĭm-pôr′tnt] *adjective*, significant, having a great value

im-por-tu-nate [ĭm-pôr′chə-nĭt] *adjective*, urging, demanding

im-pose [ĭm-pōz′] *verb*, 1) to take unfair advantage of, to compel, to force on others 2) to require something, such as a tax, be paid

im-pos-si-ble [ĭm-pŏs′ə-bəl] *adjective*, unrealizable, hopeless

im-pos-tor [ĭm-pŏs′tər] *noun*, one who practices deception by assuming a false identity

im-po-tent [ĭm′pə-tənt] *adjective*, weak, ineffective, powerless

im-prac-ti-cal [ĭm-prăk′tĭ-kəl] *adjective*, not easily done

im-pre-cate [ĭm′prĭ-kāt′] *verb*, to hope evil will happen, to curse

im-preg-na-ble [ĭm-prĕg′nə-bəl] *adjective*, invulnerable, able to withstand attack, unbeatable

im-press [ĭm-prĕs′] *verb*, 1) to affect someone's feelings or opinion in a positive way 2) to leave an imprint, to stamp

im-pres-sion [ĭm-prĕsh′ən] *noun*, 1) a sensation, an effect 2) an imitation of a person 3) a mark made on a surface of something

im-pres-sive [ĭm-prĕs′ĭv] *adjective*, evoking admiration or respect because of size, ability, etc.

im-print [ĭm-prĭnt′] *noun*, a deep impression left by pressure

im-pris-on [ĭm-prĭz′ən] *verb*, to hold someone in jail

im-prob-a-ble [ĭm-prŏb′ə-bəl] *adjective*, unlikely to happen

im-prop-er [ĭm-prŏp′ər] *adjective*, rude or inappropriate, contrary to social convention

im-pro-pri-e-ty [ĭm′prə-prī′ĭ-tē] *noun*, an inappropriate or indecent expression or act

im-prove [ĭm-prōōv′] *verb*, to make or become better, to uplift, to refine

im-prove-ment [ĭm-prōōv′mənt] *noun*, an act, state, or result of improving or bettering

im-pro-vise [ĭm′prə-vīz′] *verb*, 1) to make do with whatever is at hand 2) to perform without preparation at a moment's notice

im-pru-dent [ĭm-prōōd′nt] *adjective*, not wise, indiscreet

im-pu-dent [ĭm′pyə-dənt] *adjective*, bold, disrespectful

im-pulse [ĭm′pŭls′] *noun*, 1) a sudden desire to do something 2) a driving force 3) an electrical pulse or current

im-pul-sive [ĭm-pŭl′sĭv] *adjective*, spontaneous, without forethought

im-pu-ni-ty [ĭm-pyōō′nĭ-tē] *noun*, freedom from punishment

im-pu-ri-ty [ĭm-pyŏōr′ĭ-tē] *noun*, pollution, contamination

im-pute [ĭm-pyōōt′] *verb*, to credit, to attribute, to ascribe

in [ĭn] *adjective*, 1) being inside, *preposition*, 2) showing where 3) at or inside of something 4) during, before the end 5) wearing 6) at hand or on hand 7) near

in-a-bil-i-ty [ĭn′ə-bĭl′ĭ-tē] *noun*, lack of ability, power or capacity

in-ac-ces-si-ble [ĭn′ăk-sĕs′ə-bəl] *adjective*, 1) out of reach, unattainable 2) hard to contact

in-ac-cu-ra-cy [ĭn-ăk′yər-ə-sē]
noun, an error, being incorrect

in-ad-e-quate [ĭn-ăd′ĭ-kwĭt]
adjective, not enough

in-ad-ver-tent-ly [ĭn′əd-vûr′tnt-lē]
adverb, accidentally

in-al-ien-a-ble [ĭn-āl′yə-nə-bəl]
adjective, not to be taken away

in-an-i-mate [ĭn-ăn′ə-mĭt]
adjective, lifeless, dull

in-ar-tic-u-late [ĭn′är-tĭk′yə-lĭt]
adjective, lacking the ability to
express oneself in speech

in-au-gu-rate [ĭn-ô′gyə-rāt′]
verb, 1) to begin 2) to install into
office in a formal manner

in-can-des-cent [ĭn′kən-dĕs′ənt]
adjective, glowing or luminous
with intense heat or brightness

in-can-ta-tion [ĭn′kăn-tā′shən]
noun, singing or chanting of
words or sounds believed to
have magical effect

in-ca-pa-ble [ĭn-kā′pə-bəl]
adjective, unable, lacking skill,
ability, or temperament

in-ca-pac-i-tate [ĭn′kə-păs′ĭ-tāt′]
verb, to disable

in-car-cer-a-tion [ĭn-kär′sə-rā′shən] *noun*, imprisonment

in-car-nate [ĭn-kär′nĭt] *adjective*,
in the flesh, in human form

in-car-na-tion [ĭn′kär-nā′shən]
noun, 1) the act of assuming a
human body 2) the embodiment
of a god or spirit 3) one life
among many for those who
believe in reincarnation

in-cen-di-ar-y [ĭn-sĕn′dē-ĕr′ē]
adjective, 1) causing something
to burn, 2) tending to inflame,

noun, 3) a bomb designed to start
fires 4) an arsonist

in-cense [ĭn-sĕns′] *noun*, 1) a
substance that releases a pleasant
scent when burned, *verb*, 2) to
anger

in-cen-tive [ĭn-sĕn′tĭv] *noun*,
encouragement, stimulus

in-ces-sant [ĭn-sĕs′ənt] *adjective*,
continuing without interruption

inch [ĭnch] *noun*, a measure of
length, 1/12 of a foot

in-ci-dent [ĭn′sĭ-dənt] *noun*, 1) a
happening, a casual occurrence
2) a disturbance, a violent event

in-ci-den-tal-ly [ĭn′sĭ-dĕn′tl-ē]
adverb, casually, by chance

in-cin-er-a-tor [ĭn-sĭn′ə-rā′tər]
noun, a container or furnace
where garbage is burned

in-ci-sion [ĭn-sĭzh′ən] *noun*, a cut
or slit into body tissue, a gash

in-cite [ĭn-sīt′] *verb*, to stir up, to
stimulate to action, to provoke

in-clem-ent [ĭn-klĕm′ənt]
adjective, 1) stormy 2) lacking
mercy, unkind

in-cli-na-tion [ĭn′klə-nā′shən]
noun, 1) a preference, a tendency
2) a slant, an angle

in-cline [ĭn-klīn′]*verb*, 1) to lean, to
slant 2)to be likely to, to tend to

in-clude [ĭn-klōōd′] *verb*, 1) to
have as part of 2) to count or
think of someone or something
as a part of a group, to involve

in-clu-sive [ĭn-klōō′sĭv] *adjective*,
not leaving anyone or anything out

in-cog-ni-to [ĭn′kŏg-nē′tō]
adjective or adverb, 1) with
one's identity concealed, *noun*,
2) a secret identity

in-co-her-ent [ĭn′kō-hîr′ənt]
adjective, incomprehensible,
lacking meaningful connection

in-come [ĭn′kŭm′] *noun*, the money
a person earns from work or
investments, salary

in-com-par-able
[ĭn-kŏm′pər-ə-bəl] *adjective*,
excellent, unequaled by
comparison, unrivaled

in-com-pat-i-ble
[ĭn′kəm-păt′ə-bəl] *adjective*, not
capable of getting along or being
used together

in-com-pe-tent [ĭn-kŏm′pĭ-tənt]
adjective, not qualified, not able
to do a job or task

in-com-plete [ĭn′kəm-plēt′]
adjective, unfinished, lacking

in-con-ceiv-a-ble
[ĭn′kən-sē′və-bəl] *adjective*,
unimaginable, hard to believe

in-con-gru-ous [ĭn-kŏng′grōō-əs]
adjective, lacking harmony,
inconsistent

in-con-se-quen-tial
[ĭn-kŏn′sĭ-kwĕn′shəl] *adjective*,
having little importance

in-con-ven-ience [ĭn′kən-vēn′yəns]
noun, a problem or difficulty that
interferes with your comfort or
ability to do something in a
timely manner

in-con-ven-ient [ĭn′kən-vēn′yənt]
adjective, untimely, awkward

in-cor-po-rate [ĭn-kôr′pə-rāt′]
verb, 1) to unite into one body
2) to form into a corporation

in-cor-rect [ĭn′kə-rĕkt′] *adjective*,
not right in facts, wrong

in-crease [ĭn-krēs′] *noun*, 1) the
amount by which something gets

larger , *verb*, 2) to become
greater in size or quantity

in-cred-i-ble [ĭn-krĕd′ə-bəl]
adjective, surpassing belief,
unlikely, unbelievable

in-cred-u-lous [ĭn-krĕj′ə-ləs]
adjective, unwilling to believe,
skeptical

in-cre-ment [ĭn′krə-mənt, ĭng′-]
noun, an increase, addition

in-crim-i-nate [ĭn-krĭm′ə-nāt′]
verb, to accuse or charge with a
crime or fault, to implicate

in-crim-i-nat-ing
[ĭn-krĭm′ə-nā′tĭng] *adjective*,
showing proof of guilt

in-cu-bate [ĭn′kyə-bāt′] *verb*, 1) to
apply enough warmth to make
something hatch 2) to help
develop

in-cum-bent [ĭn-kŭm′bənt]
adjective, 1) required, obligatory,
noun, 2) an officeholder

in-cur [ĭn-kûr′] *verb*, to bring
something unpleasant upon
oneself

in-cur-a-ble [ĭn-kyōōr′ə-bəl]
adjective, irreparable, incapable
of being cured, terminally ill

in-cur-sion [ĭn-kûr′zhən] *noun*, an
invasion into enemy territory

in-debt-ed [ĭn-dĕt′ĭd] *adjective*,
under obligation to repay money
or a favor

in-deed [ĭn-dēd′] *adverb*, really,
truly, in fact, certainly

in-def-i-nite [ĭn-dĕf′ə-nĭt]
adjective, uncertain, inexact

in-def-i-nite-ly [ĭn-dĕf′ə-nĭt-lē]
adverb, without a set time frame

in-del-i-ble [ĭn-dĕl′ə-bəl] *adjective*,
unable to be removed or blotted
out, permanent

in-dem-ni-ty [ĭn-dĕm′nĭ-tē] *noun*, protection or exemption from loss or damage, security

in-dent [ĭn-dĕnt′] *verb*, 1) to set lines in from the margin 2) to form notches on the edge

in-den-ture [ĭn-dĕn′chər] *noun*, the written work agreement of a servant to a master

in-de-pend-ence [ĭn′dĭ-pĕn′dəns] *noun*, *no plural*, freedom from the control of others

in-de-pend-ent [ĭn′dĭ-pĕn′dənt] *adjective*, free, not relying on others, without bias

in-de-struct-i-ble [ĭn′dĭ-strŭk′tə-bəl] *adjective*, incapable of being destroyed

in-dex [ĭn′dĕks′] *noun*, a list, usually alphabetical, for finding reference to topics, names, etc.

In-di-an [ĭn′dē-ən] *noun*, 1) a native American 2) a native of the Asian country of India

In-di-ana [ĭn′dē-ăn′ə] *noun*, one of the 50 United States located in the Midwest, the capital is Indianapolis. The state flower of **Indiana** is the peony, and the state motto is "The crossroads of America."

in-di-cate [ĭn′dĭ-kāt′] *verb*, to show or describe, to point out

in-di-ca-tion [ĭn′dĭ-kā′shən] *noun*, something that shows a trait

in-di-ca-tor [ĭn′dĭ-kā′tər] *noun*, 1) something that points to a trait 2) an instrument for automatically showing the pressure of the working fluid in an engine

in-dict [ĭn-dīt′] *verb*, to formally charge with a crime

in-dict-ment [ĭn-dīt′mənt] *noun*, a formal accusation charging someone with a crime

in-dif-fer-ent [ĭn-dĭf′ər-ənt] *adjective*, 1) mediocre 2) unresponsive, unconcerned

in-dig-e-nous [ĭn-dĭj′ə-nəs] *adjective*, native to an area

in-di-gent [ĭn′dĭ-jənt] *adjective*, poor, destitute

in-di-gest-i-ble [ĭn′dĭ-jĕs′tə-bəl] *adjective*, unable to be swallowed, eaten or digested

in-di-ges-tion [ĭn′dĭ-jĕs′chən] *noun*, a stomach-ache, heartburn

in-dig-nant [ĭn-dĭg′nənt] *adjective*, angry because of something that is not right, resentful

in-dig-na-tion [ĭn′dĭg-nā′shən] *noun*, anger about something thought not right, rage

in-dig-ni-ty [ĭn-dĭg′nĭ-tē] *noun*, insulting or humiliating treatment

in-di-go [ĭn′dĭ-gō′] *noun*, a deep blue-violet dye made from plants

in-di-rect [ĭn′dĭ-rĕkt′] *adjective*, in a roundabout way, circuitous

in-di-rect-ly [ĭn′dĭ-rĕkt′lē] *adverb*, inadvertently, not intentionally

in-dis-creet [ĭn′dĭ-skrēt′] *adjective*, lacking prudence or discretion, unwise, not careful, imprudent

in-dis-pen-sa-ble [ĭn′dĭ-spĕn′sə-bəl] *adjective*, absolutely necessary, essential

in-dis-put-a-ble [ĭn′dĭ-spyo͞o′tə-bəl] *adjective*, undeniable, unquestionable

in-di-vid-u-al [ĭn′də-vĭj′ŌŌ-əl], *adjective*, 1) a person, 2) a single thing, an entity, one

in-di-vid-u-al-ly [ĭn′də-vĭj′ŌŌ-əl-lē] *adverb*, separately, one by one, distinctly

in-di-vis-i-ble [ĭn′də- vĭz′ə-bəl] *adjective*, 1) that cannot be divided 2) cannot be divided without leaving a remainder

in-do-lent [ĭn′də-lənt] *adjective*, lazy, inactive, slothful

in-dom-i-ta-ble [ĭn-dŏm′ĭ-tə-bəl] *adjective*, unconquerable

in-duce [ĭn-dŌŌs′] *verb*, 1) to persuade, to influence 2) to cause 3) to infer

in-duce-ment [ĭn-dŌŌs′mənt] *noun*, any motive that leads one to act

in-duc-tive [ĭn-dŭk′tĭv] *adjective*, 1) going from specific to general 2) relating to electric or magnetic induction

in-dulge [ĭn-dŭlj′] *verb*, to allow one to enjoy, to give way to

in-dul-gence [ĭn-dŭl′jəns] *noun*, the act of being too permissive or generous

in-dus-tri-al [ĭn-dŭs′trē-əl] *adjective*, commercial, related to economy, industry, or manufacturing

in-dus-tri-ous [ĭn-dŭs′trē-əs] *adjective*, hard-working

in-dus-try [ĭn′də-strē] *noun*, 1) hard work 2) commerce, enterprise, business activity

in-el-i-gi-ble [ĭn-ĕl′ĭ-jə-bəl] *adjective*, not qualified to be chosen for an office, activity, or relationship

in-ept [ĭn-ĕpt′] *adjective*, incapable of performing a task, unskilled

in-eq-ui-ty [ĭn-ĕk′wĭ-tē] *noun*, unfairness, bias

in-ert [ĭn-ûrt′] *adjective*, 1) without power, inactive 2) unable to react

in-er-tia [ĭ-nûr′shə] *noun*, the state of matter by which it tends to remain at rest unless acted upon by an external force

in-ev-i-ta-ble [ĭn-ĕv′ĭ-tə-bəl] *adjective*, unavoidable

in-fal-li-ble [ĭn-făl′ə-bəl] *adjective*, unfailing, incapable of error

in-fa-mous [ĭn′fə-məs] *adjective*, having a bad reputation

in-fan-cy [ĭn′fən-sē] *noune*, the first part of life, early childhood

in-fant [ĭn′fənt] *noun*, a very young child in the first stage of life, a baby, a newborn

in-fan-try [ĭn′fən-trē] *noun*, the ground forces of the army, foot soldiers

in-fat-u-a-tion [ĭ-făch′ŌŌ-ā′shən] *noun*, a brief but intense romantic attachment

in-fect [ĭn-fĕkt′] *verb*, to share a virus or infection with others

in-fec-tion [ĭn-fĕk′shən] *noun*, any disease caused by germs

in-fec-tious [ĭn-fĕk′shəs] *adjective*, capable of being spread or communicated, contagious

in-fer [ĭn-fûr′] *verb*, to arrive at a conclusion by logic, to deduce

in-fer-ence [ĭn′fər-əns] *noun*, a conclusion drawn from certain premises, a guess

in-fe-ri-or [ĭn-fîr′ē-ər] *adjective*, 1) lower 2) of less importance 3) inequal, subordinate

in·fer·nal [ĭn-fûr′nəl] *adjective*, referring to hell, diabolical

in·fest [ĭn-fĕst′] *verb*, to overrun in a troublesome manner

in·fil·tra·tion [ĭn′fĭl-trā′shən] *noun*, 1) the act of penetrating the pores of a substance 2) the process of joining gradually

in·fi·nite [ĭn′fə-nĭt] *adjective*, unending, total, without limit

in·fin·i·tes·i·mal [ĭn′fĭn-ĭ-tĕs′ə-məl] *adjective*, immeasurably small

in·fin·i·ty [ĭn-fĭn′ĭ-tē] *noun*, the symbol ~, that which continues indefinitely, timelessness

in·firm [ĭn-fûrm′] *adjective*, weak, sick, in poor health, ill, not well

in·fir·ma·ry [ĭn-fûr′mə-rē] *noun*, a small hospital, a first-aid facility

in·flam·ma·ble [ĭn-flăm′ə-bəl] *adjective*, easy to burn, volatile

in·flam·ma·tion [ĭn′flə-mā′shən] *noun*, swelling and redness

in·flate [ĭn-flāt′] *verb*, to fill with air, to expand

in·fla·tion [ĭn-flā′shən] *noun*, a state in which price levels rise continually

in·flict [ĭn-flĭkt′] *verb*, to force, to impose, to deal a blow

in·flu·ence [ĭn′flōō-əns] *noun*, 1) power, authority, or control 2) the gradual or unseen operation of some cause, *verb*, 3) to act upon 4) to persuade

in·flu·en·tial [ĭn′flōō-ĕn′shəl] *adjective*, able to change people's thoughts on something

in·flu·en·za [ĭn′flōō-ĕn′zə] *noun*, the flu, a disease characterized by fever, headaches, and fatigue

in·flux [ĭn′flŭks′] *noun*, the process of flowing into or coming in

in·form [ĭn-fôrm′] *verb*, 1) to tell, to notify, to advise 2) to teach

in·for·mal [ĭn-fôr′məl] *adjective*, casual, not dressy or formal

in·form·ant [ĭn-fôr′mənt] *noun*, someone who gives information

in·for·ma·tion [ĭn′fər-mā′shən] *noun*, facts, data, the things you need to know, knowledge

in·frac·tion [ĭn-frăk′shən] *noun*, a violation, the breaking of a law, rule, etc.

in·fringe·ment [ĭn-frĭnj′mənt] *noun*, an act that breaks the rules or an agreement

in·fu·ri·ate [ĭn-fyŏŏr′ē-āt′] *verb*, to make someone furious

in·fuse [ĭn-fyōōz′] *verb*, 1) to instill a principle or quality 2) to steep in water or other fluid without boiling for the purpose of extracting useful qualities

in·fu·sion [ĭn-fyōō′zhən] *noun*, 1) the act of introducing or dispersing of properties 2) a beverage or other solution obtained by steeping a substance in water or other liquid

in·ge·nu·i·ty [ĭn′jə-nōō′ĭ-tē] *noun*, skill in discovering, inventing, or planning

in·gest [ĭn-jĕst′] *verb*, to take in food or liquids

in·grat·i·tude [ĭn-grăt′ĭ-tōōd′] *noun*, unthankfulness

in·gre·di·ent [ĭn-grē′dē-ənt] *noun*, 1) a component part of any mixture 2) one of several things that are mixed together to make something

in-hab-it [ĭn-hăb′ĭt]*verb*, to make a
place a home, to live or dwell in

in-hab-it-ant [ĭn-hăb′ĭ-tənt] *noun*,
an animal or person who lives at
a location, a resident

in-hale [ĭn-hāl′] *verb*, to take a
deep breath, to breathe in

in-her-ent [ĭn-hîr′ənt] *adjective*,
existing as part of the nature of a
person or thing

in-her-it [ĭn-hĕr′ĭt] *verb*, to receive
something, usually from a
person by will or succession

in-her-it-ance [ĭn-hĕr′ĭ-təns] *noun*,
an estate, heritage, legacy

in-hib-it [ĭn-hĭb′ĭt] *verb*, 1) to
intimidate, to make someone
hold back in fear 2) to restrain

in-hi-bi-tion [ĭn′hə-bĭsh′ən] *noun*,
a painfully self-conscious feeling

in-iq-ui-ty [ĭ-nĭk′wĭ-tē] *noun*, a
gross injustice, wickedness

in-i-tial [ĭ-nĭsh′əl] *adjective*,
1) first, *noun*, 2) the first letter of
a name, *verb*, 3) to sign with
one's initials

in-i-tial-ly [ĭ-nĭsh′ə-lē] *adverb*, at
the beginning

in-i-ti-ate [ĭ-nĭsh′ē-āt′] *verb*, to
introduce, to begin or start
something, to originate

in-i-ti-a-tion [ĭ-nĭsh′ē-ā′shən]
noun, an induction, an inaugural

in-i-t-ia-tive [ĭ-nĭsh′ə-tĭv] *noun*,
1) an act that begins a series of
actions 2) the ability or will to
do something because it needs to
be done

in-ject [ĭn-jĕkt′] *verb*, 1) to
introduce, to insert 2) to give
someone a shot 3) to force
something into

in-jec-tion [ĭn-jĕk′shən] *noun*, an
insertion of medicine through a
needle into the body, a shot

in-jure [ĭn′jər] *verb*, to cause harm
of any kind, to wound

in-ju-ri-ous [ĭn-jŏŏr′ē-əs]
adjective, hurtful, harmful

in-ju-ry [ĭn′jə-rē] *noun*, 1) a
wound, harm to the body 2) an
offense, harm done

in-jus-tice [ĭn-jŭs′tĭs] *noun*, a
violation of the rights of another,
an unfair or unjust act

ink [ĭngk] *noun*, a colored liquid
used with a pen for writing, in a
printer, etc.

in-land [ĭn′lənd] *adjective*, away
from the shore or coast

in-law [ĭn′lô′] *noun*, a person
related through marriage

in-let [ĭn′lĕt′] *noun*, a channel of
water extending into the land
from a larger body of water

in-mate [ĭn′māt′] *noun*, a prisoner
or resident of a mental hospital

inn [ĭn] *noun*, a small hotel that
serves meals, a tavern

in-nate [ĭ-nāt′] *adjective*, inborn,
inherent

in-ner [ĭn′ər] *adjective*, 1) further
in or in the center 2) spiritual

in-ning [ĭn′ĭng] *noun*, the period in
a baseball game for each of two
teams to get three outs

in-no-cence [ĭn′ə-səns] *noun*, *no
plural*, 1) freedom from guilt,
2) simplicity, naivete

in-no-cent [ĭn′ə-sənt] *adjective*,
1) not guilty of a crime or sin,
blameless 2)pure,
unsophisticated

in-no-va-tion [ĭn′ə-vā′shən] *noun*,
the introduction of a new
product or method

in-no-va-tive [ĭn′ə-vā′tĭv]
adjective, featuring something
new, original

in-nu-en-do [ĭn′yōō-ĕn′dō] *noun*, a
suggestion, a hint, an insinuation

in-oc-u-late [ĭ-nŏk′yə-lāt′] *verb*, to
inject an animal or person with a
virus to prevent an infection

in-op-por-tune [ĭn-ŏp′ər-tōōn′]
adjective, poorly timed

in-or-di-nate [ĭn-ôr′dn-ĭt]
adjective, excessive, extravagant

in-or-gan-ic [ĭn′ôr-gǎn′ĭk] *adjective*,
relating to matter that does not
contain carbon atoms in its main
structure

in-put [ĭn′pŏŏt′] *noun*, anything
put in, feedback, data entry

in-quest [ĭn′kwĕst′] *noun*, judicial
inquiry or examination
especially into a death

in-quire [ĭn-kwīr′] *verb*, to ask
about, to investigate

in-quir-y [ĭn-kwīr′ē, ĭng′-] *noun*,
investigation, study, the act of
asking

in-qui-si-tion [ĭn′kwĭ-zĭsh′ən, ĭng′]
noun, formal questioning

in-quis-i-tive [ĭn-kwĭz′ĭ-tĭv]
adjective, curious, apt to ask
questions, given to research

in-sane [ĭn-sān′] *adjective*, crazy,
mentally ill

in-sa-tia-ble [ĭn-sā′shə-bəl]
adjective, incapable of being
satisfied or appeased

in-scrip-tion [ĭn-skrĭp′shən] *noun*,
an engraved or carved message

in-scru-ta-ble [ĭn-skrōō′tə-bəl]
adjective, unexplainable,
mysterious

in-sect [ĭn′sĕkt′] *noun*, a bug with
six legs and usually one or two
pairs of wings

in-sec-ti-cide [ĭn-sĕk′tĭ-sīd′] *noun*,
a poison used to kill insects

in-sen-si-ble [ĭn-sĕn′sə-bəl]
adjective, not aware,
unconscious, unable to feel

in-sep-a-ra-ble [ĭn-sĕp′ər-ə-bəl]
adjective, incapable of being
separated or disjoined

in-sert [ĭn-sûrt′]*noun*, 1) an extra
piece sewn or put in place, *verb*,
2) to put something into another
thing, to inject, to set in place

in-side [ĭn-sīd′] adjective, 1)
internal, interior, *noun*, 2) the
portion that is in the middle or
inner surface of something,
preposition, 3) lying within

in-sid-i-ous [ĭn-sĭd′ē-əs] *adjective*,
deceitful, beguiling, hidden

in-sight [ĭn′sīt′] *noun*,
understanding, perceptiveness

in-sig-ni-a [ĭn-sĭg′nē-ə] *noun*, an
emblem, a symbol, a badge

in-sig-nif-i-cance
[ĭn′sĭg-nĭf′ĭ-kəns] *noun*, lack of
importance, irrelevance

in-sig-nif-i-cant [ĭn′sĭg-nĭf′ĭ-kənt]
adjective, unimportant, trivial

in-sin-cere [ĭn′sĭn-sîr′] *adjective*,
untrue, false, disingenuous

in-sin-u-ate [ĭn-sĭn′yōō-āt′] *verb*,
to introduce artfully, to suggest,
to imply, to hint slyly

in-sip-id [ĭn-sĭp′ĭd] *adjective*,
uninteresting, dull, banal

in-sist [ĭn-sĭst′]*verb*, to say firmly with emphasis 2) to assert or demand persistently

in-so-lence [ĭn′sə-ləns] *noun*, arrogance, rudeness, impudence

in-so-lent [ĭn′sə-lənt] *adjective*, rude, insulting, disrespectful

in-sol-u-ble [ĭn-sŏl′yə-bəl] *adjective*, 1)incapable of being dissolved 2) not able to be solved or explained

in-som-ni-a [ĭn-sŏm′nē-ə] *noun*, the inability to sleep

in-spect [ĭn-spĕkt′]*verb*, to examine carefully and critically, to scrutinize, to look over

in-spec-tion [ĭn-spĕk′shən] *noun*, a careful examination

in-spec-tor [ĭn-spĕk′tər] *noun*, 1) someone who inpects things 2) a high-ranking police official

in-spi-ra-tion [ĭn′spə-rā′shən] *noun*, something that stimulates imagination and goodwill

in-spire [ĭn-spīr′] *verb*, to stimulate to think and to act, to influence

in-sta-bil-i-ty [ĭn′stə-bĭl′ĭ-tē] *noun*, lack of stability, unsteadiness

in-stall [ĭn-stôl′]*verb*, 1) to place in possession of an office, rank, or order 2) to put in place

in-stal-la-tion [ĭn′stə-lā′shən] *noun*, the act of putting something into place

in-stall-ment [ĭn-stôl′mənt] *noun*, one of a number of parts or payments

in-stance [ĭn′stəns] *noun*, an example, a case in point

in-stant [ĭn′stənt] *adjective*, 1) happening or done at once, urgent, immediate, *noun*, 2) the present or current moment

in-stan-ta-ne-ous [ĭn′stən-tā′nē-əs] *adjective*, done at that moment

in-stant-ly [ĭn′stənt-lē] *adverb*, at once, immediately

in-stead [ĭn-stĕd′] *adverb*, in place of someone or something

in-step [ĭn′stĕp′] *noun*, the arched middle portion of the human foot or of a shoe

in-sti-gate [ĭn′stĭ-gāt′] *verb*, to urge, to start, to provoke

in-still [ĭn-stĭl′] *verb*, 1) to teach, to educate, to inform 2) to saturate, to infuse, to permeate

in-stinct [ĭn′stĭngkt′] *noun*, a natural impulse that makes animals know how to take care of themselves, innate aptitude

in-stinc-tive-ly [ĭn-stĭngk′tĭv-lē] *adverb*, naturally, innately, automatically

in-sti-tute [ĭn′stĭ-tōōt′] *noun*, 1) an organization devoted to research and study, *verb*, 2) to form or establish an organization 3) to set in motion

in-sti-tu-tion [ĭn′stĭ-tōō′shən] *noun*, 1) an organization used to serve a group of people 2) a way of life, an established custom

in-struct [ĭn-strŭkt′] *verb*, to teach, to show someone how to do something, to direct

in-struc-tion [ĭn-strŭk′shən] *noun*, teaching, direction, a training manual, knowledge imparted

in-struc-tor [ĭn-strŭk′tər] *noun*, a teacher or mentor

in-stru-ment [ĭn′strə-mənt] *noun*, 1) a device, a mechanism, a tool

2) a device used to make musical sounds 3) a means to an end

in-stru-men-tal [ĭn'strə-měn'tl] *adjective*, 1) helpful, acting to get something done 2) meant to be performed on musical instruments

in-suf-fer-a-ble [ĭn-sŭf'ər-ə-bəl] *adjective*, painful, not to be endured, intolerable

in-suf-fi-cient [ĭn'sə-fĭsh'ənt] *adjective*, not enough for what is needed

in-su-late [ĭn'sə-lāt'] *verb*, to protect from heat, cold, electricity, etc., by means of a layer of protective material

in-su-la-tion [ĭn'sə-lā'shən] *noun*, a material that prevents passage of heat, electricity, or sound

in-sult [ĭn-sŭlt'] *noun*, 1) an unkind or rude remark, *verb*, 2) to treat with abuse or rudeness

in-sur-ance [ĭn-shōŏr'əns] *noun*, money paid in return for the promise of payment in the event of an accident, property damage, death, etc.

in-sure [ĭn-shōŏr'] *verb*, to guarantee, to protect

in-sur-gent [ĭn-sûr'jənt] *noun*, a person who rebels against the law or leadership

in-sur-rec-tion [ĭn'sə-rĕk'shən] *noun*, an uprising, a rebellion

in-tan-gi-ble [ĭn-tăn'jə-bəl] *adjective*, not able to be touched

in-te-ger [ĭn'tĭ-jər] *noun*, 1) a whole number 2) an intact unit

in-te-grate [ĭn'tĭ-grāt'] *verb*, to make into a whole, to combine into one unit, to merge

in-teg-ri-ty [ĭn-tĕg'rĭ-tē] *noun*, honesty, uprightness

in-tel-lect [ĭn'tl-ĕkt'] *noun*, the power to understand the mind

in-tel-lec-tu-al [ĭn'tl-ĕk'chōō-əl] *adjective*, able to reason, smart

in-tel-li-gence [ĭn-tĕl'ə-jəns] *noun*, 1) the faculty of understanding and reasoning 2) information communicated

in-tel-li-gent [ĭn-tĕl'ə-jənt] *adjective*, very smart, clever

in-tel-li-gent-ly [ĭn-tĕl'ə-jənt-lē] *adverb*, sensibly, skillfully

in-tel-li-gi-ble [ĭn-tĕl'ĭ-jə-bəl] *adjective*, capable of being understood

in-tend [ĭn-tĕnd'] *verb*, 1) to plan to do something 2) to design for a particular purpose

in-tense [ĭn-tĕns'] *adjective*, expressing strong emotion, extreme

in-ten-si-fy [ĭn-tĕn'sə-fī'] *verb*, to make greater or more intense

in-ten-si-ty [ĭn-tĕn'sĭ-tē] *noun*, great concentration of energy

in-ten-sive [ĭn-tĕn'sĭv] *adjective*, thorough, involving special effort

in-tent [ĭn-tĕnt'] *noun*, 1) purpose 2) meaning

in-ten-tion [ĭn-tĕn'shən] *noun*, aim, a plan, a purpose, a meaning

in-ten-tion-al-ly [ĭn-tĕn'shə-nəl-lē] *adverb*, purposely, deliberately

in-tent-ly [ĭn-tĕnt'lē] *adverb*, strongly, purposefully

in-ter [ĭn-tûr'] *verb*, to bury

in-ter-act [ĭn'tər-ăkt'] *verb*, to relate mutually to

in-ter-cede [ĭn'tər-sēd'] *verb*, to act on another's behalf, to mediate

in-ter-cept [ĭn'tər-sĕpt'] *verb*, to stop or seize something before it reaches its intended destination

in·ter·est [ĭn′trĭst] *noun*, 1) a concern or pleasure from learning something 2) title or share in a thing 3) a percentage rate of money paid for the use of money, *verb*, 4) to involve or gain the attention of someone

in·ter·est·ing [ĭn′trĭ-stĭng] *adjective*, able to hold the attention or curiosity of someone

in·ter·face [ĭn′tər-fās′] *noun*, 1) a surface forming a common boundary between adjacent areas 2) in computer science, the software or hardware connecting one drive or system to another

in·ter·fere [ĭn′tər-fîr′] *verb*, to prevent something from happening, to meddle

in·ter·fer·ence [ĭn′tər-fîr′əns] *noun*, obstruction, interruption

in·ter·im [ĭn′tər-ĭm] *adjective*, 1) temporary, *noun*,2)the meantime

in·te·ri·or [ĭn-tîr′ē-ər] *adjective*, 1) being within any limits, inner, inside, *noun*, 2) that which is within, an inner area

in·ter·lude [ĭn′tər-lōōd′] *noun*, 1) a pause, a lull 2) a brief play or musical piece performed between longer pieces

in·ter·me·di·ate [ĭn′tər-mē′dē-ĭt] *adjective*, in the middle between extremes

in·ter·ment [ĭn-tûr′mənt] *noun*, the burial ceremony

in·ter·mi·na·ble [ĭn-tûr′mə-nə-bəl] *adjective*, seemingly endless

in·ter·mis·sion [ĭn′tər-mĭsh′ən] *noun*, a break or recess

in·ter·mit·tent [ĭn′tər-mĭt′nt] *adjective*, coming and going at intervals, beginning again

in·ter·nal [ĭn-tûr′nəl] *adjective*, 1) occuriring inside of something, inner 2) referring to any function inside the body

in·ter·na·tion·al [ĭn′tər-năsh′ə-nəl] *adjective*, universal, global

in·ter·ne·cine [ĭn′tər-nĕs′ēn′] *adjective*, mutually destructive

In·ter·net [ĭn′tûr-nĕt] *noun*, the link to other computers, connected by a network

in·ter·pret [ĭn-tûr′prĭt] *verb*, to translate, to define, to explain

in·ter·pre·ta·tion [ĭn-tûr′prĭ-tā′shən] *noun*, an explanation of someone's art or other work, a translation

in·ter·pret·er [ĭn-tûr′prĭ-tər] *noun*, 1) one who explains or expounds 2) a translator

in·ter·ro·gate [ĭn-tĕr′ə-gāt′] *verb*, to ask questions of someone

in·ter·rupt [ĭn′tə-rŭpt′] *verb*, to stop something from continuing

in·ter·sect [ĭn′tər-sĕkt′] *verb*, to meet to form angles

in·ter·sec·tion [ĭn′tər-sĕk′shən] *noun*, 1) a point formed by two lines meeting 2) a place where two or more roads meet

in·ter·state [ĭn′tər-stāt′] *adjective*, 1) pertaining to commerce between the states, *noun*, 2) a highway that runs through two or more states

in·ter·val [ĭn′tər-vəl] *noun*, the space of time between any two points or events, a break

in·ter·vene [ĭn′tər-vēn′] *verb*, 1) to come or be between 2) to occur between points of time or events

in-ter-view [ĭn′tər-vyōō′] *noun*, a meeting in which one person or several people are questioned often by journalists or a prospective employer

in-ti-ma-cy [ĭn′tə-mə-sē] *noun*, close familiarity or association, a very personal relationship

in-ti-mate [ĭn′tə-mĭt] *adjective*, familiar, close, dear, private

in-tim-i-date [ĭn-tĭm′ĭ-dāt′] *verb*, to make someone afraid, to threaten someone, to scare

in-to [ĭn′tōō] *preposition*, toward the middle of something to the inside from outside

in-tol-er-a-ble [ĭn-tŏl′ər-ə-bəl] *adjective*, unbearable

in-tol-er-ance [ĭn-tŏl′ər-əns] *noun*, prejudice, bias, bigotry

in-to-na-tion [ĭn′tə-nā′shən] *noun*, 1) the rise and fall of a voice's pitch 2) chanting

in-tox-i-cate [ĭn-tŏk′sĭ-kāt′] *verb*, 1) to enliven, to excite, to elate 2) to make drunk

in-trac-ta-ble [ĭn-trăk′tə-bəl] *adjective*, difficult to control

in-tran-si-tive [ĭn-trăn′sĭ-tĭv] *adjective*, designating a verb in a sentence that does not need a direct object to complete its meaning

in-trep-id [ĭn-trĕp′ĭd] *adjective*, fearless, dauntless

in-tri-cate [ĭn′trĭ-kĭt] *adjective*, complicated, involved, detailed

in-trigue [ĭn′trēg′] *noun*, 1) a conspiracy, a strategy, a secret plan, *verb*, 2) to draw into, to fascinate, to arouse curiosity

in-trin-sic [ĭn-trĭn′zĭk] *adjective*, basic and essential

in-tro-duce [ĭn′trə-dōōs′] *verb*, 1) to bring into notice 2) to make known by formal announcement 3) to bring into use

in-tro-duc-tion [ĭn′trə-dŭk′shən] *noun*, 1) a piece of writing at the beginning of a book that explains something about the story 2) the exchange of names when two people first meet

in-tro-vert [ĭn′trə-vûrt′] *noun*, a loner, someone who feels self-conscious, a shy person

in-trude [ĭn-trōōd′] *verb*, to trespass, to enter uninvited

in-tru-sion [ĭn-trōō′zhən] *noun*, the act of forcing your way in without right or welcome or permission

in-tu-i-tion [ĭn′tōō-ĭsh′ən] *noun*, instinctive knowledge or feeling

in-un-date [ĭn′ŭn-dāt′] *verb*, to overflow, to flood, to overwhelm

in-ure [ĭn-yōōr′] *verb*, to accustom, to harden by use or exposure

in-vade [ĭn-vād′] *verb*, to move by force into another's country, property, house, etc.

in-va-lid [ĭn-văl′ĭd] *adjective*, 1) null and void, insupportable, [ĭn-val′ĭ-d] *noun*, 2) a person who is incapacitated by injury or illness

in-val-i-date [ĭn-văl′ĭ-dāt′] *verb*, 1) to make or show something to be wrong 2)to deprive of legal force

in-var-i-ab-ly [ĭn-vâr′ē-ə-blē] *adverb*, without fail, predictably

in-va-sion [ĭn-vā′zhən] *noun*, an attack, a raid

in-vent [ĭn-vĕnt′] *verb*, to create or design a new product

in-ven-tion [ĭn-vĕn′shən] *noun*, a design or creation of something new

in-ven-to-ry [ĭn′vən-tôr′ē] *noun*, an itemized list of stock on hand often with its estimated worth

in-verse [ĭn-vûrs′] *noun*, the opposite, the reverse in direction

in-vert [ĭn-vûrt′] *verb*, to overturn, to turn upside down

in-ver-te-brate [ĭn-vûr′tə-brĭt] *noun*, any animal without a backbone or spinal column, e.g. *a worm*

in-vest [ĭn-vĕst′] *verb*, 1) to empower 2) to provide time or money, usually in the hope of receiving more in return

in-ves-ti-gate [ĭn-vĕs′tĭ-gāt′] *verb*, to examine, to inquire

in-ves-ti-ga-tion [ĭn-vĕs′tĭ-gā′shən] *noun*, an inquiry into a matter, a thorough exploration or inspection, an examination

in-vest-ment [ĭn-vĕst′mənt] *noun*, money used to create a source of income or profit

in-ves-tor [ĭn-vĕs′tər] *noun*, one who spends money on something with a view of obtaining income or profit

in-vet-er-ate [ĭn-vĕt′ər-ĭt] *adjective*, deep-rooted, habitual

in-vig-o-rate [ĭn-vĭg′ə-rāt′] *verb*, to fill with life and energy

in-vin-ci-ble [ĭn-vĭn′sə-bəl] *adjective*, not capable of being overcome, unyielding

in-vis-i-ble [ĭn-vĭz′ə-bəl] *adjective*, not visible, not able to be seen

in-vi-ta-tion [ĭn′vĭ-tā′shən] *noun*, a request asking for someone to be present or participate in an activity

in-vite [ĭn-vīt′] *verb*, to ask someone to do something or come somewhere

in-voke [ĭn-vōk′] *verb*, 1) to call upon, to ask for 2) to cause

in-vol-un-tar-y [ĭn-vŏl′ən-tĕr′ē] *adjective*, done unwillingly

in-volve [ĭn-vŏlv′] *verb*, to take part in, to make a part of

in-vul-ner-a-ble [ĭn-vŭl′nər-ə-bəl] *adjective*, incapable of being injured

in-ward [ĭn′wərd] *adjective*, directed toward the center

in-ward-ly [ĭn′wərd-lē] *adverb*, internally

i-o-dine [ī′ə-dīn′] *noun*, a nonmetallic element isolated as a crystalline solid

i-o-ta [ī-ō′tə] *noun*, a very small quantity or degree, a particle

Io-wa [ī′ə-wə] *noun*, one of the 50 United States located in the Midwest the capital city is Des Moines. The state flower of **Iowa** is the wild rose and the state motto is "Our liberties we prize and our rights we will maintain."

i-rate [ī-rāt′] *adjective*, angry

ir-i-des-cent [ĭr′ĭ-dĕs′ənt] *adjective*, showing the rainbow-like play of colors, shimmering

irk-some [ûrk′səm] *adjective*, tedious, annoying

i-ron [ī′ərn] *noun*, 1) a magnetic gray metal 2) a heated device used to smooth the wrinkles

174

from clothes 3) an element, *verb*, 4) to press with a heated iron to remove wrinkles on clothes

i-ron-ic [ĭ-rŏn′ĭk] *adjective*, appearing to be false or contradictory, but in fact true

i-ro-ny [ī′rə-nē, ī′ər-] *noun*, 1) the outcome of events contrary to what was expected 2) the expression of the opposite of what is meant for humorous or literary effect

ir-rad-i-ate [ĭ-rā′dē-āt′] *verb*, 1) to illuminate, to enlighten 2) to expose to radiation

ir-ra-tion-al [ĭ-răsh′ə-nəl] *adjective*, absurd, unreasonable

ir-rec-on-cil-a-ble [ĭ-rĕk′ən-sī′lə-bəl] *adjective*, not able to be resolved by compromise, unfriendly

ir-reg-u-lar [ĭ-rĕg′yə-lər] *adjective*,1) not conforming to rule 2) erratic, not uniform

ir-rel-e-vant [ĭ-rĕl′ə-vənt] *adjective*, not applicable

ir-rep-a-ra-ble [ĭ-rĕp′ər-ə-bəl] *adjective*, permanently damaged

ir-re-proach-a-ble [ĭr′ĭ-prō′chə-bəl] *adjective*, blameless, above reproach

ir-re-sist-i-ble [ĭr′ĭ-zĭs′tə-bəl] *adjective*, too attractive to resist

ir-re-triev-a-ble [ĭr′ĭ-trē′və-bəl] *adjective*, lost, gone forever

ir-rev-er-ent [ĭ-rĕv′ər-ənt] *adjective*, lacking proper respect

ir-rev-o-ca-ble [ĭ-rĕv′ə-kə-bəl] *adjective*, unable to be retracted

ir-ri-gate [ĭr′ĭ-gāt′] *verb*, to supply with water by causing a stream to flow through, as in channels

ir-ri-tate [ĭr′ĭ-tāt′] *verb*, 1) to annoy, to excite to anger, to bother 2) to make skin sore, red, or swollen

ir-ri-ta-tion [ĭr′ĭ-tā′shən] *noun*, 1) something that makes a person mildly angry 2) something that causes a painful or inflamed part of the body

is [ĭz] the part of the *verb* to **be** that we use with *he, she,* and *it*

Is-lam [ĭs-läm′] *noun*, Muslim religion founded in Arabia in the 7th century based on the teaching of Muhammed as recorded in the Koran

is-land [ī′lənd] *noun*, a body of land completely surrounded by water

isle [īl] *noun*, a small island

i-so-late [ī′sə-lāt′] *verb*, 1) to separate and set apart, to place alone 2) to cut off from others

iso-la-tion [ī′sə-lā′shən] *noun*, solitude, detachment

i-sos-ce-les tri-ang-le [ī-sŏs′ə-lēz′ trī′ăng′gəl] *noun*, a triangle with two equal sides

is-sue [ĭsh′ōō] *noun*, 1) a topic on which there is disagreement 2) the condition or action of being made available, *verb*, 3) to give

isth-mus [ĭs′məs] *noun*, a neck of land bordered by water joining two larger portions of land

it [ĭt] *pronoun, plural*, **they**, 1) used of something previously named 2) used as the subject in sentences about the weather, time, and dates and other phrases

i-tal-ic [ĭ-tăl′ĭk] *noun*, type in which the letters slant

itch [ĭch] *noun*, 1) a tickling feeling in the skin that makes one want to scratch, *verb*, 2) to feel a desire to scratch and rub a sore because it is irritating

i-tem [ī′təm] *noun*, 1) a point 2) a news article 3) a single thing in a list

i-tem-ize [ī′tə-mīz′] *verb*, to list or state by particulars

itin-er-ant [ī-tĭn′ər-ənt] *adjective*, traveling from place to place

itin-er-ar-y [ī-tĭn′ə-rĕr′ē] *noun*, the detailed plan for a journey

its [ĭts] *adjective*, of it, belonging to it, the possessive of the word **it**

it's [ĭts] the *contraction* of the words **it** and **is**

it-self [ĭt-sĕlf′] *pronoun*, *plural*, **themselves**, referring to the subject of the sentence

I've [īv] the *contraction* of the words **I** and **have**

i-vo-ry [ī′və-rē, īv′rē] *noun*, hard, white substance taken from the tusks of elephants or walruses

i-vy [ī′vē] *noun*, a leafy climbing vine usually with pointed evergreen leaves

J

jack-et [jăk′ĭt] *noun*, 1) a covering worn over clothing, similar to a coat, typically of waist or hip length 2) a covering put over something

jade [jād] *noun*, a stone of a green color, but sometimes whitish, capable of a fine polish

jad-ed [jā′dĭd] *adjective*, tired, weary from having had too much of something

jag-uar [jăg′wär′] *noun*, a wild cat with a spotted coat that lives in Central or South America

jail [jāl] *noun*, a prison

jam [jăm] *noun*, 1) a sweet spread, made of boiled fruit and sugar 2) traffic that is stopped because no one can move 3) a predicament *verb*, 4) to pack tightly together, to compress, to press or push

jan-i-tor [jăn′ĭ-tər] *noun*, one who takes care of the repairs and cleaning of a building

Jan-u-ary [jăn′yoo-ĕr′ē] *noun*, the first month of the year, having 31 days

jar [jär] *noun*, a container like a bottle with a wide opening

jar-gon [jär′gən] *noun*, language used by a particular group, special terminology

jaun-dice [jôn′dĭs] *noun*, a medical condition that makes the skin look yellow

jaunt [jônt] *noun*, a short trip

jave-lin [jăv′lĭn] *noun*, a spear thrown by hand for distance as in an athletic event or used as a weapon

jaw [jô] *noun*, the bony part of the face in which the teeth are set

jazz [jăz] *noun*, a style of music using unusual tone effects on brass instruments improvised by black Americans in the 1900's

jeal-ous [jĕl′əs] *adjective*, to be unhappy because you want what someone else has, envious

jeal-ous-y [jĕl′ə-sē] *noun*, suspicious fear or watchfulness, resentment of someone's success or romantic interest in someone else

jeer [jîr] *verb*, to make fun of someone and laugh in their face, to mock, to scorn

jel-ly [jĕl′ē] *noun, no plural*, 1) any substance between liquid and solid 2) a sweet spread made of fruit and pectin

jel-ly-fish [jĕl′ē-fĭsh′] *noun*, a soft gelatinous sea creature that looks like a squishy blob

jeop-ard-ize [jĕp′ər-dīz′] *verb*, to expose to danger or even death

jerk [jûrk] *noun*, 1) a quick pull or twist movement, *verb*, 2) to pull, to push or to twist suddenly

jer-sey [jûr′zē] *noun*, clothing usually made of cotton with elastic that covers the top of the body like a shirt

jest [jĕst] *verb*, to joke, to jeer

jet [jĕt] *noun*, 1) an aircraft propelled through air by an engine, which releases a stream of hot air behind itself as it travels 2) a stream of gas, air, or liquid that spurts from a hole

jet-ti-son [jĕt′ĭ-sən] *verb*, to throw overboard, to discard

jet-ty [jĕt′ē] *noun*, a kind of wall built out into water for protection against the waves

Jew [jōō] *noun*, a member of the Jewish religion

jew-el [jōō′əl] *noun*, a precious stone used as an ornament, a gem of great value

jew-el-er [jōō′ə-lər] *noun*, one who makes, or deals in jewels, gems and precious stones, etc.

jew-el-ry [jōō′əl-rē] *noun, no plural*, ornaments like rings, earrings, necklaces made with precious or semiprecious stones, gems and metals

jilt [jĭlt] *verb*, to break up a romantic interest

jin-gle [jĭng′gəl] *verb*, 1) to make a tingling sound like the sound of bells, *noun*, 2) a catchy verse

job [jŏb] *noun*, 1) a task or responsibility 2) work done for payment 3) a position or duty

jog [jŏg] *verb*, 1) to run for exercise 2) to jolt, to bump, to shake 3) to stir into activity

join [join] *verb*, 1) to connect, to bring together, to meet 2) to become a member

joint [joint] *adjective*, 1) an endeavor involving two or more people, *noun*, 2) the part of the body where bones connect 3) the place where two things are joined or connected 4) a poor quality restaurant or night club

joke [jōk] *noun*, 1) a funny story or funny phrase spoken to amuse people, *verb*, 2) to tell funny stories or say things to make people laugh, to fool around

jolt [jōlt] *noun*, 1) a sudden and unexpected movement, *verb*, 2) to cause a sudden movement

joule [jōōl, joul] *noun*, the measurement of force or energy

jour-nal [jûr′nəl] *noun*, a book that records daily thoughts or transactions, a diary

jour-nal-ism [jûr′nə-lĭz′əm] *noun, no plural*, the job of writing for a publication or broadcasting news

jour-nal-ist [jûr′nə-lĭst] *noun*, a professional writer for a newspaper or magazine

jour-ney [jûr′nē] *noun*, the passage from one place to another, a trip

jo-vi-al [jō′vē-əl] *adjective*, joking in a friendly manner, light-hearted, joyous humor

joy [joi] *noun*, *no plural*, great happiness, delight, elation

joy-ful [joi′fəl] *adjective*, full of joy, very glad, happy

Jr. the abbreviation of the word **junior** when referring to a son who has his father's name

ju-bi-lant [jōō′bə-lənt] *adjective*, thrilled, rejoicing, great joy

Ju-da-ism [jōō′dē-ĭz′əm] *noun*, the religion of people descended from the Israelites in the Bible

judge [jŭj] *noun*, 1) one with legal authority who applies the rules of law in a court 2) the person designated to decide the winner in a contest, *verb*, 3) to make a decision, to form an opinion

judg-ment [jŭj′mənt] *noun*, 1) a decision or opinion 2) intelligence, understanding

ju-di-cial [jōō-dĭsh′əl] *adjective*, providing or relating to justice or a fair decision, just, legal

ju-di-cious [jōō-dĭsh′əs] *adjective*, sound in judgment, wise, discreet, sagacious, fair

ju-do [jōō′dō] *noun*, *no plural*, a form of martial arts that uses the body as a weapon, and bans throws and blows

jug [jŭg] *noun*, a container with a handle for holding liquids

jug-ger-naut [jŭg′ər-nôt′] *noun*, an overpowering or crushing force

jug-gle [jŭg′əl] *verb*, to throw several things into the air and keep them moving by throwing and catching them as a trick

jug-u-lar [jŭg′yə-lər] *noun*, one of the large veins returning the blood from the head

juice [jōōs] *noun*, the natural fluid that comes from fruit, vegetables or cooked meat

Ju-ly [jŏŏ-lī′] *noun*, the seventh month of the year, having 31 days

jump [jŭmp] *noun*, 1) a spring or leap, *verb*, 2) to lift the feet off the ground into the air, to leap 3) to rise suddenly

jump-er [jŭm′pər] *noun*, a sleeveless dress worn over a blouse

junc-tion [jŭngk′shən] *noun*, a place where roads or lines of railways meet and cross

June [jōōn] *noun*, the sixth month of the year, having 30 days

jun-gle [jŭng′gəl] *noun*, a thick growth of tropical bushes, vines, trees, etc., extending over a large area

jun-ior [jōōn′yər] *adjective*, 1) a student in his third year of a four-year course 2) the son named after his father

junk [jŭngk] *noun*, stuff regarded as unwanted or useless

jun-ket [jŭng′kĭt] *noun*, a trip, a short pleasure excursion

ju-ris-dic-tion [jŏŏr′ĭs-dĭk′shən] *noun*, the legal authority of a court, to apply the law

ju-ror [jŏŏr′ər, -ôr′] *noun*, one of a group of peers chosen to judge someone accused of a crime

ju-ry [jŏŏr′ē] *noun*, a group of
people chosen to decide if a
person is guilty or innocent of a
crime in a court of law

just [jŭst] *adjective*, 1) fair and right
2) normal, *adverb*, 3) to the amount
needed, but no more 4) a very short
time ago, by a short time 5) only
6) used to compare two things

jus-tice [jŭs′tĭs] *noun*, *no plural*,
fairness, equity, impartiality

jus-ti-fy [jŭs′tə-fī′] *verb*, 1) to
show or prove to be right 2) to
make even or true, as lines of
type by proper spacing

ju-ve-nile [jōō′və-nīl′] *adjective*,
1) young, youthful, *noun*, 2) a
youth, anyone under the legal
adult age of 18

K

ka-lei-do-scope [kə-lī′də-skōp′]
noun, an optical instrument
exhibiting an endless variety of
colored forms

kan-ga-roo [kăng′gə-rōō′] *noun*, a
marsupial, an animal that eats only
plants, lives in Australia, jumps
around on its large back legs

Kan-sas [kăn′zəs] *noun*, one of the
50 United States, located in the
Midwest, the capital city is
Topeka. The state flower of
Kansas is the sunflower, and the
motto is "To the stars through
difficulties."

kar-at [kăr′ət] *noun*, the unit
measure of the purity of gold

kay-ak [kī′ăk′] *noun*, a canoe that
holds one person

keel [kēl] *noun*, the bottom of the
boat, the underside

keen [kēn] *adjective*, 1) 1) having a
sharp edge 2) mentally aware,
quick to understand 3) showing a
stong interest, eager

keep [kēp] *verb*, 1) to hold
something 2) to store something,
to stock it 3) to make someone
stay someplace 4) to prevent
someone from doing something
5) to continue on

ken-nel [kĕn′əl] *noun*, a place to
keep and care for dogs

Ken-tucky [kən-tŭk′ē] *noun*, one
of the 50 United States, located
in the South, the capital is
Frankfort. The state flower of
Kentucky is the goldenrod, and
the state motto is "United We
Stand, Divided We Fall."

kept [kĕpt] *past tense* of **keep**

ker-chief [kûr′chĭf] *noun*, a
woman's scarf worn as a
covering for the head

ker-nel [kûr′nəl] *noun*, a grain or
seed, the edible part of a nut

ker-o-sene [kĕr′ə-sēn′] *noun*, thin
oil used to ignite a fire

ket-tle [kĕt′l] *noun*, a large metal pot
with a lid and a handle and a spout

key [kē] *noun*, 1) a metal
instrument used for locking and
unlocking things 2) a lever on a
musical instrument that affects
the sound 3) the piece of
information needed to make
something understood

key-board [kē′bôrd′] *noun*, a
common input device

khak-i [kăk′ē] *noun*, a tan or
brownish cotton cloth

kick [kĭk] *noun*, 1) an impulsive
move with the foot, *verb*,

2) to hit something with the foot, to move the foot suddenly

kid [kĭd] *noun*, 1) a young goat 2) a child, *verb*, 3) to tease or joke

kid-nap [kĭd′năp′] *verb*, to take someone against their will

kid-nap-per [kĭd′nă-pər] *noun*, someone who takes a person against their will

kid-ney [kĭd′nē] *noun*, one of two parts inside the body which remove waste liquid from the blood and excretes uric acid

kill [kĭl] *verb*, to make someone die

kill-er [kĭl′ər] *noun*, a person who murders or takes the life from another

kil-o-gram [kĭl′ə-grăm′] *noun*, a unit of weight equal to 1,000 grams

kil-o-me-ter [kĭ-lŏm′ĭ-tər] *noun*, a distance equal to 1,000 meters, almost 1 mile

kil-o-watt [kĭl′ə-wŏt′] *noun*, a unit of power equal to 1,000 watts

kin [kĭn] *noun*, *no plural*, family members, one's relatives

kind [kīnd] *adjective*, 1) nice, good, helpful, willing to please, *noun*, 2) a sort or particular one

kin-der-gar-ten [kĭn′dər-gär′tn] *noun*, a preschool for children before the first grade

kin-dle [kĭn′dl] *verb*, 1) to set fire, to ignite 2) to arouse, to inspire

kind-ness [kīnd′nĭs] *noun*, *no plural*, goodness, compassion

kin-dred [kĭn′drĭd] *adjective*, 1) similar in nature, comparable, alike 2) related by family

ki-net-ic [kĭ-nĕt′ĭk] *adjective*, the changes of motion produced by forces, the force of motion

king [kĭng] *noun*, a male ruler of a country, especially one who comes from a family of rulers

king-dom [kĭng′dəm] *noun*, the lands owned by a monarchy, an empire, an independent realm

kin-ship [kĭn′shĭp′] *noun*, a relationship or connection between family members

kiss [kĭs] *noun*, 1) a slight touch with the lips, *verb*, 2) to touch with the lips as a sign of affection or love

kit [kĭt] *noun*, a set of instruments needed for doing something or going somewhere

kitch-en [kĭch′ən] *noun*, the room where food is prepared and cooked and eaten

kite [kīt] *noun*, a light frame covered with fabric, plastic or paper, flown in the air at the end of a long string

kit-ten [kĭt′n] *noun*, a baby cat

knap-sack [năp′săk′] *noun*, a supply bag of canvas or leather with shoulder straps, worn on the back

knave [nāv] *noun*, an unscrupulous, dishonest person, a rascal

knead [nēd] *verb*, to manipulate by pressing and stretching to mix and remove air, to massage

knee [nē] *noun*, the joint between the thigh and the lower leg connecting the femur and tibia

kneel [nēl] *verb*, to stand on your knees, to bend down so that your calf is laying on the ground

knew [nōō] *past tense* of **know**

knife [nīf] *noun*, *plural*, **knives**, a cutting instrument consisting of a sharp blade fastened to a handle

knight [nīt] *noun*, 1) an armed soldier in the Middle Ages 2) a chess piece in the shape of a horse's head 3) an honorary title in Britain

knit [nĭt] *verb*, to join wool into a cloth using long needles

knob [nŏb] *noun*, a handle in the shape of a round lump

knock [nŏk] *noun*, 1) a noise made when something is hit *verb*, 2) to hit or strike with the fist 4) to make a noise by hitting on the surface

knoll [nōl] *noun*, a small round hill

knot [nŏt] *noun*, 1) one or more threads tied together, *verb*, 2) to tie something securely with rope or cord so that it cannot come untied

know [nō] *verb*, 1) to understand clearly, to learn 2) to be skilled in 3) to be acquainted with someone

knowl-edge [nŏl′ĭj] *noun*, something learned and remembered, gained by experience

know-ledge-a-ble [nŏl′ĭ-jə-bəl] *adjective*, familiar with, learned

known [nōn] *past participle* of **know**

knuck-le [nŭk′əl] *noun*, one of the joints in the finger or toe

Ko-ran [kə-răn′, -rän′, kô-, kō-] *noun*, the holy book of Islam containing the revelations of Muhammed

L

la-bel [lā′bəl] *noun*, 1) a slip of paper indicating contents, ownership, etc. *verb*, 2) to affix a tag or sticker on something naming what it is

la-bor [lā′bər] *noun*, 1) work 2) the pain a woman feels birthing a baby, *verb*, 3) to work hard

lab-o-ra-to-ry [lăb′rə-tôr′ē] *noun*, a place devoted to experiments in natural science

la-bo-ri-ous [lə-bôr′ē-əs] *adjective*, hardworking, tiresome, tedious

lab-y-rinth [lăb′ə-rĭnth′] *noun*, a series of intricate passageways, a maze, an inexplicable difficulty

lace [lās] *noun*, 1) a string used to tie a shoe 2) frilly threadwork used as edging or as an embroidery design, *verb*, 3) to thread through holes with a string or cord

lac-er-a-tion [lăs′ə-rā′shən] *noun*, a cut, a tear made with a knife

lack [lăk] *noun*, 1) not enough, a shortage, *verb* 2) to be without

lack-a-dai-si-cal [lăk′ə-dā′zĭ-kəl] *adjective*, half-hearted, lazy, indifferent, listless

la-con-ic [lə-kŏn′ĭk] *adjective*, brief and to the point

lac-quer [lăk′ər] *noun*, a liquid that hardens into a clear tough film

lac-tic acid [lăk′tĭk-ăs′ĭd] *noun*, a colorless, syrupy liquid, occurring in sour milk

lad [lăd] *noun*, a boy

lad-der [lăd′ər] *noun*, a device used for climbing designed with two side pieces joined together with shorter pieces called rungs that form steps

lad-en [lād′n] *adjective*, heavily loaded, full of cargo

la-dle [lād′l] *noun*, a cup-shaped spoon with a long handle, used for serving or dipping

la-dy [lā′dē] *noun*, 1) a polite and considerate woman 2) in Britain, a title for the wife or daughter of a Lord

lag [lăg] *verb*, to move at a slower pace to stay behind the others

la-goon [lə-gōōn′] *noun*, a shallow body of water near a sea, or pond-like body of water

laid [lād] *past tense* of **lay**

lair [lâr] *noun*, a den, a hole, a hideout for a wild animal

la-i-ty [lā′ĭ-tē] *noun*, someone not connected to the clergy, a layman practicing religion

lake [lāk] *noun*, a body of water with land all around

lamb [lăm] *noun*, a baby sheep

lame [lām] *adjective*, limping or disabled in a hand or joint

la-ment [lə-mĕnt′] *verb*, to mourn, to express grief or regret

lam-i-nat-ed [lăm′ə-nā′tĭd] *adjective*, arranged in layers of plastic one upon the other

lamp [lămp] *noun*, a device used to project artificial light

lam-poon [lăm-pōōn′] *noun*, a cartoon or satire in print

lance [lăns] *noun*, 1) a spear, a harpoon, a javelin, *verb*, 2) to puncture 3) to cut into with a surgical knife

land [lănd] *noun*, *no plural*, 1) the dry part of the earth, not covered by water 2) a country, region, area, *verb*, 3) to arrive on the ground from the air or water

land-fill [lănd′fĭl′] *noun*, a large outdoor site where solid waste is covered by soil

land-lord [lănd′lôrd′] *noun*, a person who owns a building which he lets others use or live in, in return for money

land-mark [lănd′märk′] *noun*, 1) an achievement, a turning point, benchmark 2) a distinctive building or geographical marker like a bend in the river

land-scape [lănd′skāp′] *noun*, a view of an area with its natural surroundings

lane [lān] *noun*, a short road

lan-guage [lăng′gwĭj] *noun*, 1) any means of conveying or communicating ideas 2) human speech 3) dialect, jargon, vocabulary used by a group

lan-guish [lăng′gwĭsh] *verb*, to lose strength, to weaken

lan-guor [lăng′gər] *noun*, a feeling of depression, nervous exhaustion, weakness of mind or body

lank [lăngk] *adjective*, 1) thin, lean 2) hanging straight or limp

lan-tern [lăn′tərn] *noun*, a portable lamp, with a protective case for lights, carried with a handle often used outdoors for light

lap [lăp] *noun*, 1) the seat created by the legs and chest when sitting 2) the distance once around a track 3) a place of rest, *verb*, 4) to drink water with a tongue, like an animal

lapel [lə-pĕl′] *noun*, the flat hanging appendage on a jacket

lapse [lăps] *noun*, 1) an interval of time in which something stops and then starts again 2) termination of policy because of non-payment of premium when due 3) a slip or error

lar-ce-ny [lär′sə-nē] *noun*, taking and carrying away of things, stealing, robbery

lard [lärd] *noun*, grease, fat

large [lärj] *adjective*, greater than average in size, number, etc., immense, big

large-ly [lärj′lē] *adverb*, mostly

lar-ger [lär′jər] *adjective*, bigger

lar-gess [lär-zhĕs′] *noun*, the generous giving of gifts

lar-va [lär′və] *noun*, *plural*, *larvae or larvas*, the second stage of an insect that goes through complete metamorphosis

lar-yn-gi-tis [lăr′ən-jī′tĭs] *noun*, infection of the larynx or upper end of the windpipe

lar-ynx [lăr′ĭngks] *noun*, the voice organ in the upper throat

la-ser [lā′zər] *noun*, a narrow beam of high-energy light that is all exactly the same color

lash [lăsh] *noun*, 1) a whip, a cane, *verb*, 2) to hit hard 3) to secure something in place with a rope

las-so [lăs′ō] *noun*, 1) a rope with a loop at the end used for catching cattle, *verb*, 2) to catch by throwing the noose of a rope around the neck or torso

last [lăst] *adjective*, 1) the end, final 2) an instance when something happens 3) to come after all others 4) to be a part of for a long time, to endure, *adverb*, 5) to stay in good condition, to be preserved

last-ing [lăs′tĭng] *adjective*, the length of time something continues, enduring

latch [lăch] *noun*, 1) a small bolt used to fasten a door, *verb*, 2) to fasten something shut

late [lāt] *adjective*, 1) after the time agreed on 2) near the end of a day, year, etc. 3) a missed opportunity 4) deceased

late-ly [lāt′lē] *adverb*, recently, a short time ago, not long since

la-tent [lāt′nt] *adjective*, hidden, present but not visible

lat-er [lāt′ər] *adverb*, after a certain amount of time, subsequently

lat-er-al [lăt′ər-əl] *adjective*, coming from the side

lat-est [lā′tĭst] *adjective*, most recent, newest, popular

lath-er [lăth′ər] *noun*, *no plural*, the bubbles created by soap

lat-i-tude [lăt′ĭ-tood′] *noun*, *no plural*, imaginary horizontal lines on a map indicating the distance of a place, measured in degrees, north or south of the earth's equator 2) freedom to act and to choose

lat-ter [lăt′ər] *adjective*, the second of two things, the last mentioned

laud [lôd] *verb*, to praise

laugh [lăf] *verb*, to make a sound showing something is funny, to express happiness

laugh-ter [lăf'tər] *noun*, *no plural*, a giggle, mirth, a chuckle

launch [lônch] *noun*, 1) a small boat propelled by an engine, *verb*, 2) to send off, to put a boat into water or send a space ship into orbit 3) to plunge boldly into action

laun-dry [lôn'drē] *noun*, dirty clothes washed together

lau-rel [lôr'əl] *noun*, an evergreen shrub with pink flowers

la-va [lä'və] *noun*, very hot melted rock that bursts out of a volcano

lav-a-to-ry [lăv'ə-tôr'ē] *noun*, a room with a toilet and a sink

lav-en-der [lăv'ən-dər] *noun*, a fragrant plant with purple flowers, classified as an herb

lav-ish [lăv'ĭsh] *adjective*, 1) extravagant, excessive, 2) giving in great amounts, *verb*, 3) to give generously

law [lô] *noun*, a written rule of conduct made and enforced by the government

law-mak-er [lô'mā'kər] *noun*, a person in government who is part of the legislature

lawn [lôn] *noun*, a piece of ground where grass is grown and is kept short in front of a building

law-yer [lô'yər] *noun*, a professional who practices law, an attorney, barrister

lax-a-tive [lăk'sə-tĭv] *noun*, a medicine or herb that induces a bowel movement

lay [lā] *verb*, 1) to place something in a horizontal position 2) when an adult female produces eggs 3) to remain, to rest

lay-er [lā'ər] *noun*, a covering that is set between two levels

la-zy [lā'zē] *adjective*, disinterested in work, slow-moving, indolent

lead [lĕd] *noun*, 1) a heavy, metallic element, having a bright luster 2) the part of a pencil used for writing, [lēd] *verb*, 3) to guide, to show someone the way

lead-er [lē'dər] *noun*, the chief, the person in charge, the ruler

lead-er-ship [lē'dər-shĭp'] *noun*, the quality of those who take charge or show the way

leaf [lēf] *noun*, *plural*, *leaves*, 1) a green part of a stem that grows off a branch of a plant 2) a sheet of paper

leaf-let [lē'flĭt] *noun*, a brochure or a small sheet of printed matter

league [lēg] *noun*, 1) an association or alliance with other individuals 2) sports teams organized to compete against each other 3) three nautical miles

leak [lēk] *noun*, 1) a crack or hole through which liquid, gas or light can ooze, *verb*, 2) to let something escape through an unintended opening such as a crack or hole

lean [lēn] *adjective*, 1) thin, without fat, *verb*, 2) to bend or incline toward 3) to rest on something for support to keep from falling, to recline

leap [lēp] *noun*, 1) a jump, *verb*, 2) to jump or spring over a hurdle or through space

leap year *noun*, a year, once every four years, in which February has 29 days instead of 28

learn [lûrn] *verb*, 1) to acquire knowledge or skill through study or experience 2) to find out, to commit to memory

learn-ing [lûr′nĭng] *noun*, knowledge, education

leash [lēsh] *noun*, a restraining device in the form of a rope or cord, chain or strap

least [lēst] *adjective*, the smallest amount, degree or size

leath-er [lĕth′ər] *noun*, skin of a dead animal prepared for use

leave [lēv] *noun*, 1) permission to be absent, *verb*, 2) to go away from, to depart, to exit 3) to allow something to remain untouched 4) to bequeath

lech-er-ous [lĕch′ər-əs] *adjective*, impure in thought and act, lustful, perverted

lec-tern [lĕk′tərn] *noun*, a podium for public speaking

lec-ture [lĕk′chər] *noun*, 1) a speech on any subject, *verb*, 2) to speak, to talk, to teach

ledge [lĕj] *noun*, a narrow shelf, such as at the bottom of a window, or a narrow, flat piece of rock, on which you can stand

ledg-er [lĕj′ər] *noun*, a book of accounts listing names and debits and credits

left [lĕft] *adjective*, 1) the side of a person or thing that is to the west when facing north, the opposite

of the right side, *verb*, 2) the *past tense* of **leave**

leg [lĕg] *noun*, 1) the body part attached to the foot or paw, used for walking 2) one of at least three pieces on a piece of furniture, used to make it stand

leg-a-cy [lĕg′ə-sē] *noun*, a gift of personal property left in a will

le-gal [lē′gəl] *noun*, based upon or in accordance with law

leg-end [lĕj′ənd] *noun*, 1) a story about someone that has no factual basis 2) a description or key accompanying a map or picture 3) an admirable person

leg-er-de-main [lĕj′ər-də-mān′] *noun*, slight of hand, magic

leg-i-ble [lĕj′ə-bəl] *adjective*, capable of being read with ease

le-gion [lē′jən] *noun*, a large group of soldiers, a multitude of people

leg-is-la-ture [lĕj′ĭ-slā′chər] *noun*, persons in a state elected by the people, having power to make, repeal or change laws

le-git-i-mate [lə-jĭt′ə-mĭt] *adjective*, 1) lawful, conforming to accepted standards 2) genuine

leg-ume [leg′yo͞om] *noun*, a plant of the pea family grown as a crop

lei-sure [lē′zhər] *noun, no plural*, free time from the demand of work or duty, spare time

lem-ming [lĕm′ĭng] *noun*, a small rat-like animal known for its mass migration into the sea

lem-on [lĕm′ən] *noun*, a yellow citrus fruit with a very sour taste, grown in tropical climates

lem-on-ade [lĕm′ə-nād′] *noun*, a beverage of sweetened lemon juice and water

lend [lĕnd] *verb*, 1) to let someone use something for a while, until they return it 2) to offer help

length [lĕngkth] *noun*, 1) the distance from end to end 2) the amount of time

length-en [lĕngk′thən-] *verb*, to make longer, drawn out

le-ni-ent [lē′nē-ənt] *adjective*, mild, merciful, not strict

lens [lĕnz] *noun*, 1) a piece of curved glass or other transparent material by which light rays meet to form an image 2) a part of the eye that focuses light rays to form an image on the retina

leop-ard [lĕp′ərd] *noun*, one of the big cats with a spotted coat, that weighs 100-175 pounds, is seven feet long and lives in Africa

le-sion [lē′zhən] *noun*, a wound, a sore, diseased tissue

less [lĕs] *adjective*, a smaller amount, a reduction

less-en [lĕs′ən] *verb*, to make smaller, to become less

les-son [lĕs′ən] *noun*, something that must be learned or studied

let [lĕt] *verb*, 1) to allow, to permit, to grant 2) to rent, to lease

le-thal [lē′thəl] *adjective*, deadly

le-thar-gy [lĕth′ər-jē] *noun*, fatigue, without energy, feeling tired, drowsy, sluggish

let's [lĕts] the *contraction* of the words **let** and **us**

let-ter [lĕt′ər] *noun*, 1) a message in writing, often sent through the mail 2) one of the characters of the alphabet

let-tuce [lĕt′əs] *noun*, a plant having succulent leaves that are used in salads

lev-ee [lĕv′ē] *noun*, an embankment, dike, dam

lev-el [lĕv′əl] *adjective*, 1) flat, with no higher or lower places, *noun*, 2) a place or position of a particular height, *verb*, 3) to make a surface flat or even

lev-er [lĕv′ər] *noun*, 1) a bar used to exert pressure or sustain weight 2) a means to an end

lev-i-ty [lĕv′ĭ-tē] *noun*, lightness of mind, high spirits, happiness

le-vy [lĕv′ē] *verb*, to put a judgment on property to collect money, to impose a tax

lewd [lood] *adjective*, obscene, indecent, lecherous, lustful

lex-i-cog-ra-pher [lĕk′sĭ-kŏg′rə-fər] *noun*, a person who writes dictionaries

lex-i-con [lĕk′sĭ-kŏn′] *noun*, a dictionary, a word list

li-a-bil-i-ty [lī′ə-bĭl′ĭ-tē] *noun*, 1) a responsibility, 2) a monetary obligation, a debt

li-a-ble [lī′ə-bəl] *adjective*, 1) legally responsible 2) likely, prone, inclined, apt

li-ai-son [lē′ā-zŏn′] *noun*, cooperation that facilitates a close working relationship between people or organizations

li-ar [lī′ər] *noun*, someone who does not tell the truth

li-bel [lī′bəl] *noun*, a false statement made about someone

lib-er-al [lĭb′ər-əl] *adjective*,
1) progressive reform
2) generous, ample, abundant

lib-er-ate [lĭb′ə-rāt′] *verb*, to free
from constraints, to release

lib-er-a-tion [lĭb′ə-rā′shən] *noun*,
freeing, emancipation

lib-er-ty [lĭb′ər-tē] *noun*, freedom,
independence from foreign rule

li-bi-do [lĭ-bē′dō] *noun*, emotional
urges behind human activity

li-brar-i-an [lī-brâr′ē-ən] *noun*,
one who has charge or care of
the materials in a library

li-brar-y [lī′brĕr′ē] *noun*, 1) a place
where books are kept for reading
and research 2) a room or
building where books and
documents are preserved for
future generations

lib-ret-to [lĭ-brĕt′ō] *noun*, the text
of an opera or other dramatic
musical work

li-cense [lī′səns] *noun*, 1) authority
given to do any act 2) excess of
liberty, *verb*, 3) to authorize

li-cen-tious [lī-sĕn′shəs] *adjective*,
unprincipled, unrestrained

li-chen [lī′kən] *noun*, a fungus that
grows like algae on rocks and
tree bark

lick [lĭk] *noun*, 1) a stroke of the
tongue over something *verb*,
2) to touch with the tongue 3) to
defeat

lic-o-rice [lĭk′ər-ĭs] *noun*, a dried
root, or an extract used in candy

lid [lĭd] *noun*, a cover for a pot or
pan, or some other container

lie [lī] *noun*, 1) the intentional
statement of an untruth, *verb*,

2) to put oneself in a reclining
position 3) to say something that
is not true, to fib

lien [lēn] *noun*, a legal claim upon
real or personal property

lieu [loō] *preposition*, in place, as
in the phrase "in lieu of"

lieu-ten-ant [loō-tĕn′ənt] *noun*,
1) a substitute for another in
performance of any duty 2) a
commissioned officer in the
military below captain

life [līf] *noun*, 1) the ability of
living organisms to grow and
reproduce 2) the period between
birth and death

lift [lĭft] *noun*, 1) a free ride in a car
or other form of transportation 2)
the means by which something is
raised, *verb*, 3) to pick up, to
raise, to elevate 4) to go up, to
ascend

lig-a-ment [lĭg′ə-mənt] *noun*, a
tough band of fibrous tissue
connecting bones, or to support
an organ in place in the body

light [līt] *adjective*, 1) buoyant, not
heavy 2) carefree, *noun*, *no
plural*, 3) the opposite of
darkness, *verb*, 4) to ignite a fire
5) to illuminate, to brighten

light-ning [līt′nĭng] *noun*, *no
plural*, flashing of light by
electricity discharged from one
cloud to another during a storm

like [līk] *adjective*, 1) similar to,
equal to, *preposition*,
2) resembling, typical of, *verb*,
3) to enjoy, to find agreeable

like-ly [līk′lē] *adjective*,
1) expected, probable, suitable,
adverb, 2) probably, certainly

like-ness [līk′nĭs] *noun*,
1) similarity, resemblance, 2) a picture of a person, a portrait

like-wise [līk′wīz′] *adverb*, in the same way, also, similarly

li-lac [lī′lək] *noun*, a shrub in the olive family that has fragrant white or purple flowers

lil-li-pu-tian [lĭl′ə-pyōō′shən] *adjective*, extremely small

lil-y [lĭl′ē] *noun*, a plant with trumpet-like flowers and thick tubular roots

limb [lĭm] *noun*, 1) a part of the body such as an arm or leg or wing 2) the large branch of a tree

lim-ber [lĭm′bər] *adjective*, flexible, elastic, easy to bend

lim-bo [lĭm′bō] *noun*, 1) a place near heaven or hell where certain souls are kept 2) a West Indian dance 3) a state of oblivion

lime [līm] *noun*, a green citrus fruit, similar to a lemon, grown on trees in warm climates

lim-it [lĭm′ĭt] *noun*, 1) that which terminates or confines 2) the full extent, *verb*, 3) to set boundaries, to restrict

lim-i-ta-tion [lĭm′ĭ-tā′shən] *noun*, shortcomings, restriction

lim-ou-sine [lĭm′ə-zēn′] *noun*, a long automobile with many seats and a permanent top

limp [lĭmp] *adjective*, 1) without stiffness, not firm, *noun*, 2) the way you walk when one leg is hurt, *verb*, 3) to walk carefully without putting too much pressure on the leg or foot

lim-pid [lĭm′pĭd] *adjective*, crystal clear, transparent

line [līn] *noun*, 1) the distance between 2 points 2) people or things arranged in a row 3) a business or vocation 4) a streak made with a pencil and ruler 5) a collection of points along a straight path that goes on and on in opposite directions 6) a boundary marker 7) dialogue in performance, *verb*, 8) to put a layer between the container and the product 9) to collect in a row, to watch or wait for something 10) to draw a thin mark

lin-en [lĭn′ən] *noun*, a thread or cloth made of flax

lin-er [lī′nər] *noun*, a first class passenger ship or airplane

lin-ger [lĭng′gər] *verb*, 1) to stay on longer than expected, to dawdle 2) to persist

lin-ge-rie [län′zhə-rā′] *noun*, lacey, silk or cotton underwear worn by women, undergarments

lin-guis-tic [lĭng-gwĭs′tĭk] *adjective*, pertaining to language

lin-i-ment [lĭn′ə-mənt] *noun*, a liquid applied to soothe the skin

lin-ing [lī′nĭng] *noun*, a fold, an overlay that forms a covering

link [lĭngk] *noun*, 1) a connection, a bond, a tie, *verb*, 2) to be joined together, to unite

li-no-le-um [lĭ-nō′lē-əm] *noun*, a washable floor covering having a base of solidified oil on a canvas foundation

lint [lĭnt] *noun*, dirt, dust, fuzz

li-on [lī′ən] *noun*, one of the big cats that lives in Africa

lip [lĭp] *noun*, one of the soft red rims round the mouth

liq-uid [lĭk′wĭd] *adjective,* 1) flowing like water, *noun,* 2) fluid, not solid or gas

liq-ui-date [lĭk′wĭ-dāt′] *verb,* to sell possessions for cash

liq-uor [lĭk′ər] *noun,* any liquid substance, an alcoholic beverage

lisp [lĭsp] *noun,* a speech impediment making it difficult to make an **S** sound

list [lĭst] *noun,* 1) names of different things written down one after another, *verb,* 2) to order things by writing them down in a sequence

lis-ten [lĭs′ən] *verb,* to pay attention to what someone is saying, to heed

list-less [lĭst′lĭs] *adjective,* lacking spirit or energy, languid, tired

lit [lĭt] *past tense* of **light**

lit-a-ny [lĭt′n-ē] *noun,* a prayer in the form of a religious song alternating with the congregation

li-ter [lē′tər] *noun,* a unit in the metric system used to measure liquid equal to 1.057 quarts

lit-er-ac-y [lĭt′ə-r′ə-sē] , *noun* the ability to listen, speak, read, write, view, represent, compute, and solve problems at levels of proficiency necessary to function in the family, in the community, and on the job

li-ter-ate:*adjective,* able to read and write

lit-er-al-ly [lĭt′ər-ə-lē] *adverb,* word for word, as stated, verbatim

lit-er-a-ture [lĭt′ər-ə-chŏŏr′] *noun, no plural,* 1) the study of writing and books 2) printed material

lithe [līth] *adjective,* pliable, bendable, limber, supple

lith-i-um [lĭth′ē-əm] *noun,* a soft, silver-white metallic element of the alkali group

lit-i-gant [lĭt′ĭ-gənt] *noun,* a person who wants to sue another

lit-i-ga-tion [lĭt′ĭ-gā′ shən] *noun,* the subject of a lawsuit, any matter before the court or a judge

lit-mus [lĭt′məs] *noun,* a coloring matter obtained from lichens, that is violet-blue, and turns red by an acid, and is restored to blue by an alkali

lit-ter [lĭt′ər] *noun,* 1) newborn baby animals, offspring 2) trash, small pieces of garbage thoughtlessly discarded, *verb,* 3) to throw trash on the ground, not in a garbage can

lit-tle [lĭt′l] *adjective,* 1) a small amount or size 2) a brief period of time

live [līv, lĭv] *adjective,* 1) performed unrehearsed, broadcasted directly 2) full of energy, *verb,* 3) to be, to exist 4) to reside in, to inhabit 5) to be active and to satisfy an ideal

live-li-hood [līv′lē hŏŏd] *noun,* the means of supporting oneself

live-ly [līv′lē] *adverb,* full of energy, very active, full of life

liv-er [lĭv′ər] *noun,* an organ inside the body which cleans the blood

live-stock [līv′stŏk′] *noun,* animals raised on a farm or ranch

livid

liv-id [lĭv′ĭd] *adjective*, 1) angry
2) lead colored, black and blue

liv-ing [lĭv′ĭng] *adjective*, 1) alive,
noun, 2) a manner of existence

liz-ard [lĭz′ərd] *noun*, a cold
blooded reptile with four short
legs and a scaly body

lla-ma [lä′mə] *noun*, a South
American ruminant animal,
related to the camel and raised
for its fleecy wool

load [lōd] *noun*, 1) something
carried by a person, vehicle or
animal 2) a burden, *verb*, 3) to
put cargo or materials on a truck
or vehicle 4) to fill a gun with
ammunition 5) to burden

loaf [lōf] *noun*, 1) the whole
amount of bread before it is
sliced, *verb*, 2) to take it easy, to
idle away time, to waste time

loan [lōn] *noun*, 1) a thing,
especially money, lent to another
person, *verb*, 2) to let someone
borrow something, to lend

loathe [lōth] *verb*, to detest, to feel
intense dislike for, to abhor

lob-by [lŏb′ē] *noun*, 1) an entrance
way, a foyer, *verb*, 2) to
influence, to pressure, to sway

lob-ster [lŏb′stər] *noun*, an edible
sea animal with a shell, a tail,
and ten legs

lo-cal [lō′kəl] *adjective*, regional,
in a confined area or place

lo-cal-i-ty [lō-kăl′ĭ-tē] *noun*, a
position, a situation, a place

lo-cate [lō′kāt′] *verb*, to find, to
search out, to come across

lo-ca-tion [lō-kā′shən] *noun*, where
something is, a certain place

lock [lŏk] *noun*, 1) a device for
fastening things like doors that
can only be opened or closed
with a key or secret code 2) a
strand of hair, *verb*, 3) to close
and make secure 4) to fasten
with a lock

lock-er [lŏk′ər] *noun*, a box often
with a lock, for keeping things

lo-co-mo-tive [lō′kə-mō′tĭv] *noun*,
a railroad engine that pulls trains

lo-cust [lō′kəst] *noun*, an insect
like a grasshopper that travels in
swarms and eats plants

lode [lōd] *noun*, vein-like deposit
of mineral ore

lodge [lŏj] *noun*, 1) a place to stay
where you pay for the service,
verb, 2) to pay to stay
someplace, like a motel or inn
3) to become embedded in
something

loft [lôft] *noun*, an upper room, a
storage area, an attic

loft-y [lôf′tē] *adjective*, very high

log [lôg, lŏg] *noun*, 1) a piece of
wood that was part of the trunk
or limb of a tree 2) a book of
records, a register of a trip

log-ic [lŏj′ĭk] *noun*, the art of
correct reasoning, especially of
inference, sound judgment

log-i-cal [lŏj′ĭ-kəl] *adjective*, in a
way that is orderly and makes
sense, reasonable

lo-go [lō′gō′] *noun*, a slogan or
symbol that represents a name

loi-ter [loi′tər] *verb*, to hang
around, to linger aimlessly, to
proceed slowly, to waste time

190

lone [lōn'] *adjective*, single, one, standing apart, isolated

lone-li-ness [lōn'lē-něs] *noun*, feeling alone, solitude

lone-ly [lōn'lē] *adjective*, 1) a sad, depressing feeling because one is alone 2) desolate, remote

long [lông] *adjective*, 1) measuring a distance from one end to another 2) farther or taller than the others 3) an extended period or time, *adverb*, 4) a time in the distant past 5) conditionally, *verb*, 6) to want something badly, to pine, to yearn

lon-gev-i-ty [lŏn-jěv'ĭ-tē] *noun*, to live the duration of a long life

long-ing [lông'ĭng] *verb*, desiring, wanting, yearning, craving

lon-gi-tude [lŏn'jĭ-tood'] *noun, no plural,* imaginary lines shown on maps that go from north to south along the earth's surface, measured in degrees east and west from the prime meridian, which runs north and south through Greenwich, England

look [look] *noun*, 1) a glance, a gaze 2) appearance, *verb*, 3) to stare, or glance at 4) to seem or appear 5) to expect, to await

loom [loom] *noun*, 1) a machine used to weave cloth from yarn, *verb*, 2) to hover over 3) likely to happen in the future

loop [loop] *noun*, a ring made by a rope or string crossing itself

loop-hole [loop'hōl'] *noun*, a way of getting around a law or legal agreement, a means of escape

loose [loos] *adjective*, 1) not fastened tightly or securely 2) free, not confined or shut in

loos-en [loo'sən] *verb*, to become unfastened, to make less tight

loot [loot] *noun*, 1) money or spoils, *verb*, 2) to steal, to rob, to pillage and plunder

lop-sid-ed [lŏp'sī'dĭd] *adjective*, hanging over to one side, uneven

lo-qua-cious [lōkwā'shəs] *adjective*, talkative, chatty, fond of talking

lord [lôrd] *noun*, 1) a person having great power or authority, a master or ruler 2) the title for a judge, bishop, or nobleman

lore [lôr] *noun*, a lesson, a teaching

lose [looz] *verb*, 1) to fail to win 2) to misplace something

loss [lôs] *noun*, 1) damage, injury, ruin 2) deprivation

lost [lôst] *adjective*, 1) confused, bewildered, disoriented 2) wasted 3) the *past tense* of **lose**

lot [lŏt] *noun*, 1) a piece of land or property 2) a large quantity of something 3) a kind or sort

lo-tion [lō'shən] *noun*, a liquid put on the skin to add moisture and make it soft or clean

lot-tery [lŏt'ə-rē] *noun*, a game of gambling in which a prize is given to the person with the matching digits drawn from a pool of numbers

lo-tus [lō'təs] *noun*, a water plant with white, yellow, blue or pink flowers, a water lily

loud [loud] *adjective*, 1) noisy, making or having a loud sound 2) offensively bright colors

Lou-i-si-ana [loo-ē-'zē-ăn'ə] *noun*, one of the 50 United States located in the South, the capital is Baton Rouge. The state flower of **Louisiana** is the flower of the magnolia tree, and the motto is "Union, justice, confidence."

lounge [lounj] *noun*, 1) a couch with little or no back 2) a room in a bar where people relax and listen to music, *verb*, 3) to rest or recline comfortably

louse [lous] *noun, plural,* **lice**, a small insect without wings that lives on the skin of animals, birds, and people

lous-y [lou′zē] *adjective*, bad

lov-a-ble [lŭv′ə-bəl] *adjective*, able to be loved, warm, deep feeling

love [lŭv] *noun*, 1) a very strong warm feeling or deep concern for someone, commitment 2) darling, sweetheart, *verb*, 3) to feel passion, or a strong affection for someone or something

love-ly [lŭv′lē] *adjective*, beautiful, having pleasing qualities

lov-ing [lŭv′ĭng] *adjective*, showing affection or fondness

low [lō] *adjective*, 1) close to the ground, not very high 2) quiet, not very loud 3) coarse, mean 4) inferior quality

low-er [lou′ər] *adjective*, 1) inferior 2) less 3) under, *verb*, 4) to make something closer to the ground 5) to diminish the volume of sound 6) to demean, to debase in estimation

loy-al [loi′əl] *adjective*, true and faithful to a person

loy-al-ty [loi′əl-tē] *adjective*, allegiance, faithfulness

lu-bri-cant [lōō′brĭ-kənt] *noun*, grease or gear oil

lu-bri-cate [lōō′brĭ-kāt′] *verb*, to make smooth or slippery

lu-cent [lōō′sənt] *adjective*, glowing with light, shining

lu-cid [lōō′sĭd] *adjective*, 1) bright, 2) easily understood, clear

luck [lŭk] *noun*, 1) something good or bad that happens by chance or accident 2) good fortune

luck-y [lŭk′ē] *adjective*, fortunate

lu-cra-tive [lōō′krə-tĭv] *adjective*, profitable, money making

lu-cre [lōō′kər] *noun*, money

lu-di-crous [lōō′dĭ-krəs] *adjective*, funny, ridiculous, absurd

lug-gage [lŭg′ĭj] *noun, no plural*, bags, suitcases, trunks and traveling accessories, baggage

luke-warm [lōōk′wôrm′] *adjective*, not very warm, but not cold, room temperature, tepid

lull [lŭl] *noun*, 1) a quiet interval, a pause, *verb*, 2) to soothe, to calm

lull-a-by [lŭl′ə-bī′] *noun*, a soft song that puts someone to sleep

lum-ba-go [lŭm-bā′gō] *noun*, rheumatic pain in the loins and small of the back

lum-ber [lŭm′bər] *noun*, 1) logs or timber cut into planks or boards, *verb*, 2) to move along slowly and heavily, to plod

lu-mi-nous [lōō′mə-nəs] *adjective*, 1) well lit, bright, radiating light 2) glowing in the dark

lump [lŭmp] *noun*, 1) a swelling on the body that becomes a mass 2) a hard form without a special shape or size, *verb*, 3) to put together in a pile

lu-nar [lōō′nər] *adjective*, having to do with the moon

lu-na-tic [lōō′nə-tĭk] *adjective*, 1) crazy, mad, psychotic, *noun*, 2) an insane person

lunch [lŭnch] *noun*, the meal you eat in the middle of the day

lunch-eon [lŭn′chən] *noun*, a midday meal enjoyed with others

lung [lŭng] *noun*, one of the two sac-like organs inside the chest with which we breathe

lunge [lŭnj] *verb*, to leap, to charge at someone suddenly

lu-pine [lōō′pən] *noun*, a plant related to peas and beans with tall spikes of flowers

lure [lōōr] *noun*, 1) something appealing, *verb*, 2) to entice, to bait, to attract, to tempt

lu-rid [lōōr′ĭd] *adjective*, horrible, sensational, shocking, gruesome

lurk [lûrk] *verb*, to wait in hiding, to watch someone without their knowledge, to go furtively

lus-cious [lŭsh′əs] *adjective*, appealing to taste or smell

lust [lŭst] *noun*, 1) a strong feeling of wanting something that would be selfish 2) sexual appetite

lus-ter [lŭs′tər] *noun*, shine, brightness, sheen or gloss

lux-u-ri-ous [lŭg-zhōōr′ē-əs] *adjective*, fine and expensive, very nice, sumptuous

lux-u-ry [lŭg′zhə-rē] *noun*, an item that adds to pleasure and comfort

lynch [lĭnch] *verb*, to hang someone in an act of mob violence

lyr-ic [lĭr′ĭk] *noun*, a poem intended to be a song

M

ma-ca-bre [mə-kä′brə] *adjective*, horrible, gruesome, ghastly

mac-a-ro-ni [măk′ə-rō′nē] *noun*, a flour paste dried in long slender tubes, pasta

ma-chet-e [mə-shĕt′ē] *noun*, a long, curved knife used for cutting tall vegetation

mach-i-na-tion [măk′ə-nā′shən] *noun*, a scheme, a plot, or plan

ma-chine [mə-shēn′] *noun*, a device made to consume energy to produce another form of energy to do some kind of work

ma-chin-er-y [mə-shē′nə-rē] *noun*, *no plural*, equipment, devices

mack-er-el [măk′ər-əl] *noun*, a fish found traveling in schools in the North Atlantic

mad [măd] *adjective*, 1) insane, crazy, out of your right mind, reckless 2) angry, enraged

mad-am [măd′əm] *noun*, a respectful way of speaking to or writing to a woman

made [mād] *past tense* of **make**

mad-ri-gal [măd′rĭ-gəl] *noun*, a folk song or ballad of the 16th and 17th century

mael-strom [māl′strəm] *noun*, a powerful whirlpool

maes-tro [mīs′trō] *noun*, an eminent composer, a master

mag-a-zine [măg′ə-zēn′] *noun*, a pamphlet or news summary published periodically

mag-ic [măj′ĭk] *noun*, *no plural*, 1) the art or pretended art of controlling forces through the use of secret charms 2) clever tricks done to outsmart people, using sleight of hand

mag-i-cal [măj′ĭ-kəl] *adjective*, enchanting, marvelous

ma-gi-cian [mə-jĭsh′ən] *noun*, one who uses tricks to do things that seem impossible

mag-is-trate [măj′ĭ-strāt′] *noun*, a public civil officer charged with administering the law, a justice of the peace

mag-nan-i-mous [măg-năn′ə-məs] *adjective*, great of mind, generous and forgiving

mag-nate [măg′nāt′] *noun*, a person of prominence and influence, a tycoon

mag-ne-si-um [măg-nē′zē-əm] *noun*, a ductile silver-white metallic element

mag-net [măg′nĭt] *noun*, 1) a combination of metals that have a force that attract metals like iron 2) something that attracts

mag-net-ic [măg-nĕt′ĭk] *adjective*, 1) possessing the properties of the magnet 2) exerting a moral attractive force or charm

mag-nif-i-cence [măg-nĭf′ĭ-səns] *adjective*, grandeur, splendor

mag-nif-i-cent [măg-nĭf′ĭ-sənt] *adjective*, wonderful, impressive

mag-ni-fy [măg′nə-fī′] *verb*, to increase the size of what you are looking at, to enlarge

mag-ni-fy-ing glass [măg′nə-fī′ĭng glăs] *noun*, a lens that enlarges something small so that it is easier to see

mag-ni-tude [măg′nĭ-tōōd′] *noun*, great in size, or extent

ma-hog-a-ny [mə-hŏg′ə-nē] *noun*, a hard, reddish wood from tropical American trees

maid [mād] *noun*, a female servant

maid-en name [mād′n-nām] *noun*, a woman's last name before she is married

mail [māl] *noun*, letters and packages sent through and delivered by the postal service

maim [mām] *verb*, to injure so that part of the body is useless

main [mān] *adjective*, chief, most important, the center piece

Maine [mān] *noun*, one of the 50 United States located in New England, the capital is Augusta. The state flower of **Maine** is the eastern white pine cone and tassel, and the motto is "Direct or guide."

main-spring [mān′sprĭng′] *noun*, the principal spring in a mechanism, as in a watch

main-stay [mān′stā′] *noun*, 1) pillar, support 2) strength

main-tain [mān-tān′] *verb*, 1) to hold or keep in any particular condition, to preserve 2) to support, to insist

main-te-nance [mān'tə-nəns]
noun, no plural, upkeep

maize [māz] *adjective,* 1) pale
yellow, *noun,* 2) corn

ma-jes-ti-cal-ly [mə-jĕs'tĭk-lē]
adverb, with grandeur and
stately dignity, regal

maj-es-ty [măj'ĭ-stē] *noun,* the title
of a sovereign power, grandeur

ma-jor [mā'jər] *adjective,* 1) chief,
most important, the largest,
noun, 2) an officer in the
military between Lieutenant
Colonel and General

ma-jor-i-ty [mə-jôr'ĭ-tē] *noun,* the
greater number, more than half

make [māk] *verb,* 1) to create or
produce 2) to force 3) to earn or
win 4) to appoint or name

mal-aise [mă-lāz'] *noun,*
uneasiness, distress, fatigue

mal-a-prop-ism
[măl'ə-prŏp-ĭz'əm] *noun,* comic
misuse of a word, *i.e., a verbal
agreement isn't worth the paper
it is written on*

ma-lar-i-a [mə-lâr'ē-ə] *noun,* a
disease produced by the bite of a
mosquito causing a fever

male [māl] *adjective,* 1) belonging
to men and boys, *noun,* 2) a
grown boy, masculine, manly

ma-lev-o-lent [mə-lĕv'ə-lənt]
adjective, wishing evil or harm

mal-ice [măl'ĭs] *noun,* a desire to
inflict bad feelings on another

ma-lign [mə-līn'] *verb,* to say bad
things about someone

ma-lig-nant [mə-lĭg'nənt]
adjective, tending or threatening
to produce death as a tumor

mal-le-a-ble [măl'ē-ə-bəl] *adjective,*
1) capable of being extended or
shaped by beating with a hammer
2) easy to influence

mal-let [măl'ĭt] *noun,* a stick, a
club, a hammer-like tool

mal-nu-tri-tion [măl'noo-trĭsh'ən]
noun, no plural, undernourishment
caused by poor diet

mal-prac-tice [măl' prăk'tĭs] *verb,*
professional misconduct especially
by a physician

mam-mal [măm'əl] *noun,* any
warm-blooded vertebrate that
nurses its young

mam-moth [măm'əth] *adjective,*
very large, gigantic, huge

man [măn] *noun, plural,* **men,**
1) a full grown male person
2) speaking of mankind in
general *verb,* 3) to supply with
people

man-age [măn'ĭj] *verb,* 1) to
succeed in getting something
done, to reach a goal 2) to
control or have power over
something 3) to function

man-age-a-ble [măn'-ĭ-jə-bəl]
adjective, governable,
submitting to control

man-age-ment [măn'ĭj-mənt]
noun, people who manage any
enterprise, an administration

man-ag-er [măn'ĭ-jər] *noun,* a
person who looks after and
directs the activities of a
business, a supervisor

man-date [măn'dāt'] *noun,* an
order, a command

man-da-to-ry [măn'də-tôr'ē]
adjective, required, imperative

man-drel [măn'drəl] *noun,* an axis
inserted to support something

mane [mān] *noun*, the long hair on the back of the neck of an animal, such as a horse or lion

ma-neu-ver [mə-nōō′vər] *noun*, 1) a military movement 2) a scheme or manipulation, *verb*, 3) to move in a skillful way

mange [mānj] *noun*, a contagious skin disease of animals marked by itching and hair loss

man-go [măng′gō] *noun*, a juicy fruit with a large seed that grows on a tree in tropical climates

ma-ni-ac [mā′nē-ăk′] *noun*, a madman, an insane person

man-i-cure [măn′ĭ-kyŏŏr′] *noun*, a grooming of hands and fingernails

man-i-fest [măn′ə-fĕst′] *adjective*, 1) something obvious or clear, *noun*, 2) an invoice of a ship's, or truck's, or plane's cargo, *verb*, 3) to show, to display, to reveal

man-i-fes-to [măn′ə-fĕs′tō] *noun*, a statement of policy and plans

man-i-fold [măn′ə-fōld′] *adjective*, having many and various kinds or features

ma-nip-u-late [mə-nĭp′yə-lāt′] *verb*, 1) to treat or work with the hands 2) to control the action of something by management

man-kind [măn′kīnd′] *noun*, *no plural*, all human beings

man-ner [măn′ər] *noun*, 1) the way in which something is done or happens, prevailing customs *plural*, 2) ways of behaving in social situations

man-or [măn′ər] *noun*, a large house, a mansion,

man-sion [măn′shən] *noun*, a large, impressive house, a castle

man-tel [măn′tl] *noun*, 1) the shelf above a fireplace 2) the earth's interior layer between the crust and the core

man-u-al [măn′yōō-əl] *adjective*, 1) done by hand, *noun*, 2) an instruction guide

man-u-fac-ture [măn′yə-făk′chər] *verb*, to assemble parts into a product in a factory

ma-nure [mə-nōōr′] *noun*, livestock excrement

man-u-script [măn′yə-skrĭpt′] *noun*, a copy of a work intended for publication

man-y [mĕn′ē] *adjective*, containing a large number of something

map [măp] *noun*, 1) a representation of the physical features of the earth, *verb*, 2) to plan, to chart, to outline

ma-ple [mā′pəl] *noun*, a hardwood tree that produces sweet sap, boiled into syrup

mar [mär] *verb*, to damage, to hurt, to disfigure, to impair, to injure

mar-ble [mär′bəl] *noun*, *no plural*, 1) a hard stone that polishes well, used in buildings 2) a small glass or stone ball used in a game

March [märch] *noun*, the third month of the year, having 31 days

march [märch] *noun*, 1) the distance of a walk using regular steps 2) a piece of music to which soldiers walk, *verb*, 3) to walk with measured steps, to advance in this manner

mare [mâr] *noun*, a female horse

mar-ga-rine [mär′jər-ĭn] *noun*, *no plural*, a butter substitute made from vegetable oils

mar-gin [mär′jĭn] *noun*, 1) the border of empty space around the text on paper 2) a deposit of a portion of the value of stocks or bonds

mar-gin-al [mär′jə-nəl] *adjective*, borderline, passable

mar-i-gold [măr′ĭ-gōld′] *noun*, a yellow or orange flower that is a member of the daisy family

ma-rine [mə-rēn′] *noun*, having to do with the sea

mar-i-on-ette [măr′ē-ə-nĕt′] *noun*, a puppet manipulated by strings

mar-i-time [măr′ĭ-tīm′] *adjective*, bordering on the sea, nautical

mark [märk] *noun*, 1) a spot or a scratch, imprint 2) a point or the total of points indicating how one has scored on an examination or in a class 3) a distinguishing feature, *verb*, 4) to indicate a line or boundary 5) to leave a spot or write something 6) to distinguish

mar-ket [mär′kĭt] *noun*, 1) a store, an outlet, a shop 2) supply and demand, commodity market, *verb*, 3) to develop ways to sell a product by making it attractive

mar-ma-lade [mär′mə-lād′] *noun*, a preserve or jam made of the pulp and rind of fruit

ma-roon [mə-rōōn′] *verb*, to leave someone isolated

mar-riage [măr′ĭj] *noun*, a wedding ceremony, the state of being married

mar-row [măr′ō] *noun*, soft tissue filling in cavities of bones

mar-ry [măr′ē] *verb*, to take someone as a husband or wife

marsh [märsh] *noun*, a low, wet place where the ground is damp and swampy, a bog

mar-shal [mär′shəl] *noun*, 1) the master of ceremonies of a parade or an event 2) an officer of justice similar to a sheriff, *verb*, 3) to manage, to direct

mar-su-pi-al [mär-sōō′pē-əl] *noun*, animals that nurse their offspring in a pouch

mar-tial [mär′shəl] *adjective*, pertaining to military affairs, war or battle, inclined to war

mar-tyr [mär′tər] *noun*, one who suffers persecution, torture or death for a cause or beliefs

mar-vel [mär′vəl] *noun*, 1) something that is remarkable or exciting, *verb*, 2) to be filled with wonder or astonishment

mar-vel-ous [mär′və-ləs] *adjective*, astonishing, causing wonder

Mary-land [mĕr′ə-lənd] *noun*, one of the 50 United States located on the east coast, the capital is Annapolis. The state flower of **Maryland** is the black-eyed susan and the motto is "Manly deeds, womanly words."

mas-cot [măs′kŏt′] *noun*, an animal or person that represents a school, team, or other group

mas-cu-line [măs′kyə-lĭn] *adjective*, of or pertaining to the male sex, manly

mash [măsh] *verb*, to make into a pulpy mass or mush

mask [măsk] *noun*, 1) a covering that hides a face or its expressions *verb*, 2) to disguise or hide, to cover, to conceal

ma-son [mā′sən] *noun*, a person
who builds with brick, stone, etc.

mas-quer-ade [măs′kə-rād′] *noun*,
1) a party at which people wear
masks and sometimes costumes,
verb, 2) to dress in costume, to
wear a disguise, to conceal

mass [măs] *noun*, 1) a quantity or
amount of something with no
particular shape or number
2) the quantity of matter that a
body contains as measured by
the force of gravity on it
3) a large gathering of people
4) in the Catholic church the
celebration of the Eucharist

Mas-sa-chu-setts [măs′ə-choo′sĭts]
noun, one of the 50 United
States, located on the east
coast, the capital is Boston. The
state flower of **Massachusetts**
is the mayflower, and the motto
is "By the sword we seek peace,
but peace only under liberty."

mas-sa-cre [măs′ə-kər] *noun*,
1) the killing of many
defenseless people, *verb*, 2) to
murder a large number of people

mas-sage [mə-säzh′] *noun*, 1) a
rubdown, kneading of the body
with the hands *verb*, 2) to rub to
stimulate circulation, to caress

mas-sive [măs′ĭv] *adjective*, heavy,
weighty, consisting of a large
amount, immense, huge

mast [măst] *noun*, a tall pole that
holds up a ship's sail

mas-ter [măs′tər] *noun*, 1) an
accomplished artist, a teacher ,
one in control 2) the title of
address in front of a boy's name,
verb 3) to accomplish a difficult
task

mas-ter-piece [măs′tər-pēs′] *noun*, a
fine example of skill or excellence

mat [măt] *noun*, 1) a floor covering
made of straw, rubber, vinyl,
etc. 2) a tangled hair mass

match [măch] *noun*, 1) a slender
piece of wood or cardboard
tipped with a flammable mixture
2) a sports contest, 3)a person or
thing equal to another *verb*, 4)
to sort similar objects, to pair up

mate [māt] *noun*, 1) an associate,
one of a male and female pair of
animals, birds, etc. *verb*, 3) to
bring together a male and
female animal to reproduce

ma-te-ri-al [mə-tîr′ē-əl] *adjective*,
1) pertaining to or composed of
matter 2) of consequence,
substantial, *noun* 3) data 4) cloth,
the fabric something is made of
5) possessions, real things not
spiritual things

ma-te-ri-al-ize [mə-tîr′ē-ə-līz′]
verb, to take form, to emerge

ma-ter-nal [mə-tûr′nəl] *adjective*,
motherly, relating to a mother

ma-ter-ni-ty [mə-tûr′nĭ-tē] *noun*,
motherhood, the time during
pregnancy, or for a mother to
care for a newborn infant

math-e-mat-ics [măth′ə-măt′ĭks]
noun, *plural*, the study of
numbers, arithmetic

ma-tin-ee [măt′n-ā′] *noun*, an
afternoon theater performance

ma-tri-arch [mā′trē-ärk′] *noun*, the
woman who rules a family or
social group, clan or tribe

mat-ri-mo-ny [măt′rə-mō′nē]
noun, marriage, wedlock

ma-trix [mā′trĭks] *noun*, 1) an
environment from which
something develops or originates
2) a mold or die

mat-ter [măt′ər] *noun*, *no plural*,
1) the substance of which
something is made 2) a situation
or affair *verb*, 3) to be of
importance, to signify

mat-tress [măt′rĭs] *noun*, a stuffed
cushion to sleep on

ma-ture [mə-tyŏŏr′] *adjective*,
fully grown or developed, adult

ma-tu-ri-ty [mə-tyŏŏr′ĭ-tē] *noun*,
adulthood, full development

maud-lin [môd′lĭn] *adjective*,
tearfully sentimental

maul [môl] *verb*, to handle
roughly, to lacerate

mau-so-le-um [mô′sə-lē′əm] *noun*,
a stately tomb, an above ground
structure for burials

mav-er-ick [măv′ər-ĭk] *noun*, a
rebel, a nonconformist

max-im [măk′sĭm] *noun*, a
proverb, wise words

max-i-mum [măk′sə-məm]
adjective, 1) greatest attainable,
most, *noun*, 2) the largest
amount possible

May [mā] *noun*, the fifth month of
the year, having 31 days

may [mā] *verb*, 1) used to show
that something is possible 2) to
be allowed or permitted to 3)
showing a hope that something
will happen

may-be [mā′bē] *adverb*, perhaps,
possibly

may-hem [mā′hĕm′] *noun*,
commotion, disturbance

may-on-naise [mā′ə-nāz′] *noun*, a
dressing for salad or sandwiches,
usually made from eggs and oil

may-or [mā′ər, mâr] *noun*, the
chief magistrate and leader of a
city or town

me [mē] *pronoun*, the form of "I"
used as an object, used by a
speaker to refer to himself or
herself

mead-ow [mĕd′ō] *noun*, a field of
grass or flowers, grassland

mea-ger [mē′gər] *adjective*, small
in amount, scant

meal [mēl] *noun*, food served and
eaten, the occasion for eating

mean [mēn] *adjective*, 1) unkind,
cruel, uncaring 2) the middle,
verb, 3) to be the same as, to
have as a definition 4) to intend
to do something 5) to denote

me-an-der [mē-ăn′dər] *verb*, to
wander around, to follow a path
with twists and turns

mean-ing [mē′nĭng] *noun*, 1) the
definition of a word 2) the
significance of an action , signs
or symbols

means [mēnz] *noun*, *plural*,
resources that help us to do
what we want to do, wealth

meant [mĕnt] *verb*, *past tense* of
mean

mean-while [mēn′hwīl′] *adverb*,
at the same time

mea-sles [mē′zəlz] *noun*, *plural*, a
contagious disease marked by
distinct red circular spots,
accompanied by a fever

meas-ure [mĕzh/ər] *noun*, 1) a standard or test 2) dimension, size, capacity 3) step, action, proceeding, maneuver, *verb*, 4) to take measurements, to gauge, to scale, to calibrate

meas-ure-ment [mĕzh/ər-mənt] *noun*, the size, weight, distance, mass, etc. of something

meat [mēt] *noun*, the parts of an animal's body used as food

me-chan-ic [mĭ-kăn/ĭk] *noun*, 1) one who repairs cars or other machines, 2) *plural*, **mechanics**, the inner workings or things, the study of how machines work

mech-an-ism [mĕk/ə-nĭz/əm] *noun*, 1) the parts of a machine taken collectively 2)any system that works like a machine

med-al [mĕd/l] *noun*, a small, award, often embossed, given for achievement

med-dle [mĕd/l] *verb*, to interfere

me-di-a [mē/dē-ə] *plural*, *noun*, see **medium**

me-di-an [mē/dē-ən] *adjective*, 1) halfway, central, *noun*, 2) the middle, center, mid-point

me-di-ate [mē/dē-āt/] *verb*, to settle a dispute as an impartial third party

med-i-cal [mĕd/ĭ-kəl] *adjective*, healing, therapeutic

me-dic-i-nal [mĭ-dĭs/ə-nəl] *adjective*, having properties that cure disease or sickness

med-i-cine [mĕd/ĭ-sĭn] *noun*, 1) the study and treatment of illness 2) a remedy to treat disease and restore good health

me-di-e-val [mē/dē-ē/vəl] *adjective*, characteristic of the Middle Ages from about the fifth to the fifteenth centuries

me-di-oc-ri-ty [mē/dē-ŏk/rĭ-tē] *noun*, the average, commonplace, ordinary

med-i-tate [mĕd/ĭ-tāt/] *verb*, to think deeply

med-i-ta-tion [mĕd/ĭ-tā/shən] *noun*, deep, solemn reflection

me-di-um [mē/dē-əm] *adjective*, 1) sized between large and small, *noun*, 2) conditions, the environment 3) a means to communicate with the dead *plural*, **media**, 4) a network of communication such as television, radio, newspapers , etc. that reaches the public

med-ley [mĕd/lē] *noun*, a mixture

meek [mēk] *adjective*, humble, gentle, patient, quiet

meet [mēt] *verb*, to come face to face, to approach, to encounter

meet-ing [mē/tĭng] *noun*, 1) a gathering to discuss an issue or idea 2) point of contact

meg-a-phone [mĕg/ə-fōn/] *noun*, a cone or electric device that amplifies the sound of a voice

mel-an-chol-y [mĕl/ən-kŏl/ē] *adjective*, 1) filled with sorrow, very sad, *noun,* 2) a feeling of sadness characterized by depression

mel-low [mĕl/ō] *adjective*, 1) good-natured, relaxed, *verb*, 2) to soften with maturity

mel-o-dy [mĕl/ə-dē] *noun*, a harmonious tune, music

mel-on [mĕl/ən] *noun*, a large juicy fruit growing on vines

melt [mĕlt] *verb*, to change to a liquid state by applying heat

mem-ber [mĕm/bər] *noun*, 1) one of the limbs of the body, such as a leg, arm, hand, etc. 2) a part of a group, a component 3) one that belongs to a certain group

mem-ber-ship [mĕm/bər-shĭp/] *noun*, the state of belonging to a certain group

mem-brane [mĕm/brān/] *noun*, a thin piece or layer of animal or vegetable tissue that serves to cover separate cells, organs, etc.

me-men-to [mə-mĕn/tō] *noun*, a token as a reminder, a souvenir

mem-oir [mĕm/wär/, -wôr/] *noun*, an autobiography

mem-o-ra-ble [mĕm/ər-ə-bəl] *adjective*, worthy of remembrance, remarkable

mem-o-ran-dum [mĕm/ə-răn/dəm] *noun*, a note made as a reminder, a written message, a memo

me-mo-ri-al [mə-môr/ē-əl] *noun*, a monument, a marker, a statue

mem-o-rize [mĕm/ə-rīz/] *verb*, to commit to memory, to learn by heart, to remember exactly

mem-o-ry [mĕm/ə-rē] *noun*, something a person remembers, the ability to remember

men-ace [mĕn/ĭs] *noun*, a danger

me-nag-er-ie [mə-năj/ə-rē] *noun*, a varied group or collection of animals, persons, or things that are strange, odd, or startling

mend [mĕnd] *verb*, 1) to repair or fix, to sew a tear, or patch a hole

2) to heal, to improve, to recover from illness 3) to set right a dispute

me-ni-al [mē/nē-əl] *adjective*, suitable for servants, low

men-in-gi-tis [mĕn/ĭn-jī/tĭs] *noun*, an infection of the three membranes that envelop the brain and spinal cord, that could be fatal

men-tal [mĕn/tl] *adjective*, of or existing in the mind

men-tal-ly [mĕn/tl-lē] *adverb*, in or using the mind, intellectually

men-tion [mĕn/shən] *noun*, 1) a reference, a notice, *verb*, 2) to remark, to refer to briefly

men-tor [mĕn/tôr/] *noun*, a trusted teacher, a wise counselor

men-u [mĕn/yoō] *noun*, 1) a list indicating the choice of meals at a restaurant 2) a list of options in a computer program

mer-chan-dise [mûr/chən-dīz/] *noun*, 1) commodities, wares, goods, *verb*, 2) to sell, to promote, to market

mer-chant [mûr/chənt] *noun*, a person who buys and sells goods

mer-ci-ful [mûr/sĭ-fəl] *adjective*, compassionate, kind-hearted

mer-ci-less [mûr/sĭ-lĭs] *adjective*, cruel, unkind, showing no compassion, inhumane

mer-cu-ry [mûr/kyoŏrē] *noun, no plural*, a heavy, silver-white metallic chemical element, liquid at ordinary temperatures

mer-cy [mûr/s *noun*, the act of sparing someone punishment shown to an offender or enemy

mere [mîr] *adjective*, not more than what is specified, only

mere-ly [mîr′lē] *adverb*, simply, hardly, barely

merge [mûrj] *verb*, to combine into one, to blend gradually

me-rid-i-an [mə-rĭd′ē-ən] *noun*, an imaginary great circle on the surface of the earth, passing through the poles and any given place on the earth's surface

mer-it [mĕr′ĭt] *noun*, 1) worth, good qualities, *verb*, 2) to deserve

mer-maid [mûr′mād′] *noun*, a mythical creature that lives in the water, having the head and torso of a woman and the tail of a fish

mer-ry [mĕr′ē] *adjective*, happy, full of laughter, joyful

me-sa [mā′sə] *noun*, a flat-topped hill with steep sides, common in dry areas

mesh [mĕsh] *noun*, 1) a net-like material of cords or wires that interlock with spaces between them, like a screen, *verb*, 2) to blend, to intertwine

mes-mer-ize [mĕz′mə-rīz′] *verb*, to hypnotize, to spellbind

mess [mĕs] *noun*, 1) many things mixed up, a jumble, *verb*, 2) to make something dirty or untidy 3) to make a muddle of

mes-sage [mĕs′ĭj] *noun*, 1) a letter or note 2) a communication transmitted from one person to another 3) a central theme

mes-sen-ger [mĕs′ən-jər] *noun*, one who does an errand, a carrier

mes-sy [mĕs′ē] *adjective*, untidy

met [mĕt] *past tense* of **meet**

me-tab-o-lism [mĭ-tăb′ə-lĭz′əm] *noun*, the chemical and physical changes in living cells that process energy in the body

met-al [mĕt′l] *noun*, 1) a chemical element such as silver or gold, or any combination of metals, such as brass, copper, or nickel

met-al-lic [mə-tăl′ĭk] *adjective*, resembling, pertaining to or consisting of metal

meta-mor-phic [mĕt′ə-môr′fĭk] *adjective*, changed in form

met-a-mor-pho-sis [mĕt′ə-môr′fə-sĭs] *noun*, a change from one form of development or shape into another

met-a-phor [mĕt′ə-fôr′] *noun*, a figure of speech in which one thing is spoken of in terms of another, *i.e., the road was a ribbon of moonlight...*

met-a-phys-ics [mĕt′ə-fĭz′ĭks] *noun*, speculative philosophy

me-te-or [mē′tē-ər′] *noun*, a fragment of solid matter that enters the earth's atmosphere and burns, leaving a bright streak in the sky

me-te-or-ite [mē′tē-ə-rīt′] *noun*, the metallic or stony remains of a body that has entered the earth's atmosphere

me-te-or-ol-o-gist [mē′tē-ə-rŏl′ə-jĭst] *noun*, a person who studies the weather

me-ter [mē′tər] *noun*, 1) a machine used for measuring 2) a measure of length equal to 100 centimeters or approximately 39 inches 3) the rhythm in a poem

meth-od [mĕth′əd] *noun*, a process or system used to do something

me-thod-i-cal [mə-thŏd′ĭ-kəl] *adjective*, systematic, orderly

Me-tho-dist [mə-thŏdĭst] *noun*, a member of the Protestant Christian denomination that developed from the teachings of John and Charles Wesley

me-tic-u-lous [mĭ-tĭk′yə-ləs] *adjective*, extremely careful

met-ric sys-tem *noun*, a system that measures length in centimeters, meters, and kilometers; capacity in liters, mass in grams and kilograms; temperature in degrees Celsius

me-trop-o-lis [mĭ-trŏp′ə-lĭs] *noun*, the chief city of a country, state or region, an urban center

met-tle [mĕt′l] *noun*, courage, spirit, fortitude, character

Mich-i-gan [mĭsh′ĭ-gən] *noun*, one of the 50 United States, located in the North, the capital is Lansing. The state flower of **Michigan** is the apple blossom and the motto is "If you seek a pleasant peninsula, look about you."

mi-cro-cosm [mī′krə-kŏz′əm] *noun*, a small world

mi-cro-or-gan-ism [mī′krō-ôr′gə-nĭz′əm] *noun*, an animal , bacterium, plant, or virus that can only be seen with a microscope

mi-cro-phone [mī′krə-fōn′] *noun*, a device that converts sounds into electrical energy signals that can then be amplified

mi-cro-scope [mī′krə-skōp′] *noun*, an optical instrument with a lens that makes it possible to see things too small to be seen with the naked eye

mi-cro-scop-ic [mī′krə-skŏp′ĭk] *adjective*, too small to be seen with a naked eye

mid [mĭd] *adjective*, halfway

mid-dle [mĭd′l] *adjective*, 1) halfway between two points, median, central, *noun*, 2) the center, the point equally distant from two sides

mid-get [mĭj′ĭt] *noun*, a small person who is fully mature

mid-night [mĭd′nīt′] *noun*, 12 o'clock at night

midst [mĭdst, mĭtst] *noun*, the middle, the central point

might [mīt] *noun*, *no plural*, 1) strength or force, *verb*, 2) *past tense* of **may**

might-y [mī′tē] *adjective*, strong, powerful, important, great

mi-grant [mī′grənt] *adjective*, one who travels from place to place in search of work

mi-grate [mī′grāt] *verb*, 1) to move from one land to settle in another 2) to make a journey each year from one place to another at the same time of year

mi-gra-tion [mī-grā′shən] *noun*, movement to leave one area to live in another

mild [mīld] *adjective*, 1) gentle in feeling 2) not severe or extreme

mile [mīl] *noun*, a measure of length equal to 5,280 feet, 1,760 yards, or 1.6 kilometers

mile-age [mī′lĭj] *noun*, 1) an allowance for the cost per mile traveled 2) the total amount of miles traveled in a given time

mile-stone [mīl′stōn′] *noun*, a turning point, a great achievement or significant event

mil-i-tant [mĭl′ĭ-tənt] *adjective*, 1) warlike, combative, *noun*, 2) a revolutionary, a violent objector, a terrorist

mil-i-tar-y [mĭl′ĭ-tĕr′ē] *noun*, the armed forces of a country

milk [mĭlk] *noun*, 1) the liquid produced by a female mammal to feed her young, *verb*, 2) to force milk from a female mammal

mill [mĭl] *noun*, a building or group of buildings in which resources such as lumber, cotton, corn and steel, are processed

mil-len-ni-um [mə-lĕn′ē-əm] *noun*, a span of one thousand years

mil-li-liter [mĭl′ə-lē′tər] *noun*, a liquid measure equal to 1/1000 of a liter, or less than .04 fluid ounces

mil-li-me-ter [mĭl′ə-mē′tər] *noun*, a measure of length, 1/1000 of a meter, or about .04 inches

mil-lion [mĭl′yən] *noun*, ten times one hundred thousand, 1,000,000

mil-lion-aire [mĭl′yə-nâr′] *noun*, a person whose property and assets total $1,000,000

mime [mīm] *noun*, 1) a performer who only uses motion and facial expression, but no voice, to communicate, *verb*, 2) to use actions instead of speech to communicate

mim-e-o-graph [mĭm′ē-ə-grăf′] *noun*, a stenciling copying device fed by an ink drum

mim-ic [mĭm′ĭk] *verb*, to copy or repeat what someone does or says, to imitate playfully

mim-ic-ry [mĭm′ĭ-krē] *noun*, an imitation, an impersonation

min-a-ret [mĭn′ə-rĕt′] *noun*, a lofty slender tower attached to a mosque

mince [mĭns] *verb*, 1) to cut into very small pieces 2) to moderate or restrain words

mind [mīnd] *noun*, 1) thoughts, a person's reason or way of feeling, *verb*, 2) to watch over, to pay attention to, to obey

mine [mīn] *noun*, 1) a large hole or tunnel deep in the ground made to reach and remove metals or other natural resources from the earth, *pronoun*, 2) something that belongs to the person who is speaking, *verb*, 3) digging into land to remove metal ore or other valuable resources

min-er-al [mĭn′ər-əl] *noun*, any inorganic substance occurring naturally in the earth

min-gle [mĭng′gəl] *verb*, to join or mix together, to blend

min-i-a-ture [mĭn′ē-ə-chŏŏr′] *adjective*, 1) very small, done on a small scale, *noun*, 2) a very small painting, especially a portrait

min-i-mum [mĭn′ə-məm] *adjective*, 1) smallest, *noun*,

2) the least quantity possible or allowable in a given case

min-is-ter [mĭn′ĭ-stər] *noun*,

1) the head of a government department in some countries 2) a representative to a foreign country ranking under an ambassador 3) a Christian member of the clergy, *verb*, 4) to give help to someone, to care for, to serve, to attend

min-is-try [mĭn′ĭ-strē] *noun*, 1) a department of government headed by a minister 2) the work of the clergy 3) the act of serving

Min-ne-so-ta [mĭn′ĭ-sō′tə] *noun*, one of the 50 United States located in the North, the capital is St. Paul. The state flower of **Minnesota**, is the pink and white lady slipper and the motto is,"The star of the north."

min-now [mĭn′ō] *noun*, a small fish

mi-nor [mī′nər] *adjective*,

1) smaller, not very important *noun*, 2) a person younger than the legal age

mi-nor-i-ty [mə-nôr′ĭ-tē] *noun*, a number, part or amount forming less than half of a whole

mint [mĭnt] *noun*, 1) a large amount of money 2) any of the plants of the mint family, used to flavor food, gum, etc.3) a candy

mi-nus [mī′nəs] *preposition*, less

min-ute [mĭn′ĭt] *adjective*, 1) very small, *noun*, 2) a period of time equal to sixty seconds

mi-nu-ti-a [mĭ-nōo′shē-ə] *noun*, *plural*, **minutiae**, very small, petty details, trifling matters

mir-a-cle [mĭr′ə-kəl] *noun*, an occurrence that is unusual and goes beyond the laws of nature

mi-rac-u-lous [mĭ-răk′yə-ləs] *adjective*, supernatural, awesome, incredible

mi-rage [mĭ-räzh′] *noun*, an unreal reflection, an optical illusion

mire [mīr] *noun*, 1) a bog, a swamp, *verb*, 2) to immerse in swampy ground, to entangle

mir-ror [mĭr′ər] *noun*, 1) a looking glass in which one can see reflections 2) something that reflects

mirth [mûrth] *noun*, laughter, glee

mis-be-have [mĭs′bĭ-hāv′] *verb*, to behave badly, to be disruptive

mis-cel-la-ne-ous [mĭs′ə-lā′nē-əs] *adjective*, consisting of several different kinds, mixed, various

mis-chief [mĭs′chĭf] *noun*, an annoying action on the part of a person, havoc, harm or damage

mis-chie-vous [mĭs′chə-vəs] *adjective*, causing petty injury or annoyance to others

mis-con-cep-tion [mĭs′kən-sĕp′shən] *noun*, a misunderstanding, a mistake

mis-con-duct [mĭs-kŏn′dŭkt] *noun*, wrongdoing, improper behavior

mis-con-strue [mĭs′kən-strōo′] *verb*, to misunderstand

mis-cre-ant [mĭs′krē-ənt] *noun*, an evil person, a lawbreaker

mis-de-mean-or [mĭs′dĭ-mē′nər] *noun*, a crime less than a felony, any minor misdeed

mi-ser [mī′zər] *noun*, a tightwad, one who hoards money

mis-er-a-ble [mǐz′ər-ə-bəl] *adjective*, unhappy, causing misery

mis-er-y [mǐz′ə-rē] *noun*, great unhappiness, or distress

mis-for-tune [mǐs-fôr′chən] *noun*, bad luck, something bad that happens, an unlucky event

mis-giv-ing [mǐs-gǐv′ǐng] *noun*, a feeling of worry, doubt about a future event, apprehension

mis-hap [mǐs′hăp′] *noun*, an unfortunate accident

mis-in-ter-pret [mǐs′ǐn-tûr′prǐt] *verb*, to confuse, to mistake

mis-judge [mǐs-jŭj′] *verb*, to mistake, to underestimate

mis-lead [mǐs-lēd′] *verb*, to lead astray, to deceive, to lie

mis-lead-ing [mǐs-lē′dǐng] *adjective*, deceptive, vague, unclear, not accurate

mis-no-mer [mǐs-nō′mər] *noun*, the wrong name, an incorrect identification

mis-place [mǐs-plās′] *verb*, to lose temporarily, to mislay

Miss [mǐs] *noun*, the title before the name of an unmarried woman

miss [mǐs] *noun*, 1) a failure, an error, a slip, *verb*, 2) to fail to make the most of an opportunity or moment 3) to notice someone's absence, to feel sad someone is gone 4) to avoid, to fail to hit, to escape 5) to omit

mis-sile [mǐs′əl] *noun*, a weapon capable of being hurled

mis-sion [mǐsh′ən] *noun*, a special service, task or duty

mis-sion-ar-y [mǐsh′ə-nĕr′ē] *noun*, one whose work is to teach others about his religion

Mis-sis-sip-pi [mǐs′ǐ-sǐp′ē] *noun*, one of the 50 United States, located in the South, the capital is Jackson. The state flower of **Mississippi** is the magnolia blossom, and the motto is "By valor and arms."

mis-sive [mǐs′ǐv] *noun*, a letter

Mis-sou-ri [mǐ-zŏŏr′ē] *noun*, one of the 50 Unieted States, located in the Midwest, the capital is Jefferson City. The state flower of **Missouri** is the hawthorn, and the motto is:"Let the welfare of the people be the supreme law."

mis-spell [mǐs-spĕl′] *verb*, to spell incorrectly

mist [mǐst] *noun*, a thin cloud of fine droplets of water vapor or fog near the ground

mis-take [mǐ-stāk′] *noun*, an error, the wrong answer or action

Mis-ter [mǐs′tər] *noun*, a title for a man, abbreviated, 'Mr.'

mis-tle-toe [mǐs′əl-tō′] *noun*, a plant that lives off another, with evergreen leaves and white berries used at Christmas for decoration

mis-tress [mǐs′trǐs] *noun*, a woman who has control over others

mis-trust [mǐs-trŭst′] *noun*, 1) suspicion, uncertainty, doubt, lack of confidence, *verb*, 2) to doubt, to question, to challenge

mist-y [mǐs′tē] *adjective*, hazy, damp, and foggy, consisting of a mass of fine droplets of water vapor in the atmosphere

mis-un-der-stand
[mĭs′-ŭn-dər-stănd′] *verb*, to
misconstrue, to mistake

mite [mīt] *noun*, 1) a small amount
2) a small, usually parasitic
arachnid, related to the tick

mi-ter [mī′tər] *verb*, to bevel the
ends for the purpose of matching
together, as a picture frame

mitt [mĭt] *noun*, a baseball glove
with padding to protect the hand

mit-ten [mĭt′n] *noun*, a glove with
a section for covering the thumb
and a larger section to cover all
four fingers

mix [mĭks] *verb*, to combine
different things to make one

mix-ture [mĭks′chər] *noun*, a
combination of different
substances

moan [mōn] *verb*, to make a sound
of pain or suffering, to complain

mob [mŏb] *noun*, a crowd, a horde

mo-bile [mō′bəl, *adjective* 1)
moveable, portable, [mō′-bīl′]
noun, 2) objects attached by a
wire that move airily

mo-bi-lize [mō′bə-līz′] *verb*, to put
into action, to move

moc-ca-sin [mŏk′ə-sĭn] *noun*, a
heelless shoe of deerskin or
other soft leather

mock [mŏk] *adjective*, 1) not real,
pretended, 2) *verb*, to make fun
of, to treat with ridicule

mode [mōd] *noun*, 1) manner
2) fashion, style

mod-el [mŏd′l] *noun*, 1) a person
who sets a good example 2) a
version of something that can be
studied, a copy, 3) someone

who wears clothes for
advertisement, *verb*, 3) to make
a copy of something 4) to wear
clothes as part of an exhibit

mod-er-a-tion [mŏd′ər-ā′shən]
noun, restraint, a happy medium

mod-ern [mŏd′ərn] *adjective*,
representative of the current
trends and fashions

mod-est [mŏd′ĭst] *adjective*,
1) humble, decent 2) simple

mod-es-ty [mŏd′ĭ-stē] *noun*, *no
plural*, humility, decency

mod-i-cum [mŏd′ĭ-kəm] *noun*, a
moderate or small amount

mod-i-fi-ca-tion
[mŏd′ə-fĭ-kā′shən] *noun*, a slight
change in form, an alteration

mod-i-fy [mŏd′ə-fī′] *verb*, to
change, to adjust, to alter

mod-u-late [mŏj′ə-lāt′] *verb*, to
adjust the sound

mo-gul [mō′gəl] *noun*, a powerful
person, especially in business

moist [moist] *adjective*, a little wet,
damp, humid, soggy

mois-ture [mois′chər] *noun*, *no
plural*, small drops of water,
wetness caused by water

mo-lar [mō′lər] *noun*, one of
several back teeth used for
chewing

mo-las-ses [mə-lăs′ĭz] *noun*, the
thick brown syrup drained from
sugar in the refining process

mold [mōld] *noun*, 1) a cast for
shapes into which a substance is
poured 2) a furry substance that
grows on clothing or food if left
damp and away from the sun, it is
a kind of small fungus, *verb*, 3)

to shape something into a form or a mold

mold-ing [mōl′dĭng] *noun*, a plane or curved narrow surface, used for ornamentation

mole [mōl] *noun*, 1) a small insectivore that makes and lives in holes underground 2) a small round brown mark on the skin

mol-e-cule [mŏl′ĭ-kyōōl′] *noun*, 1) a unit of matter consisting of two or more atoms combined 2) a particle

mo-lest [mə-lĕst′] *verb*, 1) to touch without permission 2) to annoy

molt [mōlt] *verb*, to shed the outer skin, feathers or exoskeleton

mol-ten [mōl′tən] *adjective*, made liquid by great heat, melted

mo-ment [mō′mənt] *noun*, a very brief period of time, an instant

mo-men-tar-y [mō′mən-tĕr′ē] *adjective*, fleeting, passing

mo-men-tous [mō-mĕn′təs] *adjective*, very important

mo-men-tum [mō-mĕn′təm] *noun*, the force or speed of movement

mon-arch [mŏn′ərk, -ärk′] *noun*, a king or queen 2) an orange and black butterfly

mon-ar-chy [mŏn′ər-kē] *noun*, a government headed by one person, a king or a queen

mon-as-ter-y [mŏn′ə-stĕr′ē] *noun*, a residence in which monks live

Mon-day [mŭn′dē, -dā′] *noun*, the second day of the week

mon-e-tar-y [mŏn′ĭ-tĕr′ē] *adjective*, of or pertaining to money or currency, pecuniary

mon-ey [mŭn′ē] *noun*, currency and coins issued by a government to use in exchange for goods or services

mon-i-tor [mŏn′ĭ-tər] *noun*, 1) a pupil or student given authority 2) a video screen attached to a computer, *verb*, 3) to keep watch over, to supervise, to check

monk [mŭngk] *noun*, a religious man who lives with other men who devote their lives to prayer and religion, a member of a religious order

mon-key [mŭng′kē] *noun*, a primate that usually has a long tail and lives in trees

mon-o-gram [mŏn′ə-grăm′] *noun*, initials consisting of two or more letters interwoven, usually written, embroidered, or engraved

mon-o-logue [mŏn′ə-lôg′] *noun*, a long speech, a soliloquy

mo-nop-o-lize [mə-nŏp′ə-līz′] *verb*, to have exclusive possession of something

mo-nop-o-ly [mə-nŏp′ə-lē] *noun*, exclusive control of the supply of any commodity

mon-o-the-ism [mŏn′ə-thē-ĭz′əm] *noun*, belief in one God

mon-o-tone [mŏn′ə-tōn′] *noun*, a voice that never changes in pitch

mo-not-o-nous [mə-nŏt′n-əs] *adjective*, 1) unvarying in pitch 2) repetitiously dull, being the same all the time

mon-soon [mŏn-sōōn′] *noun*, heavy rains and strong winds in southern Asia

mon-ster [mŏn′stər] *noun*, 1) an animal or person with a strange or unusual shape 2) an imaginary and usually frightening creature

Mon-tana [mŏn-tăn′ə] *noun*, one of the 50 United States located in the Northwest, the capital is Helena. The state flower of **Montana** is the bitteroot, and the motto is "Gold and silver."

month [mŭnth] *noun*, a period of 30 days, four weeks, or 1/12 of the year

mon-u-ment [mŏn′yə-mənt] *noun*, a statue or building erected as a tribute to someone who has died

mon-u-men-tal [mŏn′yə-mĕn′tl] *adjective*, massive, enormous, exceptionally great

mood [mōōd] *noun*, the way a person feels, state of mind

moon [mōōn] *noun*, the large body in the sky that shines at night, a satellite of a planet

moose [mōōs] *noun*, a large North American and Eurasian deer

moot [mōōt] *adjective*, questionable, debatable

mop [mŏp] *noun*, 1) a tool with a long handle and a sponge or fabric on the bottom used for cleaning floors, *verb*, 2) to clean the floor, usually with soap and water or to remove spilled liquids

mor-al [môr′əl] *adjective*, ethical, honest, concerned with right conduct, virtuous, upright

mo-rale [mə-răl′] *noun*, spirit, confidence, resolve,

mo-ral-i-ty [mə-răl′ĭ-tē] *noun*, virtue, righteousness, ethics

mor-al-ly [môr′ə-lē] *adverb*, in accordance with ethical duty, righteously, respectfully

mor-a-to-ri-um [môr′ə-tôr′ē-əm] *noun*, 1) a suspension, an interval 2) a legal delay of payment

mor-bid [môr′bĭd] *adjective*, depressing, having to do with disease, gruesome

more [môr] *adjective*, 1) larger in amount or number, *adverb*, 2) again, in addition

mo-res [môr′āz′] *noun*, *plural*, the customs of a society, the code of acceptable conduct

morgue [môrg] *noun*, a place where dead bodies go to be identified before burial

Mor-mon [môr mŭn] *noun,* a member of the Church of Jesus Christ of Latter-day Saints founded in the U.S. in 1830 by Joseph Smith

morn-ing [môr′nĭng] *noun*, the time from when the sun rises until noon or the time from midnight to noon

mo-rose [mə-rōs′] *adjective*, sad, dejected, gloomy or sullen

mor-phine [môr′fēn′] *noun*, a narcotic derived from opium

morse code [môrs kōd] *noun*, *no plural*, a way of sending messages using flashing lights or a pattern of sounds

mor-sel [môr′səl] *noun*, a little piece of food, a crumb

mor-tal [môr′tl] *adjective*, 1) destructive to life, fatal 2) human and therefore able to die

mor-tal-i-ty [môr-tăl′ĭ-tē] *noun,* the condition of being mortal

mor-tar [môr′tər] *noun,* 1) a mixture made of cement, lime, sand, and water, used to hold bricks or stone together 2) a short cannon used to fire shells at a high angle 3) a bowl in which substances are crushed to a powder with a pestle

mort-gage [môr′gĭj] *noun,* a legal agreement regarding property between a borrower and a lender

mor-ti-cian [môr-tĭsh′ən] *noun,* an undertaker, a funeral director

mor-ti-fy [môr′tə-fī′] *verb,* to shame, to belittle, to humiliate

mor-tu-ar-y [môr′chōō-ĕr′ē] *noun,* a place where dead bodies are kept until burial or cremation

mo-sa-ic [mō-zā′ĭk] *noun,* a surface decoration made by inlaying small pieces of variously colored material such as tile, marble, or glass

Mos-lem [mŏz′ləm] *noun, adjective,* see Muslim

mosque [mŏsk] *noun,* a holy building where Muslims worship

mos-qui-to [mə-skē′tō] *noun,* an insect capable of puncturing the skin of humans and other animals and sucking blood

moss [môs, mŏs] *noun,* a bright green plant that grows flat on wet ground and stones

most [mōst] *adjective,* 1) greatest in amount or number, *adverb,* 2) very, *noun,* 3) the largest amount or number

mote [mōt] *noun,* a small speck

moth [môth] *noun,* an insect with four wings, like a butterfly that flies at night

moth-er [mŭth′ər] *noun,* the female parent

moth-er-in-law [mŭth′ər-ĭn-lô′] *noun,* the mother of one's spouse

mo-tion [mō′shən] *noun,* the action or process of moving

mo-tion-less [mō′shən-lĭs] *adjective,* not moving

mo-ti-vate [mō′tə-vāt′] *verb,* to provide the inner drive that causes one to act

mo-ti-va-tion [mō′tə-vā′shən] *noun,* the feeling that moves one to act

mo-tive [mō′tĭv] *noun,* the reason for doing something, incentive

mo-tor [mō′tər] *noun,* a compact engine that makes things move or work

mo-tor-boat [mō′tər-bōt′] *noun,* a small boat with an engine

mo-tor-cy-cle [mō′tər-sī′kəl] *noun,* a two-wheeled vehicle without a top, moved by a motor

mot-tled [mŏt′ld] *adjective,* spotted with different colors

mot-to [mŏt′ō] *noun,* a saying or catch-phrase that expresses a belief, a guiding principle

mound [mound] *noun,* 1) a heap of earth or a small hill, a knoll 2) any small pile

mount [mount] *noun,* 1) a mountain named after someone, *verb,* 2) to rise 3) to get on 4) to ascend 5) to prepare by putting in place

moun-tain [moun′tən] *noun*, a large hill or raised part of land with steep sides that rises from the earth's surface

mourn [môrn] *verb*, to feel sadness at a loss or death of someone

mourn-ing [môr′nĭng] *noun*, *no plural*, a period of grief to honor someone who died

mouse [mous] *noun*, *plural*, **mice**, 1) a small rodent, similar to a rat 2) a hand-held device that guides the cursor or pointer on a computer

mouth [mouth] *noun*, 1) the opening through which all animals consume food 2) an entry

move [mōōv] *verb*, 1) to change position or cause something to change position 2) to go to live in a new place 3) to affect, to arouse, or influence 3) to budge, to change opionion, to go on

move-ment [mōōv′mənt] *noun*, 1) an inclination, a tendency toward change 2) action, transit, change

mov-ie [mōō′vē] *noun*, a film, a motion picture

mov-ing [mōō′vĭng] *adjective*, touching, emotional

mow [mō] *verb*, to cut grass

Mr. *noun*, a title put before a man's name

Mrs. *noun*, a title put before a married woman's name

Ms. *noun*, a title put before a woman's name

much [mŭch] *adjective*, 1) of a large amount, great. *adverb*, 2) often, to a great degree *noun*, 3) a large amount or a lot of

mucus [myōō′kəs] *noun*, spit, of or relating to mucus, a shiny substance coating the inside of the body cavities

mud [mŭd] *noun*, wet soft earth

mud-dy [mŭd′ē] *adjective*, 1) murky, dirty 2) not clear or pure

muf-fin [mŭf′ĭn] *noun*, a quick bread made from batter and baked in a cup-shaped pan

muf-fle [mŭf′əl] *verb*, to cover or suppress a sound, to tone down

muf-fler [mŭf′lər] *noun*, 1) any of various devices to deaden the noise of escaping gases or vapors 2) a scarf worn around the neck

mug [mŭg] *noun*, 1) a cup with a handle, *verb*, 2) to assault someone, usually to rob them

mug-gy [mŭg′ē] *adjective*, warm and very damp, humid

mulch [mŭlch] *noun*, a protective layer of decomposing organic matter

mule [myōōl] *noun*, an animal whose parents were a female horse and a male donkey

mul-ti-form [mŭl′tə-fôrm′] *adjective*, having many shapes or forms

mul-ti-ple [mŭl′tə-pəl] *adjective*, 1) many 2) having many parts

mul-ti-pli-ca-tion [mŭl′tə-plĭ-kā′shən] *noun*, *no plural*, the process of finding the number or quantity by repeated addition of a specified number

mul-ti-ply [mŭl′tə-plī′] *verb*, to increase by a number of times

mul-ti-tude [mŭl′tĭ-tōōd′] *noun*, a crowd, a large gathering

mum-my [mŭm′ē] *noun*, a dead body preserved with chemicals and wrapped in cloth

mumps [mŭmps] *noun*, *plural*, an illness that causes fever and swelling in the neck and throat

mun-dane [mŭn-dān′] *adjective*, commonplace, worldly as opposed to spiritual

mu-nic-i-pal [myōō-nĭs′ə-pəl] *adjective*, having a local self-government, as in a city or town

mu-ral [myōōr′əl] *noun*, a picture painted directly on a wall

mur-der [mûr′dər] *noun*, 1) the act of killing someone, either after first planning to do so or during another crime, such as a robbery, *verb*, 2) to kill a person intentionally

mur-der-er [mûr′dər-ər] *noun*, a person who intends to kill someone and does so

mur-mur [mûr′mər] *verb*, to speak very softly, to whisper

mus-cle [mŭs′əl] *noun*, an organ whose special function is to produce movement

muse [myōōz] *noun*, 1) one's inner voice as a source of creativity, **Muse**, 2) one of the nine Greek goddesses, responsible for art, music, and literature, *verb*, 3) to ponder, to meditate, to think, to reflect

mu-se-um [myōō-zē′əm] *noun*, a building that exhibits a collection of things of interest

mush-room [mŭsh′rōōm′] *noun*, a plant that is not green and is a fungus, it usually has a stem with a cap on it

mu-sic [myōō′zĭk] *noun*, the art or science of harmonic sounds

mu-si-cian [myōō-zĭsh′ən] *noun*, one who plays a musical instrument and performs

mus-ket [mŭs′kĭt] *noun*, a gun with a long barrel, used by soldiers before rifles were invented

musk-rat [mŭs′krăt′] *noun*, a rodent that lives in or near water

Mus-lim [mŭz′ləm] *noun*, a follower of the religion that believes in Allah as the one god and the teachings of Muhammed as written in the Koran

must [mŭst] *verb*, 1) used with another verb to show what is necessary or what has to be done 2) showing what is sure or likely

mus-tache [mŭs′tăsh′] *noun*, the hair covering an upper lip

mus-tang [mŭs′tăng′] *noun*, a wild horse of the American plains

mus-tard [mŭs′tərd] *noun*, 1) a plant with yellow flowers and a seed in pods 2) powder or sauce made of ground mustard seed

mu-ta-ble [myōō′tə-bəl] *adjective*, 1) changing in form 2) fickle

mute [myōōt] *adjective*, voiceless, speechless, unable to speak

mu-ti-late [myōōt′l-āt′] *verb*, to cut off or remove an essential part

mu-ti-nous [myōōt′n-əs] *adjective*, unruly, rebellious, insurgent

mu-ti-ny [myōōt′n-ē] *noun*, a revolt, a rebellion, an uprising

mu-tual [myōō′chōō-əl] *adjective*, having a common interest

muz-zle [mŭz′əl] *noun*, 1) a fastening on the mouth of an animal to prevent it from biting or eating 2) the open end of a gun from which the bullet comes out when the gun is fired, *verb*, 3) to gag, to silence, to hush, to restrain speech and expression

my [mī] *adjective*, belonging to the person speaking

my-op-ic [mī-ŏp′ĭk] *adjective*, 1) nearsighted 2) self-centered, showing lack of imagination or foresight, or intellectual insight

myr-i-ad [mĭr′ē-əd] *noun*, a very large number

my-self [mī-sĕlf′] *pronoun*, the same person as the one speaking

mys-ter-y [mĭs′tə-rē] *noun*, something not explained or beyond human comprehension

mys-ti-cal [mĭs′tĭ-kəl] *adjective*, beyond understanding, spiritual

mys-ti-fy [mĭs′tə-fī′] *verb*, to confuse, to puzzle, to bewilder

myth [mĭth] *noun*, a legendary story used to explain nature or religion and often featuring heroes or supernatural beings

my-thol-o-gy [mĭ-thŏl′ə-jē] *noun*, the study of stories and legends

N

nag [năg] *verb*, to pester, to annoy, to bother, to find faults

nail [nāl] *noun*, 1) a piece of pointed metal to be put into wood with a hammer 2) the horny tip on the ends of fingers and toes, *verb*, 3) to fasten with a hammer and nail

na-ive [nä-ēv′] *adjective*, unsophisticated, innocent

na-ked [nā′kĭd] *adjective*, without clothes, uncovered, nude

name [nām] *noun*, 1) a word given to someone or something for identification, *verb*, 2) to decide what someone or something will be called, to specify

name-ly [nām′lē] *adverb*, that is

name-sake [nām′sāk′] *noun*, one having the same name as another one, named after another

nap [năp] *noun*, 1) a short rest 2) a textured surface on fabric

nap-kin [năp′kĭn] *noun*, a piece of cloth or paper used at a meal to keep one's clothes, hands, and mouth clean while eating

nar-cot-ic [när-kŏt′ĭk] *noun*, a drug that relieves pain, blunts the senses and produces sleep

nar-rate [năr′āt′] *verb*, to make known, to tell a story, to recount

nar-ra-tive [năr′ə-tĭv] *noun*, a story, a history, a recital

nar-ra-tor [năr′āt′ ər] *noun*, a person who relates a story

nar-row [năr′ō] *adjective*, limited in width, breadth, or scope

na-sal [nā′zəl] *adjective*, associated with the nose

nas-cent [năs′ənt] *adjective*, coming into existence, the beginning

na-tion [nā′shən] *noun*, a group of people living in a particular territory under the same government, a federation

na-tion-al [năsh′ə-nəl] *adjective*, of or pertaining to a country or territory

na-tion-al-i-ty [năsh′ə-năl′ĭ-tē] *noun*, the identification of a person based on the country where he or she was born or holds citizenship

na-tive [nā′tĭv] *adjective*, 1) belonging to the place where a person is born, indigenous, *noun*, 2) a person born and raised in a certain place

nat-u-ral [năch′ər-əl] *adjective*, 1) produced by nature, not man-made 2) inborn, an innate ability

nat-u-ral-ly [năch′ər-ə-lē] *adverb*, as one would expect

na-ture [nā′chər] *noun*, *no plural*, 1) that which is not man-made, the physical world 2) traits characteristic of someone, disposition, personality

nau-se-a [nô′zē-ə] *noun*, 1) a stomach sickness accompanied by a desire to vomit 2) disgust

nau-se-ate [nô′zē-āt′] *verb*, to cause to become sick, to fill with disgust, causing a sick feeling

nau-ti-cal [nô′tĭ-kəl] *adjective*, having to do with the sea

na-val [nā′vəl] *adjective*, seafaring, nautical, relating to the navy

na-vel [nā′vəl] *noun*, the belly button, where the umbilical cord was attached before birth

nav-i-gate [năv′ĭ-gāt′] *verb*, to control in which direction a vehicle will go on a route

nav-i-ga-tion [năv′ĭ-gā′shən] *noun*, *no plural*, the ability to travel through water or plan and follow a specific route

nav-i-ga-tor [năv′ĭ-gā′tər] *noun*, one who directs and controls the course of a vehicle

na-vy [nā′vē] *noun*, the officers and personnel of warships

near [nîr] *adverb*, 1) a short distance away, *preposition*, 2) close to

near-by [nîr′bī′] *adverb*, close at hand, not far away

near-ly [nîr′lē] *adverb*, almost

near-sight-ed [nîr′sī′tĭd] *adjective*, able to see only things close by

neat [nēt] *adjective*, clean and orderly, well arranged

Ne-bras-ka [nə-brăs′kə] *noun*, one of the 50 United States, centrally located west of the Missouri River, the capital is Lincoln. The state flower of **Nebraska** is the goldenrod, and the motto is "Equality before the law."

nec-es-sar-y [nĕs′ĭ-sĕr′ē] *adjective*, needing to be done, essential

ne-ces-si-tate [nə-sĕs′ĭ-tāt′] *verb*, to demand, to require

ne-ces-si-ty [nə-sĕs′ĭ-tē] *noun*, 1) something indispensable or necessary 2) an urgent matter

neck [nĕk] *noun*, 1) the part of the body connecting the head and the torso 2) a narrow connecting part, as of a bottle

neck-lace [nĕk′lĭs] *noun*, jewelry worn around the neck

nec-tar [nĕk′tər] *noun*, a sweet liquid made by flowers

need [nēd] *noun*, 1) a lack, *verb*, 2) to lack something that is necessary or essential 3) must

nee-dle [nēd′l] *noun*, an instrument for sewing, made of steel, sharp at one end, with an eyehole for thread at the other end

need-y [nē′dē] *adjective*, poor, penniless, impoverished

neg-ate [nĕg′-āt] *verb*, 1) to deny the existence of something 2) to nullify, make ineffective

neg-a-tive [nĕg′ə-tĭv] *adjective*, 1) expressing denial, refusal or resistance, not positive, *noun*, 2) an image on developed film

ne-glect [nĭ-glĕkt′] *noun*, *no plural*, 1) disregard, carelessness, lack of care or attention, *verb*, 2) to not look after something, letting it deteriorate, to ignore

neg-li-gence [nĕg′lĭ-jəns] *noun*, failure to give the care the occasion demands

neg-li-gi-ble [nĕg′lĭ-jə-bəl] *adjective*, very small, insignificant

ne-go-ti-a-ble [nĭ-gō′shə-bəl] *adjective*, 1) transferable or able to be assigned to another person 2) able to be compromised about, open to discussion

ne-go-ti-ate [nĭ-gō′shē-āt′] *verb*, to settle, to work out, to deal or bargain with others, to compromise

neigh-bor [nā′bər] *noun*, a person who lives near another

neigh-bor-hood [nā′bər-hŏŏd′] *noun*, a small part of a community shared by a group of people who live near each other

nei-ther [nē′thər] *adjective*, *pronoun*, 1) not the one nor the other, *conjunction*, 2) not either

ne-on [nē′ŏn′] *noun*, an inert gaseous element often used in display lights

neph-ew [nĕf′yōō] *noun*, the son of a brother or a sister

nep-o-tism [nĕp′ə-tĭz′əm] *noun*, favoritism to a relative in a business situation

nerve [nûrv] *noun*, a thread in the body that carries feelings and messages to and from the brain

nerv-ous [nûr′vəs] *adjective*, very worried and a little scared

nest [nĕst] *noun*, a temporary home built by an animal or insect

nes-tle [nĕs′əl] *verb*, to be very close to someone else in a comfortable way

net [nĕt] *noun* 1) a fabric made of tying threads together in a uniform design to form a mesh 2) remaining income after deducting taxes and expenses

net-tle [nĕt′l] *noun*, 1) a weed with small thorns, *verb*, 2) to annoy, to bother, to irritate, to vex

neu-rot-ic [nŏŏ-rŏt′ĭk] *adjective*, suffering from a mental disorder characterized by anxiety and worry and phobias

neu-ter [nōō′tər] *verb*, to make sterile, to spay or castrate

neu-tral [nōō′trəl] *adjective*, 1) neither positive nor negative 2) not on either side during a war 3) in the middle 4) a position in which gears are not engaged

neu-tron [nōō′trŏn′] *noun*, an uncharged particle in an atomic nucleus

Ne-va-da [nə-văd′ə] *noun*, one of the 50 United States, located in the West, the capital is Carson City. The state flower of **Nevada** is the sagebrush, and the motto is "All for our country."

nev-er [nĕv′ər] *adverb*, not at any time, absolutely not

nev-er-the-less [nĕv′ər-thə-lĕs′] *adverb*, notwithstanding, in spite of that, yet, however

new [nōō] *adjective*, 1) not having been seen or used before 2) additional

New Hampshire [nōō hămp′shər] *noun*, one of the 50 United States located in New England, the capital is Concord. The state flower of **New Hampshire** is the purple lilac, the motto is "Live free or die."

New Jersey [nōō, jûr′zē] *noun*, one of the 50 United States located in the East, the capital is Trenton. The state flower of **New Jersey** is the purple violet and the motto is "Liberty and prosperity."

New Mexico [nōō mĕk′sĭ-kō′] *noun*, one of the 50 United States, located in the Southwest, the capital is Santa Fe. The state flower of **New Mexico** is the yucca and the motto is "It grows as it goes."

news [nōōz] *noun*, *plural*, a report of current events, things that happened recently

news-pa-per [nōōz′pā′pər] *noun*, a publication that appears daily or weekly, containing recent information

New York [nōō yôrk] *noun*, one of the 50 United States located in the Northeast, the capital is Albany. The state flower of **New York** is the rose and the motto is "Excelsior", which expresses the idea of still higher, ever upward.

next [nĕkst] *adverb*, 1) in the nearest position, without anything between 2) immediately following

nib-ble [nĭb′əl] *verb*, to eat small bites of something

nice [nīs] *adjective*, 1) kind, good 2) pleasant, socially agreeable

niche [nĭch] *noun*, 1) a small, suitable place 2) the position of a particular population in an ecological community

nick-el [nĭk′əl] *noun*, 1) five cents, equal to five pennies 2) a hard, silvery metallic element of the iron group

nick-name [nĭk′nām′] *noun*, a name given to someone which is not his real name

nic-o-tine [nĭk′ə-tēn′] *noun*, a toxic alkaloid, the addictive property of tobacco

niece [nēs] *noun*, the daughter of one's brother or sister

nig-gard-ly [nĭg′ərd-lē] *adjective*, meanly stingy, meager

night [nīt] *noun*, the time of day after the sun goes down

night-mare [nīt′mâr′] *noun*, a terrifying dream or event

nine [nīn] *adjective*, *noun*, the number 9, eight plus one

nine-teen [nīn-tēn′] *noun*, nine plus ten, written 19

nine-teenth [nīn-tēnth′]*adjective*, the number 19 in order, 19th

nine-ti-eth [nīn′tē-ĭth] *adjective*, the number ninety in order, 90th

nine-ty [nīn′tē] *noun*, written 90, 9 X 10

ninth [nīnth] *noun, adjective*, number 9 in order, 9th

nip-ple [nĭp′əl] *noun*, 1) the tip of the breast where the milk ducts discharge 2) the rubber cap on a baby bottle

nir-va-na [nîr-vä′nə] *noun*, in Buddhist teachings, the ideal state, freedom from pain and worry, perfect bliss

ni-tro-gen [nī′trə-jən] *noun*, a gas necessary for life that is colorless, tasteless and odorless

no [nō] *adjective*, 1) not any, *adverb*, 2) a word we use to answer a question, or indicate disagreement

no-bil-i-ty [nō-bĭl′ĭ-tē] *adjective*, a member of the royal circle

no-ble [nō′bəl] *adjective*, 1) aristocratic, born to wealth 2) unselfish, of good character

no-bod-y [nō′bŏd′ē] *pronoun*, no one, a person of no importance

noc-tur-nal [nŏk-tûr′nəl] *adjective*, active or functioning at night

nod [nŏd] *noun*, 1) an inclination of the head, *verb*, 2) to tip the head slightly to acknowledge something

noise [noiz] *noun*, 1) a loud harsh sound, 2) sound of any kind

no-mad [nō′măd′] *noun*, a person who travels about with a tribe and has no address or home

nom-i-nate [nŏm′ə-nāt′] *verb*, to name for an office or place

nom-i-na-tion [nŏm′ə-nā′shən] *noun*, to submit a name for an award or appointment

nom-i-nee [nŏm′ə-nē′] *noun*, a person selected or appointed to run for a position

non-cha-lant [nŏn′shə-länt′] *adjective*, showing a jaunty coolness, aloof, unconcerned

none [nŭn] *adjective*, not any, nothing, no one, not one

non-ex-ist-ent [nŏn′ĭg-zĭs′tənt] *adjective*, not real

non-fic-tion [nŏn-fĭk′shən] *noun*, a true story

non-sense [nŏn′sĕns′] *noun*, folly, silliness, absurdity, meaningless

noon [nōōn] *noun*, midday, twelve o'clock, daytime

nor [nôr; nər when unstressed] *conjunction*, a word used between two choices after neither

nor-mal [nôr′məl] *adjective*, not unusual, common, every day

nor-mal-ly [nôr′mə-lē] *adverb*, generally, ordinarily, frequently

north [nôrth] *adjective,* 1) facing or coming from the north, *adverb,* 2) to or toward the north *noun,* 3) the direction to the left of one facing east, the compass point opposite to south, **North,** 4) regions or countries north of a point that is mentioned or understood

North America [nôrth-ə-měr′ĭ-kə]
noun, one of the seven continents containing 7.9% of the world's population

North Carolina [nôrth kăr′ə-lī′nə]
noun, one of the 50 United States located in the Southeast, the capital is Raleigh. The state flower of **North Carolina** is the dogwood, the state motto is "To be rather than to seem."

North Dakota [nôrth də-kō′tə]
noun, a state located in the Northwest of the United States, the capital is Bismark. The state flower of **North Dakota** is the wild prairie rose, and the state motto is "Liberty and union, now and forever, one and inseparable."

north-east [nôrth-ēst′] *noun,* the point between north and east on a compass

north-west [nôrth-wěst′] *noun,* the point between north and west on the compass

nose [nōz] *noun,* 1) the part of the face that contains the nostrils and the organs of smell 2) the front of a plane, rocket, etc.

nose-gay [nōz′gā′] *noun,* a small hand-held fragrant bouquet

nos-tal-gia [nŏ-stăl′jə] *noun,* homesickness, a sentimental longing for something in the past

nos-tril [nŏs′trəl] *noun,* either of the external openings of the nose

not [nŏt] *adverb,* a word that forms a contradiction in a sentence

no-ta-ble [nō′tə-bəl] *adjective,* remarkable, worthy of notice

no-ta-ry [nō′tə-rē] *noun,* an officer who witnesses and verifies commercial papers and is authorized to take affidavits

no-to-ri-ous [nō-tôr′ē-əs] *adjective,* widely or commonly known, usually unfavorable

not-with-stand-ing [nŏt′wĭth-stăn′dĭng] despite, although, nevertheless

noun [*noun*] *noun,* a word that refers to a person, place, or thing

nour-ish [nûr′ĭsh] *verb,* 1) to feed or foster the growth of something 2) to keep healthy, to nurture, to strengthen

no-ta-tion [nō-tā′shən] *noun,* notes or marks to indicate something

notch [nŏch] *noun,* 1) a nick, a dent, *verb,* 2) to make a notch

note [nōt] *noun,* 1) an observation stuck in the mind 2) a bill, IOU, paper money 3) a single sound of music on the scale 4) a brief written message, *verb,* 5) to make an observation and commit it to memory 6) to mention

noth-ing [nŭth′ĭng] *adjective,* not anything, zero, insignificant

no-tice [nō′tĭs] *noun,* 1) a written warning indicating that something has happened or will happen, *verb,* 2) to observe, to become aware of

no-tice-a-ble [nō′tĭ-sə-bəl] *adjective,* capable of being observed, conspicuous

no-ti-fi-ca-tion [nō′tə-fĭ-kā′shən] *noun,* to inform someone of something, to give notice

no-ti-fy [nō′tə-fī′] *verb,* to let someone know, to inform

no-tion [nō′shən] *noun*, a general or vague idea, a thought, a whim

no-to-ri-e-ty [nō′tə-rī′ĭ-tē] *noun*, fame, renown, celebrity status

nour-ish-ment [nûr′ĭsh-mənt] *noun*, food that strengthens the body and helps it grow

nov-el [nŏv′əl] *adjective*, 1) new, unusual, *noun*, 2) a work of fiction or romance

nov-el-ist [nŏv′ə-lĭst] *noun*, a person who writes fictional stories

nov-el-ty [nŏv′əl-tē] *noun*, something new

No-vem-ber [nō-vĕm′bər] *noun*, the eleventh month of the year, having 30 days

nov-ice [nŏv′ĭs] *noun*, 1) a beginner 2) a person admitted to a religious order before taking the final vows

now [nou] *adverb*, at the present time, immediately

no-where [nō′hwâr′] *adverb*, 1) not anywhere, *noun*, 2) a place that does not exist

nox-ious [nŏk′shəs] *adjective*, harmful, deadly fumes

noz-zle [nŏz′əl] *noun*, a short outlet or pipe as of a hose, a spout

nu-ance [nōō′äns′] *noun*, a shade or trace of differences in meaning or color or tone

nu-cle-ar [nōō′klē-ər] *adjective*, using the very great power made by splitting an atom or joining atoms in nuclear fission

nu-cle-us [nōō′klē-əs] *noun*, 1) a central mass of an atom about which matter is concentrated 2) the seed of the cell is the

positively charged central region of an atom

nude [nōōd] *adjective*, naked, bare

nudge [nŭj] *noun*, 1) a gentle push, *verb*, 2) to push someone lightly

nug-get [nŭg′ĭt] *noun*, a small lump, especially of natural gold

nui-sance [nōō′səns] *noun*, anything which annoys or gives trouble, a disturbance

nul-li-fy [nŭl′ə-fī′] *adjective*, to render invalid or void

numb [nŭm] *adjective*, 1) insensitive from excessive cold 2) unable to feel pain

num-ber [nŭm′bər] *noun*, 1) a symbol representing a quantity 2) abundance, *verb*, 3) to identify with a number 4) to amount to

nu-mer-al [nōō′mər-əl] *noun*, a symbol used to represent a number

nu-mer-ous [nōō′mər-əs] *adjective*, very many, myriad, several

nun [nŭn] *noun*, a woman who gives her life to serving God

nup-tial [nŭp′shəl] *adjective*, marriage vows, a wedding

nurse [nûrs] *noun*, 1) a person who takes care of the sick and dying, *verb*, 2) to look after and attend to the needs of the sick

nurs-er-y [nûr′sə-rē] *noun*, 1) a child's room or playroom 2) a greenhouse for young plants

nur-ture [nûr′chər] *verb*, to care for, to feed and protect

nut [nŭt] *noun*, 1) the edible kernel of a seed 2) a small piece of metal with a hole in it, used to hold a bolt in place

nut-meg [nŭt′mĕg′] *noun*, the aromatic seed of an East Indian tree used as a spice

nu-tri-ent [noo′trē-ənt] *noun*, vitamins and minerals derived from food, proteins

nu-tri-tion [noo-trĭsh′ən] *noun*, a healthy diet, that nourishes the body

nu-tri-tious [noo-trĭsh′əs] *adjective*, wholesome, healthy

ny-lon [nī′lŏn′] *noun*, a strong man-made elastic thread

nymph [nĭmf] *noun*, 1) the young of an insect that has not fully developed the structural proportions and size of an adult 2) a fairy

O

oaf [ōf] *noun*, a clumsy person

oak [ōk] *noun*, a tree of hard wood bearing the acorn as a fruit

oar [ôr, ōr] *noun*, a paddle with a flat blade at the end, used to row or push a boat

o-a-sis [ō-ā′sĭs] *noun*, a fertile spot in a desert having a spring

oat [ōt] *noun*, a member of the cereal family having edible seeds such as rice, wheat or corn

oath [ōth] *noun*, a promise, a commitment, a solemn appeal

o-be-di-ence [ō-bē′dē-əns] *noun*, *no plural*, compliance with authority, submission

o-be-di-ent [ō-bē′dē-ənt] *adjective*, willing to do what one is told to do

ob-e-lisk [ŏb′ə-lĭsk] *noun*, a tall 4-sided column tapering and ending in a pyramid apex

o-bese [ō-bēs′] *adjective*, very fat

o-bey [ō-bā′] *verb*, to follow or carry out an order or law

ob-fus-cate [ŏb′fə-skāt′] *verb*, to confuse, to muddle, to obscure

o-bit-u-ar-y [ō-bĭch′oo-ĕr′ē] *noun*, an announcement of someone's death often with a short biography

ob-ject [ŏb′jĭkt] *noun*, 1) a thing, *verb*, 2) to oppose, to disagree

ob-jec-tion [əb-jĕk′shən] *noun*, a statement, a complaint

ob-jec-tive [əb-jĕk′tĭv] *adjective*, 1) not influenced by emotions, fair, *noun*, 2) a purpose or goal

ob-jur-gate [ŏb′jər-gāt′] *verb*, to scold, to rebuke severely

ob-li-ga-tion [ŏb′lĭ-gā′shən] *noun*, 1) the binding power of a promise 2) a debt of gratitude

ob-lig-a-to-ry [ə-blĭg′ə-tôr′ē] *adjective*, necessary, binding in law or conscience, mandatory

o-blige [ə-blīj′] *verb*, 1) to put under obligation, to accommodate 2) to do a favor for, to help, to assist

o-blique [ō-blēk′] *adjective*, 1) sloping or slanting 2) indirect or evasive, not explicit

ob-lit-er-ate [ə-blĭt′ə-rāt′] *verb*, to erase or blot out, to efface

ob-liv-i-on [ə-blĭv′ē-ən] *noun*, being utterly forgotten

ob-liv-i-ous [ə-blĭv′ē-əs] *adjective*, forgetful, lost in thought

ob-long [ŏb′lông′] *adjective*, a flat shape with four straight sides and four equal angles, that is longer than it is wide

ob-nox-ious [ŏb-nŏk′shəs]
adjective, annoying, offensive

ob-scure [ŏb-skyŏŏr′] *adjective*,
1) unclear, vague, unknown
2) not easily seen or heard
3) dark, hidden

ob-scu-ri-ty [ŏb-skyŏŏr′ĭ-tē] *noun*,
oblivion, no where

ob-se-qui-ous [ŏb-sē′kwē-əs]
adjective, submissive, fawning

ob-ser-vance [əb-zûr′vəns] *noun*,
1) noticing with attention 2)
compliance as a duty or custom

ob-ser-va-tion [ŏb′zər-vā′shən]
noun, the noting and recording
of facts and events

ob-serv-a-to-ry [əb-zûr′və-tôr′ē]
noun, a building equipped with
instruments for observing the
heavenly bodies, such as the
stars, moon, etc.

ob-serve [əb-zûrv′] *verb*, 1) to see
or notice 2) to comment 3) to
mark an event or day

ob-ses-sion [əb-sĕsh′ən, ŏb-] *noun*,
a fixed idea, continued brooding

ob-so-lete [ŏb′sə-lēt′] *adjective*, no
longer in use, outdated

ob-sta-cle [ŏb′stə-kəl] *noun*,
something that stands in the
way, an obstruction

ob-ste-tri-cian [ŏb′stĭ-trĭsh′ən]
noun, a physician specializing in
the delivery of babies

ob-sti-nate [ŏb′stə-nĭt] *adjective*,
not yielding to reason, stubborn

ob-struct [əb-strŭkt′] *verb*, to get
in the way of something or stop
it completely, to hinder

ob-struc-tion [əb-strŭk′shən] *noun*,
a barrier, an interference

ob-tain [əb-tān′] *verb*, to acquire or
win through effort or request

ob-tain-a-ble [əb-tān′ə-bəl]
adjective, capable of being
acquired or won

ob-trude [ŏb-trōōd′] *verb*, 1) to get
in on, to meddle, 2) to stick out

ob-tuse [ŏb-tōōs′] *adjective*, an
angle greater than 90 degrees

ob-vi-ous [ŏb′vē-əs] *adjective*,
easily seen or understood,
evident, apparent to everyone

ob-vi-ous-ly [ŏb′vē-əs-lē] *adverb*,
apparently, clearly, evidently

oc-ca-sion [ə-kā′zhən] *noun*, 1) an
event, a happening, an important
time 2) a chance, an opportunity

oc-cas-ion-al-ly [ə-kā′zhə-nə-lē]
adverb, once in a while

oc-cult [ə-kŭlt′] *adjective*, the
mysterious, secret, supernatural

oc-cu-pant [ŏk′yə-pənt] *noun*, the
inhabitant, a resident, a tenant

oc-cu-pa-tion [ŏk′yə-pā′shən]
noun, 1) a job, a way of using
time, *no plural*, 2) being in a
certain place or space

oc-cu-py [ŏk′yə-pī′] *verb*, 1) to
make or hold possession of
something 2) to live in a place

oc-cur [ə-kûr′] *verb*, 1) to happen
2) to come to mind, to appear

oc-cur-rence [ə-kûr′əns] *noun*,
something that happens

o-cean [ō′shən] *noun*, a body of
salt water covering three fifths of
the earth

o-cea-nog-ra-phy [ō′shə-nŏg′rə-fē]
noun, the study of life in the sea

221

o'clock [ə-klŏk′] *adverb*, according to the clock

Oc-to-ber [ŏk-tō′bər] *noun*, the tenth month of the year having 31 days

oc-to-pus [ŏk′tə-pəs] *noun*, a sea creature that has eight long limbs

oc-u-list [ŏk′yə-lĭst] *noun*, a doctor who treats the eyes

odd [ŏd] *adjective*, 1) any number that cannot be evenly divided by two 2) unusual, very different

odds [ŏdz] *noun*, *plural*, uncertain advantages, doubtful chances

odi-ous [ō′dē-əs] *adjective*, hateful, repulsive, repugnant

odi-um [ō′dē-əm] *noun*, repugnance, intense hatred

o-dom-e-ter [ō-dŏm′ĭ-tər] *noun*, a device in a vehicle used to measure distance traveled

o-dor [ō′dər] *noun*, a smell

o-dor-ous [ō′dər-əs] *adjective*, having a strong smell

of [ŭv] *preposition*, 1) belonging to 2) from among 3) made from 4) about 5) in relation to

off [ôf] *adverb*, 1) away from 2) not on or not working, *preposition*, 3) at a distance

of-fend [ə-fĕnd′] *verb*, to hurt someone's feelings, to insult

of-fense [ə-fĕns′] *noun*, a misdeed, an insult, a sense of insult or injury, an act of aggression

of-fen-sive [ə-fĕn′sĭv] *adjective*, 1) insulting, in poor taste, *noun*, 2) the position of an attack

of-fer [ô′fər] *noun*, 1) a proposal, a suggestion, *verb*, 2) to present to be accepted or refused

of-fice [ô′fĭs] *noun*, 1) a place in which business or professional work is done 2) a position that requires certain duties and tasks

of-fi-cer [ô′fĭ-sər] *noun*, a person lawfully invested with a position of trust or authority

of-fi-cial [ə-fĭsh′əl] *adjective*, 1) having the right or permission to do something, *noun*, 2) a person who is in charge of something 3) of or pertaining to the holding of an office

of-fi-ci-ate [ə-fĭsh′ē-āt′] *verb*, to act as an officer in performing a duty such as a minister

off-spring [ôf′sprĭng′] *noun*, descendants, children, progeny

of-ten [ô′fən] *adverb*, many times, frequently, repeatedly

o-ha-na [ōhŏna] *noun*, family, no one left behind

Ohio [ō-hī′ō] *noun*, one of the 50 United States located in the Midwest region, the capital is Columbus. The state flower of **Ohio** is the scarlet carnation and the motto is "With God all things are possible."

ohm [ōm] *noun*, the unit of electrical resistance

oil [oil] *noun*, 1) any liquid substance that does not dissolve in water 2) a nutrient derived from a pressed nut 3) a dark, thick mineral liquid, found deep in the ground 4) a substance used to burn in a lantern or lamp post, *verb*, 5) to lubricate with grease or oil

oint-ment [oint′mənt] *noun*, a
lubricant put on the skin,
containing medicine

Okla-ho-ma [ō′klə-hō′mə] *noun*,
one of the 50 United States
located in the Southwest, the
capital is Oklahoma City. The
state flower of **Oklahoma** is the
mistletoe, and the motto is
"Labor conquers all things."

old [ōld] *adjective*, 1) nót young,
having lived a long time 2) the
word we use to show our age
3) not new 4) something that has
lasted over time, antique

ol-fac-to-ry [ŏl-făk′tə-rē] *adjective*,
referring to the nose and the
sense of smell

ol-i-gar-chy [ŏl′ĭ-gär′kē] *noun*, a
government run by a few leaders

ol-ive [ŏl′ĭv] *noun*, the fruit of an
olive tree eaten as a relish

om-i-nous [ŏm′ə-nəs] *adjective*,
looking or sounding as if
something bad will happen,
portending evil or harm

o-mis-sion [ō-mĭsh′ən] *noun*,
failure to do something,
something that is left out

o-mit [ō-mĭt′] *verb*, to leave
something out, to fail to include

om-e-lette [ŏm′ə-lĭt] *noun*, eggs
beaten together and cooked in
hot fat in a flat pan

om-nip-o-tent [ŏm-nĭp′ə-tənt]
adjective, having power over all

om-ni-pres-ent [ŏm′nĭ-prĕz′ənt]
adjective, universally present at
the same time, everywhere

om-nis-cient [ŏm-nĭsh′ənt]
adjective, all-knowing

om-ni-vore [ŏm′nə-vôr′] *noun*, an
animal that eats both plants and
animals

on [ŏn] *adverb*, 1) to be precise
2) a location 3) to show time or
date 4) about 5) to continue,
preposition, 6) atop

once [wŭns] *adverb*, 1) one time
2) a long time ago

one [wŭn] *adjective*, 1) the number 1
2) the same, unified 3) act as the
same, *noun*, 4) a single thing
5) any person 6) a unit

one-self [wŭn-sĕlf′] *pronoun*, the
same person who is the subject
of the sentence

on-ion [ŭn′yən] *noun*, a garden
vegetable having an edible bulb
with pungent taste and odor

on-ly [ōn′lē] *adjective*, 1) sole, no
one else, nothing more, 2) but,
adverb, 3) merely, just

on-o-mat-o-poe-ia
[ŏn′ə-măt′ə-pē′ə] *noun*, a term
used to describe words that
actually sound like the noises
they depict such as *boom*

on-slaught [ŏn′slôt′] *noun*, a
vicious assault, a massacre

on-to [ŏn′tōō′] *preposition*, to a
place, to a position on

o-nus [ō′nəs] *noun*, 1) a burden
2) a responsibility, blame

on-ward [ŏn′wərd] *adverb*, moving
toward a point ahead, forward

ooze [ōōz] *verb*, to flow out slowly

o-pal [ō′pəl] *noun*, a precious stone
of milky hue, with a play of
iridescent colors

o-paque [ō-pāk′] *adjective*, not reflecting or giving out light, not transparent; dull, dark

o-pen [ō′pən] *adjective*, 1) not shut or covered 2) ready for business 3) not surrounded by other things 4) unbiased, free thinking, *verb*, 5) to allow entrance 6) to start, to unfold 7) to remove the cover or door 8) to undo, to untie

o-pe-ra [ŏp′ər-ə] *noun*, a dramatic presentation set to music

op-er-ate [ŏp′ə-rāt′] *verb*, to make something work or function

op-er-a-tion [ŏp′ə-rā′shən] *noun*, 1) any methodical action 2) a plan put into action 3) surgery

op-er-a-tor [ŏp′ə-rā′tər] *noun*, one who operates equipment or works as a manager

o-pi-ate [ō′pē-ĭt] *noun*, a drug which causes rest or sleep, a narcotic or sedative

o-pin-ion [ə-pĭn′yən] *noun*, a belief stronger than an impression, a point of view, a conclusion

o-pos-sum [ə-pŏs′əm] *noun*, a rodent that sleeps upside down hanging from a tree during the day, and travels at night

op-po-nent [ə-pō′nənt] *noun*, a member of the other team, an antagonist, an adversary

op-por-tune [ŏp′ər-tōōn′] *adjective*, timely, well chosen

op-por-tun-ist [ŏp′ər-tōō′nĭst] *noun*, an individual who takes advantage of a situation and ignores ethics to achieve a goal

op-por-tu-ni-ty [ŏp′ər-tōō′nĭ-tē] *noun*, a fit or convenient time, occasion, a good chance

op-pose [ə-pōz′] *verb*, to go against, to defend, to combat, to object, to resist, to fight

op-po-site [ŏp′ə-zĭt] *adjective*, 1) facing, set over against 2) one that is contrary to another

op-po-si-tion [ŏp′ə-zĭsh′ən] *noun*, against, hostile or contrary action, a negative response

op-press [ə-prĕs′] *verb*, to overpower, to subdue, to treat harshly, to hold down

op-pres-sion [ə-prĕsh′ən] *noun*, hardship, cruelty, persecution

op-pres-sive [ə-prĕs′ĭv] *adjective*, 1) unreasonably burdensome 2) tyrannical, cruel, unfair

op-tic [ŏp′tĭk] *adjective*, pertaining to the eye, light and vision

op-ti-cal [ŏp′tĭ-kəl] *adjective*, visual, seeing

op-ti-cian [ŏp-tĭsh′ən] *noun*, a person who makes glasses, a dealer in optical goods

op-ti-mal [ŏp′tə-məl] *adjective*, most favorable condition

op-ti-mist [ŏp′tə-mĭst] *noun*, one who looks on the bright side of things, positive thinking

op-ti-mis-tic [ŏp′tə-mĭs-tĭk] *adjective*, having a positive outlook, upbeat, hopeful

op-tion [ŏp′shən] *noun*, 1) a choice 2) a stock available at a certain time at a stated price

op-tom-e-trist [ŏp-tŏm′ĭ-trĭst] *noun*, one who examines eyes and fits glasses to help a person see better

op-u-lence [ŏp′yə-ləns] *adjective*, having property, wealthy, rich, affluent, luxurious

o-pus [ō′pəs] *noun*, a great creative literary or musical work

or [ôr;] *conjunction*, used to connect words when given a choice

o-ral [ôr′əl] *adjective*, 1) spoken information 2) of the mouth

or-ange [ôr′ĭnj] *adjective*, 1) a color made when red and yellow are mixed together, *noun*, 2) a sweet, juicy fruit grown on trees in tropical climates

or-a-tor [ôr′ə-tər] *noun*, a public speaker of great eloquence

or-a-to-ri-o [ôr′ə-tôr′ē-ō′] *noun*, a dramatic poem set to music

or-a-to-ry [ôr′ə-tôr′ē] *noun*, a moving or powerful speech

or-bit [ôr′bĭt] *noun*, 1) the course an object follows in space around another, *verb*, 2) to travel through space in a cycle

or-chard [ôr′chərd] *noun*, a grove where fruit trees grow for food

or-ches-tra [ôr′kĭ-strə] *noun*, 1) a band of performers on various instruments 2) the lower floor in a theater for instruments

or-chid [ôr′kĭd] *noun*, an exotic tropical flower with three petals

or-dain [ôr-dān′] *verb*, to appoint, to install, to elect, to decree

or-deal [ôr-dēl′] *noun*, an extremely stressful situation

or-der [ôr′dər] *noun*, 1) a careful arrangement 2) a special system used to organize information 3) grouping, placement 4) a request telling someone to do something, *verb*, 5) to arrange carefully 6) to issue a command, to instruct

or-di-nal num-ber [ôr′dn-əl-nŭm′bər] *noun*, a number expressing degree or order in a series such as 1st, 2nd.

or-di-nance [ôr′dn-əns] *noun*, 1) a local law, an edict or decree 2) a prescribed practice or usage

or-di-nar-i-ly [ôr′dn-âr′ə-lē] *adverb*, usually, generally

or-di-nar-y [ôr′dn-ĕr′ē] *adjective*, 1) according to custom or established order 2) regular, commonplace, normal

ore [ôr, ōr] *noun*, a kind of rock in which metal is found

Or-e-gon [ôr′ĭ-gən] *noun*, one of the 50 United States in the Northwest, the capital is Salem. The state flower of **Oregon** is the Oregon grape, and the motto is "The Union."

or-gan [ôr′gən] *noun*, 1) a musical instrument similar to a piano, with long pipes through which air travels through to make the sound 2) a part of the body that serves a specific function

or-gan-ic [ôr-găn′ĭk] *adjective*, grown naturally without pesticides or fertilizers

or-gan-ism [ôr′gə-nĭz′əm] *noun*, any individual life form

or-gan-i-za-tion [ôr′gə-nĭ-zā′shən] *noun*, an association, a group of people working together for a common purpose

or-gan-ize [ôr′gə-nīz′] *verb*, 1) to plan, to arrange and implement in an orderly way 2) to establish or construct a plan or a scheme

o-ri-en-tal [ôr′ē-ĕn′tl] *adjective*, pertaining to the Orient or East Asia

o·ri·en·ta·tion [ôr′ē-ĕn-tā′shən] *noun*, the act of getting your bearings, an introduction

or·i·fice [ôr′ə-fĭs] *noun*, a mouthlike opening, a slit, any hole in a body

or·i·gin [ôr′ə-jĭn] *noun*, the first use or the beginning

o·rig·i·nal [ə-rĭj′ə-nəl] *adjective*, the first of its kind, new and different, inventive

o·rig·i·nal·i·ty [ə-rĭj′ə-năl′ĭ-tē] *noun*, creativeness, innovation

o·rig·i·nate [ə-rĭj′ə-nāt′] *verb*, 1) to bring into existence, to initiate 2) to produce as new

or·na·ment [ôr′nə-mənt] *noun*, a decoration, beautification

or·na·men·tal [ôr′nə-mĕn′tl] *adjective*, decorative, adorned, beautiful, embellished

or·nate [ôr-nāt′] *adjective*, excessively decorated, adorned

or·ni·thol·o·gist [ôr′nə-thŏl′ə-jĭst] *noun*, one who studies birds

or·phan [ôr′fən] *noun*, a child whose parents are dead

or·phan·age [ôr′fə-nĭj] *noun*, a home for children who have no family

or·tho·dox [ôr′thə-dŏks′] *adjective*, accepted, traditional doctrine, very conservative

or·thog·ra·phy [ôr-thŏg′rə-fē] *noun*, correct spelling

os·cil·late [ŏs′ə-lāt′] *verb*, 1) to swing backward and forward, to vibrate 2) varying above or below a mean value

os·si·fy [ŏs′ə-fī′] *verb*, 1) to change or harden cartilage into bone 2) to set into a repeating pattern

os·ten·si·ble [ŏ-stĕn′sə-bəl] *adjective*, shown, professed, apparent, pretended

os·ten·ta·tious [ŏs′tĕn-tā′shəs] *adjective*, pretentious, conspicuous, showiness as an attempt to attract attention

os·tra·cize [ŏs′trə-sīz′] *verb*, to banish, to cast out from social favor or fellowship

os·trich [ŏs′trĭch] *noun*, a very large bird, with long legs, that is black and white, and cannot fly

oth·er [ŭth′ər] *adjective*, 1) not the same, a different one, *adverb*, 2) differently, *pronoun*, 3) someone or something not mentioned specifically

oth·er·wise [ŭth′ər-wīz′] *adverb*, 1) if not 2) except for that 3) of a different kind

ought [ôt] *verb*, should

ounce [ouns] *noun*, 1) a weight measurement equal to 28.35 grams 2) a tiny bit

our [our] *adjective*, belonging to us

our·selves [our-sĕlvz′] *pronoun*, referring to the subjects in a sentence, we or us

oust [oust] *verb*, to dismiss, to kick out, to expel, to force out

out [out] *adverb*, 1) not in or inside, away from 2) absent, away 3) not shining or burning 4) to bring to a conclusion 5) excluded, omitted

out·cast [out′kăst′] *noun*, a displaced person, an exile

out-come [out′kŭm′] *noun*, a possible result as in an experiment, a final product

out-doors [out-dôrz′, -dōrz′] *adjective*, not inside a building, located outside in the open air

out-doors-man [out-dôrz′mən, -dōrz′-] *noun*, a person who enjoys nature and outdoor activities

out-er [ou′tər] *adjective*, on the outside or edge of something

out-fit [out′fĭt′] *noun*, 1) clothing used for a particular purpose, *verb*, 2) to provide clothes or equipment

out-grow [out-grō′] *verb*, to change as one develops

out-growth [out′grōth′] *noun*, development, product

out-ing [ou′tĭng] *noun*, a short trip

out-let [out′lĕt′, -lĭt] *noun*, 1) an opening, 2) manufacturer

out-line [out′līn′] *noun*, 1) a line showing the shape of something 2) the plan or format for a composition, *verb*, 3) to give the main points of

out-live [out-lĭv′] *verb*, to outlast, to live or last longer than

out-rage [out′rāj′] *noun*, 1) anger caused by injury or insult 2) anything that causes resentment or anger, a wicked or brutal act or remark *verb*, 2) to fill with anger of resentment

out-side [out-sīd′] *adverb*, 1) on or to the exterior surface, *noun*, 2) the outer part or surface

out-stand-ing [out-stăn′dĭng] *adjective*, 1) very good, excellent 2) not paid or settled

o-val [ō′vəl] *adjective*, a round flat shape like an egg

ov-en [ŭv′ən] *noun*, an electric appliance like a sealed box used to bake food

o-ver [ō′vər] *adjective*, 1) in control of 2) finished, *adverb*, 3) from start to finish again 4) unused, extra 5) to go beyond the top, *preposition*, 6) covering 7) across, from one side to the other 8) in every part

o-ver-all [ō′vər-ôl′] *adjective*, including all things, as a whole

o-ver-alls [ō′vər-ôlz′] *noun*, a kind of loose trousers with a bib

o-ver-board [ō′vər-bôrd′] *adverb*, over the side of a boat into the water

o-ver-cast [ō′vər-kăst′] *adjective*, cloudy, sunless, gloomy

o-ver-coat [ō′vər-kōt′] *noun*, a coat worn over the other clothing

o-ver-come [ō′vər-kŭm′] *verb*, to beat, to conquer, to lick

o-ver-due [ō′vər-dōō′] *adjective*, delinquent, late, past due

o-ver-es-ti-mate [ō′vər-ĕs′tə-māt′] *verb*, to calculate over the actual amount

o-ver-flow [ō′vər-flō′] *verb*, 1) to pour over the edge of a container when filled 2) to flood

o-ver-haul [ō′vər-hôl′] *verb*, to restore, to repair, to rebuild

o-ver-head [ō′vər-hĕd′] *adjective*, 1) above our heads, in the sky, *noun*, *no plural*, 2) the fixed costs to maintain something

o-ver-lap [ō′vər-lăp′] *verb*, 1) to rest on top of or over something and cover part of it 2) to partially coincide

o-ver-look [ō'vər-lŏŏk'] *verb*, 1) to fail to notice 2) to excuse

o-ver-night [ō'vər-nīt'] *adjective*, 1) from one day to the next, *adverb*, 2) during the night

o-ver-seas [ō'vər-sēz'] *adjective*, across the ocean, abroad

o-ver-seer [ō'vər-sē'ər] *noun*, one who watches over an area or institution, a supervisor

o-ver-sight [ō'vər-sīt'] *noun*, an error, a blunder, a failure

o-vert [ō-vßrt'] *adjective*, open to view, not concealed

o-ver-take [ō'vər-tāk'] *verb*, to chase and catch up to

o-ver-ture [ō'vər-chŏŏr'] *noun*, a proposal, an introduction

o-ver-whelm [ō'vər-hwĕlm'] *verb*, 1) to overpower in mind and feeling 2) to engulf, to inundate

owe [ō] *verb*, 1) to have to give or pay 2) to feel grateful to someone for something

owl [oul] *noun*, a large bird that lives in the forest, it flies at night and eats small animals

own [ōn] *adjective*, 1) of or belonging to oneself or itself, *verb*, 2) to have or possess

own-er [ō'nər] *noun*, the person who has the right to something

own-er-ship [ō'nər-shĭp'] *noun*, a right of possession, a lawful claim or title

ox [ŏks] *noun*, *plural*, **oxen,** a full-grown male of domestic cattle used for farm work

ox-i-dize [ŏk'sĭ-dīz'] *verb*, to combine with oxygen

ox-y-gen [ŏk'sĭ-jən] *noun*, a colorless, tasteless, odorless, chemically active gas, the part of air that animals, plants and people need to stay alive

oys-ter [oi'stər] *noun*, an edible shellfish, a bivalve mollusk

o-zone [ō'zōn'] *noun*, a faintly blue gas obtained by the silent discharge of electricity in air

P

pace [pās] *noun*, 1) a steady step or speed that is maintained, *verb*, 2) to walk back and forth

pach-y-derm [păk'ĭ-dßrm'] *noun*, a thick-skinned animal

pac-i-fist [pə-sĭf'ĭ-st] *noun*, someone who looks for peaceful means, opposed to force

pac-i-fy [păs'ə-fī'] *verb*, to appease, to calm, to soothe

pack [păk] *noun*, 1) a bundle or a collection of things 2) a group of wild animals that hunt together, *verb*, 3) to bundle or place a group of things into a container

pack-age [păk'ĭj] *noun*, a box or bundle containing one or more objects

pact [păkt] *noun*, an agreement, a contract, a treaty, a bargain

pad [păd] *noun*, 1) a soft material used to protect a wound 2) a number of sheets of paper stuck together at one edge

pad-dle [păd'l] *noun*, 1) an ore or long stick used to row a boat, *verb*, 2) to spank, to whack on the bottom 3) to row a boat 4) to move the hands and feet in shallow water

pad-dock [păd'ək] *noun*, a field or enclosure where horses are kept

pad-dy [păd'ē] *noun*, a field for growing rice

pad-lock [păd'lŏk'] *noun*, a portable lock, jointed at one end

page [pāj] *noun*, 1) one side of a piece of paper in a book 2) a person who delivers messages *verb*, 2) to summon or call indirectly through an intercom or paging system

pag-eant [păj'ənt] *noun*, an exhibition, a show, a parade

paid [pād] *verb*, the *past tense* of **pay**

pail [pāl] *noun*, a bucket or container with a handle

pain [pān] *noun*, physical suffering from injury or illness, distress

pain-ful [pān'fəl] *adjective*, a feeling of hurt, aching

paint [pānt] *noun*, 1) a liquid in a variety of colors that is used to cover a surface to protect or decorate it, *verb*, 2) to coat or color with paint 3) to convey an image by creating it using paints

paint-er [pān'tər] *noun*, a person who paints pictures or buildings

paint-ing [pān'tĭng] *noun*, completed pictures done with paint, a representation

pair [pâr] *noun*, 1) two like things put together as a match 2) an instrument with two parts joined together, e.g. *scissors*, *verb*, 3) to separate into groups of two

pa-ja-mas [pə-jä'mə] *noun, plural*, loose fitting clothes worn to bed

pal [păl] *noun*, a friend, chum

pal-ace [păl'ĭs] *noun*, a beautiful home of a wealthy person

pal-at-a-ble [păl'ə-tə-bəl] *adjective*, 1) tasty 2) acceptable to the mind, pleasing

pa-la-tial [pə-lā'shəl] *adjective*, suitable for a palace, impressively spacious

pale [pāl] *adjective*, 1) light in color, faded, *noun*, 2) the area enclosed by a boundary

pal-ette [păl'ĭt] *noun*, a board on which a painter mixes paints

pal-i-sade [păl'ĭ-sād'] *noun*, a partition formed as a barrier

pal-lid: [păl'id] *adjective,* pale

palm [päm] *noun*, 1) a tree with a long trunk without branches and large leaves at the top 2) the wide part inside the hand

pal-pa-ble [păl'pə-bəl] *adjective*, 1) capable of being touched or felt, obvious 2) tangible

pal-pi-tate [păl'pĭ-tāt'] *verb*, to throb, to pound with emotion or exertion, to quiver, to shake

pal-try [pôl'trē] *adjective*, insignificant, petty, trifling

pam-per [păm'pər] *verb*, to coddle, to indulge, to baby, to spoil

pam-phlet [păm'flĭt] *noun*, a book of a few sheets of printed matter

pan [păn] *noun*, a round metal pot for cooking things over heat

pan-a-ce-a [păn'ə-sē'ə] *noun*, a solution to all problems or sickness, a cure-all

pan-cre-as [păng′krē-əs] *noun*, a large gland under and behind the stomach that secretes insulin to the intestine to help digest food

pan-da [păn′də] *noun*, a large black and white animal like a bear restricted to China

pan-de-mo-ni-um [păn′də-mō′nē-əm] *noun*, a wild tumult, an uproar, confusion

pan-der [păn′dər] *verb*, to cater to the low desires of others

pane [pān] *noun*, a piece of glass used in windows or doors

pan-el [păn′əl] *noun*, 1) a sunken compartment with raised margins in a ceiling 2) a complete jury 3) a group assembled to judge a contest or conduct a public discussion

pan-ic [păn′ĭk] *noun*, 1) a sudden fear which can spread quickly, *verb*, 2) to feel frightened or alarmed, filled with terror

pan-sy [păn′zē] *noun*, a flower that blooms through the winter

pant [pănt] *verb*, to breathe quickly

pan-ther [păn′thər] *noun*, one of the large wild cats, a cougar

pan-to-mime [păn′tə-mīm′] *noun*, a play in which actors use gestures without speech

pan-try [păn′trē] *noun*, a small room where food is stored

pants [pănts] *noun*, *plural*, trousers

pa-pa [pä′pə] *noun*, a father, a dad

pa-per [pā′pər] *noun*, 1) sheets of thin material used for writing, wrapping, etc. 2) a newspaper 3) paper with writing or printing on it verifying identity

pap-ri-ka [pă-prē′kə] *noun*, a Turkish red pepper

pa-py-rus [pə-pī′rəs] *noun*, a reed plant that grows in the Nile Valley once used as paper

par [pär] *noun*, average, standard, the norm, equality in value

par-a-ble [păr′ə-bəl] *noun*, a short, simple story teaching a lesson

par-a-chute [păr′ə-shōōt′] *noun*, 1) a light device made of silk or nylon, designed in an umbrella shape, used to retard the free fall from an aircraft, *verb*, 2) to eject from an aircraft by jumping out equipped with a parachute used to slow something's fall to the ground from a great height

pa-rade [pə-rād′] *noun*, 1) a number of people walking or marching together, a public procession, *verb*, 2) to walk or march with a group of people

par-a-digm [păr′ə-dīm′] *noun*, a model, an example, a pattern

par-a-dise [păr′ə-dīs′] *noun*, a place of complete happiness or beauty, like heaven

par-a-dox [păr′ə-dŏks′] *noun*, a statement that contradicts itself, but is in fact true

par-af-fin [păr′ə-fĭn] *noun*, a white wax used to make candles and seal preserves

par-a-gon [păr′ə-gŏn′] *noun*, a model of perfection

par-a-graph [păr′ə-grăf′] *noun*, a subdivision in writing, beginning with an indent on a new line

par-a-keet [păr′ə-kēt′] *noun*, a small blue or green domestic song bird

par-al-lel [pär′ə-lĕl′] *adjective*,
1) lying in the same direction and always the same distance apart, never intersecting 2)similar

par-al-lel-o-gram
[pär′ə-lĕl′ə-grăm′] *noun*, a four sided plane figure with opposite sides equal and parallel

pa-ral-y-sis [pə-răl′ĭ-sĭs] *adjective*, loss of sensation and motion of body parts, a helpless state

par-a-lyze [pär′ə-līz′] *verb*, to destroy the energy of something, to stop all movement or feeling

pa-ram-e-ter [pə-răm′ĭ-tər] *noun*, the limit, a set standard

par-a-mount [pär′ə-mount′] *adjective*, most important

par-a-noi-a [pär′ə-noi′ə] *noun*, insanity marked by delusions of persecution or glory

par-a-phrase [pär′ə-frāz′] *verb*, to restate a passage in one's own words for clarity

par-a-site [pär′ə-sīt′] *noun*, animal or plant living off another, using it as its only source of food

par-cel [pär′səl] *noun*, 1) a package wrapped in paper, for mailing or carrying, *verb*, 2) to divide into portions to hand out

parch [pärch] *verb*, to dry in the sun, to dehydrate, to scorch

parch-ment [pärch′mənt] *noun*, the skin of a goat or sheep prepared for writing

par-don [pär′dn] *noun*, *no plural*, 1) forgiveness, *verb*, 2) to excuse, to forgive, to absolve

par-don-a-ble [pär′dn-ə-bəl] *adjective*, excusable, forgivable

pare [pâr] *verb*, 1) to peel, to cut off the outer edge, 2) to reduce

par-ent [pâr′ənt] *noun*, 1) the father or mother 2) the source

pa-ren-the-sis [pə-rĕn′thĭ-sĭs] *noun*, one of the curved lines which enclose an aside ( )

par-ish [pär′ĭsh] *noun*, an area served by one church

park [pärk] *noun*, 1) a place in town designated for recreation, rest, and beauty, *verb*, 2) to put a car or vehicle in place

par-ka [pär′kə] *noun*, a heavy winter coat with a hood

par-ley [pär′lē] *noun*, a conference between two opponents, a discussion to settle a dispute

par-lia-ment [pär′lə-mənt] *noun*, an assembly in Great Britain similar to the United States Congress

par-lor [pär′lər] *noun*, a room that is usually used for talking or entertaining, a living room

pa-ro-chi-al [pə-rō′kē-əl] *adjective*, of or pertaining to a parish, a local area

par-o-dy [pär′ə-dē] *noun*, a humorous imitation, satire

pa-role [pə-rōl′] *noun*, an early conditional release from prison, free on probation

par-rot [pär′ət] *noun*, a brightly colored bird with a short curved beak that can mimic speech

par-si-mo-ny [pär′sə-mō′nē] *noun*, selfishness, stinginess

pars-ley [pär′slē] *noun*, an herb with flat or curled leaves used to flavor soups, etc., or to garnish food

par-snip [pär′snĭp] *noun*, a fleshy white root, in the carrot group

part [pärt] *noun*, 1) some of a thing or things 2) a share in an activity 3) a character in a play or film, *verb*, 4) to separate, to leave from 5) to break apart

par-tial-ly [pär′shə-lē] *adverb*, partly, somewhat, slightly

par-ti-al-i-ty [pär′shē-ăl′ĭ-tē] *adjective*, biased, inclined to favor one side

par-tic-i-pate [pär-tĭs′ə-pāt′] *verb*, to have a share in common with others, to take part, to join in

par-tic-i-pa-tion [pär-tĭs′ə-pā′shən] *noun*, the act of getting involved with others

par-ti-ci-ple [pär′tĭ-sĭp′əl] *noun*, one of two forms of a verb forming the past or future tense

par-ti-cle [pär′tĭ-kəl] *noun*, the smallest form of matter

par-tic-u-lar [pər-tĭk′yə-lər] *adjective*, relating to a part, individual, precise, specific

par-tic-u-lar-ly [pər-tĭk′yə-lər-lē] *adverb*, specifically, in detail

par-ti-san [pär′tĭ-zən] *adjective*, an adherent to a party or faction

par-ti-tion [pär-tĭsh′ən] *noun*, 1) a division, a dividing wall, *verb*, 2) to divide, to separate

part-ly [pärt′lē] *adverb*, to some extent, partially, somewhat

part-ner [pärt′nər] *noun*, 1) an associate in business 2) a companion in dancing or sports

par-ty [pär′tē] *noun*, 1) a meeting of friends to enjoy themselves 2) a group of people who have the same interests or goals, *verb*, 3) to celebrate

pass [păs] *noun*, 1) a high mountain road 2) a paper allowing you to go somewhere or have something 3) a forward gesture, *verb*, 4) to give something to someone else 5) to be allowed to advance to the next level

pas-sage [păs′ĭj] *noun*, 1) an excerpt from a chapter, a clause or quotation 2) the act or process of passing as through time or from place to place, a journey 3) a path 4) a part of a written work or a piece of music

pass-é [pă-sā′] *adjective*, behind the times, old fashioned

pas-sen-ger [păs′ən-jər] *noun*, a traveler in a vehicle such as a car, boat, bus, etc.

pas-sion [păsh′ən] *noun*, a strong feeling or desire, enthusiasm

pas-sion-ate [păsh′ə-nĭt] *adjective*, ardent in feeling or desire

pas-sive [păs′ĭv] *adjective*, to be unresponsive, not active

pass-port [păs′pôrt′] *noun*, an official permission issued to a person allowing travel out of the country and return, a document of identification

past [păst] *adjective*, 1) referring to time and events in history, *noun*, *no plural*, 2) time gone by, *preposition*, 3) to or on the further side of 4) beyond in time

pas-ta [päs′tə] *noun*, noodles made from flour, water, salt, and eggs

paste [pāst] *noun*, 1) a sticky substance that glues things together, *verb*, 2) to put in place, for example with an adhesive

pas-tel [pă-stĕl′] *noun*, a sketch or drawing of a soft color or hue

pas-teur-ize [păs′chə-rīz′] *verb*, to subject fluids to a high temperature (131 degrees Celsius, 158 degrees Fahrenheit) to prevent the growth of bacteria

pas-time [păs′tīm′] *noun*, something that you do to amuse yourself or to relax, like a hobby

pas-tor [păs′tər] *noun*, a reverend, the clergyman of a church

pas-to-ral [păs′tər-əl] *adjective*, rural, in the country, rustic

pas-try [pā′strē] *noun*, sweet baked foods, such as cakes or pies

pas-ture [păs′chər] *noun*, grassland for grazing livestock

pat [păt] *noun*, 1) a light touch with an open hand, a gentle tap, *verb*, 2) to touch lightly with a hand

patch [păch] *noun*, 1) a small piece of cloth used to mend a tear, *verb*, 2) to put a piece of material on a surface to repair a hole or strengthen a worn area

pat-ent [păt′nt] *adjective*, 1) obvious, plain, *noun*, 2) the right given to an inventor by the government, to exclusively produce a product for a number of years

pa-ter-nal [pə-tûr′nəl] *adjective*, fatherly, kind, devoted

path [păth] *noun*, a track worn by people or animals walking on it

pa-thet-ic [pə-thĕt′ĭk] *adjective*, causing pity or grief, full of pathos and sympathy

pa-thol-o-gy [pă-thŏl′ə-jē] *noun*, the science of treating disease, their natural causes, results, etc.

pa-thos [pā′thŏs′] *noun*, human or animal experience that cause feelings of pity, compassion

pa-tience [pā′shəns] *noun*, *no plural*, the act of waiting calmly for someone or something

pa-tient [pā′shənt] *adjective*, 1) able to bear quietly or wait for something calmly, *noun*, 2) a person under medical treatment

pat-i-o [păt′ē-ō′] *noun*, a paved outdoor space that is used for eating, cooking or relaxing

pa-tri-arch [pā′trē-ärk′] *noun*, 1) father and ruler of a family or tribe 2) a venerable old man

pa-tri-ot [pā′trē-ət] *noun*, one who loves and defends his country

pa-tri-ot-ic [pā′trē-ŏt′ĭk] *adjective*, public-spirited, flag-waving

pa-tri-ot-ism [pā′trē-ə-tĭz′əm] *adjective*, love of one's country

pa-trol [pə-trōl′] *noun*, 1) a small group of soldiers or police officers, *verb*, 2) to follow a route regularly looking for criminal activity

pa-tron [pā′trən] *noun*, 1) someone who provides financial support to a cause 2) a customer

pa-tron-ize [pā′trə-nīz′] *verb*, 1) to act as a supporter 2) to treat with condescension, to look down on

pat-tern [păt′ərn] *noun*, 1) anything used as a guide or model for making things 2) a repeated sequence 3) to make by following a prototype or model

pau-per [pô′pər] *noun*, destitute, a
very poor person, a beggar

pause [pôz] *noun*, 1) a break in
action of speech, *verb*, 2) to stop
briefly, to delay action or speech

pave [pāv] *verb*, 1) to cover the
surface with asphalt bricks or
cement 2) to prepare the way

pave-ment [pāv′mənt] *noun*,
highway surface, asphalt

paw [pô] *noun*, the foot of a four-
legged animal that has claws

pawn [pôn] *noun*, 1) a victim 2) a
chess piece, *verb*, 3) to sell

pay [pā] *noun*, 1) the compensation
received for work, *verb*, 2) to
give someone money for goods
and services

pay-ment [pā′mənt] *noun*,
compensation, installment

pay-roll [pā′rōl′] *noun*, the money
used to pay workers

pea [pē] *noun*, a seed from a pod
bearing vine that can be eaten

peace [pēs] *noun*, 1) a period of
harmony among nations when
there is no war 2) a calm ordered
condition,

peach [pēch] *noun*, *plural*, **peaches**
1) a juicy yellow-orange fruit
with downy skin, from an
orchard tree that has pink
flowers 2) a yellowish-pink
color

pea-cock [pē′kŏk′] *noun*, a bird
with a large brightly colored tail

peak [pēk] *noun*, 1) the pointed top
of a mountain or ridge 2) the
point of greatest development

peal [pēl] *noun*, 1) a loud ringing
of bells *verb*, 2) to resound

pea-nut [pē′nŭt′] *noun*, a legume
that bears edible pods that taste
like nuts

pear [pâr] *noun*, a juicy yellow,
brown or green fruit from an
orchard tree

pearl [pûrl] *noun*, a precious white
substance like a bead found
inside an oyster, used in jewelry

peas-ant [pĕz′ənt] *noun*, a person
who makes a living from
working the soil, especially in
poorer countries

peb-ble [pĕb′əl] *noun*, a small
stone worn by erosion

pe-can [pĭ-kän′] *noun*, the edible
kernel nut from a hickory tree
grown in the south

peck [pĕk] *noun*, 1) ¼ of a bushel,
verb, 2) to cut or lift with the
beak

pec-to-ral [pĕk′tər-əl] *adjective*,
pertaining to the chest

pe-cu-liar [pĭ-kyōōl′yər] *adjective*,
oddly different from the usual,
strange, distinctive, particular

pe-cu-ni-ar-y [pĭ-kyōō′nē-ĕr′ē]
adjective, pertaining to or
consisting of money

ped-a-gogue [pĕd′ə-gŏg′] *noun*, a
narrow-minded teacher

ped-al [pĕd′l] *noun*, 1) a lever
acted on by the foot, *verb*, 2) to
push with the feet when riding a
bicycle in order to get the
bicycle to move

ped-dle [pĕd′l] *verb*, to sell on the
street or door to door

ped-es-tal [pĕd′ĭ-stəl] *noun*, a base
or support for a column

pe-des-tri-an [pə-dĕs′trē-ən] *noun*, a person who walks, one who journeys on foot

pe-di-a-tri-cian [pē′dē-ə-trĭsh′ən] *noun*, a doctor who is an expert in children's diseases

ped-i-gree [pĕd′ĭ-grē′] *noun*, a register of a line of ancestors, descent, ancestry, lineage

peek [pēk] *noun*, 1) a glance, *verb*, 2) to look at, to catch sight of

peel [pēl] *noun*, *no plural*, 1) the outside covering of a fruit or vegetable, *verb*, 2) to cut the outside covering off of a fruit or vegetable to eat the food inside

peer [pîr] *noun*, 1) someone your own age or someone with similar interests, an equal, *verb*, 2) to take a closer look

peg [pĕg] *noun*, a wooden or metal object used as a hook when put on a wall or as a fastening

pe-jo-ra-tive [pĭ-jôr′ə-tĭv] *adjective*, a deteriorating effect on the meaning of a word, expressing disapproval

pelt [pĕlt] *noun*, 1) the furry skin of an animal 2) to strike over and over with repeated blows

pen [pĕn] *noun*, 1) an instrument for writing using ink 2) an enclosure for animals

pe-nal-ize [pē′nə-līz′] *verb*, to scold, to punish, to chastise

pen-al-ty [pĕn′əl-tē] *noun*, the suffering or fine imposed as a punishment for a violation

pen-chant [pĕn′chənt] *noun*, a strong mental leaning or attraction, a decided taste

pen-cil [pĕn′səl] *noun*, a writing instrument with a gray substance in the middle that marks paper

pend-ant [pĕn′dənt] *noun*, a hanging ornament or piece of jewelry, like a necklace

pend-ent [pĕn′dənt] *adjective*, hanging or suspended

pend-ing [pĕn′dĭng] *adjective*, 1) about to happen, imminent, *preposition*, 2) until 3) during

pen-du-lum [pĕn′jə-ləm] *noun*, a weight which swings from side to side under the combined action of gravity and momentum

pen-e-trate [pĕn′ĭ-trāt′] *verb*, 1) to enter into, 2) to affect deeply

pen-guin [pĕng′gwĭn] *noun*, a large flightless sea bird of Antarctica that has flipper-like wings

pen-in-su-la [pə-nĭn′syə-lə] *noun*, a piece of land extending from the mainland, surrounded by water on three sides

pen-i-ten-tia-ry [pĕn′ĭ-tĕn′shə-rē] *noun*, a federal prison

pen-nant [pĕn′ənt] *noun*, a flag or banner with an insignia

pen-ni-less [pĕn′ē-lĭs] *adjective*, extremely poor, without any money, destitute

Penn-syl-va-nia [pĕn′səl-vān′yə] *noun*, one of the 50 United States located in the Northeast, the capital is Harrisburg. The state flower of **Pennsylvania** is the mountain laurel and the motto is "Virtue, liberty, and independence."

pen-ny [pĕn′ē] *noun*, *plural*, **pennies**, a copper coin worth one cent

pen-sion [pĕn′shən] *noun*, an allowance of money given to someone regularly starting at retirement

pen-sive [pĕn′sĭv] *adjective*, a deep thinker, thoughtful with a hint of sadness, reflective

pen-ta-gon [pĕn′tə-gŏn′] *noun*, a shape with five equal sides

pent-house [pĕnt′hous′] *noun*, an apartment on the top floor of a building

pe-on [pē′ŏn′] *noun*, an unskilled laborer, a menial worker

peo-ple [pē′pəl] *noun*, *plural* of **person**, 1) human beings, men, women, and children 2) a nation

pep-per [pĕp′ər] *noun*, *no plural*, 1) a powder made from seeds of some plants and used to flavor food 2) the fruit of pepper plants, which can be used in cooking or eaten raw in salads

pep-per-mint [pĕp′ər-mĭnt′] *noun*, 1) oil from an herb used to give a taste of mint 2) a candy that tastes like mint

per [pûr] *preposition*, for or in each, according to

per-ceive [pər-sēv′] *verb*, to comprehend, to obtain knowledge through the senses

per-cent [pər-sĕnt′] *noun*, a number in proportion to 100

per-cent-age [pər-sĕn′tĭj] *adjective*, allowance or commission on a hundred

per-cep-ti-ble [pər-sĕp′tə-bəl] *adjective*, capable of being perceived, discernible

per-cep-tion [pər-sĕp′shən] *noun*, viewpoint, observation

perch [pûrch] *noun*, 1) a place for a bird to sit, *verb*, 2) to sit on a narrow branch or stick

per-co-late [pûr′kə-lāt′] *verb*, to pass or trickle through

per-cus-sion [pər-kŭsh′ən] *noun*, the group of musical instruments, such as a drum, whose sound is produced by striking or hitting

per-emp-to-ry [pə-rĕmp′tə-rē] *adjective*, closed to further discussion or action

per-en-ni-al [pə-rĕn′ē-əl] *adjective*, 1) lasting through the year 2) never failing

per-fect [pûr′fĭkt] *adjective*, 1) beyond improvement, having nothing wrong, *verb*, 2) to improve, to make better

per-fec-tion [pər-fĕk′shən] *noun*, the state of being without fault the highest degree of excellence

per-fect-ly [pûr′fĭkt-lē] *adverb*, completely, ideally, flawlessly

per-fi-dy [pûr′fĭd′ē] *noun*, betrayal of trust, treachery

per-fo-rate [pûr′fə-rāt′] *verb*, to make a small hole, to prick

per-form [pər-fôrm′] *verb*, 1) to act in a play or a musical event 2) to do, to carry out a task

per-for-mance [pər-fôr′məns] *noun*, a show or act presented before an audience

per-form-er [pər-fôrm′ər] *noun*, one who entertains before an audience

per-fume [pûr′fyōōm′] *noun*, *no plural*, liquid that has a sweet smell, a fragrant oil 2) a delightful odor

per-func-to-ry [pər-fŭngk′tə-rē] *adjective*, done merely as a duty with little interest or care

per-haps [pər-hăps′] *adverb*, by chance, possibly, maybe

per-il [pĕr′əl] *noun*, a danger, a grave risk, a hazard

pe-rim-e-ter [pə-rĭm′ĭ-tər] *noun*, the measurement of the distance around a two-dimensional figure

pe-ri-od [pĭr′ē-əd] *noun*, 1) an interval of time having a specific length or character 2) a punctuation mark used at the end of a sentence 3) a session in school

pe-ri-od-i-cal [pĭr′ē-ŏd′ĭ-kəl] *noun*, a publication appearing with a fixed interval between issues

pe-riph-er-al [pə-rĭf′ər-əl] *adjective*, having to do with, or situated on the outside

pe-riph-er-y [pə-rĭf′ə-rē] *noun*, the edge, usually of a round surface

per-i-scope [pĕr′ĭ-skōp′] *noun*, an optical instrument that allows observation of objects from a position not in a direct line of sight, used in submarines

per-ish [pĕr′ĭsh] *verb*, to die

per-ish-a-ble [pĕr′ĭ-shə-bəl] *adjective*, likely to spoil, something that rots in air, it has to be refrigerated to make it last

per-ju-ry [pûr′jə-rē] *noun*, false testimony under oath

per-ma-nent [pûr′mə-nənt] *adjective*, meant to last without changing, lasting, durable

per-ma-nent-ly [pûr′mə-nənt-lē] *adverb*, lasting indefinitely

per-me-a-ble [pûr′mē-ə-bəl] *adjective*, 1) capable of receiving fluids or transmitting magnetic effects 2) allowing liquids to pass through

per-me-ate [pûr′mē-āt′] *verb*, to pass through the pores of, to spread throughout, to pervade

per-mis-sion [pər-mĭsh′ən] *noun*, formal consent, authorization

per-mit [pər-mĭt′] *noun*, 1) a written notice that allows you to do something, *verb*, 2) to allow

per-ni-cious [pər-nĭsh′əs] *adjective*, destructive, ruinous, causing insidious harm

per-pen-dic-u-lar [pûr′pən-dĭk′yə-lər] *adjective*, 1) perfectly upright 2) at right angles to a horizontal plane

per-pe-trate [pûr′pĭ-trāt′] *verb*, to do or to perform, to carry through, to commit

per-pet-u-al [pər-pĕch′ōō-əl] *adjective*, never ceasing, continuing forever, endless

per-pe-tu-ate [pər-pĕch′ōō-āt′] *verb*, to continue, indefinitely

per-plex [pər-plĕks′] *verb*, to embarrass, to bewilder, to cause to doubt, to puzzle, to baffle

per-plex-i-ty [pər-plĕk′sĭ-tē] *noun*, the quality or state of being puzzled, bewilderment

per-se-cute [pûr′sĭ-kyōōt′] *verb*, to bother, to oppress, to punish

per-se-cu-tion [pûr′sĭ-kyōō′shən] *noun*, the act of persistently injuring, harassing or annoying

per-se-ver-ance [pûr′sə-vîr′əns] *noun*, the will to keep working until the job is done, persistence

per-se-vere [pûr′sə-vîr′] *verb*, to work to accomplish a goal despite difficulty

per-sist [pər-sĭst′] *verb*, to keep doing something, to persevere, to keep trying

per-sist-ence [pər-sĭs′təns] *noun,* the act of continuing to do something, not giving up

per-son [pûr′sən] *noun*, **people,** *plural,* , a human being, such as a man, woman or child, an unnamed individual

per-son-a-ble [pûr′sə-nə-bəl] *adjective*, good-natured, agreeable, charming, attractive

per-son-al [pûr′sə-nəl] *adjective*, of or concerning a particular person, concerning a person's private life, confidential

per-son-al-i-ty [pûr′sə-năl′ĭ-tē] *noun*, distinctive personal character, individuality

per-son-al-ly [pûr′sə-nə-lē] *adverb*, 1) from one's own viewpoint 2) in person

per-son-i-fi-ca-tion [pər-sŏn′ə-fĭ-kā′shən] *noun*, 1) to think of or represent as a person 2) an embodiment or example of someone

per-son-nel [pûr′sə-něl′] *noun*, the staff of an organization

per-spec-tive [pər-spěk′tĭv] *noun*, as one sees it, a point of view

per-spi-ra-tion [pûr′spə-rā′shən] *noun*, sweat, a salty water fluid secreted from the sweat glands

per-spire [pər-spīr′] *verb*, to sweat

per-suade [pər-swād′] *verb*, to influence or gain over by argument or advice

per-sua-sive [pər-swā′sĭv] *adjective*, an influential argument

pert [pûrt] *adjective*, bold, flippant, forward, impertinent, saucy

per-tain [pər-tān′] *verb*, to relate, to be connected as a part

per-ti-nent [pûr′tn-ənt] *adjective*, belonging or relating to the subject at hand, relevant

per-turb [pər-tûrb′] *verb*, to trouble, or disturb, to agitate

pe-ruse [pə-rōōz′] *verb*, to read

per-vade [pər-vā′d] *verb*, to pass through, to permeate

per-va-sive [pər-vā′sĭv] *adjective*, to become spread throughout all parts, universal, permeating

per-ver-sion [pər-vûr′zhən] *noun*, turning from right to wrong

per-vert [pər-vûrt′] *verb*, to make contrary or obstinate remarks

pes-ky [pěs′kē] *adjective*, annoying, being like a pest

pes-si-mist [pěs′ə-mĭst] *noun*, one who looks on the dark side of things and expects the worst

pes-si-mism [pěs′ə-mĭz′əm] *adjective*, belief that life is basically bad or evil

pest [pěst] *noun*, an annoying and destructive insect or person

pes-ti-cide [pěs′tĭ-sīd′] *noun*, any substance designed to kill living organisms, such as insects, plants, fungi and rodents

pes-ti-lence [pěs′tə-ləns] *noun*, any deadly contagious epidemic of a disease or virus

pet [pět] *noun*, 1) an animal you look after and keep in your house, *verb*, 2) to stroke

pet-al [pĕt′l] *noun*, one of the parts of the corolla of a flower that are usually colorful

pe-tite [pə-tēt′] *adjective*, small, little, a woman or girl of small size

pe-ti-tion [pə-tĭsh′ən] *noun*, 1) a formal request accompanied by signatures as an endorsement, *verb*, 2) to request change by making a written formal request

pet-ri-fy [pĕt′rə-fĭ′] *verb*, to turn to stone, to harden, to deaden

pet-ro-le-um [pə-trō′lē-əm] *noun*, mineral oil, a dark brown or green inflammable liquid

pet-ty [pĕt′ē] *adjective*, a small matter of little importance, insignificant, trivial

pew [pyōō] *noun*, one of a number of fixed benches, like a seat, with backs in a church

pew-ter [pyōō′tər] *noun*, an alloy consisting mainly of tin and other metals

phan-tom [făn′təm] *noun*, an apparition, a ghost, a vision

phar-ma-cy [fär′mə-sē] *noun*, a place where medicines are dispensed, a drug store

phase [fāz] *noun*, a stage in a process of development

pheas-ant [fĕz′ənt] *noun*, a game bird with long tail feathers that lives in the woods

phe-nom-e-non [fĭ-nŏm′ə-nŏn′] *noun*, *plural*, **phenomena**, a marvel, an event, a happening

phil-an-throp-ic [fĭl′ən-thrŏp′ĭk] *adjective*, love for mankind, benevolent, generous

phi-lol-o-gist [fĭ-lŏl′ə-jĭst] *noun*, the study of languages, their structure and origin

phi-los-o-pher [fĭ-lŏs′ə-fər] *noun*, a wise person, a reflective thinker, a sage

phi-los-o-phy [fĭ-lŏs′ə-fē] *noun*, the study of moral and mental sciences, metaphysics

pho-bi-a [fō′bē-ə] *noun*, dislike, an irrational fear of something

phone [fōn] *noun*, the short term for telephone

pho-net-ic [fə-nĕt′ĭk] *adjective*, the sound of letters in a word that create speech

pho-no-graph [fō′nə-grăf′] *noun*, a record player

phos-pho-res-cence [fŏs′fə-rĕs′əns] *noun*, any bright and luminous radiating light

phos-pho-rus [fŏs′fər-əs] *noun*, a nonmetallic element used in matches

pho-to-graph [fō′tə-grăf′] *noun*, 1) a picture produced using film and a camera, *verb*, 2) to take a picture with a camera

pho-to-graph-ic [fō′tə-grăf′ĭk] *adjective*, the process of photography

pho-to-syn-the-sis [fō′tō-sĭn′thĭ-sĭs] *verb*, the process by which chlorophyll-containing cells in green plants use light as an energy source to synthesize carbohydrates from carbon dioxide and water

phrase [frāz] *noun*, 1) a part of a sentence 2) an expression, a saying, *verb*, 3) to express in words or a particular way

phys-i-cal [fĭz′ĭ-kəl] *adjective*, of or pertaining to nature or the human body

phy-si-cian [fĭ-zĭsh′ən] *noun*, a doctor of medicine

phys-ics [fĭz′ĭks] *noun*, the science that deals with matter and energy such as light, motion, sound, heat, electricity, or force, and the laws that govern them

phys-i-ol-o-gy [fĭz′ē-ŏl′ə-jē] *noun*, that part of biology which studies living organisms

phy-sique [fĭ-zēk′] *noun*, the development and bodily structure or appearance of a person, the frame, figure

pi-an-ist [pē-ăn′ĭst] *noun*, a skilled performer on the piano

pi-a-no [pē-ăn′ō] *noun*, a musical instrument played by hitting its keys on a keyboard with fingers, which hit felt-covered hammers which strike metal strings

pick [pĭk] *noun*, 1) a choice or selection 2) a tool used to break the earth, *verb*, 3) to choose 4) to hold with your fingers

pick-et [pĭk′ĭt] *noun*, 1) a stake, a peg, *verb*, 2) to strike, to boycott

pick-le [pĭk′əl] *noun*, 1) any food which has been preserved in brine or in vinegar 2) an awkward situation

pic-nic [pĭk′nĭk] *noun*, a pleasure trip with a meal eaten in the open air

pic-to-graph [pĭk′tə-grăf′] *noun*, a rudimentary diagram or symbol used to represent an idea as the primitive writing of stone tablets and cave drawings

pic-ture [pĭk′chər] *noun*, 1) visual representation such as a drawing, painting, photograph, etc., *verb*, 2) to imagine in your mind, to visualize

pic-tur-esque [pĭk′chə-rěsk′] *adjective*, forming a pleasing picture, graphic, quaint

pie [pī] *noun*, a dish made with fruit, meat or vegetables, surrounded by a pastry crust on the bottom and sometimes on top

piece [pēs] *noun*, 1) a fragment or part separated from the whole, *verb*, 2) to put together, to repair

pier [pîr] *noun*, a wharf or dock extending into the water from the land used as a place to moor ships

pierce [pîrs] *verb*, 1) to pass or break through 2) to make a hole through

pierc-ing [pîrsĭng] *adjective*, very loud and shrill

pig [pĭg] *noun*, any swine raised for pork and bacon

pi-geon [pĭj′ən] *noun*, a plump bird with a small head

pig-ment [pĭg′mənt] *noun*, the color of something, a hue

pile [pīl] *noun*, 1) a heap of things laying one on another 2) the nap of a fabric 3) a post in a pier that goes into the soil beneath the water, *verb*, 4) to amass, to gather together in a heap, to accumulate, to stack

pil-grim [pĭl′grəm] *noun*, a person who journeys to pray at a holy place as an act of religious devotion

pil-grim-age [pĭl′grə-mĭj] *noun*, a journey to a holy place

pill [pĭl] *noun*, a small tablet or capsule of medicine that can be easily swallowed

pil-lage [pĭl'ĭj] *verb*, to strip of money, ransack, rob, destroy

pil-lar [pĭl'ər] *noun*, 1) a strong post 2) a column, a vertical support or structure

pil-low [pĭl'ō] *noun*, a cloth case filled with feathers or other soft material put under the head during sleep

pil-low-case [pĭl'ō-kās'] *noun*, the cloth bag put over a pillow to keep it clean

pi-lot [pī'lət] *noun*, someone who is qualified to guide or navigate a ship or a plane

pin [pĭn] *noun*, 1) a slender piece of metal or wood, sharp on one end round on the other, used to join and fasten things together, *verb*, 2) to fasten with a sharp instrument 3) to hold in a spot

pin-cers [pĭn'sərz] *noun*, an instrument or an appendage having two grasping jaws working on a pivot

pinch [pĭnch] *noun*, 1) a very small amount, *verb*, 2) to squeeze between the finger and thumb 3) to make something feel tight

pine [pīn] *noun*, 1) an evergreen tree with leaves that look like needles, *verb*, 2) to want something very badly

pine-ap-ple [pīn'ăp'əl] *noun*, 1) the fruit of a tropical plant, resembling the shape of a pinecone 2) a symbol of hospitality

pin-ion [pĭn'yən] *noun*, a cogwheel with a small number of teeth, designed to interlock its gear with a larger wheel

pink [pĭngk] *adjective*, 1) a pastel color of red and white *noun*, 2) the color made by mixing red and white

pin-na-cle [pĭn'ə-kəl] *noun*, 1) a small turret above the rest of the building 2) a lofty peak

pint [pīnt] *noun*, a liquid measurement equal to 2 cups or 16 fluid ounces

pi-o-neer [pī'ə-nîr'] *noun*, one of the first to explore an area or field of study, an innovator

pi-ous [pī'əs] *adjective*, devout

pipe [pīp] *noun*, 1) a tube, a cylinder used to convey liquid or gas 2) a device with a bowl at the end of a short straw used to smoke tobacco 3) a musical instrument through which air is blown, *verb*, 4) to make a high pitched sound

pi-quant [pē'kənt] *adjective*, 1) pleasantly tart-tasting, spicy 2) provocative

pique [pēk] *noun*, slight anger or resentment, wounded pride

pi-rate [pī'rĭt] *noun*, a person who robs ships at sea

pis-til [pĭs'təl] *noun*, the part of a flower that produces seeds

pis-tol [pĭs'təl] *noun*, a small gun like a revolver, a firearm

pis-ton [pĭs'tən] *noun*, a metal disk which moves up and down in a cylinder exerting pressure

pit [pǐt] *noun*, 1) a deep hole in the ground 2) the seed of a fruit

pitch [pǐch] *noun*, 1) a gummy substance used for sealing roads and caulking 2) a ball thrown or tossed 3) the tone of a voice or a sound, *verb*, 4) to put in place or set up 5) to toss or throw a ball 6) when a boat leans to an angle while traveling in the water

pitch-er [pǐch'ər] *noun*, 1) a container with a lip and a handle to pour liquid 2) the person who throws the ball to the batter in a baseball game

pitch-fork [pǐch'fôrk'] *noun*, a fork with a long handle used to lift and toss hay

pit-fall [pǐt'fôl'] *noun*, a trap, a snare or hazard not easily avoided, a manhole

pith-y [pǐth'ē] *adjective*, concise, short and to the point

pit-i-ful [pǐt'ǐ-fəl] *adjective*, something that causes sympathy

pit-tance [pǐt'ns] *noun*, a small amount, next to nothing

pit-y [pǐt'ē] *noun*, 1) the sadness felt when someone else is hurt or in trouble, *verb*, 2) to feel sorry for someone, to feel sympathy

piv-ot [pǐv'ət] *noun*, a fixed pin on which something turns

piz-za [pēt'sə] *noun*, a baked flat crust covered with cheese, tomato sauce, etc.

pla-cate [plā'kāt'] *verb*, to pacify, to satisfy, to please someone

place [plās] *noun*, 1) a designated area or a particular space, *verb*, 2) to put in a particular spot 3) to identify by recalling

plac-id [plăs'ǐd] *adjective*, calm, peaceful, tranquil, untroubled

pla-gia-rism [plā'jə-rǐz'əm] *noun*, the act of copying someone's work and claiming it as your own

plague [plāg] *noun*, 1) anything troublesome 2) an infectious disease, *verb*, 3) to annoy

plaid [plăd] *adjective*, a pattern on cloth with stripes of different colors that cross each other

plain [plān] *adjective*, 1) open to view, clear, easy to understand, 2) simple, *noun*, 3) a stretch of gently rolling land with few trees

plain-ly [plān'lē] *adverb*, clearly

plain-tiff [plān'tǐf] *noun*, one who commences a legal action or suit

plan [plăn] *noun*, 1) a drawing made to scale of a new building or a project 2) a scheme indicating how to accomplish something, *verb*, 3) to design, to scheme or devise

plane [plān] *noun*, 1) a hand tool used to smooth the surface of wood 2) the short term for airplane 3) any flat or level surface

plan-et [plăn'ǐt] *noun*, a large mass like the earth that revolves around the sun

plank [plăngk] *noun*, a long, flat, thin piece of wood

plank-ton [plăngk'tən] *noun*, plant and animal organisms, generally microscopic, that float and or drift in great numbers in fresh or salt water

plant [plănt] *noun*, 1) a living thing that is not a mineral or animal 2) a factory, a work place, *verb*, 3) to put into the ground to grow

plan-ta-tion [plăn-tā'shən] *noun*, a large estate or farm cultivated by workers living on it

plaque [plăk] *noun*, 1) a marker, a tablet with an inscription 2) tarter calcified on the teeth

plas-ma [plăz'mə] *noun*, the fourth state of matter, composed of broken up atoms

plas-tic [plăs'tĭk] *adjective*, 1) referring to any pliable petroleum based product, *noun*, 2) any of a group of substances made chemically and molded by heat to form, fibers, bottles, etc.

plate [plāt] *noun*, a shallow dish from which food is eaten

pla-teau [plă-tō'] *noun*, 1) an elevated plane 2) inactive period

plat-form [plăt'fôrm'] *noun*, 1) a part of a station where you get on and off trains 2) a raised stage or dais so the audience can see the speaker or performers 3) beliefs, principles

plat-i-tude [plăt'ĭ-tōōd'] *noun*, a commonplace statement

pla-ton-ic [plə-tŏn'ĭk] *adjective*, a friendly relationship

pla-toon [plə-tōōn'] *noun*, a military unit of troops

plat-ter [plăt'ər] *noun*, 1) a large serving of food 2) a large shallow plate for serving food

plau-dits [plô'dĭts] *noun*, *plural*, enthusiastic approval, applause

plau-si-ble [plô'zə-bəl] *adjective*, apparently right, seeming to be reasonable, credible

play [plā] *noun*, 1) the performance of a story on the stage, *verb*, 2) to amuse or entertain 3) to

take part in a game 4) to perform on a musical instrument

plea [plē] *noun*, 1) an appeal, an urgent request 2) a defense

plead [plēd] *verb*, 1) to ask for something that is felt to be very important, to appeal earnestly 2) to respond to a charge by a court of law

pleas-ant [plĕz'ənt] *adjective*, 1) agreeable, amiable, friendly 2) fair, mild, comfortable

pleas-ant-ly [plĕz'ənt-lē] *adverb*, agreeably, politely, kindly

please [plēz] *noun*, 1) a word added to a request to make it sound polite, *verb*, 2) to make someone happy 3) to wish

pleased [plēzd] *adjective*, glad

plea-sur-ably [plĕzh'ər-ə-bəl] *adverb*, capable of affording satisfaction, pleasant

pleas-ure [plĕzh'ər] *noun*, enjoyment or satisfaction

pledge [plĕj] *noun*, 1) a promise, a guarantee, *verb*, 2) to take an oath, to bind by a promise

plen-ty [plĕn'tē] *adjective*, enough, all that is needed

pleth-o-ra [plĕth'ər-ə] *noun*, a large or excessive amount of something, an abundance

pli-ant [plī'ənt] *adjective*, bendable

pli-ers [plī'ərz] *noun*, a small pincers with long jaws, used for bending metal rods or wire, or holding small objects

plod [plŏd] *verb*, to walk heavily, to trudge, to work steadily

plot [plŏt] *noun*, 1) a piece of land 2) a secret plan, usually to commit a crime 3) the story of a book, film, etc. *verb*, 4) to plan a secret activity, to conspire

plow [plou] *noun*, 1) a farm tool used to overturn earth for planting *verb*, 2) to turn over the soil to prepare the earth for planting 3) to move forcefully

pluck [plŭk] *verb*, to pull off or pull out 2) to grasp or grab

plug [plŭg] *noun*, 1) a stopper used to keep water from draining out of a basin 2) a device put in a wall socket to conduct electricity, *verb*, 3) to put an electric cord into a socket 4) to put a stopper into a drain hole, to fill a hole 5) to persevere

plum [plŭm] *noun*, a sweet juicy red fruit with a pit as a seed

plumb-er [plŭm'ər] *noun*, a tradesman who fits, and repairs gas and water pipes

plumb-ing [plŭm'ĭng] *noun*, *no plural*, all the water pipes, containers, etc. put in a building so that there can be running water and drainage

plume [plōōm] *noun*, a large or conspicuous feather

plum-met [plŭm'ĭt] *verb*, to fall straight down quickly

plump [plŭmp] *adjective*, a little fat, rounded in form

plunge [plŭnj] *noun*, 1) a sudden dive or fall, *verb*, 2) to fall quickly from a great height 3) to throw oneself into

plung-er [plŭn'jər] *noun*, 1) a rubber suction cup on a handle, used to clear drains 2) a piston-like part that acts with a thrusting movement in a pump

plu-ral [plŏŏr'əl] *adjective*, of or involving more than one

plus [plŭs] *preposition*, in addition to, increased by

ply-wood [plī'wŏŏd'] *noun*, sheets of wood arranged in thin layers where the grain is in opposite directions to give it strength

p.m. *adjective*, post meridian, the afternoon, the period between noon and midnight

pneu-mo-nia [nŏŏ-mōn'yə] *noun*, infection of the lungs caused by bacteria or viruses

poach [pōch] *verb*, 1) to hunt or fish illegally 2) to cook a raw egg in boiling water

pock-et [pŏk'ĭt] *noun*, an envelope made by sewing a piece of cloth into clothing to hold things

pod [pŏd] *noun*, a long, slender part of a vine plant in which the seeds grow, like a pea or bean

po-di-um [pō'dē-əm] *noun*, a pedestal, a raised platform

po-em [pō'əm] *noun*, a composition, usually in verse, with regular rhythm and sounds that express images in powerful or beautiful language

po-et [pō'ĭt] *noun*, one who writes verse in a specific form

po-et-ic [pō-ĕt'ĭk] *adjective*, pertaining to poetry, imaginative

po-et-ry [pō'ĭ-trē] *noun*, *no plural*, words written in verse

poign-ant [poin'yənt] *adjective*, touching, piercing, sharp, keen, affecting the emotions

point [point] *noun*, 1) the tip of something, usually sharp, 2) the purpose of a verbal illustration, 3) the number of goals for a team, 4) at a particular time, 5) the location of an ordered pair of numbers, *verb*, 6) to indicate

point-less [pointlĕs] *adjective*, meaningless, senseless

poise [poiz] *noun*, 1) composure, self-assurance, confidence, *verb*, 2) to balance, to keep steady

poi-son [poi′zən] *noun*, 1) any substance dangerous to life and health, *verb*, 2) to kill with toxic chemicals, 3) to ruin

poi-son-ous [poi′zə-nəs] *adjective*, deadly, toxic, noxious

poke [pōk] *verb*, to push something pointed into something, to prod

po-lar [pō′lər] *adjective*, 1) of or near the North or South Poles, 2) at opposite ends

pole [pōl] *noun*, 1) a round piece of wood, metal or plastic ,etc. a rod, 2) one end of the earth or at the end of the axis of a sphere

po-lice [pə-lēs′] *noun, no plural*, members of a department of government that maintains order and enforces the law

pol-i-cy [pŏl′ĭ-sē] *noun*, 1) a course of action adopted by an individual or group, 2) an insurance contract

po-li-o [pŏl′ē′ō] *noun*, (short for poliomyelitis) a disease caused by a virus that affects the nervous system and can result in paralysis

pol-ish [pŏl′ĭsh] *noun*, 1) a substance such as oil or cleanser used to make a surface shine when rubbed with a cloth, *verb*, 2) rubbing something to make it shine or glossy

po-lite [pə-līt′] *adjective*, showing good manners, courteous

po-lit-i-cal [pə-lĭt′ĭ-kəl] *adjective*, of or pertaining to the conduct of government or politics

pol-i-ti-cian [pŏl′ĭ-tĭsh′ən] *noun*, a person who runs for public office

pol-i-tics [pŏl′ĭ-tĭks] *noun*, the conduct of government

pol-i-ty [pŏl′ĭ-tē] *noun*, form of government of a nation or a state

poll [pōl] *noun*, 1) a survey, *verb*, 2) to interview, to canvass

pol-len [pŏl′ən] *noun*, a fine yellow dust on the anthers of seed bearing flowers, which serves as the male agent in reproduction

pol-li-nate [pŏl′ə-nāt′] *verb*, to fertilize a flower so that it will reproduce itself by conveying pollen to the stigma

pol-lute [pə-lōōt′] *verb*, to contaminate, to make dirty or unusable, to make foul

pol-lu-tion [pə-lōō′shən] *noun*, substances in the air, in water and on land that contaminate the earth

pol-y-gon [pŏl′ē-gŏn′] *noun*, a many sided plane or figure

pomp-ous [pŏm′pəs] *adjective*, arrogant, showing off

pon-cho [pŏn′chō] *noun*, a sleeveless cover for the upper body, a waterproof cloak

pond [pŏnd] *noun*, a small body of water, smaller than a lake

pon-der [pŏn′dər] *verb*, to think about something, to contemplate, to consider carefully

po-ny [pō′nē] *noun*, a small horse

pool [pōōl] *noun*, 1) any amount of still liquid, a basin 2) a collection

of things 3) billiards 4) to gather
or combine resources for mutual
benefit

poor [po͝or] *adjective*, 1) not
having much money, 2) needing
kindness or help, 3) not good

pop [pŏp] *noun*, *no plural*, 1) a
sudden noise made when air is
released, 2) part of the popular
culture of the 1960s, *verb*,
3) to make a sudden, sharp,
explosive sound

pope, Pope [pōp] *noun*, the leader
of the Roman Catholic Church

pop-py [pŏp'ē] *noun*, a red flower
that has seeds that have a
narcotic effect

pop-u-lar [pŏp'yə-lər] *adjective*,
pleasing to people in general

pop-u-lar-i-ty [pŏp'yə-lăr'ĭ-tē]
noun, *no plural*, a measurement
of how happy people are with
something

pop-u-late [pŏp'yə-lāt'] *verb*, to
occupy, to reside in

pop-u-la-tion [pŏp'yə-lā'shən]
noun, the count of people or
organisms who live in an area

pop-u-lous [pŏp'yə-ləs] *adjective*,
crowded with people

por-ce-lain [pôr'sə-lĭn] *noun*, a
delicate form of china, made
with a special clay

porch [pôrch] *noun*, a covered
platform in front of a doorway

por-cu-pine [pôr'kyə-pīn'] *noun*, a
small animal that has long spikes
all over its body for protection

pore [pôr] *noun*, a small hole in the
skin for perspiration

pork [pôrk] *noun*, *no plural*, the
meat from a pig used as food

po-rous [pôr'əs] *adjective*, a rough
surface, full of holes or texture

por-ridge [pôr'ĭj] *noun*, food made
by boiling grain in water or milk
until it is very soft, e.g., oatmeal

port [pôrt] *noun*, 1) a harbor or
community where ships and
boats dock, 2) the left handed
side of a ship when facing
forward, 3) a sweet red wine,
4) an opening in a ship for cargo

port-a-ble [pôr'tə-bəl] *adjective*,
easily carried by hand

por-tal [pôr'tl] *noun*, an entrance, a
large doorway, a gate

por-tend [pôr-tĕnd'] *verb*, to
foretell, to predict, to forecast

por-tent [pôr'tĕnt'] *noun*, a sign, an
omen, forewarning of a threat

por-tent-ous [pôr-tĕn'təs]
adjective, ominous, serious

por-ter [pôr'tər] *noun*, a person
hired to carry luggage in a hotel
or a train station or airport

port-fo-li-o [pôrt-fō'lē-ō'] *noun*, a
portable case holding papers,
prints, drawings, etc.

por-ti-co [pôr'tĭ-kō'] *noun*, a
colonnade at the entrance of a
building

por-tion [pôr'shən] *noun*, a part of
a whole, a segment, a share

port-ly [pôrt'lē] *adjective*,
overweight, heavy set, fat

por-trait [pôr'trĭt] *noun*, a painting
or photograph of someone

por-tray [pôr-trā'] *verb*, to
describe, to represent

pose [pōz] *noun*, 1) a stance or
posture, *verb*, 2) to model, to
stand, 3) to ask a question

po·si·tion [pə-zĭsh′ən] *noun*, 1) a posture, an attitude 2) a job

pos·i·tive [pŏz′ĭ-tĭv] *adjective*, 1) the affirmative, the opposite of negative 2) confident attitude

pos·sess [pə-zĕs′] *verb*, to have as property, to own, to control

pos·ses·sion [pə-zĕsh′ən] *noun*, that which one owns, property

pos·si·bil·i·ty [pŏs′ə-bĭl′ĭ-tē] *noun*, likelihood, probability, chance

pos·si·ble [pŏs′ə-bəl] *adjective*, what may happen or exist

post [pōst] *noun*, 1) a piece of wood or metal placed in the ground as a support 2) a place where a person is stationed, a job or responsibility 3) sending mail through the post office, *verb*, 4) to make known by putting notices or flyers in public places 5) to station at a place

post·age [pō′stĭj] *noun*, *no plural*, the amount of money paid for something sent through the mail

post·card [pōst′kärd′] *noun*, a small note card with a written message sent through the mail

post·er [pō′stər] *noun*, a large advertisement usually hung on a wall in a public place

pos·ter·i·ty [pŏ-stĕr′ĭ-tē] *noun*, the future generation, descendents

post·hu·mous [pŏs′chə-məs] *adjective*, occurring after death

post·pone [pōst-pōn′] *verb*, to put off, to defer to a later time

post·script [pōst′skrĭpt′] *noun*, 1) a note added to a signed letter 2) an addition to a book

pos·tu·late [pŏs′chə-lāt′] *noun*, 1) a self-evident truth, *verb*, 2) to presume, theorize, speculate

pos·ture [pŏs′chər] *noun*, a stance, an unnatural attitude, position

pot [pŏt] *noun*, a container, usually round made for cooking

pot·ash [pŏt′ăsh′] *noun*, wood ashes, potassium hydrochloride

po·tas·si·um [pə-tăs′ē-əm] *noun*, 1) a soft, white metallic element of the alkali group, 2) Vitamin K

po·ta·to [pə-tā′tō] *noun*, an underground starchy vegetable

po·tent [pōt′nt] *adjective*, powerful, effective, mighty

po·ten·tial [pə-tĕn′shəl] *noun*, the capability someone has to accomplish something

po·tion [pō′shən] *noun*, a dose of a liquid with magical powers

pot·pour·ri [pō′pŏŏ-rē′] *noun*, any miscellaneous grouping

pot·ter·y [pŏt′ə-rē] *noun*, *no plural*, ceramic dishes and pots made of baked clay

pouch [pouch] *noun*, 1) a bag, purse 2) a sack on a marsupial for their young

poul·tice [pōl′tĭs] *noun*, a compress used to heal a bruise or sprain

poul·try [pōl′trē] *noun*, any domestic fowl used as food

pounce [pouns] *verb*, to jump on something, to seize eagerly

pound [pound] *noun*, 1) a form of money in Britain and some other countries 2) a measure of weight equal to 2 cups, 16 oz. 3) a place to keep stray animals *verb*, 4) to crush something by striking it over and over

pour [pôr] *verb*, to flow or cause to flow, as in making a stream

pout [pout] *verb*, to make a long face, to sulk, to mope

pov-er-ty [pŏv′ər-tē] *noun*, the state of being poor, destitute, or without money or resources

pow-der [pou′dər] *noun*, *no plural*, fine grains of matter, like dust

pow-er [pou′ər] *noun*, the ability to do something, strength or force

pow-er-ful [pou′ər-fəl] *adjective*, strong, forceful, mighty

prac-ti-cal [prăk′tĭ-kəl] *adjective*, 1) derived from actual use and experience, virtual 2) given to action rather than to speculation

prac-ti-cal-ly [prăk′tĭk-lē] *adverb*, almost, nearly

prac-tice [prăk′tĭs] *noun*, 1) an exercise 2) an habitual action 3) the work of a profession, *verb*, 4) to perform over and over to learn a skill 5) to do something as a principle of living 6) to work at a profession

prag-mat-ic [prăg-măt′ĭk] *adjective*, practical, matter of fact, using common sense

prai-r-ie [prâr′ē] *noun*, a meadow of grassland with no trees

praise [prāz] *noun*, 1) applause, approval, admiration, *verb*, 2) to say nice things about someone, to applaud, to compliment

prance [prăns] *verb*, to frolic, to dance about in a lively manner

prank [prăngk] *noun*, a playful trick, a joke, a caper

prate [prāt] *verb*, to speak foolishly, to boast idly

pray [prā] *verb*, to talk to God or a god, often asking for something or expressing gratitude

pray-er [prâr] *noun*, words spoken aloud or silently to God

preach [prēch] *verb*, to talk to people about how they should live a better life

preach-er [prē′chər] *noun*, a person who talks about living life according to the words of the Bible, a minister

pre-am-ble [prē′ăm′bəl, prē-ăm′-] *noun*, an introduction or preface

pre-car-i-ous [prĭ-kâr′ē-əs] *adjective*, depending on the will of another, uncertain

pre-cau-tion [prĭ-kô′shən] *noun*, something that is done beforehand to guard against harm, danger, mistakes, or accidents

pre-cede [prĭ-sēd′] *adjective*, to go before, to introduce or preface

prec-e-dent [prĕs′ĭ-dənt] *noun*, 1) an authoritative example 2) preceding in time or rank serving as an example

pre-cept [prē′sĕpt′] *noun*, a principle of conduct

pre-cinct [prē′sĭngkt′] *noun*, a district with certain boundaries

pre-cious [prĕsh′əs] *adjective*, 1) of great value, much loved by someone 2) costly, expensive

prec-i-pice [prĕs′ə-pĭs] *noun*, a very high and steep cliff

pre-cip-i-tate [prĭ-sĭp′ĭ-tāt′] *adjective*, 1) headlong, rash, *noun*, 2) a solid formed in a solvent in which it will not dissolve and settles as particles, *verb*, 3) to condense from vapor and fall to the earth's surface like snow or rain

pre-cip-i-ta-tion [prĭ-sĭp′ĭ-tā′shən] *noun*, water that falls as rain or snow from the atmosphere

pre-cip-i-tious [prĭ-sĭp′ĭ- tious] *adjective*, 1) very steep 2) hasty, done without careful thought

pre-cise [prĭ-sīs′] *adjective*, exact, accurate, clearly expressed

pre-ci-sion [prĭ-sĭzh′ən] *adjective*, accuracy, exactness

pre-clude [prĭ-klo͞od′] *verb*, to prevent from happening, to hinder, to make impossible

pre-co-cious [prĭ-kō′shəs] *adjective*, showing skills at an earlier age than usual

pre-cur-sor [prĭ-kûr′sər] *noun*, forerunner, predecessor

pred-a-tor [prĕd′ə-tər, -tôr′] *noun*, an animal that eats other animals

pred-e-ces-sor [prĕd′ĭ-sĕs′ər] *noun*, one that comes before another in business or sequence

pre-dic-a-ment [prĭ-dĭk′ə-mənt] *noun*, a stressful position, dilemma, or situation

pre-dict [prĭ-dĭkt′] *verb*, to make a reasonable statement about what might happen, to foretell

pre-dic-tion [prĭ-dĭk′shən] *noun*, foretelling the future, prophecy

pre-di-lec-tion [prĕd′l-ĕk′shən] *noun*, an inclination toward something, preference

pre-dom-i-nance [prĭ-dŏm′ə-nəns] *noun*, power over someone

pre-em-i-nent [prē-ĕm′ə-nənt] *noun*, distinction above others, outstanding, superior

pref-ace [prĕf′ĭs] *noun*, an explanation to the reader at the beginning of a book

pre-fer [prĭ-fûr′] *verb*, to like one thing better than another

pref-er-a-ble [prĕf′ər-ə-bəl] *adjective*, a better choice

pref-er-ence [prĕf′ər-əns] *noun*, one thing that is liked more than another, inclination

pre-fix [prē′fĭks′] *noun*, letters added at the front of a word to alter the meaning

preg-nant [prĕg′nənt] *adjective*, having a child or offspring developing in the body

pre-his-tor-ic [prē′hĭ-stôr′ĭk] *adjective*, a time prior to recorded history

prej-u-dice [prĕj′ə-dĭs] *noun*, a strong feeling against something

prel-ude [prĕl′yo͞od′] *noun*, the introduction, forerunner

pre-ma-ture [prē′mə-tyo͞or′] *adjective*, too early, undeveloped

pre-mier [prĭ-mîr′] *adjective*, a head of government in many nations, such as Russia

pre-miere [prĭ-mîr′] *noun*, the first public showing or display

pre-mi-um [prē′mē-əm] *noun*, 1) a bonus given as an inducement to purchase products 2) the amount usually paid in installments by a policy holder for coverage under a contract

pre-mo-ni-tion [prē'mə-nĭsh'ən]
noun, a dream or image in which
one sees what is to come

prep-a-ra-tion [prĕp'ə-rā'shən]
noun, the act of doing something
beforehand to get ready for
something

pre-pare [prĭ-pâr'] *verb*, to make
or get ready for something

pre-pon-der-ance
[prĭ-pŏn'dər-əns] *adjective*,
superiority of weight, influence,
overwhelming power

prep-o-si-tion [prĕp'ə-zĭsh'ən]
noun, a word used before a noun
or pronoun to indicate where or
to express connections and
relationships

pre-pos-ter-ous [prĭ-pŏs'tər-əs]
adjective, absurd, ridiculous

pre-req-ui-site [prē-rĕk'wĭ-zĭt]
noun, an essential condition,
required beforehand

pre-rog-a-tive [prĭ-rŏg'ə-tĭv] *noun*,
an exclusive or peculiar right or
privilege of a certain rank

pres-age [prĕs'ĭj] *verb*, to foretell

pre-scribe [prĭ-skrīb'] *verb*, to give
directions to guide someone

pre-scrip-tion [prĭ-skrĭp'shən]
noun, a written direction for
preparation of a medicine

pres-ence [prĕz'əns] *noun*, the act
or state of being present

pre-sent [prĕz'ənt] *adjective*,
1) not past or future, now 2) in
attendance, being in a certain
place *noun*, 3) the present time,
right now 4) a gift, *verb*, 5) to
show, to perform 6) to introduce
one person to another 7) to give
as a gift

pres-en-ta-tion [prĕz'ən-tā'shən]
noun, exhibition, demonstration,
display or lecture

pre-ser-va-tion [prē-zûr-vā'shən]
noun, protection from harm,
danger, or rot

pre-serve [prĭ-zûrv'] *noun*, 1) an
area for the protection of wildlife
and natural resources, *verb*, 2) to
keep something in its original
form, to protect

pre-serves [prĭ-zûrvz'] *noun
plural*, fruits preserved in syrup

pre-side [prĭ-zīd'] *verb*, to control,
to lead, to manage, to oversee

pres-i-dent [prĕz'ĭ-dənt] *noun*,
1) the elected leader of the
United States government 2) the
head of a university, college or
corporation

press [prĕs] *noun*, 1) the newspaper
business or media generated
news stories, *verb*, 2) to push on
steadily with pressure 3) trying
to get someone to do something
4) pushing something to cause
an effect 5) to iron out the
wrinkles in clothing

pres-sure [prĕsh'ər] *noun*, the
action of a force against an
opposing force

pres-tige [prĕ-stēzh'] *noun*,
influence derived from past
success or reputation

pre-sume [prĭ-zoōm'] *verb*, to
assume, to conclude, to suppose

pre-sump-tion [prĭ-zŭmp'shən]
noun, an assumption

pre-sup-pose [prē'sə-pōz'] *verb*, to
assume, to consider beforehand

pre-tend [prĭ-tĕnd'] *verb*, to fake,
to make believe, to imitate

pre-tense [prē'tĕns'] *noun*, the act of pretending to be or have something you are not

pre-ten-sion [prĭ-tĕn'shən] *adjective*, when one assumes an air of superiority

pre-text [prē'tĕkst'] *noun*, a false reason to justify an action

pret-ty [prĭt'ē] *adjective*, 1) attractive, pleasing to the eye, *adverb*, 2) close to, quite, fairly

pre-vail [prĭ-vāl'] *verb*, to command, to control, to win

prev-a-lent [prĕv'ə-lənt] *adjective*, widespread, generally accepted

pre-vent [prĭ-vĕnt'] *verb*, to keep something from happening

pre-ven-tion [prĭ-vĕn'shən] *noun*, that which hinders or obstructs

pre-view [prē'vyōō'] *noun*, 1) a look at something before it is reproduced, *verb*, 2) to see in advance

pre-vi-ous [prē'vē-əs] *adjective*, existing or occurring earlier, prior, preceding

pre-vi-ous-ly [prē'vē-əs-lē] *adverb*, formerly, at one time, before

prey [prā] *noun*, any animal that serves as food for another animal

price [prīs] *noun*, the cost of something, what you have to pay

prick [prĭk] *verb*, to make a small hole with something sharp

pride [prīd] *noun*, *no plural*, the feeling of doing your personal best, self-respect

priest [prēst] *noun*, a clergyman of the Catholic Church

prim [prĭm] *adjective*, very precise and formal, exceedingly proper

pri-ma-ry [prī'mĕr'ē] *adjective*, 1) pertaining to elementary education or schools 2) first

prime [prīm] *adjective*, 1) best, choice, excellent, *verb*, 2) to prepare for operation, to make ready

prime min-is-ter [prīm-mĭn'ĭ-stər] *noun*, the head of government in the parliamentary system

prim-i-tive [prĭm'ĭ-tĭv] *adjective*, characterized by the manner of an early time, crude

prince [prĭns] *noun*, 1) the son of a king or queen 2) the ruler of a small country or state

prin-cess [prĭn'sĭs] *noun*, 1) the daughter of a king or queen 2) the wife of a prince

prin-ci-pal [prĭn'sə-pəl] *noun*, 1) occupying the first place or rank, most important 2) the person in charge of a school

prin-ci-ple [prĭn'sə-pəl] *noun*, 1) a source or origin 2) a fundamental truth or doctrine

print [prĭnt] *noun*, 1) the size and style of lettering in a book or poster, *verb*, 2) to press words and pictures on paper or cloth by machine 3) to write

print-er [prĭn'tər] *noun*, a device connected to a computer to make paper copies of a document

pri-or [prī'ər] *adjective*, earlier, before, preceding in time

pri-or-i-ty [prī-ôr'ĭ-tē] *noun*, most important

prism [prĭz'əm] *noun*, 1) a three dimensional object with all sides equal 2) a transparent solid that refracts light

pris-on [prĭz′ən] *noun*, a place where criminals are kept while they are punished

pris-on-er [prĭz′ə-nər] *noun*, a person who is guilty of a crime and must serve a sentence of time away from society, living among other criminals

pris-tine [prĭs′tēn′] *adjective*,
1) part of earlier times, primitive 2) unspoiled, spotless

pri-va-cy [prī′və-sē] *noun*, isolation, seclusion, solitude

pri-vate [prī′vĭt] *adjective*,
1) confidential, personal, secret, *noun*, 2) an enlisted soldier

pri-va-tion [prī-vā′shən] *noun*, hardship, want, lack of comfort

priv-i-lege [prĭv′ə-lĭj] *noun*, a peculiar benefit, favor, or advantage of a group

prize [prīz] *noun*, 1) a reward for winning a contest, *verb*, 2) to cherish, to hold dear

prob-a-bil-i-ty [prŏb′ə-bĭl′ĭ-tē] *adjective*, the chance an event will occur, likelihood

prob-a-ble [prŏb′ə-bəl] *adjective*, likely to occur, plausible

prob-a-bly [prŏb′ə-blē] *adverb*, very likely to prove true

pro-bate [prō′bāt′] *noun*, proof before an officer of the county that a will is valid

pro-ba-tion [prō-bā′shən] *noun*, a trial period, an experiment

probe [prōb] *verb*, to explore with a pointed object or tool

prob-lem [prŏb′ləm] *noun*, 1) a dilemma, something that needs to be solved or worked out

2) a question on a test

pro-ce-dure [prə-sē′jər] *noun*, a manner of proceeding in any action, a process, conduct

pro-ceed [prō-sēd′] *verb*, to go onward or forward, to advance

proc-ess [prŏs′ĕs′] *noun*, 1) a method of operation 2) to change by a special treatment

pro-ces-sion [prə-sĕsh′ən] *noun*, people following one another as part of a ceremony

pro-claim [prō-klām′] *verb*, to announce officially, to declare

proc-la-ma-tion [prŏk′lə-mā′shən] *noun*, an announcement

pro-cliv-i-ty [prō-klĭv′ĭ-tē] *noun*, an inclination, a natural tendency

pro-cras-ti-nate [prō-krăs′tə-nāt′] *verb*, to postpone, to put off doing something, to delay

pro-cras-ti-na-tion [prō-krăs′tə-nā′ shən] *noun*, hesitation, delaying, tarrying

prod [prŏd] *verb*, 1) to poke, to stir up, to jab 2) to urge, to nag

prod-i-gal [prŏd′ĭ-gəl] *adjective*, one who is reckless with money

pro-di-gious [prə-dĭj′əs] *adjective*, marvelous, enormous, huge

prod-i-gy [prŏd′ə-jē] *noun*, a highly gifted child, a marvel

pro-duce [prə-dōōs′] *noun*,
1) fruits of the harvest, *verb*, 2) to create, to bring forth, to provide 3) to present, to display, to exhibit 4) to cause, to make

pro-duc-er [prə-dōō′sər] *noun*, someone in charge of making a movie or film

prod-uct [prŏd'əkt] *noun,*
1) something that has an economic value such as refined natural resources or a man-made material 2) the outcome of an endeavor 3) the result of multiplying two numbers together

pro-duc-tion [prə-dŭk'shən] *noun,*
1) creation, construction 2) that which is the result of effort

pro-fane [prō-fān'] *adjective,* not sacred, irreverent, secular

pro-fan-i-ty [prō-făn'ĭ-tē] *noun,* cursing, swearing, expletive

pro-fess [prə-fĕs'] *verb,* to lay claim to, to affirm, to declare

pro-fes-sion [prə-fĕsh'ən] *noun,* an employment which needs specialized study and training

pro-fes-sion-al [prə-fĕsh'ə-nəl] *adjective,* 1) engaged in an activity as a paid job 2) highly competent

pro-fes-sor [prə-fĕs'ər] *noun,* a teacher of the highest rank in a university or college

prof-fer [prŏf'ər] *verb,* to offer, to give, to present, to submit

pro-fi-cient [prə-fĭsh'ənt] *adjective,* advanced in any occupation or study, skillful

pro-file [prō'fīl'] *noun,* a drawing or other representation of a view

prof-it [prŏf'ĭt] *noun,* 1) a monetary gain, *verb,* 2) to be of advantage, to gain, to benefit

prof-li-gate [prŏf'lĭ-gĭt] *adjective,* 1) wasteful 2) licentious

pro-found [prə-found'] *adjective,* 1) intense, intellectual 2) very deep, endless, bottomless

pro-fuse [prə-fyōōs'] *adjective,* existing in large amounts

pro-fu-sion [prə-fyōō'zhən] *noun,* plenty, abundance

prog-e-ny [prŏj'ə-nē] *noun,* children, offspring

prog-no-sis [prŏg-nō'sĭs] *noun,* foretelling the course and termination of a disease

prog-nos-ti-cate [prŏg-nŏs'tĭ-kāt'] *verb,* to predict, to plan for the future, to foretell

pro-gram [prō'grăm'] *noun,* 1) a plan of action 2) a written outline of the order of events in a public exercise presented as a leaflet 3) a set of instructions that tells a computer to do a specific job 4) a planned activity, verb 5) to use create a set of instructions for a computer

pro-gress [prŏg'rĕs'] *noun, no plural,* 1) a moving toward a goal, development, *verb,* 2) to go forward, 3) to advance to a higher stage, to improve

pro-gres-sion [prə-grĕsh'ən] *noun,* the act of moving forward

pro-gres-sive [prə-grĕs'ĭv] *adjective,* favoring reform, forward thinking

pro-hib-it [prō-hĭb'ĭt] *verb,* to prevent, to forbid, to hinder

pro-hi-bi-tion [prō'ə-bĭsh'ən] *noun,* a law forbidding the sale of alcoholic liquors

proj-ect [prŏj'ĕkt'] *noun,* 1) an activity that requires planning and materials, *verb,* [prō-jĕkt'] 2) to cause an image to be shown on a screen 3) to stick out, to protrude 4) to estimate

pro-jec-tile [prə-jĕk′təl] *noun*, an object propelled through the air

pro-jec-tion [prə-jĕk′shən] *noun*, 1) a bulge, something sticking out 2) a forecast, a prediction

pro-le-tar-i-at [prō′lĭ-târ′ē-ĭt] *noun*, a member of the working class

pro-lif-ic [prə-lĭf′ĭk] *adjective*, abundantly fruitful, plentiful

pro-logue [prō′lôg′] *noun*, an introduction to a play or a story

pro-long [prə-lông′] *verb*, to lengthen, to extend

prom-e-nade [prŏm′ə-nād′] *noun*, 1) a walk in a public place, *verb*, 2) to walk arm in arm

prom-i-nent [prŏm′ə-nənt] *adjective*, important, noticable

prom-ise [prŏm′ĭs] *noun*, 1) a declaration, binding one to do or not to do a specific act, *verb*, 2) to engage to do, to pledge

prom-is-so-ry [prŏm′ĭ-sôr′ē] *adjective*, containing or implying a promise, an informal contract such as an I.O.U. note

pro-mote [prə-mōt′] *verb*, to further, to encourage, to advance

pro-mo-tion [prə-mō′shən] *noun*, advancement in rank, improvement, support

prompt [prŏmpt] *adjective*, 1) without delay, without too much time passing, *verb*, 2) to cause to act, to urge

prompt-ly [prŏmpt′lē] *adverb*, instantly, quickly, without delay

prone [prōn] *adjective*, 1) inclined to, apt 2) lying face down

prong [prông] *noun*, a sharp projecting part, a spike

pro-noun [prō′noun′] *noun*, a word like **he**, **she**, **it**, **they**, used instead of using a noun again

pro-nounce [prə-nouns′] *verb*, 1) to assert, to declare, to proclaim 2) to speak emphasizing proper sounds and accents, to enunciate

pro-nun-ci-a-tion [prə-nŭn′sē-ā′shən] *noun*, the act of saying words with the proper sound and accent

proof [proŏf] *noun*, *no plural*, facts which prove something

prop [prŏp] *noun*, 1) an accessory, *verb*, 2) to support, to reinforce 3) to encourage

prop-a-gan-da [prŏp′ə-găn′də] *noun*, an effort to spread an idea

prop-a-gate [prŏp′ə-gāt′] *verb*, to multiply, to spread around

pro-pel [prə-pĕl′] *verb*, to impel , to cause to move or continue in motion, to push forward

pro-pel-ler [prə-pĕl′ər] *noun*, blades turned by a motor to move a boat or airplane through water or air

pro-pen-si-ty [prə-pĕn′sĭ-tē] *noun*, a natural inclination, a tendency

prop-er [prŏp′ər] *adjective*, fitting, appropriate, respectable

prop-er-ly [prŏp′ər-lē] *adverb*, correctly, rightly, absolutely

prop-er-ty [prŏp′ər-tē] *noun*, land, buildings, cars, boats, and other things people own

prop-er-ty tax [prŏp′ər-tē-tăks] *noun*, a certain amount of money paid as a tax on the land and buildings, and cars and boats a person owns

proph-e-sy [prŏf'ĭ-sī'] *noun*, 1) a prediction made after receiving a sign or a vision, *verb*, 2) to predict, to foretell, to foresee

proph-et [prŏf'ĭt] *noun*, 1) a person who predicts what is going to happen in the future 2) a person who claims to be selected by God to lead

pro-phy-lac-tic [prō'fə-lăk'tĭk] *noun*, a medicine that prevents disease, a preventive

pro-pi-tious [prə-pĭsh'əs] *adjective*, favorable conditions

pro-por-tion [prə-pôr'shən] *noun*, the relation of one portion to another in size, the ratio

pro-pos-al [prə-pō'zəl] *noun*, a formal suggestion, an offer

pro-pose [prə-pōz'] *verb*, to offer for consideration, to put forward

prop-o-si-tion [prŏp'ə-zĭsh'ən] *noun*, a plan, a scheme

pro-pri-e-tor [prə-prī'ĭ-tər] *noun*, an owner, one who has legal right to a business

pro-pri-e-ty [prə-prī'ĭ-tē] *noun*, established standards of proper behavior, appropriateness

pro-pul-sion [prə-pŭl'shən] *noun*, driving forward, thrust

prose [prōz] *noun*, ordinary language, not poetry or verse

pros-e-cute [prŏs'ĭ-kyo͞ot'] *verb*, to enforce the law by legal process, to seek justice for a crime

pros-pect [prŏs'pĕkt'] *noun*, 1) an expectation, a possibility, odds

2) a view, an outlook, *verb*, 3) to explore, to search

pros-pec-tus [prə-spĕk'təs] *noun*, a summary of a plan, an outline

pros-per [prŏs'pər] *verb*, to do well, to become rich, to succeed

pros-per-i-ty [prŏ-spĕr'ĭ-tē] *noun*, material well-being, success

pros-per-ous [prŏs'pər-əs] *adjective*, doing well

pros-the-sis [prŏs-thē'sĭs] *noun*, an artificial device to replace a missing part of the body

pros-trate [prŏs'trāt'] *adjective*, 1) lying down *verb*, 2) to stretch out full on the ground

pro-tect [prə-tĕkt'] *verb*, to guard or defend, to keep from harm

pro-tec-tion [prə-tĕk'shən] *noun*, preservation from loss, injury, or annoyance, safe keeping

pro-té-gé [prō'tə-zhā'] *noun*, one under the care and protection of another, often learning a craft under the guidance of a more experienced person

pro-tein [prō'tēn'] *noun*, a nutrient found in amino acids essential to the growth and repair of animal tissue found in eggs, meat, etc.

pro-test [prə-tĕst'] *noun*, 1) a complaint or formal disagreement, *verb*, 2) to disagree strongly, to object

Prot-es-tant [prŏt'ĭ-stənt] *noun*, *adjective*, a person belonging to a Christian church

pro-to-col [prō'tə-kôl'] *noun*, decorum, formalities, proper manners, a set of rules

pro-ton [prō′tŏn′] *noun*, a particle of matter, a part of an atom

pro-to-type [prō′tə-tīp′] *noun*, original work used as a model by others, an example

pro-trac-tor [prō-trăk′tər-] *noun*, a device for measuring angles on a plane or on paper

pro-trude [prō-trōōd′] *verb*, to stick out, to cause to jut out

proud [proud] *adjective*, a feeling of satisfaction over something one owns, is, or does

proud-ly [proud′lē] *adverb*, feeling a sense of accomplishment after doing your personal best

prove [prōōv] *verb*, 1) to show that something is true with evidence and tests 2) to turn out

prov-e-nance [prŏv′ə-nəns] *noun*, place or source of origin

pro-verb [prŏv′ûrb′] *noun*, a short saying that speaks the truth

pro-vide [prə-vīd′] *verb*, 1) to look out for in advance 2) to furnish

prov-i-dence [prŏv′ĭ-dəns] *noun*, divine direction, foresight

prov-ince [prŏv′ĭns] *noun*, part of a country, with its own government

pro-vin-cial [prə-vĭn′shəl] *adjective*, limited to a small area, parochial

pro-vi-sion [prə-vĭzh′ən] *noun*, requirement, a formal stipulation

pro-voke [prə-vōk′] *verb*, 1) to make someone angry, to annoy, 2) to incite to action

prowl [proul] *verb*, to sneak, to rove about stealthily

prox-im-i-ty [prŏk-sĭm′ĭ-tē] *noun*, nearness, neighborhood, vicinity

prox-y [prŏk′sē] *noun*, 1) a person authorized to act for another 2) a document giving such authorization

pru-dent [prōōd′nt] *adjective*, cautious, sagacious, advisory

prune [prōōn] *noun*, 1) a dried plum, *verb*, 2) to cut off branches of a plant

pry [prī] *verb*, 1) to lift off or open by pushing with leverage 2) to snoop, to spy, to search

psalm [säm] *noun*, a sacred song or poem used to praise God

pseu-do-nym [sōōd′n-ĭm′] *noun*, a fictitious name, a pen name

psy-che [sī′kē] *noun*, 1) the soul or spirit 2) the mind's force

psy-chi-a-trist [sĭ-kī′ə-trĭst] *noun*, a doctor who analyzes and treats mental problems

psy-cho [sī′kē′ō]*noun*, the mind or mental processes

psy-chol-o-gy [sī-kŏl′ə-jē] *noun*, the study of mental states, the mind and its processes

psy-cho-sis [sī-kō′sĭs] *noun*, a major mental disorder in which the personality is very seriously disorganized and one's sense of reality is usually altered

pto-maine [tō′mān′] *noun*, an alkaloid from decomposing animals that is usually poisonous

pub-lic [pŭb′lĭk] *adjective*, 1) open to everyone, *noun*, 2) the people constituting a community

pub-li-ca-tion [pŭb′lĭ-kā′shən] *noun*, published material

pub-lic-i-ty [pŭ-blĭs′ĭ-tē] *noun*, public notice and attention

pub-lish [pŭb′lĭsh] *verb*, to print and sell a manuscript

pub-lish-er [pŭb′lĭ-shər] *noun*, one who creates and offers for sale books, magazines, or newspapers

pud-ding [pŏŏd′ĭng] *noun*, a custard made of milk, sugar and eggs boiled together

pud-dle [pŭd′l] *noun*, a small pool of water on the ground

puff [pŭf] *noun*, 1) a quick burst of air, smoke, etc. *verb*, 2) to make short quick breaths of air

pu-is-sant [pwĭs′ənt] *adjective*, powerful, strong, potent

pul-chri-tude [pŭl′krĭ-tōōd′] *noun*, beauty, loveliness, charm

pull [pŏŏl] *noun*, 1) a force, a power, strength, *verb*, 2) to move something toward oneself through grasping and drawing with force 3) to put on

pul-ley [pŏŏl′ē] *noun*, a wheel used to transmit power by means of a band, rope, or chain

pul-mo-nar-y [pŏŏl′mə-nĕr′ē] *adjective*, affecting the lungs

pulp [pŭlp] *noun*, 1) a soft, moist, sticky mass of fibers made up of wood, straw, etc. and used to make paper and paperboard 2) the soft moist part of fruit that is left after the seeds and peels are removed

pul-pit [pŏŏl′pĭt] *noun*, an elevated desk or platform in a church for a preacher or orator

pul-sate [pŭl′sāt′] *verb*, to throb

pulse [pŭls] *noun*, a heart beat

pul-ver-ize [pŭl′və-rīz′] *verb*, to reduce to a fine powder or dust

pum-mel [pŭm′əl] *verb*, to beat

pump [pŭmp] *noun*, 1) a machine for making liquid or gas move by putting air into something or to extract water or other liquid from the ground using a special lever, *verb*, 2) to draw up using up and down action

pump-kin [pŭmp′kĭn] *noun*, a large orange gourd-like fruit, used in cooking

punch [pŭnch] *noun*, 1) a hit aimed squarely with a fist 2) a fruit drink, *verb*, 3) to hit someone very hard with a fist

punc-tu-al [pŭngk′chōō-əl] *adjective*, on time

punc-tu-al-i-ty [pŭngk′chōō-ăl′ĭ-tē] *adverb*, being prompt, making a point of being on time

punc-tu-ate [pŭngk′chōō-āt′] *verb*, to add proper signs and marks of grammar to writing

punc-tu-a-tion [pŭngk′chōō-ā′shən] *noun*, *no plural*, signs like ,, : , ? and ! used in writing so that the reader emphasizes certain ideas expressed on paper

punc-ture [pŭngk′chər] *noun*, 1) perforation with something pointed, *verb*, 2) to penetrate, to pierce, to make a hole

pun-dit [pŭn′dĭt] *noun*, a critic, a commentator, an expert

pun-gent [pŭn′jənt] *adjective*, powerful or strong odor or flavor

pun-ish [pŭn′ĭsh] *verb*, to discipline, to reprove, to correct

pun-ish-ment [pŭn′ĭsh-mənt] *noun*, 1) a penalty 2) rough or injurious treatment inflicted for an offense

pu-ny [pyōō′nē] *adjective*, insignificant, tiny, weak

pu-pa [pyōō′pə] *noun*, the inactive stage of development of an insect before reaching the adult, often in a cocoon or a cell

pu-pil [pyōō′pəl] *noun*, 1) a boy or girl being taught by a teacher 2) a black dot, the expanding and contracting opening in the iris of the eye, in the middle of the eye that receives light

pup-pet [pŭp′ĭt] *noun*, a small doll that looks like a person or an animal that is moved by wires or with hands on a small stage

pup-py [pəpē] *noun*, a young dog

pur-chase [pûr′chĭs] *noun*, 1) something that has been paid for, an acquisition, *verb*, 2) to acquire for a price, to buy

pure [pyōōr] *adjective*, without anything mixed into it, clean, unpolluted, spotless

pur-ga-to-ry [pûr′gə-tôr′ē] *noun*, 1) a place where a sinner makes amends 2) limbo

purge [pûrj] *verb*, 1) to clean by removing impurities 2) to remove all criminal charges from public record

pu-ri-fy [pyōōr′ə-fī′] *verb*, to make clean, to free from imperfection

pu-ri-ty [pyōōr′ĭ-tē] *noun*, cleanliness, pureness, innocence

pur-loin [pər-loin′] *verb*, to steal

pur-ple [pûr′pəl] *adjective*, 1) the color of violets, *noun*, 2) a color made by mixing red and blue pigments

pur-pose [pûr′pəs] *noun*, the reason for which something exists or has been done

purse [pûrs] *noun*, 1) a small hand bag to hold money and personal items 2) prize money from a race

pur-sue [pər-sōō′] *verb*, to follow with a view to overtake, to persecute, to capture

pur-suit [pər-sōōt′] *noun*, an aim, an objective, a search

pur-vey-or [pər-vā′ər] *noun*, someone who provides food

push [pŏŏsh] *noun*, 1) a shove, a rigorous effort, *verb*, 2) to press or lean against, so as to move

put [pŏŏt] *verb*, 1) to move, to place 2) to impose, to assign

pu-trid [pyōō′trĭd] *adjective*, foul, rotten, decayed, disgusting

put-ty [pŭt′ē] *noun*, an adhesive, glue, compound to seal something

puz-zle [pŭz′əl] *noun*, 1) a picture cut into many pieces to be put back together 2) a game designed to make it difficult for you to finish, *verb*, 3) to exercise one's mind 4) to perplex

pyg-my [pĭg′mē] *noun*, a dwarf, a very small person in Africa

pyr-a-mid [pĭr′ə-mĭd] *noun*, 1) a solid shape with a square base and pointed top, whose faces are triangles with a common corner 2) huge monuments in the desert of Egypt, built as burial vaults for ancient Egyptian kings

py-ro-ma-ni-ac [pī′rō-mā′nē-ăk′] *noun*, a person who likes to set fires and watch them burn

Q

quack [kwăk] *noun*, 1) an imposter, a fake, *verb*, 2) to make noises like a duck

quad-ri-lat-er-al [kwŏd′rə-lăt′ər-əl] *noun*, a four-sided polygon

quad-ru-ped [kwŏd′rə-pĕd′] *noun*, a four-footed animal

quad-ru-ple [kwŏ-drōō′pəl] *verb*, to multiply by four

quaff [kwŏf] *verb*, to drink with enthusiasm

quag-mire [kwăg′mīr′] *noun*, a bog, a marsh, muddy soil

quail [kwāl] *noun*, 1) a game bird that lives in the woods, *verb*, 2) to cower in fear

quaint [kwānt] *adjective*, pleasing in an unusual way, peculiar, odd

quake [kwāk] *verb*, to shake, to shudder, to tremble, to quiver

qual-i-fi-ca-tion [kwŏl′ə-fĭ-kā′shən] *noun*, special training or knowledge

qual-i-fy [kwŏl′ə-fī′] *verb*, 1) to meet the set criteria 2) to make less harsh or strict

qual-i-ty [kwŏl′ĭ-tē] *noun*, 1) a characteristic that distinguishes one person or thing from another 2) a degree of excellence

qualm [kwäm] *noun*, misgiving, remorse, uneasiness

quan-ti-ty [kwŏn′tĭ-tē] *noun*, an amount of something

quar-an-tine [kwôr′ən-tēn′] *noun*, 1) separation of people with a contagious disease, *verb*, 2) to be separated from society while

suffering from an infectious disease in order to prevent the disease from spreading

quar-rel [kwôr′əl] *noun*, 1) an angry dispute, *verb*, 2) to argue or disagree, to fight with words

quar-ry [kwôr′ē] *noun*, 1) a deep pit where stone is cut out of the gound to use for buildings 2) prey, an animal that is being hunted

quart [kwôrt] *noun*, a liquid measurement equal to 32 ounces, 1.13 liters, ¼ of a gallon, 2 pints

quar-ter [kwôr′tər] *noun*, 1) a coin worth 25 cents 2) one of four equal parts, one fourth

quar-ters [kwôr′tərz] *noun*, *plural*, a place where people live, especially if they live where they work

quar-tet [kwôr-tĕt′] *noun*, a group of musicians or singers, also, a piece of music for four instruments or voices

quartz [kwôrts] *noun*, a mineral compound of silica

queen [kwēn] *noun*, 1) the wife of the king 2) any woman who rules a country born to that title, a female monarch 4) any woman who is very important

queer [kwîr] *adjective*, odd, different in a strange way

quell [kwĕl] *verb*, to put down, to quiet, to suppress, to pacify

quench [kwĕnch] *verb*, 1) to satisfy one's thirst or appetite 2) to extinguish, to put out

que-ry [kwîr′ē] *noun*, 1) a question, *verb*, 2) to doubt or question, to interrogate

quest [kwĕst] *noun*, a search, a journey, an exploration

ques-tion [kwĕs'chən] *noun*, 1) an inquiry, *verb*, 2) to ask, to inquire 3) to doubt, to quiz

ques-tion mark [kwĕs'chən-märk] *noun*, the sign ? used at the end of a sentence which asks a question

ques-tion-naire [kwĕs'chə-nâr'] *noun*, a survey submitted to obtain information, a printed set of questions

queue [kyōō] *noun*, a line of people waiting for something

quib-ble [kwĭb'əl] *verb*, to equivocate, to play with words

quick [kwĭk] *adjective*, very fast,

quick-en [kwĭk'ən] *verb*, to hurry, to rush, to hasten, to accelerate

quick-ly [kwĭk'lē] *adverb*, in a hurry, fast, promptly

qui-et [kwī'ĭt] *adjective*, 1) making little or no sound, not moving , still, *noun*, 2) silence

qui-et-ly [kwī'ĭt- lē] *adverb*, calmly, peacefully, silently

quill [kwĭl] *noun*, 1) a large feather from a bird's tail or wing 2) a sharp spine of a porcupine

quilt [kwĭlt] *noun*, a blanket made by sewing small pieces of fabric together in a design

quince [kwĭns] *noun*, a bitter fruit resembling a large yellow apple

quin-tes-sence [kwĭn-tĕs'əns] *noun*, the purest and highest essence of something

quip [kwĭp] *noun*, a taunting remark, a witty remark

quit [kwĭt] *verb*, to give up, to surrender, to depart, to leave

quite [kwīt] *adverb*, completely, entirely, actually, really

quiv-er [kwĭv'ər] *noun*, 1) a case for holding arrows 2) a trembling, *verb*, 2) to shake a little, to tremble nervously

quix-ot-ic [kwĭk-sŏt'ĭk] *adjective*, romantically idealistic

quiz [kwĭz] *noun*, 1) a small test, *verb*, 2) to ask a few questions

quo-rum [kwôr'əm] *noun*, the number of members of any body legally necessary to transact business

quo-ta [kwō'tə] *noun*, the amount, quantity, proportion

quo-ta-tion [kwō-tā'shən] *noun*, 1) words spoken or written lifted from their context 2) the naming or publishing of the current prices of stocks, bonds, etc., the price named

quote [kwōt] *verb*, to say or write something that has been said before by another person

quo-tient [kwō'shənt] *noun*, the product from the division of one number by another

R

rab-bi [răb'ī] *noun*, the leader or teacher of the Jewish religion

rab-bit [răb'ĭt] *noun*, a small furry animal with long ears and long back legs that burrows holes and lives underground

rab-ies [rā'bēz] *noun*, disease caused by organisms called a virus that attacks the nervous system

rac-coon [ră-kōōn′] *noun*, a large black and white nocturnal rodent that lives in trees

race [rās] *noun*, 1) a competitive event, a contest 2) a part of humanity, an ethnic background, *verb*, 3) to run in a dash or compete in a contest

ra-cial [rā′shəl] *adjective*, pertaining to ethnic differences

rac-ism [rā′sĭz′əm] *noun*, narrow-mindedness, intolerance, bigotry

rack [răk] *noun*, 1) a frame on which things are hung or kept, *verb*, 2) to cause pain

rack-et [răk′ĭt] *noun*, 1) a light bat with a netted hoop 2) a loud or confused noise

ra-dar [rā′där] *noun*, *no plural*, the ability to find the position of something using radio waves

ra-di-ant [rā′dē-ənt] *adjective*, shining, luminous, bright

ra-di-ate [rā′dē-āt′] *verb*, to give off energy or rays of light

ra-di-a-tor [rā′dē-ā′tər] *noun*, a device used to cool a liquid

rad-i-cal [răd′ĭ-kəl] *adjective*, unconventional, odd

ra-di-o [rā′dē-ō] *noun*, 1) the use of electromagnetic waves to carry messages without the use of wires, *verb*, 2) to send or transmit messages in this manner

ra-di-o-act-ive waste
[rā′dē-ōăk′tĭvwāst] *noun,* waste left over from creating nuclear power or atomic energy which gives off radiant energy in rays

or particles by the disintegration of the atomic nuclei such as found in radium and uranium

ra-di-um [rā′dē-əm] *noun*, a metallic element found in minute quantities, capable of spontaneously emitting rays

ra-di-us [rā′dē-əs] *noun*, the distance from the center of a circle to its perimeter

raft [răft] *noun*, large pieces of wood joined to make a flat floating surface

raft-er [răf′tər] *noun*, a crossbeam

rag [răg] *noun*, 1) an old torn garment 2) a piece of cloth used to clean, polish or dust

rage [rāj] *noun*, fierce anger that continues with great force

raid [rād] *noun*, 1) a surprise attack, *verb*, 2) to invade, to attack, to assault

rail [rāl] *noun*, 1) a bar extending horizontally between two posts as in a fence or railroad ties, *verb*, 2) to scold, to rant and rave

rail-ing [rā′lĭng] *noun*, a fence or partition to keep people or animals from straying into places they should not go

rail-road [rāl′rōd′] *noun*, a road or track built with parallel steel rails and used by trains

rain [rān] *noun*, 1) part of a weather pattern when water droplets fall from the sky *verb*, 2) to fall as water in drops from the sky 3) to fall like rain

rain-bow [rān′bō′] *noun*, an arc-shaped spectrum of colors seen in the sky, caused by sunlight refracted by raindrops

rain-coat [rān′kōt′] *noun*, a coat that protects a person from getting wet

rain-fall [rān′fôl′] *noun*, the amount of water falling within a given time or area

raise [rāz] *noun*, 1) an increase in salary, *verb*, 2) to lift up, to elevate 3) to grow or cultivate

rai-sin [rā′zĭn] *noun*, a dried grape

rake [rāk] *noun*, 1) a long-handled tool with teeth used to gather leaves on the ground, *verb*, 2) to use a tool to gather fallen leaves or to smooth soil

ral-ly [răl′ē] *noun*, 1) a mass meeting, an assembly, a gathering, *verb*, 2) to restore, to recover, to renew 3) to counter attack

ram [răm] *noun*, a male sheep

ram-ble [răm′bəl] *verb*, 1) to wander in a leisurely manner 2) to chatter, to babble

ram-i-fi-ca-tion [răm′ə-fĭ-kā′shən] *noun*, 1) branching out, a diversion 2) a complicated outcome of a statement or plan

ramp [rămp] *noun*, a slanted walk or roadway that connects a lower to a higher place

ram-page [răm′pāj′] *noun*, a rage, violent behavior, a tantrum

ramp-ant [răm′pənt] *adjective*, unruly, furious, unrestrained

ram-part [răm′pärt′, -pərt] *noun*, a defensive mound of earth

ran [răn] *past tense* of **run**

ranch [rănch] *noun*, a rural estate where livestock are raised

ran-cid [răn′sĭd] *adjective*, rotten, an unpleasant smell or taste

ran-cor [răng′kər] *noun*, bitterness, hatred, malice, ill will

ran-dom [răn′dəm] *adjective*, without order or logic

range [rānj] *noun*, 1) a line of mountains or hills 2) an extensive variety of different things 3) the distance something can travel on its own

rang-er [rān′jər] *noun*, an enforcement agent assigned to patrol a certain region

rank [răngk] *adjective*, 1) bad smell, *noun*, 2) a class thought of as higher or lower than other groups, *verb*, 3) to classify in a group 4) to arrange in a row

ran-kle [răng′kəl] *verb*, to make someone annoyed and mad

ran-sack [răn′săk′] *verb*, to search a house thoroughly

ran-som [răn′səm] *noun*, the release of a person in return for payment

rant [rănt] *verb*, to talk wildly, to speak bombastically

rap [răp] *verb*, 1) to knock, to tap, to thump 2) to talk, to chat

rap-id [răp′ĭd] *adjective*, very fast, quick, swift, often, speedy

rap-id-ly [răp′ĭd-lē] *adverb*, quickly, hurriedly, swiftly

rap-ids [răp′ĭdz] *noun*, *plural*, a place in the river where the river descends creating swift currents producing white water

rap-ture [răp′chər] *noun*, joy, delight, bliss, exhilaration

rare [râr] *adjective*, unusual, uncommon, hard to come by

rare-ly [râr′lē] *adverb*, once in a great while, very seldom

ras-cal [răs′kəl] *noun*, a deceitful person, a mischievous child

rash [răsh] *adjective*, 1) acting quickly without thinking about the results, reckless, *noun*, 2) a patch of red spots on the skin, indicating an allergy

rasp-ber-ry [răz/bĕr′ē] *noun*, a red or purple berry that grows on a bush

rat [răt] *noun*, 1) a small rodent, larger than a mouse, that lives on grain 2) an informer

rate [răt] *noun*, 1) a relative amount 2) the speed of something, *verb*, 3) to evaluate, to rank, to grade, to consider

rath-er [răth′ər, ră′thər] *adjective*, preferable, instead, somewhat

rat-i-fy [răt′ə-fī′] *verb*, to approve formally, to endorse, to confirm

ra-tio [rā′shē-ō′] *noun*, the relation between quantity, degree or rate between one thing and another

rati-oci-na-tion [răsh′ē-ŏs′ə-nā′shən] *noun*, reasoning logically, the process of exact thinking

ra-tion [răsh′ən, rā′shən] *noun*, 1) a fixed amount of something that is given or allowed, *verb*, 2) to limit the amount of resources to each person or group

ra-tion-al [răsh′ə-nəl] *adjective*, reasonable, intelligent, sensible

ra-tion-al-i-za-tion [răsh′ə-nə-lĭ-zā′shən] *noun*, bringing into conformity with reason, logical thinking

ra-tion-al-ize [răsh′ə-nə-līz′] *verb*, to explain away, to make excuses, to justify

rat-tle [răt′l] *noun*, 1) a toy with beads inside that makes a noise when shaken, *verb*, 2) to shake, to clatter, to move noisily

rau-cous [rô′kəs] *adjective*, rough in sound, harsh, strident

rav-age [(răv′ĭj] *verb*, to plunder, to destroy or wreck, to ruin

rave [rāv] *verb*, to speak enthusiastically about something

rav-en-ous [răv′ə-nəs] *adjective*, extremely hungry

ra-vine [rə-vēn′] *noun*, a long, deep ditch or valley in the earth with steep sides, a gorge

raw [rô] *adjective*, 1) uncooked, bloody 2) something in its natural, unadulterated state 3) cold and damp

ray [rā] *noun*, 1) a thin beacon of light 2) part of a line that has an endpoint and goes on and on in one direction 3) a trace, hint

ray-on [rā′ŏn] *noun*, a fine cloth that looks like glossy silk

raze [rāz] *verb*, to level to the ground, to destroy completely

ra-zor [rā′zər] *noun*, a keen edged cutting instrument especially used for shaving

reach [rēch] *noun*, *no plural*, 1) the distance that can be attained 2) grasp, *verb*, 3) to stretch out to touch or take something 4) to get to a place, to arrive at

re-act [rē-ăkt′] *verb*, to act because of something that has happened

re-ac-tion [rē-ăk′shən] *noun*, a direct response

re-ac-tion-ar-y [rē-ăk′shə-nĕr′ē] *adjective*, someone who is against progress

read [rēd] *verb*, to look at words and understand them

read-i-ly [rĕd′ə-lē] *adverb*, easily, willingly, without hesitating

read-i-ness [rĕd′ē-nĭs] *adjective*, willingness, eagerness, ease

re-ad-just [rē′ə-jŭst′] *verb*, to adapt, to fine tune

read-y [rĕd′ē] *adjective*, 1) willing, able, prepared 2) at hand

re-al [rē′əl, rēl] *adjective*, factual, actually existing, true

re-al-ism [rē′ə-lĭz′əm] *noun*, a philosophy that regards external objects as the most fundamentally real things, and perceptions or ideas as secondary

re-al-ist [rē′ə-lĭst] *noun*, 1) someone with a practical outlook 2) an attempt to make art and literature resemble life

re-al-i-ty [rē-ăl′ĭ-tē] *noun*, fact, truth, real things, actuality

re-al-i-za-tion [rē′ə-lĭ-zā′shən] *noun*, a perception, an awareness

re-al-ize [rē′ə-līz′] *verb*, 1) to understand, to make real, to become aware of 2) to achieve

re-al-ly [rē′ə-lē′] *adverb*, truly, very, genuinely, indeed

realm [rĕlm] *noun*, region, sphere, domain or province, kingdom

ream [rēm] *noun*, in the paper business, 500 sheets of paper

reap [rēp] *verb*, to gather the harvest by cutting

rear [rîr] *adjective*, 1) at the back, behind, *noun*, 2) the back part, *verb*, 3) to raise children or livestock until they grow up

rea-son [rē′zən] *noun*, 1) the answer or explanation given as part of a belief 2) a cause for acting, thinking, or feeling a special way, *verb*, 3)) to think things through to present an opinion, to conclude, to infer

rea-son-a-ble [rē′zə-nə-bəl] *adjective*, governed by reason, not excessive, logical

rea-son-a-bly [rē′zə-nə-blē] *adverb*, adequately, fairly, sufficiently, logically

rea-son-ing [rē′zə-nĭng] *noun*, the thought process, logic

re-as-sure [rē′ə-shŏŏr′] *verb*, to help feel safe and comfortable

re-as-sur-ance [rē′ə-shŏŏr′əns] *noun*, restoring confidence

re-bate [rē′bāt′] *noun*, a deduction offered on a purchase in the form of a refund

re-bel [rĕb′əl] *noun*, 1) someone who fights against the leadership of a government, *verb*, 2) to defy any authority, to revolt

re-bel-lion [rĭ-bĕl′yən] *noun*, a revolt, resistance, mutiny

re-bel-lious [rĭ-bĕl′yəs] *adjective*, someone who resists the law, defying authority

re-bound [rē′bound′] *verb*, 1) to bounce back, to move like a boomerang 2) to recover

re-buff [rĭ-bŭf′] *noun*, 1) a sharp rejection, a snub, *verb*, 2) to drive back or repel 3) to refuse bluntly, to reject, to snub

re-build [rē-bĭld′] *verb*, to repair, to put in working order

re-but-tal [rĭ-bŭt′l] *noun*, an argument introduced by the other side in a debate

re-cal-ci-trant [rĭ-kăl′sĭ-trənt] *adjective*, obstinately stubborn

re-call [rĭ-kôl′] *verb*, 1) to summon or call back, 2) to remember

re-cant [rĭ-kănt′] *verb*, to withdraw a previous statement

re-ca-pit-u-late [rē′kə-pĭch′ə-lāt′] *verb*, to repeat the principal points in a program

re-cede [rĭ-sēd′] *verb*, to move back, to retreat, to withdraw

re-ceipt [rĭ-sēt′] *noun*, a written acknowledgment that something was received

re-ceive [rĭ-sēv′] *verb*, to take in, to come into possession of, accept

re-cent [rē′sənt] *adjective*, something that happened a little while ago, prior to the present

re-cent-ly [rē′sənt-lē] *adverb*, a short while ago

re-cep-ta-cle [rĭ-sĕp′tə-kəl] *noun*, 1) a container 2) a contact device in an electrical outlet

re-cep-tion [rĭ-sĕp′shən] *noun*, 1) a greeting, a welcome 2) a social gathering 3) receiving television or radio wave frequencies

re-cess [rē′sĕs′] *noun*, 1) a short intermission 2) a space formed by indentation, a niche

re-ces-sion [rĭ-sĕsh′ən] *noun*, an economic slow down

characterized by high unemployment

re-cid-i-vism [rĭ-sĭd′ə-vĭz′əm] *noun*, habitual return to crime

rec-i-pe [rĕs′ə-pē′] *noun*, a list of ingredients and directions for preparing something

re-cip-i-ent [rĭ-sĭp′ē-ənt] *noun*, the person who accepts something

re-cip-ro-cal [rĭ-sĭp′rə-kəl] *adjective*, mutual, exchangeable, interacting, given in return

re-cip-ro-cate [rĭ-sĭp′rə-kāt′] *verb*, to return the favor for something done or given, to respond in kind

re-cit-al [rĭ-sīt′l] *noun*, a program of music or dance before an audience

re-cite [rĭ-sīt′] *verb*, to repeat from memory, to narrate in detail

reck-less [rĕk′lĭs] *adjective*, careless and dangerous

reck-on [rĕk′ən] *verb*, to come to terms with, to settle matters

re-claim [rĭ-klām′] *verb*, to bring back, to restore, to recover

re-cline [rĭ-klīn′] *verb*, to lean back

rec-luse [rĕk′lōōs′] *noun*, a hermit

rec-og-ni-tion [rĕk′əg-nĭsh′ən] *noun*, 1) acknowledgment of something done or given 2) acknowledgment of acquaintance

rec-og-nize [rĕk′əg-nīz′] *verb*, 1) to acknowledge formally 2) to identify as previously seen or known 3) to greet, to accept

re-coil [rĭ-koil′] *verb*, to retreat, or drawback, to shrink back

rec-ol-lect [rĕk′ə-lĕkt′] *verb*, to call to mind, to remember

rec-ol-lec-tion [rĕk′ə-lĕk′shən] *noun*, something remembered

re-com-mend [rĕk′ə-mĕnd′] *verb*, to present favorably, to urge or suggest, to advise

re-com-men-da-tion [rĕk′ə-mĕn-dā′shən] *noun*, a suggestion for what is most suitable

rec-om-pense [rĕk′əm-pĕns′] *noun*, 1) compensation, payment, *verb*, 2) to pay for service received

rec-on-cil-able [rĕk′ən-sĭl′ə-bəl, rĕk′ən-sĭ′-] *adjective*, capable of being restored to friendship

re-con-cile [rĕk′ən-sīl′] *verb*, 1) to restore to friendship 2) to settle a quarrel 3) to be resigned to accept things as they are

rec-on-dite [rĕk′ən-dīt′] *adjective*, hard to understand, profound, hidden from view, abstruse

re-con-nais-sance [rĭ-kŏn′ə-səns] *noun*, a survey of the enemy by soldiers, reconnoitering

re-con-struct [rē′kən-strŭkt′] *verb*, to put something together or make it again, to rebuild

re-cord [rĭ-kôrd′,rĕk′ərd] *noun*, 1) a written account of what happened 2) a plastic disk on which sounds are recorded, *verb*, 3) to write down something that has happened 4) to register on a disk in a permanent form

re-cord-er [rĭ-kôr′dər] *noun*, 1) an office worker, a secretary 2) a wooden or plastic flute played like a whistle

re-count [rĭ-kount′] *verb*, 1) to tell a story, to narrate 2) to count again

re-course [rē′kôrs′] *noun*, resorting to help when in trouble

re-cov-er [rĭ-kŭv′ər] *verb*, 1) to get back to a normal state, to get well, to recuperate 2) to get back what was lost or stolen

re-cov-er-y [rĭ-kŭv′ə-rē] *noun*, a return to good health

rec-re-a-tion [rĕk′rē-ā′shən] *noun*, sports or play as a form of enjoyable relaxation

re-crim-i-na-tion [rĭ-krĭm′ə-nā′shən] *noun*, an accusation in response to another, a countercharge

re-cruit [rĭ-krōōt′] *noun*, 1) a new member who agrees to join a group, *verb*, 2) to enlist, to attract new members

rec-tan-gle [rĕk′tăng′gəl] *noun*, a flat shape with four straight sides and four right angles, the opposite sides of which are parallel

rec-ti-fy [rĕk′tə-fī′] *verb*, to correct, to make better

rec-ti-tude [rĕk′tĭ-tōōd′] *noun*, uprightness, moral virtue

re-cu-per-ate [rĭ-kōō′pə-rāt′] *verb*, to recover, to restore to health

re-cur [rĭ-kûr′] *verb*, to return again and again as an event

re-cur-rent [rĭ-kûr′ənt] *adjective*, returning repeatedly or coming again to mind

re-cy-cle [rē-sī′kəl] *verb*, to process materials so they can be made into new products

red [rĕd] *adjective*, 1) crimson, cherry, ruby, *noun*, 2) one of the three primary colors: blue, yellow and red

re-deem [rĭ-dēm′] *verb*, 1) to recover, 2) to buy back 3) to exchange 4) to fulfill

red-o-lent [rĕd′l-ənt] *adjective*, 1) fragrant, a pleasant odor 2) strongly reminiscent

re-dress [rĭ-drĕs′] *verb*, to set right, to make amends for, to remedy

re-duce [rĭ-dōōs′] *verb*, to diminish, to make smaller or use less

re-duc-tion [rĭ-dŭk′shən] *noun*, 1) the act of making less 2) the amount by which something is diminished

re-dun-dant [rĭ-dŭn′dənt] *adjective*, superfluous, excessively wordy, repetitious

reed [rēd] *noun*, 1) a small, thin, flat piece of wood, metal, or plastic used in the mouthpiece of some musical instruments, such as the clarinet 2) a tall sturdy grass that grows in the water

reef [rēf] *noun*, a ridge of sand, rocks, or coral, off shore but close to the water's surface

reek [rēk] *verb*, to give off an odor

reel [rēl] *noun*, 1) a spool that turns, winding or unwinding a fishing line 2) a Scottish dance *verb*, 3) to feel happy, elated with excitement

re-enact [rē′ĕn-ăkt′] *verb*, to perform as if for the first time

re-fer [rĭ-fûr′] *verb*, 1)to recommend someone go to see someone for help 2) to use a resource for help

ref-er-ee [rĕf′ə-rē′] *noun*, a sports official with final authority for conducting a game

ref-er-ence [rĕf′ər-əns] *noun*, 1) a specific direction of the attention 2) a written statement of the qualifications of another 3) a resource such as a, dictionary, encyclopedia, thesaurus

re-fine [rĭ- fīnd] *verb*, to reduce to a fine, unmixed, or pure state by removing all unwanted matter

re-fined[rĭ-fīn′d] *adjective*, 1) in a pure state 2) having good manners and good taste

re-fin-er-y [rĭ-fī′nə-rē] *noun*, a factory where resources like oil or sugar are made ready for use

re-flect [rĭ-flĕkt′] *verb*, 1) to throw or cast back the sun's rays 2) to think, to ponder, to meditate

re-flec-tion [rĭ-flĕk′shən] *noun*, 1) an image bounced back from a shiny surface 2) an object seen in a mirror 3) serious thought, thinking back on something

re-flec-tor [rĭ-flĕk′tər] *noun*, a polished surface that reflects light, heat or sound

re-flex [rē′flĕks′] *adjective*, mechanical, unthinking, habitual

re-form [rĭ-fôrm′] *noun*, 1) a change, an improvement, *verb*, 2) to correct, to revise, to renew

re-form-a-to-ry [rĭ-fôr′mə-tôr′ē] *noun*, a jail or prison

re-frac-tion [rĭ-frăk′shən] *noun*, the bending of a ray of light

re-frain [rĭ-frān′] *noun*, 1) a chorus, a verse, *verb*, 2) to abstain, to keep oneself from doing something

re-fresh [rĭ-frĕsh′] *verb*, to revive with rest or food, to renew

re-fresh-ment [rĭ-frĕsh′mənt]
noun, food and drink

re-frig-er-a-tor [rĭ-frĭj′ə-rā′tər]
noun, an appliance that preserves
food in cool temperatures

ref-uge [rĕf′yo͞oj] *noun*, a safe
place, a place to hide

ref-u-gee [rĕf′yo͞o-jē′] *noun*, an
exile, someone forced to leave
his country

re-fund [rĭ-fŭnd′] *noun*,
1) reimbursement, repayment,
verb, 2) to give back, to
reimburse, to repay

re-fur-bish [rē-fûr′bĭsh] *verb*, to
repair and make useful

re-fus-al [rĭ-fyo͞o′zəl] *noun*, a
denial, a refusal

ref-use [rĭ-fyo͞oz′] *noun*, 1) a
general term for solid waste
materials, also called garbage or
trash, *verb*, 2) to deny, not to
allow or agree, to decline to do

re-fute [rĭ-fyo͞ot′] *verb*, to prove
false, to disprove, to rebut

re-gain[rĭ- gān] *verb,* to get back

re-gal [rē′gəl] *adjective*, royal,
majestic, stately, splendid

re-gale [rĭ-gāl′] *verb*, to entertain

re-gard [rĭ-gärd′] *noun*, *plural*,
1) respect, concern, *verb*, 2) to
think of or see 3) to relate to

re-gard-ing [rĭ-gär′dĭng]
preposition, about, concerning

re-gard-less [rĭ-gärd′lĭs] *adverb*,
without concern for problems or
objections, despite, although

re-gat-ta [rĭ-gä′tə] *noun*, a boat or
yacht race

re-gen-er-ate [rĭ-jĕn′ə-rāt′] *verb*, to
renew, to reconstitute

re-gen-er-a-tion [rĭ-jĕn′ə-rā′shən]
noun, a spiritual rebirth

re-gime [rā-zhēm′] *noun*, character
of government or of a prevailing
social system

reg-i-men [rĕj′ə-mən] *noun*, a
systematic plan usually to
improve health

reg-i-ment [rĕj′ə-mənt] *noun*, 1) an
infantry unit 2) to systematize

re-gion [rē′jən] *noun*, an indefinite
area, a territory, a district

reg-is-ter [rĕj′ĭ-stər] *noun*, 1) an
entry in a book or record, *verb*,
2) to enter one's name on the
list, catalogue, record

reg-is-trar [rĕj′ĭ-strär′] *noun*, a
keeper of records

reg-is-tra-tion [rĕj′ĭ-strā′shən]
noun, enrollment

re-gret [rĭ-grĕt′] *noun*, 1) an
apology, a feeling of remorse,
verb, 2) to feel sadness for doing
something wrong

re-gret-ta-ble [rĭ-grĕt′ə-bəl]
adjective, unfortunate, sad

reg-u-lar [rĕg′yə-lər] *adjective*,
habitual, customary, routine

reg-u-lar-i-ty [rĕg′yə-lăr′ĭ-tē]
noun, *no plural*, uniformity,
constancy, on a regular basis

reg-u-late [rĕg′yə-lāt′] *verb*, to
control or direct by a rule

reg-u-la-tion [rĕg′yə-lā′shən]
noun, a rule of conduct, a law

re-gur-gi-tate [rē-gûr′jĭ-tāt′] *verb*,
to spit out food that has been
swallowed, to vomit

re-ha-bil-i-tate [rē′hə-bĭl′ĭ-tāt′]
verb, to restore to proper
condition, i.e., good health

re-hears-al [rĭ-hûr′səl] *noun*, a practice performance

re-hearse [rĭ-hûrs′] *verb*, to practice in preparation for a performance, to try out

reign [rān] *noun*, 1) the period of time when a king or queen rules, *verb*, 2) to rule or govern

re-im-burse [rē′ĭm-bûrs′] *verb*, to make restoration, to repay

rein [rān] *noun*, 1) a strap of a bridle for governing a horse or other animal, *verb*, 2) to pull back or control, to check

rein-deer [rān′dîr′] *noun*, a large deer of arctic regions used to pull a cart or sled

re-in-force [rē′ĭn-fôrs′] *verb*, to strengthen, to stiffen, to fortify

re-it-er-ate [rē-ĭt′ə-rāt′] *verb*, to repeat, to say or do again

re-ject [rĭ-jĕkt′] *verb*, to refuse to accept or use

re-joice [rĭ-jois′] *verb*, to celebrate, to be joyful, to delight

re-ju-ve-nate [rĭ-jo͞o′və-nāt′] *verb*, to make more lively or youthful

re-lapse [rĭ-lăps′] *noun*, 1) a set back 2) to return to a former state, to regress, to revert

re-late [rĭ-lāt′] *verb*, to tell, to connect in thought and meaning

re-la-tion [rĭ-lā′shən] *noun*, 1) a member of the same family 2) an association or friendship

re-la-tion-ship [rĭ-lā′shən-shĭp′] *noun*, 1) the association between things, the affect one thing has on another 2) kinship

rel-a-tive [rĕl′ə-tĭv] *adjective*, 1) in relation to or compared to, *noun*, 2) a person connected by blood or marriage, kin

re-lax [rĭ-lăks′] *verb*, 1) to rest, to be at ease 2) to make less rigid

re-lax-a-tion [rē′lăk-sā′shən] *noun*, *no plural*, a time of rest or ease, leisure, recreation

re-lay [rē′lā] *verb*, 1) to send, to give out, to beam 2) to convey

re-lease [rĭ-lēs′] *noun*, 1) freedom from confinement, *verb*, 2) to let go, to set free, to liberate, to untie 3) to relieve

rel-e-gate [rĕl′ĭ-gāt′] *verb*, to banish, to consign to an inferior position, place or condition

re-lent [rĭ-lĕnt′] *verb*, to become less strict, to become more forgiving

rel-e-van-cy [rĕl′ə-vəns-ē] *noun*, reference to the case at hand

re-li-a-ble [rĭ-lī′ə-bəl] *adjective*, dependable, trustworthy

re-li-ance [rĭ-lī′əns] *adjective*, confidence, something dependent on something else

rel-ic [rĕl′ĭk] *noun*, that which remains or is left, anything valued as a memento

re-lief [rĭ-lēf′] *noun*, *no plural*, 1) assistance, aid, help 2) comfort, ease, cheer 3) the contour of the front of a building

re-lieve [rĭ-lēv′] *verb*, to free from worry, to alleviate, to ease

re-lig-ion [rĭ-lĭj′ən] *noun*, possessing beliefs concerning the nature and purpose of the universe and the supernatural

re-li-gious [rĭ-lĭj′əs] *adjective*, 1) possessing pious beliefs in a God or gods 2) dedicated, devout

re-lin-quish [rǐ-lǐng′kwǐsh] *verb*, to abandon, to leave alone

rel-ish [rĕl′ǐsh] *noun*, 1) a condiment made of vegetables and herbs 2) great enjoyment, *verb*, 3) to savor, to appreciate, to like, to enjoy, to delight in

re-luc-tance [rǐ-lŭk′təns] *noun*, unwillingness or aversion marked by hesitation

re-luc-tant [rǐ-lŭk′tənt] *adjective*, unwilling to participate

re-ly [rǐ-lī′] *verb*, to depend confidently, to trust

re-main [rǐ-mān′] *verb*, to stay

re-main-der [rǐ-mān′dər] *noun*, 1) the fraction left over after a number has been divided 2) what is left over, remnant, residue

re-mains [rǐ-mānz′] *noun*, *plural*, parts which are left behind exposed to air, a corpse

re-make [rē-māk′] *noun*, something that has been redone or given a different form

re-mark [rǐ-märk′] *noun*, 1) something spoken, *verb*, 2) to take notice of, to observe

re-mark-a-ble [rǐ-mär′kə-bəl] *adjective*, uncommon, extraordinary, unusual

re-mark-a-bly [rǐ-mär′kə-blē] *adverb*, notably, especially

re-me-di-al [rǐ-mē′dē-əl] *adjective*, intended to improve poor skills

rem-e-dy [rĕm′ǐ-dē] *noun*, 1) a cure 2) a solution to the problem

re-mem-ber [rǐ-mĕm′bər] *verb*, to keep in your mind, to not forget

re-mem-brance [rǐ-mĕm′brəns] *noun*, a recollection, a memory

re-mind [rǐ-mīnd′] *verb*, to help someone remember

rem-i-nisce [rĕm′ə-nǐs′] *verb*, to think back or talk about past experiences, to recollect

rem-i-nis-cence [rĕm′ə-nǐs′əns] *noun*, the act of recalling the past, recollection, memory

rem-i-nis-cent [rĕm′ə-nǐs′ənt] *adjective*, suggestive, remindful

re-miss [rǐ-mǐs′] *adjective*, negligent, careless, neglectful

re-mit [rǐ-mǐt′] *verb*, to send money usually as a payment

re-mit-tance [rǐ-mǐt′ns] *noun*, the sending of money, bills, etc, money transmitted

rem-nant [rĕm′nənt] *noun*, something left over

re-mon-strate [rǐ-mŏn′strāt′] *verb*, to plead in protest, to argue repeatedly in opposition

re-morse [rǐ-môrs′] *noun*, deep regret for wrongdoing

re-mote [rǐ-mōt′] *adjective*, far away, a great distance from everyone, slight, aloof

re-mov-al [rǐ-mōō′vəl] *noun*, to take something away

re-move [rǐ-mōōv′] *verb*, to take and move somewhere else

re-mu-ner-a-tion [rǐ-myōō′nə-rā′shən] *noun*, compensation, reward

ren-ais-sance [rĕn′ǐ-säns′] *noun*, a rebirth, revival, renewal

rend [rĕnd] *verb*, 1) to split, to tear apart with violence 2) to disturb

rend-er [rĕn′dər] *verb*, to cause to become, to provide, to perform

ren-dez-vous [rän′dā-vōō′] *noun*, a meeting place, an appointment

ren-di-tion [rĕn-dĭsh′ən] *noun*, the artistic interpretation of a song or dance and how it is performed

ren-e-gade [rĕn′ĭ-gād′] *noun*, a person who deserts a cause to join another, an outlaw

re-new [rĭ-nōō′] *verb*, 1) to bring up to date 2) to start again

re-new-al [rĭ-nōō′əl] *noun*, a new start, recurrence, a revival

re-nounce [rĭ-nouns′] *verb*, to abandon, to discontinue, to disown, to repudiate

ren-o-vate [rĕn′ə-vāt′] *verb*, to make repairs, to redecorate

re-nown [rĭ-noun′] *adjective*, fame, widespread recognition

rent [rĕnt] *noun*, 1) money paid to use property, *verb*, 2) to pay someone to use something that they own, to lease

re-pair [rĭ-pâr′] *noun*, 1) the result of renewing or reconditioning something, *verb*, 2) to fix or mend, to make new again

re-par-a-tion [rĕp′ə-rā′shən] *noun*, compensation demanded by a victorious nation from a defeated nation, amends

rep-ar-tee [rĕp′ər-tē′,] *noun*, a clever reply

re-pay [rĭ-pā′] *verb*, to give someone money owed to them

re-peal [rĭ-pēl′] *noun*, 1) retraction, withdrawal, *verb*, 2) to cancel

re-peat [rĭ-pēt′] *verb*, to cause to happen again, to duplicate

re-peat-ed-ly [rĭ-pē′tĭd-lē] *adverb*, said or done again and again

re-pel [rĭ-pĕl′] *verb*, to drive back, to oppose, to ward off

re-pel-lent [rĭ-pĕl′ənt] *adjective*, offensive, disgusting, repugnant

re-pent [rĭ-pĕnt′] *verb*, to express regret, to feel contrite

re-pent-ance [rĭ-pĕn′təns] *noun*, sorrow for what one has done or omitted to do, regret

re-per-cus-sion [rē′pər-kŭsh′ən, rĕp′ər-] *noun*, the effect of something said or done

rep-er-toire [rĕp′ər-twär′] *noun*, a list of musical scores which a company or a person has thoroughly rehearsed and is prepared to perform

rep-e-ti-tion [rĕp′ĭ-tĭsh′ən] *noun*, doing or saying something over and over

re-place [rĭ-plās′] *verb*, 1) to take the place of 2) to make good

re-place-ment [rĭ-plās′mənt] *noun*, a person or thing that takes the place of another, a substitute

re-plen-ish [rĭ-plĕn′ĭsh] *verb*, to fill again, to supply anew

re-plete [rĭ-plēt′] *adjective*, filled to capacity, abundantly supplied

rep-li-ca [rĕp′lĭ-kə] *noun*, a copy

re-ply [rĭ-plī′] *noun*, 1) an answer, a response, *verb*, 2) to give an answer, to reply

re-port [rĭ-pôrt′] *noun*, 1) an oral or written account containing information in an organized form, *verb*, 2) to give an account of something

re-port-er [rĭ-pôr′tər] *noun*, 1) a person who reports legal proceedings or legislative debates 2) a person who gathers information and writes reports for a newspaper, magazine, etc.

re-pose [rĭ-pōz′] *noun*, 1) a state of calm *verb*, 2) to be in a state of rest or relaxation

re-pos-i-to-ry [rĭ-pŏz′ĭ-tôr′ē] *noun*, a storehouse, a vault where things are kept

rep-re-hen-si-ble [rĕp′rĭ-hĕn′sə-bəl] *adjective*, wicked, deceitful

rep-re-sent [rĕp′rĭ-zĕnt′] *verb*, 1) to portray, to stand for something 2) to act or speak for someone or something

rep-re-sen-ta-tion [rĕp′rĭ-zĕn-tā′shən] *noun*, something that expresses a point of view or represents something else, a portrayal

rep-re-sen-ta-tive [rĕp′rĭ-zĕn′tə-tĭv] *adjective*, 1) typically characteristic, *noun*, 2) one acting in the place of another

re-press [rĭ-prĕs′] *verb*, to check, to overpower, to keep down

re-prieve [rĭ-prēv′] *noun*, 1) a delay, *verb,* 2) to postpone, to delay the punishment of

rep-ri-mand [rĕp′rə-mănd′] *verb*, to censure, to scold

re-pris-al [rĭ-prī′zəl] *noun*, retaliation, an act short of war by which a nation seeks to redress a wrong committed against it by another nation

re-proach [rĭ-prōch′] *noun*, 1) blame, censure, *verb*, 2) to blame someone, to criticize

re-pro-duce [rē′prə-dōōs′] *verb*, 1) to produce offspring or create babies 2) to make a copy of something, to duplicate

re-prove [rĭ-prōōv′] *verb*, to reprimand someone for doing something wrong, to correct someone, to rebuke, to chide

rep-tile [rĕp′tĭl] *noun*, a cold-blooded, egg laying vertebrate, such as a lizard or snake

re-pub-lic [rĭ-pŭb′lĭk] *noun*, government in which people elect their representatives

re-pub-li-can [rĭ-pŭb′lĭ-kən] *noun*, a person who advocates a republican government, one who believes in government elected by representatives

Re-pub-li-can Par-ty *noun*, A U.S. political party that developed in the 1850s from those who opposed slavery and that elected Abraham Lincoln as the first Republican president

re-pu-di-ate [rĭ-pyōō′dē-āt′] *verb*, to disown, to renounce, to reject

re-pug-nant [rĭ-pŭg′nənt] *adjective*, disgusting, vulgar, offensive, objectionable

re-pulse [rĭ-pŭls′] *verb*, 1)to offend 2) to drive back, to repel

re-pul-sion [rĭ-pŭl′shən] *noun*, a feeling of aversion or disgust

rep-u-ta-tion [rĕp′yə-tā′shən] *noun*, what people generally think about a person or thing

re-quest [rĭ-kwĕst′] *noun*, 1) something that is asked for, *verb*, 2) to ask for something

re-quire [rĭ-kwīr′] *verb*, to have need of, to insist or compel

re-quire-ment [rĭ-kwīr′mənt] *noun*, a condition that must be met to satisfy a need, something needed, a necessity

req-ui-site [rĕk′wĭ-zĭt] *noun*, a
demand, something required

req-ui-si-tion [rĕk′wĭ-zĭsh′ən]
noun, an official written request
for something

re-quite [rĭ-kwīt′] *verb*, to repay, to
seek revenge, to get even

re-scind [rĭ-sĭnd′] *verb*, to cut off
or remove, to cancel or abolish

res-cue [rĕs′kyōō] *noun*, 1) help or
aid offered to save someone,
verb, 2) to aid or save from
danger or confinement

re-search [rĭ-sûrch′] *noun*, *no
plural*, 1) a careful study
conducted to learn and discover
something new, *verb*, 2) to
investigate or study something,
to make a careful inquiry

re-sem-blance [rĭ-zĕm′bləns] *noun*,
similarity, likeness

re-sem-ble [rĭ-zĕm′bəl] *verb*, to
have similar qualities and
likeness, to be like

re-sent [rĭ-zĕnt′] *verb*, to feel angry
with someone because they were
unfair, to feel indignant

re-sent-ment [rĭ-zĕnt′mənt] *noun*,
exasperation, ill will, anger

res-er-va-tion [rĕz′ər-vā′shən]
noun, 1) a commitment to hold a
space for someone 2) hesitation,
qualm 3) land the government
gave Indians to live on

re-serve [rĭ-zûrv′] *noun*,
1) restraint, *verb*, 2) to hold
something for someone

res-er-voir [rĕz′ər-vwär′] *noun*,
1) a place where a large supply
of anything is built up over time
2) a body of water stored for use

re-side [rĭ-zīd′] *verb*, to live, to
inhabit, to remain, to dwell in

res-i-dence [rĕz′ĭ-dəns] *noun*,
living or dwelling in a place for
some time, a home

res-i-dent [rĕz′ĭ-dənt] *noun*,
someone who resides in a place

res-i-den-tial [rĕz′ĭ-dĕn′shəl]
adjective, where people live

re-sid-u-al [rĭ-zĭj′ōō-əl] *adjective*,
effects remaining after the
principal action

res-i-due [rĕz′ĭ-dōō′] *noun*, the
remainder of something

re-sign [rĭ-zīn′] *verb*, 1) to
relinquish, to withdraw from an
office or position 2) to calmly
accept an unpleasant outcome

res-ig-na-tion [rĕz′ĭg-nā′shən]
noun, *no plural*, 1) reluctant
acceptance of something 2) a
formal statement to leave a job

re-signed [rĭ-zīnd′] *adjective*,
unresisting, patiently submissive

re-sil-ient [rĭ-zĭl′yənt] *adjective*,
the ability to return to the same
size and condition after
excessive stress and strain

res-in [rĕz′ĭn] *noun*, in plastics
manufacturing, the different
compounds used to create the
different forms of plastic

re-sist [rĭ-zĭst′] *verb*, to oppose, to
refuse to comply, to withstand

re-sist-ance [rĭ-zĭs′təns] *noun*, the
act of resisting or opposing, any
opposing force

res-o-lute [rĕz′ə-lōōt′] *adjective*,
determined, purposeful, earnest

res-o-lu-tion [rĕz′ə-lōō′shən] *noun*,
a firm decision, a course of
action decided on

re-solve [rĭ-zŏlv′] *noun,*
1) determination, conviction,
verb, 2) to decide to take action

res-o-nant [rĕz′ə-nənt] *adjective,*
echoing, , vibrant, deep in sound

re-sort [rĭ-zôrt′] *noun,* 1) a
luxurious place visited for rest
and relaxation, *verb,* 2) to turn to
for help or support

re-source [rē′sôrs′] *noun,* 1) a
source of help or supply 2) a
supply or form of wealth

re-source-ful [rē′sôrs′ fəl]
adjective, able to deal promptly
and effectively with difficulties

re-spect [rĭ-spĕkt′] *noun,* 1) an
aspect 2) consideration for
someone, *verb,* 3) to have a good
opinion of someone, look up to

re-spect-a-ble [rĭ-spĕk′tə-bəl]
adjective, honorable, well
thought of, worthy of respect

re-spect-ful [rĭ-spĕkt′fəl] *adjective,*
polite, well-mannered, civil

re-spect-ful-ly [rĭ-spĕkt′fə-lē]
adverb, in a civil manner,
courteously, politely

re-spec-tive [rĭ-spĕk′tĭv] *adjective,*
in relation to one another

re-spec-tive-ly [rĭ-spĕk′tĭv-lē]
adverb, for each separately in
precisely the order given

res-pi-ra-tion [rĕs′pə-rā′shən]
noun, the emission of vapor,
exhaling, breathing

res-pite [rĕs′pĭt] *verb,*
postponement or delay

re-splend-ent [rĭ-splĕn′dənt]
adjective, brilliant, lustrous

re-spond [rĭ-spŏnd′] *verb,* to
answer, to act in return

re-spond-ent [rĭ-spŏn′dənt] *noun,*
one who answers actions in a
civil case, the defendant

re-sponse [rĭ-spŏns′] *noun,* an
answer, a reaction, something
said or done in reply

re-spon-si-bil-i-ty
[rĭ-spŏn′sə-bĭl′ĭ-tē] *noun,* a
person or thing that one is
obligated to take care of

re-spon-si-ble [rĭ-spŏn′sə-bəl]
adjective, 1) the willingness to
respond appropriately
2) trustworthy, reliable

rest [rĕst] *noun,* 1) a quiet time for
relaxation 2) those remaining or
left behind, *verb,* 3) to relax and
feel at ease 4) to lean or put
something on something else

res-tau-rant [rĕs′tər-ənt] *noun,* a
public eating establishment

res-ti-tu-tion [rĕs′tĭ-tōō′shən]
noun, an agreement as terms of a
settlement to pay for loss or
damage

rest-less [rĕst′lĭs] *adjective,* not
relaxed, eager to do something
else, uneasy, fitful, anxious

re-store [rĭ-stôr′] *verb,* 1) to revive
2) to bring back to a former
condition, to reinstate 3) to give
back, to return

re-strain [rĭ-strān′] *verb,* 1) to hold
back with force 2) to limit

re-straint [rĭ-strānt′] *noun,* a
means of holding back from
action, a check, a control

re-strict [rĭ-strĭkt′] *verb,* to
confine, to keep within limits

re-stric-tive [rĭ-strĭk′tĭv] *adjective,*
confining, limiting, inhibiting

re-sult [rĭ-zŭlt′] *noun*, 1) the product or consequence of an action, the outcome, *verb*, 2) to have been the cause of something, to end up

re-su-me [′rez-ə-mā] *noun*, 1) a summary of personal or work history [rĭ-zōōm′] *verb*, 2) to start again after stopping for a period of time

res-ur-rec-tion [rĕz′ə-rĕk′shən] *noun*, 1) the act of rising from the dead 2) renewal, revival

re-sus-ci-tate [rĭ-sŭs′ĭ-tāt′] *verb*, to revive, especially from apparent death, to restore to consciousness

re-tail [rē′tāl′] *verb*, to sell goods directly to the consumer

re-tain [rĭ-tān′] *verb*, 1) to keep in place or hold 2) to have

re-tal-i-a-tion [rĭ-tăl′ē-ā′shən] *noun*, to repay like for like, especially evil for evil

re-tard [rĭ-tärd′] *verb*, to delay the progress of, to hinder

re-ten-tion [rĭ-tĕn′shən] *noun*, 1) holding something 2) having a good memory, retaining

ret-i-cence [rĕt′ĭ-səns] *noun*, not revealing your thoughts or feelings openly

ret-i-na [rĕt′n-ə] *noun*, the light-sensitive colored circle of an eye

re-tire [rĭ-tīr′] *verb*, 1) to withdraw to a place of privacy 2) to remove from active service

re-tire-ment [rĭ-tīr′mənt] *noun*, the period at the end of a career when a person stops working to relax and enjoy their savings

re-tort [rĭ-tôrt′] *verb*, a response

re-tract [rĭ-trăkt′] *verb*, 1) to draw back as claws or fangs 2) to disavow, to recant, to disclaim

re-treat [rĭ-trēt′] *noun*, 1) a place to rest and relax, a place of safety *verb*, 2) to turn around and go back, to withdraw

re-trench [rĭ-trĕnch′] *verb*, to cut down, to economize, to reduce

ret-ri-bu-tion [rĕt′rə-byōō′shən] *noun*, vengeance, compensation, punishment for offenses

re-trieve [rĭ-trēv′] *verb*, 1) to get and bring back 2) to recover

ret-ro-ac-tive [rĕt′rō-ăk′tĭv] *adjective*, that which takes effect from a time in the past

ret-ro-grade [rĕt′rə-grād′] *verb*, going or inclined to go backward

ret-ro-spect [rĕt′rə-spĕkt′] *noun*, looking back on things past

re-turn [rĭ-tûrn′] *noun*, 1) to go to a place and come back from it 2) the income from an investment, *verb*, 3) to give or put something back 4) to go back to the same place 5) to reply

re-use [rē-yōōz′] *verb*, to use again, to recycle

re-veal [rĭ-vēl′] *verb*, 1) to make known, to tell, to disclose, to admit 2) to bring into view

re-veil-le [rĕv′əl lē]*noun*, a signal on a bugle, drum, etc. early in the morning to wake soldiers

rev-e-la-tion [rĕv′ə-lā′shən] *noun*, a sign from heaven, a disclosure

rev-el-ry [rĕv′əl-rē] *noun*, boisterous merrymaking

re-venge [rĭ-vĕnj′] *noun*, 1) a form of getting even, retribution, *verb*, 2) to administer punishment

rev-e-nue [rĕv′ə-nōō] *noun*, 1) the return from an investment 2) an item of income 3) the taxes collected by a government

re-ver-ber-ate [rĭ-vûr′bə-rāt′] *verb*, to echo, to resound

re-vere [rĭ-vîr′] *verb*, to regard with respect, to admire, to look upon with awe, to honor

rev-er-ence [rĕv′ər-əns] *adjective*, honor or respect given to someone because of position

rev-er-end [rĕv′ər-ənd] *noun*, the title of the leader of a church

rev-er-ie [rĕv′ə-rē] *noun*, a daydream, a musing

re-verse [rĭ-vûrs′] *adjective*, 1) opposite, backward, *noun*, 2) a lever that makes a machine go backward, *verb*, 3) to turn around 4) to evoke or annul

re-vert [rĭ-vûrt′] *verb*, to return to a former habit, practice or belief

re-view [rĭ-vyōō′] *noun*, 1) an examination or inspection 2) a critical essay 3) a periodical, *verb*, 4) to go over or examine critically 5) to look back upon

re-vile [rĭ-vīl′] *verb*, to denounce using abusive language

re-vise [rĭ-vīz′] *verb*, to review and make changes in order to bring up to date, to correct, to improve

re-vi-sion [rĭ-vĭzh′ən] *noun*, the changed version of writing, or work, or doctrine

re-vive [rĭ-vīv′] *verb*, to bring back to life or to regain strength

re-volt [rĭ-vōlt′] *noun*, 1) a planned attack on a government or its leaders, *verb*, 2) to fight as a mass of rebels against leaders

3) to offend someone by making them feel ill or disgusted

rev-o-lu-tion [rĕv′ə-lōō′shən] *noun*, 1) the motion of a body about a center or axis 2) the overthrow of a government or system by those who are governed, usually by force, a rebellion 3) a radical change

rev-o-lu-tion-ar-y [rĕv′ə-lōō′shə-nĕr′ē] *noun*, an activist who promotes change

re-volve [rĭ-vŏlv′] *verb*, 1) to orbit the way the Earth moves slowly around the sun 2) to rotate 3) to recur in cycles

re-volv-er [rĭ-vŏl′vər] *noun*, a firearm with a cylinder of several chambers to be discharged repeatedly

re-vul-sion [rĭ-vŭl′shən] *noun*, a sickening feeling, a negative reaction

re-ward [rĭ-wôrd′] *noun*, 1) something given to praise good work, kindness or bravery, *verb*, 2) to give a prize in appreciation of good work

rhap-so-dize [răp′sə-dīz′] *verb*, to speak or write enthusiastically

rhap-so-dy [răp′sə-dē] *noun*, delight, happiness, enthusiasm

rhet-o-ric [rĕt′ər-ĭk] *noun*, the art of using language effectively

rheu-ma-tism [rōō′mə-tĭz′əm] *noun*, a painful disease of the muscles and joints, accompanied by swelling and stiffness

rhi-noc-er-os [rī-nŏs′ər-əs] *noun*, a large wild animal with tough skin and two large horns on its nose, which lives in Africa

Rhode Island [rōd-ī′lənd] *noun*, one of 50 United States located on the east coast, the capital is Providence. The state flower of **Rhode Island** is the violet and the motto is "Hope."

rhom-bus [rŏm′bəs] *noun*, a form with four equal sides in the shape of a diamond

rhu-barb [rōō′bärb′] *noun*, acid leafstalks of a coarse herb, used for sauce or pie

rhyme [rīm] *noun*, 1) correspondence of sounds in words, *verb*, 2) to end the line of a verse with the same sound

rhythm [rĭth′əm] *noun*, 1) repetition of a beat played throughout a musical piece 2) the recurrence of stress or a sound at regular intervals

rib [rĭb] *noun*, one of many narrow bones surrounding the chest

rib-ald [rĭb′əld] *adjective*, wanton, indecent, offensive, vulgar

rib-bon [rĭb′ən] *noun*, a narrow fabric usually of silk, used to trim a dress or a present

rice [rīs] *noun*, a grain in the cereal family from a grass-like plant grown in warm climates

rich [rĭch] *adjective*, 1) wealthy, having many resources 2) plentiful, abundant

rich-es [rĭch′ĭz] *noun*, *plural*, treasures, things worth a lot of money, valuable possessions

rid [rĭd] *verb*, to dispose of

rid-dance [rĭd′ns] *noun*, a cleaning up or out, relief or deliverance

rid-dle [rĭd′l] *noun*, 1) a clever question with an unexpected answer, a puzzling thing, *verb*, 2) to pierce with many holes

ride [rīd] *verb*, to travel on an animal or in a vehicle to go somewhere

rid-er [rī′dər] *noun*, 1) modification of a law, by adding a clause to legislation 2) a passenger on a journey

ridge [rĭj] *noun*, a long narrow raised part of the hill, a crest

rid-i-cule [rĭd′ĭ-kyōōl′] *noun*, 1) taunts, jeers, *verb*, 2) to sneer at, to mock, to make fun of

ri-dic-u-lous [rĭ-dĭk′yə-ləs] *adjective*, unworthy of serious consideration, absurd

rife [rīf] *adjective*, prevalent, common or frequent in occurrence, widespread

ri-fle [rī′fəl] *noun*, 1) a firearm with a long barrel, *verb*, 2) to search hurriedly through

rift [rĭft] *noun*, an opening, a break

rig [rĭg] *noun*, 1) heavy equipment, 2) a vehicle used to haul large shipments, *verb*, 3) to equip

rig-ging [rĭg′ĭng] *noun*, the ropes used to raise and hold the sails of a ship

right [rīt] *adjective*, 1) of or located to the opposite of left **2)** what is fair and good 3) correct, *adverb*, 4) correctly 5) straight to, without stopping *noun*, 6) a freedom allowed by law

right triangle [rīt-trī′ăng′gəl] *noun*, a triangle that has one right angle in it, the opposite side is the hypotenuse

right-eous [rī′chəs] *adjective*, just, virtuous, acting in a moral way

rig-id [rĭj′ĭd] *adjective*, hard, fixed, immovable, not flexible

rig-or [rĭg′ər] *noun*, severity

rig-or-ous [rĭg′ər-əs] *adjective*, strict, severe discipline

rim [rĭm] *noun*, the often-curved edge of something, a border

rind [rīnd] *noun*, the tough outer skin of fruit or cheese that protects it from air

ring [rĭng] *noun*, 1) small circular band worn on the finger 2) a circular object with a vacant center 3) an area where fights are held 4) a small group 5) the sound created by a bell, *verb*, 6) to make a sound like a bell

rink [rĭngk] *noun*, a playing field, a ring, a smooth floor

rinse [rĭns] *verb*, to wash lightly, to cleanse with water after washing

ri-ot [rī′ət] *noun*, 1) unrestrained fighting, vandalism, *verb*, 2) to fight in an angry crowd

ri-ot-ous [rī′ət-əs] *adjective*, unrestrained, tumultuous

rip [rĭp] *verb*, to tear away

ripe [rīp] *adjective*, completely mature, ready to be eaten, aged

rip-en [rī′pən] *verb*, to grow to maturity or when ready to eat

rip-ple [rĭp′əl] *noun*, 1) a little wave, *verb*, 2) to cause little waves of sound or movement

rise [rīz] *noun*, 1) an increase, *verb*, 2) to stand up 3) to move upward 4) to move in a positive direction 5) to get up out of bed

risk [rĭsk] *noun*, 1) a sense or chance of danger involved with

doing something, *verb*, 2) to take a chance of injury or loss

rite [rīt] *noun*, a formal ceremony, a ritual, a custom

rit-u-al [rĭch′ōō-əl] *noun*, a set action or series of actions

ri-val [rī′vəl] *noun*, a competitor

ri-val-ry [rī′vəl-rē] *noun*, a contention, a contest, jealousy

riv-er [rĭv′ər] *noun*, a large natural stream of fresh water that flows into the ocean

riv-et [rĭv′ĭt] *noun*, 1) a metal pin for passing through holes in two or more pieces to hold them together, *verb*, 2) to hold attention firmly, to engross

roach [rōch] *noun*, a cockroach or small insect that eats food

road [rōd] *noun*, a route used for vehicles to travel, an avenue or thoroughfare, a street

roam [rōm] *verb*, to wander about, to travel aimlessly

roar [rôr, rōr] *noun*, 1) a deep angry sound, a loud growl or snarl, *verb*, 2) to growl in a loud voice 3) to laugh loudly

roast [rōst] *noun*, 1) a piece of meat that has been cooked over fire or will be, *verb*, 2) to cook without water over a fire or in an oven, to expose to great heat

rob [rŏb] *verb*, to deprive, to steal from someone, to defraud

rob-ber [rŏb′ər] *noun*, a thief, someone who steals

robe [rōb] *noun*, a piece of clothing that covers most of the body worn for lounging or relaxing

rob-in [rŏb'ĭn] *noun*, a brown song bird with a red breast found in North America

ro-bot [rō'bət] *noun*, a programmed machine designed to do the work of a person

ro-bust [rō-bŭst'] *adjective*, vigorous, strong, healthy

rock [rŏk] *noun*, 1) a hard, natural material of mineral origin, a stone 2) the mineral matter that makes up a large portion of the earth's crust *verb*, 3) to move back and forth or from side to side

rock-et [rŏk'ĭt] *noun*, 1) a missile, a spacecraft, *verb*, 2) to shoot into space 3) to move swiftly

rod [rŏd] *noun*, a thin pole

rode [rōd] *past tense* of **ride**

ro-dent [rōd'nt] *noun*, a small furry four-legged animal, like a squirrel, mouse or rat

ro-de-o [rō'dē-ō'] *noun*, a contest for people like cowhands to show their skill

rogue [rōg] *noun*, a scoundrel

role [rōl] *noun*, a part played by an actor, a characterization

roll [rōl] *noun*, 1) a long, drawn out noise 2) a small rounded portion of bread, *verb*, 3) to move along by turning over and over 4) to make something flat by pressing it with a roller

ro-man nu-mer-als [rō-män'nōō'mər-əlz] *noun*, *plural*, the number symbols used by Romans 2,500 years ago

ro-mance [rō-mǎns'] *noun*, 1) the state of being in love 2) a story about love between people, *verb*, 3) to court romantically

ro-man-tic [rō-mǎn'tǐk] *adjective*, 1) not based in fact, fanciful 2) thoughts of love and adventure

roof [rōōf] *noun*, 1) the external cover of a building 2) the top of the mouth

rook-ie [rōōk'ē] *noun*, a beginner

room [rōōm] *noun*, 1) one of the parts of a house separated by walls and doors 2) space

roost [rōōst] *noun*, 1) a perch, *verb*, 2) to sleep or rest on a perch

roost-er [rōō'stər] *noun*, a domestic male fowl, a cock

root [rōōt] *noun*, 1) the part of the plant that grows in the ground, it's purpose is to hold it in the earth, to absorb moisture and to store nourishment, *verb*, 2) to dig up with the nose or snout 3) to cheer for a team

rope [rōp] *noun*, a heavy cord

rose [rōz] *noun*, 1) a shrub with a beautiful sweet smelling flower, *verb*, 2) the *past tense* of **rise**

ros-ter [rŏs'tər] *noun*, a list

ros-trum [rŏs'trəm] *noun*, a stage for public speaking, a pulpit

rot [rŏt] *verb*, to decompose, to decay gradually, to spoil

ro-ta-ry [rō'tə-rē] *noun*, rotating parts turning on an axis

ro-tate [rō'tāt] *verb*, to turn around a center or axis, to revolve

ro-ta-tion [rō-tā'shən] *noun*, 1) a revolution, turning in a full circle 2) the growing of different crops in the same place usually in regular order

rote [rōt] *noun*, learning through repetition and memorization

rot-ten [rŏt′n] *adjective*, no good

ro-tun-da [rō-tŭn′də] *noun*, a round building or rooms

rough [rŭf] *adjective*, 1) not smooth, uneven, difficult 2) not calm or gentle 3) unfinished, crude, coarse to the touch

rough-ly [rŭf-lē] *adverb*, approximately

round [round] *adjective*, 1) in the shape of a circle or a ball, circular, *noun*, 2) a circle, an orb, a globe 3) a course, a cycle, a series, *verb*, 4) to turn a bend or corner 5) to express a number to the nearest whole number

round-a-bout [round′ə-bout′] *adjective*, 1) not direct or straightforward, *noun*, 2) a traffic circle

rouse [rouz] *verb*, to stimulate, to spur, to wake up, to excite

rout [rout] noun1) a disorganized retreat from an attack, *verb*, 2) to drive out, to defeat decisively

route [rōōt, rout] *noun*, a road for traveling ffrom one place to another

rou-tine [rōō-tēn′] *adjective*, 1) habitual, 2) unoriginal, *noun*, 3) a regular course or procedure

row [rō] *noun*, 1) an arrangement set in a line 2) a quarrel or fight, *verb*, 3) to propel with oars

roy-al [roi′əl] *adjective*, 1) of a king or queen 2) fit for a king or queen

roy-al-ty [roi′əl-tē] *noun*, 1) a member of the monarchy 2) a

payment to the owner for the use of copyright material

rub [rŭb] *verb*, 1) to create friction by moving something back and forth 2) to massage

rub-ber [rŭb′ər] *noun*, *no plural*, a mix of chemicals to form a pliable substance

rub-bish [rŭb′ĭsh] *noun*, *no plural*, refuse, garbage, trash

rub-ble [rŭb′əl] *noun*, pieces or fragments of large objects

ru-by [rōō′bē] *noun*, a precious stone of deep red

rud-der [rŭd′ər] *noun*, a steering mechanism at the back of a boat

rud-dy [rŭd′ē] *adjective*, reddish, healthy-looking

rude [rōōd] *adjective*, not polite, unkind, discourteous behavior

ru-di-men-ta-ry [rōō′də-mĕn′tə-rē] *adjective*, the first undeveloped state, unrefined, imperfect

ruf-fi-an [rŭf′ē-ən] *noun*, a person who is rough and dirty

ruf-fle [rŭf′əl] *noun*, 1) trimming, frill, *verb*, 2) to make uneasy

rug [rŭg] *noun*, a floor covering made of woven fibers or wool

rug-ged [rŭg′ĭd] *adjective*, 1) rough and wild 2) full of rocks with a jagged surface

ruin [rōō′ĭn] *noun*, 1) destruction, damage, *verb*, 2) to destroy

ru-in-ous [rōō′ə-nəs] *adjective*, destructive, harmful

rule [rōōl] *noun*, 1) a law, a guide for conduct or procedure, *verb*, 2) to have power and control over someone 3) to decree

rul-er [rōo'lər] *noun*, 1) someone who governs a body of people 2) an instrument used to measure and draw straight lines

rum-ble [rŭm'bəl] *noun*, 1) a loud sound, like earth moving, *verb*, 2) to make a continuous loud, low noise, like thunder

ru-mi-nate [rōo'mə-nāt'] *verb*, 1) to chew the cud 2) to ponder, to think about, to meditate

rum-mage [rŭm'ĭj] *noun*, 1) odds and ends, miscellany, *verb*, 2) to look for, to rifle through

ru-mor [rōo'mər] *noun*, gossip, common talk, hearsay

run [rŭn] *noun*, 1) the distance traveled, a journey 2) a score in a baseball game 3) movement that is quicker than walking, *verb*, 4) to move quickly or swiftly 5) to work or make work 6) to go over 7) to escape, to retreat 8) to ooze or pour out

rung [rŭng] *noun*, 1) a rod on a ladder that is a step, *verb*, 2) *past participle* of **ring**

run-ner [rŭn'ər] *noun*, 1) a long ski on the bottom of a sled used on snow and ice 2) a person who runs errands 3) a carpet or decorative cover placed on a walk way

rup-ture [rŭp'chər] *noun*, 1) a fracture, a breach, *verb*, 2) to break, to fracture, to split

ru-ral [rōor'əl] *adjective*, having to do with, in, or like farmland, country people, or life in the country, rustic

ruse [rōos] *noun*, a trick, gimmick

rush [rŭsh] *noun*, *no plural*, 1) rapid movement, haste 2) reeds that grow near the water, *verb*, 3) to move quickly or fast as in a hurry 4) to charge, to attack

rust [rŭst] *noun*, *no plural*, 1) a corrosive red-brown substance that forms on iron when it has been exposed to water and oxygen, *verb*, 2) to become covered with the corrosive element 3) to deteriorate

rus-tic [rŭs'tĭk] *adjective*, referring to country people, rural

rus-tle [rŭs'əl] *verb*, to make a soft rubbing sound, to crackle

rut [rŭt] *noun*, a deep narrow groove in the ground

ruth-less [rōoth'lĭs] *adjective*, cruel, harsh, merciless

rye [rī] *noun*, a grass with seeds that are made into flour

S

Sab-bath [săb'əth] *noun*, a holy day, a day of rest

sack [săk] *noun*, a large bag made of woven material strong enough to carry things

sa-cred [sā'krĭd] *adjective*, holy, worshipped, religious

sac-ri-fice [săk'rə-fīs'] *noun*, 1) an offering, the surrender of anything, *verb*, 2) to give up something, to forfeit

sac-ro-sanct [săk'rō-săngkt'] *adjective*, most sacred, holy

sad [săd] *adjective*, unhappy, sorrowful, affected by grief

sad-dle [săd′l] *noun*, 1) a seat made of leather that fits over the back of a horse, *verb*, 2) to burden

sa-dis-tic [sə-dĭs′tĭk] *adjective*, pleasure in being cruel

sa-fa-ri [sə-fär′ē] *noun*, a journey into the jungles and plains of Africa, to look at wild animals

safe [sāf] *adjective*, 1) not in danger, protected, secure, *noun*, 2) a vault, a chest, a repository

safe-ty [sāf′tē] *noun*, a way of preventing damage to workers or a machine, protection

sag [săg] *verb*, 1) to hang down, to droop 2) to decline in value

sa-ga [sä′gə] *noun*, any legend, a long drawn out story

sa-ga-cious [sə-gā′shəs] *adjective*, shrewd, wise, knowledgeable

sage [sāj] *noun*, a wise man

said [sĕd] *past tense* of **say**

sail [sāl] *noun*, 1) a large cloth used to catch the wind and move a boat, *verb*, 2) to travel on water 3) to navigate a ship equipped with sails 4) to glide

sail-or [sā′lər] *noun*, a seaman, someone who works on a ship

saint [sānt] *noun*, a person who has lived a religious life and has been recognized by a group of religious leaders for good work

sake [sāk] *noun*, used with **for**, to show purpose or reason

sal-ad [săl′əd] *noun*, a preparation of vegetables, fruit, fish, or meat, dressed with vinegar, oil, etc.

sal-a-ry [săl′ə-rē] *noun*, fixed wages for a year, quarter, or month, for services

sale [sāl] *noun*, 1) the exchange of goods for money 2) when merchandise is sold at a reduced price 3) an auction

sales-man [sālz′mən] *noun*, one whose occupation is to sell goods or merchandise

sales tax [sālz-tăks] *noun*, a tax people pay for purchases

sa-li-ent [sā′lē-ənt] *adjective*, standing out, conspicuous, striking, noticeable, obvious

sa-line [sā′lēn′] *adjective*, salty

sa-li-va [sə-lī′və] *noun*, a fluid secreted in the mouth to help digest food, spit

salm-on [săm′ən] *noun*, a species of fresh-water fish

sa-loon [sə-lōōn′] *noun*, a bar or tavern, a large public room

salt [sôlt] *noun*, a white crystal compound of chlorine and sodium found in sea water, used to flavor food and preserve meat

sa-lu-bri-ous [sə-lōō′brē-əs] *adjective*, promoting health

sal-u-ta-tion [săl′yə-tā′shən] *noun*, a greeting, something uttered

sal-u-tar-y [săl′yə-tĕr′ē] *adjective*, beneficial, wholesome

sa-lute [sə-lōōt′] *noun*, 1) a sign of respect for a superior officer *verb*, 2) to hold up the right hand to the forehead

sal-vage [săl′vĭj] *noun*, 1) property saved from destruction, *verb*, 2) to save, to recycle, to recover, to rescue

sal-va-tion [săl-vā′shən] *noun*, saved from harm or loss, deliverance from evil

salve [săv] *noun*, a medicinal ointment, a lotion, a balm

same [sām] *adjective*, 1) having the same identifying characteristics, identical 2) not different

sam-ple [săm′pəl] *noun*, 1) a part of anything shown as quality, a specimen, *verb*, 2) to try or test

san-a-to-ri-um [săn′ə-tôr′ē-əm] *noun*, a place where chronically ill patients receive the care they need until they recover

sanc-ti-fy [săngk′tə-fī′] *verb*, to bless, to make holy, to anoint

sanc-tion [săngk′shən] *noun*, 1) coercive measures directed against a nation that has violated international law, *verb*, 2) to approve, to support, to confirm

sanc-tu-ar-y [săngk′chōō-ĕr′ē] *noun*, church, a place of refuge

sand [sănd] *noun, no plural*, fine grains made of rocks usually found near the sea or in deserts

san-dal [săn′dl] *noun*, a kind of shoe consisting of a sole strapped to the foot

sand-wich [sănd′wĭch, săn′-] *noun*, slices of bread with something between them such as meat, cheese or jelly

sane [sān] *adjective*, reasonable, sensible, sound in mind

sang [săng] *past tense* of **sing**

san-i-tar-y [săn′ĭ-tĕr′ē] *adjective*, very clean, antiseptic, hygiene

san-i-ta-tion [săn′ĭ-tā′shən] *noun*, the maintenance of keeping things clean

san-i-ty [săn′ĭ-tē] *noun*, a healthy outlook, a state of being sane

sank [săngk] *verb, past tense* of **sink**

sap [săp] *noun, no plural*, 1) the fluid in a plant that gives nourishment, *verb*, 3) to take strength from something, to weaken gradually

sapi-ent [sā′pē-ənt] *adjective*, wise, shrewd, showing great wisdom

sap-ling [săp′lĭng] *noun*, a young tree, a sprout of a tree

sap-phire [săf′īr′] *noun*, a precious gemstone of a blue color

sar-casm [sär′kăz′əm] *noun*, scornful remarks, ridicule

sar-cas-tic [sär-kăs′tĭk] *adjective*, taunting, satirical, scornful

sar-coph-a-gus [sär-kŏf′ə-gəs] *noun*, a coffin, a casket

sar-dine [sär-dēn′] *noun*, a small herring preserved in olive oil

sash [săsh] *noun*, a wide ribbon worn around the waist or over the shoulder

sat-el-lite [săt′l-īt′] *noun*, 1) a small, heavenly body orbiting around a planet 2)an artificial object launched to orbit the earth or other celestial bodies

sa-ti-ate [sā′shē-āt′] *verb*, to satisfy fully, to supply to excess

sat-ire [săt′īr′] *noun*, a form of writing that makes fun of habits, ideas or customs

sat-is-fac-tion [săt′ĭs-făk′shən] *noun*, the feeling of having what you need and want

sat-is-fac-to-ry [săt′ĭs-făk′tə-rē] *adjective*, sufficient, fulfilling all requirements, adequate

sat-is-fy [săt′ĭs-fī′] *verb*, 1) to be enough or good enough, to meet a need 2) to make sure

sat-u-rate [săch′ə-rāt′] *verb*, to become thoroughly soaked

Sat-ur-day [săt′ər-dē′]*noun*, the seventh day of the week

sauce [sôs] *noun*, a liquid of a variety of ingredients eaten with food to improve its taste

sauc-er [sô′sər] *noun*, a small plate put under a cup to catch the drips

saun-ter [sôn′tər] *verb*, to stroll, to walk slowly, to meander

sau-sage [sô′sĭj] *noun*, minced and seasoned meat, commonly enclosed in an edible casing

sav-age [săv′ĭj] *adjective*, wild, untamed, uncivilized

sa-van-nah [sə-văn′ə] *noun*, a grassy plain that has very few trees in a tropical climate

sa-vant [să-vänt′] *noun*, a scholar, a learned person, a sage

save [sāv] *verb*, 1) to rescue from harm or danger 2) to set aside for future use, to store

sav-ings [sā′vĭngz] *noun*, *plural, no singular*, money set aside to use in the future, reserve funds

sav-ior [sāv′yər] *noun*, someone who saves others from danger

sa-vor [sā′vər] *noun*, 1) a taste or aroma, *verb*, 2) to taste or enjoy a distinctive flavor, smell or quality, to appreciate

saw [sô] *noun*, 1) a tool with a jagged blade and handle used to cut wood, *verb*, 2) *past tense* of *see* 3) to cut with a serrated blade or saw

say [sā] *verb*, to speak something

say-ing [sā′ĭng] *noun*, a wise statement that is full of truth like a proverb or aphorism

scab [skăb] *noun*, 1) a hard covering of coagulated blood on a wound 2) a worker who stays on the job while others go on strike

scaf-fold [skăf′əld] *noun*, 1) a temporary platform built to hold laborers while working on a building 2) the gallows

scald [skôld] *verb*, 1) to injure or burn with hot liquid 2) to heat to just below the boiling point

scale [skāl] *noun*, 1) a balance to measure weight 2) a range, degree, or progression 3) a protective crust *verb*, 4) to adjust to a standard of measure 5) to climb or ascend

sca-lene tri-an-gle [skā′lēn′ trī′ăng′gəl] *noun*, a triangle with unequal sides

scal-lop [skăl′lŏp]*noun*, 1) a kind of mollusk with two deeply grooved, curved shells, that swims by rapidly snapping its shells together 2) any of a series of curves forming an ornamental edge on cloth, lace, etc.

scalp [skălp] *noun*, 1) the skin and hair of the head, *verb*, 2) to remove the hair from someone

scam-per [skăm′pər] *verb*, to scurry, to run quickly

scan [skăn] *verb*, to look over, to review, to examine closely

scan-dal [skăn′dl] *noun*, an incident which offends conscience or moral feelings

scape-goat [skāp′gōt′] *noun*, someone who bears the blame for others

scar [skär] *noun*, 1) a mark left where a wound has been, *verb*, 2) to make a deep cut or to cause deep unforgettable pain

scar-ab [skăr′əb] *noun*, a large beetle with a dark shell

scarce [skârs] *adjective*, hard to find or come by, not plentiful

scarce-ly [skârs′lē] *adverb*, with difficulty, barely, hardly

scare [skâr] *noun*, 1) a sudden fright, *verb*, 2) to make someone afraid, to frighten, to terrify

scarf [skärf] *noun, plural,* **scarves,** a triangular or rectangular piece of cloth worn around the head, neck, or shoulders

scat-ter [skăt′ər] *verb*, to throw things everywhere, to disperse

scav-en-ger [skăv′ən-jər] *noun*, collector of garbage, an animal that devours refuse

scene [sēn] *noun*, 1) a setting, a view 2) a specific place 3) a shocking incident, a fight

scen-er-y [sē′nə-rē] *noun, no plural*, the setting of a place or landscape, the panorama

sce-nic [sē′nĭk] *adjective*, full of natural splendors, breathtaking

scent [sĕnt] *noun*, a smell that characterizes things

sched-ule [skĕj′ool] *noun*, 1) a written formal list or inventory, *verb*, 2) to arrange tasks to fit into a specific time frame

scheme [skēm] *noun*, 1) a plan, purpose, arrangement, *verb*, 2) to make secret plans, to plot

schol-ar [skŏl′ər] *noun*, a person who studies a particular subject at great length, a student

schol-ar-ship [skŏl′ər-shĭp′] *noun*, money granted to a worthy student to pay for their education

scho-las-tic [skə-lăs′tĭk] *noun*, pertaining to a school or education

school [skool] *noun*, 1) a place of instruction 2) a style, manner, method 3) a company of fish

schoon-er [skoo′nər] *noun*, a sailing ship with fore and aft rigging

sci-ence [sī′əns] *noun*, classified knowledge of the physical world

sci-en-tif-ic [sī′ən-tĭf′ĭk] *adjective*, in conformity to the principles of the physical world

sci-en-tist [sī′ən-tĭst] *noun*, a person who studies information about natural phenomena

scis-sors [sĭz′ərz] *noun*, a tool with two blades and handles, pivoted together that is used for cutting

scoff [skŏf] *verb*, to ridicule or make fun of, to deride, to jeer

scold [skōld] *verb*, to angrily tell someone they did something wrong, to reprimand

scoop [skoop] *noun*, 1) a large spoonful, *verb*, 2) to take some from the whole thing with a spoon or the hands

scoot [skoot] *verb*, to move quickly

scope [skōp] *noun*, 1) a range of one's mind 2) opportunity to function, capacity

scorch [skôrch] *verb*, to burn lightly leaving a brown stain

score [skôr] *noun*, 1) the points you get on a test or in a game 2) the reason, the purpose 3) a copy of a musical composition showing all parts for instruments and voices 4) a period of twenty years, *verb*, 5) to make points in a game 6) to achieve success

scorn [skôrn] *noun*, 1) disrespect, disdain, hate, *verb*, 2) to act like someone is worthless

scor-pi-on [skôr'pē-ən] *noun*, an arachnid that kills with its poisonous tail

scoun-drel [skoun'drəl] *noun*, a villain, a rascal, a mean person

scour [skour] *verb*, 1) to search an area thoroughly 2) to clean and polish by rubbing

scout [skout] *noun*, a person sent out ahead to obtain information

scowl [skoul] *noun*, 1) an angry, disgusted expression on the face, *verb*, 2) to make an angry expression showing disapproval

scram-ble [skrăm'bəl] *verb*, to move quickly on hands and knees, to hurry along

scrap [skrăp] *noun*, waste with some value, particularly material left over from construction or manufacturing suitable for reprocessing

scrap-book [skrăp'bŏŏk'] *noun*, a blank book filled with mementos, cards and souvenirs

scrape [skrăp] *noun* 1) a predicament, *verb*, 2) to take something off by rubbing it with a sharp edge 3) to make a grating sound

scratch [skrăch] *noun*, 1) a mark or wound made with something

pointed, *verb*, 2) to make marks with something pointed 3) to remove a layer by rubbing

scream [skrēm] *noun*, 1) a loud, shrill cry made in pain or fear, *verb*, 2) to make a sharp cry

screech [skrēch] *noun*, 1) a loud high-pitched noise, *verb*, 2) to make a harsh shrill noise

screen [skrēn] *noun*, 1) a portable covered framework in the nature of a partition 2) a grating of fine wire 3) protection, *verb*, 4) to eliminate applicants

screw [skrōō] *noun*, 1) a cylinder, grooved in an advancing spiral on its surface, *verb*, 2) to turn around and around

scrib-ble [skrĭb'əl] *verb*, to write or draw in an unintelligible manner

scrim-mage [skrĭm'ĭj] *noun*, a football or soccer practice

script [skrĭpt] *noun*, 1) a form of handwriting that connects the letters in a word 2) written words to be spoken from a text

scrip-ture [skrĭp'chər] *noun*, any sacred writing or book

scroll [skrōl] *noun*, 1) a rod with a roll of paper attached, *verb*, 2) to move a cursor smoothly, vertically or sideways, to review data on a computer screen

scrub [skrŭb] *verb*, to rub with a hard brush to clean off a spot

scru-pu-lous [skrōō'pyə-ləs] *adjective*, careful, cautious, exact, punctilious, precise

scru-ti-nize [skrōōt'n-īz'] *verb*, to examine closely and critically

scru-ti-ny [skrōōt'n-ē] *noun*, close examination, minute inspection

sculpt [skŭlpt] *verb*, to make or shape a statue

sculp-tor [skŭlp′tər] *noun*, one who carves or cuts wood or stone into statues

sculp-ture [skŭlp′chər] *noun*, works of art made from stone, clay or metal, a statue

scythe [sīth] *noun*, a long, curved-blade instrument for cutting grass by hand

sea [sē] *noun*, part of an ocean that is partially surrounded by land

sea-gull [sē′gŭl′] *noun*, a bird that lives near the ocean and scavenges for food

seal [sēl] *noun*, 1) an emblem affixed to a document to prove authenticity 2) a mammal with sleek skin, and limbs in the form of flippers, that lives in the water and on land, *verb*, 3) to close tightly so that something cannot be opened

seam [sēm] *noun*, 1) the stitches joining two pieces of cloth together 2) a fissure

search [sûrch] *noun*, 1) a careful investigation, a hunt, *verb*, 2) to look for someone or something

sea-son [sē′zən] *noun*, 1) a special time of year devoted to a certain activity 2) one of the four divisions of the year: fall, winter, spring, summer, *verb*, 3) to flavor or add zest to food

seat [sēt] *noun*, 1) a place to sit or a cushion to sit on 2) a location

se-cede [sĭ-sēd′] *verb*, to withdraw from association or fellowship

se-ces-sion [sĭ-sĕsh′ən] *noun*, withdrawal

se-clu-sion [sĭ-klo͞o′zhən] *noun*, 1) hiding, isolation 2) privacy

sec-ond [sĕk′ənd] *adjective*, 1) coming directly after the first, *noun*, 2) a very short period of time, a moment, *verb*, 3) to endorse, to support a motion

se-cre-cy [sē′krĭ-sē] *noun*, keeping things quiet without the knowledge of others

se-cret [sē′krĭt] *adjective*, 1) kept from the knowledge of most people, *noun*, 2) something known only to oneself or a few

sec-re-tar-y [sĕk′rĭ-tĕr′ē] *noun*, 1) a person who writes letters, files documents 2) a government officer who is a member of the President's Cabinet

se-crete [sĭ-krēt′] *verb*, to produce a liquid discharge

se-cre-tion [sĭ-krē′shən] *noun*, a fluid emitted from a gland

sec-tion [sĕk′shən] *noun*, a piece of the whole, a portion, a part

sec-tor [sĕk′tər, -tôr′] *noun*, region, area, zone, a distinct part

sec-u-lar [sĕk′yə-lər] *adjective*, worldly, not pertaining to church matters, temporal, earthly

se-cure [sĭ-kyo͝or′] *adjective*, 1) safe 2) strong and fixed firmly, *verb*, 3) to assure

se-cu-ri-ty [sĭ-kyo͝or′ĭ-tē] *noun*, 1) safety, assurance, freedom from danger 2) stocks and bonds

se-date [sĭ-dāt′] *adjective*, dignified, composed, calm

sed-a-tive [sĕd′ə-tĭv] *noun*, a tranquilizer, a narcotic

sed-en-tar-y [sĕd′n-tĕr′ē]
adjective, accustomed to sitting
most of the day

sed-i-ment [sĕd′ə-mənt] *noun*, the
solid matter that settles to the
bottom in a liquid

se-di-tion [sĭ-dĭsh′ən] *noun*,
resistance to authority,
insubordination

sed-ul-ous-ly [sĕj′ə-ləs-lē]
adjective, diligently, loyally

see [sē] *verb*, 1) to perceive or
acknowledge with the eye 2) to
understand, to comprehend 3) to
go and look 4) to meet 5) to
think about something and to act
if necessary

seed [sēd] *noun*, a small grain from
which a plant grows

seek [sēk] *verb*, to look for

seem [sēm] *verb*, to appear to be
true or probable

seen [sēn] past perfect of **see**

seep [sēp] *verb*, a liquid flowing
slowly or leaking through

seg-ment [sĕg′mənt] *noun*, any part
which separates from the whole

seg-re-ga-tion [sĕg′rĭ-gā′shən]
noun, the act of setting groups
apart, separation, racial
discrimination

seis-mic [sīz′mĭk] *adjective*,
pertaining to an earthquake

seize [sēz] *verb*, 1) to grasp
suddenly, to take possession of
by force

sel-dom [sĕl′dəm] *adjective*, rarely,
not often, infrequently

se-lect [sĭ-lĕkt′] *adjective*, 1) first
rate, *verb*, 2) to choose, to pick

se-lec-tion [sĭ-lĕk′shən] *noun*, a
collection of things chosen

self [sĕlf] *noun*, your person, what
you are, individuality

self-ish [sĕl′fĭsh] *adjective*, to think
only of oneself and not others

self-ish-ness [sĕl′fĭsh- nĭs] *noun*,
pettiness, being small-minded

sell [sĕl] *verb*, 1) to offer in
exchange for money 2) to deal in

sem-blance [sĕm′bləns] *noun*,
likeness, resemblance, similarity

se-mes-ter [sə-mĕs′tər] *noun*,
either of two terms into which
the period of instruction is
divided in an academic year

sem-i-cir-cle [sĕm′ĭ-sûr′kəl] *noun*,
the shape of half a circle

sem-i-co-lon [sĕm′ĭ-kō′lən] *noun*, a
mark of punctuation (;) used to
separate two independent clauses
when there is no conjunction, as
*When you make a mistake, admit
it; learn from it and don't repeat
it. Bear Bryant*

sen-ate [sĕn′ĭt] *noun*, one of the
groups that constitutes the
legislative government

sen-a-tor [sĕn′ə-tər] *noun*, an
elected representative who
serves in the Senate

send [sĕnd] *verb*, to cause
something or someone to go
somewhere, to dispatch

se-nil-i-ty [sĭ-nĭl′ĭ-tē] *noun*, feeble
mindedness of old age

sen-ior [sēn′yər] *adjective*,
1) older, *noun*, 2) a student in the
final year of a four year course

sen-sa-tion [sĕn-sā′shən] *noun*,
1) a feeling 2) excited interest

sense [sĕns] *noun*, 1) reason or understanding 2) a reasonable meaning 3) a feeling, *verb*, 4) to recognize, to detect

sense-less [sĕns′lĭs] *adjective*, stupid, unconscious

sen-si-bil-i-ty [sĕn′sə-bĭl′ĭ-tē] *noun*, awareness, understanding

sen-si-ble [sĕn′sə-bəl] *adjective*, reasonable, possessing good sense, smart, perceptive

sen-si-tive [sĕn′sĭ-tĭv] *adjective*, quick to notice or feel, easily affected by slight change

sen-su-ous [sĕn′shōō-əs] *adjective*, exuding sexuality, appealing

sen-tence [sĕn′təns] *noun*, 1) a combination of words which express a thought, beginning with a capital letter, ending with a period 2) the judgment of a court, *verb*, 3) to pass judgment on, to inflict punishment

sen-ti-ment [sĕn′tə-mənt] *noun*, feelings, thoughts, emotions

sen-ti-men-tal [sĕn′tə-mĕn′tl] *adjective*, expressing feelings of love, pity, etc. to excess

sen-ti-nel [sĕn′tə-nəl] *noun*, a soldier set to guard an army from surprise, a sentry

sen-try [sĕn′trē] *noun*, a lookout, guard, watchman, a soldier

sep-a-rate [sĕp′ə-rāt′] *adjective*, 1) not together, not joined, *verb*, 2) to divide, to disconnect, to keep apart

sep-a-ra-tion [sĕp′ə-rā′shən] *noun*, time apart from each other

Sep-tem-ber [sĕp-tĕm′bər] *noun*, the ninth month of the year, having 30 days

sep-tic [sĕp′tĭk] *adjective*, decaying, putrid or toxic, rotten

sep-ul-cher [sĕp′əl-kər] *noun*, a tomb, a burial place

se-quel [sē′kwəl] *noun*, the continuation of a story

se-quence [sē′kwəns] *noun*, a succession, a following or coming after in a series

se-ques-ter [sĭ-kwĕs′tər] *verb*, to go into isolation, to remove, to seclude, to set apart

sere-nade [sĕr′ə-nād′] *verb*, to court, to play music under a window to charm a sweetheart

ser-en-dip-i-tous [sĕr′ən-dĭp′ĭ-t əs] *adjective*, fortunate discoveries made by accident

se-rene [sə-rēn′] *adjective*, calm, tranquil, placid, clear, peaceful

se-ren-i-ty [sə-rĕn′ĭ-tē] *noun*, tranquility, peace

ser-geant [sär′jənt] *noun*, a noncommissioned officer ranking next above a corporal

se-ries [sîr′ēz] *noun*, a number of things connected in a sequence

se-ri-ous [sîr′ē-əs] *adjective*, 1) grave in manner or disposition, earnest, solemn, sincere 2) weighty

se-ri-ous-ly [sîr′ē-əs-lē] *adverb*, thoughtfully, sincerely

ser-mon [sûr′mən] *noun*, a talk given by a religious leader

ser-pent [sûr′pənt] *noun*, a snake

ser-pen-tine [sûr′pən-tēn′] *adjective*, winding, twisting

ser-rat-ed [sĕr′ā′tĭd] *adjective*, having a saw-toothed or jagged edge

se-rum [sîr′əm] *noun*, the watery protein of an animal fluid

serv-ant [sûr′vənt] *noun*, one who works for another especially in a home to perform chores

serve [sûrv] *verb*, 1) to do work for other people, to give assistance or help 2) to offer food to someone 3) to answer a purpose

serv-ice [sûr′vĭs] *noun*, 1) a job that one performs for others 2) a church ceremony

ser-vile [sûr′vəl] *adjective*, subservient, groveling, cringing

ses-sion [sĕsh′ən] *noun*, the sitting of an organized body for the transaction of business, a term

set [sĕt] *noun*, 1) a group of things thought of together, *verb*, 2) to put in a place 3) to make something happen, to begin 4) to sink in the sky below the horizon

set-ting [sĕt′ĭng]] *noun*, 1) the position of something, as a dial, that has been set 2) time and place, environment, etc. of an event, story, play, etc. 3) actual physical surroundings, real or artificial

set-tle [sĕt′l] *verb*, 1) to go and live in a place 2) to make comfortable 3) to come to a mutual agreement, to decide

set-tle-ment [sĕt′l-mənt] *noun*, 1) an agreement 2) a new place for people to live, a colony

sev-en [sĕv′ən] *adjective, noun*, the number 7, one plus six

sev-en-teen [sĕv′ən-tēn′] *adjective, noun*, the number 17, 7 + 10

sev-en-teenth [sĕv′ən-tēnth′] *adjective, noun*, number 17 in order, written 17th

sev-enth [sĕv′ənth] *adjective, noun*, number 7 in order, 7th

sev-en-ti-eth [sĕv′ən-tē-ĭth] *adjective, noun*, number 70 in order, written 70th

sev-en-ty [sĕv′ən-tē] *noun, adjective*, the number 70, 7 X 10

sev-er [sĕv′ər] *verb*, to cut off, to separate, to disconnect

sev-er-al [sĕv′ər-əl] *adjective*, 1) separate or distinct, *pronoun*, 2) being more than two but fewer than many

se-vere [sə-vîr′] *adjective*, 1) strict in judgment or discipline, harsh 2) hard to deal with

se-ver-i-ty [sə-vĕr′ĭ-tē] *noun*, harshness, intensity

sew [sō] *verb*, to bind two pieces of cloth together with a needle and thread, to repair with a thread

sew-age [sōō′ĭj] *noun*, liquid waste from homes and businesses transported away by sewers

sew-er [sōō′ər] *noun*, 1) a gutter, a disposal system 2) one who works with needle and thread

sex [sĕks] *noun*, to be male or female

shab-by [shăb′ē] *adjective*, old, cheap, dirty, falling apart

shack-le [shăk′əl] *noun*, 1) chains, handcuffs, *verb*, 2) to confine, to restrain with chains

shade [shād] *noun, no plural*, 1) shelter from the sun or light, *verb*, 2) to cut off from a bright light 3) to dim or darken

shad-ow [shăd′ō] *noun*, 1) the image cast on a surface when something blocks the light 2) a faint indication

shaft [shăft] *noun,* 1) a long thin pole 2) a long hole leading to a mine 3) a ray or beam

shake [shāk] *verb,* 1) to move quickly up and down or from side to side 2) to tremble

shall [shăl] *verb,* 1) a word used instead of will with *I* and *we,* to indicate something is going to happen 2) used with *I* and *we* in questions when asking or offering to do something

shal-low [shăl′ō] *adjective,* 1) not deep 2) superficial, with little seriousness or deep thought

sham [shăm] *noun,* a farce

sham-bles [shăm′bəlz] *noun, plural,* a scene of disorder

shame [shām] *noun,* 1) dishonor, guilt, humiliation, *verb,* 2) to humiliate or embarrass

sham-poo [shăm-pōō′] *noun,* 1) a liquid soap used to wash hair, *verb,* 2) to wash hair with soap

shape [shāp] *noun,* 1) the outline or form of something, 2) a form or condition in which something exists, *verb,* 3) to mold or give form to something

share [shâr] *noun,* 1) a portion of something after it has been divided, *verb,* 2) to use, experience, or enjoy with others 3) to participate in 4) to disclose to others

shark [shärk] *noun,* a large predatory fish with a huge jaw

sharp [shärp] *adjective,* 1) having a thin cutting edge 2) the ability to see things far away that are small 3) severe or intense, having a strong odor or flavor 4) alert 5) quick and forceful

sharp-en [shär′pən] *verb,* 1) to make a pointed edge 2) to make acute or more sensitive to feeling

sharp-ly [sharp-lē] *adverb,* clearly, suddenly, distinctly

shat-ter [shăt′ər] *verb,* to break into many pieces or fragments

shave [shāv] *verb,* to cut very close

shawl [shôl] *noun,* a long piece of cloth worn over the shoulders and head

she [shē] *pronoun,* the female person or subject in the sentence

sheaf [shēf] *noun,* 1) a quantity of grain bound together 2) any bundle of things such as papers

shear [shîr] *verb,* to cut wool from a sheep, to cut hair, to clip

shears [shîrz] *noun, plural,* large-sized scissors

sheath [shēth] *noun,* a case that holds a sword or dagger

sheathe [shēth] *verb,* to put into a case or covering

shed [shĕd] *noun,* 1) a hut for tools, *verb,* 2) to let something fall or come off naturally 3) to pour forth, to stream out

sheep [shēp] *noun, no plural,* an animal that is kept for meat and wool from its thick, fleecy coat

sheep-ish-ly [shē′pĭsh-lē] *adverb,* with a feeling of embarrassment

sheer [shîr] *adjective,* 1) totally, entirely 2) transparent

sheet [shēt] *noun,* 1) a large flat piece of something such as paper or cloth 2) a rope used to secure a ship's sail

shelf [shĕlf] *noun, plural,* **shelves,** a board attached to a wall to put things on it

shell [shĕl] *noun*, the hard protective covering of fruit, eggs or some fish and reptiles

shel-lac [shə-lăk′] *noun*, a wood finishing such as varnish, lacquer or polyurethane

shell-fish [shĕl′fĭsh′] *noun*, any fish with a hard armor such as crabs, lobsters, or oysters

shel-ter [shĕl′tər] *noun*, 1) a safe place, a place to hide, *verb*, 2) to hide someone, to guard or keep safe from harm, to protect

shep-herd [shĕp′ərd] *noun*, a person who herds and tends sheep, goats, or livestock

sher-bet [shûr′bĭt] *noun*, flavored dessert ice

sher-iff [shĕr′ĭf] *noun*, a law enforcement officer of a county

shib-bo-leth [shĭb′ə-lĭth] *noun*, a slogan, a catchword

shield [shēld] *noun*, 1) a piece of defensive armor carried on the arm, protection, *verb*, 2) to defend or protect 3) to conceal

shift [shĭft] *noun*, 1) a set of people who work together at one time 2) the length of time that one group works, *verb*, 3) to move, to transfer, to displace

shil-ling [shĭl′ĭng] *noun*, English currency equal to a dollar

shim-mer [shĭm′ər] *verb*, to glimmer intermittently, to glisten

shin [shĭn] *noun*, the part of the leg between the knee and the ankle

shine [shīn] *verb*, to give off light

shin-gle [shĭng′gəl] *noun*, a tile made of wood or tar used to protect a roof or wall

ship [shĭp] *noun*, a boat which travels in deep water like the sea

ship-ment [shĭp′mənt] *noun*, the act of sending goods by air, water, or, on the road

shirt [shûrt] *noun*, a garment which covers the upper part of the body consisting of a collar, sleeves, and buttons, similar to a blouse

shiv-er [shĭv′ər] *verb*, to shake from feeling cold or afraid

shoal [shōl] *noun*, 1) a sandbar or piece of rising ground in shallow water 2) a school of fish

shock [shŏk] *noun*, 1) the feeling caused by a horrible unpleasant surprise 2) a pain caused by electricity going through the body, *verb*, 3) to startle, to disturb or surprise

shod-dy [shŏd′ē] *adjective*, not genuine, inferior quality

shoe [shoō] *noun*, an outer covering for the foot consisting of a sole and a covering made of leather, vinyl, or cloth

shoot [shoōt] *noun*, 1) new growth, a sprout, *verb*, 2) to discharge a weapon 3) to move quickly, to dart 4) to photograph or film

shop [shŏp] *noun*, 1) a place to go and buy different things that you need, *verb*, 2) to visit stores to make purchases

shore [shôr] *noun*, 1) land bordering water such as a lake or the sea, *verb*, 2) to prop up

short [shôrt] *adjective*, 1) the opposite of tall, small 2) not long, brief, concise

short-age [shôr′tĭj] *noun*, not enough, a deficiency

short-en [shôr′tn] *verb*, to cut down

short-en-ing [shôr′tn-ĭng] *noun*, lard or oil used in cooking

shorts [shôrts] *noun, plural,* pants worn above the knee

shot [shŏt] *noun,* 1) injection with a hypodermic needle 2) a try, an attempt 3) lead for a shotgun

should [shŏŏd] *verb,* obligated to do something, ought to

shoul-der [shōl′dər] *noun,* 1) part of the body between the neck and the chest, connected to the arms, *verb,* 2) to carry a burden

shouldn't [shŏŏd′nt] the *contraction* of the words **should** and **not**

shout [shout] *noun,* 1) a sudden cry in a loud voice, *verb,* 2) to speak or yell in a loud voice

shove [shŭv] *noun,* 1) a push, *verb,* 2) to push roughly or rudely

shov-el [shŭv′əl] *noun,* 1) a broad scoop with a long handle for lifting dirt, *verb,* 2) to lift things from the ground or another surface with a shovel

show [shō] *noun,* 1) a display in which things are gathered for people to see 2) a performance for an audience, *verb,* 3) to let someone see something

show-er [shou′ər] *noun,* 1) precipitation from clouds in the form of rain 2) a bath in which water is sprayed from a nozzle, 3) a party to honor someone, *verb,* 4) to pour down or fall on 5) to bestow

shred [shrĕd] *noun,* 1) a small amount, *verb,* 2) to tear or cut into small pieces

shrew [shrōō] *noun,* 1) a scolding woman, a nag 2) a mouse-like rodent with a long snout

shrewd [shrōōd] *adjective,* clever in business, sharp-witted

shriek [shrēk] *noun,* 1) a high-pitched scream, *verb,* 2) to utter a shrill cry, to scream

shrill [shrĭl] *adjective,* having a high-pitched sound, piercing

shrimp [shrĭmp] *noun,* a shellfish that is considered a delicacy

shrine [shrīn] *noun,* 1) a place for worship and keeping sacred relics 2) a saint's tomb

shrink [shrĭngk] *verb,* 1) to withdraw, to pull away from 2) to lessen, to make smaller

shriv-el [shrĭv′əl] *verb,* to contract in size, to shrink and wrinkle

shrub [shrŭb] *noun,* a bush

shrug [shrŭg] *verb,* 1) to raise the shoulders to show uncertainty about something 2) to disregard

shud-der [shŭd′ər] *noun,* a quick, light shaking motion, a shiver

shuf-fle [shŭf′əl] *verb,* 1) to walk dragging your feet 2) to rearrange the order, to mix together like a deck of cards

shun [shŭn] *verb,* to deliberately avoid, to stay away from

shut [shŭt] *verb,* to close, to adjust something so that it is not open

shut-ter [shŭt′ər] *noun,* 1) a wooden cover for a window 2) a mechanical device for opening and closing the aperture of a camera lens to expose the film

shy [shī] *adjective,* bashful, wary

sib-ling [sĭb'lĭng] *noun*, a brother or sister

sick [sĭk] *adjective*, not feeling well

sick-ness [sĭk'nĭs] *noun*, illness, nausea, ailment, disease

side [sīd] *noun*, 1) the right or left portion of the body 2) the surface of something flat that has a top and bottom 3) the boundaries of a surface or image 4) a perspective, a way of looking at something, an aspect

siege [sēj] *noun*, a continued attempt of an army to gain possession around a fortified place to compel its surrender

sieve [sĭv] *noun*, a bowl with holes in the bottom to let water drain out, or used to separate fine matter from the coarser materials

sigh [sī] *noun*, 1) a deep breath indicating that you are tired, sad, etc, *verb*, 2) to let out a deep breath, to exhale

sight [sīt] *noun*, 1) the ability or power to see 2) something worth seeing 3) a scene, an incident

sign [sīn] *noun*, 1) a gesture which sends a message to the person who sees it 2) an indication 3) a plaque with a message, *verb*, 4) to write your name 5) to hire or transfer by written agreement

sig-nal [sĭg'nəl] *noun*, 1) a movement or thing which tells you what to do, *verb*, 2) to warn someone, or send another message through motions

sig-na-ture [sĭg'nə-chər] *noun*, 1) a name written in ink, in cursive, as an endorsement to an agreement 2) the printed sheet so marked as to leave an imprint

sig-net [sĭg'nĭt] *noun*, an emblem

sig-nif-i-cance [sĭg-nĭf'ĭ-kəns] *noun*, *no plural*, the meaning

sig-nif-i-cant [sĭg-nĭf'ĭ-kənt] *adjective*, expressive or suggestive, important

sig-ni-fy [sĭg'nə-fī'] *verb*, to indicate, to signal, to denote

si-lence [sī'ləns] *noun*, *no plural*, 1) complete quiet 2) secrecy

si-lent [sī'lənt] *adjective*, making no sound, quiet, speechless

si-lent-ly [sī'lənt-lē] *adverb*, quietly, without a sound

sil-hou-ette [sĭl'ōō-ĕt'] *noun*, an outline of something against a light background

sil-i-con [sĭl'ĭ-kən, -kŏn'] *noun*, a nonmetallic element, very abundant in nature

silk [sĭlk] *noun*, a fine fabric made by the threads from a silkworm

sill [sĭl] *noun*, the rim on a window

sil-ly [sĭl'ē] *adjective*, not serious, or reasonable, playful, foolish

silt [sĭlt] *noun*, sediment of fine particles that hangs in stagnant water or forms on the bottom left there by running water

sil-ver [sĭl'vər] *adjective*, 1) the color of this metal, *noun*, *no plural*, 2) a soft shiny gray metal used for jewelry, coins, and ornaments

sim-i-an [sĭm'ē-ən] *adjective*, like a monkey or an ape

sim-i-lar [sĭm'ə-lər] *adjective*, somewhat like, nearly, corresponding, resembling

sim-i-lar-i-ty [sĭm'ə-lăr'ĭ-tē] *noun*, likeness, resemblance

sim-i-le [sĭm/ə-lē] *noun*, a phrase comparing unlike subjects using like or as, i.e., *he is as slow as a turtle; she sings like a bird*

sim-ple [sĭm/pəl] *adjective*, 1) easy to understand 2) plain, common, not complicated, not showy

sim-plic-i-ty [sĭm-plĭs/ĭ-tē] *adjective*, freedom from duplicity, absence of excess

sim-pli-fy [sĭm/plə-fī/] *verb*, to make easier to understand

sim-ply [sĭm/plē] *adverb*, only, or merely, absolutely

sim-u-late [sĭm/yə-lāt/] *verb*, to feign, to pretend, to fake

si-mul-ta-ne-ous [sī/məl-tā/nē-əs] *adjective*, occurring at the same time, concurrent

si-mul-ta-ne-ous-ly [sī/məl-tā/nē-əs-lē] *adverb*, happening at the same time

sin [sĭn] *noun*, 1) an act that harms someone, *verb*, 2) to err, to violate a moral principle

since [sĭns] *adverb*, 1) between a moment in the past and now, *conjunction*, 2) because, *preposition*, 3) after, from a certain time until the present

sin-cere [sĭn-sîr/] *adjective*, being in reality what it appears to be, genuine 3) free of hypocrisy

sin-cere-ly [sĭn-sîr/lē] *adverb*, honestly, truly

sin-cer-i-ty [sĭn-sĕr/ĭ-tē] *adverb*, honesty, truthfulness

sin-ew [sĭn/yōō] *noun*, 1) a tendon, a muscle 2) strength, power

sing [sĭng] *verb*, to make music with the voice

singe [sĭnj] *verb*, to scorch or burn the surface or ends

sin-gle [sĭng/gəl] *adjective*, 1) consisting of only one person or thing, alone, *noun*, 2) in baseball, a hit in which the batter reaches first base

sin-gu-lar [sĭng/gyə-lər] *adjective*, 1) when speaking of one, *noun*, 2) unique, particular, individual

sin-is-ter [sĭn/ĭ-stər] *adjective*, dishonest, indicative of lurking evil, wicked, menacing

sink [sĭngk] *noun*, 1) a basin that holds water, *verb*, 2) to go down 3) to become submerged in water 4) to permeate the mind

sin-ner [sĭn/ər] *noun*, one who does wrong to others

sip [sĭp] *noun*, 1) a small amount of liquid swallowed, *verb*, 2) to drink a very small amount

si-phon [sī/fən] *noun*, a bent tube, having one end longer than the other, used for drawing liquids from a higher to a lower level

sir [sûr] *noun*, 1) the title of a knight 2) a respectful term to use when talking to a man

si-ren [sī/rən] *noun*, a device that makes a loud warning sound

sis-ter [sĭs/tər] *noun*, 1) a girl who shares the same parents with a sibling 2) the title for a nun

sit [sĭt] *verb*, to rest in a chair or on the floor, with the back straight

site [sīt] *noun*, a particular piece of land or a building whose location has a specific use

sit-u-ate [sĭch/ōō-āt/] *verb*, to put in place, to position, to locate

sit-u-a-tion [sĭch′o͞o-ā′shən] *noun*, 1) circumstances, the state of affairs, a case 2) a position

six [sĭks] *adjective, noun*, the number 6, five plus one

six-teen [sĭk-stēn′] *adjective, noun*, the number 16, six plus ten

six-teenth [sĭk-stēnth′] *adjective, noun*, the number 16 in order, written 16th

sixth [sĭksth] *adjective, noun*, the number 6 in order, written 6th

six-ti-eth [sĭk′stē-ĭth] *adjective, noun*, number 60 in order, 60th

six-ty [sĭks′tē] *adjective*, the number 60, six times ten

size [sīz] *noun*,) the amount of space that something takes up

skate [skāt] *noun*, 1) a runner or set of wheels with a frame to fit the shoe, *verb*, 2) to glide over the ground with shoes fit with a runner or wheels

skel-e-ton [skĕl′ĭ-tn] *noun*, the bones of a person or animal that show its size and structure

skep-tic [skĕp′tĭk] *noun*, a doubter, a cynic, a questioner

skep-ti-cal [skĕp′tĭ-kəl] *adjective*, distrustful, not convinced

sketch [skĕch] *noun*, 1) a drawing that lacks detail, an image, *verb*, 2) to draw in a rough manner

ski [skē] *noun, plural*, **skis**, one of a pair of long, flat, wood or metal runners used for gliding on snow or water *verb*, 2) to slide over snow on blades using poles for balance

skid [skĭd] *noun*, 1) a pallet to elevate something off the ground, *verb*, 2) to slip on a wet surface 3) to lose traction

skill [skĭl] *noun*, having the ability and knowledge to do something

skil-let [skĭl′ĭt] *noun*, a small metal pan with a handle, a frying pan

skill-ful [skĭl′fəl] *adjective*, very good at doing something

skill-ful-ly [skĭl′fə-lē] *adverb*, intelligently, sensibly

skim [skĭm] *verb*, 1) to read over quickly 2) to take off the floating layer 3) to glide in a sail boat

skimp [skĭmp] *verb*, to hold back, to offer small portions

skin [skĭn] *noun*, 1) the covering of the body, or fruit, often covered with hairs, *verb*, 2) to remove the outer layer of something

skip [skĭp] *verb*, 1) to move by alternately hopping or stepping, to move with light steps 2) to omit, to pass over, to miss

skirt [skûrt] *noun*, 1) woman's clothing that hangs from the waist, *verb*, 2) to avoid

skit [skĭt] *noun*, a short play or theatrical performance

skit-tish [skĭt′ĭsh] *adjective*, lively, frisky, nervous

skulk [skŭlk] *verb*, 1) to move slyly and secretly in a sneaking manner 2) to lie in hiding

skull [skŭl] *noun*, the bony structure of the head enclosing the brain

skunk [skŭngk] *noun*, a rodent with black fur distinguished by a white strip that goes down its back and tail and sprays a horrible smell when scared

sky [skī] *noun*, the space above the Earth which can be seen when you look up

sky-scrap-er [skī′skrā′pər] *noun*, a very tall building

slack [slăk] *adjective*, 1) lazy, slow, barely moving 2) a mixture of small pieces of coal, dust, and dirt left from screening coal

slacks [slăks] *noun*, *plural*, pants or trousers for casual wear

slain [slān] *past tense* of **slay**

slam [slăm] *verb*, 1) to fling or put down violently, with a loud noise 2) to shut, to close

slan-der [slăn′dər] *noun*, 1) a malicious, false statement made about a person, *verb*, 2) to lie about someone, to malign

slang [slăng] *noun*, *no plural*, language used in conversation, that is crude, disrespectful, or inappropriate, an expletive

slant [slănt] *verb*, to lean or slope

slap [slăp] *noun*, 1) the blow or hit caused by something flat, *verb*, 2) to hit with something flat, such as an open hand

slate [slāt] *adjective*, 1) a gray color, *noun*, 2) a fine-grained metamorphic rock used as a roof tile or writing tablet with chalk

slaugh-ter [slô′tər] *noun*, *no plural*, 1) a killing of a large number of people or animals, *verb*, 2) to kill animals or people as a group

slave [slāv] *noun*, a person owned as property, subject to the will of his owner

slav-er-y [slā′və-rē] *noun*, *no plural*, the concept of owning people as property

slay [slā] *verb*, to kill or murder

slea-zy [slē′zē] *adjective*, low class

sled [slĕd] *noun*, a wooden device with runners on the bottom used to carry people or things on snow or ice as a vehicle

sleek [slēk] *adjective*, smooth, neat, glossy, well-groomed

sleep [slēp] *noun*, *no plural*, 1) a time of rest, when not awake and alert, *verb*, 2) to rest semi-unconscious with eyes closed

sleet [slēt] *noun*, 1) a combination of ice and rain falling from the sky, *verb*, 2) to shower frozen rain

sleeve [slēv] *noun*, the part of clothing that covers the arm

sleigh [slā] *noun*, a horse drawn vehicle with runners used for carrying people over snow

sleight [slīt] *noun*, skill, cunning

slen-der [slĕn′dər] *adjective*, 1) slim, thin, narrow 2) meager

slice [slīs] *noun*, 1) a piece cut from the whole, a share, *verb*, 2) to cut a flat piece off from a whole

slick [slĭk] *adjective*, 1) a surface that is slippery when wet 2) clever, deceitful

slide [slīd] *noun*, 1) a piece of playground equipment you can sit on and slip on the surface, an image for projection on a screen, *verb*, 3) to move smoothly along a surface, to slip

slight [slīt] *adjective*, of a small degree, of little importance

slim [slĭm] *adjective*, slender, thin, lean, narrow, meager

slime [slīm] *noun*, mire, mud

sling [slĭng] *noun,* 1) a piece of cloth holding something in place, *verb,* 2) to throw

slip [slĭp] *noun,* 1) a piece of paper 2) a garment worn under a dress 3) a mistake 4) a stall to keep something 5) a cutting from a plant, *verb,* 6) to lose your balance and fall off your feet 7) to enter or exit unobserved 8) to escape, to pass from

slip-per [slĭp'ər] *noun,* a light shoe which may be slipped on easily

slip-per-y [slĭp'ə-rē] *adjective,* 1) smooth and slick or slimy, hard to grip 2) devious, not trustworthy, shifty

slit [slĭt] *noun,* 1) a long narrow opening, *verb,* 2) to make a small cut as an opening

slith-er [slĭth'ər] *verb,* to move, walk or slide like a snake

slo-gan [slō'gən] *noun,* a catch phrase, a motto

slope [slōp] *noun,* 1) a surface which is higher on one side than the other, *verb,* 2) to lean on an incline, to slant up or downward

slot [slŏt] *noun,* a long, narrow opening for receiving something

sloth [slôth] *noun,* a lazy person

slov-en-ly [slŭv'ən-lē] *adjective,* untidy, careless in work habits

slow [slō] *adjective,* 1) to move without much speed, not fast 2) behind others, sluggish

slow-ly [slō'lē] *adverb,* to crawl or move sluggishly, not quickly

slug [slŭg] *noun,* 1) a soft, slimy creature without bones or legs that eats plants 2) a false coin, *verb,* 3) to hit with a fist

sluice [slōōs] *noun,* an artificial channel for water with a gate

slum [slŭm] *noun,* a poor neighborhood, a ghetto

slum-ber [slŭm'bər] *noun,* 1) a deep sleep, a long nap, *verb,* 2) to sleep, to doze

slump [slŭmp] *noun,* 1) a drop, a decline, a decrease, *verb,* 2) to sink, to slouch, to stoop

slur [slûr] *noun,* 1) a disrespectful remark, *verb,* 2) to insult, to offend 3) to garble, to speak unintelligibly

slush [slŭsh] *noun,* partially melting snow or ice

sly [slī] *adjective,* clever and deceiving, calculating

smack [smăk] *noun,* 1) a kiss, a pat, a peck, *verb,* 2) to hit with a hand as a slap 3) to put the lips together after a tasty meal

small [smôl] *adjective,* 1) little, not big 2) mean-spirited, petty

small-er [smôl'ər] *adjective,* not as big, shorter, less, fewer

small-est [smôl'ĕst] *adjective,* tiny, very little

smart [smärt] *adjective,* 1) intelligent, bright 2) well dressed, attractive, fashionable, *verb,* 3) to feel a painful, stinging sensation

smash [smăsh] *verb,* to break violently into many pieces

smat-ter-ing [smăt'ər-ĭng] *noun,* slight knowledge, a few facts

smell [smĕl] *noun,* 1) the identifying scent that distinguishes something, *verb,* 2) to use one of the five senses to recognize a scent

smelt [smĕlt] *verb*, to melt in a furnace, to purify an ore

smile [smīl] *noun*, 1) an expression formed by the upward curve of the mouth, to show pleasure, amusement, etc., 2) to look pleased, happy, or amused

smirk [smûrk] *noun*, a twisted smile, a smug expression

smog [smŏg] *noun*, a mixture of pollutants, principally ground-level ozone, produced by chemical reactions in the air

smoke [smōk] *noun*, 1) visible fumes, *verb*, 2) to puff or inhale the vapor from a lit cigarette, 3) to make fumes come from fire

smol-der [smōl′dər] *verb*, 1) to burn without flame 2) anger, liable to break out at any moment

smooth [smōōth] *adjective*, 1) even, level, without bumps 2) calm, composed, unruffled

smoth-er [smŭth′ər] *verb*, to hide or suppress, to suffocate

smudge [smŭj] *noun*, 1) a dirty mark, a smear, *verb*, 2) to make dirty with streaks, to blur

smug-gle [smŭg′əl] *verb*, to bring things across borders secretly or illegally to avoid tariffs or border police

snack [snăk] *noun*, 1) food eaten between meals, *verb*, 2) to eat when you are hungry

snail [snāl] *noun*, a slug in a spirally coiled shell

snake [snāk] *noun*, 1) a cold-blooded reptile without legs that slithers on the ground, *verb*, 2) to move like a snake by slithering and sliding

snap [snăp] *noun*, 1) the sharp sound of something breaking 2) a clothing fastener like a button that locks together, *verb*, 3) to make a crackling sound 4) to try to nip or bite someone

snare [snâr] *noun*, 1) a trap that entangles its victim, *verb*, 2) to trap with a noose, to entangle

snarl [snärl] *verb*, 1) to make an angry noise with bared teeth 2) to talk in a vicious tone

snatch [snăch] *verb*, to take something directly from someone in a rough manner

sneak [snēk] *noun*, 1) a cheater, a rascal, *verb*, 2) to creep, to slink

sneer [snîr] *verb*, to laugh at someone to make fun of them

sneeze [snēz] *noun*, to blow air through the nose and mouth without warning

sniff [snĭf] *verb*, to breathe in, to inhale, to get a whiff, to smell

snif-fle [snĭf′əl] *verb*, to gasp as if to hold back tears

snob [snŏb] *noun*, someone who thinks he is better than others

snore [snôr] *verb*, to make a loud guttural noise in the nose or throat when sleeping

snout [snout] *noun*, the part of an animal's head projecting forward containing the nose and jaws

snow [snō] *noun*, *no plural*, 1) precipitation that forms in the cloud as ice and falls to the ground as white crystals, *verb*, 2) a flurry of crystals or snowflakes falling to the earth from the sky

snug [snŭg] *adjective*, close fitting, comfortable, cozy, compact

so [sō] *adverb*, 1) in such a way, to such a point 2) also 3) very, very much 4) therefore 5) in order that 6) the same thing 7) used to show agreement 8) factual

soak [sōk] *verb*, to leave something immersed in liquid for awhile

soap [sōp] *noun*, a substance used for cleaning, manufactured as bars, flakes, or liquid, mixed with water

soar [sôr] *verb*, to fly or ascend quickly and easily upward

sob [sŏb] *verb*, to cry aloud in large gasps, to weep convulsively

so-ber [sō′bər] *adjective*, serious, somber, not gay or laughing

so-bri-e-ty [sə-brī′ĭ-tē] *noun*, self-restraint, recovery from abusing alcohol, not drunk

so-bri-quet [sō′brĭ-kā′] *noun*, a nickname, a pet name

soc-cer [sŏk′ər] *noun*, *no plural*, a game of football as played in South America and Europe

so-cial [sō′shəl] *adjective*, pertaining to men as living in society, friendly, gregarious

so-cial-ism [sō′shə-lĭz′əm] *adjective*, a communist philosophy of equal sharing

so-ci-e-ty [sə-sī′ĭ-tē] *noun*, a group of persons associated together

so-ci-ol-o-gy [sō′sē-ŏl′ə-jē] *noun*, the science of the development of human society

sock [sŏk] *noun*, 1) a short stocking made of soft material to cover the foot, *verb*, 2) to punch

sock-et [sŏk′ĭt] *noun*, any device that holds a complementary part

sod [sŏd] *noun*, earth, dirt, soil

so-da [sō′də] *noun*, a carbonated beverage flavored with syrup

so-di-um [sō′dē-əm] *noun*, a silver-white, metallic element of the alkali group, also known as salt

so-fa [sō′fə] *noun*, a long couch, usually upholstered and having a back and arms

soft [sôft] *adjective*, 1) tender 2) not hard 3) low volume, not loud 4) smooth or silky

soft-en [sô′fən] *verb*, 1) to ease, to relax, 2) to melt

soft-ly [sôft′lē] *adverb*, 1) quietly 2) mildly, gently

soft-ware [sôft′wâr′] *noun*, instructions that allow a computer to do specific tasks

soil [soil] *noun*, 1) the earth where plants and organisms grow, the top layer of the earth, *verb*, 2) to make something dirty

so-journ [sō′jûrn′] *noun*, 1) a brief stay, *verb*, 2) to stay temporarily

sol-ace [sŏl′ĭs] *noun*, comfort in trouble, or sorrow, or distress

so-lar [sō′lər] *adjective*, referring to or relating to the sun

sold [sōld] *verb*, *past tense* of **sell**

sol-der [sŏd′ər] *noun*, a metal or a metallic alloy used to join by fusing metallic surfaces together

sol-dier [sōl′jər] *noun*, a man or woman enlisted in the army

sole [sōl] *adjective*, 1) single, one *noun*, 2) the part of the shoe on which the bottom of the foot rests 3) an edible flat fish

sole-ly [sōl′lē] *adverb*, the only one

sol-emn [sŏl′əm] *adjective*, serious, grave, formal and dignified

so-le-noid [sō′lə-noid′] *noun*, a cylindrical round coil

so-lic-it [sə-lĭs′ĭt] *verb*, to ask someone to buy something or commit themselves

so-lic-i-tor [sə-lĭs′ĭ-tər] *noun*, the law officer of a city or government

sol-id [sŏl′ĭd] *adjective*, 1) not hollow, hard, firm, *noun*, 2) any substance that cannot flow, takes up space and has a definite shape and volume

sol-id-ify [sə-lĭd′ə-fī′] *verb*, to change from liquid to solid

so-lil-o-quy [sə-lĭl′ə-kwē] *noun*, the act of talking to one's self, a monologue in a drama

sol-i-taire [sŏl′ĭ-târ′] *noun*, 1) a gem set by itself 2) a card game involving one person

sol-i-tar-y [sŏl′ĭ-tĕr′ē] *adjective*, living or being by one's self, single, alone, secluded

sol-i-tude [sŏl′ĭ-tōōd′] *noun*, state of being alone, a lonely place

so-lo [sō′lō] *noun*, 1) something accomplished by one person 2) an unaccompanied performance

sol-stice [sŏl′stĭs] *noun*, either of two times a year when the sun is farthest from the equator, June 21 and December 22

sol-u-ble [sŏl′yə-bəl] *adjective*, something that dissolves

so-lu-tion [sə-lōō′shən] *noun*, 1) a liquid containing another

substance dissolved in it 2) the answer found

solve [sŏlv] *verb*, to find the answer by studying the problem

sol-vent [sŏl′vənt] *adjective*, 1) debt free, able to pay one's debts, *noun*, 2) a usually liquid substance in which another substance can dissolve

som-ber [sŏm′bər] *adjective*, gloomy, serious, melancholy

some [sŭm] *adjective,* 1) an amount of, not all, *pronoun,* 2) referring to people or things without saying exactly who or what

some-bod-y [sŭm′bŏd′ē] *pronoun*, any person, an unknown or unnamed individual

some-how [sŭm′hou′] *adverb*, in some unknown way

some-one [sŭm′wŭn′] *pronoun*, a person or an individual

some-place [sŭm′plās′] *noun*, a location, somewhere

som-er-sault [sŭm′ər-sôlt′] *noun*, the act of turning upside down with your head between your legs as though rolling in a ball

some-thing [sŭm′thĭng] *pronoun*, an unknown amount or identity

some-time [sŭm′tīm′] *adverb*, a time in the past or future

some-times [sŭm′tīmz′] *adverb*, occasionally, not always

some-what [sŭm′hwŏt′] *adverb*, slightly, to some degree

some-where [sŭm′hwâr′] *adverb*, in or to, in an unspecified space

som-nam-bu-list [sŏm-năm′byə-lĭst] *noun*, a sleepwalker

son [sŭn] *noun*, a male child, or offspring

song [sông] *noun*, 1) a piece of music with words 2) poetry

son-net [sŏn′ĭt] *noun*, a poem, fourteen lines in iambic pentameter

soon [sōōn] *adverb*, something that will happen in a short time from now, promptly, quickly

soon-er [sōō′nər] *adjective*, before long, earlier than

soot [sŏŏt] *noun, no plural*, a black powder separated from fuel during combustion, smoke residue, cinders, ash

soothe [sōōth] *verb*, 1) to ease or comfort 2) to quiet, to pacify

so-phis-ti-ca-tion [sə-fĭs′tĭ-kā′shən] *noun*, intelligence, social grace, elegance, style, good taste

soph-o-more [sŏf′ə-môr] *noun*, a student in his second year of a four-year course

so-pran-o [sə-prăn′ō] *noun*, a singer who can reach the high notes in music

sor-cer-ess [sôr′sər-ĭs] *noun*, a magician, a witch

sor-did [sôr′dĭd] *adjective*, filthy, base, vile, squalid, selfish

sore [sôr, sōr] *adjective*, 1) hurting, painful, *noun*, 2) a painful, injured place on the body

so-ror-i-ty [sə-rôr′ĭ-tē] *noun*, a society or club of girls or women

sor-row [sŏr′ō] *noun*, sadness

sor-ry [sŏr′ē] *adjective*, feeling pity or sorrow, regret

sort [sôrt] *noun*, 1) a special kind, *verb*, 2) to separate into different categories, to classify

sought [sôt] *past tense* of **seek**

soul [sōl] *noun*, the part of you that is not body, and that some people think does not die with your body, the spirit of a person

sound [sound] *adjective*, 1) healthy, strong 2) deep or undisturbed, *noun*, 3) something heard from transmitted vibrations, *verb*, 4) to make a noise

soup [sōōp] *noun*, a liquid food made by boiling meat, fish, or vegetables and seasonings

sour [sour] *adjective*, 1) having a sharp, biting, acid taste, tart, tangy, 2) soured, curdled

source [sôrs] *noun*, 1) the thing or place from which something comes 2) someone who provides information 3) a reference book

south [south] *adjective*, just opposite the north

South America [south-ə-mĕr′ĭ-kə] *noun*, one of the seven continents, containing 5.9% of the world's population

South Carolina [south-kăr′ə-lĭ′nə] *noun*, one of the 50 United States, located in the Southeast, the capital is Columbia. The state flower of **South Carolina** is the yellow jasmine, and the motto is "Prepared in mind and resources." or "While I breathe I hope."

South Dakota [south-də-kō′tə] *noun*, one of the 50 United States, located in the Northwest, the capital is Pierre. The state flower of **South Dakota** is the pasque flower and the motto is "Under God the people rule."

sou-ve-nir [sōō'və-nîr'] *noun*, that which serves as a reminder, a keepsake, a memento

sov-er-eign [sŏv'ər-ĭn] *adjective*, highest in power, chief

sow *noun*, 1) [sou] *noun*, an adult female pig, [sō]*verb*, 2) to scatter seeds over the ground where they will grow to produce a crop

soy-bean [soi'bēn'] *noun*, a bean plant grown for its edible, nutritious seeds

space [spās] *noun*, 1) the limitless three-dimensional area all around 2) an empty place or unoccupied time

space-ship [spās'shĭp'] *noun*, a rocket orbiting the earth

spa-cious [spā'shəs] *adjective*, vast in extent, roomy, sizeable

spade [spād] *noun*, 1) a small hand-held shovel 2) one of the four suits in a deck of cards

spa-ghet-ti [spə-gĕt'ē] *noun*, a variety of macaroni made in cords of small diameter

span [spăn] *noun*, a stretch, the measure, the distance

spare [spâr] *adjective*, 1) kept in addition to what is already available, *verb*, 2) to give something extra, to share 3) to omit, to leave out

spark [spärk] *noun*, 1) a tiny burning particle, *verb*, 2) to stimulate, to set in motion

spar-kle [spär'kəl] *verb*, to shine with bright points of light

spark plug [spärk'plŭg'] *noun*, a device with two electrodes between which an electric jump spark is made

spar-row [spăr'ō] *noun*, a small brownish-gray bird

sparse [spärs] *adjective*, not thick, thinly scattered or distributed

spasm [spăz'əm] *noun*, a seizure, a fit, a convulsive movement

spa-tial [spā'shəl] *adjective*, relating to space

spat-u-la [spăch'ə-lə] *noun*, an instrument with a broad blade used for spreading or mixing

spawn [spôn] *verb*, to lay eggs

spay [spā] *verb*, to remove the reproductive organs, to castrate

speak [spēk] *verb*, to say words aloud, to talk, to express ideas

speak-er [spē'kər] *noun*, 1) the one talking 2) an orator, a lecturer

spear [spîr] *noun*, a long thin weapon with a pointed end

spe-cial [spĕsh'əl] *adjective*, 1) individual, peculiar, particular, different from the others 2) extra nice, distinct 3) having a particular function or purpose

spe-cial-ist [spĕsh'ə-lĭst] *noun*, one who studies a subject at great length, an expert, an authority

spe-cial-ize [spĕsh'ə-līz'] *verb*, to focus on a particular profession

spe-cies [spē'shēz] *noun, plural,* 1) a distinct sort, kind, or variety 2) a group of living things that can breed together

spe-cif-ic [spĭ-sĭf'ĭk] *noun*, special, explicit, precise, peculiar

spec-i-fy [spĕs′ə-fī′] *verb*, to designate, to name explicitly, to indicate, to point out in detail

spec-i-men [spĕs′ə-mən] *noun*, a part of anything to show the quality of the whole

spe-cious [spē′shəs] *adjective*, something false that appears to be true, deceptively attractive

speck [spĕk] *noun*, a small piece or particle of something

spec-ta-cle [spĕk′tə-kəl] *noun*, 1) a public scene that attracts a lot of attention 2) a display, a show

spec-ta-cles [spĕk′tə-kəlz] *noun*, *plural*, glasses for the eyes to improve vision set in a frame that rests on the nose and ears

spec-tac-u-lar [spĕk-tăk′yə-lər] *adjective*, impressive, amazing, breath-taking, dramatic

spec-ta-tor [spĕk′tā′tər] *noun*, one who looks on and watches, an observer, a bystander

spec-ter [spĕk′tər] *noun*, any object of dread, a ghost, an apparition

spec-tro-scope [spĕk′trə-skōp′] *noun*, an optical instrument

spec-trum [spĕk′trəm] *noun*, a broad range or sequence, especially of light separated into its constituent colors

spec-u-late [spĕk′yə-lāt′] *verb*, 1) to gamble, to buy and sell on the market 2) to consider, to contemplate, to hypothesize

spec-u-la-tion [spĕk′yə-lā′shən] *noun*, theory, hypothesis, conjecture, contemplation

speech [spēch] *noun*, 1) a long talk usually prepared in advance 2) language, words, dialect

speed [spēd] *noun*, 1) the rate at which something moves, *verb*, 2) to quicken, to hasten

speed-om-e-ter [spĭ-dŏm′ĭ-tər] *noun*, an instrument for indicating speed or velocity

spell [spĕl] *noun*, 1) a charm that captivates some and holds their attention 2) a short period of time, *verb*, 3) to indicate the correct arrangement of letters in a word 4) to be a sign of

spell-ing [spĕl′ĭng] *noun*, the correct use of the proper letters composing a word

spend [spĕnd] *verb*, 1) to give money for something 2) to use or consume energy or time

spent [spĕnt] *past tense* of **spend**

sphere [sfîr] *adjective*, 1) a social position, *noun*, 2) a ball or globe

spher-i-cal [sfîr′ĭ-kəl] *adjective*, globular, round like a ball

spice [spīs] *noun*, a seed or root of a plant used to add flavor to food

spi-der [spī′dər] *noun*, a bug that uses threads from its body to make a web to capture insects

spill [spĭl] *noun*, 1) a fall, *verb*, 2) to accidentally allow a liquid to flow out of a container

spin [spĭn] *verb*, 1) to whirl quickly 2) to twist into a thread from wool or other natural fibers

spin-ach [spĭn′ĭch] *noun*, an edible green leafy vegetable

spine [spīn] *noun*, the long row of bones in your back

spi-ral [spī′rəl] *noun*, helical, like the thread of a screw

spire [spīr] *noun*, the pointed top of a tower or steeple

spir-it [spĭr′ĭt] *noun*, 1) a mysterious part of you which is not the body, the soul 2) an eager state of mind, enthusiasm 3) a supernatural being such as a ghost or a fairy 4) an alcoholic drink such as liquor

spir-it-u-al [spĭr′ĭ-choo-əl] *adjective*, airy, motivated by the soul, holy, religious

spit [spĭt] *noun*, 1) saliva, *verb*, 2) to spray water or saliva out of the mouth

spite [spīt] *noun*, *no plural*, hatred, feelings of malice, wanting to hurt or annoy another person

splash [splăsh] *noun*, 1) the sound made when a solid falls into liquid, *verb*, 2) to make a wave of water in a pool

splen-did [splĕn′dĭd] *adjective*, excellent, magnificent, very fine

splice [splīs] *verb*, to insert a shoot, to join, to graft, to unite

splint [splĭnt] *noun*, a board used to keep a thing from bending, a way of protecting a broken limb

splin-ter [splĭn′tər] *noun*, a thin piece of wood split off from a larger piece, a sliver

split [splĭt] *noun*, 1) a tear or a break, *verb*, 2) to break lengthwise 3) to share

spoil [spoil] *verb*, 1) to damage or injure, to ruin 2) to become rotten or decayed 3) to overindulge or corrupt by coddling someone

spoke [spōk] *noun*, 1) one of the bars joining the rim of a wheel to the center to support weight, *verb*, 2) *past tense* of **speak**

sponge [spŭnj] *noun*, 1) a substance that absorbs water, used to clean and wipe 2) a primitive marine animal having a soft elastic skeleton with many pores, *verb*, 3) to live off the generosity of others

spon-sor [spŏn′sər] *noun*, 1) a patron, supporter, mentor, backer, *verb*, 2) to offer financial support for a program

spon-ta-ne-i-ty [spŏn′tə-nē′ĭ-tē] *noun*, acting at the spur of the moment, impromptu

spon-ta-ne-ous [spŏn-tā′nē-əs] *adjective*, 1) acting on impulse, a result of natural law 2) energy

spool [spōol] *noun*, a round object used to wind thread or wire

spoon [spōon] *noun*, a utensil consisting of a shallow bowl with a long handle attached to it, used for eating or stirring

spoon-ful [spōon′fŏol′] *noun*, the quantity that sits in a spoon

spo-rad-ic [spə-răd′ĭk] *adjective*, occurring irregularly

spore [spōr] *noun*, a cell that reproduces itself such as fungus, fern, or bacterium

sport [spōrt] *noun*, 1) games and exercises done for pleasure 2) a rascal 3) a teammate

spot [spŏt] *noun*, 1) a small mark, drop, or blemish 2) a location, *verb*, 3) to see something

spouse [spous] *noun*, a partner in marriage, husband or wife

spout [spout] *noun*, 1) the lip of a container from which liquid is poured, *verb*, 2) to spurt, to discharge, to gush forth

sprain [sprān] *verb*, to strain a body part by twisting it, causing it to swell

sprawl [sprôl] *verb*, to stretch, to spread out, to extend

spray [sprā] *noun*, 1) liquid dispersed in very fine drops 2) a small branch of flowers or foliage, *verb*, 3) to blow or scatter liquid in very fine drops

spread [sprĕd] *verb*, 1) to cover a surface with a thin layer 2) to unfold or stretch out 3) to circulate, to disseminate 4) to extend over a large area

spring [sprĭng] *noun*, 1) a river or pond coming up from the ground 2) a piece of wire twisted into a spiral 3) the season following winter, when plants begin to grow, *verb*, 4) to jump 5) to come from 6) to grow

sprin-kle [sprĭng′kəl] *verb*, 1) to spatter, to disperse in drops 2) to drizzle 3) to dust lightly

sprint [sprĭnt] *noun*, 1) a short fast run, *verb*, 2) to dash at top speed

sprock-et [sprŏk′ĭt] *noun*, a projection shaped so as to engage with a chain

sprout [sprout] *verb*, to grow out of a seed, to start to grow

spruce [sprōōs] *noun*, one of the softwood evergreen trees

sprung [sprŭng] *past tense* of **spring**

spry [sprī] *adjective*, vigorous, quick, energetic, agile

spun [spŭn] *past tense* of **spin**

spur [spûr] *noun*, 1) a short side track connecting with the main railroad 2) a sharp blade on the back of a boot used to urge horses to run faster 3) an impetus, a cause to action, *verb*, 4) to urge, to goad, to stimulate

spu-ri-ous [spyŏŏr′ē-əs] *adjective*, counterfeit, false, not genuine

spurn [spûrn] *verb*, to reject, to scorn, to despise, to shun

spy [spī] *noun*, *plural*, **spies** 1) an agent hired to secretly obtain information *verb*, 2) to see or catch sight of 3) to keep secret watch

squad [skwŏd] *noun*, a small group of soldiers who work, train, and fight together 2) a sports team

squad-ron [skwŏd′rən] *noun*, armed military aircraft

squal-id [skwŏl′ĭd] *adjective*, dirty through neglect, foul, filthy

squan-der [skwŏn′dər] *verb*, to spend money or resources without being accountable

square [skwâr] *noun*, 1) a surface with four equal sides and right angle corners 2) an open area in the center of town surrounded by stores and businesses

square number [skwâr- nŭm′bər] *noun*, the product of two equal factors, e.g., 12 x 12 = 144

squash [skwŏsh] *noun*, 1) a vegetable that grows on a vine 2) a game similar to racquetball, *verb*, 3) to repress 4) to flatten by pressing or from pressure

squat [skwŏt] *adjective*, 1) wide, stocky, *verb*, 2) to stoop

squeak [skwēk] *noun*, 1) a very sharp, high-pitched sound, *verb*, 2) to make a short high-pitched sound

squeal [skwēl] *noun*, 1) a shrill cry, *verb*, 2) to make such a sound 3) to turn informer

squeeze [skwēz] *verb*, to press hard upon 2) to put pressure on to extract liquid 3) to force one's way 4) to crowd

squid [skwĭd] *noun*, a sea creature similar to an octopus

squint [skwĭnt] *verb*, to scrunch one's eyes to strain to see

squirm [skwûrm] *verb*, to wiggle

squir-rel [skwûr′əl, skwŭr′-] *noun*, a small rodent with a bushy tail that lives in trees

sta-bil-i-ty [stə-bĭl′ĭ-tē] *adjective*, firmness, constancy, strength

sta-ble [stā′bəl] *adjective*, 1) firm, steady, *noun*, 2) a building in which horses are kept

stac-ca-to [stə-kä′tō] *adjective*, music played in a quick, abrupt manner

stack [stăk] *noun*, 1) a large pile arranged in some sort of order 2) a chimney, *verb*, 3) to pile up

sta-di-um [stā′dē-əm] *noun*, an open arena where concerts, sports, or events are held

staff [stăf] *noun*, a long stick carried in the hand for support

stag [stăg] *noun*, a male deer

stage [stāj] *noun*, 1) a raised floor or platform in a theatre or auditorium 2) a period of time or a step in development

stage-coach [stāj′kōch′] *noun*, a carriage on wheels pulled by horses on a fixed route

stag-ger [stăg′ər] *verb*, to stand or walk unsteadily, to reel

stag-nant [stăg′nənt] *adjective*, not moving or flowing, motionless

stag-nate [stăg′nāt′] *verb*, to be or become stagnant, motionless, to become impure or foul

staid [stād] *adjective*, sober, sedate

stain [stān] *noun*, 1) a mark that changes the appearance of something, a blot, *verb*, 2) to make a strong mark that cannot be removed 3) to disgrace

stair [stâr] *noun*, a step connecting different levels, *plural*, **stairs**, a series or flight of steps

stake [stāk] *noun*, 1) a pointed post in the ground 2) a gamble, a risk

stale [stāl] *adjective*, 1) old, dry, not fresh, tasteless 2) dull, bored

stale-mate [stāl′māt′] *noun*, a deadlock, a situation in which no side may take action

stalk [stôk] *noun*, 1) the long part of a plant that supports leaves or flowers, *verb*, 2) to follow someone with the intention of harming them 3) to pursue prey

stall [stôl] *noun*, 1) a small open room, as in a barn or a market place, *verb*, 2) to stop due to a mechanical failure

stal-lion [stăl′yən] *noun*, a male horse used for breeding

stal-wart [stôl′wərt] *adjective*, 1) sturdy, strong 2) brave 3) firm, steadfast

stam-i-na [stăm′ə-nə] *noun*, the power to endure, strength

stamp [stămp] *noun*, 1) a small piece of paper purchased to put on an envelope or package to send it through the mail 2) the imprint left from a device used to leave a mark, *verb*, 3) to mark with a special sign or design 4) to set the foot down heavily

stam-pede [stăm-pēd′] *verb*, to rush wildly in a group

stance [stăns] *noun*, 1) posture 2) political or social position

stand [stănd] *verb*, 1) to be your feet 2) to take a position 3) to mean or signify, to represent

stand-ard [stăn′dərd] *adjective*, 1) regular, official, basic, *noun*, 2) a fixed quality by which things are compared

stands [stăndz] *noun*, *plural*, the bleachers where spectators watch sports events

stan-za [stăn′zə] *noun*, a verse in a poem, a song, or a refrain

sta-ple [stā′pəl] *noun*, 1) principle commodity, an essential element 2) a wire used to attach things together such as cloth or paper, *verb*, 3) to bond two things together with staples applied by a stapler

star [stär] *noun*, 1) a point of light that can be seen in the sky at night 2) a five-pointed shape, *verb*, 3) to stand out in a positive way, to be outstanding

star-board [stär′bərd] *adjective*, the right-hand side of a ship as one faces the bow

starch [stärch] *noun*, a carbohydrate, that turns into sugar in the body

stare [stâr] *verb*, to look at someone or something with a steady gaze, to glare

stark [stärk] *adjective*, extremely

simple or severe, bleak

start [stärt] *noun*, 1) an act of beginning, *verb*, 2) to begin

star-tle [stär′tl] *verb*, to surprise, to greet unexpectedly, to shock

star-va-tion [stär-vā′shən] *noun*, to suffer from hunger and lack of food or nourishment

starve [stärv] *verb*, to be hungry, unfed, deprived of food

state [stāt] *noun*, 1) the condition of something 2) a mood 3) a group of people living under an independent government, that is part of a country or federal union which governs itself as a republic or commonwealth, *verb*, 5) to say, to declare

state-ment [stāt′mənt] *noun*, 1) a spoken or written commitment 2) a summary of an account showing the balance

states-man [stāts′mən] *noun*, a leader of government

stat-ic [stăt′ĭk] *noun*, applicable to electricity not in motion

sta-tion [stā′shən] *noun*, a stopping place for the convenience of passengers, a depot

sta-tion-ar-y [stā′shə-něr′ē] *adjective*, fixed in a place, not changing, not moving

sta-tion-er-y [stā′shə-něr′ē] *noun*, writing paper, pens, and ink

sta-tis-tic [stə-tĭs′tĭk] *noun*, a fact stated as a number or in tables

stat-ue [stăch′ōō] *noun*, replica of a figure, real or imaginary made of plaster, bronze, marble, etc.

stat-ure [stăch′ər] *noun*, 1) a person's status or place in the community 2) the height of a person or animal

sta-tus [stā′təs] *noun*, position, high standing, prestige

stat-ute [stăch′o͞ot] *noun*, a law enacted by a legislature

stat-u-to-ry [stăch′ə-tôr′ē] *adjective*, authorized, made as a law, regulated by statute

stay [stā] *verb*, to continue to be

stead-fast [stĕd′făst′] *adjective*, firmly fixed or established, unwavering, constant

stead-i-ly [stĕd′ə-lē] *adverb*, constantly, continually, regularly

stead-y [stĕd′ē] *adjective*, 1) regular 2) firm, immovable

steak [stāk] *noun*, a thick flat piece of meat or fish

steal [stēl] *verb*, 1) to take or carry away without permission 2) to move or pass very quietly without making noise

stealth [stĕlth] *noun*, secrecy, sneakiness, surreptitious

steam [stēm] *noun*, 1) the vapor created by boiling water, *verb*, 2) to cook using the intense heat of steam 3) to expose to steam

steel [stēl] *noun*, a hard metal made of specially treated iron, used in machines, knives, hardware, etc.

steep [stēp] *adjective*, 1) having a sharp incline or slope, *verb*, 2) to soak in liquid, to saturate

stee-ple [stē′pəl] *noun*, a free-standing column or tower

steer [stŭr] *noun*, 1) a form of long horned cattle, *verb*, 2) to drive, to fly, to conduct, or navigate

stel-lar [stĕl′ər] *adjective*, 1) star-like, referring to heavenly bodies, celestial 2) outstanding

stem [stĕm] *noun*, 1) the stalk of a plant that supports the flower and leaves, *verb*, 2) to develop from 3) to stop the flow of

sten-cil [stĕn′səl] *noun*, a thin sheet with perforations in the form of a design through which ink or paint may be forced

step [stĕp] *noun*, 1) a stair 2) the movement with a foot 3) one of a series of events in a program, *verb*, 4) to walk or go on foot

ster-e-o [stĕr′ē-ō′] *noun*, an electronic device that makes sounds or plays music

ster-e-o-type [stĕr′ē-ə-tīp′] *noun*, 1) a typical example or pattern 2) a conventional, oversimplified conception

ste-rile [stĕr′əl, -īl′] *adjective*, clean, antiseptic, germ free

ster-i-lize [stĕr′ə-līz′] *verb*, 1) to render incapable of germination, 2) to disinfect, to clean

ster-ling [stûr′lĭng] *adjective*, 1) genuine, superior, excellent, of the highest quality *noun*, 2) made of pure silver

stern [stûrn] *adjective*, 1) unsympathetic, firm, strict 2) the back of the boat

steth-o-scope [stĕth′ə-skōp′] *noun*, an instrument used to convey to the ear, sounds produced by the body, especially in the chest

stew [sto͞o] *noun*, 1) a thick soup, *verb*, 2) to cook in liquid

stew-ard [sto͞o′ərd] *noun*, 1) one who watches over something

2) one in charge of provisions and dinner arrangements

stew-ard-ess [stōō'ər-dĭs] *noun*, a woman who serves passengers on an airplane, a flight attendant

stick [stĭk] *noun*, 1) a short branch or twig, *verb*, 2) to make something adhere to a surface 3) to push in or out 4) to stay with something, to persevere

stiff [stĭf] *adjective*, 1) something that cannot be moved or bent easily 2) difficult or hard to accomplish 3) sore

stiff-en [stĭf'ən] *verb*, to harden, to brace, to become rigid

stig-ma [stĭg'mə] *noun*, 1) the apex of a flower pistil where pollen is placed 2) a disgraceful blot

stig-ma-tize [stĭg'mə-tīz'] *verb*, to brand, to mark as wicked

still [stĭl] *adjective*, 1) without movement, *adverb*, 2) up to this or that time 3) even so

still-ness [stĭl'nĭs] *noun*, the state of being still or without sound

stim-u-late [stĭm'yə-lāt'] *verb*, to rouse to action, to excite

stim-u-lus [stĭm'yə-ləs] *noun*, an incentive, an impetus

sting [stĭng] *noun*, 1) the pain or wound of an insect or bug bite 2) a sharp or smarting pain 3) the attack of an insect on its prey or an enemy

stin-gy [stĭn'jē] *adjective*, not generous, miserly

stink [stĭngk] *noun*, 1) an unpleasant or awful odor, *verb*, 2) to give off a bad smell

sti-pend [stī'pĕnd'] *noun*, payment given for services

stip-u-late [stĭp'yə-lāt'] *verb*, to bargain, to specify as a condition of an agreement

stir [stûr] *verb*, to mix or blend

stir-ring [stûr'ĭng] *adjective*, moving, touching, exciting

stitch [stĭch] *noun*, 1) a needle and thread, piercing cloth and then coming out again to form a link of thread in a fabric 2) a loop added to a knitting needle, *verb*, 3) to sew, to mend

stock [stŏk] *noun*, goods kept on hand, merchandise

stock-ade [stŏ-kād'] *noun*, a barricade, a fence, an obstacle

stock-hold-er [stŏk'hōl'dər] *noun*, an owner of stocks or shares in a corporation

stock-ing [stŏk'ĭng] *noun*, a sheer leg covering made of nylon

sto-ic [stō'ĭk] *noun*, one who is indifferent to pleasure or pain, stern, impassive, cold

stoke [stōk] *verb*, to provide with fuel, to feed abundantly

stole [stōl] *past tense* of **steal**

stom-ach [stŭm'ək] *noun*, a large muscular bag in the body that receives food, digests some of it, and passes it on, to the intestines

stone [stōn] *noun*, 1) a small piece of rock, *verb*, 2) to pelt or kill

stool [stōōl] *noun*, 1) a seat with three or four legs and no back 2) a bowel movement

stoop [stōōp] *verb*, 1) to bend or squat the body over forwards 2) to lower oneself, to condescend

stop [stŏp] *verb*, 1) to end, to make something come to an end 2) to prevent something from happening, moving, etc. 3) to complete the action

stor-age [stôr′ĭj] *noun*, the act of keeping things for future use

store [stōr] *noun*, 1) supply of things saved for use later 2) a shop, a place to buy things, *verb*, 3) to put away for later use

stork [stôrk] *noun*, a large bird with long legs and a large beak

storm [stôrm] *noun*, a period of high winds, possibly thunder and lightning, rain, or snow

sto-ry [stōr′ē] *noun*, 1) telling of events with words spoken or written in a book 2) an account of something either true or fictitious, a report, a description 3) the floor of a building

stout [stout] *adjective*, 1) short, heavy-set 2) resolute, firm

stove [stōv] *noun*, an appliance which is heated and used for cooking or heating

stow [stō] *verb*, to store, to put away for future use

straight [strāt] *adjective*, 1) not curved, *adverb*, 2) without going anywhere else or doing anything else 3) moving on a path that is unchanged 4) without delay, *noun*, 5) a poker hand of 5 cards in consecutive order

straight-en [strāt′n] *verb*, to fix or arrange in order

strain [strān] *noun*, 1) the change of a body produced by an external force 2) a new species or breed 3) a suggestion, a hint, a

trace, *verb*, 4) to cause stress, to stretch to reach

strait [strāt] *noun*, a narrow channel between two bodies of water, an inlet

strand [strănd] *noun*, 1) seashore, waterfront 2) a piece of something long and thin like a rope or a piece of hair

strange [strānj] *adjective*, unusual, odd, unfamiliar, exotic

strange-ly [strānj′lē] *adverb*, unusually, seldom, rarely

stran-ger [strān′jər] *noun*, a person you do not know, an outsider

stran-gle [străng′gəl] *verb*, 1) to kill by suffocating 2) to suppress

strap [străp] *noun*, 1) a narrow piece of leather, plastic, cloth, etc, used for fastening something, *verb*, 2) to fasten something on with a tie

strat-e-gy [străt′ə-jē] *noun*, a plan

strat-o-sphere [străt′ə-sfîr′] *noun*, the upper atmosphere extending 12-30 miles above the earth's surface, the ozone

stra-tum [strā′təm] *noun*, *plural* **strata**, a layer of the earth's surface, sedimentary rock

straw [strô] *noun*, 1) a dry stem 2) something that people use to suck a drink out of a glass

straw-ber-ry [strô′běr′ē] *noun*, the edible red berry of a small plant, that grows on the ground

stray [strā] *adjective*, 1) anything that does not seem to be part of a group, *verb*, 2) to wander away from home or the rest of the group 3) to digress

streak [strēk] *noun*, 1) a long mark like a band or a stripe, *verb*, 2) to draw stripes on something in a wild pattern

stream [strēm] *noun*, 1) a small river, a small body of running water 2) a steady or continuous flow, *verb*, 3) to flow, to pour

street [strēt] *noun*, a public paved road as in a town or city

strength [strĕngkth] *noun*, power, capacity for exertion or endurance, force in numbers

strength-en [strĕngk/thən] *verb*, to reinforce, to make stronger

stren-u-ous [strĕn/yo͞o-əs] *adjective*, characterized by vigorous exertion, difficult

stress [strĕs] *noun*, 1) anxiety, tension, *verb*, 2) to apply force, to cause strain 3) to emphasize

stretch [strĕch] *noun*, 1) an expanse, a range or reach, *verb*, 2) to exaggerate 3) to extend across a given space 4) to extend one's body or limbs to be limber

stretch-er [strĕch/ər] *noun*, a framework consisting of two poles with a cloth fastened between them used to carry an injured person

strict [strĭkt] *adjective*, close adherence to the rules

stride [strīd] *noun*, 1) a large step or movement, *verb*, 2) to step

stri-dent [strīd/nt] *adjective*, loud and harsh in sound, grating

strike [strīk] *noun*, 1) an unsuccessful attempt by a batter to hit a ball 2) a protest of wages that stops work in order to bargain for better working conditions, *verb*, 3) to hit or attack 4) to refuse to work because of a pay dispute 5) to discover, to uncover 6) to eliminate 7) to find, to reach

string [strĭng] *noun*, 1) a thin twine made by twisting several threads together 2) a fine piece of wire used in some musical instruments, *verb*, 3) to thread a bead onto a string

strin-gent [strĭn/jənt] *adjective*, strict, inflexible, exacting

stripe [strīp] *noun*, a long thin line

strive [strīv] *verb*, to exert oneself, to try, to make a strenuous effort

stroke [strōk] *noun*, 1) a mild heart attack, *verb*, 2) to caress, to rub

stroll [strōl] *verb*, to walk leisurely

strong [st rŏng] *adjective*, 1) able to take stress or strain 2) intense in degree 3) physically powerful

struck [strŭk] *verb*, *past tense* of **strike**

struc-ture [strŭk/chər] *noun*, 1) the framework of something, 2) a complete building

strug-gle [strŭg/əl] *noun*, 1) the fight, the effort, *verb*, 2) to continue to endure set backs

strut [strŭt] *verb*, to swagger, to walk with bravado

stub-born [stŭb/ərn] *adjective*, unwilling to give in or compromise, obstinate

stuck [stŭk] *verb*, *past tense* of **stick**

stu-dent [sto͞od/nt] *noun*, a person enrolled at a school or college

stud-y [stŭd/ē] *noun*, 1) a room to read and write 2) a subject or area of learning, *verb*, 3) to apply the mind to the effort to learn by reading and thinking

stuff [stŭf] *noun*, 1) substance, material, *verb*, 2) to fill by crowding, to push or crowd in

stum-ble [stŭm′bəl] *verb*, to walk unsteadily so that you appear to be about to fall, to trip while running 2) to come upon unexpectedly 3) to stammer

stump [stŭmp] *noun*, 1) what is left of a tree after it has been cut down, *verb*, 2) to perplex

stun [stŭn] *verb*, to astonish, to amaze, to confound, to shock

stunt [stŭnt] *noun*, 1) a performance, a skit, an act, *verb*, 2) to suppress, to retard the growth of something

stu-pen-dous [stoō-pĕn′dəs] *adjective*, astonishing, wonderful, amazing

stu-por [stoō′pər] *noun*, a state of apathy, a daze, lack of awareness

stur-dy [stûr′dē] *adjective*, very strongly built, durable

stut-ter [stə′tər] *verb*, to speak with difficulty, to stammer

sty [stī] *noun*, 1) a painful red swelling on the end of an eyelid 2) a pig pen

style [stīl] *noun*, 1) the fashion or design 2) elegance or flair

sty-mie [stī′mē] *verb*, to present an obstacle, to stump, to hinder

suave [swäv] *adjective*, smoothly, agreeable, courteous, polite

sub-due [səb-doō′] *verb*, to calm down, to bring under control

sub-ject [sŭb′jĭkt] *adjective*, 1) owing obedience to 2) likely to be affected by, *noun*, 3) an area of study 4) a person under the authority or control of another 5) in a sentence the word about which the predicate makes a statement, *verb*, 6) to expose to

sub-jec-tive [səb-jĕk′tĭv] *adjective*, based on personal feelings or opinions

sub-lime [sə-blīm′] *adjective*, great, noble, majestic, superior

sub-lim-i-nal [sŭb-lĭm′ə-nəl] *adjective*, affecting the subconscious, below the threshold of consciousness

sub-ma-rine [sŭb′mə-rēn′] *noun*, a naval warship armed with torpedoes and missiles that operates under water

sub-merge [səb-mûrj′] *verb*, to put or sink under water

sub-mis-sive [səb-mĭs′ĭv] *adjective*, to take orders without questioning authority

sub-mit [səb-mĭt′] *verb*, 1) to put something forward for someone else's reaction 2) to give in to someone or something

sub-or-di-nate [sə-bôr′dn-ĭt] *adjective*, 1) being in a lower rank or class, subject to another's authority *noun*, 2) one lower in rank, inferior

sub-poe-na [sə-pē′nə] *noun*, a writ commanding a person listed in it to appear in court

sub-scribe [səb-scrīb′] *verb*, 1) to sign up for something 2) to give permission or consent

sub-scrip-tion [səb-skrĭp′shən] *noun*, money paid as a form of membership for service

sub-se-quent [sŭb'sĭ-kwĕnt']
adjective, following, after

sub-ser-vi-ent [səb-sûr've-ənt]
adjective, useful in an inferior
capacity, subordinate

sub-side [səb-sīd'] *verb*, to settle
down to become calm

sub-si-dize [sŭb'sĭ-dīz'] *verb*, 1) to
add to 2) to provide financial aid

sub-si-dy [sŭb'sĭ-dē] *noun*, direct
financial aid by the government

sub-stance [sŭb'stəns] *noun*, the
material something is made of

sub-stan-tial [səb-stăn'shəl]
adjective, 1) strong 2) having
considerable property

sub-stan-ti-ate [səb-stăn'shē-āt']
verb, to verify, to support

sub-stan-tive [sŭb'stən-tĭv]
adjective, essential, pertaining to

sub-sti-tute [sŭb'stĭ-tōōt'] *noun*,
1) a person or thing put in place
of another, a replacement *verb*,
2) to act in place of another

sub-ter-fuge [sŭb'tər-fyōōj'] *noun*,
a device or plan by which one
can hide an objective

sub-ter-ra-ne-an [sŭb'tə-rā'nē-ən]
adjective, 1) under the earth's
surface 2) hidden, secret

sub-tle [sŭt'l] *adjective*, difficult to
to detect, not obvious, slight

sub-tle-ty [sŭt'l-tē] *noun*, cunning,
delicately understated

sub-tract [səb-trăkt'] *verb*, to take
away one number from another

sub-trac-tion [səb-trăk'shən] *noun*,
an equation in which one
number is taken from another

sub-urb [sŭb'ûrb'] *noun*, a
residential community on the
outskirts of a city or town

sub-ur-ban [sə-bûr'bən] *adjective*,
pertaining to a smaller district
next to a city or town

sub-ver-sive [səb-vûr'sĭv]
adjective, tending to overthrow
or ruin, corruption

sub-way [sŭb'wā'] *noun*, an
underground electric train or
urban transit system

suc-ceed [sək-sēd'] *adjective*, to
attain a desired object or goal

suc-cess [sək-sĕs'] *noun*, a person
who accomplishes a difficult
task or meets a goal

suc-cess-ful [sək-sĕs'fəl] *adjective*,
gaining a desired object or goal

suc-ces-sion [sək-sĕsh'ən] *noun*,
sequence, order, descent

suc-ces-sive [sək-sĕs'ĭv] *adjective*,
following one after another in a
line or series, consecutive

suc-ces-sor [sək-sĕs'ər] *noun*,
someone appointed to a title or
position to replace another

suc-cinct [sək-sĭngkt'] *adjective*,
concise, terse, brief, to the point

suc-cor [sŭk'ər] *noun*, aid, help,
assistance, relief

suc-cul-ent [sŭk'yə-lənt] *adjective*,
1) juicy 2) delicious, tasty

suc-cumb [sə-kŭm'] *verb*, 1) to
yield, to give way 2) to die

such [sŭch] *pronoun*, 1) of this or
that kind 2) used in some
phrases to mean like

suck [sŭk] *verb*, to draw into the
mouth by action of the lips and
tongue when inhaling

suc-tion [sŭk'shən] *noun*, the
pulling force of a partial vacuum

sud-den [sŭd′n] *adjective*, when something happens unexpectedly

sud-den-ly [sŭd′n-lē] *adverb*, happening at once without warning, unexpectedly

sue [soō] *verb*, to ask a court to solve a problem legally

suede [swād] *noun*, a leather made when the flesh, or underside of the leather is buffed or sandpapered to produce a nap

suf-fer [sŭf′ər] *verb*, 1) to feel pain or hurt 2) to tolerate, to allow

suf-fer-ing [sŭf′ər-ĭng] *noun*, enduring pain and sadness

suf-fice [sə-fīs′] *verb*, 1) to be enough for 2) to satisfy a need

suf-fi-cient [sə-fĭsh′ənt] *adjective*, adequate for the purpose

suf-fix [sŭf′ĭks] *noun*, letters added to the end of a word, to change the meaning

suf-fo-cate [sŭf′ə-kāt′] *verb*, 1) to smother, to choke 2) to kill by depriving of oxygen

suf-frage [sŭf′rĭj] *noun*, the right to vote, a vote

sug-ar [shōōg′ər] *noun*, a sweet substance made from sugar cane or sugar beets and used in food products

sug-gest [səg-jĕst′] *verb*, 1) to bring up or call to mind, to propose for consideration 2) to imply, to indicate

sug-ges-tion [səg-jĕs′chən] *noun*, 1) a proposal, an idea, advice, a recommendation 2) a slight trace, a hint, an implication

su-i-cide [soō′ĭ-sīd′] *noun*, the act of taking one's own life

suit [soōt] *noun*, 1) a set of clothes made from the same fabric, *verb*, 2) to adapt, to perform

suit-a-ble [soō′tə-bəl] *adjective*, fitting, proper, appropriate

suit-case [soōt′kās′] *noun*, a rectangular piece of luggage

suite [swēt] *noun*, a number of rooms connected together

suit-or [soō′tər] *noun*, a beau, a man who courts a woman

sul-fur [sŭl′fər] *noun*, a nonmetallic yellow element used in gunpowder, matches and medicine

sulk [sŭlk] *verb*, to pout and feel angry or sorry for yourself

sul-len [sŭl′ən] *adjective*, silent from anger or hurt, moody, indulging in self-pity

sul-ly [sŭl′ē] *verb*, 1) to disgrace, to tarnish someone's character 2) to soil, to stain

sul-try [sŭl′trē] *adjective*, sweltering, hot and humid

sum [sŭm] *noun*, the total of different amounts added together

sum-ma-ry [sŭm′ə-rē] *noun*, a shorter version of an article

sum-ma-tion [sə-mā′shən] *noun*, the act of finding the total

sum-mer [sŭm′ər] *noun*, the third season of the year, between spring and autumn

sum-mit [sŭm′ĭt] *noun*, 1) the top leaders, the highest point 2) the top of a mountain

sum-mon [sŭm′ən] *verb*, 1) to call, to send for by command 2) to gather, to call forth

sum-mons [sŭm′ənz] *noun*, a formal letter requesting a response in court

sump-tu-ous [sŭmp′chōo-əs] *adjective*, luxurious, splendid

sun [sŭn] *noun*, the central star of the solar system around which the planets revolve which gives off light, heat and energy

sun-dae [sŭn′dē] *noun*, a dish of ice cream covered with toppings such as chocolate syrup, nuts and whipped cream

Sun-day [sŭn′dē] *noun*, the first day of the week, observed as the Sabbath by most Christians

sun-der [sŭn′dər] *verb*, to separate, to cut apart

sun-dry [sŭn′drē] *adjective*, various, more than one or two

sun-flow-er [sŭn′flou′ər] *noun*, a plant with large yellow-rayed flower heads that produces edible seeds that yield an oil

sun-rise [sŭn′rīz′] *noun*, the early morning, the crack of dawn

sun-set [sŭn′sĕt′] *noun*, close of the day, twilight

sun-shine [sŭn′shīn′] *noun*, *no plural*, bright light, day light

su-per [sōo′pər] *adjective,*
1) outstanding, exceptionally fine,
2) great, extreme or excessive

su-perb [sōo-pûrb′] *adjective*, exceptional, extraordinary

su-per-cil-i-ous [sōo′pər-sĭl′ē-əs] *adjective*, lofty with pride, haughty, contemptuous

su-per-fi-cial [sōo′pər-fĭsh′əl] *adjective*, 1) relating to the surface or appearance only

2) actions thoughtlessly done, insincere, shallow

su-per-flu-ous [sōo-pûr′flōo-əs] *adjective*, excessive, more than needed, unnecessary

su-per-in-tend-ent [sōo′pər-ĭn-tĕn′dənt] *noun*, one having oversight and direction of some place or agency

su-pe-ri-or [sōo-pîr′ē-ər] *adjective*, 1) beyond power or influence of another 2) greater in number or amount 3) above average

su-per-mar-ket [sōo′pər-mär′kĭt] *noun*, a large store with shelves that have a variety of household products, a large grocery store

su-per-nat-u-ral [sōo′pər-năch′ər-əl] *adjective*, beyond what is explainable by natural law, metaphysical

su-per-sede [sōo′pər-sēd′] *adjective*, to come to take the place of something that is not as modern, efficient,or appropriate

su-per-son-ic [sōo′pər-sŏn′ĭk] *adjective*, faster than sound

su-per-sti-tion [sōo′pər-stĭsh′ən] *noun*, reverence for that which is unknown or mysterious

su-per-sti-tious [sōo′pər-stĭsh′əs] *adjective*, awe of that which is unknown or mysterious based on an irrational belief

su-per-vise [sōo′pər-vīz′] *verb*, to direct, to watch over

su-per-vi-sion [sōo′pər-vĭzh′ən] *noun*, *no plural*, overseeing someone's work

su-per-vi-sor [sōo′pər-vī′zər] *noun*, a person who oversees a department of workers

sup-per [sŭp'ər] *noun*, dinner, a meal eaten in the evening

sup-ple [sŭp'əl] *adjective*, 1) flexible, pliant, bending easily without breaking 2) limber

sup-ple-ment [sŭp'lə-mənt] *noun*, a part added, an appendix

sup-ply [sə-plī'] *noun*, 1) a resource, *verb*, 2) to provide something needed

sup-port [sə-pôrt', -pōrt'] *noun*, 1) aid, assistance 2) an abutment, a brace, a stay, *verb*, 3) to advocate, to back, to uphold 4) to provide food and clothing and other necessities

sup-pose [sə-pōz'] *verb*, to hold that something is true, to assume that something is true

sup-posi-tion [sŭp'ə-zĭsh'ən] *noun*, presumption, theory, principle

sup-press [sə-prĕs'] *verb*, to subdue, to quell, to inhibit, to keep from being known

su-preme [soo-prēm'] *adjective*, highest in authority, highest in degree, above all

Su-preme Court [soo-prēm'kôrt] *noun*, the most important court in the United States, consisting of 9 members appointed by the President

sure [shoor] *adjective*, certain beyond question, having no doubt

sure-ly [shoor'lē] *adverb*, certainly

surf [sûrf] *noun, no plural*, 1) the waves of the sea as they hit the shores, *verb*, 2) to ride a surfboard 3) to search the Internet on a computer

sur-face [sûr'fəs] *noun*, 1) a plane, the outside or topside face 2) the top of the water, *verb*, 3) to rise to the top of a body of water

sur-feit [sûr'fĭt] *noun*, 1) excess *verb*, 2) to over-indulge, to give to use in excess

surge [sûrj] *noun*, 1) a rush, a flow, *verb*, 2) to swell, to pour out

sur-geon [sûr'jən] *noun*, one whose profession it is to cure diseases or injuries by performing an operation

sur-ger-y [sûr'jə-rē] *noun*, an operation when a doctor cuts into a person's body with instruments to help cure them

sur-ly [sûr'lē] *adjective*, rude, cross

sur-mise [sər-mīz'] *noun*, 1) a guess, speculation, likelihood, *verb*, 2) to assume, to guess, to suppose, to conjecture

sur-mount [sər-mount'] *verb*, to be overcome, to prevail over

sur-name [sûr'nām'] *noun*, a person's last name

sur-pass [sər-păs'] *verb*, to exceed, to do better, to go beyond

sur-plus [sûr'pləs, -plŭs'] *noun*, the amount that is more than needed

sur-prise [sər-prīz'] *noun*, 1) something sudden and unexpected, *verb*, 2) to cause to feel astonished

sur-real [sûr'rēl] *adjective,* seeming like a dream; something that is real but feels imaginary or impossible, bizarre

sur-ren-der [sə-rĕn'dər] *verb*, to give up, to yield

sur-rep-ti-tious [sûr'əp-tĭsh'əs] *adjective*, kept secret (especially if it would not be approved of), hidden, unauthorized

sur-ro-gate [sûr′ə-gĭt] *adjective*, substitute, replacement

sur-round [sə-round′] *verb*, to encircle, to enclose on all sides

sur-round-ings [sə-roundĭngs] *noun, plural,* the conditions or things around a person or place

sur-veil-lance [sər-vā′ləns] *noun*, a close watch over something

sur-vey [sər-vā′] *noun*, 1) a study, a poll, a review, *verb*, 2) to examine, to inspect, to watch

sur-vey-or [sər-vā′ər] *noun*, 1) one who collects data 2) one whose business it is to measure land

sur-viv-al [sər-vī′vəl] *noun, no plural*, what one needs to stay alive or exist

sur-vive [sər-vīv′] *verb*, to continue to exist, to live longer

sur-vi-vor [sər-vīv′ər] *noun*, the one to make it when the others died or failed

sus-cep-ti-ble [sə-sĕp′tə-bəl] *adjective*, capable of being affected emotionally

sus-pect [sə-spĕkt′] *noun*, 1) a person who is believed to have done something wrong, *verb*, 2) to suppose that something is true

sus-pend [sə-spĕnd′] *verb*, 1) to hang 2) to stop temporarily

sus-pend-ers [sə-spĕn′dərz] *noun*, two adjustable bands or straps arranged to pass over the shoulders to hold the trousers up

sus-pense [sə-spĕns′] *noun, no plural*, a pause or delay which leaves people anxious

sus-pen-sion [sə-spĕn′shən] *noun*, a delay, postponement

sus-pi-cion [sə-spĭsh′ən] *noun*, 1) distrust, doubt, 2) trace

sus-pi-cious [sə-spĭsh′əs] *adjective*, having a feeling that something is wrong, distrustful

sus-tain [sə-stān′] *verb*, to bear, to hold up, to keep going

sus-te-nance [sŭs′tə-nəns] *noun*, that which supports life, a food or nourishment

su-ture [sōō′chər] *noun*, stitches sewn to hold the cut edges of a wound or incision

swag-ger [swăg′ər] *verb*, to walk in a boastful and proud manner

swal-low [swŏl′ō] *noun*, 1) a small bird with a tail split into two parts, *verb*, 2) to consume food through the mouth into the stomach, to take in

swamp [swŏmp, swômp] *noun*, 1) wet, boggy ground which is always soft, wet land, *verb*, 2) to overwhelm with too much of something, to inundate

swan [swŏn] *noun*, a large white bird with a long neck that lives in the water and on land

swap [swŏp] *verb*, to exchange

swarm [swôrm] *noun*, 1) a large group of insects or bugs, *verb*, 2) to travel in a large group, to teem, to crowd

swarth-y [swôr′thē] *adjective*, having a dark complexion

swat [swŏt] *verb*, to hit, to whack

sway [swā] *verb*, to swing gently

swear [swâr] *verb*, 1) to curse 2) to promise, to make a solemn declaration

sweat [swĕt] *noun*, 1) moisture which comes out of the skin due to exertion, *verb*, 2) to give off water through the skin

sweat-er [swĕt'ər] *noun*, a wool or woven garment worn over the top of the body

sweep [swēp] *noun*, 1) a continuous search, *verb*, 2) to clean or clear with a brush or broom

sweet [swēt] *adjective*, 1) tasting like sugar or honey 2) a pleasant or kind personality 3) having a pleasant smell

swell [swĕl] *verb*, to become larger

swel-ter [swĕl'tər] *verb*, to be tired by the heat, to perspire, to sweat

swept [swĕpt] *past tense* of **sweep**

swerve [swûrv] *verb*, to move suddenly to one side when you are moving along

swift [swĭft] *adjective*, very fast or quick to act, nimble, prompt

swim [swĭm] *noun*, 1) the act of staying afloat or traveling in water, *verb*, 2) to move through the water by using movements of the body

swin-dle [swĭn'dl] *verb*, to cheat, to deceive or defraud

swing [swĭng] *noun*, 1) a seat hanging on ropes or chains, *verb*, 2) to move freely from a fixed point, to pivot, to turn

swirl [swûrl] *noun*, 1) a spiral, *verb*, 2) to turn in a circular motion

switch [swĭch] *noun*, 1) a device that can be used to turn something on or off, *verb*, 2) to exchange 3) to turn something

on or off 4) to change as in direction, to shift, to transfer

swiv-el [swĭv'əl] *verb*, to turn or pivot on a bolt or pin

swol-len [swō'lən] *adjective*, inflamed, puffed up, enlarged

swoon [swōōn] *noun*, 1) a fainting spell, *verb*, 2) to faint

swoop [swōōp] *verb*, to fly down very quickly like a bird

sword [sôrd] *noun*, a weapon similar to a knife with a very long blade

swore [swôr] *past tense* of **swear**

syl-la-ble [sĭl'ə-bəl] *noun*, a combination of letters indicating a sound in a word

syl-lo-gism [sĭl'ə-jĭz'əm] *noun*, logical formula using a major premise, a minor premise leading to a conclusion

sym-bol [sĭm'bəl] *noun*, anything that stands for or represents something else

sym-met-ri-cal [sĭ-mĕt'rĭ-kəl] *adjective*, alike on both sides, proportional

sym-me-try [sĭm'ĭ-trē] *noun*, the balance of things on opposite sides, excellence of proportion

sym-pa-thet-ic [sĭm'pə-thĕt'ĭk] *adjective*, kind, warm, compassionate, tender

sym-pa-thize [sĭm'pə-thīz'] *verb*, to feel sorry for another, to share in a feeling

sym-pa-thy [sĭm'pə-thē] *noun*, the understanding of another person's feelings, pity

sym-pho-ny [sĭm'fə-nē] *noun*, a musical composition performed by an orchestra

symp-tom [sǐm′təm] *noun*, a sign indicating the presence of an illness or something

syn-a-gogue [sǐn′ə-gŏg′] *noun*, a house of worship, a temple

syn-chro-nic-i-ty [sǐng′krə-nǐs′ǐ-tē] *noun*, the simultaneous occurrence of unrelated events

syn-chro-nize [sǐng′krə-nīz′] *verb*, to agree in time, to move together simultaneously

syn-di-cate [sǐn′dǐ-kǐt] *verb*, a network of businesses that sell news to the media

syn-er-gy: [sǐn′ər-jē] *noun,* the interaction or cooperation of two or more organizations, substances, or other agents to produce a combined effect greater than the sum of their separate effects

syn-o-nym [sǐn′ə-nǐm′] *noun*, a word that means the same as another

syn-op-sis [sǐ-nŏp′sǐs] *noun*, a general view of a whole, an abstract or summary

syn-the-sis [sǐn′thǐ-sǐs] *noun*, combining parts into a whole

syn-thet-ic [sǐn-thĕt′ǐk] *adjective*, produced by artificial processes, not real or genuine

sy-ringe [sə-rǐnj′] *noun*, an instrument with a needle used to inject a fluid into the blood stream through a vein

syr-up [sǐr′əp] *noun*, a sugar liquid

sys-tem [sǐs′təm] *noun*, a network of things working together as a functioning unit

sys-tem-at-ic [sǐs′tə-mǎt′ǐk] *adjective*, methodical, proceeding according to method

T

ta-ble [tā′bəl] *noun*, 1) a piece of furniture with a flat top and legs used for placing things on or using as a work space 2) a list, often using lines or boxes to arrange facts

tab-leau [tăb′lō′] *noun*, a scene of persons in costume remaining silent and motionless

ta-ble-cloth [tā′bəl-klôth′] *noun*, a decorative cloth spread over the top of a table

tab-let [tăb′lǐt] *noun*, a hard flat piece or block of something

ta-boo [tə-bōō′] *adjective*, 1) forbidden, banned by religion or custom, *noun*, 2) a restriction, a ban or prohibition

tac-it [tăs′ǐt] *adjective*, implied or indicated, but not expressed

tac-i-tur-n [tăs′ǐ-tûr′n] *adjective*, habitually silent, not given to conversation, saying little

tack [tăk] *noun*, a small nail with a broad, flat head on it

tack-le [tăk′əl] *noun*, 1) ropes and pulleys arranged for hoisting or pulling 2) equipment used for fishing 3) downing a player 4) a football player, *verb*, 5) to undertake, to get down to business to solve a problem 6) to bring to the ground

tact [tăkt] *noun*, *no plural*, to do or say the right thing at the right time, diplomacy

tac-tic [tăk′tǐk] *noun*, a maneuver

tac-tile [tăk′təl, -tīl′] *adjective*, referring to the sense of touch

tag [tăg] *noun*, 1) a small identifying card or label 2) a game children play in which one player chases the others, *verb*, 3) to follow along

tail [tāl] *adjective*, 1) coming from behind, *noun*, 2) the part of an animal which sticks out at the end of its back

tai-lor [tā'lər] *noun*, one who cuts out and makes clothes

taint [tānt] *noun*, 1) a trace of something bad, *verb*, 2) to contaminate, to corrupt

take [tāk] *verb*, 1) to get hold of something 2) to carry something or go with someone to another place 3) to swallow something 4) to travel 5) to accept

tak-en [tā'kən] *adjective*, 1)held, seized 2) accepted

tale [tāl] *noun*, a story

tal-ent [tăl'ənt] *noun*, a natural ability, aptitude

tal-is-man [tăl'ĭs-mən] *noun*, an amulet or lucky charm

talk [tôk] *verb*, to speak or be able to speak, to consult or confer

talk-a-tive [tô'kə-tĭv] *adjective*, inclined to talk a lot, loquacious

tall [tôl] *adjective*, above average height, high

tal-ly [tăl'ē] *noun*, 1) a mark made to keep score or to count, *verb*, 2) to keep track of an account

tal-on [tăl'ən] *noun*, a claw, especially of a bird of prey

tame [tām] *adjective*, 1) trained to live with man, not wild, *verb*, 2) to make a wild animal obedient and friendly to people

tan [tăn] *adjective*, 1) light brown, tawny 2) to convert into leather

tan-gent [tăn'jənt] *noun*, a straight line that touches a curve without intersecting it

tan-ge-rine [tăn'jə-rēn'] *noun*, a variety of a small-sized orange

tan-gi-ble [tăn'jə-bəl] *adjective*, capable of being touched, real

tank [tăngk] *noun*, 1) a large container to hold liquid or gas fuel 2) an armed vehicle used in combat 3) the metal box in the back of the car to hold gasoline

tan-ta-lize [tăn'tə-līz'] *verb*, to tease, to tempt, to promise by offering a reward

tan-ta-mount [tăn'tə-mount'] *adjective*, equal in value

tan-trum [tăn'trəm] *noun*, an exaggerated display of anger, a fit of irritability, bad temper

tap [tăp] *noun*, 1) the faucet attached to a pipe to release liquid or gas, *verb*, 2) to hit or touch lightly 3) to drain by making a hole 4) to draw from

tape [tāp] *noun*, 1) a narrow piece of cloth or other material, *verb*, 2) to bind or secure with an adhesive material 3) to record

tap-er [tā'pər] *verb*, to decrease in amount or size by becoming narrower or smaller

tap-es-try [tăp'ĭ-strē] *noun*, a heavy, decorative, woven fabric used especially for wall hangings

tap-i-o-ca [tăp'ē-ō'kə] *noun*, cassava, a coarse granular preparation used in puddings

tar [tär] *noun*, a thick black liquid made from heating coal or wood

ta-ran-tu-la [tə-răn′chə-lə] *noun*, a hairy, large, poisonous spider

tar-get [tär′gĭt] *noun*, 1) somebody or something aimed at 2) an objective, a goal, *verb*, 3) to make the focus or object of something

tar-iff [tăr′ĭf] *noun*, a tax on goods exported or imported

tar-nish [tär′nĭsh] *verb*, 1) to dull the luster of metal 2) to taint

tart [tärt] *adjective*, 1) sour to the taste, *noun*, 2) a piece of pastry with fruit cooked on top of it

task [tăsk] *noun*, a chore or small job that must be done

tas-sel [tăs′əl] *noun*, a pendant ornament ending in a tuft of loose threads

taste [tāst] *noun*, 1) a preference, liking 2) the sense that distinguishes the flavor of things placed in the mouth 3) a flavor itself, *verb*, 4) to sample a food by taking it in the mouth

tat-too [tă-tōō′] *noun*, a design on the skin made using a needle filled with dye

taught [tôt] *past tense* of **teach**

taunt [tônt] *verb*, to tease or make fun of someone, to ridicule

taut [tôt] *adjective*, stretched tight

tau-tol-o-gy [tô-tŏl′ə-jē] *noun*, needless repetition of an idea in different words

taw-dry [tô′drē] *adjective*, cheap and showy or flashy, gaudy

tax [tăks] *noun*, 1) a sum of money to be paid to the government imposed by the elected leaders, *verb*, 2) to put a fee on service or goods that are given to the government

tax-i [tăk′sē] *noun*, a car for hire to take people from one place to another

tax-i-der-mist [tăk′sĭ-dûr′mĭst] *noun*, one who prepares dead animals to look life-like

tea [tē] *noun*, 1) prepared dried leaves of a plant 2) a small meal or snack in the afternoon 3) a cup of a beverage made with leaves steeped in hot water

teach [tēch] *verb*, to show someone how to do something

teach-er [tē′chər] *noun*, a person whose occupation is to instruct

team [tēm] *noun*, 1) persons working or playing together as a group 2) two or more animals harnessed together to pull a vehicle

tear [tîr] *noun*, 1) a drop of water that comes out of the eye 2) a hole or cut in material, *verb*, 3) to make a hole in material by pulling on it

tease [tēz] *verb*, to make fun of someone, to annoy

tea-spoon [tē′spōōn′] *noun*, a small spoon used to measure

tech-ni-cal [tĕk′nĭ-kəl] *adjective*, having knowledge of a mechanical or scientific subject

tech-ni-cian [tĕk-nĭsh′ən] *noun*, a person who works with machines or instruments

tech-nique [tĕk-nēk′] *noun*, a procedure used to perform a task

tech-nol-o-gy [tĕk-nŏl′ə-jē] *noun*, the use of science to produce useful things for practical purposes that improve life

te-di-ous [tē'dē-əs] *adjective*, tiresome, dull, boring

tel-e-phone [tĕl'ə-fōn'] *noun*, 1) an instrument for reproducing sounds at a distance, *verb*, 2) to call to someone on an instrument that communicates voices through airwaves or wires

tel-e-scope [tĕl'ĭ-skōp'] *noun*, an optical instrument for viewing distant objects

tel-e-vi-sion [tĕl'ə-vĭzh'ən] *noun*, a set used to transmit visual images onto a screen

tell [tĕl] *verb*, 1) to speak to someone, to inform, to narrate 2) to deduce, to differentiate

tell-er [tĕl'ər] *noun*, a bank employee who handles customer transactions

tem-per [tĕm'pər] *noun*, 1) a person's state of mind, mood, *verb*, 2) to tone down, to moderate, to bring under control

tem-per-a-ment [tĕm'prə-mənt] *noun*, the physical and mental character of an individual

tem-per-ance [tĕm'pər-əns] *noun*, habitual moderation of the appetites and passions

tem-per-a-ture [tĕm'pər-ə-chŏŏr'] *noun*, the degree of heat or cold

tem-ple [tĕm'pəl] *noun*, 1) a holy building 2) the part of the head above and in front of the ear

tem-po [tĕm'pō] *noun*, the rate of speed of a musical passage

tem-po-ral [tĕm'pər-əl] *adjective*, not lasting forever, limited by time, the present

tem-po-rar-y [tĕm'pə-rĕr'ē] *adjective*, intended to last a short period of time, not permanent

tempt [tĕmpt] *verb*, to entice someone to do something unwise or wrong, to provoke

temp-ta-tion [tĕmp-tā'shən] *noun*, an instant urge or desire

ten [tĕn] *noun*, the number 10, one plus nine

te-na-cious [tə-nā'shəs] *adjective*, holding fast, stubborn

te-nac-i-ty [tə-năs'ĭ-tē] *noun*, firmness, persistency

ten-ant [tĕn'ənt] *noun*, someone who lives in a house or apartment, an occupant

tend [tĕnd] *verb*, 1) to be likely to, to do something habitually 2) to take care of something

ten-den-cy [tĕn'dən-sē] *noun*, inclination, propensity, leaning

tend-er [tĕn'dər] *adjective*, 1) kind and gentle 2) sensitive to touch or movement 3) cooked so that the food is easy to eat, *noun*, 4) a car attached to a train for carrying food and water

ten-der-ness [tĕn'dər-nĭs] *noun*, affection, gentleness

ten-e-ment [tĕn'ə-mənt] *noun*, a building divided into flats

ten-et [tĕn'ĭt] *noun*, doctrine, dogma, belief, conviction

Ten-nes-see [tĕn'ĭ-sē'] *noun,* one of the 50 United States located in the South, the capital city is Nashville. The state flower of **Tennessee** is the iris, and the motto is "Agriculture and commerce."

ten-nis [tĕn'ĭs] *noun*, a game played on a court by two or four people in which a ball is hit over a net with rackets

ten-or [tĕn'ər] *noun*, 1) a tendency, a trend 2) the highest range of the male singing voice

tense [tĕns] *adjective*, 1) full of excitement 2) tightly stretched, taut, *noun*, 3) the form of a verb that shows when the action happens – past, present, or future

ten-sion [tĕn'shən] *noun*, 1) act of stretching, 2) mental or nervous state or condition of strain

tent [tĕnt] *noun*, a shelter of canvas or nylon, supported by poles

ten-ta-cle [tĕn'tə-kəl] *noun*, a long, arm-like structure growing out of an animal's body, used for movement or catching food

ten-ta-tive [tĕn'tə-tĭv] *adjective*, experimental, based on trials

tenth [tĕnth] *adjective*, the number after nine in series, written 10th

ten-u-ous [tĕn'yoō-əs] *adjective*, weak and unconvincing

ten-ure [tĕn'yər] *noun*, the period of time during which an office is held, occupation

te-pee [tē'pē] *noun*, a cone shaped tent in which some Indians live

tep-id [tĕp'ĭd] *adjective*, 1) not hot or cold, lukewarm 2) showing little enthusiasm

term [tûrm] *noun*, 1) a fixed amount of time 2) an expression or form of language 3) a condition or stipulation

ter-min-al [tûr'mə-nəl] *adjective*, 1) end, final, concluding, *noun*, 2) a depot where buses or trains make connections 3) a conducting circuit arranged for connection in an electrical circuit

ter-mi-nate [tûr'mə-nāt'] *verb*, to end, to finish, to cancel

ter-mi-na-tion [tûr'mə-nā'shən] *noun*, the ending

ter-mi-nol-o-gy [tûr'mə-nŏl'ə-jē] *noun*, vocabulary used in a specialized subject

ter-race [tĕr'ĭs] *noun*, 1) a level area cut out from the side of a hill 2) a flat area outside a house

ter-rain [tə-rān'] *noun*, the features of an area of land

ter-rar-i-um [tə-râr'ē-əm] *noun*, a transparent container in which land animals or plants are kept

ter-res-tri-al [tə-rĕs'trē-əl] *adjective*, of the earth

ter-ri-ble [tĕr'ə-bəl] *adjective*, appalling, dreadful

ter-rif-ic [tə-rĭf'ĭk] *adjective*, awesome, wonderful

ter-ri-fy [tĕr'ə-fī'] *verb*, to fill or overwhelm with fear or horror

ter-ri-to-ry [tĕr'ĭ-tôr'ē] *noun*, a portion of land belonging to someone else, a region

ter-ror [tĕr'ər] *adjective*, fear

terse [tûrs] *adjective*, concise, abrupt, a short answer

ter-ror-ist [tĕr'ər] *noun*, one who uses violence to intimidate

tes-sel-la-tion [tĕs'ə-lā'shən] *adjective*, a mosaic pattern

test [tĕst] *noun*, 1) a trial 2) an examination to assess the level of knowledge of a subject, *verb*,

3) to try something out to see how it works 4) to examine

tes-ta-ment [tĕs′tə-mənt] *noun*,1) a will 2) scripture from the Bible

tes-ti-fy [tĕs′tə-fī′] *verb*, to establish some fact, under oath to serve as evidence

tes-ti-mo-ny [tĕs′tə-mō′nē] *noun*, the statement of a witness under oath, evidence or proof

tet-a-nus [tĕt′n-əs] *noun*, a painful, often fatal, infectious disease, marked by painful spasms of the muscles, frequently of the jaw

teth-er [tĕth′ər] *noun*, 1) a cord, a link, a supply line, *verb*, 2) to tie up with a rope, to hitch, to fasten

Tex-as [tĕk′səs] *noun*, one of the 50 United States located in the Southwest, the capital city is Austin. The state flower of **Texas**, is the bluebonnet, and the motto is "Friendship."

text [tĕkst] *noun*, the words used in a book, a written work

text-book [tĕkst′bŏŏk′] *noun*, an instruction book, a manual

tex-tile [tĕks′tīl′] *noun*, fabrics such as cotton, wool, linen, silk, rayon, and polyester

tex-ture [tĕks′chər] *noun*, the feel or appearance of something – soft, smooth, rough, etc.

than [thăn] used as a *conjunction*, to introduce the second part of a comparison

thank [thăngk] *verb*, to express gratitude and appreciation

thank-ful [thăngk′fəl] *adjective*, to be grateful, to show appreciation or praise

thanks [thăngks] *noun*, an acknowledgment of a kindness, favor, or the like

Thanks-giv-ing [thăngks-gĭv′ĭng] *noun*, a national holiday celebrated the fourth Thursday in November

that [thăt] *pronoun, plural*, **those,** 1) the one singled out 2) used instead of which 3) used to join two parts of a sentence 4) so 5) used to show the result

that's [thăts] the *contraction* of the words **that** and **is**

thatch [thăch] *noun*, bundles of straw woven together

thaw [thô] *verb*, to pass from a frozen to a liquid state

the [thē before a vowel, thə before a consonant] *article*, a word that usually goes before a noun

the-a-ter [thē′ə-tər] *noun*, a building where dramatic performances are presented

the-at-ri-cal [thē-ăt′rĭ-kəl] *adjective*, dramatic, eloquent

thee [thē] *pronoun*, the objective case of thou

theft [thĕft] *noun*, the act or instance of stealing

their [thâr] *pronoun*, belonging to them, a form of the possessive case of **they** used attributively, e.g., *their school*

theirs [thârz] *pronoun*, showing personal ownership

them [thĕm] *pronoun*, the objective case of **they** , *plural*, **them-selves,** the same people, animals, or things mentioned in the sentence as the subject

theme [thēm] *noun*, the subject on which one writes or speaks

then [thĕn] *adverb*, 1) at another time, not now 2) afterwards, next 3) if that is true

the-ol-o-gy [thē-ŏl′ə-jē] *noun*, the science of God or of religion

the-o-rem [thē′ər-əm] *noun*, a principle, a theoretical proposition, a thesis

the-o-ret-i-cal [thē′ə-rĕt′ĭ-kəl] *adjective*, depending on conjecture, speculative

the-o-ry [thē′ə-rē] *noun*, an abstract plan, an hypothesis

ther-a-peu-tic [thĕr′ə-pyōō′tĭk] *adjective*, curative, healing, good for personal growth and health

ther-a-py [thĕr′ə-pē] *noun*, exercises and treatment designed to rehabilitate a person

there [thâr] *adverb*, 1) referring to that place 2) referring to at that moment

there's [thârz] the *contraction* of the words **there** and **is**

there-fore [thâr′fôr′] *adverb*, for that reason, as a result

ther-mal [thûr′məl] *adjective*, pertaining to heat

ther-mo-dy-nam-ics [thûr′mō-dī-năm′ĭks] *noun*, the relationship between heat and other forms of energy

ther-mom-e-ter [thər-mŏm′ĭ-tər] *noun*, a device for measuring how hot or cold something is

ther-mos [thûr′məs] *noun*, a vacuum bottle for keeping liquids hot or cold for hours

ther-mos-tat [thûr′mə-stăt′] *noun*, a mechanical device used to control temperature

the-sau-rus [thĭ-sôr′əs] *noun*, a dictionary of synonyms and antonyms

these [thēz] *pronoun, adjective,* the *plural* of **this**

the-sis [thē′sĭs] *noun*, an essay presented by a candidate for a degree or diploma

they [thā] *pronoun*, the *plural* of **he, she** or **it**

they'll [thāl] the *contraction* of the words **they** and **will**

they're [thâr] the *contraction* of the words **they** and **are**

thick [thĭk] *adjective*, 1)occupying much space in depth or from side to side, measuring between sides 2) a dense fluid

thief [thēf] *noun, plural,* **thieves,** one who steals

thigh [thī] *noun*, the thick part of the leg above the knee and below the hip

thim-ble [thĭm′bəl] *noun*, a metal cap put over the finger to keep it from being pricked by a needle

thin [thĭn] *adjective*, 1) not thick, slender 2) lacking volume or density 3) sparse, insufficient, inadequate, flimsy

thing [thĭng] *noun*, 1) an object, a creature, a form of life 2) conditions 3) an act or event

think [thĭngk] *verb*, 1) to form or have on the mind 2) to use the power of reason 3) to believe, to suppose

third [thûrd] *adjective, noun*, the number three in order after second, written 3rd

thirst [thûrst] *noun, no plural*, the need to drink something

thirst-y [thûr'stē] *adjective*, needing something to drink

thir-teen [thûr-tēn'] *adjective, noun*, the number 13, 3+10

thir-teenth [thûr-tēnth'] *adjective, noun*, number 13 in order, 13th

thir-ti-eth [thûr'tē-ĭth] *adjective, noun*, number 30 in order, 30th

thir-ty [thûr'tē] *adjective, noun*, the number 30, ten times three

this [thĭs] *adjective*, 1) being the one present, near or just mentioned 2) being the one nearer or last mentioned, *adverb* 3) the thing the speaker is talking about, *pronoun*, 4) the one nearer than that one in time or space 5) what is in the present or being talked about

this-tle [thĭs'əl] *noun*, a plant with prickly leaves and stems and a purple flower

thorn [thôrn] *noun*, a sharp projection on a stem

thor-ough [thûr'ō] *adjective*, complete, perfect, absolute

thor-ough-ly [thûr'ō-lē] *adverb*, completely done

those [thōz] *pronoun*, the ones over there, the ones further away than this one

thou [thou] you

though [thō] *adverb,* 1) however, *conjunction*, 2) although

thought [thôt] *noun*, 1) an idea, the process of thinking 2) intention

3) attention, *verb*, 4) the *past tense* of **think**

thought-ful [thôt'fəl] *adjective*, showing consideration for others, kind, discreet

thou-sand [thou'zənd] *noun, adjective*, the number 1,000, ten times 100

thread [thrĕd] *noun*, 1) a fine string made of cotton, linen, or silk, *verb*, 2) to wind through openings 3) to pass a thread through the eye of a needle

threat [thrĕt] *noun*, a warning, that one may do harm

threat-en [thrĕt'n] *verb*, to torment, to scare, to pose a danger

three [thrē] *adjective, noun*, the number 3, one plus two, 3

thresh-old [thrĕsh'ōld'] *noun*, a piece of timber which lies under a door, an entrance

thrift [thrĭft] *noun*, the practice of being careful with money

thrift-y [thrĭf'tē] *adjective*, careful about money, economical

thrill [thrĭl] *noun*, 1) an excited feeling, *verb*, 2) to fill with excitement

thrive [thrīv] *verb*, 1) to grow abundantly 2) to prosper, to flourish, to succeed

throat [thrōt] *noun*, the passage inside of the neck attached to the mouth, lungs, and stomach

throb [thrŏb] *verb*, to beat strongly, to pulsate steadily

throne [thrōn] *noun*, a special chair for a king or queen

throng [thrông, thrŏng] *noun*, a crowd of people, a multitude

throt-tle [thrŏt′l] *noun*, 1) a lever
or pedal that helps an engine
start and run, *verb*, 2) to strangle,
to suppress 3) to regulate the
speed of an engine

through [thrōō] *adjective*,
1) finished, *adverb*, 2) from one
side or end of something to the
other, *preposition*, 3) in one side
and out the other 4) by the
agency of, by way of, via 5)
among or between 6) past or
beyond, in the midst of

through-out [thrōō-out′]
preposition, all over, from end to
end, from inside and out

throw [thrō] *noun*, 1) the distance
something is tossed, cast or
projected, *verb*, 2) to toss, fling,
or hurl something through the air

thrust [thrŭst] *verb*, to push
suddenly and hard

thud [thŭd] *noun*, a dull sound
made when something heavy
falls and lands

thumb [thŭm] *noun*, the short,
thick finger on the hand which is
separate from the others

thun-der [thŭn′dər] *noun*, *no
plural*, the loud sound heard in
the sky during a storm

Thurs-day [thûrz′dē] *noun*, the
fifth day of the week

thus [thŭs] *adverb*, in this way

thy [thī] *pronoun*, your

thyme [tīm] *noun*, a pungent
aromatic plant used in seasoning

tick [tĭk] *noun*, 1) the sound made
by a clock 2) a check mark 3) a
small parasite that sucks blood
from animals and people, *verb*,
4) to make a soft, steady,
rhythmic sound 5) to check off

things on a list that fit a certain
criteria

tick-et [tĭk′ĭt] *noun*, 1) the ballot of
a political party 2) an admission
3) a fine 4) a price tag

tick-le [tĭk′əl] *noun*, 1) a tingling
sensation, *verb*, 2) to touch a
person lightly to make them
laugh 3) to delight, to amuse

tid-al [tīd′l] *adjective*, action of the
sea caused by the tides

tide [tīd] *noun*, regular rise and fall
of the ocean caused by the pull
of the sun and the moon

ti-dy [tī′dē] *adjective*, 1) neat and
orderly 2) substantial, more than
enough, *verb*, 3) to make neat
and well organized

tie [tī] *noun*, 1) a narrow piece of
cloth used as a man's dress
accessory worn around the neck
with a shirt, a necktie 2) a bond
3) a standoff, *verb*, 4) to fasten
something with string or rope
5) to come out equal in a contest

tier [tîr] *noun*, one of several levels

ti-ger [tī′gər] *noun*, a fierce animal,
one of the big cats, which has
yellow fur with black stripes

tight [tīt] *adjective*, 1) so close in
structure that air cannot pass
through 2) drawn close together

tight-en [tīt′n] *verb*, to draw closer
together, to squeeze

tight-ly [tīt′lē] *adverb*, pulled
closely together, tautly

tile [tīl] *noun*, a flat piece of baked
clay that has been painted with
glaze or linoleum used as a floor
covering

till [tĭl] *adverb*, 1) before, up to,
noun, 2) a cash box, a place to
store money, *verb*, 3) to plow

till-er [tĭl′ər] *noun*, a handle used to steer a boat

tilt [tĭlt] *verb*, to make something lean so that it is not straight

tim-ber [tĭm′bər] *noun*, a piece of wood, lumber, hardwood

tim-bre [tăm′bər] *noun*, quality of a musical tone produced by a musical instrument

time [tīm] *noun*, 1) minutes, hours, days, weeks, months, years, etc. 2) a limited duration 3) a period or event 4) a certain hour or part of the day 5) a moment, *verb*, 6) to measure how long it takes to do something 7) a number multiplied by another

time-ly [tīm′lē] *adjective*, prompt, well-timed, favorable

tim-id [tĭm′ĭd] *adjective*, shy, afraid, uncertain, hesitant

tim-id-i-ty [tĭm′ĭ-dĭ-tē] *noun*, lack of self-confidence or courage

tim-or-ous [tĭm′ər-əs] *adjective*, fearful and hesitant

tin [tĭn] *noun*, *no plural*, a soft white metal mixed with alloys

tinc-ture [tĭngk′chər] *noun*, a slight quality added to anything, a trace or tinge, pigment

tin-gle [tĭng′gəl] *verb*, 1) to get excited 2) to have a prickling sensation

tin-ker [tĭng′kər] *verb*, to fool around, to dabble, to putter

tin-sel [tĭn′səl] *noun*, showy or flashy decorations

tint [tĭnt] *noun*, 1) the color, shade, hue, *verb*, 2) to color, to shade

ti-ny [tī′nē] *adjective*, very small

tip [tĭp] *noun*, 1) a point, a peak 2) a hint, advice, a pointer 3) compensation for a service, gratuity, *verb*, 4) to tilt, to list, to lean to one side, to slant 5) to give someone money for a small service 6) to cause something to fall over and become unbalanced

tip-toe [tĭp′tō′] *noun*, 1) the tip of the toe, *verb*, 2) to walk on toes so that the step is not heard

ti-rade [tī′rād′] *noun*, extended scolding, denunciation

tire [tīr] *noun*, 1) a rubber, air-filled part of a car or bicycle wheel that cushions the ride, *verb*, 2) to make someone feel that he needs to rest 3) to become bored, fatigued

tir-ed [tīrd] *adjective*, feeling sleepy, needing rest

tis-sue [tĭsh′o͞o] *noun*, very thin paper that feels soft

ti-tan-ic [tī-tăn′ĭk] *adjective*, gigantic, of great size or power

tithe [tīth] *noun*, a payment of one tenth of an income given to the church

ti-tle [tīt′l] *noun*, 1) the name of a story, a book, a film, etc. 2) a word used in front of a person's name 3) a sport's championship

to [to͞o; tə when unstressed] *adverb*, 1) in a direction toward *preposition*, 2) in the direction of 3) as far as 4) on or against 5) until 6) used to show why 7) used with the infinitive of a verb 8) for the purpose of, in order to 9) belonging to

toad [tōd] *noun*, an animal that looks like a frog but does not live in water

toast [tōst] *noun*, 1) sliced bread broiled to make it crisp, *verb*, 2) to praise someone when raising your drink in a glass 3) to brown by the heat of a fire

to-bac-co [tə-băk′ō] *noun*, the dried leaves of a plant used for smoking and chewing

to-bog-gan [tə-bŏg′ən] *noun*, a very long, flat-bottomed sled used to glide on snow

to-day [tə-dā′] *adverb*, 1) on or for this very day, *noun*, 2) modern times, present day, contemporary

toe [tō] *noun*, 1) one of the five digits at the end of the foot 2) the part of a shoe or sock that covers this end of the foot

tof-fee [tô′fē] *noun*, a hard, chewy candy made of caramel candy, brown sugar and butter

to-ga [tō′gə] *noun*, Roman outer robe of free born men

to-geth-er [tə-gĕth′ər] *adverb*, 1) at the same time 2) in conjunction, with each other, in cooperation

toil [toil] *verb*, to work very hard

toi-let [toi′lĭt] *noun*, an instrument to flush human waste into a sewage system, a bathroom

to-ken [tō′kən] *noun*, 1) a sign or symbol or gesture to indicate something 2) a souvenir 3) a coin used as a currency for travel

told [tōld] *past tense* of **tell**

tol-er-ance [tŏl′ər-əns] *noun*, compassion, open-mindedness

tol-er-ant [tŏl′ər-ənt] *noun*, broad minded, liberal, accepting

toll [tōl] *noun*, 1) the charge for a privilege or a service 2) the number lost or taken, *verb*, 3) to ring a bell slowly

to-ma-to [tə-mā′tō] *noun*, a red berry with seeds and a pulpy fruit eaten as a vegetable

tomb [tōōm] *noun*, a sacred place where a dead person is buried

tomb-stone [tōōm′stōn′] *noun*, the carved stone with an inscription identifying the person on a grave

tome [tōm] *noun*, a large volume

to-mor-row [tə-môr′ō] *adverb* 1) the day after today, *noun*, 2) sometime in the future

ton [tŭn] *noun*, the weight of measure of a very heavy quantity, e.g., 2,000 pounds

tone [tōn] *noun*, 1) the sound of a voice or a musical instrument 2) manner, expression

tongs [tôngz] *noun*, *plural*, (pair of) a tool with two legs used to pick up or.to hold something

tongue [tŭng] *noun*, 1) the organ of speech covered by taste buds 2) the flap of leather or cloth under the lacing of a shoe 3) the language spoken 4) dialect

ton-ic [tŏn′ĭk] *noun*, a refreshing drink that invigorates

to-night [tə-nīt′] *adverb*, 1) the night following today, *noun,* 2) on or during the night of today

too [tōō] *adverb*, 1) also 2) more than is needed or wanted

took [tŏŏk] *past tense* of **take**

tool [tōōl] *noun*, an instrument used to do work or make repairs

tooth [tōōth] *noun*, *plural* **teeth**, 1) a white bony material that grows in the mouth, set in sockets around the jaw, used for chewing 2) the projections on a blade

tooth-ache [tōōth′āk′] *noun*, a pain in the mouth due to an infection from a tooth

top [tŏp] *adjective*, 1) best, first, chief, *noun*, 2) the highest part of something 3) the lid or cover of something 4) a toy that spins quickly on a point

to-paz [tō′păz′] *noun*, a precious stone, usually yellow or tan

top-ic [tŏp′ĭk] *noun*, the subject of a conversation, speech, or essay

to-pog-ra-phy [tə-pŏg′rə-fē] *noun*, detailed representation of the features of a region

top-ple [tŏp′əl] *verb*, to make or become unsteady and fall over

torch [tôrch] *noun*, an instrument that gives off a very hot flame

tor-ment [tôr′mĕnt′] *noun*, 1) abuse, agony, chaos, *verb*, 2) to torture, to annoy, to abuse, to afflict with mental suffering

tor-na-do [tôr-nā′dō] *noun*, a storm with a strong wind which spins very fast, a violent windstorm

tor-pe-do [tôr-pē′dō] *noun*, a self-propelled underwater missile containing explosives fired through the water from a ship to destroy another ship

tor-pid [tôr′pĭd] *adjective*, dormant, dull, lethargic

tor-rent [tôr′ənt] *noun*, a fast flow of water or energy

tor-ren-tial [tô-rĕn′shəl] *adjective*, a rushing, violent stream of water

tor-rid [tôr′ĭd] *adjective*, 1) passionate 2) tropical, sweltering, oppressively hot

tor-so [tôr′sō] *noun*, the trunk of a statue with head and limbs missing, the upper part of the human body

tort [tôrt] *noun*, a civil wrong, independent of a contract

tor-toise [tôr′tĭs] *noun*, a very large turtle that lives on the land

tor-tu-ous [tôr′chōō-əs] *adjective*, winding, full of curves

tor-ture [tôr′chər] noun1) 1) the act of causing great pain or suffering 2) distress of mind or body, *verb*, 3) to inflict pain on someone mercilessly, in order to dominate and control

toss [tôs, tŏs] *verb*, 1) to throw 2) to move about up and down

to-tal [tōt′l] *adjective*, 1) making up the whole, *noun*, 2) the sum of numbers in addition, entire

to-tal-ly [tōt′l-ē] *adverb*, wholly, entirely, completely

touch [tŭch] *noun*, 1) one of the five senses that communicates texture, temperature, and density to the brain through feeling, *verb*, 2) to make physical contact with something or someone

tough [tŭf] *adjective*, 1) yielding to force without breaking, strong 2) brave 3) difficult to chew

tour [tōōr] *noun*, 1) a journey that ends where it starts, *verb*, 2) to make a trip through a place

tour-ist [tōōr′ĭst] *noun*, a person traveling for pleasure

tour-na-ment [tōōr′nə-mənt] *noun*, a set number of contests that includes many teams or players and produces one winner

tow [tō] *verb*, to pull or haul with a rope or a chain

to-ward [tôrd] *preposition*, 1) in the direction of, in relation to 2) facing from the opposite direction

tow-el [tou/əl] noun, a piece of cloth or paper used for wiping or drying

tow-er [tou/ər] *noun*, 1) a tall building or structure that stands above the rest 2) a turret or spire attached to a building or fortress, *verb*, 3) to stand or reach above everything

town [toun] *noun*, buildings creating a hamlet, larger than a village and smaller than a city

tox-ic [tŏk/sĭk] *adjective*, poisonous, harmful

toy [toi] *noun*, an ornament or article that children play with

trace [trās] *noun*, 1) a small amount of something, *verb*, 2) to draw an image using paper to duplicate it 3) to try to follow the path of someone by using evidence that indicates what they are doing or have done

track [trăk] *noun*, 1) a mark left by something that has passed 2) a path or roadway, *verb*, 3) to follow or trace, to trail

trac-ta-ble [trăk/tə-bəl] *adjective*, 1) obedient, willing, compliant 2) easily shaped, malleable

trac-tion [trăk/shən] *noun*, adhesive friction of being drawn or pulled, the grip of the wheels on the ground

trac-tor [trăk/tər] *noun*, a machine used to plow and to till soil

trade [trād] *noun*, *no plural*, 1) the exchange of goods 2) a form of business or enterprise 3) a specific type of work that requires training, *verb*, 4) to buy and sell goods, to barter

tra-di-tion [trə-dĭsh/ən] *noun*, a custom or belief passed within families or other groups from one generation to another

tra-di-tion-al [trə-dĭsh/ə-nəl] *adjective*, following a custom that has been handed down through generations

traf-fic [trăf/ĭk] *noun*, 1) commerce, trade, the interchange of goods 2) the movement of cars and people on streets or of planes and ships

trag-e-dy [trăj/ĭ-dē] *noun*, 1) drama that deals with sad or terrible themes, as opposed to comedy 2) a fatal or unfortunate event

trag-ic [trăj/ĭk] *adjective*, very sad, dreadful, unfortunate

trail [trāl] *noun*, 1) the marks or evidence left behind in a place by someone or something that was there earlier, *verb*, 2) to follow someone, to track

train [trān] *noun*, 1) railroad cars for people or freight pulled by an engine, *verb*, 2) to teach someone or yourself to do something difficult that is considered a skill

train-ing [trā/nĭng] *noun*, preparation, instruction

trait [trāt] *noun*, a distinguishing characteristic or feature

trai-tor [trā′tər] *noun*, one who betrays a cause or any trust

tra-jec-to-ry [trə-jĕk′tə-rē] *noun*, a path taken by a projectile, or a flying object in its flight

tramp [trămp] *noun*, a person with no home or job who travels from place to place begging, a vagrant

tram-ple [trăm′pəl] *verb*, to crush into the ground, to walk heavily on something

trance [trăns] *noun*, a dream-like state of deep relaxation

tran-quil [trăng′kwəl] *adjective*, calm, peaceful, quiet, serene

tran-quil-li-ty [trăng-kwĭl′ĭ-tē] *noun*, calmness, composure

tran-quil-iz-er [trăng′kwə-līz′ər] *noun*, a sleeping pill, sedative

trans-ac-tion [trăn-săk′shən] *noun*, the doing of any business

tran-scend [trăn-sĕnd′] *verb*, to rise above and beyond the ordinary limits, to surpass, to exist independent of

tran-scen-den-tal [trăn′sĕn-dĕn′tl] *adjective*, beyond understanding, supernatural, spiritual

trans-con-ti-nen-tal [trăns′kŏn-tə-nĕn′tl] *adjective*, spanning a continent

tran-scribe [trăn-skrīb′] *verb*, to write out a spoken message

tran-script [trăn′skrĭpt′] *noun*, a written copy of a broadcast or a student's academic record

trans-fer [trăns-fûr′] *noun*, 1) the act of moving something from one place to another, *verb*, 2) to convey from one place to another

trans-fer-a-ble [trăns-fûr′ə-bəl] *noun*, capable of being moved from one place to another

trans-form [trăns-fôrm′] *verb*, 1) to change the form or appearance of something 2) to glorify

trans-form-er [trăns-fôr′mər] *noun*, a device that transfers electrical energy from one circuit to another

trans-fu-sion [trăns-fyōō′zhən] *noun*, the introduction into a person's bloodstream of blood from another

trans-gres-sion [trăns-grĕsh′ən] *noun*, violation of law, a going beyond some limit

tran-sient [trăn′shənt] *adjective*, of short duration, not permanent

tran-sis-tor [trăn-zĭs′tər] *noun*, an electrical device like a radio that sends and amplifies voices

tran-sit [trăn′sĭt] *noun*, 1) a passage 2) the state of being carried 3) a surveyor's instrument for measuring angles

tran-si-tion [trăn-zĭsh′ən] *noun*, going from one state of action or position to another

tran-si-tive [trăn′sĭ-tĭv] *adjective*, when the action of a verb is done to something or somebody

tran-si-to-ry [trăn′sĭ-tôr′ē] *adjective*, temporary, brief, lasting only a short time

trans-late [trăns-lāt′] *verb*, to pass along the message from one language to another

trans-la-tion [trăns-lā′shən] *noun*, the conversion of a message into another language

trans-lu-cent [trăns-lōō′sənt] *adjective*, a material that lets light in diffusively, but cannot be seen through

trans·mis·sion [trăns-mĭsh'ən] *noun*, 1) the apparatus by which the power is transmitted from high-speed motor power to the wheels 2) the sending of pictures or sounds through the air, as by radio or television

trans·mit [trăns-mĭt'] *verb*, 1) to send information over wires or air waves 2) to convey or send from one person or place to another 3) to pass along

trans·mit·ter [trăns-mĭt'ər] *noun*, the part of a telegraph or telephone instrument used to send a message

trans·mute [trăns-myo͞ot'] *verb*, to change, to convert from one substance to another

trans·par·ent [trăns-pâr'ənt] *adjective*, easily or capable of being seen through, clear

tran·spire [trăn-spīr'] *verb*, 1) to exhale 2) to happen, to occur

trans·plant [trăns-plănt'] *verb*, 1) to take out of the ground to plant somewhere else 2) a medical operation that exchanges a body organ

trans·port [trăns-pôrt'] *noun*, 1) a means of carrying people or goods, *verb*, 2) to carry

trans·por·ta·tion [trăns'pər-tā'shən] *noun*, the act of carrying things from one place to another

trans·pose [trăns-pōz'] *verb*, 1) to switch 2) to put into a different key in music

trap [trăp] *noun*, 1) a device used to capture someone or something 2) a strategy used to capture or entrap someone, *verb*, 3) to capture something or someone so that they cannot escape

tra·peze [tră-pēz'] *noun*, a short horizontal bar suspended by two parallel ropes, one at each end

trap·e·zoid [trăp'ĭ-zoid'] *noun*, a closed figure of four sides, two sides are parallel but unequal in length

trash [trăsh] *noun*, something considered worthless that is thrown away, garbage

trau·mat·ic [trou'măt'ĭk] *adjective*, upsetting, stressful, disturbing

tra·vail [trə-vāl'] *noun*, 1) painful labor, hard work 2) anguish

trav·el [trăv'əl] *noun*, 1) taking a trip, seeing the world, *verb*, 2) to go from one place to another 3) to be transmitted

trav·erse [trə-vûrs'] *verb*, to cross in traveling, to pass over

trawl·er [trô'lər] *noun*, a fishing boat which drags a cone-shaped net across the floor of the ocean

tray [trā] *noun*, a flat shallow receptacle with raised edges on which things can be carried

treach·er·ous [trĕch'ər-əs] *adjective*, dangerous

trea·cle [trē'kəl] *noun*, syrup obtained in refining sugar

tread [trĕd] *noun*, 1) the part touching the ground, *verb*, 2) to stand on, to walk on, to step

trea·son [trē'zən] *noun*, *no plural*, the crime of helping the enemy of a group or country one is loyal to

treas-ure [trĕzh/ər] *noun*, 1) an accumulation of wealth such as money or jewels, *verb*, 2) to regard as precious, to cherish

treas-ur-er [trĕzh/ər-ər] *noun*, one who is in charge of the disbursement of money

treas-ur-y [trĕzh/ə-rē] *noun*, a place to store and control money such as a bank

treat [trēt] *noun*, 1) something that gives pleasure or enjoyment, *verb*, 2) to behave toward 3) to deal with, to serve 4) to give medicine as a doctor

trea-tise [trē/tĭs] *noun*, an article treating a subject systematically and thoroughly

treat-ment [trēt/mənt] *noun*, 1) handling, processing 2) therapeutic care

trea-ty [trē/tē] *noun*, a formal agreement between two or more nations

tree [trē] *noun*, a large plant with a trunk, branches, and leaves

trek [trĕk] *verb*, to travel with hardship, a difficult journey

trem-ble [trĕm/bəl] *verb*, to shake, to feel nervous, to quiver

tre-men-dous [trĭ-mĕn/dəs] *adjective*, 1) marvelously great 2) very large 3) extraordinary

trem-or [trĕm/ər] *noun*, trembling, involuntary shaking of the body

trem-u-lous [trĕm/yə-ləs] *adjective*, quivering, wavering

trench [trĕnch] *noun*, a long narrow ditch, dug into the earth

trench-ant [trĕn/chənt] *adjective*, cutting, sarcastic, critical, keen

trench-er-man [trĕn/chər-mən] *noun*, a person with a hearty appetite

trend [trĕnd] *noun*, the popular course, direction, tendency

trep-i-da-tion [trĕp/ĭ-dā/shən] *noun*, fear, apprehension

tres-pass [trĕs/pəs] *noun*, 1) an intrusion, *verb*, 2) to encroach on another's right 3) to unlawfully enter land of another

tri-al [trī/əl] *noun*, 1) when people in a court of law decide whether a person is guilty of a crime 2) a test to see if something is good or bad 3) suffering or adversity

tri-an-gle [trī/ăng/gəl] *noun*, a plane figure with three sides and three angles

tri-an-gu-lar [trī-ăng/gyə-lər] *adjective*, having three points like a triangle

tribe [trīb] *noun*, a group of people descended from a common ancestor who practice the same traditions, customs, and rituals, lead by a chief, a clan

trib-u-la-tion [trĭb/yə-lā/shən] *noun*, distress, suffering

tri-bu-nal [trī-byōō/nəl] *noun*, a court or forum for justice

trib-u-tar-y [trĭb/yə-tĕr/ē] *adjective*, 1) under another's control, *noun*, 2) a stream or river that flows into a larger river

trib-ute [trĭb/yōōt] *noun*, a gesture to show respect for someone, an accolade, a statement of praise

trick [trĭk] *noun*, 1) a clever prank, a sly or ingenious feat, *verb*, 2) to deceive by cunning

trick-le [trĭk′əl] *verb*, to flow in a small, gentle stream

tri-cy-cle [trī′sĭk′əl] *noun*, a light three-wheeled vehicle

tried [trīd] *verb, past tense* of **try**

tri-fle [trī′fəl] *noun*, 1) a small amount, *verb*, 2) to play or toy

tri-fling [trī′flĭng] *adjective*, of little value or importance

trig-ger [trĭg′ər] *noun*, 1) the firing mechanism on a gun, *verb*, 2) to set something off

trig-o-nom-e-try [trĭg′ə-nŏm′ĭ-trē] *noun*, measuring the sides and angles of triangles

tril-lion [trĭl′yən] *noun*, a million million: 1,000,000,000,000

tril-o-gy [trĭl′ə-jē] *noun*, a novel or play in three separate works that are closely related

trim [trĭm] *noun*, 1) ornaments or decorations, *verb*, 2) to decorate 3) to cut back to make tidy

tri-o [trē′ō] *noun*, a set of three

trip [trĭp] *noun*, 1) a journey, a jaunt, an excursion, a pilgrimage, *verb*, 2) to skip, to stumble 3) to release a lever suddenly

tri-ple [trĭp′əl] *adjective*, three-way, multiplied three times

tri-pod [trī′pŏd′] *noun*, a stand or support with three legs

trite [trīt] *adjective*, 1) trivial, insignificant 2) hackneyed

tri-umph [trī′əmf] *noun*, 1) exultation over success, *verb*, 2) to gain victory

tri-um-phant [trī-ŭm′fənt] *adjective*, feeling thrilled and happy about winning

triv-i-a [trĭv′ē-ə] *noun*, small, unimportant matters, trifles

triv-i-al [trĭv′ē-əl] *adjective*, of little worth or importance

trol-ley [trŏl′ē] *noun*, a public bus that travels on a train track

troop [trōōp] *noun*, 1) a collection of people 2) a body of cavalry

tro-phy [trō′fē] *noun*, something as a prize or award, given to show success in an activity

trop-ic [trŏp′ĭk] *noun*, a place between the two imaginary lines that run parallel above and below the equator, where it is hot and humid all year long

trop-i-cal [trŏp′ĭ-kəl] *adjective*, temperatures of a jungle or warm climate near the equator

trot [trŏt] *verb*, to keep at a steady pace, to canter, to gallop

trou-ble [trŭb′əl] *noun*, 1) a problem, a difficulty 2) a dangerous or difficult situation 3) extra work or effort, *verb*, 4) to impose on 5) to distress

troupe [trōōp] *noun*, a troop or company of musicians or performers

trou-sers [trou′zərz] *noun, plural*, loose fitting pants

trout [trout] *noun*, a small fresh-water fish in the salmon family

trow-el [trou′əl] *noun*, 1) a hand-held spade 2) a tool with a flat blade used to apply mortar or cement

tru-ant [trōō′ənt] *noun*, 1) absent from school without good reason or permission 2) neglectful

truce [trōōs] *noun*, a peace agreement, cease-fire

truck [trŭk] *noun*, a large, heavy vehicle with at least four wheels used to transport heavy materials or large quantities

true [trōō] *adjective*, 1) honest, real, based on fact 2) loyal

tru-ism [trōō′ĭz′əm] *noun*, a self-evident obvious truth

tru-ly [(trōō′lē] *adverb*, in fact or in truth, sincerely, really

trump [trŭmp] *verb*, 1) to fabricate or invent 2) to beat someone's hand in bridge

trum-pet [trŭm′pĭt] *noun*, a horn, one of the brass instruments with several keys and a flaring bell

trunk [trŭngk] *noun*, 1) a chest, a storage box 2) the main stem of a tree 3) a compartment in a car 4) the snout of an elephant

trust [trŭst] *noun*, 1) belief in someone's goodness and integrity, *verb*, 2) to believe that someone will do as they say

trust-ee [trŭ-stē′] *noun*, one entrusted to administer the property of another

truth [trōōth] *noun*, the facts, what actually happened, reality

try [trī] *verb*, 1) to attempt, to make an effort 2) to sample

try-ing [trī′ĭng] *adjective*, difficult, straining one's patience

tryst [trĭst] *noun*, an appointed meeting, a rendezvous

tsu-nami [tsōō-nä′mē] *noun*, a giant, fast-moving ocean wave produced by an earthquake

tub [tŭb] *noun*, a container used to take a bath or wash clothes

tu-ba [tōō′bə] *noun*, the lowest-pitched of the brass instruments

tube [tōōb] *noun*, 1) a pipe made of metal, plastic 2) a glass usually used to conduct liquids or gases

tu-ber-cu-lo-sis [tōō-bûr′kyə-lō′sĭs] *noun*, a disease due to the presence of small granular tumors in an organ marked by coughing

tuck [tŭk] *noun*, 1) a pleat, fold or gather, *verb*, 2) to wrap snugly

Tues-day [tōōz′dē] *noun*, the third day of the week

tuft [tŭft] *noun*, a cluster, a clump

tug [tŭg] *verb*, to jerk, to yank, to pull with force or effort

tu-i-tion [tōō-ĭsh′ən] *noun*, the price paid for instruction

tu-lip [tōō′lĭp] *noun*, a flower grown from a bulb in a variety of colors, in the shape of a cup

tulle [tōōl] *noun*, a thin, fine net of acetate, silk or rayon, often used for veils or a tutu

tum-ble [tŭm′bəl] *verb*, 1) to turn over and over 2) to fall down

tu-mult [tōō′mŭlt′] *noun*, commotion, a riot, noise

tu-mul-tu-ous [tōō-mŭl′chōō-əs] *adjective*, wild, chaotic

tu-na [tōō′nə] *noun*, a large fish that lives in the ocean

tun-dra [tŭn′drə] *noun*, the vast treeless plains in Siberia and arctic North America

tune [tōōn] *noun*, 1) musical notes arranged as a medley, *verb*, 2) to put the right amount of tension on a stringed instrument so that it gives a certain sound 3) to be in sync, to put in harmony

tung-sten [tŭng′stən] *noun*, a hard, brittle, whitish-gray metal with an extremely high melting point at 6100 degrees Fahrenheit

tun-nel [tŭn′əl] *noun*, 1) a long passageway dug underground, *verb*, 2) to dig, to burrow

tur-ban [tûr′bən] *noun*, a man's headdress having no brim

tur-bid [tûr′bĭd] *adjective*, muddy, having the sediment disturbed

tur-bine [tûr′bĭn] *noun*, a machine that uses the gas from liquid to turn a shaft

tur-bu-lence [tûr′byə-ləns] *noun*, 1) wind currents that move very quickly 2) confusion, excited activity

tur-bu-lent [tûr′byə-lənt] *adjective*, 1) agitated, violent, stormy 2) full of disorder

tu-reen [tōō-rēn′] *noun*, a deep table dish for holding soup

tur-key [tûr′kē] *noun*, a bird of the pheasant family, originally found wild in North America

tur-moil [tûr′moil′] *adjective*, a state of great confusion, agitation or disturbance

turn [tûrn] *noun*, 1) a chance or opportunity to participate 2) a bend, a twist or a bend in the road 3) a reversal, *verb*, 4) to cause to rotate or revolve 5) to change or to transform

tur-nip [tûr′nĭp] *noun*, a thick, edible, roundish root in the mustard family, eaten when boiled

tur-pen-tine [tûr′pən-tīn′] *noun*, a thin flammable oil made from certain pine trees used as a solvent to thin paint

tur-quoise [tûr′kwoiz′] *noun*, a bluish green or greenish gray mineral used as a gem

tur-tle [tûr′tl] *noun*, a reptile with a soft body protected by a hard shell covering, into which it can draw its head, legs and tail

tusk [tŭsk] *noun*, a long pointed tooth, as of an elephant or walrus

tu-tor [tōō′tər] *noun*, a private teacher

tweed [twēd] *noun*, a soft, flexible fabric made of wool

tweez-ers [twē′zərz] *noun*, *plural*, a pincer-like tool for picking up small things

twelfth [twĕlfth] *adjective*, the ordinal of twelve, written 12th

twelve [twĕlv] *noun*, *adjective*, the number 12, the number after eleven

twen-ti-eth [twĕn′tē-ĭth] *adjective*, the number 20 in order, 20th, the ordinal of 20

twen-ty [twĕn′tē] *adjective, noun*, the number 20, ten times two

twice [twīs] *adverb*, two times, in double amount or degree

twig [twĭg] *noun*, a small outshoot of a branch or stem

twi-light [twī′līt′] *noun*, the light as the sun sets from the west

twin [twĭn] *adjective*, 1) two of the same, matched 2) an identical couple 3) either of two offspring brought forth at birth

twine [twīn] *noun*, 1) a strong cord of threads twisted together, *verb*, 2) to wrap around

twinge [twĭnj] *verb*, to feel a sharp physical or mental pain

twin-kle [twĭng′kəl] *verb*, to sparkle, to shimmer, to flicker

twins [twĭnz] *noun, plural*, two children born at the same time from the same mother

twirl [twûrl] *verb*, to whirl or spin in a circle, to rotate rapidly

twitch [twĭch] *verb*, to jerk or make spastic movements

two [tōō] *adjective, noun*, the number that follow one, written 2, one plus one

type [tīp] *noun*, 1) the letters in different fonts used to print words 2) category, sort, *verb*, 3) to use a keyboard to write words printed on a computer

type-writ-er [tīp′rī′tər] *noun*, an instrument for writing by means of type

ty-phoid [tī′foid′] *noun*, a fever which eats up the walls of the intestines causing internal bleeding

ty-phoon [tī-fōōn′] *noun*, a cyclone in the region of the Philippines or the China Sea

typ-i-cal [tĭp′ĭ-kəl] *adjective*, representing something by a model, characteristic

ty-rant [tī′rənt] *noun*, an absolute ruler who is usually cruel

U

u-biq-ui-tous [yōō-bĭk′wĭ-təs] *adjective*, being everywhere at the same time, omnipresent

UFO [yōō′ĕf-ō′] *noun*, Unidentified Flying Object, a thing in the sky that seems too strange to be real

ug-ly [ŭg′lē] *adjective*, revolting to look at, unattractive

ul-cer [ŭl′sər] *noun*, a sore on the skin filled with pus and infection that is painful, a lesion

ul-te-ri-or [ŭl-tîr′ē-ər] *adjective*, intentionally concealed

ul-ti-mate [ŭl′tə-mĭt] *adjective*, 1) final, supreme 2) farthest

ul-ti-mate-ly [ŭl′tə-mĭt-lē] *adverb*, finally, at the end, totally

ul-ti-ma-tum [ŭl′tə-mā′təm] *noun*, a final proposition or condition offered to end a dispute

um-brage [ŭm′brĭj] *noun*, resentment, anger, a sense of injury or insult, offense

um-brel-la [ŭm-brĕl′ə] *noun*, a covering held in the hand as protection from the rain

um-pire [ŭm′pīr′] *noun*, the judge or referee in a baseball game

un-a-ble [ŭn-ā′bəl] *adjective*, not capable of doing something

un-alienable [ŭn-āl′yə-nə-bəl] *adjective*, cannot be taken away

u-nan-i-mous [yōō-năn′ə-məs] *adjective*, being of one mind, showing complete agreement

u-nan-i-mous-ly [yōō-năn′ə-məs-lē] *adverb*, with all voters voting the same way

un-as-sum-ing [ŭn′ə-sōō′mĭng] *adjective*, modest, simple, plain

un-a-void-a-ble [ŭn′ə-voi′də-bəl] *adjective*, inevitable

un-bear-a-ble [ŭn-bâr′ə-bəl] *adjective*, not capable of being endured, intolerable

un-bri-dled [ŭn-brīd′ld] *adjective*, not restrained, uninhibited

un-can-ny [ŭn-kăn′ē] *adjective*, strange, mysterious, seeming to have a supernatural basis

un-cer-tain-ty [ŭn-sûr′tn-tē] *noun*, doubtfulness, not reliable

un-cle [ŭng′kəl] *noun*, the brother of one of your parents, or the husband of the sister of one of your parents

un-com-fort-a-ble [ŭn-kŭm′fər-tə-bəl] *adjective*, uneasy, causing discomfort

un-com-mon [ŭn-kŏm′ən] *adjective*, not usual, unique, odd

un-con-cern [ŭn′kən-sûrn′] *adjective*, indifference, lack of interest, freedom from anxiety

un-con-scion-a-ble [ŭn-kŏn′shə-nə-bəl] *adjective*, unscrupulous, something done that shows no conscience, excessive, unreasonable

un-con-scious [ŭn-kŏn′shəs] *adjective*, not knowing what is happening, lacking awareness

un-cov-er [ŭn-kŭv′ər] *verb*, 1) to take something from on top of something 2) to find out

un-der [ŭn′dər] *adjective*, 1) less than 2) working for or obeying, *preposition*, 3) below, beneath the surface

un-der-es-ti-mate [ŭn′dər-ĕs′tə-māt′] *verb*, to undervalue, to minimize

un-der-go [ŭn′dər-gō′] *verb*, 1) to experience 2) to suffer or endure

un-der-grad-u-ate [ŭn′dər-grăj′ōō-ĭt] *noun*, a student at a college who has not received a bachelor's degree

un-der-ground [ŭn′dər-ground′] *adjective*, 1) in the recesses of the earth 2) in secrecy

un-der-growth [ŭn′dər-grōth′] *noun*, *no plural*, thickly growing plants underneath trees

un-der-line [ŭn′dər-līn′] *verb*, to put a line under a word or words

un-der-neath [ŭn′dər-nēth′] *adverb*, down from below

un-der-rate [ŭn′dər-rāt′] *verb*, to evaluate too low, to undervalue

un-der-stand [ŭn′dər-stănd′] *verb*, 1) to grasp the nature of 2) to know what something means

un-der-take [ŭn′dər-tāk′] *verb*, to take upon oneself as a task

un-der-tak-er [ŭn′dər-tā′kər] *noun*, one whose business is to take charge of funerals

un-der-tak-ing [ŭn′dər-tā′kĭng] *noun*, a duty, an obligation, a job, a task

un-der-wear [ŭn′dər-wâr′] *noun*, the garments worn next to the skin under outside clothing

un-der-write [ŭn′dər-rīt′] *verb*, to insure, to guarantee

un-do [ŭn-dōō′] *verb*, 1) to untie or unfasten 2) to reverse or annul

un-doubt-ed-ly [ŭn-dou′tĭd-lē] *adverb*, certainly, indeed

un-du-late [ŭn′jə-lāt′] *verb*, to move with a wave-like motion

un-earth [ŭn-ûrth′] *verb*, to dig up

un-eas-y [ŭn-ē′zē] *adjective*, a little afraid, worried, uncomfortable

un-em-ployed [ŭn′ĕm-ploid′]
adjective, having no paid work

un-equal [ŭn-ē′kwəl] *adjective*,
unmatched, not even

un-e-quiv-o-cal [ŭn′ĭ-kwĭv′ə-kəl]
adjective, plain, obvious

un-err-ing-ly [ŭn-ûr′ĭng-lē]
adverb, correctly, precisely

un-e-ven [ŭn-ē′vən] *adjective*, not
level or flat, not uniform

un-ex-pect-ed [ŭn′ĭk-spĕk′tĭd]
adjective, sudden, coming
without warning, unforeseen

un-fair [ŭn-fâr′] *adjective*, unjust,
unethical, biased, dishonest

un-faltering [ŭn-fôl′tər-ĭng]
adjective, steadfast

un-fas-ten [ŭn-făs′ən] *verb*, to
undo, to detach, to separate

un-fit [ŭn-fĭt′] *adjective*, made
unsuitable, not prepared or
adapted, not competent

un-fold [ŭn-fōld′] *verb*, 1) to open
out 2) to explain, to evolve

un-for-tu-nate [ŭn-fôr′chə-nĭt]
adjective, unlucky, regrettable

un-for-tu-nate-ly
[ŭn-fôr′chə-nĭt-lē] *adverb*,
having bad luck, unsuccessful

un-friend-ly [ŭn-frĕnd′lē]
adjective, not nice, unkind

un-grate-ful [ŭn-grāt′fəl]
adjective, thankless

un-hap-py [ŭn-hăp′ē] *adjective*,
dissatisfied, not content, sad

un-health-y [ŭn-hĕl′thē] *adjective*,
1) ill, sickly 2) food or habits
that make a person feel tired

u-ni-corn [yōō′nə- kôrn] *noun*, a
mythical horse-like animal with
a horn growing from the center
of its forehead

u-ni-form [yōō′nə-fôrm′]
adjective, 1) unvaried, regular,
constant, *noun*, 2) clothes worn
for a special job or school

u-ni-form-i-ty [yōō′nə-fôrm′ĭ-tē]
noun, sameness, consistency,
identical with others

u-ni-fy [yōō′nə-fī′] *verb*, to
combine, to integrate, to connect

u-ni-lat-er-al [yōō′nə-lăt′ər-əl]
adjective, one sided

un-im-ag-i-na-tive
[ŭn-ĭ-măj′ə-nə-tĭv] *adjective*,
uninspired, common, everyday

un-impeach-a-ble
[ŭn′ĭm-pē′chə-bəl] *adjective*,
blameless and exemplary

un-im-por-tant [ŭn′ĭm-pôr′tnt]
adjective, 1) trivial, trite
2) extraneous, irrelevant

un-in-hib-it-ed [ŭn′ĭn-hĭb′ĭ-tĭd]
adjective, not restrained by
convention, free and easy

un-in-tel-li-gi-ble
[ŭn′ĭn-tĕl′ĭ-jə-bəl] *adjective*, not
capable of being understood

un-ion [yōōn′yən] *noun*, 1) a
coming together 2) a group of
people who join to support a
cause 3) a combination, **Union**
4) the army fighting for northern
states during the Civil War

u-nique [yōō-nēk′] *adjective*,
single in kind or excellence

u-ni-son [yōō′nĭ-sən] *noun*, unity
of pitch, complete accord

u-nit [yōō′nĭt] *noun*, 1) a complete
set 2) a specific amount, a form of
measurement 3) a single entity

u-nite [yōō-nīt′] *verb*, to join, to
connect, to put together as one

United States
[yōō-nī'tĭd-stāts-ŭv-ə-měr'ĭ-kə]
noun, the country made up of the
land between the Pacific Ocean
and the Atlantic Ocean, between
Canada and Mexico, including
Alaska and Hawaii, the capital,
is the District of Columbia

u-ni-ver-sal [yōō'nə-vûr'səl]
adjective, mutual understanding,
totally accepted everywhere

u-ni-verse [yōō'nə-vûrs'] *noun*, all
existing things including the
earth and all of space

u-ni-ver-si-ty [yōō'nə-vûr'sĭ-tē]
noun, an institution of higher
learning empowered to confer
degrees in the arts and sciences

un-just [ŭn-jŭst'] *adjective*, unfair,
biased, unworthy

un-kempt [ŭn-kĕmpt'] *adjective*, a
messy, uncared for appearance

un-kind [ŭn-kīnd'] *adjective*,
indifferent, unfeeling, rude

un-known [ŭn-nōn'] *adjective*,
1) unfamiliar 2) unexplored

un-less [ŭn-lĕs'] *adjective*, under
different conditions, or else

un-like [ŭn-līk'] *adjective*,
dissimilar, different

un-load [ŭn-lōd'] *verb*, 1) to take
something off a vehicle such as
cargo 2) to dispose of

un-luck-y [ŭn-lŭk'ē] *adjective*,
unsuccessful, unfortunate

un-mis-tak-a-ble [ŭn'mĭ-stā'kə-
bəl] *adjective*, clear, obvious

un-mis-take-a-bly
[ŭn'mĭ-stā'kə-blē] *adverb*,
undoubtedly, obviously

un-nec-es-sar-y [ŭn-něs'ĭ-sěr'ē]
adjective, uncalled for, needless

un-ob-tru-sive [ŭn'əb-trōō'sĭv]
adjective, not noticeable

un-pleas-ant [ŭn-plěz'ənt]
adjective, disagreeable

un-prec-e-dent-ed
[ŭn-prĕs'ĭ-děn'tĭd] *adjective*,
novel, unparalleled

un-pre-pare-ed [ŭn'prĭ-pârd']
adjective, unaware, not ready

un-rav-el [ŭn-răv'əl] *verb*, to
untangle, to unwind, to unfold

un-rea-son-a-ble [ŭn-rē'zə-nə-bəl]
adjective, absurd, illogical, not
guided by sound judgment

un-re-li-a-ble [ŭn'rĭ-lī'ə-bəl]
adjective, not dependable

un-ru-ly [ŭn-rōō'lē] *adjective*,
disobedient, lawless

un-safe [ŭn-sāf'] *adjective*,
hazardous, dangerous, risky

un-sat-is-fac-to-ry
[ŭn-săt'ĭs-făk'tə-rē] *adjective*,
not good enough, inadequate

un-scru-pu-lous
[ŭn-skrōō'pyə-ləs] *adjective*,
unprincipled, devious, deceptive

un-seem-ly [ŭn-sēm'lē] *adjective*,
unbecoming, inappropriate

un-so-phis-ti-cat-ed
[ŭn'sə-fĭs'tĭ-kā'tĭd] *adjective*,
innocent, showing inexperience

un-stead-y [ŭn-stěd'ē] *adjective*,
1) not safe 2) unsure, wavering

un-suit-a-ble [ŭn-sōō'tə-bəl]
adjective, inappropriate,
unsatisfactory, something that
does not fit in, irregular

un-sure [ŭn-shŏŏr] *adjective*, uncertain, doubtful

un-ten-a-ble [ŭn-tĕn′ə-bəl] *adjective*, not able to be maintained or supported against criticism

un-ti-dy [ŭn-tī′dē] *adjective*, messy, cluttered, not orderly

un-tie [ŭn-tī′] *verb*, to unfasten a string or rope, to loosen

un-til [ŭn-tĭl′] *conjunction*, 1) up to the time that, or when, *preposition*, 2) up to the time of, as far as, before

un-to-ward [ŭn-tôrd′] *adjective*, unfortunate, annoying

un-true [ŭn-trōō′] *adjective*, false, incorrect, deceptive, disloyal

un-u-su-al [ŭn-yōō′zhōō-əl] *adjective*, strange, odd

un-veil [ŭn-vāl′] *verb*, to remove the covering from something

un-well [ŭn-wĕl′] *adjective*, ill, sick, upset, ailing

un-wield-y [ŭn-wēl′dē] *adjective*, not easily carried, bulky

un-will-ing [ŭn-wĭl′ĭng] *adjective*, reluctant, resistant, averse

un-wind [ŭn-wīnd′] *verb*, 1) to undo something, to loosen 2) to relax, to get rid of tension

un-wise [ŭn-wīz′] *adjective*, not reasonable or sensible

un-wit-ting [ŭn-wĭt′ĭng] *adjective*, unintentional, not knowing

un-wrap [ŭn-răp′] *verb*, to remove the protective covering on a package or product

up [ŭp] *adverb*, 1) to put in a higher place, *preposition*, 2) to position something so that it is standing 3) toward

up-braid [ŭp-brād′] *verb*, to scold, to reproach, to criticize

up-heav-al [ŭp-hē′vəl] *noun*, an eruption, a change, a quake

up-hold [ŭp-hōld′] *verb*, to maintain, to support, to sustain

up-hol-ster-y [ŭp-hōl′stə-rē] *noun*, furniture with stuffing, springs, covers or trim

up-lift [ŭp-lĭft′] *noun*, 1) upgrade, restoration, *verb*, 2) to raise up 3) to improve socially or morally

up-on [ə-pŏn′] *adverb*, 1) on, *preposition*, 2) on top of something

up-per [ŭp′ər] *adjective*, 1) in a higher position, further up 2) the part of the shoe above the sole

up-right [ŭp′rīt′] *adjective*, 1) straight up and down 2) righteous, honest, honorable

up-set [ŭp-sĕt′] *verb*, 1) to knock over 2) to make unhappy or worried 3) to spoil something that was planned, to disrupt

up-stairs [ŭp′stârz′] *adverb*, 1) up the steps, *noun*, *plural*, 2) the next level, the upper level

up-ward [ŭp′wərd] *adjective*, to a higher place or position

u-ra-ni-um [yŏŏ-rā′nē-əm] *noun*, a rare radioactive, metallic element found in certain minerals used in nuclear weapons

ur-ban [ûr′bən] *noun*, characteristic of a city

ur-bane [ûr-bān′] *adjective*, suave, refined, elegant, sophisticated, charming, courteous, polite

ur-chin [ûr'chĭn] *noun*, a needy or mischievous child

urge [ûrj] *noun*, 1) a strong wish, *verb*, 2) to try to make someone do something, to push along

ur-gen-cy [ûr'jən-sē] *adverb*, calling for quick action

ur-gent [ûr'jənt] *adjective*, pressing, calling for immediate attention or action, insistent

us [ŭs] *pronoun*, the person who is speaking, and the others mentioned in the sentence, the objective case of **we**

us-age [yōō'sĭj] *noun*, a long continued practice, a custom

use [yōōz] *noun*, 1) a purpose, *verb*, 2) to find a purpose for something, to utilize

used to [yōōst-tōō] *adjective*, 1) knowing what something or someone is like, familiar 2) something done in the past but is not done now

use-ful [yōōs'fəl] *adjective*, helpful, serviceable

use-less [yōōs'lĭs] *adjective*, hopeless, valueless, vain

u-su-al [yōō'zhōō-əl] *adjective*, something that happens regularly, not uncommon

u-su-al-ly [yōō'zhōō-əl-lē] *adverb*, almost always, frequently

u-surp [yōō-sûrp'] *verb*, to seize, to take possession of by force or without right or authority

u-sur-pa-tion [yōō'sər-pā'shən]. *noun*, the act of seizing power and rank of another

u-su-ry [yōō'zhə-rē] *noun*, interest in excess of a legal rate

Utah [yōō'tô'] *noun*, one of the 50 United States, the capital is Salt Lake City. The state flower of **Utah** is the sego lily; and the motto is "Industry."

u-ten-sil [yōō-těn'səl] *noun*, a tool, a dining instrument

u-til-i-ty [yōō-tĭl'ĭ-tē] *noun*, a company that provides products such as gas, water, or electricity

u-ti-lize [yōōt'l-īz'] *verb*, to make use of something

ut-most [ŭt'mōst'] *adjective*, the furthest or most extreme

u-to-pi-a [yōō-tō'pē-ə] *noun*, heaven on earth, an ideal place

ut-ter [ŭt'ər] *verb*, to speak

ut-ter-ance [ŭt'ər-əns] *noun*, vocal expression, articulation, speech

ut-ter-ly [ŭt'ər-lē] *adverb*, completely, entirely, without doubt, totally, absolutely

V

va-can-cy [vā'kən-sē] *noun*, 1) emptiness 2) an unfilled place, job or position 3) an opening

va-cant [vā'kənt] *adjective*, empty

va-cate [vā'kāt'] *verb*, 1) to leave, to empty, to abandon 2) to annul

va-ca-tion [vā-kā'shən] *noun*, time away from work for rest, amusement, and relaxation

vac-ci-nate [văk'sə-nāt'] *verb*, to inoculate with a vaccine as a form of protection

vac-ci-na-tion [văk'sə-nā'shən] *noun*, a remedy which is the injection of the virus itself

vac-cine [văk-sēn] *noun*, a weakened germ of a virus used to protect a person from the often fatal or debilitating effects of a virus

vac-il-late [văs/ə-lāt/] *verb*, to change one's mind often, to waffle, to waver

vac-u-um [văk/yōō-əm] *noun*, 1) the absolute absence of matter 2) an appliance used to rid carpets of dust and litter 3) a kind of bottle that keeps liquids hot or cold, such as a thermos

vag-a-bond [văg/ə-bŏnd/] *noun*, a tramp, an outcast, a vagrant

va-grant [vā/grənt] *adjective*, 1) wandering, begging, *noun*, 2) one who wanders around outside from place to place

vague [vāg] *adjective*, not clearly understood, indistinct

vain [vān] *adjective*, 1) conceited, too proud of the way one looks 2) fruitless, unsuccessful

vale [vāl] *noun*, valley, lowland

val-en-tine [văl/ən-tīn/] *noun*, a love poem, a card expressing love and affection

val-et [văl/ĭt] *noun*, a manservant who takes care of the clothes and personal needs of his employer

val-iant[văl/yənt]*adjective*, full of courage, brave

val-iant-ly [văl/yənt-lē] *adverb*, unafraid of danger, boldly, courageously, bravely

val-id [văl/ĭd] *adjective*, 1) significant, sound 2) legally effective or binding

val-i-date [văl/ĭ-dāt/] *verb*, to confirm, to ratify, to substantiate

va-lid-i-ty [və-lĭ/dĭ-tē] *noun*, confirmation that proves something is what it says it is

val-ley [văl/ē] *noun*, a region of low land situated between hills or mountains, a dale

val-or [văl/ər] *noun*, bravery, courage, boldness

val-u-a-ble [văl/yōō-ə-bəl] *adjective*, precious, of considerable worth, costly

val-ue [văl/yōō] *noun*, 1) what something is worth, what someone will pay, *verb*, 2) to think that something is important and meaningful 3) to say how much something is worth on the market, to rate

valve [vălv] *noun*, any device by which the flow of liquid, air, or gas may be regulated

van [văn] *noun*, a small, covered truck carrying goods or passengers or animals

van-dal-ism [văn/dl-ĭz/əm] *noun*, willful destruction of property

vane [vān] *noun*, a piece of metal or cloth set up high to swing with the wind to tell which way the wind is blowing

va-nil-la [və-nĭl/ə] *noun*, a flavoring made from the beans of the vanilla plant

van-ish [văn/ĭsh] *verb*, to disappear, to dissolve, to end

van-i-ty [văn/ĭ-tē] *noun*, 1) too proud of oneself 2) a small table for putting on makeup

van-quish [văng/kwĭsh] *verb*, to conquer, to overcome, to overpower in battle

van-tage [văn′tĭj] *noun*, the position giving an advantage

va-por [vā′pər] *noun*, 1) condensation 2) a substance in the gaseous state such as fog

var-i-a-ble [vâr′ē-ə-bəl] *noun*, changeable, liable to vary

var-i-ance [vâr′ē-əns] *noun*, degree of difference, disagreement

var-i-a-tion [vâr′ē-ā′shən] *noun*, a change in form, position, or condition

va-ri-e-ty [və-rī′ĭ-tē] *noun*, many different things, assortment

var-i-ous [vâr′ē-əs] *adjective*, , several different kinds, diverse

var-nish [vär′nĭsh] *noun*, 1) a liquid that hardens into a clear, tough film, *verb*, 2) to paint with a clear protective sealant

var-si-ty [vär′sĭ-tē] *adjective*, a principal team in sports representing a school or college

var-y [vâr′ē] *verb*, to change

vase [vās] *noun*, a decorated pot for cut flowers or for decoration

vas-sal [văs′əl] *noun*, in feudalism, one who held land of a superior lord

vast [văst] *adjective*, limitless, expansive, very great in size, quantity or degree, widespread

vat [văt] *noun*, a large container for liquids, a barrel

vaude-ville [vôd′vĭl′] *noun*, a theatrical performance with music, songs, and dance

vault [vôlt] *noun*, 1) a room constructed to protect its contents, *verb*, 2) to jump or leap over with hands holding a pole

veer [vîr] *verb*, to change in direction or position

veg-e-ta-ble [vĕj′tə-bəl] *noun*, an edible plant grown for food

veg-e-tate [vĕj′ĭ-tāt′] *verb*, to live in a monotonous, inactive way

veg-e-ta-tion [vĕj′ĭ-tā′shən] *noun*, plant growth, foliage, flowers

veg-e-tar-i-an [vĕj′ĭ-t′ər ′ē-ən] *noun,* one who does not eat meat, one who believes in a vegetable diet as best for people

ve-he-ment [vē′ə-mənt] *adjective*, fervent, impassioned, fiery

ve-hi-cle [vē′ĭ-kəl] *noun*, something used to carry or transport people or things

veil [vāl] *noun*, a piece of transparent material worn to hide or protect the face, a cover

vein [vān] *noun*, 1) one of the vessels which conveys blood back to the heart 2) a crack in a rock filled with mineral matter

vel-lum [vĕl′əm] *noun*, a form of paper made out of animal skin that will hold ink

ve-loc-i-ty [və-lŏs′ĭ-tē] *noun*, speed, rapidity of motion

vel-vet [vĕl′vĭt] *noun*, *no plural*, a type of cloth with a soft surface

ven-det-ta [vĕn-dĕt′ə] *noun*, revenge for a dispute

ven-dor [vĕn′dər] *noun*, someone who sells something, a merchant

ve-neer [və-nîr′] *noun*, 1) a thin layer of finished wood, glued on a cheap surface 2) a superficial show of quality

ven-er-a-ble [vĕn′ər-ə-bəl] *adjective*, deserving high respect

ven-er-a-tion [věn′ə-rā′shən] *noun*, deep, respectful love, adoration

venge-ance [věn′jəns] *noun*, retribution, revenge, reprisal

ve-ni-al [vē′nē-əl] *adjective*, capable of being forgiven

ven-i-son [věn′ĭ-sən] *noun*, deer meat used for food

venn di-a-gram [věn-dĭ′ə-grăm′] *noun*, a tool to indicate the relationship of elements

ven-om [věn′əm] *noun*, poison stored in some animals

ven-om-ous [věn′ə-məs] *adjective*, poisonous, deadly, toxic

vent [věnt] *noun*, a small opening or outlet to let out air

ven-ti-late [věn′tl-āt′] *verb*, to cause fresh air to circulate through, to admit air into

ven-tril-o-quist [věn-trĭl′ə-kwĭst] *noun*, one who can make a voice seem to come from another person or thing

ven-ture [věn′chər] *noun*, 1) doing something that involves the risk of a loss *verb*, 2) to dare to go, to do or to say

ven-tur-ous [věn′chər-əs] *adjective*, daring, bold

ven-ue [věn′yōō] *noun*, an agreed place where something will take place, the scene of an event

ve-rac-i-ty [və-răs′ĭ-tē] *noun*, habitual observance of truth, truthfulness, accuracy

ve-ran-da [və-răn′də] *noun*, a long porch with a roof along the outside of a building

verb [vûrb] *noun*, the word expressing action in a sentence

ver-ba-tim [vər-bā′tĭm] *adverb*, word for word, literal

ver-bi-age [vûr′bē-ĭj] *noun*, a pompous array of words

ver-dant [vûr′dnt] *adjective*, green with vegetation

ver-dict [vûr′dĭkt] *noun*, the decision of a jury given to the court, a judgment or decision

verge [vûrj] *noun*, 1) the point beyond which something begins, the brink, *verb*, 2) to tend to incline

ver-i-fy [věr′ə-fī′] *verb*, to prove to be true, to confirm, to ascertain

ver-i-si-mil-i-tude [věr′ə-sĭ-mĭl′ĭ-tōōd′] *noun*, appearance of truth, likelihood

ver-i-ty [věr′ĭ-tē] *noun*, truth, reality, a statement that is true

ver-mi-cel-li [vûr′mĭ-chěl′ē] *noun*, a pasta dried in a slender tube form, like spaghetti

ver-mic-u-lite [vər-mĭk′yə-līt′] *noun*, slivers of mica that expand when heated, used for insulation, and water absorption

Ver-mont [vər-mŏnt′] *noun*, one of the 50 United States located in New England, the capital is Montpelier. The state flower of **Vermont** is the red clover, the motto is "Freedom and unity."

ver-nal [vûr′nəl] *adjective*, of or occurring in spring

ver-sa-tile [vûr′sə-təl′] *adjective*, having the capability of doing many different things

verse [vûrs] *noun*, 1) lines of writing which have a rhythm often a rhyme 2) a few lines of this from a longer piece called a poem 3) a small part of the Bible, the Jewish Koran, or Talmud

ver-sion [vûr′zhən] *noun*, a description from a particular point of view, a standpoint

ver-sus [vûr′səs] *preposition*, against, in contrast with

ver-te-brate [vûr′tə-brĭt] *noun*, an animal with a backbone

ver-tex [vûr′tĕks′] *noun*, 1) the point where two planes intersect to form an angle 2) the highest point

ver-ti-cal [vûr′tĭ-kəl] *adjective*, straight up and down, perpendicular to the horizon

verve [vûrv] *noun*, enthusiasm, liveliness, energy, vitality

ver-y [vĕr′ē] *adjective*, 1) the same 2) the right or appropriate one, *adverb*, 3) to emphasize the word to make it stronger

ves-sel [vĕs′əl] *noun*, 1) a hollow utensil for holding anything 2) a boat 3) a channel for delivering blood, a vein or capillary

vest [vĕst] *noun*, a sleeveless top worn over a shirt with pockets

ves-ti-bule [vĕs′tə-byōōl′] *noun*, foyer, lobby, entry way

ves-tige [vĕs′tĭj] *noun*, a trace or visible sign of something gone

vet-er-an [vĕt′ər-ən] *noun*, experienced, old in service, especially in military life

vet-er-i-nar-i-an [vĕt′ər-ə-nâr′ē-ən] *noun*, a doctor who specializes in animal health and surgery

ve-to [vē′tō] *noun*, 1) a denial, a rejection, *verb*, 2) to deny, to reject, to turn down

vex [vĕks] *verb*, to annoy, to distress, to irritate

vex-a-tion [vĕk-sā′shən] *noun*, irritation, a cause of trouble or disquiet, annoyance

vi-a [vī′ə, vē′ə] *preposition*, traveling through, by way of

vi-a-ble [vī′ə-bəl] *adjective*, capable of maintaining life

vi-a-duct [vī′ə-dŭkt′] *noun*, a bridge for carrying a road, resting on masonry arches, often in water to allow boats through

vi-and [vī′ənd] *noun*, food, provision

vi-brate [vī′brāt′] *verb*, 1) to shake, to quiver or tremble 2) to echo, to reverberate, to move to and fro

vi-bra-tion [vī-brā′shən] *noun*, the movement caused by shaking

vi-car-i-ous-ly [vī-kâr′ē-əs-lē] *adverb*, acting as a substitute, done in place of another

vice [vīs] *noun*, a weakness, personal faults or foibles

vice president [vīs′prĕz′ĭ-dənt] *noun*, the person chosen to replace the president

vi-cin-i-ty [vĭ-sĭn′ĭ-tē] *noun*, the region near or close by

vi-cious [vĭsh′əs] *adjective*, corrupt, wicked, mean

vi-cis-si-tude [vĭ-sĭs′ĭ-tōōd′] *noun*, change or succession from one thing to another

vic-tim [vĭk′tĭm] *noun*, 1) someone who suffers from an illness or action 2) a person who is deceived or cheated

vic-to-ri-ous [vĭk-tôr′ē-əs] *adjective*, conquering, triumphant in war, winning

vic-to-ry [vĭk′tə-rē] *noun*, winning a contest or a battle, a triumph

vict-uals [vĭt′lz] *noun, plural*, food for human beings, provisions

vid-e-o [vĭd′ē-ō′] *noun*, film for showing on a television set

vie [vī] *verb*, to contend, to strive in competition, to struggle

view [vyōō] *noun*, 1) ideas, beliefs, opinion 2) something you see

vig-i-lance [vĭj′ə-ləns] *noun*, watchfulness, caution

vi-gnette [vĭn-yĕt′] *noun*, a scene depicting a moment in time

vig-or [vĭg′ər] *noun*, physical or mental strength, stamina, energy

vig-or-ous [vĭg′ər-əs] *adjective*, exhibiting strength, powerful, energetic, intense, robust

vig-or-ous-ly [vĭg′ər-əs-lē] *adverb*, very fast, with a great deal of energy, healthy, spirited

vile [vīl] *adjective*, disgusting

vil-i-fy [vĭl′ə-fī′] *verb*, to slander, to malign, to slur, to revile

vil-lage [vĭl′ĭj] *noun*, a group of houses that form a community, usually smaller than a town

vil-lain [vĭl′ən] *noun*, one capable or guilty of great crimes, a rascal

vin-di-cate [vĭn′dĭ-kāt′] *verb*, to support or maintain as true, to free from suspicion

vin-dic-tive [vĭn-dĭk′tĭv] *adjective*, revengeful, retaliatory, mean

vine [vīn] *noun*, a name given to some plants with climbing stems

vin-e-gar [vĭn′ĭ-gər] *noun*, a sour liquid made by fermentation of wine or cider

vi-o-late [vī′ə-lāt′] *verb*, 1) to break the rules, to disregard as a promise 2) to break in on

vi-o-lence [vī′ə-ləns] *noun*, commotion, disorder, outrage, brutality, intense force

vi-o-lent [vī′ə-lənt] *adjective*, brutal, vicious, forceful, rough

vi-o-lent-ly [vī′ə-lənt-lē] *adverb*, harshly, with destructive force

vi-o-let [vī′ə-lĭt]) *adjective*, 1) the color that is a combination of blue and red, *noun*, 2) a purple flower that grows wild as a ground cover

vi-o-lin [vī′ə-lĭn′] *noun*, one of the small stringed instruments played with a bow

vi-o-lin-ist [vī′ə-lĭn′ĭst] *noun*, a person who plays a violin

vi-per [vī′pər] *noun*, a poisonous snake, a serpent

vir-gin [vûr′jĭn] *adjective*, pure, chaste, unused

Vir-gin-i-a [vər-jĭn′yə] *noun*, one of the 50 United States located in the Southeast, the capital is Richmond. The state flower of **Virginia** is the flowering dogwood and the motto is "Ever thus to tyrants."

vir-ile [vîr′əl] *adjective*, manly, showing masculine strength

vir-tue [vûr′chōō] *noun*, uprightness, moral excellence

vir-tu-ous [vûr′chōō-əs] *adjective*, righteous, honest, moral

vi-rus [vī′rəs] *noun*, an group of infectious submicroscopic agents that cause various diseases in plants or animals

vis-age [vĭz′ĭj] *noun*, the face, countenance, or look of a person

vis-cer-al [vĭs′ər-əl] *adjective*, felt in one's inner organs

vis-cous [vĭs′kəs] *adjective*, thick and sticky in consistency

vise [vīs] *noun*, a clamp, clasp, grip

vis-i-ble [vĭz′ə-bəl] *adjective*, as seen by the eye, in view

vi-sion [vĭzh′ən] *noun*, 1) something imagined, as in a dream, 2) a look into the future, unusual foresight 3) eyesight

vi-sion-ar-y [vĭzh′ə-nĕr′ē] *noun*, existing only in the imagination

vis-it [vĭz′ĭt] *noun*, 1) a social call, an appointment, *verb*, 2) to go to see someone 3) to chat casually

vis-i-tor [vĭz′ĭ-tər] *noun*, one who comes and goes to see another

vi-sor [vī′zər] *noun*, a sunshade or shield to block out glare

vi-su-al [vĭzh′ōō-ə-l] *adjective,* of or used in seeing, pleasing to the sight

vi-su-al-ize [vĭzh′ōō-ə-līz′] *verb*, 1) to imagine 2) to see something in the mind

vi-tal [vīt′l] *adjective*, necessary to life, important, indispensable

vi-tal-i-ty [vī-tăl′ĭ-tē] *noun*, spirit, energy, the capacity to develop

vi-ta-min [vī′tə-mĭn] *noun*, nutrients that give the body nourishment to help balance the metabolism

vi-ti-ate [vĭsh′ē-āt′] *verb*, to spoil the effect of something, to make less effective or imperfect

vit-ri-ol-ic [vĭt′rē-ŏl′ĭk] *adjective*, mean, causing bad feelings

vi-tu-per-a-tive [vī-tōō′pər-ə-tĭv] *adjective*, abusive, scolding

vi-va-cious [vĭ-vā′shəs] *adjective*, lively, sprightly, energetic

viv-id [vĭv′ĭd] *adjective*, easy to see, life-like, bright, colorful

vo-cab-u-lar-y [vō-kăb′yə-lĕr′ē] *noun*, the words of a language

vo-cal [vō′kəl] *adjective*, 1) voiced, outspoken 2) expressed by singing 3) relating to the sound made by the voice

vo-ca-tion [vō-kā′shən] *noun*, a job, employment or occupation, a profession

vogue [vōg] *adjective*, fashionable, in style, popular

voice [vois] *noun*, 1) the sounds coming through a person's mouth made by the respiratory system 2) to express an idea in writing or speaking

void [void] *noun*, an empty space

vol-ca-no [vŏl-kā′nō] *noun*, an opening in the earth's crust where melted rock, lava, gases, and ash are thrust onto the land

vo-li-tion [və-lĭsh′ən] *noun*, the act of making a conscious choice

vol-ley [vŏl′ē] *noun*, 1) a barrage, a bombardment, *verb*, 2) to return a ball before it hits the ground

vol-ley-ball [vŏl′ē-bôl′] *noun*, *no plural*, a game in which a large ball is knocked back and forth across a net, by hand

volt [vōlt] *noun*, 1) a measure of electricity, the unit of electromotive force 2) a turning movement of a horse, sideways around a center

vol-ume [vŏl′yōōm] *noun*, 1) a single book, *no plural*, 2) the space something occupies 3) the amount of sound something makes, loudness of a sound

vo-lu-mi-nous [və-lōō′mə-nəs] *adjective*, bulky, large

vol-un-tar-y [vŏl′ən-tĕr′ē] *adjective*, proceeding from the will, to give or perform freely

vol-un-teer [vŏl′ən-tîr′] *noun*, 1) one who offers his services of his own free will, *verb*, 2) to give freely of your time

vo-lup-tu-ous [və-lŭp′chōō-əs] *adjective*, shapely, full in form

vom-it [vŏm′ĭt] *noun*,1) something from the stomach that comes out of the mouth, *verb*, 2) to throw up, to regurgitate food

vo-ra-cious [vô-rā′shəs] *adjective*, 1) someone who has a large appetite 2) exceedingly eager

vor-tex [vôr′tĕks′] *noun*, whirlpool, a whirling mass of water

vote [vōt] *noun*, 1) a choice made during an election, *verb*, 2) to decide by general consent

vot-er [vōt′ər] *noun*, a person registered to participate in an election

vouch [vouch] *verb*, to certify, to assure, to provide proof

vouch-er [vou′chər] *noun*, a document exchangeable for certain goods or services

vow [vou] *noun*, 1) an oath, a solemn pledge, *verb*, 2) to promise something important

vow-el [vou′əl] *noun*, the letters – a,e,i,o,u, and sometimes y

voy-age [voi′ĭj] *noun*, a long journey by sea, water, air or space from one place to another

vul-gar [vŭl′gər] *adjective*, rude or rough in behavior, taste, etc, lacking good taste or refinement

vul-ner-a-ble [vŭl′nər-ə-bəl] *adjective*, capable of being easily harmed or injured

vul-ture [vŭl′chər] *noun*, a large bird that eats as a scavenger of dead animals

W

wade [wād] *verb*, to walk through a substance such as water or snow

waf-fle [wŏf′əl] *noun*, 1) a cake baked in an iron skillet, *verb*, 2) to change one's mind often

waft [wäft] *verb*, to move or be moved lightly over water or air, to drift

wag [wăg] *verb*, to move or cause to move briskly from side to side or up and down

wage [wāj] *noun*, 1) money paid for work or services, salary, *verb*, 2) to carry on (a war or campaign)

wa-ger [wā′jər] *noun*, the amount of money or property risked in an uncertain event, a bet

wag-on [wăg′ən] *noun*, a vehicle with four wheels that is pulled

waif [wāf] *noun*, a homeless child or animal, an orphan

wail [wāl] *verb*, to make a long cry showing sadness or pain, to sob

waist [wāst] *noun*, the part of the body between the ribs and the hips where the stomach is

wait [wāt] *noun*, 1) a time of anticipation, *verb*, 2) to expect, to anticipate, to be ready

wait-er [wā'tər] *noun*, a person hired to serve meals

waive [wāv] *verb*, to give up temporarily, to yield

waiv-er [wā'vər] *noun*, the act of giving up a right or claim

wake [wāk] *noun*, 1) the ripple of waves created by the motion of a boat, *verb*, 2) to stop sleeping, to be aroused from sleep

walk [wôk] *noun*, 1) a journey on foot, *verb*, 2) to take one step at a time, to proceed along

wall [wôl] *noun*, 1) a partition made of bricks or stone that separates space 2) one of the sides of a room or building, *verb*, 3) to divide, to partition

wal-let [wŏl'ĭt] *noun*, a small flat case for money, cards, etc., usually carried in a pocket

wal-low [wŏl'ō] *verb*, to tumble in the mud 2) move slowly

wall-pa-per [wôl'pā'pər] *noun*, *no plural*, decorative paper used to cover walls of a room

wal-nut [wôl'nŭt'] *noun*, 1) a hard, dark-colored wood, valuable for furniture 2) the nut or seed from the walnut tree in a hard shell

wal-rus [wôl'rəs] *noun*, a sea animal like the sea lion and the seal, with outside ears and tusks

waltz [wôlts] *verb*, a dance with four beats per measure

wand [wŏnd] *noun*, a baton, a rod, a fairy's magic stick

wan-der [wŏn'dər] *verb*, 1) to travel from place to place with no plan or purpose in mind
2) to slip easily off the subject

wane [wān] *verb*, to grow gradually smaller or decrease in strength, to decline, to dwindle

wan-gle [wăng'gəl] *verb*, to bring about by manipulation or trickery, to scheme

want [wŏnt] *noun*, 1) a need, lack, not having something necessary, *verb*, 2) to desire or feel a need for something, to require

wan-ton [wŏn'tən] *adjective*, unruly, wild, excessive

war [wôr] *noun*, a deadly conflict

war-ble [wôr'bəl] *verb*, to sing melodiously, to trill as a bird

ward [wôrd] *noun*, 1) a child in the care of someone other than his family 2) a district, a division, *verb*, 3) to fend off, to avert

war-den [wôrd'n] *noun*, the chief administrator of a prison

ward-robe [wôr'drōb'] *noun*, a closet of clothes

ware [wâr] *noun*, a product, merchandise, stock

ware-house [wâr'hous'] *noun*, a storehouse for wares or goods

war-i-ly [wâr'ĭ-lē] *adverb*, in a watchful and suspicious way

warm [wôrm] *adjective*, 1) a temperature between hot and cold, moderately hot, *verb*, 2) to add heat to make something no longer cold

warmth [wôrmth] *noun*,
1) friendship, 2) bodily heat

warn [wôrn] *verb*, 1) to inform
someone that something bad will
happen or of impending danger
2) to admonish, to exhort

warn-ing [wôr'nĭng] *noun*, the act
of telling someone to proceed
with caution, notification

warp [wôrp] *verb*, 1) to twist out of
shape, to distort 2) to pervert

war-rant [wôr'ənt] *noun*, 1) a
written request by a judge to
make an arrest, *verb*, 2) to be
sure of something, to justify

war-ran-ty [wôr'ən-tē] *noun*, a
guarantee that a contract will be
carried out by a manufacturer

war-ri-or [wôr'ē-ər] *noun*, a man
engaged in war, a soldier

wart [wôrt] *noun*, a small growth
or lump that looks like a blemish
on skin often caused by a virus

war-y [wâr'ē] *adjective*, very
cautious, on guard, watchful

was [wŭz] *verb*, *past tense* of **be**,
used in the 3rd singular, **he**, **she**
or **it**

wash [wŏsh] *noun*, 1) a batch of
clothes that are to be or have
been washed, *verb*, 2) to clean
with soap and water

wash-er [wŏsh'ər] *noun*, 1) a
machine for washing clothes or
dishes 2) a round piece of metal
put under a bolt to reinforce it

Wash-ing-ton [wŏsh'ĭng-tən]
noun, one of the 50 United
States located in the Northwest,
the capital is Olympia. The state
flower of **Washington** is the

coast rhododendron and the
motto is "By and by."

wasn't [wŭz'ənt] the *contraction* of
the words **was** and **not**

wasp [wŏsp] *noun*, a flying insect
like a bee, the female inflicts the
sting

waste [wāst] *adjective*, 1) useless,
noun, 2) anything discarded that
is not considered useful, *verb*,
3) to throw away, to spend or
use carelessly, to squander

waste-ful [wāst'fəl] *adjective*,
squandering or spending in a
needless manner

waste-wa-ter [wāst'wô'tər] *noun*,
water that has been used either
to manufacture a product or in
the home, which requires
treatment and purification before
it can be used again

watch [wŏch] *noun*, 1) a small
clock worn on the wrist or hung
from a chain, *verb*, 2) to observe,
to look at attentively 3) to guard,
to be on the lookout

wa-ter [wô'tər] *noun*, 1) a
molecule made of one oxygen
atom and two hydrogen atoms,
that covers 75% of the earth's
surface, *verb*, 2) to moisten or
soak with water 3) to dilute

wa-ter-fall [wô'tər-fôl'] *noun*, a
cascade of water coming down
from a precipice or cliff

wa-ter-way [wô'tər-wā'] *noun*, a
body of water that ships can use

wa-ter-wheel [wô'tər-hwēl] *noun*,
a wheel turned by water running
against or falling on paddles or
steps, used as a source of power

watt [wŏt] *noun*, a measure of electrical power equivalent to one joule per second

wave [wāv] *noun*, 1) a breaker, a surge, surf, *verb*, 2) to greet

wa-ver [wā'vər] *verb*, 1) to be unsteady and show signs of falling or giving way 2) to be indecisive

wax [wăks] *noun*, a substance made from fats and oils that melts when heated

way [wā] *noun*, 1) the manner, custom, style 2) means, process 3) a passage, a road

way-ward [wā'wərd] *adjective*, unruly, disobedient, willful

we [wē] *plural*, *pronoun*, referring to one or more people, including oneself and others

weak [wēk] *adjective*, not strong, fragile, feeble, lacking strength

weak-ness [wēk'nĭs] *noun*, inclination, tendency

wealth [wĕlth] *noun*, riches, abundance of property

wealth-y [wĕl'thē] *adjective*, rich

wean [wēn] *verb*, 1) to accustom a baby not to nurse 2) to give up a cherished activity or habit

weap-on [wĕp'ən] *noun*, an instrument used for attack or defense in combat

wear [wâr] *noun*, 1) the diminished value caused by use, *verb*, 2) to put on, to carry on the body or over the body 3) to exhibit a certain expression on the face 4) to diminish through friction 5) to cause someone to be weary or exhausted 6) to impair by use

wear-y [wîr'ē] *adjective*, 1) tired, fatigued, physically or mentally exhausted 2) bored or resigned

weath-er [wĕth'ər] *noun*, 1) the condition of the atmosphere with regard to temperature, moisture, wind, etc., *verb*, 2) to endure the elements and the conditions outside in the atmosphere

weath-er-ing [wĕth'ər-ĭng] *noun*, the effects of the elements such as wind and water on rock surfaces, and homes or buildings

weave [wēv] *verb*, 1) to interlace threads into cloth 2) to wind or curve in and out

web [wĕb] *noun*, an entanglement, a mesh, an intricate network

web-li-og-ra-phy [wĕb'lē-ŏg'rə-fē] a bibliography of Internet sites used for research

we'd [wēd] the *contraction* of the words **we** and **would**

wed [wĕd] *verb*, to join in marriage

wed-ding [wĕd'ĭng] *noun*, the ceremony when two people are married

wedge [wĕj] *noun*, 1) a flat edge used to split objects or to lift them up 2) a chunk or a block of something, *verb*, 3) to force something to split apart 4) to press in closely, to cramp

Wednes-day [wĕnz'dē, -dā'] *noun*, the fourth day of the week

weed [wēd] *noun*, 1) an unwanted or unwelcome plant, *verb*, 2) to remove as being undesirable

week [wēk] *noun*, the seven days between Sunday and Saturday

weep [wēp] *verb*, 1) to cry, to shed tears 2) to grieve, to mourn 3) to exude liquid

weigh [wāt] *verb*, to measure the heaviness of someone or something by use of a scale

weight [wāt] *noun*, 1) the force with which a body is attracted to the earth or other celestial bodies 2) how heavy a thing is

weight-less [wāt'lĭs] *adjective*, having little or no weight

weird [wîrd] *adjective*, strange

wel-come [wĕl'kəm] *verb*, to receive gladly or hospitably

weld [wĕld] *verb*, 1) to join or connect by fusing two metals with heat 2) to unite

wel-fare [wĕl'fâr'] *noun*, assistance from the government, a state of well-being, health, happiness

well [wĕl] *adjective*, 1) healthy, strong, fit, *adverb*, 2) in a thoroughly manner, *noun*, 3) a narrow, deep hole made in the ground to reach water, oil, or natural gas, *verb*, 4) to rise to the surface and flow out

welt [wĕlt] *noun*, a large blister caused by heat or a beating

went [wĕnt] past participle of **go**

were [wûr] *past tense* of the *verb* **to be** used with **we, you** and **they**

west [wĕst] *noun*, the direction in which the sunsets

west-ern [wĕs'tərn] *adjective*, of or typical of Europe and the Americas

West Vir-gin-i-a [wĕst- vər-jĭn'yə] *noun*, one of the 50 United States, located in the Southeast, the capital is Charleston. The state flower of **West Virginia** is the great rhododendron, and the motto is "Mountaineers are always free."

wet [wĕt] *adjective*, 1) covered with water, moistened, *verb*, 2) to soak with water

wet-lands [wĕt'lăndz'] *noun*, *plural*, a habitat of swamps and marshes for wildlife

whale [hwāl] *noun*, the largest animal in the sea, it is not a fish, it feeds its young with milk

wharf [hwôrf] *noun*, a dock along a shore where boats moor and wait to load or unload

what [hwŏt, hwŭt, wôt] *adjective*, 1) used to ask about the identity of a person, object, or matter 2) how remarkable, *adverb*, 3) how, in what way? *pronoun*, 4) which thing, an event, etc. 5) used to ask a question

what-ev-er [hwŏt-ĕv'ər] *pronoun*, anything that, so what

what's [hwŏts] the *contraction* of the words **what** and **is**

wheat [hwēt] *noun*, one of the cereal plants used to make flour

whee-dle [hwēd'l] *verb*, to coax

wheel [hwēl] *noun*, 1) a circular frame or disk attached to an axis that rolls, *verb*, 2) to move on rollers or wheels, to turn

wheel-bar-row [hwēl'băr'ō] *noun*, a hand cart with three wheels

when [hwĕn] *adverb*, at what time

when-ev-er [hwĕn-ĕv'ər] *adjective*, any time, no matter when

where [hwâr] *adverb*, 1) to or toward a certain place 2) at or in what place

wher-ev-er [hwâr-ĕv'ər] *adjective*, at or any place at all

whet [hwĕt] *verb*, 1) to sharpen by friction 2) to stimulate, to stir

wheth-er [hwĕth'ər] *conjunction*, used to express two choices

which [hwĭch] *noun*, the one, that

while [hwīl] *noun*, a period of time

whim-per [hwĭm'pər] *verb*, to pout, to whine, to cry

whim-si-cal [hwĭm'zĭ-kəl] *adjective*, capricious, given to fanciful notions, playful

whine [hwīn] *verb*, 1) to make a high and sad sound 2) to complain in an annoying manner

whip [hwĭp] *noun*, 1) an instrument made with a handle attached to a long lash made of leather or rope used to hit animals, *verb*, 2) to strike with a lash, to flog 3) to beat to a froth 4) to defeat

whirl [hwûrl] *verb*, to move or make something move around and around very fast

whisk [hwĭsk] *noun*, 1) a cooking utensil used to mix ingredients, *verb*, 2) to move quickly

whisk-er [hwĭs'kər] *noun*, 1) hair growing on the sides of a man's face 2) one of the long stiff hairs that grow near the mouth of dogs, cats, rats, etc.

whis-per [hwĭs'pər] *noun*, 1) a murmur, *verb*, 2) to speak very softly, to murmur quietly

whis-tle [hwĭs'əl] *noun*, 1) an instrument that makes a shrill, musical sound, *verb*, 2) to make a clear, high-pitched sound by forcing breath through the teeth or by pursing the lips, or using a device

white [hwīt] *adjective*, the color of snow, the absence of pigment

whit-tle [hwĭt'l] *verb*, 1) to shape by carving or sculpting 2) to reduce gradually, to diminish

who [ho͞o] *pronoun*, 1) the person or people 2) that 3) what persons?

who-ev-er [ho͞o-ĕv'ər] *pronoun*, any one that

whole [hōl] *adjective*, 1) total, complete, *noun*, 2) the total amount of a thing or entity

whole-some [hōl'səm] *adjective*, sound, healthy, beneficial

whom [ho͞om] *pronoun*, objective case for **who**

whose [ho͞oz] *pronoun*, of whom, possessive case of who

why [hwī] *adverb*, 1) for what reason or purpose, *noun*, 2) the cause or interaction

wick [wĭk] *noun*, the string in a candle or oil lamp that burns the flame, the fuse

wick-ed [wĭk'ĭd] *adjective*, evil, very bad, sinful, vicious

wide [wīd] *adjective*, 1) broad, expansive 2) to be fully open or accessible, of great scope

wid-ow [wĭd'ō] *noun*, a woman whose husband is dead

wid-ow-er [wĭd'ō-ər] *noun*, a man whose wife is dead

width [wĭdth] *noun*, the distance across, the breadth

wield [wēld] *verb*, to control, to sway, to manage, to use

wife [wīf] *noun*, *plural*, **wives**, a married woman

wig [wĭg] *noun*, a covering for the head, hair from other people or animals, a toupee, a hairpiece

wig-gle [wĭg'əl] *verb*, to move around, to squirm

wild [wīld] *adjective*, untamed or domesticated, a natural state

wil-der-ness [wĭl'dər-nĭs] *noun*, a tract of land undeveloped and uninhabited by people

wild-life [wīld'līf'] *noun*, any species of animals living in their natural habitat

will [wĭl] *noun*, 1) power in the mind or character, what we want to do 2) a declaration by a person concerning their estate, *verb*, 3) used with other verbs to show something is going to happen 4) used in questions when asking to do something

will-ful [wĭl'fəl] *adjective*, 1) determined, intentional, deliberate 2) obstinate, stubborn

will-ing [wĭl'ĭng] *adjective*, ready, given or done gladly

wil-low [wĭl'ō] *noun*, a tree with long drooping branches

wilt [wĭlt] *verb*, 1) to wither, to lose freshness 2) to lose strength

wil-y [wī'lē] *adjective*, sly, clever

win [wĭn] *verb*, 1) to achieve victory over others 2) to receive an award for a performance

wind [wĭnd] *noun*, 1) currents of air moving quickly with force, [wīnd] *verb*, 2) to wrap around

over and over 3) to turn round and round, to move in curves and bends, not a straight line

win-dow [wĭn'dō] *noun*, 1) a pane of glass 2) an opening with a transparent cover that allows light in

win-dow-sill [wĭn'dō-sĭl'] *noun*, a shelf or ledge below a window

wine [wīn] *noun*, an alcoholic drink made from fermented grapes

wing [wĭng] *noun*, 1) one of the two limbs of a bird or insect with which it flies 2) a side projection of an airplane 3) an extension of a building

wink [wĭngk] *noun*, 1) one eye closed and one eye open as a gesture of approval, *verb*, 2) to close and open one eye quickly

win-now [wĭn'ō] *verb*, to sift, to separate good parts from bad

win-some [wĭn'səm] *adjective*, agreeable, gracious, engaging

win-ter [wĭn'tər] *noun*, the first season of the year, between autumn and spring, when the earth is farthest from the sun

wipe [wīp] *verb*, to make dry or clean with a cloth

wire [wīr] *noun*, 1) a metal thread or strand, *verb*, 2) to connect

Wis-con-sin [wĭs-kŏn'sĭn] *noun*, one of the 50 United States located in the North,, the capital city is Madison. The state flower of **Wisconsin** is the violet, and the motto is "Forward."

wis-dom [wĭz'dəm] *noun*, learning and the capacity to use it

wise [wīz] *adjective*, showing good judgment, intelligent

wish [wĭsh] *noun*, 1) a desire that is beyond your reach, *verb*, 2) to desire, to long for, to want

wist-ful [wĭst'fəl] *adjective*, hopeful, yearning, longing

wit [wĭt] *noun*, cleverness, quickness of mind, ingenuity

witch [wĭch] *noun*, a woman who is believed to have magic powers

with [wĭth] *preposition*, 1) in the company of 2) using it 3) having 4) because of 5) next to

with-draw [wĭth-drô'] *verb*, to retreat, to go back on or to take back an offer, to remove

with-drawn [wĭth-drôn'] *adjective*, 1) taken back, removed 2) shy, introverted, retiring

with-er [wĭth'ər] *verb*, to shrivel, to fade, to lose freshness

with-hold [wĭth-hōld'] *verb*, to restrain, to hold back

with-in [wĭth-ĭn'] *adverb*, 1)inside, *preposition*, 2) in, not beyond

with-out [wĭth-out'] *adverb*, 1) outside, *preposition*, 2) lacking, wanting, not having

wit-ness [wĭt'nĭs] *noun*, 1) a spectator, an onlooker, a person who sees something, *verb*, 2) to see, to observe, to hear

wiz-ard [wĭz'ərd] *noun*, someone who performs sorcery and magic

woe [wō] *noun*, self-pity, sadness

wolf [wŏolf] *noun*, *plural,* **wolves,** a wild dog similar to a coyote

wom-an [wŏom'ən] *noun*, *plural*, **women**, a female, a lady

won-der [wŭn'dər] *noun*, 1) a feeling of surprise and admiration, amazement, *verb*, 2) to express a wish to know

won-der-ful [wŭn'dər-fəl] *adjective*, extra special, very good, remarkable, marvelous

won-drous [wŭn'drəs] *adjective*, amazing, astonishing, marvelous

wont [wônt] *adjective,* 1) apt or likely, *noun,* 2) custom, habitual procedure

won't [wônt] the *contraction* of the words **will** and **not**

wood [wŏod] *noun*, 1) the material which comes from trees 2) a small forest

wood-land [wŏod'lənd] *noun*, the forest, land covered with trees

wood-peck-er [wŏod'pĕk'ər] *noun*, a black and white bird with a red head that pecks at wood with its bill to find bugs to eat

wood-winds [wŏod'wĭndz'] *noun*, musical instruments, usually made of wood or metal, that you blow into or use a reed to play such as a clarinet

wool [wŏol] *noun*, the, soft, thick fur on a sheep often used for yarn or fabric

word [wûrd] *noun*, 1) speech, sound or symbol used to communicate 2) a message 3) a promise 4) news, information

work [wûrk] *noun*, 1) a job, a form of labor, a duty 2) a deed, an accomplishment, *verb*, 3) to do a job, to labor, to perform a duty

world [wûrld] *noun*, the Earth and its people and all living things

world-ly [wûrld'lē] *adjective*, known all over, cosmopolitan

worm [wûrm] *noun*, a thin creature without bones or legs that lives in the earth

wor-ry [wûr′ē] *verb*, to fret, to show concern, to feel anxious

worse [wûrs] *adjective*, to go from bad to a more damaged condition, inferior, less good or well

wor-ship [wûr′shĭp] *noun*, 1) ardent devotion, *verb*, 2) to pray to or show reverence or respect for someone

worth [wûrth] *noun*, the value or importance of something

worth-less [wûrth′lĭs] *adjective*, without worth, valueless

wor-thy [wûr′thē] *adjective*, admirable, deserving, noble

would [wŏŏd] future perfect tense of the *verb* be

wouldn't [wŏŏd′nt] the *contraction* of the words **would** and **not**

wound [wōōnd] *noun*, 1) an injury, *verb*, 2) to injure, to hurt 3) to disturb or upset someone

wrap [răp] *noun*, 1) a removable covering, *verb*, 2) to cover with a substance usually to protect something, to enclose

wrath [răth] *noun*, anger, fury

wreak [rēk] *verb*, to produce rage, to perpetuate, to inflict

wreath [rēth] *noun*, a ring of flowers and leaves

wreck [rĕk] *noun*, 1) the remains of something partially destroyed like a car, building, or ship, *verb*, 2) to destroy or damage something, to tear down

wren [rĕn] *noun*, a brown-grey bird that lives in the south

wrench [rĕnch] *noun*, 1) a tool used to grip a bolt or a nut 2) a forcible twist, *verb*, 3) to pull or turn suddenly with a violent twist, to damage or injure

wrest [rĕst] *verb*, 1) to pull away 2) to take away by force, to seize, to wrench away

wres-tle [rĕs′əl] *verb*, to struggle hand to hand, to grapple

wretch [rĕch] *noun*, a vile, disgusting person

wrig-gle [rĭg′əl] *verb*, to squirm or twist like a worm, to writhe

wring [rĭng] *verb*, to twist, to squeeze by twisting tightly

wrin-kle [rĭng′kəl] *noun*, 1) a crease or fold, *verb*, 2) to pucker into folds and creases

wrist [rĭst] *noun*, the joint between the hand and the forearm

write [rīt] *verb*, to use an instrument such as a pencil to draw symbols to communicate

writer [rī′tər] *noun*, author, journalist, newsperson

writhe [rīth] *verb*, to twist or move as if in pain, to thrash

wrong [rông *adjective*, 1) in error, mistaken, incorrect 2) contrary to morality or laws

wrote [rīt′n] *past tense* of **write**

Wy-o-ming [wī-ō′mĭng] *noun*, one of the 50 United States, located in the Northwest, the capital is Cheyenne. The state flower of **Wyoming** is the indian paintbrush and the motto is "Equal rights."

X

xeno-phile [zĕn′ə-fīl′] *noun*, one attracted to foreign people, manners, and styles

xeno-pho-bi-a [zĕn′ə-fō′bē-ə] *noun*, fear and hatred of foreigners or strangers

xy-lem [zī′ləm] *noun*, the system of a woody tissue that transports water in a plant

xy-log-ra-phy [zī-lŏg′rə-fē] *noun*, the art of engraving on wood

x-ray [ĕks′rā′] *noun*, 1) a photograph of a part of the inside of your body, *verb*, 2) to take a picture of the inside of the body

xy-lo-phone [zailəfoun] *noun*, a percussion instrument played by striking horizontal wooden bars with small wooden hammers

Y

yacht [yät] *noun*, a boat used either for private pleasure or as a vessel of state to convey people from one place to another

yam [yăm] *noun*, a sweet potato, the root of a potato plant

yard [yärd] *noun*, 1) a length of measure equal to 36 inches 2) the lawn or property around someone's house

yarn [yärn] *noun*, 1) knitting thread, spun wool 2) a story, a fictional account

yawn [yôn] *verb*, to open the mouth wide and breathe deeply as if tired or bored

year [yîr] *noun*, 365 days, or each cycle that the earth rotates around the sun divided, into 12 months, 52 weeks, and 4 seasons

yearn [yûrn] *verb*, to desire something, to long for

yeast [yēst] *noun*, a fungus which produces fermentation, used as a leavening agent in dough

yell [yĕl] *verb*, to shout, to scream

yel-low [yĕl′ō] *noun*, one of the primary colors, the color of corn

yen [yĕn] *noun*,1) the currency of Japan 2) a longing, an urge

yes [yĕs] *interjection*, a word of agreement, an affirmative reply

yes-ter-day [yĕs′tər-dā′] *adverb*, 1) on the day before today, *noun*, 2) the day before today

yet [yĕt] *conjunction*, until now

yield [yēld] *verb*, 1) to give way to, to submit, to surrender 2) to produce, to supply, to give forth

yo-ga [yō′ga] *noun*, an exercise by which one seeks union with the universal soul through deep mediation, prescribed postures, controlled breathing, etc.

yo-gurt [yō′gərt] *noun*, a dairy product that is thicker than milk and has a slightly sour taste

yolk [yōk] *noun*, the yellow and principal part inside an egg

you [yōō] *pronoun*, the person or persons spoken to

you'd [yōōd] the *contraction* of the words **you** and **would**

you'll [yōōl] the *contraction* of the words **you** and **will**

young [yŭng] *adjective*, the early stage of life, not old

your [yŏŏr] *pronoun*, belonging to
you

you're [yŏŏr] the *contraction* of
the words, **you** and **are**

yours [yŏŏrz, yôrz, yōrz] *pronoun*,
belonging to you

your-self [yŏŏr-sĕlf'] *pronoun*, a
form of you for emphasis when
the object of a verb and the
subject are the same

youth [yŏŏth] *noun*, a young
person, an adolescent

Z

za-ny [zā'nē] *adjective*, crazy,
whimsically comical

zeal [zēl] *noun*, ardor in pursuit of
anything, fervor, eagerness

zeal-ous [zĕl'əs] *adjective*,
enthusiastic, eager, devoted

ze-bra [zē'brə] *noun*, an African
wild animal like a horse which
has brown and white stripes all
over its body

Zen Buddhism [zĕn- bŏŏ'dĭz'əm]
noun, a faith in which Buddha is
the embodiment of the superior
man and followers seek
enlightenment through
meditation and intuition instead
of the traditional scriptures

ze-nith [zē'nĭth] *noun*, the point
directly overhead in the sky, the
summit, the highest point

zeph-yr [zĕf'ər] *noun*, a gentle
breeze, the west wind

ze-ro [zîr'ō] *noun, plural,* **zeros** or
zeroes, 1) the numberical symbol 0
2) nothing 3) the temperature on
a scale indicated by this symbol

zest [zĕst] *noun*, feeling of
enjoyment, excitement

zinc [zĭngk] *noun*, a bluish white
metallic element often mixed
with other metals

zip-per [zĭp'ər] *noun*, a slide
fastener for clothing, briefcases,
and other objects, with two sets
of interlocking teeth

zone [zōn] *noun*, a division of an
area that differs or is
distinguished in some respect
from adjoining areas

zoo [zŏŏ] *noun*, a place where
different animals are kept for
people to look at

zo-ol-o-gy [zō-ŏl'ə-jē] *noun*, the
science of animals

zy-gote [zī'gōt'] *noun*, the single
cell resulting from the union of
an egg and a sperm

Weights and Measures

ENGLISH

Length

12 inches	=	1 foot
3 feet	=	1 yard
5280 feet	=	1 mile
1760 yards	=	1 mile

Area

144 square inches	=	1 square foot
9 square feet	=	1 square yard
4840 square yards	=	1 acre
640 acres	=	1 square mile

Volume

1728 cubic inches	=	1 cubic foot
27 cubic feet	=	1 cubic yard

Capacity (Dry)

2 pints	=	1 quart
8 quarts	=	1 peck
4 pecks	=	1 bushel

Capacity (Liquid)

16 fluid ounces	=	1 pint
2 pints	=	1 quart
4 quarts	=	1 gallon (8 pints)

Mass

16 ounces	=	1 pound (7000 grains)
20 cwt	=	1 ton
2000 lbs	=	1 ton

Troy Weights

12 ounces	=	1 pound (5760 grains)

Measures

16 fluid ounces	=	1 pint

__METRIC__

__Length__
1 millimeter	=	1000 micrometers
1 centimeter	=	10 millimeters
1 meter	=	1000 millimeters
1 meter	=	100 centimeters
1 kilometer	=	1000 meters

__Area__
1 square centimeter	=	100 square millimeters
1 square meter	=	10,000 square centimeters
1 square meter	=	1,000,000 square millimeters
1 square kilometer	=	1,000,000 square meters

__Volume__
1 milliliter	=	1 cubic centimeter
1 liter	=	1000 milliliters
1 liter	=	0.001 cubic meter

__Mass__
1 gram	=	1000 milligrams
1 kilogram	=	1000 grams
1 metric ton	=	1000 kilograms

__Volume__
1 cubic inch (in^3) = 16.39 cubic centimeters (cm^3)
1,728 cubic inches = 1 cubic foot = 0.02832 cubic meters (m^3)
27 cubic feet (ft^3) = 1 cubic yard (y^3) = 0.7646 cubic meters

__Temperature Conversions__
°C Celsius = 5/9 (°F −32)   °F Fahrenheit = (9/5 °C) +32

__Square Measure__
100 sq. meters = 1 sq. decameter = 119.6 sq. yards
100 sq. decameters = 1 sq. hectometer = 2.471 acres
100 sq. hectometers = 1 sq. kilometer = 0.386 sq. miles or
                                                    247.1 acres

Words for Large Numbers

Term	Calculation	# of Zeros
Ten	10 Ones	1
One Hundred	100 Ones	2
One Thousand	1,000 Ones	3
One Million	1,000 Thousands	6
One Billion	1,000 Millions	9
One Trillion	1,000 Billions	12
One Quadrillion	1,000 Trillions	15
One Quintillion	1,000 Quadrillions	18
One Sextillion	1,000 Quintillions	21
One Septillion	1,000 Sextillions	24
One Octillion	1,000 Septillions	27
One Nonillion	1,000 Octillions	30
One Decillion	1,000 Nonillion	33

Big Words

HIPPOPOTOMONSTRASESQUIPPEDALIOPHOBIA
The fear of long words.

PNEUMONOULTRAMICROSCOPICSILICOVOLCANOCONIOSIS
This word is forty-five letters and its definition is a lung disease
caused by breathing in certain particles.

ANTITRANSUBSTANTIATIONALIST
One who doubts the validity of transubstantiation.

FLOCCINAUCINIHILIPILIFICATION
The estimation of a thing as worthless.

...TABLISHMENTARIANISM
of those who oppose the link between Church and State.

...RAGILISTICEXPIALIDOCIOUS
to say when you don't know what to say.

Roman Numerals

I	1
II	2
III	3
IV	4
V	5
VI	6
VII	7
VIII	8
IX	9
X	10
XX	20
XXX	30
XL	40
L	50
LX	60
LXX	70
LXXX	80
XC	90
C	100
CC	200
CD	400
D	500
DC	600
DCC	700
DCCC	800
CM	900
M	1,000
$\overline{V}$	5,000
$\overline{X}$	10,000
$\overline{L}$	50,000
$\overline{C}$	100,000
$\overline{D}$	500,000
$\overline{M}$	1,000,000